Selections from the Papers of the London Corresponding Society 1792–1799

EDITED WITH AN INTRODUCTION
AND NOTES BY
MARY THALE
University of Illinois, Chicago

CAMBRIDGE UNIVERSITY PRESS
Cambridge
London New York New Rochelle
Melbourne Sydney

CAMBRIDGE UNIVERSITY PRESS
Cambridge, New York, Melbourne, Madrid, Cape Town, Singapore, São Paulo, Delhi

Cambridge University Press
The Edinburgh Building, Cambridge CB2 8RU, UK

Published in the United States of America by Cambridge University Press, New York

www.cambridge.org
Information on this title: www.cambridge.org/9780521243636

First published 1983
This digitally printed version 2008

A catalogue record for this publication is available from the British Library

Library of Congress Catalogue Card Number: 82–9503

ISBN 978-0-521-24363-6 hardback
ISBN 978-0-521-08987-6 paperback

Contents

July 1792: 'As to your *twopenny Club*, it is almost beneath Ridicule   I hope you have nothing to do
with it . . .'
[Letter from A. T. to John Richter]

September 1802: '[I] t is certainly very singular in ye history of interior politics that a society so obscure
in its origin, so obscure from ye situation of ye
members of wch it was composed, should have
risen into so much importance as to have rung
ye political changes from one end of ye kingdom to ye other.'
[Letter from J. D. Collier to Thomas Hardy]

Preface

In 1792 when the founder of the London Corresponding Society, Thomas Hardy, showed the first manifesto of the Society to his American friend, Col. Smith, the response was, 'Hardy, the Government will hang you.' The government did not, but they certainly wanted to, for they accused this obscure shoemaker of high treason for his activities in the Corresponding Society. Smith's near-prophecy and the government's trial of Hardy – he was acquitted – suggest one major importance of these records of the London Corresponding Society: they reveal a dangerous challenge to the established government – and that in a period of English history which a contemporary, Francis Place, likened to the Reign of Terror. Unlike many groups which set out to demand their political or social rights but which scattered as soon as they encountered opposition, the Corresponding Society met openly for over six years despite harassment by police magistrates, interference from press gangs, vilification in newspapers, attacks in Parliament, introduction of repressive laws, arrests of members, expensive trials and even prolonged detention without trial or sentence. The blow from which they could not recover was the 1799 Act of Parliament specifically outlawing the Society by name – and thereby acknowledging its importance.

Besides their historical significance, these records are of considerable value in helping us to understand the workings of protest and reformist societies. They show us the conditions which enable one society to outlive similar societies, the dogged persistence of some members and the giving-up of others, the handling of dissension within a society, the treatment of schismatic groups, the unofficial change in goals by some members, the use of a society as a cover for illegal activities and the correlation between fiscal mismanagement and the decline of a society.

What first interested me in the London Corresponding Society was Francis Place's assertion that the Society was responsible for the moral and intellectual improvement of hundreds of members. These records of LCS meetings do show conditions which helped men redirect their lives: the orderly procedure of meetings, the insistence on a pattern of approved behaviour by members, the emphasis on argument and reconciliation rather than quarrelling. Paradoxically, what later came to fascinate me about these documents is their picture of government spies at work. They subtly recommended measures which would provide their employers with more details: one spy urged that every motion be accompanied by the name of the mover. The spies frequently rose to positions of importance, and they did not escape the complexities of their position: a spy who was a lawyer was asked by the LCS to defend a member he was prepared to testify against in the treason trials; another spy, dramatically protesting his innocence when accused of spying, said, 'there cannot exist a Man more zealous in the cause of the L. C. Society than the good & injured Citizen who stands accused'. Still another spy, James Powell, was so successful that he was never uncovered and continued spying on LCS members in England and on the continent even after the dissolution of the Society.

Thanks to the hoarding instincts of both government and certain LCS members, there still exists a large number of LCS papers, both printed and manuscript. The printed papers fall into three groups: (1) those intended for members only, dealing with internal affairs of the Society; (2) documents about the Society printed for members, other reformers and the general public; (3) educational pamphlets which were printed and sold by the LCS.

(1) The printed papers intended for members of the Society include circular letters and newspaper advertisements summoning members to meetings, especially in times when attendance was flagging; the constitutions; regulations to bring the Society into compliance with the Sedition Act of December 1795; the financial statement of the Society for 1796 and explanation of the Society's indebtedness (1797); monthly treasurer's reports from July 1796 to January 1798.

(2) The papers by LCS members or about the LCS which were printed for the public as well as for the members include the frequently reprinted *Addresses and Regulations* (1792); the *Address . . . to the Inhabitants of Great Britain, on the Subject of a Parliamentary Reform* (1792); *Address . . . to the Other Societies of Great Britain, United for the Obtaining a Reform in Parliament* (1792); *A Letter to the Right Hon. Henry Dundass* (1792);

the addresses, petitions, resolutions and narratives of the general meetings of July 1793, January and April 1794, June, October and November 1795, and July 1797; addresses to Maurice Margarot and to Thomas Muir and Thomas Fyshe Palmer 1794 (an address to Joseph Gerrald is printed in the narrative of the general meeting of April 1794); *An Account of the Seizure of Citizen Thomas Hardy* (1974); *A Vindication of the London Corresponding Society* (1974); *Reformers No Rioters* (1794); *The Reply of the London Corresponding Society to the Calumnies propagated by Persons in High Authority* (1795); *An Explicit Declaration of the Principles and Views of the London Corresponding Society* (1795); *Thoughts on Mr. Grey's Plan of Reform* (1797); *Address . . . to the Irish Nation* (1798). Although not officially published by the LCS, *Revolutions Without Bloodshed* (1794), written by LCS member James Parkinson, was discussed in the general committee and was published at LCS expense.

At the end of 1795 the Society published *The Correspondence of the London Corresponding Society*, consisting chiefly of letters written during that year. They also printed circular letters to other reform societies inviting them to participate in a convention (1794), urging them to persevere (1796), requesting donations for the support of the LCS missionaries (1796–7) and recommending general meetings (1797).

Finally, the LCS published a great many newspaper advertisements giving LCS resolutions, thanking barristers for their defence of LCS members, praising reform-minded Members of Parliament, requesting donations for the families of imprisoned reformers and advertising the *Moral and Political Magazine*.

(3) As part of their aim of educating the people in their rights, the Society reprinted parliamentary speeches by Philip Francis, John Wharton and Lord Stanhope; an excerpt from *Peace and Union* by William Frend; *The Englishman's Right* by Sir John Hawles; a compressed edition of *The State of the Representation of England and Wales*, a work first published by the Friends of the People. Hardy, in his account of the LCS, named several other works as published by the Society, but there is no other evidence connecting the LCS with any known copies of these works.

The LCS issued two periodicals which contain material by or about the Society as well as excerpts or works by outside authors. *The Politician*, an eight page weekly published four times between 13 December 1794 and 3 January 1795, contained letters on the importance of liberty, on party names, on national degeneracy, against universal suffrage, for universal suffrage; also the speech John Thelwall intended to deliver at his trial and verses written in his cell. *The Moral and Political Magazine of the London Corresponding Society*, a forty-eight page monthly magazine issued twelve times between June 1796 and May 1797, contained letters to and from the Society, speeches by Charles James Fox and John Horne Tooke, extracts from books, book reviews, poems, anecdotes, Thelwall's political lectures, brief essays and accounts of domestic and foreign transactions.

During the years of the LCS Thelwall published speeches he delivered at general meetings. In 1796 two of the victims of the pop-gun plot published accounts of events in the general committee which led to the accusation that they plotted regicide: *High Treason! ! ! Narrative of the Arrest, Examination . . . Imprisonment &c. of P. T. Lemaitre*; and *Assassination of the King . . . by John Smith*. Also in 1796 John Gale Jones published an account of his first trip as a deputy from the LCS: *Sketch of a Political Tour Through Rochester, Chatham, Maidstone, Gravesend, &c. . . .*

Most printed LCS documents can be found in the British Library or the Public Record Office. A few exist only in Nuffield College Library, the Bishopsgate Institute, John Rylands Library. The *Politician* and the *Moral and Political Magazine* are in Columbia University Library. The major repositories of LCS manuscripts are the British Library and the Public Record Office. In the British Library there are eight volumes of manuscripts collected first by Hardy and then by Place, each of whom intended to write a history of the LCS.[1] These volumes include the first draft of the plan of the LCS; rough drafts of Hardy's 1792–3 letters about the LCS; the journal of the general committee from 2 April 1792 to 2 January 1794; a copy by Hardy of his LCS letters and of the journal;[2] minutes of the general committee from 2 July to 10 September 1795; letters to and from the Society from 2 July 1795 to 15 December 1796; miscellaneous letters and records of financial transactions; John Richter's contemporary account of his arrest and imprisonment in 1794; letters, narratives and financial records pertinent to the 1798 arrests and subsequent

1 Additional Manuscripts 27808, 27811–17. Hereafter Add MSS.
2 Another MS copy of this journal is said to exist.

detention of LCS members; Hardy's history of the Society and his correspondence about publishing it; Place's 'Notes respecting the London Corresponding Society', which was a draft of a chapter of his autobiography; and Paul Thomas Lemaitre's 'Remarks' on the Pop-Gun Plot. Throughout these volumes there are many printed documents issued by the LCS or relating to the Society (e.g. LeMaitre's petition to the House of Commons about the disabilities he suffered as a result of the Pop-Gun Plot). These volumes also contain much tangential material such as lists of the jurors in trials of LCS members and over 400 folios on the dispute between LCS member Maurice Margarot and three other transported reformers.

Besides these LCS papers Place compiled three scrapbooks on reform activities of this period.[3] These contain chiefly newspaper cuttings, but also some printed LCS documents, such as the 1795 constitution, and a few manuscripts.

In addition to the manuscripts and printed documents in the British Library, there is a mass of LCS material in the Public Record Office. These papers (mostly manuscript) fall into five categories:

(a) Documents seized in 1794 and 1798, when government arrested several LCS members. In 1794, Bow Street officers stuffed the papers of Hardy, Thelwall and Richter into bags or tied them up in large handkerchiefs (the arresting officers also hauled off the papers of the Society for Constitutional Information members Tooke and Daniel Adams). The LCS papers include letters, bills, receipts, lists of members, vouchers for delegates from the various divisions and printed documents of the LCS and other reform societies. Almost nothing was too small or insignificant to be saved. The arrests of 1798 produced the same types of papers, but fewer of them (possibly the Society had learned to retain fewer papers and to hide them). Most of the papers from this mass arrest were taken from the committee room at Wych St or from the home of John Bone, a former secretary of the Society.

(b) Reports from spies or men who attended LCS meetings with the intent of informing the government of the proceedings. There are a few reports from Bow Street officers who attended division meetings in the autumn of 1792 and the general meeting of 14 April 1794. Most of the reports are from spies who passed themselves off as loyal members and who, by their assiduity, were often elected

3 British Library: Place Collection, vols. 36–8.

delegates. George Lynam started reporting in October 1792, John Taylor in January 1794, John Groves in February 1794, William Metcalfe in April 1794 and Edward Gosling in May 1794. Their reports stopped at various points in 1794 when they were identified as spies. From 1795 on most of the spy reports are from James Powell. There is one report in 1794 from J. Tolfrey and a few in 1798 and 1799 from William Gent and John Tunbridge.

(c) Depositions and records of questioning by the Privy Council. The depositions from LCS members, their acquaintances, even from a woman who claimed to have seen Hardy in another city, date mostly from 1794, as do the extensive records of interrogation by the Privy Council. From the mass arrests of 1798 all that remain are two depositions, and four examinations (only one from a leading member).

(d) Materials assembled by the government, mostly about the state prisoners of 1794 and 1798–1801. The earliest of these compilations are lists of 'republican' clubs in and around London, dated November and December 1792. The documents about the state prisoners of 1794 include indices of papers found in the possession of Hardy, Richter, Thelwall, Tooke and Adams, as well as indices of all the papers pertaining to the LCS and the Society for Constitutional Information. There are also lists of the evidence against each of the men arrested in 1794, as well as copies of the letters to and from the Society for each year. For the state prisoners of 1798–1801 there are again indices of papers seized, some lists of the evidence against the men, and numerous lists of the men arrested, the prisons they were sent to, the charges against them and the dates of arrest and release.

(e) Orders and letters from the Secretary of State for Home Affairs, the Duke of Portland, and his aides to police magistrates and commanders of troops, directing their actions with respect to LCS meetings and members.

Between 1799 and 1851 three members of the LCS wrote autobiographies which give accounts of their activities in the Society: *Memoir of Thomas Hardy* (1832), mostly written in 1799; *The Autobiography of Francis Place* (1972), written 1823–35; and *Recollections of the Life of John Binns* (1854), written in 1851. *The Life of John Thelwall* (1837) by his widow also contains material about the LCS which was unmistakably written by Thelwall himself.

These four writers force us to face the question of the reliability of these documents. Each of these men tends, understandably, to spotlight his own role in the LCS. All four of them also tend to recall the past in terms of their biases. The cautious Place, for example, reported that the 'leading men were none of them . . . hot headed revolutionists but sedate men' (p. 196); whereas the United Irishman Binns recalled that 'the wishes and hopes of many of its [the LCS's] influential members carried them to the overthrow of the monarchy and the establishment of a republic' (p. 45). Because they wrote after the suppression of the Society, they occasionally err in detail. Also, Place, after leaving the LCS in 1797, was out of touch with reform societies for several years; he is wrong, for example, in his statements about the size of the United Englishmen and about the LCS never meeting after 19 April 1798.

Whereas Place and Hardy stress the educational nature of the LCS, the government's *Reports of the Committee of Secrecy* (1794 and 1799) tend to attribute to the whole Society the occasional assertions by individuals about arming, invasion and revolution. These reports warrant Place's charge that they would seriously mislead a future historian who had no other information about the LCS.

Thanks to the foresight of Hardy and Place and the habits of government archivists, we have this rich collection of first-hand accounts of LCS meetings, accounts which are generally accurate. Where there are duplicate accounts of a meeting, one in the journal or in minutes kept by a loyal member and another in a report by a spy, they correspond closely in points of fact. The spy reports sometimes give different figures for money collected or members present, but such differences are not substantial. The official accounts of meetings often minimize dissent within the Society. For example, the 1793 'trial' of Lynam as a spy is only tangentially touched upon in the journal; our knowledge of it comes from notes seized at Hardy's house.

The spy reports of conversations with LCS members outside the meetings are less susceptible of verification; but when the Privy Council questioned LCS members about such conversations, the bulk of their testimony usually corroborated the spy's version of events. A case in point is Gosling's account of talks on 17 May 1794 with Hillier, Hayward and Bennett. There are, of course, some disputed versions of events. Did Thelwall, slashing off the head of a tankard of porter, say 'This is the way I would serve all tyrants' or 'This is the Way I would serve Kings'? Did Green sell a switchblade knife openly, or did he hide the

transaction from his wife, whom he called 'a damned aristocrat'? We cannot know which version of events is correct, but the smallness of the number of such contradictions suggests that the spies were, on the whole, reliable reporters of conversations.

The documents in this edition comprise about a third of the records of the Corresponding Society. These documents have been selected to show how the Society functioned from its inception in 1792 until its suppression in 1799. The edition includes the following documents:

all existing reports of division meetings;

all existing reports of general committee meetings;

all existing reports of executive committee meetings;

all existing reports of *ad hoc* committee meetings;

all existing spy reports of LCS meetings.[4]

motions from divisions to the general committee which are not included in existing reports of meetings.

a few depositions and spy reports of conversations with LCS members which provide evidence of the more revolutionary plans of some LCS members who allegedly were speaking for the LCS.

excerpts from Hardy's accounts of the origin of the Society and of his arrest.

excerpts from John Richter's narrative of LCS activities in May 1794.

most authorized narratives of general (i.e. public) meetings of the LCS. The speeches and petitions read at these meetings are summarized or excerpted. These last documents, which are often lengthy (Thelwall's speech at the meeting on 26 October 1795 has 10,000 words), caused no change in the aims or direction of the Society.[5]

circular letters from the general committee or executive committee to all members.

4 For any of these five groups of documents, when there are duplicate reports which contain much repetition, the most complete one is printed and the others summarized or cited in notes.

5 Anyone wishing to read speeches and addresses which are here abbreviated will find many of them in the *First and Second Reports of the Committee of Secrecy, 1794*, and in the *Report of the Committee of Secrecy, 1799*. The edition of Hardy's trial by William Ramsey reprints as an appendix the documents read at Hardy's trial; Howell's *State Trials*, vol. 24, prints them throughout the trial record. Many LCS documents are also printed in the *History of Two Acts*, 1796.

letters from individual members or groups of members concerning the whole society.

a few circular letters from the LCS to other reform societies. Other letters to and from the LCS are summarized or cited in notes, as are the other documents of the Society, such as vouchers and financial records.[6]

The documents in this edition are transcriptions of the earliest manuscript or printed document. Where there exists a draft and a final copy, the latter is used, and significant variants are noted. If there is only a government copy of a document, that is printed (wherever there are both government copies and LCS originals, the government copy is always accurate except that spelling and punctuation are regularized).

My aim in the Introduction is not to offer an interpretative history of the London Corresponding Society but to present information which will help readers to follow the day-to-day workings of the Society and to construct their own interpretations of it. Thus, except for a few brief paragraphs I have offered no general account of the political climate and issues of the 1790s nor of the relationship of the radicalism of the LCS to that of other contemporary societies or subsequent ones.[7] So also I have offered only the briefest outline history of the LCS. What I have done is synthesize a good deal of routine material from the text so that readers can follow these documents with a minimum of confusion. This information bears on such matters as the organization of the Society, its growth and the size of the membership. In the sections on class, education and connection of reformers, however, I have attempted to assist readers by synthesizing information which cannot be found in these LCS documents but which should be of use in interpreting them.

6 From the lists of extant LCS material mentioned on pp. vii–ix, one can see what has been excluded from this edition. The exclusions I most regret are the printed financial records of July 1795 to Jan. 1798, the constitutions proposed in 1794 and 1795, and the 1792 and 1794 lists of members of a few divisions.

7 Two outstanding works which provide contexts for the activities of the LCS are E. P. Thompson's *The Making of the English Working Class*, 1963, and Albert Goodwin's *The Friends of Liberty*, 1979. Another important work, J. Ann Hone's *For the Cause of Truth: Radicalism in London 1796–1821* (1982), was published too recently to be used extensively in this edn.

Acknowledgements

For permission to publish these documents, I am grateful to the Public Records Office, the British Library, Nuffield College Library and Columbia University Library. For their assistance I thank the librarians and attendants at these libraries and those at the Bishopsgate Institute, Guildhall (London), Bodleian, John Rylands, University of London, and the Institute of Historical Research.

I am indebted to the University of Illinois Research Board for grants which enabled me to have these documents photocopied and transcribed and for leaves of absence to work on this edition. To the National Endowment for the Humanities I also give thanks for a research fellowship during 1976. The Department of English at the University of Illinois, Chicago, has, over several years, suported my work on this edition with assistance in photocopying, typing and copy-reading. I am pleased to express my gratitude for this assistance.

For suggestions on the scope and shape of the edition I owe thanks to E. P. Thompson and Jerome Thale. For help with typing and copy-reading, I am especially grateful to Kathleen Edwards and Rosalie Kirk. Rosemarie Thale and Christopher Thale made valuable suggestions about the introduction. Most deeply, I am indebted to Brian Thale for many many months of his wisdom and his devotion to the Corresponding Society.

Rules of transcription

The spelling of the original documents has been retained. Since many of the manuscript reports of meetings were recorded as heard, there are sometimes different spellings of the same name, for example, Main and Mayne.

The capitalization and punctuation in the manuscripts are faithfully transcribed, with three exceptions: (1) incomplete quotation marks are supplied; (2) sentences ending without punctuation have been given terminal points when necessary for clarity; (3) raised letters have been lowered.

Illegible words are so identified in square brackets. Conjectured words are given in diamond brackets.

Words accidentally omitted in the manuscript are added in square brackets when essential for coherence. Incomplete words are also completed in square brackets when necessary.

Deleted words are given in the notes if they represent a significant change in meaning. For LCS documents which the Society reprinted, only significant changes are noted.

Editorial apparatus

For convenience in referring to these documents, they are numbered consecutively. Following the number, each document has a heading, indicating the contents.

Below the number and heading, the head-note gives the location of the manuscript used. In the case of printed documents, the location is given if the document is found in only one place. Printed documents are so identified either by italicized heading or in the headnote. All other documents are transcribed from manuscripts.

Abbreviations

Add MSS	Additional Manuscripts
BL	British Library
FoP	Society of the Friends of the People
HO	Home Office Papers
MC	*Morning Chronicle*
MP	*Morning Post*
MPM	*Moral and Political Magazine of the London Corresponding Society*
PC	Privy Council Papers
PRO	Public Record Office
SCI	Society for Constitutional Information
ST	*A Complete Collection of State Trials*, comp. T. B. Howell and T. J. Howell (1809–26)
TS	Treasury Solicitor's Papers

Add MSS are in the BL. HO, PC and TS are in the PRO.

Editor's introduction

The London Corresponding Society (1792–99) was the most controversial and most famous of the reform societies in Great Britain during the 1790s. According to Burke, Pitt, Dundas and many other speakers in Parliament, the LCS consisted of wretches, vagabonds and evil-minded men who were inflaming the minds of the ignorant, secretly providing them with arms, seditiously plotting to destroy the government of king, Lords and Commons in order to replace the constitution with French anarchy. In short, the LCS was a monster to be destroyed, and eventually government did crush it.

But to contemporary admirers the LCS was 'a small society of citizens that at the conclusion of the Eighteenth century had the courage to resist the system of oppression adopted in this country'.[1] To a famous member, Francis Place, the LCS was 'the very best school for good teaching which probably ever existed' and 'a great moral cause of the improvement which has since taken place among the People'.[2] A generation after the suppression of the LCS, R. C. Fair connected it with the impending Reform Bill: 'That Society certainly can claim the glory of first organizing the moral power of the people in support of those principles of constitutional liberty which I trust are now approaching their consummation.'[3]

Besides connecting with the Reform Bill, the Corresponding Society touches on major movements and men of an earlier period. The American Revolution led the founder of the LCS, Thomas Hardy (no relation to the novelist), to adopt the principles on which he based the Society;[4] and in selecting the name Corresponding Society Hardy may well have had in mind the American committees of correspondence which replaced the established government in the colonies. The French Revolution provided the LCS with an immediate example of political reform, to which they frequently alluded. One of their first public acts was sending the French National Convention a congratulatory address and having it printed in the newspapers. They also advertised in the newspapers their approbation of anyone in Parliament who proposed acknowledging the new French regime. In imitation of the French, the members addressed each other as 'Citizen'. (The French in their turn were aware of the LCS and planned that a conquered Britain should have Thomas Hardy as minister of police and another prominent LCS member, John Thelwall, as one of the five members of an English *Directoire*.[5]

The Society attracted the attention of the American reformer Joel Barlow and of Thomas Paine, Barlow sending them copies of his works (including *A Letter to the National Convention of France*) and Paine offering to write their first address (unfortunately he did not have time). Paine's works were of special importance to the LCS. As soon as the Society learned that Paine had been indicted for *The Rights of Man*, they started a defence fund. In order to disseminate the *Age of Reason* among the divisions of the Society, a bookbinder was persuaded by leading LCS members to publish a cheap edition, or so alleged an ex-member.

Although most of the leading members were obscure men, John Thelwall was a well-known lecturer and poet and a close friend of Wordsworth and Coleridge; the 'Citizen Wordsworth' who contributed in 1794 to the support of families of arrested LCS members may have been the poet. Another poet, Lord Byron, later contributed £10 to the fund for the LCS member, Maurice Margarot, who had been transported to Botany Bay for activities as an LCS emissary. The famous Polish general and reformer Kosciuszko met LCS members and reported that LCS publications were being read in 'the closest dungeons of Russia'.[6]

This Society, whose influence extended even to the Tsar's prisons, was a reform organization composed chiefly of artisans, mechanics and small shopkeepers who were convinced that most of the misfortunes and

---

1 Letter, J. D. Collier to Thomas Hardy, 6 Sept. 1802, Add MSS 27817, fo. 91v.
2 Letter to George Rogers, 15 Jan. 1832, quoted by Norman E. Himes in his edn of Place's *Illustrations and Proofs of the Principle of Population* (1930), p. 315; Mary Thale (ed.), *Autobiography of Francis Place* (1972), p. 200.
3 Letter to Place, 9 March 1831, Add MSS 27808, fo. 319.
4 *Memoir of Thomas Hardy* (1832), pp. 8–9.

5 Simon Maccoby, *English Radicalism, 1782–1832*, vol. 2: *From Paine to Cobbett* (1955), p. 123.
6 See p. 434.

evils of the kingdom would disappear if parliamentary representatives were elected every year by all men over the age of 21 (except lunatics and criminals). Their goal and their slogan was 'Universal Suffrage and Annual Parliaments'. To accomplish this goal, which they described as a radical reform of Parliament, they believed it necessary first to educate people so they knew their political rights and then to have hundreds of thousands of these men throughout the kingdom call for parliamentary reform. Their educational aim was pursued within the Society by their reading and discussing political pamphlets (such as *The State of the Representation*) and outside the LCS by their publishing and sending out large quantities of their addresses and of tracts such as the seventeenth-century treatise on juries, *The Englishman's Right*. With dues of only a penny a week, the LCS attracted large numbers of men eager for personal improvement as well as political reform.

Interest in parliamentary reform was not new, for in the 1780s it had been urged by groups of educated and articulate men. In London these men formed the Society of Constitutional Information (1780–94), which in the early 1780s published short tracts explaining the principles of the 1688 constitution, the present abuses of it and the need for reform. In 1788 many of these men formed the London Revolution Society to celebrate the centenary of the 'Glorious Revolution' of 1688.

But by the end of the 1780s it appeared that parliamentary reform had come no nearer as a result of these publications, these societies and these meetings. A few hundred men of good principles throughout the land could not persuade the majority of the members of the House of Commons that they should jeopardize their comfortable ways by any change in the method of selecting representatives (in 1785 Pitt introduced a motion for parliamentary reform which was dismissed almost without debate). What might persuade Parliament was a demand from the people as a whole.

It was to create this demand that the London Corresponding Society and other societies of artisans and mechanics were formed. Of these societies, the LCS is the most important because it became the leader of the other societies, sending members to other cities to address reform-minded citizens and encourage them to form societies; providing newly formed groups with copies of the LCS regulations for their adoption; maintaining a correspondence with these societies and trying to stimu-

late them when they were lagging; and attempting to coordinate the activities of all the reform societies in sending petitions and addresses and in holding meetings. The dynamism which made the LCS assume and retain leadership of the popular societies also made them outlast the other reform groups of the 1790s.

These popular reform societies of 1791–9 were new phenomena and their members knew it. They saw themselves as 'the people' to be contrasted with 'the aristocrats' (i.e. men of property who held power in society). They saw themselves taking over where the well-meaning reformers of the 1780s had failed, leading the way to the restoration of what they believed to be the rights of Saxon times, of the Magna Carta, of the 1688 constitution. 'Would not all the evil be done away at once by the People assembled in Convention?' asked one reformer.[7] There was no precedent – not even among the seventeenth-century levellers – for shoemakers, tailors and plumbers organizing under the assumption that they – men without property – had a right to decide who should vote or how parliamentary seats should be allotted. A typical attitude was that of a judge who dismissed universal suffrage as 'a most ridiculous and absurd doctrine . . . nothing can be so absurd'.[8] What made larger numbers of men in London, Sheffield, Manchester and other cities suddenly discover in 1791 and 1792 that they had these rights was a group of causes, including the example of the American war, the reading of the pamphlets published by the Society for Constitutional Information, the 1788 celebrations of the English Revolution, the enthusiasm for the French Revolution, the reading of Paine's *Rights of Man* and attendance at or participation in debating societies.[9] Hardy attributed his decision to form the LCS to his rereading in November and December 1791 the political pamphlets which he had first read during the American war.

At the first meeting of the LCS in January

7 Letter, P. W. Frost of the Stockport Society of the Friends of Universal Peace and the Rights of Man to Hardy, 27 Sept. 1792, TS 11/965/3510A.
8 Lord Eskgrove at the trial of William Skirving, *A Complete Collection of State Trials*, comp. T. B. Howell, vol. 23 (1813), col. 597. Hereafter this work is cited as *ST*.
9 H. T. Dickinson also adds the influence of Godwin's notion of the natural rights of man and Bentham's utilitarian ethic (*Liberty and Property: Political Ideology in Eighteenth-Century Britain*, 1977, p. 246).

1792 nine men were present. Two weeks later twenty-four attended. By May the Society had grown so large that they organized themselves into nine divisions, each of which sent a delegate to a general committee meeting on Thursday evenings.[10] In June they extended their scope by asking the older, more prestigious Society for Constitutional Information to admit six LCS members. In October they persuaded five other reform societies to join them in sending the address of appreciation to the French National Convention. The Society continued to grow until late November when John Reeves, with government support, founded the Association for the Preservation of Liberty and Property against Republican and Levellers, and landlords were threatened with loss of licence if they allowed LCS divisions to meet at their houses.

In 1793 the direction of the French Revolution (execution of the king, England's declaration of war, dominance of the Jacobins, increasing use of the guillotine) made many Englishmen terrified of any group which seemed to support or imitate the French. During that year the LCS merely maintained their membership. They gained some notoriety by being condemned in Parliament when they presented a petition for parliamentary reform (as did many other societies). Public acquaintance with the LCS further i ːcreased in October when they held an outdoor meeting – their first – to choose delegates to a convention of reformers in Edinburgh. At this meeting, which attracted the attention of several hundred curious bystanders, they elected Maurice Margarot and Joseph Gerrald. These able but unfortunate men were arrested in Edinburgh early in December 1793, were convicted of sedition early the next year, and sentenced to fourteen years' transportation to New South Wales.

Faced with these savage punishments of their members, early in 1794 the LCS planned to hold a convention of delegates from all the reform societies in Great Britain. Before any convention was organized they held an outdoor meeting on 14 April 1794 at Chalk Farm which attracted large numbers of the committed and the curious. By this time government had at least four spies sending regular reports of LCS activity, as well as accounts of arming societies started by several LCS members. With the spy reports of a possible union of all reform societies, of a convention which might try to replace Parliament, of arming in Shef-

field and London, of plans to murder Pitt and the royal family, government arrested leading reformers throughout England and Scotland. These arrests started with that of Thomas Hardy at 6.00 a.m. on 12 May and continued for three weeks. Although some of the men arrested were released in a few days, others were imprisoned for six and seven months, the Habeas Corpus Act having been suspended. Hardy and twelve other men, members of the LCS or SCI (or both), were indicted for high treason.

Hardy, who was tried first, was acquitted on 5 November 1794, after a trial of unprecedented length – eight days. John Horne Tooke, a promoter of the SCI, was tried next and acquitted on 22 November. The last trial, which ended in acquittal on 5 December, was that of the poet John Thelwall, the LCS member who had been giving political lectures in aid of Margarot and Gerrald. (For the next forty-eight years on or near 5 November Hardy's acquittal was celebrated at dinners where toasts were drunk to the LCS. At the first dinner in 1795 800 attended; by the time of the last, in 1842, most of the members were dead, and another generation toasted the memory of this remarkable society.)

Understandably, the arrests and trials of 1794 frightened away many members; but by the middle of 1795 the Society began to increase, sometimes enrolling more than two hundred new members a week. During the year they held two public meetings which drew large crowds, one in St George's Fields, Southwark, at the end of June and the other at Copenhagen House in St Pancras Parish at the end of October. Although both meetings were peaceable, government anticipated violence and ordered out horse and foot guard, police officers and military forces from the Tower and the Savoy. On 29 October, a few days after the meeting at Copenhagen House, the window of the king's state carriage was broken (probably by a stone) as he was on his way to open Parliament, and the door of his plain carriage was opened or attempted as he was returning. These 'outrages', as they were called, were immediately blamed on the LCS, which was accused in Parliament and in the pro-government press of having inflamed the minds of the ignorant at the recent public meeting.

To repress the LCS and other such societies, two bills were introduced in Parliament on 6 and 10 November. (Many people believed tʌat the attack on the king had been arranged by government to provide a pretext for introducing repressive laws.) Despite two public

10 Because the members usually met in public houses, they were contemptuously labelled 'Pothouse Reformers'.

meetings organized by the LCS to oppose these bills and despite numerous petitions against them, the Treason and Sedition Bills – also known as the Two Acts – received the royal assent on 18 December 1795. Since the Sedition Act made it difficult and cumbersome to hold a public meeting of more than forty-nine persons, the LCS, with 73 divisions, were forced to reorganize. They divided London into four districts, each with a district committee to which every division in that district sent a delegate; each district committee then elected from their members delegates to the general committee. This extra layer of committees (which had little function) and the alarm stirred up throughout the country by Parliament and the pro-government press ended the growth and started the decline of the Society.

Other societies also shrivelled or died. In an attempt to keep alive the reform spirit in other cities, the LCS in February 1796 sent two delegates, John Binns and John Gale Jones, on trips to Portsmouth, Maidstone, Rochester and other cities in the south. They were so well received that on their return they were sent to Birmingham to invigorate reformers there. On 16 March, a few days after their arrival, they were arrested and charged with using seditious words. Months later, in separate trials, Jones was convicted but never sentenced, and Binns was acquitted.

These arrests, with the ensuing legal expenses, further drove the LCS downhill. In June 1796 the Society accelerated their decline by starting an unprofitable monthly periodical, *The Moral and Political Magazine of the London Corresponding Society*. To help pay for the impending trials of Binns and Jones, the LCS appealed to other societies and reformers, but much of the money they received from this subscription was spent on the magazine, which had been started to swell the fund it was draining. As the Society went deeper in debt, quarrels arose over the management of money. Moreover, the Society seemed to be doing nothing to promote parliamentary reform except publishing their magazine. Many members wanted the Society to be more active; others thought they should remain quiet and restrict themselves to political education. The activists prevailed, and in July 1797 a large outdoor meeting was held, or was attempted. After less than twenty minutes, the Riot Act was read and the crowds dispersed (under the new laws, failure to disperse within an hour of the reading of the Riot Act was punishable by death). The mounting debt, the objections to a general meeting – each caused some members to drop out.

Moreover, about 1797 a society committed to action was formed – the United Englishmen (also called United Britons and True Britons), modelled on the militant United Irishmen. These men, enrolled with an illegal oath, were intent on arming for revolution. Some members of the LCS left the Society to join the United Englishmen; some others belonged to both societies. Still other members, alarmed by the toleration of United Englishmen and United Irishmen in the LCS withdrew from the Society.[11]

In April 1798, when government encouraged volunteers to arm against a possible invasion by the French, one division of the LCS proposed that the Society should participate in this patriotic activity. At a meeting of the general committee on 19 April where the proposal was to be discussed, Bow Street officers entered and arrested fifteen men (a sixteenth escaped), including at least one former member who attended only to speak against the LCS arming. The previous evening thirteen men had been arrested at a meeting where the secretary of the LCS, who was also active in the United Englishmen, intended to administer the UE oath to members of his LCS division and their friends. During the next week others members and former members of the two societies were arrested.

With the Habeas Corpus Act again suspended, these men were imprisoned without charge, some of them for almost three years, until March 1801. Despite these mass arrests, a few groups of LCS members continued to meet during the rest of 1798 and early in 1799. The Society was officially banned by name in July 1799 in 'An Act for the more effectual suppression of societies established for seditious and treasonable purposes; and for better preventing treasonable and seditious practices'.

This society – which ended with such notoriety, which caused the Habeas Corpus Act to be suspended twice in four years (as opposed to twice in the previous fifty years), which drew the public wrath of such notables as Burke and Pitt – was intended for the least notable, the 'unrepresented', that is, men who

11 William Hamilton Reid, *The Rise and Dissolution of the Infidel Societies in this Metropolis* (1800), p. 109. The causes of the dissolution of the LCS, Reid stated, also include their espousal of deistic writings and principles, leading to the secession of many devout Christians; their alienation from wealthy liberals after the LCS refused to join the Whig Club; and the increase in the cost of provisions, which prevented the lower classes from going to the public houses where the LCS met.

did not own property or who otherwise were not wealthy enough to meet the qualifications for voting. These were men of lower classes than the members of the Society for Constitutional Information, as is indicated by the lowness of the LCS dues – a penny a week, as opposed to the SCI's guinea a year. By occupation they were, as Hardy said, tradesmen, mechanics and shopkeepers. Unfortunately, we know the employment of only 347 of the thousands who joined the LCS. The list of their occupations shows a predominance of artisans, with the three largest categories of members being shoemakers or workers in allied trades (43), weavers or men connected with weaving (27), and tailors and breechesmakers (24).[12] Of the most active members in the Society, about half were artisans (Ashley, Baxter, Binns, Hardy, Hodgson, Lemaitre, Place); the others include a clerk (Richter), a lecturer (Thelwall), a mechanic (Galloway), a merchant (Margarot) and a surgeon (Jones).

The spy Groves characterized the leading members, the men he encountered in the general committee, as a few 'who possess strong but unimproved faculties', others of a lower order who 'seem to possess no abilities' and 'the most numerous [who are] of the very lowest order of Society . . . filthy & ragged . . . wretched looking blackguards'. From Groves's description – and from Gillray's caricatures of LCS meetings – we might expect that most of the members were illiterate or barely literate. There is, in fact, very little evidence of illiteracy in the documents, which include vouchers and motions written by many obscure members (admittedly, men of limited literacy were not likely to become division secretaries). The spelling and syntax in LCS documents indicate that the authors had at least a minimum education.

From the memoirs of Place, Hardy, Thelwall and John Binns we know that the sons of ambitious tradesmen attended school until thirteen or fourteen; but the learning was usually restricted to reading, writing and simple arithmetic, and often the only book the students used was the Bible.[13] Thelwall and Binns, from a slightly higher class in society, did study books other than the Bible, but even their superior education was deficient. Thelwall's widow described his education as 'conducted upon that narrow scale which, at that time . . . was regarded as alone consistent with the training of a youth designed for the ordinary occupations of trade'.[14] The intellectual interests which some members brought to the LCS may owe something to the occasional teacher, but not to the system of schooling designed for them. Thelwall himself often used to say that 'it was an established maxim among tradesmen of the first class, that if a youth were ever seen studying any other book than his father's ledger, he must be looked upon as a ruined man'.[15]

The leading LCS members were or had been youths studying books other than ledgers (and government would have agreed that they were ruined). In Hardy (1752–1832) and Ashley (c. 1762?–1829) – each a secretary of the

12 There is some overlapping of occupations in the list inasmuch as one occupation may be named in two ways. Sometimes one man was listed with two occupations, the total, therefore, exceeds 347: accountant (1), apothecary (2), artist (1), attorney (8), auctioneer (1), baker (8), barrister (4), bedsteadmaker (2), bookbinder (3), bookseller (10), bootcloser (1), bootmaker (1), bracemaker (1), breechesmaker (3), bricklayer (5), broker (1), butcher (3), cabinetmaker (7), calenderer (1), carpenter (7), carver (3), casemaker (1), tallow chandler (2), wax chandler (1), cheesemonger (2), chemist (1), china burner (1), china man (1), clerk (11), clock case maker (1), clock maker (4), coachmaker (1), gentleman's coachman (1), coffee-room keeper (1), print colourer (2), compositor (1), cook-shop keeper (1), cooper (1), cordwainer (8), currier (2), dancing master (1), dyer (3), enameller (1), engraver (1), fish-hook maker (1), founder (1), framework knitter (3), master gardener (1), gentleman (5), gilder (1), glass cutter (1), glazier (2), glover (1), grinder (1), grocer (2), greengrocer (1), gun maker (4), hackney man (1), hairdresser (8), hatter (5), hosier (2), ironmonger (2), jack maker (1), japanner (1), jewel case maker (1), labourer (1), lace and fringe maker (3), leather seller (1), lecturer (1), linen draper (6), locksmith (1), mathematical instrument maker (2), mattress maker (1), mercer (3), merchant (6), miller (1), musician (2), muslin dresser (1), military officer (2), painter (1), botanic painter (1), paper hanger (2), perfumer (4), peruke maker (1), physician (3), plasterer (1), plumber (2), printer (12), publican (5), pump maker (1), rag dealer (1), ribbon dresser (2), ribbon weaver (2), saddler (1), sailmaker (1), saloop shopkeeper (1), scale maker (1), scowerer (1), gentleman's servant (2), shoemaker (23), shopman (3), shorthand writer (1), silversmith (5), smith (6), solicitor (1), stationer (2), staymaker (3), gentleman's steward (1), stocking weaver (2), stone mason (1), surgeon (5), tailor (21), tin man (1), tin plate worker (1), tobacconist (1), truss maker (1), turner (1), undertaker (1), upholsterer (1), victualler (1), warehouseman (3), watch case maker (2), watch face painter (1), watch spring maker (1), watch maker (10), watchman (1), weaver (12), whitesmith (1), wire worker (1).

13 Place, *Autobiography*, pp. 40-1.

14 Mrs Thelwall, *The Life of John Thelwall* (1837), p. 9.

15 ibid., p. 9.

Society for two years – we see the intellectual interests often attributed to shoemakers at that time. Before starting the LCS, Hardy used his leisure (no doubt forced upon him when he opened his own shop after seven years as foreman to another shoemaker) to re-read the short political tracts published in the 1780s by the SCI. After reading an account of the unjust representation in Parliament, he formed the plan of a society for 'All classes and descriptions of men'. At the second meeting Hardy read the members extracts from Cartwright's *Give Us Our Rights*. His intellectual interests were sufficiently well-known that friends (i.e. better educated men) often sent him political papers to be distributed among the members.[16] Less is known of John Ashley's intellectual background. Place characterized him as 'a serious thinking man' whose customers allowed him to use their 'considerable collections of books'.[17]

Place himself (1771–1854) left an account of the reading he did before joining the LCS. His intellectual interests appeared as early as thirteen when he borrowed a sex manual in order to compare its information with the accounts of Christ's conception recorded in Matthew and Luke (with the result that 'reason was too strong for superstition').[18] While he was an apprentice breechesmaker Place was reading histories of Greece and Rome, translations of classical authors and the essays of Hume. As a newly married journeyman, he borrowed from his landlady Blackstone's *Commentaries* and other law books. Reading Godwin's *Political Justice* in 1793 determined him to rise from journeyman to a state of independence. This determination was made at a time when no master would hire him because he had managed a breechesmakers' strike. During the next eight months of unemployment Place read Adam Smith and Locke, reread Hume two or three times and taught himself algebra and geometry. On 28 April 1794 Place came upon part one of Paine's *Age of Reason*. 'I read it with delight', he declared.[19] He encountered the book in the room of his landlord, a cabinetmaker and LCS member. '[T]he quantity and kind of books I found in his room made me desirous of his acquaintance.' That acquaintance led Place a few weeks later to join the LCS.

In the Society Place attended the Sunday night reading and discussion meetings. In addition he and two other LCS members hired an emigrant priest to teach them French. Through the LCS Place became acquainted with John Binns, who used to come to Place's room and read aloud while Place worked. 'Thus we both obtained knowledge at the same time.'[20]

John Binns (1772–1860), like Place, had an interest in serious reading which continued after he left school at age fourteen to be apprenticed to a soap-boiler. While still at school (he recalled his formal education as defective in not providing him with a systematic course of study), he used to read aloud to his mother, who corrected his pronunciation and explained difficult passages. These readings included the *Spectator, Rambler*, Hume's *History of England* and Rollin's *History of the World*. From boyhood until well after the LCS years, he always read after going to bed.[21] His intellectual inclinations may also be presumed by his conducting a debating room with two other LCS members, John Gale Jones and William Wright.

John Baxter, a silversmith, must also have had a background of intellectual interests and training. In 1795 he published a lecture he had given to a splinter LCS group[22] and in 1796 he wrote and published *A New and Impartial History of England from the most Early Period of Genuine Historical Evidence to the Present Important and Alarming Crisis*.[23]

John Thelwall (1764–1834), who helped support the LCS delegates to Edinburgh by giving lectures and who was often the principal speaker at public meetings of the Society, is another self-educated leader with a background as shopkeeper and artisan. After two years behind the counter in his family's silk shop (starting at thirteen), one and a half more as an apprentice tailor, three and a half as a clerk to an attorney, at twenty-two he turned for a living to literature, which had long been his chief interest. He was also active in debating societies, and before joining the LCS in late 1793 he was a member of a reform society in Southwark, the Friends of the People. In 1790 he volunteered to work for the candidacy of John Horne Tooke, a stranger who soon became his mentor and financial supporter.[24]

16 Add MSS 27814, fo. 50.
17 *Autobiography*, p. 143.
18 ibid., pp. 45–6.   19 ibid., p. 126.

20 ibid., pp. 143–4.
21 *Recollections of the Life of John Binns* (1854), pp. 18–19, 23–4.
22 *Resistance to Oppression, the Constitutional Right of Britons*.
23 An advertisement for the first instalment (of 50) indicated that Baxter was '[a]ssisted by Several Gentlemen, distinguished friends to Liberty and a Parliamentary Reform' (*Cambridge Intelligencer*, 13 Feb. 1796, p. 1.
24 *Public Characters of 1800–1* (1802), p. 215;

Tooke (1736–1812), who was not a member, plays a curious role in the LCS, a role which raises the issue of leadership by educated men of higher class. The view of government was that Tooke and other men of position and property were manipulating the low and ignorant LCS members. The LCS, of course, prided themselves on their being 'the people', self-educated and self-determining. As William Skirving explained in contrasting the popular reform societies such as the LCS with the societies composed of men from the higher classes: '[W]e are the People themselves, and we are the first to shew that the People can both judge and resolve, if undirected by Faction, with both Wisdom and Moderation.'[25] The shadowy presence of Tooke in the first years of the LCS hints that 'the people' did have direction from men of higher status.

Tooke was a well-educated (Eton, Cambridge) reformer who has been active in politics since the 1760s, had published reform pamphlets in the 1780s and had been an energetic member of the SCI. In his treason trial and in Hardy's, the government charged that he organized and directed the LCS. The chief evidence for this charge was the draft of the first LCS address and resolutions which contained minor corrections in Tooke's hand and the signature 'Thomas Hardy' also in Tooke's hand. After his acquittal Tooke, in a speech to the court, minimized his connection with the LCS. After asserting that he did not know a single member of the country reform societies, he added:

nor should I have known any thing whatever of the London Societies, but from the circumstance of my having been Candidate for the City of Westminster. In that character I visited them, and, to take care of a very honest, though not a very able man, I perused such papers as he brought me, and, when I found that they were intended for publication, struck out what appeared to me to be libellous, and corrected what appeared to be bad English – a trifling favour which I never refused to any person who applied to me.[26]

What was trifling assistance in Tooke's opinion was much greater when seen from the LCS's perspective.

Tooke's name first appears in LCS documents in a letter received on 19 March 1792 from the Sheffield Society for Constitutional Information, recommending that the LCS 'enter into connexion with the Men in the Society for Constitutional Information in London, of whom Mr Horne Tooke is one'. Tooke, the letter continued, 'will be the true Friend & advocate in our Cause, consistent with his principles hitherto manifested both in Public and private'.[27] On 27 March, eight days after the Sheffield letter reached the LCS, Hardy wrote Tooke a letter which revealed that some LCS members had already entered into connection with Tooke and discussed with him the address which was to be the first printed manifesto of the LCS:

Sir I am sorry to inform you of our defeat last night at the Society. The address was not r025ieved . . . Those of us whom you saw yesterday morning means to bring it [another draft] forward in the society . . . I am sorry to trouble you but I am well assured it is a business you highly approve of.[28]

Hardy's explanation of Tooke's handwriting on the LCS address and resolutions supports the hypothesis that the LCS looked to the better-educated reformers for support: the LCS committee charged with drafting the address and resolutions ordered Hardy to send a copy of the document to the SCI for its approbation before sending it to the printer. Expecting an answer, Hardy did not sign the paper. After the SCI meeting at which the members approved the address and resolutions, Tooke, without consulting the LCS, signed the name 'Thomas Hardy' and gave the paper to the proprietor of the Argus to publish.[29]

The LCS turned to Tooke again in September 1792 when Margarot conceived the plan of uniting several societies to send an address to the French National Convention. On 15 September Margarot wrote, submitting his plan 'to Mr Horne Tooke's consideration',

Register of the Times, vol. 2, pp. 353–8; John Watkins and Frederick Shoberl, A Biographical Dictionary of the Living Authors of Great Britain and Ireland (1816); Mrs Thelwall, The Life of John Thelwall, pp. 9, 14, 16, 23, 24, 33, 74–6.
25 Letter to Hardy, 25 May 1793, TS 11/956/3501.
26 Quoted in Morning Chronicle, 24 Nov. 1794, p. 4 (hereafter MC). Tooke was inaccurate in implying that he encountered the LCS in his campaign for

a seat in Parliament. That election took place in Nov. 1790, more than a year before the founding of the LCS.
27 TS 11/965/3510A.
28 Add MSS 27811, fo. 6.
29 Letter, Hardy to Place, 7 July 1831, in Report from Committee of Secrecy, 1794, in BL C.61. b.16.

and the next day Hardy wrote to Tooke, asking his 'opinion of that proposition he [Margarot] has submitted to your judgment'.[30] Tooke's judgment must have been sought again in 1794, for the resolutions read and affirmed at the general meeting of the whole Society on 20 January were in his handwriting,[31] and he reputedly helped write the address voted on at that meeting. He was also said to be assisting in the composition of an address for the large outdoor meeting on 14 April.

In his history of the LCS Hardy acknowledged the role of men like Tooke: 'Much political information I frequently received from gentlemen experienced in the cause of Reform which was communicated to the Society and received with great approbation, and which was of much use in regulating their conduct as a Society – Inexperienced people are very liable to be led into error, and injudicious conduct, by designing men.'[32]

Besides assistance from outsiders 'experienced in the cause of reform' the LCS received direction from well-educated members who were not perceived by their fellow members as belonging to a higher class. Maurice Margarot (1745–1815) was such a leader. He was an early member of the Society, a delegate until his departure for the Edinburgh convention, a member of the committee to form a constitution, the author of LCS addresses and its chairman. Next to Hardy he was the most active member during the first two years of the Society. He seems to fit preeminently into Skirving's description of the people resolving wisely. No reference to him by the LCS, either official or unofficial, gives evidence that he was anything except *primus inter pares*. Yet at his trial, the prosecutor emphasized his superior status: 'Is it not an aggravation of this man's offence, that with superior education, intellect, and information, he encouraged a set of low, ignorant mechanics in their criminal courses.'[33] This appraisal of his status is supported by his background. Margarot had received a classical education in England and had finished his studies in Geneva. His father's house in Castle Street, Leicester Square, had been a meeting place for Wilkes, Townsend, Sawbridge, Beckford and other reformers whom Margarot would have known. Apparently, then, Margarot looked like an equal to insiders and a superior to outsiders.

Joseph Gerrald (1763–96) presents the same double picture. What records there are of him in the LCS before the Edinburgh convention give no indication he might be considered different from the rest of the members. After his conviction, while in Newgate, he seems to have associated as an equal with such visiting LCS members as Green the perfumer. Yet he had been educated under the famous Dr Samuel Parr in his academy at Stanmore, had been admitted to the bar in Pennsylvania and had written a reform pamphlet (*A Convention the Only Means of Saving Us from Ruin*). His defence speech at his trial is the most impressive of all the speeches at the state trials of 1794. To outsiders he seemed superior to other LCS members. William Beloe, who knew him, lamented, 'His principles gave way, either to the contagion of the low and mean herd, with whom he finally associated, or were made subservient to his political schemes and projects.'[34]

As the presence of educated men like Margarot and Gerrald shows, the LCS was not limited to artisans, mechanics and shopkeepers familiar only with other journeymen, small masters and shopkeepers. Even before the LCS was started some of the men who became prominent members had connections with well-known men. After the Society was founded, the artisan members often met and associated with men of established reputation.

Before starting the LCS Hardy knew Thomas Brand Hollis, a wealthy man who had been active in the SCI since 1780, a member of the Revolution Society of 1788 and a member of the elite Friends of the People in 1792. He was also acquainted with O. Equiano, the African abolitionist who lectured and wrote under the name of Gustavus Vasa. Hardy described himself as being 'very intimate' with Col. Smith, the private secretary to John Adams when he was US Ambassador.[35] A more notorious if less admirable connection was with Lord George Gordon, with whom Hardy was also 'very intimate', although he opposed Gordon's 'wild schemes'.[36] During 1792 Hardy's activities in the LCS made him acquainted with Major John Cartwright, the founder of the SCI; with John Horne Tooke; and with Daniel Stuart, the secretary of the Friends of the People. Stuart began to call on Hardy 'once, twice or more times in a week'.[37] Thelwall, as men-

30 TS 11/951/3495.   31 *ST* vol. 25, col. 511.
32 Add MSS 27814, fo. 12.
33 *ST* vol. 23, col. 696.

34 *Sexagenarian* (1817), vol. 1, pp. 261–2.
35 On seeing the first LCS address, Smith commented, with near-prophecy, 'Hardy, the Government will hang you' (*Memoir*, p. 57n).
36 ibid., p. 8.   37 *ST* vol. 24, cols. 995–6.

tioned above, had been a protégé of Tooke since 1790, dined at his house every two or three weeks, submitted everything he published for Tooke's sanction and regarded Tooke as 'his intellectual and political father'.[38] John Richter, another LCS member indicted for treason, was friendly with the rising barrister Felix Vaughan, who wrote him many letters from France and Geneva in 1790 and 1791. From these letters, it appears that Richter also knew Tooke.[39] Tooke often invited LCS members (and other reformers) to Sunday supper at his house in Wimbledon. It was here that Hardy met Major Cartwright.[40] Paul Thomas Lemaitre, another leading LCS member, described himself as a frequent guest at Tooke's table. Place refused to attend. 'I never believed that he was an honest man . . . I was several times at his desire invited to his house but I never accepted the invitation.'[41]

Although he rebuffed Tooke, Place associated with other educated men he met through the LCS, and they would come to his home and converse while he worked. Thomas Holcroft, the author; Col. Edward Despard, former administrator of the Yucatan; William Frend, fellow of Christ's College, Cambridge; Col. William Bosville, a Harrow-educated, rich Whig – were among the 'remarkable men' who spent their time up in the single room where Place sewed stuff breeches and Mrs Place took care of their children.[42]

From the evidence of these members, it appears that there was considerable interpenetration of LCS members and what Place calls 'men of superior talents'. It was taking place before the LCS was formed, but the Society may have accelerated the pace by bringing together aspiring artisans and reform-minded men of education.

Such aspiring artisans, mechanics and shopkeepers formed a small percentage of the thousands who joined the Society between 1792 and 1799. The exact number who did join has been a matter of much conjecture, for there are no accurate records. The members who estimated the size of the Society tended to be more wishful than realistic. In

1794 John Martin told his cellmate in Newgate that there were 28,000 members ready to take up arms.[43] In reality there were probably fewer than 1000 active members at that time; and rather than being ready to take up arms, three-quarters of them were about to desert the LCS. At the forty-third anniversary of Hardy's acquittal, Alexander Galloway made the incredible assertion that there had once been 80,000 members.[44]

It is difficult to establish realistic figures on membership. Although the divisions submitted lists of members in 1792 and 1794, only a few of these lists survive; and they show such variations in size that no useful total could be projected by averaging. These lists do indicate that some men came, paid once, were entered on the membership list, but never returned. The July 1792 list for Division 8 contains 52 names and a statement by the secretary that there were 37 members. Of these 37, only eleven voted on an important proposition. Some men attended without paying dues (although the constitution provided for their expulsion); some paid dues but attended irregularly; some paid more than a penny a week; some attended more than one division meeting a week (about half of the men at meetings of Division 2 from June to October 1794 did not belong to that division). Accordingly, numbers of men at division meetings and records of dues collected do not indicate accurately the number of members. Nor do the numbers of votes cast show the size of the membership, for the number of members present at the meetings is regularly larger than the number of votes cast. For example, in the week of 3 September 1795, when 1841 members were reported present, only 869 votes were tallied on a question. Some divisions reported the number of members present, but not the number of votes cast; other divisions probably counted the members at the end of the meeting, thus including men who arrived after the votes were taken.

Imperfect as the evidence is, it does show great fluctuations in the size of the Society. Before the arrest of the delegates and the consequent withering of the Society, the lowest points were the months after Hardy's arrest (when only 241 paid for membership) and the early months of 1798. The zenith was in

38 Tooke's testimony at his trial, cited in *MC* 4 Dec. 1794, p. 4; Mrs Thelwall, *Life of John Thelwall*, p. 76.
39 TS 11/953/3497.
40 *Life and Correspondence of Major John Cartwright* (1826), vol. 2, p. 290n.
41 Add MSS 27850, fo. 107.
42 Add MSS 35145, fos. 28-9.

43 Information of Evan Evans, 11 Sept. 1794, TS 11/958/3503.
44 Unidentified newspaper cutting in Add MSS 27817, fo. 164. In 1797 Galloway described a meeting of no more than 20,000 as having been attended by 150,000.

the autumn of 1795 when the weekly attendance was over 1500 and was once reported
to be 3576.[45] For each year I estimate that
the Society had the following maximum number of active (i.e. paid-up) members:

1792:	650[46]
1793:	650
1794	
Jan.–June:	800
July–Dec.:	250
1795	
Jan.–June:	300
July–Dec.:	3000
1796	
Jan.–June:	1500–2000
July–Dec.:	1000
1797:	600
1798:	400

Before the size of the Society increased beyond the confines of a single room – that is,
for their first eight or ten weeks – the members
met on Monday nights at The Bell public
house in Exeter Street. By the end of April
1792 they were too numerous for one room,
and they separated into nine divisions, each of
which met weekly on any night except Thursday or Sunday. For the next six years of their
existence the Society continued to be organized into divisions, each of which sent a
representative to a general committee meeting
on Thursday nights. The division was supposed to consist of thirty members; when it
grew to forty-six, a new division was to be
formed from the surplus sixteen.[47] In
practice some of the divisions were much
larger than thirty or forty-six. Division 29, in
February 1794, had a membership list of 170,
with 60 paid up. Since 70 of the defaulters
were only one quarter in arrears, some of
them must also have been active members. We
may assume that this division had about 100
committed members. Division 2, Hardy's
division, was even larger.

The division meetings began at 8.00 p.m.

45 I cannot believe all these men were paying members. Consternation over the impending Treason
   and Sedition Acts may have brought many secessionists to these meetings.
46 A spy reported that 350 joined during the week
   of 24 Nov.; and during a previous week spies
   counted about 680 men at division meetings. But
   from Michaelmas 1792 to Jan. 1793 the LCS collected £34 11s 9d; if dues accounted for all of
   this, there were 639 members.
47 A constitution in effect briefly in 1795 raised the
   size of the divisions to sixty.

First came the admission of new members,
each of whom was recommended by two
members who vouched for the 'Civism and
Morals' of the prospective members. (This
rule was not always observed carefully, and
spies had no difficulty gaining entry.) Before
admission the new member had to answer
correctly three questions about the need for
parliamentary reform and his willingness to
work for it. On his admission the new member
paid dues for the ensuing quarter or month,
depending on which constitution was in force.
He then received a ticket of admission, which
entitled him to attend any division (but to
vote only in his own).

After new members had been admitted, the
delegate reported the proceedings of the previous meeting of the general committee of
delegates. The division then voted on questions which had been referred by the general
committee to the whole membership of the
LCS. These referred questions dealt with such
matters as the election of six members to
affiliate with the SCI, the desirability of holding a general meeting, of admitting apprentices
as members and of electing a chairman of the
general committee quarterly instead of weekly.
Most of these questions originated in the divisions and were brought to the general committee by the delegate. A new motion submitted by a division and read at the general
committee might lead to other divisions (which
learned of it from their delegate) sending
motions supporting or contradicting the first.
Such a flurry of motions for and against a
proposal was likely to occur when a division
proposed an outdoor meeting.

Four times a year the division elected one
of their members to be the delegate to the
weekly meetings of the general committee.
After 1793 they also elected a subdelegate,
who represented the division when the delegate was unable to attend the general committee. Both these representatives were elected
by secret ballot, the names of those eligible
being read at the end of one meeting and the
ballots collected at the next. Though it was
recommended that the same men not serve
for successive quarters, the delegates tended
to be re-elected. Francis Place, for example,
became a delegate soon after joining in June
1794 and was re-elected regularly until he
resigned in March 1797. Every quarter the
division also elected a secretary, who kept
lists of the members, wrote vouchers certifying the election of delegate and subdelegate,
drew up motions to be presented to the
general committee by the delegate, collected
and recorded the dues, gave the delegate the

money for the general commitee (and presumably paid the rent for the meeting room, which was not to exceed 1s 6d per week), and even, in later years, voted in the general committee if both delegate and subdelegate were absent. From mid-1794 on, each division also elected tything men, whose duties were to tell their assigned members if the place of meeting was changed, to call on members whose dues were in arrears and to notify their tything of any last-minute changes in plans for a general meeting.

Besides attending to their official business, the division members often listened to the reading of a reform pamphlet or a newspaper account. The trial of Thomas Walker at Manchester was read from the *Courier*. 'Fast Day at Sheffield', the parliamentary speeches of Stanhope and newspaper reports of French victories were also among the readings. Thelwall sent the general committee twelve copies of his book *The Rights of Nature, Against the Usurpations of Establishments* (1796) with the recommendation 'that twelve readers be appointed by the Committee to read them to the respective divisions, & that the books be of course given to the readers as a trifling compliment for their trouble'.[48] It is unlikely that any division had time for such a long reading (94 pp.), inasmuch as the division meetings were scheduled to end at 10 p.m. Often there must have been no time for readings. The constitution adopted in 1795 stipulated that the readings take place after the meeting 'if there is time'. A constitution proposed but not adopted in 1794 set the first hour of the meeting (8–9 p.m.) for reading – probably an indication that then as now members did not arrive at meetings on time.

Two other activities at division meetings are mentioned in spy reports: the selling of political broadsides and pamphlets or books such as *The Guillotine* or *The Rights of Man* and the singing of reform songs, which the spies always characterized as seditious. A former member maintained that deistical books were sold in all the divisions. It is not possible to determine whether these activities were considered part of the division meeting or private amusements and enterprises after the official meeting.

The general committee, originally called the committee of delegates, consisted of one representative from each division. Their function was to coordinate the activities of the divisions, that is, to provide a centre, and to elect the officers of the Society. Every Thurs-

day they met (at first in a public house, then in a rented room) at 8.00 or 8.30 p.m. and conducted their business sometimes until 3.00 or 3.30 a.m., although the constitutions stipulated that the meetings end at 11.00 or 12.00.

At the beginning of the meeting each delegate reported the numbers of new members and of members present in his division. Then deputies were assigned to visit the unrepresented divisions. Large divisions applied to subdivide, and experienced members were appointed to show the new division how to conduct their meetings. Next, letters to the Society were read, and replies (drafted by a designee) were approved, as were any publications issued in the name of the LCS. If a question had been referred to the whole Society, the delegates then reported the votes of their divisions. After that, motions from the divisions were read. Finally, the secretary and treasurer announced the totals of new and present members and the amount of money taken in.

The executive committee was formed early in 1794 as a committee of secrecy, in part to prevent spies from being able to name the author of any letter or address issued by the Society. The notion of secrecy was immediately attacked, and the committee became known as the correspondence committee and then the executive committee. It consisted of six members whose principal duty was to reply to letters and to write any notices, addresses or petitions sent out in the name of the LCS. To prevent this committee from dominating the general committee and virtually replacing it as the decision-making body, the members were not allowed to speak at meetings of the general committee. The members of the executive committee must have given much of their spare time to LCS work, for the committee met two or three times a week. In addition, since most of the members were also delegates, they attended the general committee meeting on Thursday and their division meeting on another night. Not surprisingly, meetings of the executive committee were sometimes cancelled for lack of a quorum, and there were unscheduled midquarter elections to replace a resigning member.

Still other LCS meetings, and those of great importance, were the Sunday night reading and discussion sessions and debate meetings. Neither the minutes, the correspondence, nor the constitutions describe this area of LCS activity; but to Place these sessions were as valuable as the official meetings

48 Letter, 15 Dec. 1796, Add MSS 27815, fos. 142, 143v.

in educating the members. 'The discussions in the divisions, in the sunday evening readings, and in the small debating meetings, opened to them views which they had never before taken. They were compelled by these discussions to find reasons for their opinions and to tolerate others.'[49] Place recalled that these meetings, which were held at the homes of members who could accommodate a number of persons, followed a pattern: the chairman (a different man each Sunday) read aloud a chapter of a book. During the ensuing week, the book was passed around for the men to read at home. The next Sunday the chairman read the chapter again, pausing three times for comments. No one was to speak more than once during the reading, and anyone who had not spoken during the first two pauses was expected to speak at the end. After that there was a general discussion during which no one could speak on a subject a second time until everyone who wished had spoken once. '[T]hese were very important meetings and the best results to the parties followed.'[50]

At all LCS meetings certain rules of decorum were enforced. No one 'in liquor' was admitted, and habitual drunkenness was cause for expulsion from the Society. The members had to remove their hats. When a man spoke he had to stand and address the chairman. No one could speak a second time until everyone who wished had spoken once; and no one could speak more than twice to a question. The duties of the chairman, as presented in the various constitutions, included making sure that everyone was seated and not walking around the room, that no member was interrupted when speaking (unless he wandered from the question), and that no one uttered intemperate aspersions or used seditious language.

These regulations, which seem hardly noteworthy, must have been bred of experiences at the meetings. In July 1793 Hardy wrote to a correspondent that it had become necessary to introduce some of these rules. In the constitution proposed in February 1794 noisy and contentious behaviour was reprobated so often that there must have been a tendency toward unruliness. According to this constitution, '[i]t is the duty of every member to study concord, and for that purpose to moderate his own passions, particularly his personal attachments and aversions'. When voting, a member should show one hand. 'The practice of shewing both hands, or of calling all! all! or other such exclamations are [sic]

tumultuous, indecent, and utterly unwarrantable.' Even approbation should be expressed silently (by holding up a hand), for '[a]ll noise is interruption'. As for disapproval, '[t]o attribute the conduct or opinion of any member to factious combination, or other improper motive, is disorderly, as are also all invectives and declamatory remarks'. The section headed 'Order' ends with the warning, 'A noisy disposition is seldom a sign of courage, and extreme zeal, is often a cloak of treachery.' Besides rules to restrain noisiness, this constitution proposed a regulation to curb verbosity: No one was to speak more than ten minutes at one time. Lest anyone forget this restriction, '[o]ver the seat of the President in each meeting of this Society, shall be suspended a label with these words, BEWARE OF ORATORS'.[51]

Place believed that the discipline and self-respect instilled in the members changed the direction of many lives: 'The moral effects of the Society were considerable. It induced men to read books, instead of wasting their time in public houses, it taught them to respect themselves. . . . It gave a new stimulus to an immense number of men who had been but in too many instances incapable of any but the grossest pursuits.'[52]

The orderly functioning of the Society – indeed their remarkable continuance for over six years – owed much to the members' adherence to rules of procedure. The first of these sets of rules, or the first constitution, was drawn up by Hardy before there were twenty members – perhaps before there were any. After a brief preamble (150 words) on the unequal representation in Parliament, this rough draft then lists eight rules and resolutions, most of them derived from the rules and practices of the SCI. These eight rules institute 'The Corasponding Society of the unrepresented part of the people of Great Briton &c.', a society which is to be 'unlimited in its numbers'. Its members are to pay 'at least one penny towards its expence' weekly. '[A]s soon as twenty members are associated a General meeting shall be called when all the several laws or regulations already agreed to shall be read over and confirmed alterd or annulled and at the meeting there shall be elected a president, Treasurer, and Secretary.'

51 The revised version of this constitution, presented in May 1794, omitted all these strictures. Possibly their inclusion was seen as giving evidence to their enemies that the LCS did consist of men not fit to participate in the government of the country.

52 *Autobiography*, pp. 198–9.

An elected committee is to correspond with similar societies in Great Britain. A new member must be proposed by one member and seconded by another. The names and addresses of members are to be recorded, as are 'all proceedings of the Society and its committee'. Finally, no one under age twenty may be a member nor anyone 'who has not resided in this country for one year'.

These rules differ from those of the SCI in the membership consisting of the unrepresented people, consequently in the lowness of the dues, and in the requirements of age and residency in Great Britain. These three regulations reflect the unique character of the LCS with its members – many of them young – drawn largely from what were called 'the lower orders'.

A slightly altered version of this document was written about March 1792. But almost as soon as they were agreed upon these eight rules were inadequate, for they made no provisions for organizing divisions, electing delegates and conducting meetings. Early in May, a month after the divisions and general committee were established, a committee was elected to write a new constitution. The resulting ten rules – which remained the official constitution of the LCS until 1795 – specify that a new member be proposed by two members and that he answer correctly three questions on parliamentary reform; that the divisions consist of between twenty and forty members who meet weekly on any evening except Thursday; that each member pay one penny per week; that the delegate give this money to the treasurer for postage, printing and stationery; that the delegates, elected quarterly, meet every Thursday (two-thirds of them constituting a quorum) to communicate the wishes of their divisions and to authorize answers to correspondence needing immediate attention; and that the delegates report these transactions to their divisions.

Further regulations were added as needed in 1792 and 1793. Four rules introduced in February 1793 were necessitated by a temporary slackening in attendance at the general committee (five delegates to constitute a quorum, a list to be made of absent delegates and their divisions to be notified, the meeting to open at 8.00). The need for a new constitution and the difficulties of producing it are indicated by the appointment in 1793 of three successive committees of constitution, in March, in July and again in October. The last of these committees published a constitution in February 1794, *The Report of the Committee of Constitution of the London*

Corresponding Society, containing 218 numbered items. The provision for two new committees, a select committee and a council, reflects the difficulty of dealing with the business of the Society. In 1792 and 1793 most of the correspondence from other societies was answered by Hardy or Margarot, financial records were kept by Hardy, and addresses, petitions and other publications were drafted by an appointed individual or a temporary committee. The proposed select committee, a large body containing a minimum of half the number of delegates and a maximum of the same number as there were delegates, were to be in charge of prospective publications of the Society. The proposed council, consisting of a treasurer, a secretary and not less than four assistant secretaries, were to audit financial records, record laws and answer letters.

The final section of this constitution reflects a problem the Society faced in July 1793 and evidently expected to face again – the charge that a member was a government spy. This section set forth seventeen steps to be followed in the accusation and trial of a member alleged to be 'unworthy'.

This constitution was not accepted; on the contrary it gave rise to acrimonious discussions in both the general committee and some divisions. The spy Groves explained to government the basis of the objections to this proposed constitution:

> The Report of that Commee & the Form of Government recommended gave rise to great Jealousies & Animosities, as founded on principles incompatible with that Liberty which the Society was seeking for in the National System of Governmt. and as investing Powers & creating Offices & Officers among themselves which would infallibly render the Division a Cypher, and the whole management & Controul be placed in the hands of a few, & thereby their Government be Monarchical or something worse.'[53]

A new committee, again consisting of one member from each division, was appointed to revise this constitution. By 21 April 1794 their version, containing only 77 numbered points and subpoints, was printed as *Report of the Committee Appointed to Revise and Abridge a Former Report of the Constitution of the London Corresponding Society*. In place of the two new levels of officialdom proposed in February (the council and the special committee), this constitution would

53 TS 11/965/3510.

have a four-member committee of correspondence, charged only to answer letters, and three undersecretaries, who would see that the decisions of the general committee were carried out.

This constitution was discussed in the divisions at the end of April and the beginning of May. Consideration of it was dropped after the arrest of Hardy and other members, but at the end of June the general committee voted to adopt it. Several divisions promptly protested against the general committee's 'cramming' it down their throats. The general committee then rescinded their vote, and the Society continued to function according to the 1792 constitution.

With the revelation at Hardy's trial that delegates and even a member of the committee of correspondence were spies, the LCS felt the need for stricter rules on admitting prospective members. At the end of 1794 or beginning of 1795 Joseph Burks proposed six such rules to the general committee. John Bone objected to the wording of these rules and offered to draw up some rules by the next meeting. To the committee's astonishment he brought a whole new constitution (47 articles then; 45 as printed). The general committee must have felt a great need to have a new constitution, for that night they discussed sixteen of the articles, and the next week between midnight and 2.00 a.m. they finished the discussion, having locked the door to prevent delegates from leaving. The divisions were persuaded to accept this constitution without detailed discussion. But quarrels over the method of presenting the constitution to the Society led three divisions to secede and form two new societies.

This constitution, adopted about March 1795, is similar to that proposed in May 1794. Every quarter the general committee elected a secretary (who also acted as treasurer) and an assistant secretary. A six-man executive committee (two members of which were rotated every month) 'presided over' all writings bearing the Society's name and carried out the orders of the general committee. In the interests of openness, all letters sent to the executive committee and their replies were to be published quarterly and distributed without charge to the members.

The remarkable growth of the Society during the middle of 1795 led to difficulties in conducting meetings of a general committee consisting, sometimes, of well over one hundred delegates and subdelegates. In August and September several proposals were made for managing the business of the general committee more efficiently. Many of these proposals were incorporated in a new constitution. The divisions were enlarged from thirty to sixty members. The offices of secretary and treasurer were separated, and the power of the executive committee was increased. The financial accounts were to be printed monthly (a practice started several months later, in July 1796).

The passage of the Two Acts on 18 December 1795 made it necessary to modify this constitution, for the Seditious Meetings Act limited the size of unadvertised political meetings to 49 persons. Even before this Act was given the royal assent, the LCS introduced rules restricting the size of meetings. They established four district committees which funnelled delegates from the divisions (again limited to thirty members) to the general committee.

At the beginning of 1796 a member was deputed to draw up a new constitution. This final constitution was presented to the executive committee on 17 February and to the general committee and divisions on 21 March. At the end of June the general committee approved a short address to head the new regulations. According to the spy Powell, the new articles were much like the old ones except for the provision of a doorkeeper to ensure that no more than forty-nine entered a meeting.

As the preceding discussion indicates, a good deal of LCS energy was spent on constitutions. Sometimes the only activity at division meetings for several weeks was the discussion of a few articles of a proposed constitution. To the LCS a constitution was not only a way of establishing orderly procedures for meetings, but also a way of educating the members so that they could exercise their rights responsibly when Parliament and society were reformed and a way of showing the world a model of a just society.

Their punctiliousness in scrutinizing proposed constitutions, in observing the regulations and in modifying them as needed accounts in part for the surprising longevity of the LCS. Another factor contributing to their survival was their missionary attitude; they sought out reform groups in other cities, wrote when there was only a hint of a new society, wrote again if a society lapsed into silence. They sent missionaries to other cities to stir up zeal for reform. They were convinced that they were needed, that they must act as the centre of the popular reform societies. With a similar centripetal movement, they worked to keep their own members within the division and the divisions within the Society: the tythingmen were to keep their ten members active in the division. Divisions which were not represented at the general committee received a visit from deputies whose real goal was to keep the division within the fold. Divisions which seceded and formed separate societies were treated with friendliness and encouraged to return to the LCS (many individuals did). Paradoxically, differences of opinion, although they sometimes led as far as secession, also contributed to the long life of the LCS: controversial issues were frequently discussed; the members' opinions were sought; their votes mattered. In such an atmosphere a man could disagree without becoming an outcast. Consensus, begetting apathy and alienation, would have made them what the SCI became, a token reform society evaporating under the heat of the 1794 persecution.[54]

54 The size of London also helped the LCS outlast popular societies of other cities: it was difficult for magistrates to harass every division or to threaten every publican; it was harder for the 'Scrats' (aristocrats) to identify the 'Citizens' and punish them in the pocket. Possibly, too, there were more Irish and Scottish immigrants in London than in other English cities. The two Binnses and Crossfield were Irish; Hardy and Watson were Scottish; and a spy reported that one division seemed to consist entirely of Scottish shoemakers.

PART ONE

1792

Chronology

1792

Jan. ?	23	First meeting LCS
	31	Parliament opens
Feb.	16	Publication of *Rights of Man*, part 2
March–April		LCS begin correspondence with Manchester, Sheffield and Borough Friends of the People
Apr.	2	First LCS address
	11	Friends of the People founded
	20	France declares war on Austria
	30	Grey announces intention to move for parliamentary reform
May	21	Royal proclamation against seditious writings
	24	*Address of the LCS to the Nation at Large*
June	15	Parliament prorogued
July	24	Prussia declares war on France
	27	Duke of Brunswick's manifesto
Aug.		LCS *Address . . . on the Subject of a Parliamentary Reform*
	10	Insurrection in Paris; leads to imprisonment of royal family
Sept.	2	September massacres in Paris
	20	French National Convention meets Battle of Valmy begins period

Sept.		of French victories and conquests LCS decision to address French National Convention
	21	France declared a republic
Nov.	1	LCS *Address to French National Convention* delivered
	16	French declare Scheldt open in violation of treaties
	19	French promise aid to all peoples fighting oppression
	20	Reeves's Association for Preserving Liberty and Property founded
	29	LCS address in reply to Reeves
Dec.	1	Alarm over rumours of insurrection; militia called out
	4	Letter to Dundas
	5	Arrest of Carter, the billsticker
	11–13	Convention of Scottish Friends of the People in Edinburgh
	11–15	Anti-reform riots in Cambridge and Manchester
	13	Parliament opens Dublin Catholic convention, so-called Back Lane Parliament, meets
	18	Paine convicted for *Rights of Man*

1. Thomas Hardy's account of the origin of the London Corresponding Society (1799) (excerpts)[1]

Source: BL Add MSS 27814, fos. 1–38

In the Months of Novr. and Decr. 1791 my leisure hours were employed in looking over, and reading some political tracts which I had formerly perused with much pleasure during the American War. Among whom were a great variety published *gratis* by the Society for Constitutional Information[2] at that time. And some excellent pamphlets written by *Grenville Sharp, Major Cartwright, Dr. Jebb, Dr. Price, Thomas Day,*[3] *Revd. Mr. Stone, Capel Loft, John Horne Tooke, John Trenchard, Thomas Gorden, Lord Somers, Duke of Richmond, Sir William Jones, Davenant,* . . . From the small tracts and pamphlets written by those *realy* great men, much political information was diffused through the nation at that period, by their benevolent exertions. . . . After reading, and attentively considering the short state of the representation which was then published by the society for constitutional information, although it was an imperfect statement, yet it was very evident that a *radical reform in parliament* was quite necessary. (I at first imagined that it might be possible to begin a society in London of those who had no vote for a member to represent them in parliament.) Such as the populous parishes of St. Giles's, Mary Le Bone, Bloomsbury, and all those in every parish in London, Westminster, and Southwark, who were not housekeepers, but who were arived at the years of maturity, and who had an *inherent* right to a vote, but were unconstitutionaly deprived of it by an arbitrary statute Enacted in the eighth year of Henry the Sixth. I supposed that such a laudable scheme only wanted a beginning, and by persevering, to obtain it. Upon farther investigation of the subject, I found that it was impossible to establish a society to have any *effect*, upon so narrow a scale, for it is as clear as a mathematical axiom that the whole Mass of the people are unrepresented, or misrepresented. Therefore I relinquished that ideal plan, and formed another on a larger scale, which included all classes and descriptions of men (*criminals, insane, and infants excepted*) agreeable to the plan of the Duke of Richmond,[4] Major Cartwright, Dr. Jebb &c. . . .

This plan of a society I read to an intimate acquaintance who approved of it, and a few days afterwards two more friends and him met me at supper where I took the opportunity of reading it to them. They all were pleased with it as a groundwork. And it being a new thing we were anxious about putting it in practice. I proposed that we should have a meeting next Monday night at a public house the sign of the Bell in Exeter St. strand. It was agreed to, and each of us was to invite as many of our acquaintance as we thought would agree to the measure. Mr. Boyd the Landlord with whom I

1 Thomas Hardy, the founder of the London Corresponding Society, began a history of the Society in 1799. He described the founding of the Society in 1792 and its history up to the last general meeting before his arrest on 12 May 1794. Later Hardy used portions of this history in his autobiography.
2 In his *Memoir* Hardy says that these political tracts had been given to him by Thomas Brand Hollis, a member of the Society for Constitutional Information (p. 12). The educational aim of these pamphlets is well indicated by the title of one collection: *Tracts published and distributed gratis by the Society for Constitutional Information, with a design to convey to the minds of the People a Knowledge of their rights; principally those of representation* (1783). Most of the seven tracts in this collection are short (2–11 pp.), as are thirty-three others which the SCI ordered published in 1782. The authors include most of the men named in the next sentence.
3 According to the 1795 *New Annual Register*, Hardy was motivated to found the LCS by reading one of Day's pamphlets ('British and Foreign History', p. 164). Day, the author of *Sanford and Merton*, also wrote *Reflections upon the Present State of England, and the Independence of America* and *A Dialogue Between a Justice of the Peace and a Farmer*.
4 This plan of annual Parliaments and universal manhood suffrage was laid down by Richmond (Charles Lennox) in a work which became the bible for the LCS, *A Letter from His Grace the Duke of Richmond to Lieutenant Colonel Sharman, Chairman to the Committee of Correspondence Appointed by the Delegates of Forty-Five Corps of Volunteers, Assembled at Lisburn in Ireland (1783)*. At Hardy's trial in 1794 this letter was read as evidence that the aims of the LCS had a reputable ancestry. Ironically, Richmond, who handed a copy of his letter to the defence counsel, no longer believed in universal suffrage.

was acquainted, and who I knew was a friend to freedom was quite agreeable that a society for a reform of parliament should meet at his house,[5] ... previous to *this first meeting*[6] I had prepared and ruled a book for the purpose of every man putting down his name if he approved of the measure. I had prepared tickets also written upon them *London Corresponding Society* No. 1.2.3. A great deal of conversation was about giving a name to the society, whether the patriotic club – The reformation society – constitutional society. As it was difficult to decide which to adopt, I showed them the book and the Tickets, which I had prepared, with *London Corresponding Society* written upon them – That name was immediately adopted, as more appropriate to the object of the Society, which was to correspond with individuals, and societies of men who wished for a reformation, and to collect the opinion and sense of the nation as far as possible by that means. I took the idea from that admirable letter of the Duke of Richmond to Coll. Sharman Chairman of the Committee of Correspondance at Lisborn in Ireland.

This [first] meeting of the society took place on the evening of the *25th Jan. 1792.*[7] After the business of the day was ended they retired as was customary for tradesmen

to do to a public house and after supper conversation followed, condoling with each other on the miserable and wretched state the people were reduced to, merely as we believed, from the want of a fair, and equal representation in the commons house of parliament – We considered what was best to be done to remedy this evil, I had copied several extracts from different Authors respecting a reform of parliament which was read to the company present – And a short state of the representation as given in a table at the end of an excellent Book written by Major Cartwright, intitled *Give us our Rights*[8] They were astonished at such a state of Mock representation. ... which determined them instantly to commence operation, upon the plan that was just read to them, and which they cordially approved of as an excellent foundation whereon to rear a goodly edefice. I then presented the book to them, which was previously prepared, and requested them to subscribe their names, some were for defering it until the next meeting, but I endeavoured to show the propriety of their immediate subscribing their names, and making a small deposit, which I considered would give them an interest in promoting the success of the society. Having got eight to put their names down and to pay one penny each, the first meeting night,[9] then I gave each one a ticket with his name written upon the back of it. The next thing which they considered was to choose from among themselves some trusty servants to conduct the business of that friendly and well meaning company. They appointed me Treasurer and Secretary. There they stumbled at the threshold. *Two very important offices filled by one person.* The amount of cash in the Treasurers had the first meeting was *Eight Pence.* Although we were at first but few in number and humble in situation and circumstances, yet we wished to take into our consideration how to remedy the many defects and abuses which had crept into the administration of government. And in our enquiries we soon discovered that gross ignorance and prejudice of the bulk of the nation was the

5 In a 'History of the Society' written in 1796, the institution of the LCS was attributed to 'Robert Boyd, Thomas Hardy, and George Walne, each of whom had acquired, by long and close attention to political transactions, a thorough knowledge of the encouragement which they had to expect, and the difficulties they had to encounter' (*The Moral and Political Magazine of the London Corresponding Society*, vol. 1 (Sept. 1796), p. 182; hereafter *MPM*). Hardy told the Privy Council in 1794 that he had been introduced to the Society by a young man who had since died (TS 11/963/3509, fo. 23v). This was probably William Gow or Gough, a watchmaker, described in the 1796 'History' as one of three other members 'who contributed to give vigour to the infancy of the Society' (Maurice Margarot and Robert Thompson were the other two). Probably, then, Hardy read his plan of the society to Walne, his brother-in-law; afterwards he and Walne met with Gow and Boyd, and the four agreed to start a club. Gow, being dead, might safely be named to the Privy Council.

6 In the margin next to this line Hardy wrote '1791', perhaps an indication that he had prepared for the Society in 1791.

7 Originally Hardy called this the first meeting. The second meeting after this is called the third meeting. This first meeting of nine men could not have been on Monday, 25th Jan., nor could the second meeting have been, as Hardy wrote, on Monday, 1 Feb. Both those dates were Wednesdays. Inasmuch as the society met on Mondays in March, it is likely that the first two meetings were also on

Mondays and that the London Corresponding Society was instituted on 23 Jan.

8 Hardy read them these works as well as a parable by William Frend about 'certain brethren dwelling together in one house and having all things in common'. This parable so impressed Hardy that he quoted it at the end of this history.

9 According to an earlier draft (interleaved with this version), 'they all entered their names and paid one penny except one person who cautiously took another week to consider of it'.

greatest obstacle to the obtaining redress Therefore our aim was to have a well regulated and orderly society formed for the purpose of dispelling that ignorance and prejudice as far as possible, and instill into their minds by means of the press a sense of their rights as freemen, and of their duty to themselves, and their posterity, as good citizens, and heridatory guardians of the liberties transmitted to them by their forefathers. On the Monday following, which was the *first of Feb*: there were eight more added to our number, and encreased the funds of the society to *two shillings*. The Third meeting nine more were added, which made the number of the society amount to twenty five[10] and the sum in the *treasury, four shillings and one penny*. a mighty sum!

On the *second* night of meeting there was a Chairman appointed for the *third meeting* – when the following questions were proposed for discussion viz.

First   Is there any necessity for a reformation of the present State of the Representation in the British House of Commons?

Second   Would there be any Utility in a parliamentary reform? – or in other words – Are there any just grounds to believe that a reformation in parliament will be of any essential service to the Nation?

Third   Have *we* who are Treadsmen – Shopkeepers and mechanicks any right to seek to obtain a parliamentary reform?

The above questions were debated in the society for five nights successively – in all points of view that we were capable of handling the subject – and after due deliberation, and discussion, they were all decided in the affirmative.

It is necessary that I should here take notice of the first Letter that I had written to Sheffield respecting the society[11]. . . .

When I recieved the answer to the foregoing Letter I then read the copy of the Letter with the Answer, and the packet of papers which I recieved at the same time – *not* as an official Letter from the Society – but as a private one – it was written in haste without consulting one individual about it There were at that time in the room I think about 50 persons They were very much pleased with the Answer and the printed Addresses which accompanyed it – it animated them with additional ardor – when they were informed that others in a distant part of the nation had *thought* – and had also *begun* to *act* in the same way with themselves – The communication being quite unexpected – they had not before heard that any such Society existed at Sheffield, at that time – nor that any Letter had been written to them – The Society being so well satisfied of course I recieved their unanimous thanks for opening so important a correspondance[12] —— A Committee of six was that night appointed to revise alter or amend the laws and regulations – and to prepare something to be published as an Address to the Nation – The outlines of two or three excellent Addresses were presented by different members of the Committee but not approved of by the Society – The same committee however obtained leave of another week to prepare one – About this time Mr. Maurice Margarot became a member of the Society – he was added to the Committee that night A short address with some resolutions were drawn up by him and after some little alteration they were agreed to by the Society and ordered to be printed – "Who should put the Bell about the cats neck?" Who was to Sign this address became the next question? some objected because they were serving Masters who might perhaps discharge them from their employment – others that if their names appeared to any Address and

10 Peter Macbean recalled that there were twenty men present, including Hardy, Margarot, Black, Gow, Merry, Dowling and himself (testimony at the trial of Hardy, *ST* vol. 24, cols. 1002–3).

11 On 8 March 1792, Hardy – on his own initiative – wrote to a Rev. Bryant, an abolitionist, who he assumed would belong to a reform society in Sheffield, the existence of which Hardy had just learned from the newspaper. Hardy described the LCS and asked the Sheffield society for advice (Add MSS 27811, fos. 4v–5v). Bryant gave the letter to the Sheffield Society for Constitutional Information, which had been in existence since 1791. In a letter which Hardy received on 19 March, the Sheffield SCI gave an account of their method of dividing the society (2000 members) into groups of ten with delegates attending a monthly general meeting. They recommended

that the LCS adopt this plan and that they 'enter into connexion with the Men in the Society for Constitutional Information in London, of whom Mr. Horne Tooke is one'. Tooke, the letter continued, 'will be the true Friend & advocate in our Cause, consistent with his principles hitherto manifested both in Public and private' (TS 11/965/3510A).

12 During the next month, April, Hardy opened a correspondence about the LCS with the Manchester Society for Constitutional Information and with the Borough Society of the Friends of the People, both recently organized. He wrote to Samuel Favell, a founder of the Borough Society on the very day (18 April) it was officially inaugurated (Add MSS 27811, fos. 7, 9; Add MSS 27814, fos. 173–4; TS 11/965/3510A.)

resolutions of any society for a reform of parliament, they might lose their Customers – Margarot was asked to sign them – he objected also for this reason, that he at that time had connections with some Merchants in the City (Thullisons and others) closely connected with the Administration he was in expectation at that time of some employment from some of them – by taking a conspicuous part in the Society it might be injurious to him in his prospects if it were known that he belonged to any society of that kind

Although he assured us that he should promote the object which the Society had in View to the utmost of his power, as a private Member, but he could not by any means suffer his name to appear – at least for that time – As it was necessary to have a name to the Address that it might appear genuine – it was next proposed to me to sign it – the only objection that I could possibly have was – that being an obscure individual – my name could add no consequence to it – but I being the most independant in the Society at that time having nothing to hope nor fear from any *party* or *class* of Men whatever – I readily agreed – . . . . My name appeared *singly* to the first address and resolutions on the 2d. of April 1792

A copy of the Address and resolutions were ordered to be sent to the *London Constitutional Society*[13] which they afterwards printed in the newspapers – After that time the *London Corresponding Society* became public – Likewise a copy was ordered to be sent to the *Constitutional Society* of *Manchester* and *Sheffield* who were also by this time known to the public – In return we recieved their addresses and rules and regulations &c. . . . .

Several thousands of the first printed Address and resolutions were distributed *gratis* throughout the Nation which we were enabled to do (and which in fact was the original design of the first promoters of the Society) from the fund raised by the penny a week from each member – As our plan was *Universal Suffrage* and *annual parliaments*, The Society admitted journeymen treadsmen of all denominations into it – A class of Men who deserve better treatment than they generaly meet with from those who are fed, and cloathed, and inriched by thier labour, industry, or ingenuity.

Many of that description of Men are unmarried, and whose practice is to go to a public house from their workshops after the labour of the day, to have their supper, and then

13 The Society for Constitutional Information.

regale themselves with a pint or pot of Beer, and smoak thier pipes, and convers about the news of the day – the hardness of the times – the dearness of provisions, and of every necessary and comfort in life & c. which directs thier conversation a little farther by inquiring into the *cause* of all those calamities of which they complain – . . . . By admitting all upon the principle of universal suffage, the society increased rapidly – . . . .

When L. Daer became a member some one proposed that he should be chairman next meeting night it seemed to be the wish of many present – I objected to him being chairman upon this ground that it would still appear to be a party business and might prevent the people exerting themselves in their own cause and depend implicitly (as formerly) upon the mere ipse dixit of some NobleMan or great Man without the least trouble of examining for themselves – none were better pleased than I was on his becoming a member – nor none esteemed him more highly. . . .

We were so scrupulous about the admission of any of those of the higher ranks that when any of them offered to pay more than we usually demanded on the admission of a new member We would not recieve it but told them that we had money sufficient for all necessary purposes Viz for printing, postage of Letters, and stationary – . . . . – Every three Months new Officers were elected by ballot or the old ones rechosen if they found it convenient – There was a uniform rule by which all Members were admitted high and low rich and poor – After the three following questions were proposed to them and answered in the Affirmative thier names and residences were entered into a book kept for that purpose (*but not their titles*) each member had a ticket given to him with a copy of the rules and orders and the Addresses of the Society

Question first.   Are you convinced that the parliamentary Representation of this Country is at present inadequit and imperfect?

Question 2d.   Are you thoureoughly perswaded that the welfare of these kingdoms requires that every person of *Adult* years in possession of his reason and not incapacitated by crimes should have a vote for a Member of parliament?

Question 3d.   Will you endeavour by all justifiable means to promote such reformation in parliament.

By this time we were under the necessity of haveing printed tickets – for the members multiplied so fast that the business of the society was retarded by writing the tickets –

printed tickets were talked of for several weeks before they were ordered to be printed – what is every bodys business is no bodys business (an old proverb) – At last I gave the form of a ticket into the committee for their approbation with this Motto *"Unite, persevere, and be free"* I remember Margarot objecting to that Motto at first as liable to be construed to our injury – however the next day when he called upon me (which was his practice every day) he said that it would do very well it was very proper –

Members entered so quickly that it was found expedient to divide the society into separate bodies and class them so that it might be more convenient for the members and be as neighbourly meetings (which was the original design before any meeting at all took place) and each division to send one of their number as delegate to form a committee in some central place for conducting the business of the society and when that committee amounted to 60 Members to be divided again into six parts each part or division to appoint one of their number to form another committee – At this time the society was divided into nine parts – each part appointed a representative to meet in a committee with instructions to revise – correct or alter the rules and regulations of the society and to prepare another address to the Nation – which was done brought forward to the society – agreed to – ordered to be printed and the Chairman and Secty. Margarot and myself to sign it – on the 24th. May 1792 – Margarot had not the same objection which he had before – . . . .

About this time we began to be a little more particular about the admission of people into the room where the divisions of the society met on account of several improper persons intruding and intriguing to get into the room as members and afterwards endeavouring to disturb the harmony of the Society by thier noisy and virulent declamations designing thereby to through them into confusion and anarchy that they might become an easy prey to thier evil designs – The method which we adopted in order to counteract as much as possible the nefarious designs of those men was this – In each of the divisions it was agreed to appoint a Chairman every meeting night, by acclamation or a Show of hands – on the next meeting night the Chairman was to descend to become door keeper in rotation It was not deemed any degradation to the man who filled that high and elevated Station of *president*, to stoop to take upon him the *lowest office* in Society, *door-keeper*, when it was for the express purpose of promoting, and securing happiness, order, and Tranquillity in the Society.

[One of the early activities of the Corresponding Society was the drafting of the address announcing their existence and expressing their principles. A letter which Hardy wrote to John Horne Tooke on 27 March reveals that the LCS had difficulty agreeing upon an address and that Hardy sought advice from Tooke:

'I am sorry to inform you of our defeat last night in the Society The address was not ricieved for one reason, it was not animated enough and another some of the sentiments were too low and contemptable to appear to the publick from the principle City in the Nation. For example Where it says 'Men less indebted to Education than Nature – for the plain Common sense they possess' some of the amendments were agreed to others were rejected the same Committee were allowed another week to finily settle upon a Declaration but I have my doubts about it for we are so full of self importance that we will not concede to each other when we have a good thing before us – The Committee meets tomorrow night – Mr. Paine was so good as to offer to draw up something for us if he had a little more time we have 'till next Monday if he cannot before tomorrow night favour us with his thoughts as an address to the publick Those of us whom you saw yesterday morning means to bring it foreward in the society after the other is read if there is another can be agreed to by the Commee'[14]

The issue was not raised at the Monday night meeting because on 28 or 29 March (Wednesday or Thursday) the committee agreed to adopt the address written by Maurice Margarot and to send a copy to the Society for Constitutional Information. Hardy sent it on 30 March with a request from the committee to enter into correspondence with the SCI 'if it is not too much presumption in us to expect such an honour'.[15] The SCI, meeting that evening, recorded the LCS resolutions in their minutes and directed their secretary 'to assure them [LCS] of our desire to correspond and co-operate with them'.[16]

14 Add MSS 27811, fo. 6.
15 TS 11/952/3496. A copy of this early version of the address is in TS 11/951/3495.
16 Minutes, TS 11/951/3495. Tooke made minor changes in the address, signed Hardy's name, and

9

At the next meeting of the LCS, on Monday, 2 April, Margarot's address was presumably accepted by the members.]

2. First Address of the LCS, 2 April 1792[17]

Source: printed copy in Place Collection, vol. 36, fo.5; earlier MS copy in TS 11/951/3495; MS copy in Add MSS 27812, fos. 2–4v, is the first entry in the 'Journal of the London Corresponding Society'

Man as an Individual is entitled to Liberty – it is his Birth-right.

As a Member of Society, the Preservation of that Liberty becomes his indispensable Duty.

When he associated, he gave up certain Rights, in order to secure the Possession of the remainder;

But, he voluntarily yielded up only as much as was necessary for the common Good:

He still preserved a Right of sharing in the Government of his Country; – without it, no Man can with Truth call himself FREE.

Fraud or Force, sanction by Custom, withholds that Right from (by far) the greater Number of Inhabitants of this Country.

The few with whom the Right of Election and Representation remains, abuse it, and the strong Temptations held out to Electors, sufficiently prove that the Representatives of this Country seldom procure a Seat in Parliament, from the *unbought* Suffrages of a Free People.

The Nation at length perceives it, and testifies an ardent Desire of remedying the Evil.

The only Difficulty, therefore, at present is, the ascertaining the true Method of proceeding.

To this end, different and numerous Societies have been formed in various Parts of the Nation.

Several likewise have arisen in the Metropolis, and among them, (though as yet in its Infant State) the *Corresponding Society*, with Modesty intrudes Itself and Opinions, on the Attention of the Public, in the following Resolutions:

Resolved, – That every Individual has a

Right to Share in the Government of that Society of which he is a Member – unless incapacitated:

Resolved, – That nothing but Non-age, Privation of Reason, or an Offence against the general Rules of Society, can incapacitate him.

Resolved, – That it is no less the *Right* than the *Duty* of every Citizen, to keep a watchful Eye on the Government of his Country; that the Laws, by being multiplied, do not degenerate into *Oppression*; and that those who are entrusted with the Government, do not substitute *Private Interest* for *Public Advantage*.

Resolved, – That the People of Great Britain are not *effectually* represented in Parliament.

Resolved, – That in Consequence of a *partial, unequal,* and therefore *inadequate Representation*, together with the *corrupt* Method in which Representatives are elected; *oppressive Taxes, unjust Laws, restrictions of Liberty,* and *wasting of the Public Money,* have ensued.

Resolved, – That the only Remedy to those Evils is a fair, equal, and impartial Representation of the People in Parliament.

Resolved, – That a fair, equal, and impartial Representation can never take Place, until all *partial Privileges* are abolished.

Resolved, – That this Society do express their *Abhorrence* of Tumult and Violence, and that, as they aim at Reform, not Anarchy, Reason, Firmness, and Unanimity are the only Arms they themselves will employ, or persuade their Fellow-Citizens to exert, against *Abuse of Power.*

Ordered, – That the Secretary of this Society do transmit a Copy of the above to the Societies for Constitutional Information, established in *London, Sheffield,* and *Manchester.*

By Order of the Committee,
April 2, 1792.   T. HARDY, Secretary.

[When these resolutions were reprinted with the *Address to the Nation* of 24 May, the preamble was revised by expansion. The new preamble starts, 'Assured that man, Individual man, may justly claim Liberty as his birthright, we naturally conclude that, as a member of Society; it becomes his indispensable duty to preserve inviolate that Liberty for the benefit of his fellow citizens and of his and their posterity'[18]]

sent the document to be printed in the *Argus* newspaper. Tooke's signing Hardy's name was later regarded by the government as evidence that Tooke and the SCI created and manipulated the LCS.

17 The printed copy differs from the earlier version chiefly in non-significant changes in diction.

18 Printed copy in BL 8135.b.8.

3. Journal: LCS General Committee, 3–22 May 1792[19]

Source: Add MSS 27812, fos. 1–4v (later copies in Add MSS 27814, fos. 89–90)

Thursday 3d May 1792

The nine appointed Delegates met, and after a reciprocal production & examination of their vouchers,[20] formed themselves into a Committee.

The Committee, thus formed, proceeded to business in choosing a Chairman and Secretary by ballot.

Mce Margarot having a Majority of votes was appointed Chairman.

Thos Hardy, already acting Secretary & Treasurer was next confirmed in those offices without a dissentient vote.

Thursday 10 May

The Committee took into consideration a rough draught produced by the Delegates of an address to the nation from the London Corresponding Society & ordered a dozen proofs of it to be struck off, that each Delegate might communicate with the division thereon.

Sat. 22 May (a special Committee)

The Committee completed the address to the nation; it was signed by the Chairman & Secretary and one thousand copies of it were ordered to be printed,[21] & that it be at full length on their Journal.

A Letter was received from the Constitutional Society of Manchester containing many expressions of friendship; a short account of the proceedings in that part of the country, & a book of their Rules, with sundry other papers.

4. Address of the LCS to the Nation at Large, 24 May 1792[22]

Source: printed copy in BL 8135b. 8 (1); MS in Add MSS 27812, fos. 4v–9 (Journal)

Whereas it is notorious, that very numerous, burthensome, and unnecessary Taxes are laid on the persons and families of us and others, the Industrious Inhabitants of Great Britain, an exceedingly great Majority of whom are, notwithstanding, excluded from all Representation in Parliament:

And whereas, upon inquiry into the Cause of this Grievance, which is at once an Obstruction to our Industry and a Diminution of our Property, we find that the Constitution of our Country (which was purchased for us at the expence of the lives of our Ancestors) has, by the Violence and Intrigue of Criminal and Designing Men, been injured and undermined in its most essential and important parts; but particularly in the House of Commons, where the whole of the supposed Representation of the People is neither more nor less than an Usurped Power, arising either from Abuses in the Mode of Election and Duration of Parliaments, or from a Corrupt Property in certain decayed Corporations, by means of which the Liberties of this Nation are basely bartered away for the private profit of Members of Parliament:

And whereas it appears to us, that until this Source of Corruption shall be cleansed by the Information, Perseverance, Firmness, and Union of the People at large, we are robbed of the Inheritance so acquired for us by our Fore-Fathers; and that our Taxes, instead of being lessened, will go on increasing, in as much as they will furnish more Bribes, and Places, and Pensions, to our Ministers and Members of Parliament.

---

19 The Journal of the LCS contains the minutes of meetings from 3 May 1792 to 2 January 1794. It occupies the entire volume Add MSS 27812, fos. 1–83v. After the arrest of Hardy in 1794, someone (perhaps Felix Vaughan to whom it had been entrusted by John Pearce) ripped out several pages which the government might find incriminating. Several years after the trial, Hardy, preparing a history of the LCS, copied the Journal. This later copy, which occasionally clarifies a statement in the original, is in Add MSS 27814, fos. 89–155.

20 The vouchers, or government copies, for Divs. 1–8 (all signed by Robert Boyd) show that the delegates were William Gow, Thomas Hardy, Felix Vaughan, George Walne, Alexander Rogers, John Richter, Maurice Margarot and John Martin (TS 11/953/3497, TS 11/958/3503, TS 11/965/3510A).

21 'printed and distributed gratis' – later copy.

22 Reprinted (with small changes), together with Resolutions of 2 April 1792 and Address of 6 August 1792, in TS 11/959/3505; MS notation at end: 'In Mr. Margarott's of 4 Decr. 1792/ J H/E T'. A copy of the reprint was issued with date of July 1794 (TS 11/956/3501). The reprint of this address, together with the resolutions of 2 April and the preamble starting, 'Assured that man . . .'. were marked for revision in 1794. Non-significant revisions of punctuation will not be noted here.

Now it is resolved by us, the Members of this Society, to form ourselves into one firm and permanent Body, for the purpose of informing ourselves and others of the exact State of the Present Parliamentary Representation – for obtaining a peaceful but adequate Remedy to this intolerable Grievance – and for corresponding and co-operating with other Societies united for the same Objects. And to this end we adopt the following Regulations, for the internal order and government of our Society.

I. That every person, before he is admitted into our Body, shall be proposed by Two Members, and shall agree to the Declaration following, viz.

[The three questions on parliamentary reform are presented in declaratory form.]

II. That the whole Body shall go under one common name of *The London Corresponding Society, United for the Reform of Parliamentary Representation.*

III. That for the more easy and orderly proceeding of the Society, it be separated into as many Divisions as there shall be Twenty Members,[23] to make up the number requisite for such Division. And that no Division shall divide again, till it shall amount to double such number of Members; at which time notice shall be given to the Committee of Delegates hereafter mentioned, by the then Delegate of such Division.

IV. That each Division shall meet Weekly, on any Evening (Thursdays excepted) at some house to be chosen by themselves, and shall appoint a Chairman for the good order thereof: and also shall name a Delegate, as hereafter mentioned.

V. That each Member shall pay to the Chairman of his Division One Penny per Week, which shall be credited to the Account of such Member in a Book to be kept for that purpose. That all Money so paid, shall be transmitted Monthly, by the Delegate of such Division, to the Treasurer, who is to account with the Body of Delegates for the same, at the four usual Quarter Days.

VI. That the Sums so paid to the said Treasurer shall form one Common Stock, to be applied by the said Delegates in the Postage of Letters, in Stationary, and in Printing such matters as may be good for the Information of the Society. But that before any expence whatever shall be incurred, the said Delegates

shall inquire of the Treasurer what Balance he has in hand, in order that the said Stock may never be exhausted.

VII. That the Delegates so appointed shall meet on Thursday in every Week, and shall continue in Office for Three Months; subject, however, to be recalled by their several Divisions before the expiration of that time, if thought necessary. That being assembled, they shall name a Chairman and Secretary, who shall both sign the Register which shall be kept of their Proceedings.[24]

VIII. That such Delegates, so assembled, shall, in the first place, communicate the Wishes of their several Divisions, relative to any objects of the Society. That they shall be authorised to answer any Correspondence, which may require immediate attention; and afterwards, that each Delegate shall report the same to his respective Division. Also, that they shall consider of the general state of the Society; but shall on no account publish any New Set of Principles, until they shall be approved by a Majority of the Individual Members of the Society at large.

IX. That it shall be necessary for Two Thirds of the said Delegates to form a Quorum for the Dispatch of Business.

X. That these Resolutions and Regulations be printed for the Members of the Society, and that a Copy be given to each Member, on his admission.

MAUR. MARGAROT, *Chairman.*
THOMAS HARDY, *Secretary.*

Forasmuch as it is possible that the grounds of our Complaint may be denied, and that our Views and Principles may be misrepresented, we desire that every one will seriously consider and treasure in his memory the state of scandalous facts which follow. – Let him then ask himself, whether it be the part of a good Citizen to sit quiet under such abuses, which have not only increased, but are at this moment increasing; and which ought therefore to be remedied without delay.

Till the Reign of Henry the VI. it was not necessary for the Inhabitant of a County to have a Freehold Estate of 40s. a Year, in order to vote for the Representative of his County. But the Statute of that King, passed in the year 1429, under pretence of preventing Disputes at Elections, most unjustly deprived a great part of the Commons of this Nation of the right of consenting to those Taxes, which, notwithstanding, they were compelled to pay

23 Reprint: 'thirty Members'.

24 Reprint substitutes, 'who shall both sign all the public Acts of the Society'.

just as if such right had not been taken from them.

Till the reign of Queen Anne, it was not necessary for the Inhabitant of a County to have 600l. a Year, Freehold or Copyhold Estate, in order to his being elected the Representative of his County. But the Statute of that Queen, passed in the year 1710, under pretence of the Freedom of Parliament, excluded all persons not possessed of such a property from our Representation, whatever be their Principles, their Abilities, or their Integrity.

Till the Reign of William III. Parliaments were of right to be called *Once a Year*, or oftener if need be. But the Statute of that King, passed in the year 1694, under pretence of calling them more frequently, enacted, that they 'should be holden once in *Three Years* at the least.'

Till the Reign of George I. Parliaments were therefore of Three Years Duration. But the Statute of that King, passed in the year 1715, under pretence of a "restless[25] Faction" then existing in the Nation, usurped a power of enacting, that "Parliaments should respectively have Continuance for Seven Years."

As for the supposed Representation of the People, which is called the "Commons of England in Parliament assembled;"

The County of Cornwall contains in itself alone the privilege of sending *Forty-Four* Members to Parliament, which is just one less in number than those of the whole Kingdom of Scotland, containing near Three Millions of People.

Of these Forty-Four supposed Representatives, two are elected by the Freeholders of the County: the rest sit for Twenty-One Corporation Towns; of which,

	Electors	
Launceston *has only*	10	*& is the property of* Lord Elliot
Leskeard, - -	9	- - - - - - - Ditto
Lestwithiel, - -	7	- - - - - - - D. of Northumberland
Truro, - -	13	- - - - - - - Lord Falmouth
Bodmyn, - -	18	- - - - - - - Sir Francis Basset
Helston, - -	3	- - - - - - - D. of Leeds, &c.
Saltash, - -	16	- - - - - - - Sir Francis Basset
East Loe, - -	20 ⎫	- - - - - - - Judge Buller
West Loe, - -	20 ⎭	
Grampound, - -	30	- - - - - - - Lord Somers, &c.
Camelford, - -	6	- - - - - - - Lord Camelford
Penryhn, - -	50	- - - - - - - Sir Francis Basset
Tregony, - -	50	- - - - - - - Lord Hertford
Bossiney, - -	20	- - - - - - - Lord Bute
St. Ives, - -	60	- - - - - - - Mr. Praed
Fowey, - -	26	- - - - - - - Prince of Wales
St Germains, - -	6	- - - - - - - Lord Elliot
St. Mitchell, - -	14	- - - - - - - D. of Northumberland
Newport, - -	30	- - - - - - - Lord Lovaine
St. Mawes, - -	15	- - - - - - - Marq. of Buckingham
Callington, - -	30	- - - - - - - Lord Falmouth

Electors 453   Members 42

To these we might add, of the same description, twenty-eight Corporations, consisting of 354 Electors, which send 56 Members to that House of Commons, which is so frequently and so falsely called the Democracy of the Nation: while the Towns of Sheffield, Manchester, Birmingham, Leeds, Wolverhampton, &c. containing above three hundred thousand people, have no Electors or Representatives whatever.

Upon the whole it appears, that 257 supposed Representatives of the People, making a Majority of the House of Commons, are returned by a Number of Voters not exceeding the thousandth part of the Nation.

But as Providence has kindly furnished men, in every station, with faculties necessary for judging of what concerns themselves, shall we, the Multitude, suffer a few, with no better right than ourselves, to usurp the power of governing us without Controul? Surely no ! – Let us rather unite in one common Cause, to

25 MS in Journal adds 'popish'.

13

cast away our Bondage, being assured, that in so doing, we are protected by a Jury of our Countrymen, while we are discharging a duty to ourselves, to our Country, and to Mankind.

Ordered

That the Secretary of this Society do transmit Copies of the above to all the Societies in the Nation, engaged in the same Cause.

Bell, Exeter Street, }
May 24, 1792.

5. Journal: LCS General Committee, 24 May–21 June 1792

Source: Add MSS 27812, fos. 9–12 (later copies in Add MSS 27814, fos. 90–2)

Thursday 24 May

The King having thought proper, by the advice of his Privy Council to send forth a proclamation, couched in terms so vague that they applied directly to no particular man, writing, or assembly, yet manifestly tending to alarm & prejudice all ranks of men against certain (asserted to be) wicked, seditious & inflammatory writings, complaints, men & measures[26] – The Committee after prudent deliberation thereon resolved, that in their next letter to the London Constitutional Society, some notice should be taken of it.

Report was made to the Committee that the Division No. 8 having encreased to forty five members prayed that leave might be granted them to divide again – the consideration of this report was postponed.

[The first evidence of dissension within the Society dates from this week. On 28 May John Kidder (or Redder) wrote to the 'President' of the LCS, saying that he had received a letter directing him to meet the delegates that night and that 'some of the leading Members' knew he had withdrawn from the LCS and knew his motives for doing so. He left the LCS with regret, he continued, and owned that there were 'many Members who will ever command my Admiration & Esteem'.[27] Since 28 May was a Monday and the regular meetings of the delegates were on Thursdays, he must have been summoned to a special meeting.]

Thursday 31st. May

The Committee perused &[28] the rough draught of a letter, to the London Constitutional Society, containing thanks for their friendly communications and remarks on the King's Proclamation.[29] –

The above letter signed by the Chairman and the Secretary was ordered to be sent.

By direction of the Committee the Chairman issued an order to the Division No. 8 to divide and that, the said new division being No. 10 should choose a Delegate.

Thursday 7th. June

The Committee heard different reports of the effect of the King's Proclamation on the minds of the weak and the ignorant, and of the abuses the said proclamation had caused in giving birth to the Mount Street disturbances,[30] and in bringing forward the time-serving Test & bare-faced Abuse of entrusted power, in certain magistrates who thinking every measure legal in consequence of a King's Proclamation &, in their hurry, stumbling over

26 The proclamation commanded magistrates to discover the authors, printers and sellers of 'divers wicked and seditious writing . . . tending to excite tumult and disorder . . . respecting the laws and happy constitution . . . established in this country'. The magistrates were also commanded to 'take the most immediate and effectual care to suppress and prevent all riots, tumults, and other disorders' ('His Majesty's Proclamation for Preventing Seditious Meetings and Writings, May 21, 1792'). This proclamation became the basis of numerous prosecutions, especially against printers and sellers of Paine's works.

27 TS 11/958/3503.
28 Originally '& recieved'.
29 The SCI on 18 May agreed to send the LCS and other reform societies a series of resolutions against the proclamation. The next week the SCI voted to send copies of a letter from Paine announcing a cheap edition of the *Rights of Man* (an edition prompted by rumours of a prosecution against the work), and a series of resolutions on Paine's letter, ending with an affirmation of the SCI's willingness to support freedom of the press and Paine (*ST* vol. 25, cols. 152–3). The LCS reply, dated 31 May, approved Paine's proposed publication and argued that the king's proclamation expressed the desire shared by the LCS of 'abiding by the constitution in its pure & uncorrupt state' (TS 11/952/3496).
30 On 6 June the watch-house in Mount St, Grosvenor Sq., was nearly demolished by forty enraged servants of fashionable people. The servants, who had merely been celebrating the king's birthday, were arrested and detained all night in the watch-house. When released, they vented their anger; the military were called out, and quiet was not restored until after 'repeated firings' (*Annual Register*, 1792).

he Brothels, the Gaming Houses, and the
eceptacles of public depredation, fostered (in
manner) under their wing, dared to threaten
iarmless Publicans with putting a stop to
heir licences, if they admitted into their
iouses any sober industrious body of Trades-
nen, presuming to discuss political subjects.
Thus, under a worse political tyranny than
:hat of Venice, several Divisions found them-
;elves at a loss for houses to meet at.

Thursday 14th. June

The Committee drew up & sent to the
London Constitutional Society a letter, stating,
that in consequence of the mention made of a
Proclamation against Mr. Thomas Paine, a
subscription had been opened in different
divisions of the London Corresponding Society
in his behalf &c.[31] and further expressing a
desire that six of their members might be
admitted into the London Constitutional
Society upon the same footing as those of the
Manchester & Sheffield Societies.[32]
This day the Committee assembled for the
last time at the Bell in Exeter Street.[33]

Thursday 21 June

The Committee received a protest as under
from Mce. Margarot Delegate of the 7th.
Division against the proceedings of the preceding night, and further the Committee was
made acquainted with the approbation the
Division No. 7 had given to their Delegate for
having so protested.

31 According to the letter to the SCI, a division
which met on Monday (11 May) heard Paine's
letter to Dundas read aloud and immediately
started the subscription, to which every one of
the twenty persons present signed his name; on
Tuesday Div. 5 also began a subscription; and on
Thursday the delegates voted to recommend the
subscription to all the divisions (letter of 14 June
[misdated 14 March] in TS 11/952/3496). In the
end the subscription amounted to no more than
£10 (Hardy's testimony to the Privy Council, TS
11/963/3509, fo. 37).
32 Also the Norwich Society, as the later copy
states. Earlier in the week Hardy had broached
affiliation with the Southwark, or Borough,
Friends of the People, asking if LCS members
might visit them (letter of 9 June, in TS
11/965/3510A).
33 The king's proclamation had led the magistrates
to threaten the Bell's publican, Boyd, with the
loss of his licence – a loss of £1,000 to him if he
continued to let the LCS meet at his house. The
committee and the divisions which had been
meeting at the Bell now moved to private houses
or auction rooms (letter, Hardy to Lord Daer,
14 July 1792, Add MSS 27811, fos. 14v–15).

A letter from the Editors of the Patriot was
read as was likewise the answer thereto, which,
signed by the Chairman & Secretary was
ordered to be sent.[34]
A letter from the London Constitutional
Society, in answer to our last was likewise
read. It informed the Committee that the
London Constitutional Society granted our
request & was willing to admit six of our
Members to become honorary Members of
their Society.
The new Division No. 10 sent James Styles
to the Committee as their Delegate
Visitor this meeting
Mr. Sinclair of the Constitutional Society.
Copy of the Protest

6. Letter: Maurice Margarot to Committee of Delegates of the LCS, 18 June 1792[35]

Source: TS 11/965/3510A

Monday 18 June 1792

Gentlemen
With surprize I read in the Argus of to day,
a letter to the Society for Constitutional
Information drawn up & sent them by the
Committee of Delegates of the Lond. Corresp.
Society on Thursay last
Considering Unanimity as the Strength &
Basis of our Society & at all times entertaining
a just diffidence of my own opinion when
opposed to that of the Committee, it grieves
me much to be oblidged in the present instance
to dissent from them, but unfortunately
absent on that day & no previous notice
having been given of that business I was
unable untill now of opposing what I deem to
be inconsistent with the Honour advantage &
Safety of the Society
first, I conceive the request made in that
letter to the Society for Constitutional Information for the admission of Six of our Members &a &a to be, an Assumption of power in
the Delegates, they not having previously
taken the opinion & approbation of their

34 The anonymous editors (actually, Matthew
Campbell Browne) wrote on 14 June, recommending their magazine; and the LCS replied
on 18 June, thanking them for the six issues and
expressing optimistic reform sentiments (TS
11/965/3510). The *Patriot* was issued fortnightly
in Sheffield from 3 April 1792 to 30 July 1793
and irregularly for two more issues. Priced at 3d,
it contained about 36 pp. of editorials, essays and
extracts from earlier books.
35 Margarot's letter was copied in the Journal, and
the original filed.

Several Divisions and moreover premature in that no Official Invitation thereto from the Constitutional Society had been made; the Delegates therefore, whatever private excitement they may have received from Individuals desirous of such a union, may be said to have incautiously exposed the London Corresp. Society to the Mercy of the Constitutional Society to admit or to reject their *Petition* & thereby making this junction assume the appearance of a favor rather than an Act of mutual expediency & public Utility.

Secondly, I object to the manner of mentioning in that letter (& by its publication now gone forth as the Act & deed of the London Corresp. Society) of a Subscription entered into by the Society, for the defence of the prosecution commenced against Mr. Thos. Paine in consequence of his valuable production "entitled Rights of Man", as thereby we seem to make our Society a party concerned in Mr. Paynes works & while yet ignorant on what part thereof the Prosecution may be grounded we declare our Approbation of the whole & of every sentence therein; which I cannot conceive to be the sentiment of the Majority of our Members and the expression in consequence of his valuable production entitled &a &a is liable to be twisted by Malignant persons into an unwarrantable setting our face against the Laws & their execution instead of what the subscription is really meant to be a preventative against any abuse of power in the enforcing those laws & a gratefull tribute of Assistance to a worthy Man who by his Philanthropic writings has exposed himself to the revengeful wrath of Despotism. the Constitutional Society have by not adopting our expression sufficiently censured it & have more cautiously substituted in their resolutions *that a Subscription be opened for the benefit of Mr. Thos. Paine Author of the Rights of Man.*

Finally, the Subscription so noticed having taken place only in two divisions, cannot untill it has become more general be called the Subscription of the London Corresp. Society & even then in conveying the information to the Constitutional Society I must ever protest against the admission of the word, Duty.

Thus aggreing in the substance but objecting to the mode I beg you will admit this as my protest against so much of the proceedings of the Committee on thursday last.

I am Gentlemen with all sincerity & esteem
Your humble Servt.
Mce. Margarot
To the Committee of Delegates of the London Corresp. Society.

7. Journal: LCS General Committee, 28 June–16 August 1792

Source: Add MSS 27812, fos. 12–20 (later copies in Add MSS 27814, fos. 92–4)

Thursday 28 June

The Committee, this evening, postponed settling the accounts of the different Delegates, because some of the division had not yet appointed new Delegates.

The mode of electing the six members to be incorporated in the London Constitutional Society was determined on in the manner following.

> *Resolved* that each Division elect six Members of the London Corresponding Society to associate with the Constitutional Society. That a return of the members so elected be laid before the Delegates at their next meeting. That those who appear to have the majority of voices be elected.

The Committee next read a letter from the Chairman of the Friends of the People in Southwark inviting the London Corresponding Society to a closer & more frequent intercourse. – An answer was ordered to be written [36] and to be conveyed to them, by the Secretary and deputation of six Delegates.

Thursday 5th. July

The Committee took into consideration the friendly reception their deputation had met with from the Friends of the People, in Southwark & a farther deputation of Messrs. Gow, & Margarot was agreed upon for next Tuesday.

Several of the Delegates[37] settled their accounts with

36 This answer stated the belief 'that as public good is the Basis on which all Societies for a reform in Parliament, are instituted so a consolidation of them all must take place before that reform can be effected or deemed the Sense of the Nation'. Government, which seized the LCS draft of the letter in 1794, annotated this statement: 'This shows a Consolidation of Clubs reckoning themselves *The Nation*' (letter, 28 June 1792, TS 11/965/3510A.)

37 The ten delegates for the third quarter of 1792 had now been elected: William Gow, Thomas Hardy, George Walne, Robert Lyttlejohn, Andrew Murray, Francis Dowling, Maurice Margarot, James Black, Alexander Grant and James Styles (vouchers or government copies in TS 11/965/3510A and TS 11/958/3503).

[The next page of the Journal, containing the rest of this entry, was cut out. It must have contained the result of the elections of six LCS members to associate with the SCI. The tally of the divisions shows that the following men received votes from more than one division: Richter (63); Margarot (61); Grant (59); Lyttlejohn (59); Hardy (49); Rogers (48), his name subsequently crossed out; Gow (41); Murray (31); Cowie (17). Nine other men received votes from single divisions, probably their own. On the day after this meeting of delegates Hardy wrote to the SCI announcing the names of the men chosen for admission to the SCI.[38]

The tally indicates an active membership of 168.]

[Thursday 12 July] [39]

and unanimously agreed to.

Resolved That the Committee of the London Corresponding Society be always open to such members of the Southwark Society of the Friends of the People as find it convenient to visit them.

The Committee gave up the idea of making a public dinner on the fourteenth of July, the anniversary of the French Revolution.

Thursday 19 July

The Committee audited the Treasurer's accounts unto this day, & found the receipts of the Society had amounted to £9 .. 5 .. 1
The Expences to   6 .. 7 .. 11
And there remained in
the Treasurers hand a
Balance of   £2 .. 17 .. 2

The Committee next gave orders for the purchase of such books & stationary as would be wanted.

The consideration of bye-laws for the Committee, next took place: & after some discussion they were referred until the next meeting.

The Journal was revised & given to the Secretaries to be fairly entered in the Societies books.

A letter was read from the secretary of the Constitutional Society informing us that the six members proposed by our Society had all been approved of at their last meeting.

Thursday 26 July. 1792

The Committee postponed the further examination of the bye-laws, as also the report concerning the Divisions No. 5 & 9.

By the accounts of the different Delegates respecting their different divisions it appeared the Society was rapidly encreasing.

Such members as attended for the first time in their places at the London Constitutional Society gave an account of the cordial reception they there met with.

An address to the public was read in the Committee but no resolution was taken thereon.

Thursday 2d. Augt. 1792

Some of the Delegates accounted with the Treasurer, & the others promised to do the same on the next committee night.

The Committee came to the following resolutions with regard to the division No. 5.

Resolved That the Delegates of the three Divisions No. 1, 2 & 3 which meet together at the Unicorn, Covent Garden shall propose to their respective Divisions to draught out a certain number of their members to be sent to reinforce the Division at No. 5. meeting at the Marquis of Granby, Castle Street Oxford Market,[40] and that the said members being there assembled shall proceed to choose a Chairman, who shall be empoured to convoke all the members of that division by a special summons for the purpose of electing a Delegate.[41]

Thursday 9th Augt. 1792

The Delegates finished settling their accounts with the Treasurer.

The Committee heard the address again read, & ordered proof sheets to be printed for the Delegates to take the opinions of their different Divisions thereon.

The correspondence of the Society was taken into consideration & it was resolved to delay writing to any society until the address could be printed.
    Visitor
        Mr. Sinclair.

Thursday 16th Augt. 1792

The Committee received the assent of all the Divisions to the publication of the Address

40 In later copy some members 'who live contiguous to Oxford Market' are 'to be requested to transfer' to Div. 5.
41 'to summon the absent Members and choose a new Delegate that the division may be revived' – later copy.

38 Tally in TS 11/966/3510B; letter of 6 July 1792, TS 11/952/3496.
39 Folio containing first part of account cut out.

to the Inhabitants of Great Britain, and in consequence therof ordered two thousand copies to be printed.[42]

[The address is then copied out]

They also approved of the printing a circular letter for the use of the society whenever a general call of the society should be deemed necessary.

The three following bye laws for the use of the committee were unanimously approved of & passed (viz)

I   A question being under the consideration of the Committee the Delegates shall deliver their opinions by rotation.

II   No Delegate shall speak out of his turn, nor more than twice to one question unless to explain or to retract

III   Visitors should be at liberty to deliver their sentiments subject to the same regulations as the Delegates, but upon no account to give a vote.

8. Address from LCS to the Inhabitants of Great Britain on the Subject of a Parliamentary Reform, 16 August 1792 (excerpts) [43]

Source: BL 8135.b.8(3); copy from same typesetting (with typographical errors corrected) in TS 11/957/3505

FELLOW CITIZENS,
Of every rank and every situation in life, Rich, Poor, High or Low, we address you all as our Brethren, on a subject of the highest importance and most intimately connected with the welfare of every Individual who deems Liberty a Blessing. . . . we entreat you to examine cooly and impartially the numerous abuses that prevail [in the British Government], their destructive consequences on the poor, and their evil tendency on all. . . . We next submit to your examination an effectual mode of putting a stop to them and of thereby restoring to our no less boasted than impaired Constitution its pristine vigour and purity; and we thereunto warmly solicit the junction of your efforts with ours. This great end however we believe attainable, solely, by the whole nation deeply impressed with a sense of its wrongs uniting, and as it were with one voice demanding of those to whom for a while it has entrusted its Sovereignty, a Restoration of ANNUALLY ELECTED PARLIAMENTS, UNBIASSED AND UNBOUGHT ELECTIONS, AND AN EQUAL REPRESENTATION OF THE WHOLE BODY OF THE PEOPLE. . . . The only resource. . . . will be found in those Societies which, instituted with a view to the public Good, promote a general instruction of our rights as men, expose the abuses of those in power, and point out the only constitutional, the only effectual means of . . . obtaining a complete redress. . . .

[R]eform one abuse, and the others will all disappear – if we once regain an Annually elected Parliament, and that Parliament to be fairly chosen by all, the people will again share in the Government of their Country and their then unbought unbiassed suffrages must undoubtedly select a majority of Honest Members. . . .

Let no man imagine himself unconcerned in the proposed reform – let no one think so meanly of his situation or abilities, as to suppose his coming forward will be of no service to the Cause of Liberty! Numbers, Union and Perseverance must in the end be crowned with success. . . .

Soon then should we see our Liberties restored, the Press free, the Laws simplified, Judges unbiassed, Juries independant, Needless Places and Pensions retrenched, Immoderate Salaries reduced, the Public better served, Taxes diminished and the Necessaries of life more within the reach of the poor, Youth better educated, Prisons less crowded, old Age better provided for, and sumptuous Feasts, at the expence of the starving poor, less frequent.

Look not upon this, Dear Countrymen, as an enthusiastic vision, but rather let us together take a calm and reasonable review of such an Honest Parliament assembled. . . . Contested Elections none, or very few, and soon determined; Party Debates, none, the

42 'ordered in the *first place* 2000 copies to be printed and distributed *gratis*' – later copy.
43 Reprinted (with a few changes) together with resolutions of 2 April 1792 and address of 24 May 1792, dated July 1794, in TS 11/956/3501. All printed copies of the Address give the date as 6 August. But on 8 Aug. Hardy wrote to Horne Tooke that they intended to print the Address before 13 Aug., and the general committee accepted it and ordered it printed only on 16 Aug. Margarot wrote this address, according to a MS obituary (Add MSS 27816, fo. 217).
   At the trial of Hardy the Attorney General said that this address 'first developes . . . the determination of those societies to work what they call a reform without any communication whatever with that parliament, which they held to be incompetent to bring about the business' (*ST* vol. 24, col. 307; see also col. 1238).

Interest of the People being one; Long Speeches much diminished, Honest Men seeking reason, not oratory; No placemen in the Senate, Corrupt Influence dies away, and with it all tedious, obstinate Ministerial opposition to measures calculated for the public good. . . .

Recalling to their mind that wise and wholesome provision of the 12th of William III. Chap. 2. enacting that *All resolutions taken in the Privy Council shall be signed by such of the Privy Council as shall advise and consent to the same.* They would call for an immediate renewal of that long suspended Law, and by so doing all destructive secret Influence would be rooted up, and the people could then, at all times, discover who were their friends, and who their foes. . . .

Numerous other Reforms would undoubtedly take place, even in the first Session of Parliament so elected. . . . Every transaction would tend to reform, and a strict Œconomy its natural consequence, might soon enable us to reduce our Taxes, and by the Integrity of Parliament, that reduction would light upon such objects as best might relieve the Poor. . . .

Therefore Britons, Friends and fellow Citizens, with hand and heart unite, claim what is your Right, persevere and be Free, for who shall dare withstand our Just demands! – Oppression already trembling at the voice of Individuals, will shrink away and disappear for ever, when the Nation United shall assert its privileges, and demand their Restoration.

Signed by Order,
M. MARGAROT, Chairman.
T. HARDY, Secretary.

Ordered, that the Secretary of this Society, do transmit Copies of the above to all the Societies in the Nation, engaged in the same cause.

London, 6th August, 1792,

9. Journal: LCS General Committee, 23 August–20 September 1792

Source: Add MSS 27812, fos. 20–2v (later copies in Add MSS 27814, fos. 95–7)

Thursday 23d. Augt. 1792

The Committee received the assent of the different divisions to the following law

"Ordered that no Delegate, nor member of this Society do presume to *publish* or send to any news paper, any letter pamphlet or writing communicated to the Society, by any individual or society, unless by an express order

from the Committee under the penalty of expulsion."[44]

Orders were given to the secretary to transmit a number of copies of the address to all the associations in Great Britain.

Thursday 30 Augt. 1792

Report was made to the Committee that Alexr. Grant, Delegate for the division No. 9 had been superseded by his Division & that Wm. Wilson was appointed in his room.

Robert Thomson appeared in the Committee as the pro tempore Delegate of Division No 5 *deserted* by Andrew Murray.

A general quarterly meeting of the Society, was proposed & debated but as the Committee was divided in opinion, the further consideration of its expediency was postponed to that day month.

Visitor Mr. Sinclair

Thursday 6 Septr. 1792

The Committee was informed by Robt. Thomson that the Division No. 5 had confirmed him in the office of Delegate.[45]

On enquiring it appeared to the Committee that the Secretary had, according to order, written to the following

The Londn. Constitutional Society with	12 copies
The Manchester Do.	12
Sheffield Do.	50
The Borough Do. of the Friends of the People	50
The Editors of the Patriot	12
& Edinburgh[46]	6

The Committee instructed him to write with all possible dispatch to every other Society in the Kingdom.

It was proposed in the Committee that the first set of Resolutions should be reprinted annexed to the address to the nation at large *mutatis mutandis*, but on account of the

44 Three delegates had ordered a song by a member to be printed at LCS expense. See p. 20.
45 'Robert Thompson produced his voucher as Delegate from Divn. No. 5 in the room of Andrew Murray who had for several weeks deserted that Divn' – later copy, with marginal note: 'Thompson composed several patriotic songs which he afterwards published in a book but the Strong arm of power forced him into a foreign land – him and his family are now in paris prospering.'
46 Later copy adds to this list 'The Aldgate Society of friends of the people . . . The London Constitutional Whigs . . . The London Revolution Society . . . The Norwich Revolution Society'.

lateness of the hour, this and several other proposals were postponed to the next Committee night.

A motion was made that *a law be enacted to enforce* the immediate payment of the whole quarter, & that at whatever period of the quarter a member was admitted he should pay the whole without deduction –
negatived

Thursday 13th. Septr. 1792

The Committee received the proposal of sundry fresh regulations drawn up by Robert Watson a member of Division No. 7.

"They were ordered to ly on the table."

The reprinting the address was next taken into consideration, and after certain amendments had been adopted[47] two thousand copies were ordered to be printed.

The Secretary was directed to write to a new Society formed at Stockport under the title of the friends of *Universal Peace* & the *Rights of Man*.[48]

The Delegates of the Divisions No. 1, 2 & 9 assembling at the Unicorn in Covent Garden were directed to severely reprimand their respective divisions for a late undue assumption of power in ordering a song to be printed at the expence & in the name of the Society at large.[49]

The Borough Society of the Friends of the People wrote to the Committee to acquaint them that they met on the Tuesday following – The Chairman was authorized to return them an answer.

Thursday 20th. Septr. 1792

The Committee examined a proof copy of the 2d. edition of the Ist & IId. addresses, and ordered another proof to be struck off, and authorized the Chairman & Secretary to examine it, & give the necessary orders relative thereto.

In order the better to inforce the observance of the law respecting the dividing of the Society into small bodies to meet at separate houses, the Committee came to the resolution of admitting in future but one Delegate from each place of meeting.

The Chairman reported to the Committee, that accompanied by William Gow he had visited the Borough Society of the *Friends of*

the People, that the Committee had received them kindly & had promised to attend our Committee occasionally.

A message was received from the independent Whigs[50] informing the Committee, that having received an address from the Jacobin Club at Cherbourg they had printed a certain number of them, and that the Types being set, the Committee might if they chose avail themselves of it. – Accordingly orders were given for the printing of 500 Copies of the said letter for the use of the Society.

An address to the French Constituent Assembly was proposed; the Delegates were directed to represent the measure to their divisions; the Secretary to write circular letters mentioning it to the several Societies with whom we are in correspondence, & the Chairman was required to draw up the rough draught of it for the consideration of the Committee.

A Motion was made by the Delegate of division No. 7.[51] to the following purport.

"That the new Delegates be enjoined to deliver in together with their Vouchers an exact account of the number of members in their several divisions, with an accurate list of their names, the time of their admission, their places of abode, their numerical ranks in their Divisions, & the names of those members who proposed them for admission." *Negatived* –

James Black Delegate of Division No. 8 informed the Committee that their Landlord of the Blue Posts, in the Hay-market had been threatened with the loss of his licence if he permitted that Division to assemble any longer at his house. Accordingly they moved to the *Rising Sun in Bedford Bury*.

10. *The Address to the French National Convention*, 27 September 1792[52]

[If the LCS's first step towards leadership of the English reform societies was initiating correspondence with other societies as soon as their existence became known to the LCS, their second was organizing several of the societies to sign the LCS's laudatory Address to the French National

47 'and after enquiring at the Treasurer the state of the funds' – later copy.
48 The letter had been written two days earlier.
49 'The song was composed by R. Thompson, its title, "*God save the Rights of Man*" ' – marginal note in later copy.

50 'Constitutional Whigs' – later copy.
51 'Robert Watson' is written above this, in another hand.
52 The text of the LCS address is not reproduced here. See n. 57 for source.

Convention. This was the first venture in which societies outside London cooperated with the LCS, in effect the first step towards a union of all reform societies in England.

The LCS had a precedent for addressing the French in friendly terms. In 1789 the London Revolution Society, celebrating the English Revolution of 1688, sent an Address of Congratulation to the French National Convention. The impetus for the LCS address in 1792 was, according to Hardy, the Duke of Brunswick's 'wicked and cruel manifesto' of July 1792, threatening to destroy Paris and the approach to it unless the royal family were set at liberty. [53]

The plan of an address from several societies originated with Margarot, who wrote to Tooke on 15 September, asking 'whether a plan might not be adopted for obtaining the Assent of all the different Societies throughout the Nation, to an Animated (but safe) Declaration, assuring the French that we entertain the most friendly dispositions &c &c towards them and that we will, to the utmost of our power discountance all Hostile attempts on the part of Ministry'. Such a declaration would 'quiet French jealousies with regard to the English & would encourage them in their arduous struggle'; and the numbers of signatures to the declaration would 'check . . . Ministerial attempts'.[54] The next day Hardy wrote to Tooke asking his opinion of Margarot's plan, adding that 'Ten or Twenty Thousand signatures would have more weight than as many Thousand Pounds for ten men might subscribe that sum'.[55]

After the committee of delegates approved the plan of an address on 20 September, Margarot began writing to the other reform societies inviting them to add the names of their members to this address. He wrote to the SCI, the Borough Friends of the People, the Constitutional Whigs and Independent Friends of the People, all in London; to the societies in Derby, Edinburgh, Manchester (two societies), Norwich, Stockport and Sheffield. As a result of these efforts by the LCS, four other societies joined their names to this address – the Constitutional Whigs, Manchester Constitutional Society, Manchester Reformation Society and the Norwich Revol-

ution Society – and one other, the Stockport Friends of Universal Peace and the Rights of Man, sent resolutions approving the French Revolution. After the LCS sent the address, eleven other groups, including the SCI and the Sheffield Society for Constitutional Information, sent separate addresses.[56] Without the initiative of the LCS these other societies probably would not have addressed the French National Convention.

The LCS address, written by Margarot, is headed with a list of the co-signing societies – 'united in one common cause' – and their officers.[57] It opens with the statement that 'while foreign robbers are ravaging your territories . . . the oppressed part of mankind' are praying for the French cause, 'so intimately blended with their own'. Although 'an oppressive system of controul' has brought the English almost to a state of slavery, the signers think it their duty to swear 'an inviolable Friendship' to the French, 'our Fellow Citizens of the World and our Brethren by the same Heavenly Father'. The real enemy is the 'all-consuming Aristocracy – Wisely have you acted in expelling it from France.' The signers cannot assist with arms because the English government has pledged neutrality, but their hearts are with the French and they 'fondly anticipate the numerous blessings' mankind will enjoy if the French succeed, 'as we ardently wish'. The final paragraph of the address, written after the rest and after the French defeat of Brunswick's force, congratulates the French on their 'success unparalleled' and explains that this address, dated 27 September, has been delayed one month by 'the desire of having the concurrence of different Country Societies'.

After the Address had been engrossed on

53 Add MSS 27814, fo. 45.
54 TS 11/951/3495.   55 ibid.

56 Letters to and from these societies: 21, 26 Sept.; 10, 11, 15, 16, 17, 18, 19, 25, 27 Oct.; 3 Nov.; in TS 11/952/3496, TS 11/953/3497, TS 11/958/3503, TS 11/965/3510A. Albert Goodwin, *Friends of Liberty* (1979), has a thorough discussion of these addresses, pp. 244 ff. and Appendix 2.
57 Printed copy from a newspaper, in Add MSS 27814, fo. 46, is annotated by Hardy, 'The following printed Address to the French National Convention is a true copy.' The version in *ST* vol. 24, cols. 312–13, contains several slight variants and one significant change: 'five thousand British Citizens' is substituted for 'a few thousands' as the number signing the address.

vellum and signed by Hardy and Margarot, the committee of delegates deputed Hardy, Margarot, Martin and Walne to arrange its transmittal to France. On 31 October Hardy called at the Portman Square residence of the French ambassador, Chauvelin, and asked if he would convey it to the French National Convention. Chauvelin ordered the deputation to come the next morning at 11.00. At that meeting, on 1 November, Margarot read the Address to Chauvelin, who approved it and dispatched it to the Convention, where it was read aloud on 7 November and ordered published in the newspapers.[58]]

11. Journal: LCS General Committee, 27 September–4 October 1792

Source: Add MSS 27812, fos. 22v–3v (later copies in Add MSS 27814, fos. 97–8)

Thursday 27th September 1792

The secretary laid before the Committee three letters, the first from the Stockport Society of the *Friends of Universal Peace*, & of the Rights of Man in answer to ours of the [11th] inst, with which we transmitted to them some of our addresses.[59]

The second was from the President of the *Constitutional Whigs Independent & Friends of the People*, acquiescing to our proposal of an address to the French Constituent Assembly, but with restrictions.[60]

And the third was from Robert Watson a Member of the Division No. 7. but on account of the impropriety of his conduct, the Committee passed to the order of the day.

It was agreed that the Delegates should so manage that their respective divisions might choose their delegates before next Committee night.

Visitors

Mr. Scheffer, Secretary to the Committee of the Friends of the People in the Borough[61] –

Thursday 4 Octr. 1792

The new chosen Delegates met & produced their respective returns signed by the chairman of their Division (Viz)

Division	Number of Members[62]
No. 1	
2 Thomas Hardy	61
3 Robert Lyttlejohn	30
4 George Walne	21
5 Robert Thomson	42
6 John Jackson	34
7 Maurice Margarot	44
8 John Martin	41
9 William Wilson	
10 John Tindall	54

Thomas Hardy Delegate of Division No. 2 prayed for leave to divide – Granted.[63]

58 Add MSS 27814, fo. 46; *Memoir*, p. 117; letter, J. P. Rabaud de St Etienne to Margarot, 8 November 1792, TS 11/965/3510A. Ironically, the French translation omits all mention of the LCS, although it does include the names of Hardy and Margarot at the end (*Adresse à la Convention Nationale de France, Par des Sociétés de Bretons uniés dans une cause commune, c'est à dire pour obtenir une représentation juste, égale & impartiale dans Parlement*, Paris. 1792).

59 The Stockport society thought these addresses too tame: 'the Sentiments hardly arise to that Height which we expect from Men sensible of their full claim to absolute and uncontrollable liberty i.e. unaccountable to any Power which they have not immediately constituted and appointed. . . . would not all the evil be done away at once by the People assembled in convention?' At Hardy's trial the Attorney General argued that the failure of the LCS to disavow these notions showed that they agreed with them (letter, P. W. Frost to Hardy, received 27 Sept. 1792, TS 11/965/3510A; *ST* vol.24, col. 309).

60 They wanted the right to pass judgment of the parts of the address, and they objected to having

individual signatures because there was not time to obtain them all. Hardy and Margarot dealt with these reservations in a visit to the society on 9 Oct. (letter, George Puller to Chairman of LCS, 26 Sept. 1792, TS 11/965/3510A.)

61 'Mr Scheffer, Secretary . . . Borough some communication to the Committee – some others of his friends was recieved as visitors' – later copy.

62 The three extant vouchers for this election give higher numbers of members: Div. 3, 52 members; Div. 4, 25; Div. 10, 62. The lower numbers in the Journal probably represent paid-up members. On 7 Nov., Div. 9 reported 10 members on the voucher listing William Baxter as the new delegate. This change of delegates and the low number of members suggest that the division was not prospering. Despite a good membership (41 on 14 Nov.), Div. 1 seems to have had difficulty finding a man willing to be a delegate. Not until mid-November did it elect Robert Bell; and apparently he was the third man tapped, for on the voucher two other names (Wm Spence and Josh Blake) are crossed out.

On 20 Nov. Div. 10 elected a new delegate, John Copely (vouchers in TS 11/953/3497).

Jackson of Div. 6 is Thomas, not John.

63 Fifteen members left to form Div. 11, which met the next day and elected Edward Evans delegate (voucher in TS 11/953/3497).

The Committee thus formed proceeded to choose their Officers for the ensuing quarter, when no complaint arising against any of the former they were continued in their office (Viz)

Maurice Margarot, Chairman
Thos. Hardy, Treasurer & Secretary
and Robert Lyttlejohn assistant Secretary

Robert Watson a member of the 7th. Division presented himself before the Committee as member of a Division, which had formed itself in an irregular manner, the Chairman, authorized by the Committee, reprimanded him for his unjustifiable behaviour, and sent him back to his own Division.

Some of the Delegates accounted with the Treasurer, but others not being prepared to do the same the Accounts of the Treasurer could not be audited.

The Address to the National Convention of France was read, corrected, approved, & the different Delegates instructed to read the same at their several Divisions the Secretary was ordered to make out a certain number of copies of the same.

12. Letter: Anonymous informer to Lord Grenville, 7 October 1792[64]

Source: TS 11/959/3505

My Lord
In the absence of the Rt Honble Mr Dundas I have the honor to address your Lordship – as I understand officially the business I have to communicate is in his department.

I am a member of the London Corresponding Society –

That the views of these combined associations are hostile to the present government admits not the smallest doubt the firmness, unanimity and secresy which are the peculiar characteristics of this society their great number and extensive correspondence renders it a *serious* concern to those who wish well to our excellent Constitution –

The minds of the People are constantly kept in a state of fermentation, by the most seditious and treasonable writings, which are read to the different divisions every evening – the sacred character of His Majesty is held up to Public ridicule, His Ministers are constantly calumniated, and every principle on which they act, misrepresented.

Mr Paine, Horne Tooke, his Nephew Mr Vaughan, lend no small assistance towards exciting the people to *rebellion* by visiting the different divisions – there are many other popular demagogues who from their superior abilities attract the attention of the multitude.

From my situation in the Society, I am enabled from time to time to acquaint your Lordship with all their proceedings – their correspondence with Sheffield, Birmingham, Wolverhampton, Isle of Wight, et cetera – Scotland, Ireland, *Chorbourg* and even the present National Convention of France – . . . .

If you think these hints worthy your Lordships attention, you will be pleased to signify the same in the most guarded manner in the Daily Advertiser I will immediately wait on your Lordship, and expect the strictest secresy –

I have the honor to be, My Lord,
Yr Lordships
Most obedient
humble servant
Mercator

Octr 7th. 1792
The Rt Honble Lord Grenville

14. Journal: LCS General Committee, 11–18 October 1792

Source: Add MSS 27812, fo. 23v (later copy in Add MSS 27814, fos. 98-9)

Thursday 11 Octr. 1792

The Committee changed the place of their meeting. The Delegates reported the assent of all the several divisions to the address to the French National Assembly; the Secy. was therefore ordered to send copies of it to the different country Societies, and to the Society for Constitutional Information in London requesting their concurrence in the measure.

Several letters were received and read – among them one from Joel Barlow presenting the Society with a copy of his works. The Committee thereupon

Resolved that the Secretary be ordered to return the thanks of the Committee to Joel Barlow for his present,[65] & polite attention to the London Corresponding Society.

Visitors

Mr. Scheffer the Secy. and other Gentlemen

64 Government description: '7th Octo: 1792/ (Anonymous)/Rx 8' There are no other spy reports in this handwriting.

65 On 6 Oct. Barlow sent the LCS copies of *A Letter to the National Convention of France, on the defects of the constitution of 1791* and *Advice to the Privileged Orders* (TS 11/965/ 3510A).

Members of the Borough Society of the Friends of the People.

Thursday 18 Octr. 1792

The Committee audited the Treasurer's accounts unto this day and found that the receipts for the last quarter had amounted with the balance brought from[66]

[At this point in the Journal there is an excision which removed the rest of this account, all of the accounts of meetings of 25 October and 1 November, and part of the report of the meeting of 8 November.]

14. Report from spy Lynam: LCS Division 2 (government paraphrase), 29 October 1792[67]

Source: TS 11/959/3505

[The first report from the spy George Lynam consisted of a list of LCS meeting

66 'and found that the receipts was considerably more than the expenditure' – later copy.
67 Government description: 'Houses of meeting / 29 Octo. 1792'. Lynam, an ironmonger, joined Div. 12 in Oct. 1792, was elected a delegate of Div. 23 in Nov., and provided government with numerous reports of the activities of the Society. In June 1793 he was accused of being a spy, but was acquitted. His role as a spy was not revealed until after the arrest of Hardy in May 1794.
    At the trial of Hardy Lynam described his first acquaintance with the LCS: 'I was at the sign of the Mansion-house, when the division No. 12, had a meeting there; I knew nothing at all of it, but the landlord had one of their printed resolutions [the Address to the Nation and the Resolutions of 24 May 1792] given to him, and I requested the favour of looking at it, and upon seeing it, my remark to him was, that it was a society formed for overturning the constitution of this country, and I advised him by no means to suffer them to meet there any more, for if he did, he would certainly have his licence taken away. . . . I went up to the society the same evening along with two other gentlemen that were there. I understood that any person might go into the room; there had been two or three had attempted it, therefore they appointed a door keeper to admit none but those that were members; one of the society endeavoured to turn me out, however I went in, and had some conversation with the president, whose name was Watson, and who was at that time supposed to be secretary to lord George Gordon; we were

places and an account of a meeting of Division 2. The original account of this meeting is missing; the paraphrase given here was made in 1794.[68]]

29 Octr. – The Witness [Lynam] was present at a Meeting of Division 2 at the Unicorn in Henrietta Street Covent Garden – The Meeting consisted of between 70 & 80

charged with interrupting the company; I asked pardon of the society, saying, I did not mean to do any thing of the kind, but understanding the society was on a public ground, I should be much obliged to them for one of their resolutions, and then I should leave them to their own deliberations.' Lynam became a member at the next meeting of Div. 12, which (as a consequence of Lynam's advice to the publican of the Mansion House) took place at the Crown in Newgate Street (*ST* vol. 24, cols. 763 & 805). Since Div. 12 met on Wednesdays, Lynam joined on 24 Oct. at the latest.
    He promptly began sending reports of the meetings to Evan Nepean, Under Secretary of State for Home Affairs. The connection between Nepean and Lynam is unclear. At Hardy's trial, Lynam testified that he described the 'societies about London' to 'a gentleman that I had received friendship from at the west end of the town; he recommended me by all means to make a report of it, I did make a report of it, and have done' (col. 807). Since Lynam was upheld in his refusal to name the gentleman or the recipient of the reports, it is uncertain whether Nepean was both. The court held that 'those persons who are the channel by means of which that detection [of crimes] is made, should not be unecessarily disclosed' (col. 808). Inasmuch as an Under Secretary of State is by definition a 'disclosed' channel, there may have been an intermediary who introduced Lynam to Nepean. For Nepean's connection with the spy Groves see p. 113, n. 40.
68 TS 11/954/3498. The 'Evidence of George Lynam as to the proceedings of the London Corr Society from Octobr. 1792 to February 1794' is a 17pp. document paraphrasing many of Lynam's reports of LCS meetings. A comparison of the paraphrases with the original reports (where they exist) reveals that the paraphrase omits material of the original report which was not considered pertinent to the impending treason trials. What it does present is accurate. References to Lynam as 'the witness' suggest that the paraphrase was made in Oct. 1794 between the indictment and the trial of Hardy. A 29 pp. copy of these paraphrases, in TS 11/956/3501, starts, 'Mr. George Lynam of Walbrook Ironmonger will prove. . . .' There is still another set of paraphrases of Lynam's reports (12 pp.) in TS 11/966/3510. Finally, there is an 8 pp. summary of these reports in ibid.

Persons. . . . [69] Hardy who had been Elected a Delegate for the Division on the 1st. of that month . . . reported from the General Committee that Mr. Paines address to the French People had been ordered to be published & Delivd. out in all the Divisions[70] that his Letters to the People of France had been already Published & delivd. out in the Divisions[71] – That a Letter had been recvd. from the Sheffd. Constl. Society Stating that an address to the French Convention had been drawn up & only waited the Sanction of the Genl. Meeting which as soon as it had recived it shod. be transmitted to the London Corr. Society with all possible Dispatch –

Mr. Margarot . . . communicated a Letter from the Manchester Reformation Society dated the 27th. of Octr. approving the address of the London Corr. Society to the French Convention . . . & accompaning a Transcript of the address signed by all the Members of the Society in order to its being transmitted to France –

The Resolutions of the Society for Constl. Informn. . . . approvg the spirit of the London Corr. Societys address but resolving to send a seperate one were also reported to the Division – [72]

15. Report from spy Lynam: LCS Division 12 (government summary), c. October 1792[73]

Source: TS 11/959/3505

Lynam's Account of the Meeting of Division 12 at the Crown in Newgate Street – Read the

Copy of the Address to the French Convn. which was first proposed by the Meeting at the Unicorn & brought forward the 27 Septr. last

[During the first week of November, four new divisions (13, 14, 15, 16) were authorized. They elected as delegates John Grice, John Tindall, Richard Gay and John Baxter. Division 13 had 11 members; Division 14, 16 members; Division 15, 17 members; Division 16, 31 members.[74] This rapid increase continued during November, with seven more divisions established during the following three weeks. 'The increase of new Members', wrote Hardy, 'was so rapid that the Secretary could not enter their names and residences fast enough on the night they came to be inrolled into the society but were necessitated to defer it untill he had an opportunity in the course of the week before the next meeting night.'[75] Newly formed divisions were initiated by members of older divisions. According to the 1796 'History of the Society' Gough (Gow), Thompson and Margarot 'were indefatigable in their exertions in visiting and instructing new divisions'.[76]

16. Report from spy Lynam: LCS Division 11 (government summary), 2 November 1792[77]

Source: TS 11/959/3505

Lynam's Account of the Meeting at the Rainbow Report from the Delegates – A Company at Stockport had wrote their Approbation of the Meetings held in different Parts to the Sheffield Meeting – The Editor of the

reading of the address to the French National Convention (*ST* vol. 24, col. 765).

He did not note that William Freemantle was elected delegate (voucher in TS 11/953/3497). Since it was customary to elect the delegate at the first meeting of a newly formed division, this should have been the first meeting of Div. 12. But the number of members listed on the voucher – 58 – is remarkably large for a new division, and Lynam's testimony indicates at least two earlier meetings of this division. Div. 12 was probably established early in Oct.

69 The ellipses in these reports indicate the omission of government's notes (e.g. 'Vide Hardy's Papers Bundle B') or of extended quotations from documents Lynam had heard read at meetings. Such quotations could not have been part of Lynam's original reports.
70 By 1 Nov. 2000 copies were printed at a cost of £3 (receipted bill, TS 11/965/3510A).
71 Addition in other paraphrase: 'The Rights and Duties of Man to be continued weekly' (TS 11/966/3510).
72 'The Constitutionl: Society think the more addresses the better – & will Address separately' – paraphrase in TS 11/966/3510. At the trial Lynam added one item: the delegate reported that over 2000 people at Norwich had signed the LCS address to the French National Convention.
73 This is from a document entitled 'Index to Bundle G', a government bibliography of 1792 papers about the LCS and SCI. At Hardy's trial Lynam, consulting his notes, testified that he noted nothing about this meeting except the

74 Vouchers in TS 11/953/3497.
75 Add MSS 27814, fo. 38.
76 *MPM*, vol. 1 (Sept. 1796), p. 183.
77 Short summary in TS 11/966/3510 lists this as a meeting of Div. 11.

Sheffield Paper wrote that it wd. be a good Plan to Send London Delegates into the Country to instruct the Farmers
Letter from the Delegates to a new Society at Nottingham[78] 6 Honorary Members admitted to Crown & Anchor

17. Journal: LCS General Committee, 8 November 1792[79]

Source: Add MSS 27812, fos 24–4v (later copy in Add MSS 27814, fo. 19)

Three Orders were signed this Evening for three new Divisions as follows,

From Division No. 5 - Granted - No. 17
No. 2 - - - - - - 18
No. 6 - - - - - - 19[80]

The Delegate of No. 2 made a Motion for printing the Names and Places of Abode of all the Delegates, and the Places of Meeting of all the Divisions.

Rejected Unanimously.

A Letter was read from the Sheffield Constitutional Society, who instead of concurring in our Address send the Committee one of their own, desiring them to forward it – The Chairman was authorized to wait upon Mr. Chauvelin with it.

The Treasurer recieved the Delegates first Payment.

A Letter was read from the Associated Friends of the People in Edinburg, cautiously declining joining in the Address,[81] but giving a very favorable Account of the Spirit of Liberty in those Parts.

A Letter from the Stockport Friends of Universal Peace, &c gave us to understand that our Correspondence with them was watched, and that some of our Letters had been intercepted.

The Chairman was authorized to answer the above Letters, and the Editors of the Patriot.[82]

"It was resolved that in future all Absentees from the Committee pay the same Share of Expences as if present."

18. Report from spy Lynam: LCS Division 2 (government summary), 14 November 1792[83]

Source: TS 11/959/3505

Lynam's Account of the General Meeting of the Corr. Society at the Unicorn –

The first Meeting was 2d. April 1792 at Mr. Robt. Boyds the Bell Exeter Street Strand – but he was afraid of losing his Licence & would not let them continue there there are printed Articles of that Date

The Delegates reported a Letter from Major Johnston at Edinburgh – they do not approve of an Address to France so soon – are forming the Plan of a Paper to inform the Public upon Politics –

The Address to the Convention had been ordd. to be published & sent to the 83 Departments – Sheffield sent up their Address to be forwarded – which was done

a Correspondence between Sheffield & Stockport[84]

An Account also of a Meeting the same Day

78 Lynam's testimony: the letter was from the Nottingham Society to the delegates of the LCS. Lynam thought the letter was not read (*ST* vol. 24, col. 765).

79 As noted above, the first part of this account was cut from the Journal. The later copy, which combines this entry with that for 18 Oct., includes a paragraph not found in the original: 'More copies of the Address to the Nation were ordered to be printed and distributed gratis. Mr. Schieffer and other members of the Borough Society of the friend of the people were visitors.'

80 Delegate of Div. 17 unknown. Joseph Field elected delegate of Div. 18 on 14 Nov. (voucher in TS 11/953/3497). John Richter elected delegate of Div. 19 at its first meeting (at the Friend at Hand, Little North St, Knightsbridge) on 26 Nov. (*ST* vol. 24, col. 574).

81 'We do not conceive that it would be either Wise, politic or prudent to enter into a correspondence with France . . . as it might be productive of mischief and misconstruction at home' (W. Johnston to Hardy, 31 Oct. 1792, TS 11/965/3510A).

82 The anonymous editors announced their intention to publish the LCS *Address to the Nation*, their approval of the plan to address the French National Convention, and their request that the LCS encourage a new society at Stockport. In a lengthy reply (a month later) the LCS sent a copy of the *Address to the FNC* for possible inclusion in the *Patriot*. Although the editors had offered to publish anything the LCS wished the public to know, they did not publish this (editors to Hardy, 15 Oct. 1792, TS 11/965/3510A; committee of LCS to editors, 15 Nov. 1792, TS 11/958/3503).

83 Short summary in TS 11/966/3510 lists this as a meeting of Div. 2, as does Lynam's testimony at Hardy's trial.

84 At Hardy's trial Lynam gave further details of this meeting: 'There was read a letter, written by Mr. Barlow – his address to the [French National] Convention, very inflammatory, and there were very loud plaudits at the reading. . . .

at the Crown in Newgate Street – Same Letter from Edinburgh

17 Novr. Favel in Tooley Strt. avows himself Paine's Supporter[85]

19. Report from spy Munro, 14 November 1792[86]

Source: TS 11/959/3505

The first Club I visited was the Cock and Crown kept by one Burton at the Corner of Cock Court Villers Street, this Scociety meets for what they are pleased to term the reformation of Government and particularly a more equal representation in Parliment, it is the fifteenth Division and sends one Deligate to the Scociety of Deligates, which notwithstanding every art I used, I could not learn when it was held. the person I spoke most to was the only man in the Club that had common information, he was young and told me he was the Deligate of the Scociety he had a large bundle of papers before him which he would not oppen till I was gone and would not admit me a Member without being proposed, and recomended by two of the Members; he however as well as the rest of the Members was extremely civil, the whole of them except the Deligate appeared to me to be the very lowest tradesmen, they were all smoaking pipes and drinking porter.

The next I visited was the Red Lion Brownlow Street long Acre, this house is kept by one Lee, and Division 13th is held here, the company appeared more decent than at Division 15th but were also extremely low, the Deligate with whom I spoke, was very civil, but made the same objections as the other did respecting

The next is a report by somebody to the meeting that the London Corresponding Society in London, in number, was six thousand; that the division, No. 14, meeting at Spitalfields, was increased, and would soon be equal in number to all the rest of the divisions of the society' (ST vol. 24, col.766).

85 Samuel Favel (Favell), a tea merchant (called 'slop seller') was active in the Revolution Society in 1789, in the SCI from 1786 until June 1792, and in the Borough FoP from its inception in April 1792. His support of Paine may be inaccurately reported here: He ceased attending the SCI when it voted to collect funds for Paine's defence; and in Dec. 1792 he wrote to government denying that he supported Paine.

86 Government description: 'London Corresponding Society / Capt. Munro., 14 Nov. 1792'. George Munro of George Street, Manchester Sq., was a captain in the army.

admitting stranger Members. the house and the people that were in it impress'd me with much horror, as the people below stairs seemingly consisted of nothing but Thieves and pickpockets.

The third I visited was the Marquis of Granby kept by one Pride this is the 5th Division, there were a vast number of Scotchmen in this, it seem'd the best attended and best conducted, the Deligates Name was Thomson, discovering I was a Countryman of his (for he was Scotch) I was admitted a Member of this Division with little difficulty, and have the honor of accompanying this with one of their printed papers, which will give you a clear Idea of the nature of these Scociety's who's intentions seem that of corrupting the minds of the lower order of the people by inflaming their imaginations with imaginary grievances, and working them up to comit some great excess which may alarm and throw the Country with the greatest confusion. There are at present Twenty two or Twenty three Divisions. Division 5th has sent forth three Divisions for when they exceed Sixty they detach a part of their body to establish another Division in some other Quarter of the Town.

London 14th Novr. 1792

20. Report from spy Munro, 15 November 1792[87]

Source: TS 11/959/3505

Division No. 10 which I had the hon'or of remarking Yesterday I was to late to attend on Thursday evening met that evening at the Scotch Arms round Court in the Strand, it was attended by more than one hundred people, but quarelling amongst them selves the seperated, and the Majority have agreed to meet at the Buking Streets Court in the Strand, which is almost adjoining round Court next Wednesday.

After obtaining this information I visited the Scociety held at the Nags head Orange Court where the 6th Division meets this Club was thinly attend there not being more than twelve Members present and neither Deligate or Deputy Deligate present

From this I went to the Green Dragon Kings Street Golden Square here the 3d Division meets and was attended by more than Two hundred people; a Mr Frost almost the

87 Government description: '1792 Nov 15 / Capt Munro's Information'.

only decent Man I have seen in any of their Divisions made a long inflamatory speech, which he concluded by recomending to the members to deffend their oppinions with their lives and property, this man seem'd very popular.

The meeting at the one Tun, Tun Court in the Strand is the 1st Division and met there for the first time last Night, this Division was attended by more than one hundred and Twenty a Mr. Hardy seem'd the leading Man, this club was beginning to break up before I came.

I understand the Divisions best attended is No. 2 held at the Unicorn Covent Garden and No. 8 held at the Sun Windmill Street which meet on Mondays.

I beg leave to remark that all the Divisions I have seen are attended by the very lowest tradesmen, and the most of them seem Scotch Shoemakers

Lond. 15th Novr.

21. Journal: LCS General Committee, 15 November 1792

Source: Add MSS 27812, fo. 24v (later copy in Add MSS 27814, fo. 100)

Thursday 15th. Novr. 1792.

Joseph Field the New Delegate for Division No. 18 produced his voucher.

Five Orders for as many fresh Divisions were granted   Viz.

To the Delegate of No. 2 three Orders were given for to take the Names of No. 20. 21 & 22.

One Order to the Delegate of Division No. 12 to take the Name of No. 23.

And One Order to the Delegate of No. 3 to take the Name of No. 24.[88]

The Chairman reported to the Committee his having waited on Mr. Chauvelin with the Address from the Sheffield Constitutional Society –

Some Conversation took Place about our Address –

A Letter was read from Mr. Rabaud,[89] and the Chairman was directed to procure further Information

[The rest of this entry, all of that for 22 November and most of the entry for 29 November have been cut out of the Journal.]

22. Report from spy Kennedy, c. 20 November 1792[90]

Source: TS 11/959/3505

1 Division
One Ton   Strand   Evans delegate – on Wednesdays heard nothing of any consequence only a few Letters in the public Papers which was read over by the Delegate[91]

2d division
Unicorn   Henrietta St.   Evans delegate.

88 Delegates of Div. 20 and 22 unknown. John Prothero elected delegate of Div. 21 (at the Red Lyon, King St, Golden Sq.) on 26 Nov..(government copy of voucher, TS 11/958/3503). George Lynam, delegate of Div. 23 (at the Ship, Finsbury Place, Moorfields), 11 members, on 26 Nov. (voucher in TS 11/953/3497). Baker, delegate of Div. 24 on 29 Nov. (government list of delegates, TS 11/966/3510B).

89 Announcing the receipt of the Address and thanking the LCS for their confidence and courage. The salutation to Margarot: 'Mon cher Concityon de Monde' (8 Nov. 1792, TS 11/965/3510A).

90 Government description: 'Novr 1792 / Mr Kennedy'. Christopher Kennedy, of Cross Court, Broad Court, Long Acre, was both a carpenter and a constable attending the public office in Bow Street.

91 An undated government compilation gives two columns of details about the divisions, presumably from two spies, for the information is sometimes conflicting. For Div. 1 it adds: 'Near 100 on the 14th Nov., Delegate Mr Thompson / ... 25' (TS 11/959/3505). Apparently '25' is the number present at a different meeting of the division. Besides the data given below on Divs. 2–15, the report lists three other divs.: 'Black Swan   Brown's Lane   Spital fields Monday / No. 17 Est. 6 Nov. meet on that day & on the 13. but not suffered to remain[.] Friend at Hand   North Street   Knightsbridge – Wednesday K[ennedy] / No. unknown [Div. 19]. Est. 31 Oct. abt. 30 – Tedmouth keeps the House. Wheatsheaff Marylebone Street Tuesday – K[ennedy] / Established 13 Nov. Mr Thompson Del.'
If the Thompson listed here as delegate of Divs. 1, 5 and an unnumbered one was Robert Thompson, the misidentification indicates that this man who hardly figures in the minutes of meetings was, as the 1796 'History of the Society' says, one of the most energetic of the early members. Thompson fled to France a few weeks later. Kennedy and other spies were probably ordered to include names of publicans so that magistrates knew whom to threaten with loss of licence.

Mr Ritcher Clerk to Sir Robt. Herries –
Presidt   The making uncommonly numerous
more so than at any other division.
The chief Questions in agitation where the
defending Paine in the Action brought ags't
him by the Attorney Gen'l towards which
several liberrally subscrib'd. Also the sacred
Character of his Majesty was treated very contemptuously & the Majority in Gen'l was
totally in favor of Mr. Paines conduct respecting the reform   Mr Taylor. M. P. was present
on the 19th of Novr. last[92]

3 division
Little Jno. Delegate
Their principle conversation was respecting the
reform & each firmly resolv'd to support each
other in the business to see themselves righted
but without any violence, whatever   a Letter
from Stockport was going to be read but was
not it being thought of no consequence.[93]

4 division
Crown & Thistle   Peter St   Westr
Partly of the same Tenor

5 division
Marquis Granby   Oxford Market
Thompson delegate
Their conversation exactly the same as the 3d
division

6 division
Orange Court
Nothing particular happd[94]

7 divn.
Black dog   Oxford Market
Margarot delegate
Same as the first division[95]

8 divisn
Sun   Windmil St
Evans delegate
On entring into the room was immediately
suspected and was very ill treated being not
only abus'd by the President but was threatend
to be turn'd out if I did not immediately
depart after some altercation they was somewhat appeas'd & they inform'd me it was
resolv'd that no man in Office whatever was

suffer'd to enter the room words again arose
a Gentleman present kept up the contention &
insisted on my being turn'd out to prevent
which I withdrew & as I was going I rec'd a
Kick in the Side on the Stairs

10th division
There is shortly to be a meeting of the Military
near Grosvenor Square[96]

11 division
3 Herrings   Bell yard
Mr Paine gave £1000 to the Society for constitutional information since then £2000 has
been Subscrib'd to prevent information and to
defend Actions &c[97]

12 divisn
Crown   Newgate St.
Heard the Society was to be remov'd to
Finsbury Square on Tuesdays – Also that Mr
Erskine was to be council in behalf of Mr
Paine[98]

13 Divisn
Red Lyon   Brownlow St.
Nothing particular happen'd[99]

14 divisn
Scotch Arms   Rd. Court
Nothing materially occurr'd
Little John delegate[100]

15 divisn
Sign of the Cock   Cock Ct.   New St.
Golden Sqe.
Partly the same as the first division[101]

16 divisn
Crown   Air St.   Wednesday
Piccadilly
Was not there

Sir
    Those are the particulars as nigh as I can
guess[102]

92 '2d & 9th Divisions both Monday . . . 250 on the
    13'
93 'near 50   14 Nov./ Green Dragon King Street
    Goulden Square   35 No.   Wednesday'
94 'Naggs head . . . Friday'
95 'upwards of 40 – 13 Nov./ . . . Mondays'
96 'Mr. Tindall Delegate near 30 on the 14 / Scotch
    arms Round Court on the Strand   Mr Styles
    30 Tuesdays'
97 'Rainbow Fleet Street now Fridays / Mr Baxter
    Delegate No. 11 near 40.   ab 30 the 16th.'
98 'Freemantle Del. . . . abt. 40 peope   14 Nov'
99 'Red Lyon . . . kept by Lee / near 25 – 14 Nov'
100 'Wednesdays / Did not meet on the 14th
    removed to [undecipherable word] in Hewitts
    Court'
101 'Tuesdays / Mr. Day [Gay] Delegate, ab 40
    people on the 13th.
102 Written on the verso.

[To counteract the reform societies, on 20 November 1792, John Reeves and Charles Philip Yorke founded The Association for Preserving Liberty and Property Against Republicans and Levellers. The Association soon affiliated with other anti-republican societies throughout the country. The first publication of the Association (dated 20 November 1792) so alarmed the LCS that they promptly issued a retort in an *Address . . . to the Other Societies of Great-Britain United for the Obtaining a Reform in Parliament* (dated 29 November 1792). The document which provoked the LCS to such instant action opens as follows:

At a Meeting of Gentlemen at the Crown and Anchor Tavern in the Strand, November 20, 1792,
John Reeves, Esq. in the Chair.

The following Considerations and Res-olutions were entered into and agreed upon:
Considering the danger to which the Publick Peace and Order are exposed by the circulating of mischievous Opinions, founded upon plausible but false reasoning; and that this circulation is principally carried on by the industry of Clubs and Societies of various denominations in many parts of the kingdom:
It appears to us, that it is now become the duty of all Persons, who wish well to their Native Country, to endeavour, in their several neighbourhoods, to prevent the sad effects of such mischievous industry; and that it would greatly tend to promote these good endeavours, if Societies were formed in different parts of the Kingdom, whose object should be to support the Laws, to suppress seditious Publications, and to defend our Persons and Property against the innovations and depredations that seem to be threatened by those who maintain the mischievous opinions before alluded to.[103]]

23. Thomas Hardy's account of government interference with the LCS, *re* 20 November 1792

Source: excerpted from Hardy's history of the LCS, Add MSS 27814, fos. 39–43, 48

This Address of theirs Alarmed the Nation very much being supported by government and

all their venal agents. . . . The publicans and Tavern keepers were threatned with the loss of their Licence if they suffered any of these reforming societies to meet in their Houses
The poor publicans were obliged to submit – There was no appeal – for the Magistrates on Licen[c]ing day have it in their power to stop their Licenc[e] without giving a reason why – They succeeded so far in their alarm and threats that not one publick house – tavern nor Coffee House would recieve a branch of the society that professed a reform in parlia-ment, . . . All that hubbub and noice through-out the country disorganized the *London Corresponding Society* very much – Many of the Members were also alarmed and fled to different parts of the country – some went to America – others who were great declaimers in the society slunk into holes and corners and were never heard of more – others of the violent orators deserted and joined the Stan-dard of the enemy. . . . The few comparatively few who remained firm and true to their first principles and determined to *persevere* – were obliged to hire private houses and Auction rooms at great expence[104] – the members were obliged to double[105] their weekly pay and also to double their dilligence. . . .
The scattered remains of the society still met regularly every week – except one – and that was the week when Reeve's Association published their declaration & overawed the publicans so much that none of them would admit us into their houses (as a society). . . . The Committee did not meet two nights in one place for several weeks afterwards but shifted their place of meeting every week in order to avoid the interruption of police officers who were prowling about seeking whom they might devour – we knew they could not legally interrupt us – but by their clamour and threats they might prevent us from quietly meeting together and impede us in regulating and doing the business of the Society – We met in one anothers houses alternatly and sometimes in publick houses

104 By 12 Dec. only two private houses had been hired, one in Old Round Court and one in Compton St; the Society were looking for three other meeting rooms (government account, 'Societies in and about London', TS 11/959/3505).
105 'One half of the weekly subscription was alloted for providing places of meeting to accomodate the Divisions of the Society after being driven out of public Houses – paying for room rent – fire and candles The other half went as usual to pay for printing postage of the letters and stationary' – Hardy's note.

103 Quoted in *The British Political Tradition. Book Two: The Debate on the French Revolution 1789–1800*, ed. Alfred Cobban (1950), pp. 276–7.

privately that were friendly to the cause and not much affraid of losing their licence

24. Report from spy Lynam: LCS Division 12 (government paraphrase), 21 November 1792

Source: TS 11/954/3498

21 Novr. – The Witness [Lynam] was present at the Meeting of Division No. 12 at the Crown in Newgate Street when the report was made from the Committee of Delegates of the Letter having been received from Norwich ... enquiring whether the London Correspg Society ment to rest Satisfied with the Duke of Richmonds Plan only or whether it was their private intention to rip Monarchy by the Roots & place Democracy in its stead, –
    The Delegates suspected this might be some scheme to draw them into some unwarrantable expressions & declined answering – .... [106]
    The Delegate also reported that a Letter had been written to Sheffield. ... [107]

[The minutes of the meeting of the general committee for 22 November have been cut out of the Journal. These minutes must have dealt with the declaration by Reeves's

106 Shortly after the Norwich letter of 11 Nov. reached the LCS on the 15th, Margarot wrote a private letter to John Cozens at Norwich, asking about the men who had signed the Norwich letter. Cozens received this letter on the 17th and answered on the 20th, saying that the three men (i.e. George Knapp, Isaac Saint and Anthony Caddiwould) were 'industrious & respectable' (TS 11/965/3510A). This letter did not reach the LCS until the 28th, but on the 26th Margarot had answered the new Norwich society, asking for more information about them, explaining that the aims of the LCS were presented in their addresses, and advising Norwich on the organization of their society (TS 11/958/3503). His advice includes the admonition to 'leave Monarchy Democracy & even Religion entirely aside, never dispute on those Topicks'.

107 Paraphrase in TS 11/966/3510B adds: 'Colonel Semple of the Guards belongs to the Society – Wrote to Sheffield and Edinburgh.' At Hardy's trial Lynam gave further details of this meeting: 'It was at this division mentioned, that there was talk of a congress to be held in Scotland. The next thing that was done, was to read judge Ashurst's charge to the grand jury.' At this meeting several members branched off to form the new division, No. 23, which first met on 27 Nov. (*ST* vol. 24, col. 767).

Association and with the appointment of a subcommittee to write an answer to it. Presumably the authorization to form Division 25 was given at this meeting; for their delegate, George Bowden, was elected on 27 November, and the division had not been authorized at the previous meeting of the general committee.[108]]

25. Report from spy Lynam: LCS Division 23 (government summary), 27 November 1792[109]

Source: TS 11/959/3505

Lynam's Report of Meeting of a new Division at the Ship Moorfields – himself chosen Deligate Recommended to inform the Public that the London Corr Society are not Levellers – & advised Members to avoid Riot – [110]

26. Journal: LCS Committee of Delegates, 29 November 1792[111]

Source: Add MSS 27812, fos. 25-7v

    The Chairman moved that Leave might be given him to write a Letter to H Dundass Esqr. to demand for the Society the Protection of his Majesty's Ministers; but it being a late Hour the Consideration of that Matter was adjourned.

108 Voucher in TS 11/953/3497.
109 Div. 23 was an offshoot of Div. 12.
110 In answer to a question from Lord Chief Justice Eyre at Hardy's trial, Lynam explained that the division made this recommendation because 'on account of the magistrates interfering with their meetings, and some of the publicans had been threatened to have their licences taken away'. Lynam added that it was reported at this meeting 'that in Edinburgh, the first characters belonged to the cause, had formed themselves into a society, and called themselves a Convention of Delegates, and it was resolved to subscribe for the defence of any prosecuted member and his family' (*ST* vol. 24, col. 767).
111 The first part of the entry has been cut out. The excision is followed by a copy, in fair hand, of the Address to the other Societies of Great-Britain (see 28).
    Lynam's report of this meeting (next document) supplies missing material. One detail omitted in both accounts is the reading of a letter from the SCI announcing that Mr Sharp was engraving a print of Paine from a portrait by Romney (letter, Margarot to Daniel Adams, 29 Nov. 1792, TS 11/952/3496).

27. Report from spy Lynam: LCS General Committee (government paraphrase), 29 November 1792[112]

Source: TS 11/954/3498

29 Novr. The Witness [Lynam] was present at the Meeting of Delegates consisting of 22 when the Sub Committee brought forward a Draft of an Answer to the Declaration of the Crown & Anchor Association which was ordered to be referred back to be revised – but this was prevented by Mr. Vaughan the Counsel who came as a visitor from the Constl. Society & offered a Draft of an address which

being read was approved – after some alterations had been made in it particularly by rejecting the words "Dying in the Cause &c. tho' some thing was said in Justification of those Words by a Quotation from an expression used by Brewer in the time of Oliver Cromwell – . . . .

It was Ordered that this Address should be inserted in the Sunday Newspaper if it could be got in & that 500 large Copies of it shod. be printed to be stuck up in the streets & sent to each Division

Mr. Vaughan most strongly recommended good order & peaceable conduct

It was said if the Society's finances were low they might send to the Constitutional Society who wod. print for them and it was determined to be firm in a Parliamentary reform to be peaceable and quiet to use good words & observe order in all the Meetings

Margarot moved that a Letter shod. be written to Mr. Pitt & the Attorney General submitting the Meetings to them & that if they were declared illegal he would surrender himself & take his Trial but this was overruled

It was agreed to support all prosecuted Members & the same recommended to all the Divisions[113]

28. Printed handbill: *Address of the London Corresponding Society, to the other Societies of Great-Britain, united for the obtaining a REFORM IN PARLIAMENT* (excerpts). 29 November 1792[114]

Source: Add MSS 27814, fo. 42

'We know . . . that the Wages of every Man are his Right; that *Difference of Strength, of*

---

112 A summary of the report is in 'Index to Bundle G' (the papers relative to the LCS and SCI in 1792), in TS 11/959/3505. It is similar to this in information but not consistently written in sentences. It adds that the committee met at the Sun in Windmill St. This was the first time that Lynam, now a delegate, attended the general committee. He made notes from which he wrote his reports to Nepean and from which he delivered his oral reports to his division. At the trial of Hardy, Lynam was asked whether it was the custom to take notes on all that passed.
   Lynam replied: 'That was always a regular rule. . . . . Sometimes there was a communication which has been conceived by the chairman not proper to be communicated to the divisions; and Margarot has said, you must not communicate this; . . . the delegates were allowed to take reports or information, whether from the chairman, or any of the delegates, either with regard to a letter, or any other matter. The chairman has said, though you are informed such a thing has been wrote or has happened, though you are allowed to take a minute of it, we tell you it is not fit it should be communicated to the divisions; but that notes were allowed to be taken at all times is true. . . . I have heard of some reports made by other people; this circumstance might strike me, and another circumstance might strike another, which I might not take particular notice of, or think it worthwhile to put down. . . . I do conceive that a delegate being sent to know what business the society was transacting, that he should take the best account of it that he possibly could. . . . I put down every thing I possibly could; but I did not put down every thing that did pass, nor was it in the power of any of the delegates to do so; but it was the invariable practice of the delegates to make minutes either upon paper, or in books, for the purpose of communicating what had been transacted at the meeting of delegates at the next division, at their meetings, on different nights, from Thursday to Thursday' (*ST* vol. 24, cols. 821–2).

113 At Hardy's trial Lynam testified that the committee also agreed to change the place of meeting weekly. He added that Div. 11 'had received twenty visitors from Islington; a society was intended to be formed there'. Upon questioning he attributed to Vaughan the statement that the SCI would print for the LCS. 'It was then reported that many enemies to the society had endeavoured to get into the society. – At this meeting it was reported that five divisions had been scouted, that is prevented meeting at the places where they usually had met' (*ST* vol. 24, cols. 768–9).

114 The handbill was signed by Margarot and Hardy but written by Felix Vaughan. This copy was annotated by Hardy.
   Alexander Grant printed 500 posting bills

Talents, and of Industry, do and ought to afford proportional Distinctions of Property, which, when acquired and confirmed by the Laws, *is sacred and inviolable. . . .*

'If our Laws and Constitution be just and wise in their Origin and their Principle, every Deviation from them as first established must be injurious to the People, whose Persons and Property were then secured; if, at the Revolution, this Country was adequately represented, it is so no longer, and therefore calls aloud for *REFORM*.'

What formerly made Britons superior to the French was our more limited monarchy, smaller aristocracy, and trial by jury. Now the French have broken their chains. 'If during this Conflict with military Assassins and domestic Traitors, Cruelty and Revenge' have arisen among a few in Paris, let us not attribute their acts to a whole nation.

'Let us then continue with Patience and Firmness, in the Path which is begun; let us then wait and watch the ensuing Sessions of Parliament, from whom we have so much to hope and little to fear. The House of Commons may have been the Source of our Calamity, it may prove that of our Deliverance. Should it not, we trust we shall not prove unworthy of our Forefathers, WHOSE EXERTIONS IN THE CAUSE OF MANKIND SO WELL DESERVE OUR IMITATION.'

29. Journal: LCS Special Committee of Delegates, 4 December 1792

Source: Add MSS 27812, fos. 27v-9 (later copy in Add MSS 27814, fo. 100)

Special Committee.[115]
Tuesday 4th. Decr.
1792.
Illegal Persecution having disturbed all our Meetings, the Chairman summoned a Special

Committee for the Purpose of taking into Consideration the following Letter to the Secretary of State.

[There follows Margarot's letter of 4 December to Henry Dundas,[116] announcing that, on behalf of many of his countrymen, he is officially transmitting two addresses giving their reasons for associating; and calling on the king's ministers to protect them in the pursuit of their constitutional rights, so that their 'lawful and well-regulated Assemblies' will be no more interrupted. 'At your Hands, Sir, I therefore demand Justice and Protection for the Society, against all ruffians, who, let loose on the Public, have dared, or shall henceforth dare, like the Satellites of ancient sanguinary tyrants, assume to themselves the double office of making laws and executing them.' Mr Pitt and the Duke of Richmond have 'traced out the path we now pursue'. But since things appear different to them now that they are in power, 'severities may be had recourse to, to quell that desire for Reform which they themselves have raised. Should that be the Case, I beg it as a favor, or rather, being in the foremost rank, I claim it as my Right, that the attack may commence upon me.']

Which, after being read and agreed to, was sent by a Deputation of three Delegates to the General Post-office.

30. Journal: LCS General Committee, 6 December 1792

Source: Add MSS 27812, fo. 29v (later copy in Add MSS 27814, fo. 100)

Journal.

General Committee.
Thursday 6th. Decr. 1792.
Such Delegates as had not attended the Special Committee of the 4th. were made

for 2 gns, but he later refused to print an additional 500 large and 1,000 small posting bills of this address ('Information of Alexander Grant', TS 11/956/3501; Grant's testimony at Hardy's trial, *ST* vol. 24, cols. 402-3). At Hardy's trial the Attorney General asserted that this address, which replies to charges made by Reeves's Association, particularly the charge of levelling, taken with the other addresses and with the failure of the LCS to disavow the sentiments of the other societies, 'meant that, if parliament did not give them redress, they would have it by their own force' (col. 323).

115 At Hardy's trial Lynam read his summons to the meeting: 'Citizen Lynam, you are requested to meet the Special Committee this evening, at

seven o'clock, at the Nag's-head, Orange-street, Leicester-fields. - I am your fellow citizen, / Thomas Hardy. / Please to inform any of the delegates near you that you know, but no one else' (*ST* vol. 24, col. 769).

116 Printed and reprinted as *Letter to the Right Hon. Henry Dundass, Secretary of State for the Home Department By the London Corresponding Society, United for the Purpose of Obtaining a Reform in Parliament.*

acquainted with what had passed therat.

Messrs. Field, *Lynam*[117] and Bell the three deputed Delegates gave an Account to the Committee of their having delivered the Chairman's Letter to the Secretary Dundass at the Post-office, and brought a Reciept from the attending Clerk.[118]

The Committee read and approved two Letters to be sent, the one to the Society for Constitutional Information, the other to the Crown and Anchor Association.[119]

Most of the Delegates reported that their Meetings had been interrupted; the Committee therefore came to the Resolution that private Rooms must be hired, by the different Divisions.

Report was made that the Bill-sticker appointed to post up the Answer to the Place and Pension Club, had been taken up and committed to Tothill Fields by the Bow-street Magistrats – he was ordered to be bailed, and a Subscription was begun in Behalf of the Cause; the Committee judging it to be a most[120]

117 'the spy' inserted above the line, obviously much later; omitted in later copy.
118 According to Lynam, it was Margarot's suggestion that instead of delivering the letter to the Secretary of State's office they should put it into the general post office 'and then there was no doubt that it would go safe' (*ST* vol. 24, cols. 770–1).
119 'Reeves Chairman' – addition in later copy. Both letters accompanied copies of the 29 Nov. reply to Reeves's Association. The letter to the SCI also contained MS copies of the letter to Dundas and that to Reeves (Margarot and Hardy to Adams; Hardy to Reeves; both 6 Dec. 1792, both TS 11/952/3496).
120 Several pages are cut out at this point. The next Journal entry is for 11 Jan. 1793.

The excised material must have included more discussion of the bill-sticker, for a hand-bill soliciting subscriptions for him was published, dated the next day, 7 Dec. (reprinted in pamphlet-size edn of 29 Nov. address, in BL). William Carter, an illiterate porter, watchman and bill-sticker, was hired on 5 Dec. to post copies of the address. He should have been instructed to post them at night; instead he was ordered to post them in the morning. He was arrested by a Bow Street runner, detained in the watch-house, and ordered held for trial. A month later, on 7 Jan. 1793, Carter was sentenced to six month's imprisonment for sedition ('The Case of William Carter a Bill Sticker', TS 11/965/3510A).

At this meeting of the general committee Div. 5 was authorized to divide and form Div. 27 (government copy of authorization, 6 Dec. 1792, TS 11/958/3503). The authorization to form Div. 26 was given either at this meeting or

31. Report from spy Lynam: LCS Division 23 (government summary), 11 December 1792[121]

Source: TS 11/959/3505

Lynam's Report of Meeting of Division 23
Davis went to a Serjt. at the Tower & made a Convert of him & several Soldiers[122] – 3 Members of this Division offered to stick up the Society's Address to other Societys[123]

32. Report from spy Lynam: LCS Committee of Delegates (government summary), 13 December 1792[124]

Source: TS 11/959/3505

Meeting of Delegates – 18
Baxter was at a Meeting at Shoreditch Church   he opposed the Meeting & was taken to the Watch House for it & throwing amongst them 2 of the Society's Rules – [125] admitted to Bail
Places of Meeting of different Divisions

at the previous one; on 14 Dec. the twenty-one members chose James Moore as delegate (voucher, TS 11/956/3501).
121 According to the paraphrase in Lynam's 'Evidence', the meeting was at the Brown Bear in Moorfields.
122 Government evidently started watching Davis, for on 20 Dec. Nepean wrote to Major General Leake that a shoemaker named Davis of 15 Cannon Street had been disseminating seditious doctrines among the soldiers at the Tower, that Davis intended to visit his sergeant friend that day and distribute the Rules and Regulations of the LCS and possibly a mischievous publication, 'The Soldiers Friend' (HO 42/23).
123 At the trial of Hardy Lynam, consulting his minutes of this meeting, added further details: 'There were no new members admitted. . . . It was reported that colonel Dalrymple, of Edinburgh, was determined to have a parliamentary reform; it was reported likewise, that the Irish were scouted, as we had been; that they had applied to the council [the Privy Council in Dublin], who had declared their meetings to be legal. . . . A motion was then made that as the finances of the divisions are low, as they cannot print the Address, the divisions are recommended to subscribe' (*ST* vol. 24, cols. 769–70).
124 According to the 'Evidence of George Lynam', the meeting was held at the Two Pillars in New Round Court, Strand.
125 When Baxter opposed this meeting in support of 'the constitution of the country . . . he was laid hold of; and . . . in consequence of that, seeing he could not resist, he put his hand into his pocket, and pulled out many of the society's

Little John in Dukes Court was Assistant Secretary to Hardy[126] – James[127] Field chosen in his Place

Ridgway to publish Margarott's Letter to Mr. Dundas & the Receipt given to Lynam Field & Bell unless the latter declines – then to be inserted by 3 Delegates[128]

A Committee to consider of Cases of prosecuted Members & who should be defended – Lynam – Baxter – Vaughan – Martin – Smith – Bowden – Richter[129]

New Tickets issued – Members all to pay Arrears before they have the new Tickets

Recd. Letter from Norwich[130] – from Paisley – & from Edinburgh – to concur in the Opinion of calling a Convention in Scotland[131]

addresses, and threw them with a great deal of exultation among the people assembled there, and he complained that he was very ill-used, his coat torn, and he struck several times in the church-yard' (Lynam's testimony, *ST* vol. 24, col. 770).

126 Because the magistrates were after him, Lyttlejohn was going to Scotland; hence his resignation (Lynam's testimony, *ST* vol. 24, col. 750).

127 Joseph – paraphrase.

128 The letter was 'to be put into the Post Office in the presence of the Witness [Lynam] Field & Bell who were to take a Receipt for it from the Postmaster' – paraphrase. At Hardy's trial Lynam explained: it was Margarot's suggestion that instead of delivering the letter to the Secretary of State's office, they should put it into the general post office 'and then there was no doubt but that it would go safe' (*ST* vol. 24, cols. 770–1). At the end of the published letter is an account of posting it to Dundas and a statement that the Committee waited fifteen days for a reply before ordering its publication.

129 The committee was also 'to protect those who had not provoked prosecution by rash words or being concerned in any tumult' – paraphrase. The paraphrase substitutes 'Waln a Taylor' for 'Vaughan'.

130 The Norwich letter asked if the LCS members were going to sign the declaration of attachment to the present constitution, which, in Norwich at least, was being carried from door to door for signatures. According to Lynam's testimony, Margarot directed 'that this letter should not be taken notice of to any of the divisions'. On the day after this meeting, Margarot replied to Norwich: 'I am authorized to answer you in the Name of our Society that not one of our Members will affix his Signature to any Declaration or profession of being fully satisfied with the existing Abuses engrafted on our Constitution' (John Cozens to Hardy, 12 Dec. 1792; Margarot to Cozens, 14 Dec. 1792; both in TS 11/958/3503).

131 The letters from Paisley and Edinburgh have

Letter by Margarot to Stuart Secy. to the Friends of the People Frith Street[132]

33. Report from spy Lynam: LCS General Committee (government paraphrase), 20 December 1792[133]

Source: TS 11/966/3510B, shorter summary and paraphrase of Lynam's reports

20 Decr. – Meeting of 18 Delegates
No. 31 Compton Street

disappeared; all that is known of them is found in Lynam's testimony at Hardy's trial: 'Then there was a letter dated the 15th from Paisley, that they were willing to correspond with us – twelve societies formed in August for a parliamentary reform. Then there was a letter from Edinburgh, of the 11th of December, to call a convention of all Scotland, to be of the same opinion; the title of that Society was, "The Friends of the People". Archibald East Hodge, president; W. Reed, secretary' (*ST* vol. 24, col. 773).

132 'It was recommended by several delegates to correspond with the Friends of the People at Free-mason's tavern' (Lynam's testimony, *ST* vol. 24, cols. 773–4). The Society of the Friends of the People (1792–5) was formed on 11 April by reform-minded men of position and influence, including twenty-three MPs. With annual dues to two and a half guineas, the FoP were financially as well as socially separated from most LCS members. Not surprisingly, FoP plans for parliamentary reform did not extend to universal male suffrage. Although one of the early resolutions of the FoP was to confer with deputies from other reform societies, they had not approached the LCS. On 14 Dec. the LCS wrote, soliciting their correspondence and enclosing copies of their addresses, resolutions and letter to Dundas (TS 11/958/3503). In the reply, dated 28 Dec., the FoP urge the LCS to impress on the minds of workmen and labourers that they should preserve the public peace (TS 11/956/3501).

At the trial Lynam added further details throughout his report of this meeting: Div. 4 made a motion that a letter should be written by the secretary to the common council of London. The motion was referred to the secretary. 'Division, No. 1, recommended, that it be represented to the public that confusion may be expected, but that if riots ensue our societies will aid the magistrates, and that copies be sent to the magistrates; but take care that we say that there is not the least disposition appears of committing any riot, and that we will persevere in a parliamentary reform.' The general committee approved this recommendation (*ST* vol. 24, cols. 770–3).

133 In the official Journal of the Society, the pages recording this meeting were cut out. At the trial of Hardy, Lynam added some

Answer to Norwich read by Margarot with several Publications to be sent thither[134] Motion by Division 24 That it is the opinion

of this Society that We publish the Resolution of this Society to assist the Magistrates & that We will persevere in a Reform[135]

Carter to stick up Bills in the Evening instead of the Morning[136]

further information about this meeting: 'Two members deputed from the Constitutional Whigs to know if the London Corresponding Society would address the Friends of the People. Baxter recommended to take his case into consideration, he being prosecuted for his resistence at the meeting at Shoreditch church. Division No. 12 recommended to petition parliament before Mr. Grey brings in his bill for a parliamentary reform. . . . [Baxter] was not [supported], but his matter was brought forward afterwards; inquiry was made, whether we corresponded with the societies formed at Ipswich and at Woodbridge, the answer was, no. Mr. Martin recommended not to publish anything, the times won't do; he says that you cannot oppose the treasury. Then Baxter brought forward a motion from his division, No. 16, for the delegates to consult and to determine whether they will sign the Crown and Anchor address [from Reeves's society] – it was determined to be left to the discretion of each individual, but it was recommended to avoid signing it if possible. . . . A motion was made by division 16, that each division present a ticket gratis, to any soldier that will be agreeable to enter, but caution them at the same time when they were admitted of the danger – this was not agreed upon, but referred for a week. . . . There was an intimation at that time that Ridgeway would publish any thing the society should send to him – he mentioned the duke of Richmond's letter, and said that he would print that or any thing they sent. . . . Baxter's business was brought forward again; Martin informed him that his recognizance was not entered at Hick's Hall; he was ordered to withdraw his recognizance himself, and then he could not be held himself again to bail in that action, but there was not any thing done in that; it was then said [by Margarot] that Mr. Fox had gone as far as we can expect, but we do not look upon him to be more honest than others, and think he has been forced to avow himself so strongly in the House, and it is necessary to have a head [for the plan of parliamentary reform]' (*ST* vol. 24, cols. 774–5).

The committee also authorized Div. 12 to divide and form Div. 29 (authorization, 20 Dec. 1792, TS 11/956/3501). The committee admitted a new delegate from Div. 5, Herbert Milbourne, succeeding Robert Thompson (voucher, 18 Dec. 1792, TS 11/953/3497). Thompson, threatened with prosecution for his political poems, went to France.

134 'There was an answer sent to . . . the Norwich Society, . . . they sent a reply, that they had sent five guineas in order to have Mr. Fox's speech

34. Report from spy Lynam: LCS General Committee (government paraphase), 27 December 1792

Source: TS 11/954/3498

27 Decr. The Witness [Lynam] was present at a Meeting of the Delegates at No. 31 Compton Street 14 attending

It was directed on the Motion of Baxter that each Delegate shod. take the sense of his Division as to Admitting Soldiers into the Society and on what Terms they were to be admitted

The red Tickets ordered on the 13th. of Decr. were delivered out

[in the House of Commons, on parliamentary reform] sent down by the Expedition . . . . They are to publish some hand-bills, and show that they are not disheartened, and are determined not to sign but persevere. Five hundred copies of Mr. Fox's speech; fifty of Margarot's letter to Dundas; fifty of John Bull to Thomas Bull were sent down' (Lynam's testimony, *ST* vol. 24, col. 774). The Norwich order for five guineas' worth of publications must have been in a letter, now lost, written after 14 Dec. (when Margarot sent them a few papers) and before 25 Dec. (when they thank the LCS for the receipt of the parcel of papers, TS 11/958/3503). The missing letter presumably established the safe means of communication which Margarot suggested in his letter of 14 Dec.

135 Margarot was to draw up a resolution for the next meeting (testimony of Lynam at the trial of Hardy, *ST* vol. 24, col. 775).

136 'There came forward a petition from William Carter, who was employed to stick those bills up, that he had lost a place of twelve shillings a week. . . . He says he was confined three days and two nights, but Martin says only one day. . . . Martin was employed for the defence of William Carter, and there was a subscription then made for that defence; at that time division, No. 12, subscribed a guinea and a half; No. 18, fifteen shillings; No. 11, five shillings. . . . Gay, a printer belongs to the society, but he denies it; he employed William Carter to stick up the large bills in the morning, instead of the evening, which was the reason why he was taken up – this was reported at that time by Martin' (Lynam's testimony, *ST* vol. 24, col. 775).

PART TWO

1793A

(January–May)

Chronology

1793

Jan.	7	Carter the bill-sticker convicted
	21	Louis XVI executed
Feb.	1	France declares war on England
March	13	Division 12 secedes; forms Society of British Citizens
	18	Battle of Neerwinden; period of French military reversals begins
Apr.	26	French peace offers delivered
	30	Opening of second meeting of Scottish Convention
May	2–6	Reform petitions introduced in Parliament
	6–7	Grey's reform motion debated and defeated
May 31–June 2		Girondins overthrown in Paris
Summer		French reign of terror begins
July		Irish convention bill passed
	8	LCS general meeting held; *Address to the Nation*
Aug.	28	British occupy Toulon
Aug. 30–1		Muir tried and convicted; sentenced to 14 years' transportation
Sept.	2	LCS general meeting; address to the king
	12–13	Palmer tried and convicted; sentenced to 7 years' transportation
Oct.	24	LCS open air meeting elects delegates to convention in Edinburgh; Briellat arrested
Oct. 29–Nov. 6		Edinburgh convention meets
Nov.	7	LCS delegates arrive in Edinburgh
	19	Edinburgh convention reconvenes
Dec.	5	Margarot, Gerrald and Skirving arrested
	6	Convention dispersed
	19	French recapture Toulon

35. Notebook: LCS Minutes of Division 23, 1 January 1793[1]

Source: TS 11/951/3495

Mr Salter – President Mr Soups elected
                                    Secretary
  Lynam – Delegate and acting Secretary
                   chosen
Mr. Goff – Member[2]
                          Mr Davis owes me 13
Mr Cobham – Member

Being all the Member's assembled this 1st.
Day of Jany 1793 have elected officers &c &
transacted the business of yd Division No 23,
but sho'd what they have done not be con-
firmd by the next meeting on yd 8th. of
January, the Electon to be conciderd void and
of no effect –

Soldier's as other member's –
Quaere to Petition if dont do it many wont
belong Society

36. Report from spy Lynam: LCS General Committee (government paraphrase), 3 January 1793[3]

Source: TS 11/954/3498

3 Janry – The Witness [Lynam] was present
at a Meeting of the Delegates at No. 31 Compton Street   16 attending when Mr. Margarot

1 This document is in a small notebook which also
   contains the financial accounts of Div. 23 for 1
   Jan. to 21 Feb. and a list of the members of the
   division. In the hand of Lynam.
2 Crossed out: 'Owes Me 13d'.
3 At the trial of Hardy, Lynam added further details of this meeting: 'It was proposed that each
   member should pay a penny each night if he introduced a visitor, to pay at the division he
   attends, and then to be discharged, paying at his
   own division. Mr Durant, a stranger acquainted us
   of Thomson's distress. [Thomson was] a man
   that lived by Coventry-street, I forget the name
   of the place; he was gone off to France at that
   time, I think. [His distress, or rather] the wife's
   distress [was] in consequence of his being obliged to leave London, being one belonging to
   this society, a very violent man, and he was
   therefore sought after; it was represented that the
   rent was not paid, and that she was quite distressed with three children, Thomson gone to France,

was chosen President & Hardy Secretary &
Field sub Secretary for the ensuing Quarter
It was resolved to publish a Declaration of
their Principles

[At Hardy's trial, Lynam testified about a
meeting of Division 23 on 8 January at
No. 33, Crown-street, Moorfields: 'I have it
down here, that the declaration, which is,
I suppose the declaration mentioned before
[at meeting of delegates on 3 Janaury] . . .
it is the opinion of this division that it
should be rejected – it was agreed, likewise,
not to address the king at all . . . . it was
said that Mr. Grey would not bring forward
his motion for a reform, unless petitions
were sent to parliament; agreed to petition
parliament by all means, and not to address
them.'[4]

37. Journal: LCS General Committee, 10 January 1793

Source: Add MSS 27812, fos. 29v–30v
(later copy in Add MSS 27814, fo. 101)

[The first part of this entry was cut from
the Journal.]

the rent owing, nine guineas – Mr. Harvey, an
attorney of the Temple, her friend – sixteen
delegates met, and collected in the whole 12s 6d.
for her, and it was to be recommended to each
division, but as a body they do not assist any
body – There was a motion came forward then,
for a declaration to the public, but objected to
by two divisions, saying power supersedes the
laws, or, as it suits them, leaves those laws dormant – rather have a constitution without a king
than a king without a constitution. . . . I do not
think any thing was done in it . . . . Mr. Margarot
then reported, that we had no letters for two
months, except one he had received that day,
but the seal was opened and it was sealed again;
it was then mentioned there were five delegates
from the Roman Catholics, that they were of the
same meaning with us, and it was agreed to try
and see if we could not settle a correspondence
with them. [They were not present at the meeting, but] it was reported that they were in London, Irish Roman Catholics' (ST vol. 24, cols
775–6).
4 ST vol. 24, col. 774.

41

weaker minded Members began to subside.

The Motion respecting Soldiers was left to be finally determined next Committee Night because some Delegates had not had the Opportunity of consulting their Divisions on it's Propriety.[5]

A Motion for printing an Explanation of the Word Equality was negatived . . . . but the Delegates agreed to furnish their Divisions with such as were already printed, at their own Expence.[6]

Two other Motions were presented and refer'd.

A provisional Regulation was proposed and unanimously carried, respecting the Admission of Manuscript Papers into the Committee, viz,

That no written Papers shall be recieved by the Committee of Delegates in future, except transmitted to them by the Delegate of a Division or by the Secretary of the Society.

A Letter was recieved and read from the Friends of the People, signifying their Acceptance of our proffered Correspondence, their Regard and Veneration of the original Principles of our Constitution – and a friendly Admonition to us to abstain from the Intermixture of Foreign Correspondence and domestic Reform – After the Discussion of the above mentioned Letter, some conversation took Place respecting the situation of Mrs. Thomson,[7] and also respecting the Bill-sticker – but the Committee adopted no Resolution relating to either Case.

38. Report from spy Lynam: LCS General Committee (government paraphrase), 10 January 1793

Source: TS 11/954/3498

10th. Janry. – The Witness [Lynam] was present at a Meeting of the Delegates at No. 31 in Compton Street – 17 attended
The Letter written to the Society of Friends of the People at Freemasons Tavern . . . with the Answer of that Society . . . were read and it was resolved to discontinue any correspondence with them because they never had declared explicitly how far they meant to go Bell one of the Delegates said that the address of the London Corr. Society to the French Convention proved that they wished to have the French Laws here – this was assented to by the rest of the Company but Margarot said they must be cautious.[8]

tuted: he was however extensively admired, in the Society, and probably would have experienced a similar degree of approbation from the country at large, had not persecution nearly suppressed his works, and compelled him to seek refuge in France, where we are happy to learn he has since succeeded well as a bookseller' ('History of the Society', *MPM*, vol. 1 (June 1796), p. 183).

8 At the trial Lynam was questioned about the response to Bell's statement; he said that Margarot replied, 'no doubt', that no one objected to it, that 'it passed with the silent assent of the rest of the company'.

Lynam added further details of this meeting: 'Mr. Margarot then reported, that the country correspondence did not shine . . . . That there were but very few letters. At that time they were under a good deal of difficulty, being disturbed in their meetings, and a vast deal of very strong language had been held both then and at former times, and afterwards to . . . . it was observed by some one of the delegates, that Mr. Pitt's plan to add a hundred members to the House of Commons would not do, for that would still give them more advantage, and keep us from a proper reform; Mr. Gerrald then said, he knew a person of the name of Dolon, who was secretary, and one of the Irish delegates too, and that he was gone off to Ireland; that he knows his address; he explained to him our endeavours, of which he approved, and he proposed to correspond with him; he said the Catholics had succeeded entirely; Bell had a friend that he knew, whose name was Devereux, one of the delegates, and he agreed to correspond by the post – however, that was said to be dangerous, as no letters go through the post-office' (*ST* vol. 24, cols. 777–8).

5 'A Motion respecting the gratuitous admission of Soldiers into the Society was proposed and discussd and refered to the different divisions for their approbation at last it was negatived' – later copy.

6 Later copy: 'A motion for printing an Excellent explanation of the word equality – but cautious of not running the Society into debt – it was negatived – but each of the delegates agreed to subscribe and have it printed and distributed at their own expence.' The four page pamphlet, aptly titled *An Explanation of the Word Equality*, was another refutation of the charge of levelling made by the Reeves association.

7 As reports of 24 Jan. indicate, her house was searched in the night, and she believed she had a claim on the LCS for monetary assistance. Her husband, Robert Thompson or Thomson, who had fled to France, had been one of the most active members of the LCS, going nightly to instruct new divisions. 'Thompson, an auctioneer by business, possessed a lively poetical genius, which did not exactly accord with the calm prudential principles on which the Society was insti-

39. Report from spy Lynam: 14 January 1793[9]

Source: TS 11/958/3503

Jany 14

Ld. Semple at Rigways

- - - - -

a Gentn. came in for the Jockey club, to go to france this evening *price 12/* shewd me first volume took yd Gentleman's direction to send it in one hour

- - - - -

20, 21, 22 dont exist believed did not meet 27 & 28 never met

- - - - -

Coffeehouse shire Lane a good room – if can be allow'd will send another Div: there

- - - - -

Hardy's Divis: meets strong No 8 Queen Street a Woman keeps the House

- - - - -

Hardy send's 50 Address's[10] 12, Kersaint's, speach[11] this night to different correspondents, but dont send who they come from

- - - - -

Ridgway dines with Fox this day

Jany 12

Sheilds was in company with 11 People at a Coffee house west end of town 6 of them Officers one declared, if a French Army was to arrive here he wo'd join them the others same opinion & meet to communicate such principles

9 Government description: 'Information 14 Jany. 1793'. According to Lynam's testimony at the trial of Hardy, the information of this report was gained from Hardy at his house (*ST* vol 24, col. 778).

10 Lynam identified this as 'the original address of the society'.

11 *The Speech of Kersaint to the French National Convention, with the Resolutions of that Body Respecting a War with England*, 1793. Gui-Pierre de Coetnempren, Comte de Kersaint, an early supporter of the French Revolution and a member of the Jacobin Club, asserted that the actions of the English government against the French did not represent the will of the English people and that if England started a war she would lose both trade and colonies. Kersaint was guillotined during the reign of terror (4 Dec. 1793).

40. Journal: LCS General Committee, 17 January 1793

Source: Add MSS 27812, fos. 30v–1v (later copy in Add MSS 27814, fos. 102–3)

Thursday 17 Janry. 1793.

The Treasurer's Accounts for the Last Quarter were audited up to this Day, when the Reciepts and Ballance of the last Quarter together amounted to 34.11.9
And the Expenditure to this Day . 27. 3.1

Consequently there remained in his Hands a Ballance in our favor of 7. 8.8

A Correspondence was ordered to be opened by the first Opportunity with Bath,[12] Glascow, Durham, Bamf and Dundee.

A Letter and Resolutions from the United Societies in Norwich were read and ordered to be communicated to the different Divisions.

The Petition of Carter the Bill-sticker presented on the 20th. Decr. came on by Order for Discussion, and as almost all the Divisions had instructed their Delegates to move for a special Committee of Enquiry upon his Case, the Committee resolved itself into a General-special Committee to meet on the ensuing Saturday to examine and conclude thereon.

Several Motions were debated.

The 1st. from Division No. 15 on the Propriety of giving to each Member an additional Number of our Addresses to disperse among his Acquaintance, as a Proof of the Purity of our Principles, and the Legality of our Intentions.

It appearing that the Secretary had 3000 Copies now lying useless by him, he was ordered to distribute 2000 to the different Delegates and reserve one Thousand for the future Wants of the Society.

The 2nd. from No. 23 for granting permission to Lowe to print for Sale our Addresses.

An amendment was made that Mr. Ridgeway's Name should also be inserted in the Permission, and the original Motion was carried thus, that Ridgeway and Lowe[13] be permitted to print any Number of our Addresses not exceeding 10,000, for their conjoint Use and Profit, provided to prevent Errors or Interpolations a proof Sheet be submitted to

12 The letter to Bath had been written a week earlier. However, as Lynam reports (next document), Margarot told the delegates that he had already written to Bath.

13 James Ridgway and William Low in later copy.

the Inspection of the Chairman of the Committee.

The Motion relative to the gratuitous Admission of Soldiers was withdrawn.

The Motion from No. 4 presented on the 13th. of Decr. and praying that the Livery of London might be addressed by the Society, in Vindication of it's Principles – was negatived unanimously.

It was proposed and agreed that an open Committee free to every Individual of the Society should be established on Saturday Evenings, and commence on Saturday the 26th. Instant.

41. Report from spy Lynam: 15, 17 January 1793[14]

Source: TS 11/958/3503

Sir

Can Sheild's be known

20, 21, & 22 believe never met
27 & 28 never met

15 Jany Crown Street[15]

Recommended to address Ourselve's to Persevere & Publish L– C– Societys resolution's, to refute the charge of being Levelor's Ridgway & Low to Print Ten thousand of L– C– Societys Rules address & resolution's

Compton Street   17 Jany[16]

Division 26 meets here
Robins Coffee house Shire Lane a very good room,   29 meets there, and will take any of yd Division's on Monday & Friday nights – 29 first meeting here, expect to meet very strong

No's 2 & 7 expect to meet very strong Compton Street
No 2 are to make 20 new member's next meeting
No 7 are to make 10 Do
Division No 17 done away
19 Divison's kept up – 2 & 3 of them meet together
3d Division are going to debate political question's,   the first question whether the age of 18 or 21 is yd propper age for voting for a member of Parliament – at 18 liable to be call'd out as a Malitia Man
Deligate 18 – recomendd, to appoint a committee to report the expence of Carter's case &c[17]
Division 5   same as 18
The motion of Division 4 to address Common Council &c rejected.
Division No 12 recommended to Deligates to concider of a Public meeting to discuss a Parliamentary Reform – refer'd back
Division 15, recommend that each member sho'd have 4 or 5 of L– C– Societys addresses to deliver out to the Public
- - - - -
Deligate 29 – inform'd that a Quaker had given Genl. Raineford of Soho Square one of the addresses & that he requestd 10 more, as the one he had, he took to Court & was much approved – Genl R– wanted the Quaker to go before Lord Grenville, he wo'd not but said he was convinced of the necessity of a reform & had wrote Mr. Pitt thereon, but received no answer
- - - - -
Deligate Division 4 made a motion of thanks to be sent to Mayor & Majestrate's of Glasgow, Dundee, Banff, & Durham for uniteing with Us in our intention's;   Voted thanks unnecessary but to correspond with them – M M If any thanks are due, it is to Benjn. Hobhouse Esqre Bath who has found a Society there agreable to Our's;   wrote to him last friday post, if no answer, then to send some addresses Directed to him thro' Mr Richard's Bookseller – and from time to time inform him how we go on
- - - - -
  Carter's imprisonment look upon for Life on account of yd Securitys – Agreed a special

14 Government description: '20th January 1793. / Clubs & Meetings; / Intelligence relative to the proceedings in Crown Street and Compton Street on the 15 and 17 Jany 1793.' At the trial of Hardy, when Lynam was supposedly consulting these minutes, he testified that sixteen delegates were present at the meeting.
15 Presumably this is an account of the meeting of Div. 23, of which Lynam was the delegate. However, the decision to let Ridgway and Low print 10,000 copies of the rules etc. was not made until two days later, 17 Jan. at the weekly meeting of the general committee. Lynam may be confusing the two meetings. At Hardy's trial Lynam did not report his minutes of this meeting.
16 The rest of this report is Lynam's version of the weekly meeting of the general committee, held at 31 Compton St.

17 At the trial Lynam explained that the committee was to report on the money necessary for the support of Carter's family. Lynam also reported that a petition from Carter was presented, that he had been sentenced to six month's imprisonment plus a fine and sureties for good behaviour (*ST* vol. 24, col. 778).

Committee of all yd Deligates sho'd meet every Saturday – and send for Mr. Vaughan to know why he did not defend his own writeing, for Martin to know the expence &c – for Grant to know why he employd Carter in the Day instead of night – 9 to sit on business 31 Compton Street – when this is finishd then all the Deligates and every member to meet there of Saturday evenings to discuss Politics,[18] and if Possible to get a report of yd Debates in yd House.

- - - - -

Letter read signd Blake from Norwich, saying they admired Our spirited conduct, had wrote to Mr Grey yd 11 Jany. and had recd. a letter from the Friends of the People, who Propose a mild reformation, and beg to be inform'd if they are Friends; *Their* Societys are numerous, but in the Country they Majestrate's Prevent their encreasing. They recommend Us to correspond with them thro' yd means of yd Bell Society of Norwich

Treasurer's account to this day
From Michaelmas 1792 to this
		day Recd	27-9-2
Do	Do	Do Expended	27-3-1
		Ball:	6-1

Each Division's Payments as I co'd take down down –

[There follows a list of payments from Divisions 4–6, 9–12, 14–17, 21, 23, 25, totalling £21 5s 9d. Individual payments range from 3s 6d (Div. 21) to £6 10s 10d (Div. 6).]

42. Journal: LCS General Committee, 19, 24 January 1793

Source: Add MSS 27812, fos. 31v–2v (later copy in Add MSS 27814, fos. 103–4)

Special Committee 19th. Janry.
1793.

The Committee on the Case of the Bill-sticker could not proceed to Business on Account of the Absence of all the Evidences; who however had been severally summoned by the Assistant Secretary – They therefore made it the Order of the day. for the next Committee – Thursday the 24th.

18 At this meeting they were to pay a penny each for the room.

Thursday 24th. Janry.

The Reports this Evening were more favorable than heretofore. Division No. 15 requested Leave to divide – Granted to take the vacant Number 28.

The Business of the Evening was rather impeded by the irregular Admission of a Petition from Mrs. Thomson which was rejected; the Comittee informing the Petitioner that collectively it could not take Cognizance of any Thing of the Kind.[19]

The Come. resolved into a special Comittee upon the Case of Carter the Bill-sticker. Herbert Milbourne in the Chair – John Martin Sollicitor to the Society gave a clear and satisfactory Account of the Manner in which the Business had been conducted previous to and during the Trial: by which it appeared that the Attorney General had duped the Jury into a Verdict, and that the Prisoner was convicted under the Idea of a lenient Punishment being to be inflicted.

The Solictor took upon himself the whole and sole Management of providing for the Prisoner's Support during his Confinement, and observed that as he intended pushing forward a Subscription for him in another Society (the Society for Constitutional Information) he should not trouble this Society for further pecuniary Assistance.[20]

The Come. having resumed itself Two Motions were discussed and agreed to –

The 1st. from Division 16 – That a Correspondence should be opened with the Friends of the Liberty of the Press.

The 2nd. from Division 23 for printing our 8 primitive Resolutions in the Paper – together with an explicit temporary Address intended to make our Aims as public as possible, and to prove the Constitutionality of our Proceedings.

19 '– although after the business was ended the delegates each subscribed something towards her support – and they likewise mentioned her case to the divisions although not oficially from the Come' – later copy.

20 'It appears by a small Book partly in Martin's Hand Writing & partly in Hardy's that a Subscription had been opened for Carter while in Prison under his Sentence to which the Prisoners Martin Hardy & Richter had contributed 10/6 each' – government gloss to paraphrase of Lynam's report on this meeting (TS 11/956/3501). The total subscription amounted to £17 4s 10d (marginal note in government summary of Lynam's report of this day, in 'Index to Bundle F', TS 11/953/3497).

43. Reports from spy Lynam: 22, 24 January 1793[21]

Source: TS 11/958/3503

Sir

Crown Street   Moorfield's   22 Jany

Made one Member

31 Compton Street   24 Jany

Two Gentlemen came with a Petition very proudly drawn up in behalf of Mrs. Thompson, supposed by Mr Harvey of the Temple – it states her house was search'd in the Dead of night & rely's on support by promise – *We say no such promise* –, She wants to go to France, but wants large necessaryes & Payment of some debts of a Peculiar nature – One of yd above Persons formerly Deligate for Division No 11[22] – the other supposed to be Harveys clerk – Mr. Hardy gave her £2..6..6, the 15th. Inst – Mr. Martin thought it sho'd be rejected, agreed[23] – He said he had an Ex officio from the Attorney General, & that he might be as much an object.

Examination of Mr. Marten
Marten drew up a very long brief, & shew'd it to Mr. Vaughan who had no objection to defend it, afterwards declined it being a delicate matter to defend his own writeing & wish'd it might not be known.

He recommended Mr. Erskine who declined, then Garrow, found him against Us, Fielding declined, He then recomended Warren, who was wishfull of it – Marten then said Grant was the cause of Carter's Punishment, as he had undertaken to have them stuck up at night, & did not.
Grant has got the manuscript & declines giving it Up
Martin call'd to have it burnt,   Field sub

secretary to apply to him & if he dont give it up, to expell him the society,   the consequence wo'd be expulsion from the Crown & Anchor as one of Our honorary visitors, – LittleJohn is one likewise.[24]

Carter said he had in his Pocket that which wo'd do for the Deligate's – determined he sho'd not receive his guinea per week after this, unless he asks Pardon & the manuscript given up by Grant.

- - - - -

12th. Division now meet at No 10 White house court White X street Friday's

- - - - -

Deligate Division No 13 not attended this quarter

- - - - -

19 Division branchd from No 6

- - - - -

20, 21, & 22 never met

- - - - -

29 made one member   21 now joind 18

- - - - -

24 meet Mary le bon lane

- - - - -

| Division 15 Divide & take No 28, 15 meet Compton Street |
| 28 Ove the water   17 Done away |

- - - - -

Division 11 made 2 member's

- - - - -

Division 23 Motion to address Ourselve's agreable to the times & to extract Our 8 resolution's underneath – to be brought forward on saturday evening Compton Street at a general meeting, & this meeting to be continued

- - - - -

Motion Division 14[25] Address a letter to Friends of the Press for their exertion at yd Crown & Anchor,   They are the same People as meet their under constitutional information

- - - - -

A letter from Norwich to be answerd – was not read

- - - - -

21 Government description: 'Proceedings at the Meetings in Crown Street & Compton Street on the 22 & 24 Jany. 1793'.
22 Evans.
23 At the trial Lynam expanded this passage: 'Martin thought it should be rejected, but it was agreed to – Martin then reported, that he had an *ex-officio* from the attorney-general, and he might be as much an object of the support of the delegates, and of the divisions, as she' (*ST* vol. 24, col. 779). An *ex officio* information was a method of proceeding in a criminal case which permitted the authorities to dispense with the grand jury and to hold a trial before a handpicked special jury rather than an impartial common jury.
24 Lynam's version at the trial: 'it was mentioned then that Littlejohn, likewise, was an honorary member [of the SCI], and that he would also be expelled' (col. 778).
25 At the trial Lynam identified this as a motion from Div. 16. On 19 Jan. the Friends of the Liberty of the Press met at the Crown and Anchor tavern where Erskine made a speech denouncing the associations formed for the avowed purpose of suppressing and prosecuting writings.

Letter from Richter, he dare not attend, but may depend upon his being a stauch friend – He carried yd address to Grant
- - - - -
Hardy stated he had not brought forward the ballance of cash in his hand's of last quarter. Viz. £6..18..7 makeing neat ballance this quarter £7..4..8
- - - - -
Deligates meet next thursday at No 8 Queen Street 7 dials
- - - - -
Deligate (I think No 5) going to France, got 2 Setts Payne's books – He recd. a letter tuesday night last 12 OClock, saying a hint to the wise – You will all be taken up, yd Deligates
- - - - -
From Lowe – Ridgway Publishing one more of Paynes work's, to come out 26 Jany
- - - - -
a Meeting at 53 Dean Street believe friends of the People
- - - - -
Lowe has got a situation 16/ per week in Clerkenwell
- - - - -
7-2-& 5 met. 50 Each
- - - - -
Whitehead Perpetual foreman of exchecquer Jury
- - - - -
Shield's translater of French to Courier

44. Journal: LCS General Committee, 31 January 1793

Source: Add MSS 27812, fos. 32v–3 (later copy in Add MSS 27814, fo. 104)

Janry. 31st. 1793.

The Delegates Reports of this Week were favorable.

Charles Turner produced his Voucher as Delegate for No. 5 Vice Mr. Melbourne.

A Motion from No. 7 to print Mr. Laws Letter of Secession from the Place and Pension Association was rejected.[26]

A Circular Letter was read from Sheffield desiring to know our Opinion on the best Method of obtaining a radical Reform and also our Opinion of the Friends of the People. The Chairman was instructed to return a tem-

porary Answer, till such Time as we had collected the Sense of our Divisions whether they concurred in Opinion with the People of Sheffield that a Petition to Parliament was the likeliest Method to pursue.

A Letter to the Friends of the People was read and approved of, in Answer to their Reply to our first.[27]

45. Report from spy Lynam: LCS General Committee (government paraphrase), 31 January 1793

Source: TS 11/954/3498

31 Janry   The Witness [Lynam] was present at a Meeting of the Delegates at No. 5 Queen Street seven Dials – 13 attended

A Letter from the Society of the ffriends of the people at the ffreemasons Tavern was read & the reply . . . apparently drawn by Margarot was read to the Committee[28] and Ordered to be sent. . . .

It appeared to be apprehended by the Delegates that they should make a Breach with this Society as the Consl. Society had done before.[29]

The Circular Letter from Sheffield . . was also read in this Meeting. . . .

Margarot then said, we are getting on fast again, & a petition is not the mode.[30] –

26 On 24 Jan. the *Morning Chronicle* published a letter from Thomas Law criticizing Reeves's Association for Preserving Liberty and Property against Republicans and Levellers for heeding anonymous letters (cutting in Place Collection, vol. 36, fo. 25).

27 This letter asked the FoP the questions that had been raised in the Sheffield letter and in previous meetings of the committee of delegates: 'what measures [do] you mean to pursue, when [do] you mean to begin & how far [do] you intend carrying your proposed Reform' (1 Feb. 1793, TS 11/956/3501).

28 At Hardy's trial, Lynam was asked if the actual letter to be sent to the FoP was read to the delegates. 'I will not be confident of that . . . there were several letters that were wrote by Margarot himself without being shown to the delegates, and after he had wrote them, when he came to the meeting of delegates he reported that he had wrote such a letter, and he gave the heads of such letter' (*ST* vol. 24, col. 781).

29 At the trial of Hardy, Lynam summarized the letter and added: 'then a remark was made that we are very apprehensive of creating a breach between them, as is the case between them and the Constitutional Society; there was a good deal of conversation in consequence of that letter, that the Society of the Friends of the People did not go so far in their idea as the London Corresponding Society did, for all along it was held as an invariable idea that it must eventually come to a struggle' (*ST* vol. 24, col. 782).

30 Lynam's testimony at Hardy's trial: 'A letter from Sheffield of the 16th of January, 1793,

47

signed David Martin president, Horsefall secretary, recommending a communication with all the societies in the kingdom, to form a constitutional meeting, and all to agree upon the same thing – asked how far we mean to proceed at this time – A reform nugatory, unless univeral right is established, and they advise a general petition to the House of Commons, on the present inadequate representation – they want to know if the Friends of the People are true friends – Margarot says we are getting on too fast, and that petition was not the mode . . . . but at the same time it was agreed upon by him and the rest of the delegates, that petitions should be presented for the sake of keeping the public mind agitated with a reform.'

At the trial Lynam added further details, some of which he admitted, under questioning, were from recollection rather than from his minutes of the meeting: 'A motion brought forward by the delegate of division No. 16, which was Baxter, wishing that six-pence [of the quarterly dues of 13d] may be paid only to the society, and the other seven-pence to go towards the expense of their room, it was agreed that this might be a very proper measure to be adopted for poor divisions; it was particularly remarked that at that time the people round Spitalfields were exceedingly numerous, and supposing that they should come to any open resistance these were divisions that ought particularly to be encouraged. [On request, Lynam repeated this material, with a slight rephrasing of the last part:] it was remarked at that time, and it was assented to by the whole meeting of delegates, that supposing there should be an opposition, or that the two parties in fact should come to an open declaration, an open rupture, that it was absolutely necessary to give encouragment to the divisions meeting in Spitalfields, for that they in general were very poor, and very numerous, and it was very necessary to keep them together. There was a good deal of conversation upon the necessity, and the propriety of it . . . . I have made a remark before of these divisions, that they increase so fast, that they were well satisfied that, in these divisions alone, very shortly they would have as many in number as there were in number in all the other divisions besides. A motion was made by the delegate of division No. 7, that Mr. Law's letter to Mr. Reeves, giving his reason for withdrawing himself from them, be published, to show the infamy of their proceedings, that the society was falling away very fast; but this motion was rejected, and instead of that, to publish extracts from 'The War, or who pays the Reckoning?' deferred the selection for one week . . . . It was then recommended that all the divisions should go to No. 52, in Frith-street, and sign the address of the Friends of the Liberty of the Press; – that is, every delegate was to recommend it to his division, at the next meeting. – In the course of the meeting, Margarot made a remark, that our address to Mr. Reeves was not liable to any punishment, or he and Mr. Hardy would have been taken up. Mar-

[At Hardy's trial, Lynam testified about a meeting of Division 23 on 5 February 1793: 'Bambridge read a minute that there are sixty friends to the cause, who decline at present meeting the society; but they are good friends, and sincerely wish them success; and some of them say, if they want money, they are ready to contribute. – He says, there are certain religious societies in the kingdom, almost in every town, whose sentiments lead them strictly to republicanism; they are numerous in Birmingham, Leeds, Liverpool, Bristol, Manchester, Hull, Derbyshire, and particularly in London. The society in London are just now beginning to organize themselves agreeable to the principles of France – their meetings are Mondays and Thursdays. – It was then said that Tom Paine's Works had been published in Sweden.'[31]]

46. Journal: LCS General Committee, 7 February 1793

Source: Add MSS 27812, fos. 33-4 (later copy in Add MSS 27814, fos. 104-5)

Thursday Febry. 7th. 1793.

Lambert produced his Voucher as Delegate for No. 28.

Jarvoise produced his Voucher as Sub-Delegate[32] for No. 25.

Evans produced his Voucher as Sub-Delegate for No 11 – incorporated with No. 15.

On a Motion from No. 16 the Delegates Resolved.

That in Consequence of the Poverty of Divisions Nos. 16 and 25 the Delegates of those Divisions shall have a discretionary

garot said, he meant to invite sir Sampson Wright to his division, or any one that he might send to the divisions, to show the legality of them' (cols. 780–2).

31 *ST* vol. 24, cols. 782–3.
32 The concept of a subdelegate appointed for a whole quarter first appeared on 28 Dec. when Div. 4 elected a delegate and a subdelegate for the next quarter. However this was the only division to elect a subdelegate. (On two previous occasions – 15 Nov. and 5 Dec. – a subdelegate had been elected to attend the general committee for one night.) For the next quarter (April–June 1793) six divisions elected subdelegates. Later the subdelegate as well as the delegate attended meetings of the general committee, but was allowed to vote only in the absence of the delegate (vouchers in TS 11/953/3497 and TS 11/956/3501; list of delegates in TS 11/954/3498).

Power of appropriating Part of the Society's Quarterage towards defraying the Deficiency of Room-rent.

A Letter was read from Sheffield enclosing the Circular Letter mentioned and read last Week; requesting the Society to transmit the said enclosed Circular Letter to every Society for Reform in London.

The Purport of the Circular Letter was that they had determined to petition Parliament; and that all Reform would in their Opinion be useless which did not restore universal Suffrage, and annual Elections.

In Consequence of these Letters the Committtee resolved to request a Conference upon the Subject of parliamentary Reform with every patriotic Society in London. And the Secretary was ordered to advertise a Request to all the Members to be punctual in their Attendance upon their separate Divisions to consider the following Question "Which are the most effectual Steps to be pursued at the present Juncture of Affairs for obtaining an effectual, immediate, and radical Reform in Parliament."

The following Regulations were agreed upon for the Committee.

1st. That 5 Delegates be sufficient to proceed to Business.

2nd. That the Chair be taken at 8 O Clock precisely.

3rd. That the Names of Absentees at 9 O Clock be taken down by the Secretary.

4th. That the Committee appoint a Delegate from among those present to report the Absentee to his Division next night and to make the Report for him.

47. Report from spy Lynam: LCS General Committee, 7 February 1793

Source: TS 11/958/3503

Feby 7 No 8 Queen Street
Law's for Deligate's

[The four new regulations are given.]

Division 3 joind 7 – Divi: 11 joind 15
Order'd the Deligates visit 15 as they are disorderly
Field met Div: 28 at their first meeting St. Georges Fields and made 3 new member's
Division 25 met 4 or 5 – falling off
Division 5 met 30 and brought forward 6 old member's by (inviting), this method to be adopted by all Divisions, and will soon get strong again

Reported that there are Parson's visit in their vesty room's – about 250 in number
Deligate 14 declined & now joind No 10
Copely Del: for 10
Division 9 joind 29
Division 2 very numerou's fill'd 2 room's and next night to have many more
Division 1 nearly lost   some of them joind 2
Division 28 met 11 in number last night
Field Deligate for 18 first meeting at yd
Crown Air Stt Piccadilly
Division 19 met first at Knightsbridge done away
Do 25 & 16 joind
Surplus of Quarterage of other Division's to Pay for Room of 16[33] & 25 – they being poor – We must Preserve these Divisions   will be of great service if there sho'd be a war this from M M[34]
Bath letter gone 14 Days and no answer
No letters this week
A Letter from Sheffield 26[35] Jany 93   By order of Society for constitutional information to convey to all Societys their desire of knowing how far they mean to go – They are of opinion all sho'd be of one opinion & Petition parliament this Session, it will give strength to yd cause, They say restoration of right of election sho'd not be under 21 — By doing this shall know how far can support Mr Grey's motion, no time to be lost. Hardy proposes a Deligate from each Society and Division to agree how to proceed – Mr Fox has said in the House the People have a right to alter the Government when they please The Scotch & Irish have done it[36]

33 'Baxters' written above '16'.
34 At Hardy's trial Lynam was asked to affirm that Divs. 16 and 25 were the Spitalfield divisions. He was also asked to affirm that Margarot had used the word *war*. By *war*, Lynam understood 'that the country would rise against the present government . . . . and it was mentioned by several of the delegates, that it was eventually expected that there would certainly be a rising in the country'.
35 '16' written above '26'. This is the circular letter discussed at the previous meeting of the general committee of delegates.
36 On 1 Feb. Fox, speaking in the House of Commons against the possibility of a war with France, asserted 'that the people are the sovereigns in every State; that they have a right to change the form of their government, and a right to cashier their Governors for misconduct, as the people of this country cashiered James II, not by a Parliament, or any regular form known to the Constitution, but by a Convention speaking the sense of the People' (*Parliamentary Register*, vol. 34 (1793), cols. 417-8).

London corresponding Society first form'd to send Deligate's to all other Societys in the Kingdom to determine the best way of re-form[37] — The Friends of the People in the Boro yet exist, orderd to communicate Our letter's to them and all other Societys to enquire their sentiments,[38] determined to have a meeting of 2 or 3 from every Society and for a Plan of Proceeding   Then to com-municate with the Country -, Write to Shef-field will write them upon this very soon — how We mean to proceed[39]

Each Division to debate upon the best way of Proceeding – Advertize this Saturday Sun-day & Monday

15 Deligates met

48. Journal: LCS General Committee, 14 February 1793

Source: Add MSS 27812, fos. 34-5 (later copy in Add MSS 27814, fos. 105-6)

Thursday Febry. 14th. 1793.

The Delegate of No. 23 requested Leave of Precedence to make an extraordinary Report. - stating - That Division No. 12 had chosen Mr. Godfrey Delegate, upon the Resignation of Mr. Freemantle – that the said Mr. Godfrey being Attorney to Lord George Gordon, and under the supposed Influence of his Principles was an improper Person to be recieved as Delegate of any Division of the Society[40] – He had therefore the Authority of his Division to request the Committee would postpone the Reception of Mr. Godfrey till a Deputation had waited on Division No. 12 and reasoned with them on the probable bad Consequences

37 One of the delegates made this statement.
38 '7 Febry 1793' written above this phrase.
39 Paraphrase: 'It was resolved that this Letter from Sheffield should be referred to the Friends of the People in the Boro' & the other Societys that their Sentiments should be enquired & a Plan of proceedg. being agreed upon it should be com-municated to the Society at Sheffield in the mean time a Letter should be written to that Society expressive of these Intentions.'
40 The LCS would be especially uneasy about any connection with Gordon, the instigator of the anti-Catholic riots in 1781; for Gordon had attracted public attention on 29 Jan., on the expiration of his five-year jail sentence, when he appeared in court with 'a beard of enormous length' and 'a large slouched hat', which he refused to remove on the ground that he had been converted to ' "the holy covenant of cir-cumcision" '. (*New Annual Register*, 1793, 'Occurrences', p. 5).

of electing a Person as their Delegate who was in Habits of Connection with any Party-leader.

This Report was interrupted at the Com-mencement by the Entry of Mr. Godfrey into the Committee – as the Committee were not at his Entrance in full Possession of the Ob-jections made against him, the Chairman was desired to request Mr. Godfrey to with-draw – To this Mr. Godfrey objected – The Question was then put rotatively to each Individual and was carried unanimously for Mr. Godfrey to with-draw – The Chairman then informed Mr. Godfrey that if he would with-draw for half an Hour till the Committee had heard and discussed the Objections made to his Admis-sion, he would be then allowed to reenter the Committee-room and reply . . . –

[The rest of this entry was cut from the Journal, except the last line, which appears at the top of a folio:]

Behaviour and Conduct of the Committee.[41]

49. Report from spy Lynam: LCS General Committee, 14 February 1793[42]

Source: TS 11/958/3503

Meeting of Del. 14 feby 1793
No 8 Queen Street

14 Del: met –   Division No 14 first met
Scotch Arm's Crown St. Strand
Tindal Del: for No 10 – Stiff Del: for 13 –
Moor Del: for 26
Division No 12 met at Godfry's an Attorney
No 38 Fore Street and chose him Deligate,
Rejected being Ld. G. Gordon's Attorney –
Reject all connected wth. L. G. G.[43] –

41 In his later copy Hardy summarized the missing material: 'on his re admission into the room some little altercation took place between Mr. G and the Come   however a deputation took place to divn. 12'.
42 Address: 'E. Nepean Esqr. / Whitehall'. Govern-ment description: 'Proceedings of the Delegates / 14 Feby. 1793 / Rx 15'.
43 Lynam's explanation at the trial of Hardy: 'They were determined to have nothing at all to do with any person that had any connexion with lord George Gordon; and the division No. 12, had a person of the name of Watson, supposed to be secretary to lord George Gordon, that attended them; and it was intimated that lord George

This Div: to meet in Newgate Street next wednesday or at Robins's[44] –

To be agreed next night if You Petition Parliament, it will engage Public attention for yd Present –

Division No 16 met in No 25 & made 3 new member's

No 2 met from ⟨80⟩ to 100 – other's met 37–50. 18–14 & No 29 met strong

16 Division's kept up – Div: 24 to be revived

Baker Del: run away

McGregor a publican joind Div: No 7

Agreed to demand a conferance of Constitutional Society   They are drawing up a state of representation, & go as far as We do

Friends of yd People & the Boro' do *not* Holborn Society declare themselves for republicanism[45]

Aldgate Society continued & call'd yd Botheram Society[46] a Meeting 3 Tuns Boro' – Friends of People at yd Circus

These about 6 Societys to confer with

Friends of People not yet answerd our Letter

A Letter sent to Constitutional Wigs at Sheffield saying We are about a general conferance and shall write them

There are 2 Societys at Norwich United Constitutional Societys   Wrote them to Persevere & assured them We are firm, & mean to collect a general opinion

3 Questions for concideration, if Petition King or Parliament or call a convention[47] –

Gordon was by some means acquainted with what was going on; that he made use of this Watson by way of bringing forward different things; they conceived he would be very troublesome, and that if his name was connected with the Corresponding Society, it would make them disrespectful in the eyes of the public; they then rejected him' (*ST* vol. 24, cols. 784–5). As noted before, Hardy 'was very intimate with Lord George Gordon', but disapproved of the 'wild schemes . . . of that misguided but much injured man' (*Memoir*, p. 8).

44 'Division No. 12 to meet next Wednesday at the Crown in Newgate-street; but if refused at the Crown, to go to Robins's coffee-house in Shire-lane, who would take in any of the divisions' (Lynam's testimony).

45 Asked what had become of the Holborn Society, Lynam testified that 'it is broke up; and the greatest part of the members have joined the Corresponding Society since'.

46 Printed as 'Bother'em' in the trial of Hardy. Lynam explained that the society had 'broke up'.

47 This topic was to be discussed in each division during the week.

Decline coming to any resolution till the whole Nation are agree'd[48]

M.M. says neither Petition or remonstrance, it will be unconstitutional

– Aldgate Society sent thanks to Mr Fox for his speach saying People may alter Constitution without giving reason's

A Mr Jones says he knows 3 People employd by Government who correspond wth. Jacobin's in France –

50. Report from spy Lynam: LCS Division 23, 19 February 1793[49]

Source: TS 11/958/3503

Feby 19   Crown Street

One Vote for 18 Year's of Age for electing, 10 for 21 Year's & One for housekeeper's

Resolv'd that Printed copie's of L C. Society Petition to Parliament be Printed, and distributed out to yd World[50]

51. Journal: LCS General Committee, 21 February 1793

Source: Add MSS 27812, fos. 35–5v (later copy in Add MSS 27814, fos. 106–7)

Thursday Febry. 21st. 1793

The Committee having met and Mr. Godfrey attending, the deputed Delegates gave an Account of their Mission – by which it appeared that George Lynam had not attended[51] his Duty, but that Thos. Stiff and Joseph Field had waited on and communicated to the Division the Resolution of the Committee, that the Division had treated it with Levity almost with Contempt, and had unanimously re-elected Mr. Godfrey as Delegate, with Instructions to deny the positive Right of the Committee to object to the Admission of any Delegate fairly elected. –

Mr. Godfrey having produced a Letter to

48 This was a remark by one delegate, not an affirmed resolution.

49 Address: 'E. Nepean Esqr / Whitehall'. Government description: 'Proceedings at the Meetings at Crown Street & Compton Street on the 19 & 21 & 23 Feby. / 1793'. This is on the same sheet as the report of the meetings of the general committee on 21 and 23 Feb.

50 'That means that they had come to a determination to petition parliament, not to petition the King, nor to call a convention' (Lynam's testimony, *ST* vol. 24, col. 786).

51 'Lynam although deputed and the accuser of Godfrey also had not attended . . .' – later copy.

the Secretary from Division 12, coinciding with the above Report, the Chairman having read it to the Committee, proceeded to take the Sentiments of such Divisions upon the Business as had their Delegates present, when it appeared that Six Divisions approve the Conduct of the Committee, two submit the whole Affair to their better Judgement, and three have not determined –

A Motion was next made, and carried unanimously that Mr. Godfrey be further suspended till the Sense of the Society be taken universally upon the Propriety or Impropriety of absolutely rejected him –

Mr. Godfrey utterly denied the Right of the Committee or the Power of Interference in the separate Divisions – and being requested to with-draw, persisted that as he concieved he there represented the twelfth Division, he there would stay unless induced to with-draw from the Fear of personal Violence being offered to him. –

In Consequence of this Pertinacity the Committee being unable to proceed to the Business of the Evening adjourned to Saturday the 23rd. Instant.

52. Report from spy Lynam: LCS General Committee, 21 February 1793

Source: TS 11/958/3503

Feby 21st Compton Street

Field met Division No 12 at yd Crown Newgate Street, They where refused a room 2 Common Council being there saying they wo'd take away the licence if entertain'd – They then whent to Godfreys & rechose him Deligate – rejected him & as he wo'd not leave the room – Adjourn'd to Saturday evening to 57 Charles Street

53. Journal: LCS General Committee, 23 February 1793

Source: Add MSS 27812, fos. 35v–6 (later copy in Add MSS 27814, fo. 107)

Adjourned Committee Saturday
23rd. Febry. 1793.

A Letter from the Friends of the People was read, and much approved – [52]

52 Lynam summarizes the approved sections of this letter (see next document). Other parts of the letter and the politely hostile tone of the whole may not have been approved, for the LCS reply is wholly defensive (e.g. 'we are sorry that you

It was determined to recommend to our Country Correspondents to petition the House of Commons separately; and that ourselves should petition but not precipitately.

The Chairman announced a Letter from Edward Farley respecting a Publication of his on the Illegality of Imprisonment for debt[53] – but the Consideration of it's Contents was postponed to the next Meeting.

The Secretary sent Word of his having recieved 12 Copies of the "State of the Representation of England and Wales" from the Friends of the People.[54]

54. Report from spy Lynam: LCS General Committee, 23 February 1793

Source: TS 11/958/3503

Feby 23 Charles Street

Reported a great number of Deligates from Scotland are in Town upon a reform – A

should appear to be hurt by the plain questions We put to you in our last – to ask of you what measures you mean to pursue in a matter which concerns us all is certainly no ways calling upon you to surrender up to our Society or even to the public at large your discretion', etc.). The first two letters from the FoP are patronizing: in their first, they advised the LCS – then almost a year old – to behave peaceably. They make it clear that they feel no kinship with the LCS as fellow reformers; for example, to the request for their opinion of the LCS publications, they reply, 'we are not called upon to pronounce any judgment on the publications of individuals or societies' (Edward Jer. Curteis to Hardy, 15 Feb. 1793; undated draft of reply; both in TS 11/956/3501).

53 Farley presented the LCS (also the SCI) with a copy of his pamphlet: *Imprisonment for Debt Unconstitutional and Oppressive, proved from the fundamental principles of the British Constitution and the rights of nature* (Farley to delegates, 21 Feb. 1793, TS 11/956/3501).

54 *The State of the Representation of England and Wales, Delivered to the Society of the Friends of the People, Associated for the Purpose of Obtaining a Parliamentary Reform, on Saturday the 9th of February 1793.*

Hardy described the dissemination of these pamphlets (he recalled receiving 300): 'they were proportionably distributed among the different divisions each division lent to a class of their members to read for one week – they returned them the next meeting night And another class had them to read another week and they returned them also . . . &c.' (Add MSS 27814, fos. 54–5).

The LCS so valued this 38 pp. pamphlet, with

Letter from Southampton approving yd Plan & want Our addresses to form a Society there & will correspond with us – a letter & addresses to be sent them[55]

Constitutional Society ajournd to 15 March supposed to be to see what Mr Grey brings forward
All the Societys Town & Country to be wrote to send up a Petition from each and no time to be lost – Ours to be drawn up immediately and engage it will be sign'd by 20 thousand; If they are all rejected desire them to continue, as then will be the time for all to unite and Petition the King

The Friends of the People approve Mr Greys remonstrance[56]   it is a leading feature – Reported that yd serious stopages from the Bank refusing discounts will assist the cause by the failures which must follow

A Letter from E Farley Esqre. upon the illegality of arrest for debt, he has been 5 Years writeing a treatise upon it, and wants Us to subscribe, Extracts may be made from it to be very serviceable
A Letter from friends of the People dated 15th feby in answer to Our's of yd 1st sign'd E. Jerh. Carter[57] Chairman, saying very soon their Plan wo'd come forward to reform all yd abuse's existing, Mr Reeve's Society is unconstitutional; & their object is to form a new organ to speak to the legislation, They will not give up their Power of action to any Society, but say the time of action may not be very distant

I think I can get this letter for Your Perusal, if agreable

French Preists are informer's to yd Minister – An order has been sent to a Frenchman who has resided 21 Year's here to depart – no reason but asking one of these Preists for a debt of 15s

Answer'd Norwich Society   We believe Friends of yd People are sincere

Agreed to write Bath Society of yd steps taking 12 Deligates met[58]

Private information that a Private meeting is held in Bishopgate Street – a Mr. Christie of Devonshire Square sent 50 £ to yd Convention for supporting the Warr; tis supposed he has meetings

55. Journal: LCS General Committee, 28 February 1793

Source: Add MSS 27812, fos. 36–7v (later copy in Add MSS 27814, fos. 107–9)

Thursday Febry. 28th. 1793

James Brown produced his Voucher as Sub Delegate for Division 26.

From the Report of the Delegates it appeared that a large Majority of the Society approved the utter Rejection of Mr. Godfrey; and the Secretary recieved Orders to communicate that Information to the Division 12 – and to desire them to proceed to the Election of another Delegate.

The following Resolution was resolved to be submitted to each Division for their Confirmation; in Consequence of the Case of Mr. Godfrey –

Resolved   That when an Objection is made against the Admission or Continuance of any Delegate chosen by any of the Divisions of this Society; and it shall appear that a Majority of the Delegates are against the Admission or Continuance of such Delegate he may be rejected from his Office by the Delegates; who may direct that the Division by which such Delegate is elected shall proceed to elect another Delegate.

A Motion of Thanks to Charles James Fox, the Earl of Lauderdale and the virtuous Minority in both Houses of Parliament who have exerted themselves so ably tho' unsuccessfully in the Cause of the People to avert a War with France, was unanimously carried –   The Secretary recieved Instructions to insert the foregoing Motion in the public Papers.

A printed circular Letter was recieved from Sheffield containing several Resolutions passed in their Societies – expressive of their Abhorrence of War as destructive of the Interests of a trading, manufacturing and commercial Country – and returning their

its statistics on the small number of electors who selected various MPs, that they published a shorter version in 1795. More than forty years later, Francis Place still praised it as a significant reform document (Add MSS 27789, fos. 384–7).

55 To be sent by Div. 28 (Lynam's testimony, *ST* vol. 24, col. 786).
56 On 21 Feb. Grey moved that Parliament send the king an address asking him to ignore the councils which had recommended the war and to restore peace. Motion rejected by 109 to 21.
57 'Curteis' written above in a less polished manner. At the trial Lynam identified him as Carter and was told that the correct name was Curteis.

58 At Hardy's trial Lynam added one detail not found in his report: 'A motion to be debated at each division, if they gave the delegates power to reject any delegate on good reasons' (*ST* vol. 24, col. 787).

Thanks to Messrs Fox, Erskine, Grey Lambton, and to the Duke of Norfolk, Marquiss of Lansdowne, Earls Stanhope, Lauderdale, and Derby, for their Exertions in the Cause of Freedom both in and out of Parliament.

A letter to Sheffield was approved, and ordered to be sent informing them of our Resolution to petition,[59] and recommending them to lose no Time in pursuing the same course.

Mr. Farley's Letter was read requesting Subscriptions in Support of Measures for proving the Illegality of Imprisonment for Debt, and effecting it's total Abolition The Committee ordered their Secretary to return for Answer, that as a Society they could support nothing by pecuniary Assistance which was not closely connected with the Object of their Association viz a reform in parliament; but that the Members of the Committee would individually recommend his Production

A Petition to Parliament was produced and read by Mr. Gerald – as was also one by Mr. Farley, read by Mr. Margarot – The prior Petition seemed to meet the Approbation of the Committee but the Lateness of the Hour was the Occasion of their being both refered to the next Meeting.

56. Report from spy Lynam: LCS General Committee, 28 February 1793[60]

Source: TS 11/958/3503

Meeting of Deligates 28 feby 1793
at Mr. Stiffs   Paternoster Row

Little John bringing forward his division again[61]
Division 26 made 7 new Member's
Rejected Godfrey from being deligate, and all People concerned wth. Ld G. Gordon
249 Member's met last week in yd different division's
Agreed[62] to Publish thanks to Mr. Fox & minority & to Lord Lauderdale for their

opposition to yd War to be put in the Morning Chronocle, Morning Post & Eyre's Sunday Paper
Observed by Martin
Report that it is yd Minister's war to divert yd mind's of the People
36 Societys at Paisley, sent 3 or 4 letter's none recd
Letter from Sheffield by order of Committee for constitutional information, say War the greatest evil ever introduced to the Trade of Brittain &c to Publish their thanks to Mr Fox && in all the Paper's both Town & Country – same to Mr. Erskine M. M. to write to them to Petition Parliament derectly & to request all Society's to do yd same, and altho they may be thrown out, it will answer a good Purpose, as yd cause will be agetated every week – likewise to continue and afterwards all unite in one General one to the King[63]
Stiff Deligate for Division 13
The L. C. Society's Petition drawn up by Mr. Gerrold to be agreed upon next Thursday, and to be left at different Place's for signatures – Gerrald had applied to Mr. Mackintosh who agreed to go with him to Mr Fox to get him to present it

I shall have the letter of the Friends of People to L. C. S. in yd. course of 2 or day's to read to Division

I have got yd state of Representation of England & Wales drawn up by a Committee of Friends of People & Deliverd to them 9th. Feby, it is too large to enclose – Printed by order of the Society for D. Stuart No 52 Frith St. Soho

57. Journal: LCS General Committee, 7 March 1793

Source: Add MSS 27812, fos. 37v-8v (later copy in Add MSS 27814, fo. 109)

Thursday March 7th.
1793.

From the Report of the Delegates it appeared that the Society would not confirm the Committee's Resolution of the last Evening.

On a Motion from No. 14 that all Reports from the Divisions be brought to the Committee in Writing, the Comittee passed to the Order of the Day.

A Motion for leaving the Committee the

---

59 'to petition the house of commons' – later copy. Letter to William Camage, 4 March 1793, TS 11/965/3510A.
60 Address: 'E. Nepean Esqr. / Whitehall'. Government description: 'Proceedings of the Delegates of the London Corresponding Society / 28 Feby. 1793'.
61 Div. 14.
62 Inserted after report was written: 'on Martin's Motion'. At Hardy's trial, Lynam testified that Margarot made the motion (*ST* vol. 24, col. 787).
63 Lynam is wrong: the letter does not speak of a petition to the king. At Hardy's trial Lynam (who had by then been able to see the letter in print) omitted this statement.

Power of Suspending a Delegate, till the General Sense of the Society was collected, was presented – but withdrawn as it was clearly understood that the Committee already possessed that Power. –

A Motion was presented by the Delegate of No. 9 including a regular Process to be observed in Cases similar to that of Mr. Godfrey, but it was withdrawn upon Account of it's requiring serious Consideration, and the Business of the Petition being more momentous at that Time.

The Petition was then read – Some Amendments were made, and a postscript Clause expressing our Notions of parliamentary Reform was added by the Chairman and agreed to.

A certain Number of the Petition was ordered to be printed for the Use of each Delegate; and an Advertisement to summon the Members of each Division to attend to hear it read and discussed, was ordered to be inserted in the public Papers.

58. Letter: W. Williams of the British Citizens, formerly Division 12, to LCS, 13 March 1793[64]

Source: TS 11/965/3510A

Gentlemen

A Letter signed Thos. Hardy secretary of the London Coresponding society of which a Copy is Subjoined.[65] has been laid before the Committee of the society of British Citizens. by the Member to whom it was addressed

The Committee in this as in every other instance – regulating their deliberations by that principle of fraternity – which requires a Citizen to Judge Charitably of all Men – will not pass by with Contempt – but regard with Candour, the Subject to which that Letter has reference – and being from unquestionable Authority informed of the several Circumstances – they will by accurate and unequivocal Observation Consider them –

It appears to the Committee

First – That on the 6th. day of February. 1793. the 12th. Division of the London Cores-

ponding society Elected Mr. Saml. Godfrey their Delegate – on this the Committee of British Citizen have to observe – that they have referred to the Constitution of the London Coresponding Society – and they find that by such Election of a Delegate the Division exercised a Right unquestionably given to it by that Constitution – and there does not appear any power declared or implied which does Controvert or Controul that Right –

Secondly – That persons calling themselves a Committee of Delegates of the London Coresponding society – voted – first a Suspension – and afterwards an exclusion of such Elected Delegate – the Committee of British Citizens are under the necessity of describing the persons so voting as persons calling themselves a Committee – because by the obvious Construction of the same Constitution it is clear, that the suspension or exclusion of any one or more Delegates – must render those which remained a self-Elected body – who having violated the principle of one Election had abandoned the principles of all – and by their infractions could no longer be considered in any of the Capacities which they Collectively – and Collectively only – held from the respective Divisions of the Society – Election violated renders all it's Delegation and Authority void – and it follows, that any partial Majority of Delegates excluding a Member Contrary to the fundamental Rights of a free choice – might with a Majority on every other Occasion – and with equal reason, exclude every Member, who thought differently with themselves – here the Committee of British Citizens must lament the short sighted policy of Men – avowing themselves the friends of Parliamentary Reform but evidently betraying a total ignorance of the first Right of Representation – and at a loss to Comprehend what is meant by a free choice –

Hence it is that the Committee of British Citizens will not descend to any particular examination of the narrow – not to say the Ridiculous exceptions – under which those Men have endeavoured to Shelter their Opposition to the Admission of the Elected Delegate into that Committee to which he was Constituted – and intitled to sit – we observe generally that the Moment his Election by the Division had passed – in that Moment by the same fair Construction. of the before mentioned Constitution he became an unexceptionable Member of that Committee – for your Constitution points out no second Election nor any Refusal or Revision of the first – neither warranting any interference of other Delegates or of other Divisions or Assemblies –

64 Address: 'To the London Corresponding Society'. Annotated: 'Wrote by Godfree's Clerk'.

65 The letter, addressed to Mr J Wood, informs Div. 12 that 'it is the Opinion of a great Majority of the several divisions that Mr. Godfrey ought not to be admitted as a Delegate' and requests the division to elect another delegate.

We do not find then, that the shadow of exception rests on the Character of this BRITISH CITIZEN who was unanimously delegated by the 12th. Division of the London Coresponding society and therefore we his fellow Citizens have forbid him to answer those Frivolity's which were called exceptions – he shall not descend to combat by ⟨Arguments⟩ that vote of exclusion which is in direct hostility to common sence –

GENTLEMEN –
We lament your diminished. numbers – we feel for the impotent and degraded state into which your Society is Reduced – under the influence of a few individuals who either have a *secret* Interest in your Circumvention or whose dull and inactive line of Conduct has placed you so far behind the rest of your Countrymen that while every County and Corner of the Kingdom is actually engaged in Measures to effect the Just Rights of a Parliamentary Representation you being in the midst of the Metropolis – but having your laudable intentions perplexed and preverted by that improper influence are Confessedly at a loss to understand the Common Rights which are necessary to regulate your own little Committee –

Signed by Order of the Committee
W. Williams

Committee Room
Fore Street   Moregate
March 13th. 1793

59. Journal: LCS General Committee, 14 March 1793

Source: Add MSS 27812, fo. 38v (later copy in Add MSS 27814, fo. 109)

Thursday March 14th. 1793.

From the Delegate's Reports it appeared that the Society had made a considerable Encrease the last Week.

Two Motions were presented   the first from No. 5

That the Delegates be requested to frame general Rules for the Government of the whole Society – Made the Order of the Day for the ensuing Meeting.

The Second from No. 1 That an Abstract, which appeared in a late Manchester Herald respecting the Evil Conseçuences of War on the Poor, from a Publication of the Revd. Mr. Frend of Cambridge, should be printed for the

Use of the Members of the Society [66] – Passed unanimously.

John Lowe produced his Voucher as Sub-Delegate for Division 13.

The Petition was next taken into Consideration: various Amendments were proposed by different Divisions – after much Dis-

[Two folios are cut from the Journal at this point.]

60. Report from spy Lynam: LCS General Committee, etc., 14 March 1793 [67]

Source: TS 11/953/3497

Sir

March 7th. 93   Compton Street

14 Deligates met
Number of all meeting this week in all yd Divisions 238
Read the Petition to Parliament and engaged all yd evening [68]

March 12   Crown Street

Met 11   2 Visitors, made 2 Member's

March 14 Compton Street

Division 29 made 3. No 10 made 1 – No 23 made 2 – No 7. made 3   No 5 made 1 – No 2

66 This three page document reports the complaints of two poor women at being 'sconced' a fourth of their labour to support war (*Extracts from the Appendix of a Pamphlet Entitled Peace and Union, Recommended to the Associated Bodies of Republicans and Anti-Republicans*, 1793). For publishing *Peace and Union*, which recommends reforms in parliamentary representation, law and religion, William Frend was excluded from Cambridge after a lengthy trial in the court of the Vice Chancellor and after an unsuccessful appeal in the civil court. In London he became one of the public men who assisted the LCS: in 1795 he addressed an outdoor meeting called by the LCS; later he organized a subscription for the men arrested in 1798; and in 1823 he started a subscription for Hardy.

67 Government description: 'March 7th 1793. / Seditious Societies'. At Hardy's trial Lynam conflated the 7 and 14 March reports of the general committee of delegates. On 12 March Div. 23 met.

68 The petition, entitled 'The Inhabitants of London, Westminster and their Vicinity', was referred to the individual divisions for their consideration (paraphrase of Lynam's reports, TS 11/950/ 3501).

made 3 – No 16 made 5 – No 4 made 4. No 13 made 2

Encreased this week – 24

Bells Divison agreed to remove from 8 Queen Street to Robins's

New Deligates to be chose 28 March

Agreed that the Essay on War, wrote by Mr. Friend of Cambrige Published in yd Manchester Paper, should be Printed and deliverd to all the Divisions, and the Public

The Petition to be made out on Rolls of Parchment for each Deligate to get signatures by yd 21st. Inst

To try what Coffee house will take it in, Reported believe that Osborn's Hotel will take it in

Division 12. Meet at Godfreys 50 and encrease under the title of British Citizen's

I do not know how to act respecting the being a Deligate for the ensuing quarter, nor about signing the petition I shall think myself very much honourd in Your direction herein

61. Report from spy Lynam: LCS General Committee, 23 March 1793[69]

Source: TS 11/965/3510

Sir

The late Division No 12 Meet at Godfreys under the Title of British Citizen's & meet from 40 to 50

The interpreter at yd Queen Square Police office, Whitehead, and 2 other's meet on Sundays at Mile end, They are most violent Democrats

March 21   Compton Street

Division No. 8 made 1   No. 13 made 1   No 18 made 1   No 28 made 1   No 29 made 1 No. 1 made 3   No. 16 & 25 made 7   No. 7 made 3

Made by 14 Divisions this week   18

Petition signd this week Vizt.

No	8,	13,	29,	10,	5,
	35,	26,	16,	24,	21,
No.	25,	2,	7,	1,	11
	40,	50,	40,	17,	12,

Whole number signing   281

69 Address: 'E. Nepean Esqr/ Whitehall'. Government description: '23 March 1793/ Mr Lynam'. The official record of this meeting was cut out of the LCS Journal.

Each Deligate to have a roll and to go round for signatures

Division No 1 met at Robins's very full indeed

Divisions 16 & 25, were visited by some Constables, but being so numerous they dare not go amongst them – [70]

Mr. William's of Smithfield applied to Margarot for & has a roll to get signatures he will get 500

Ridgway has one –   Spencer Holborn Do

Dawson Covent garden has one

Letter from Birmingham dated 15 March intitled Society for constitutional information signd John Harrison Begins Citizen Hardy, Request to correspond, to strengthen the love of human nature, restore Representation &c – Enclosed one of their printed petitions, addressed to Journimen Workmen and others, complains of the venal mode of election, of Poor rates, Tythes, and the dearness of Provisions, determined to think & speak for themselves, to Petition Parliament, speak unite and it will be done

J. Harrison

This letter came   Post directed to Hardy, the place of his residence in St. Martins Lane before he took his house Piccadilly

The Friends of People have had 2 letter's from them directed to Stewart

Agreed to make extracts from Friends, address to Republicans and Antirepublicans

Grant & Littlejohn were dischd from the London Corr. Society   Grant for employing Carter in the Day & Littlejohn for neglecting his Division

agreed to write to the Const Society & ask for other honorary Members to sit in their Room.[71]

70 Baxter reported that the constables came to disperse the meeting; 'they left word that they would come in greater force' (Lynam's testimony, *ST* vol. 24, col. 788).

71 Government paraphrase of this meeting adds: 'Baxter reported that he had recd a Letter dated 28th. ffeby saying – as you meet to overturn the Constitution you are warned that warrants will be taken out agt. every Member

'It was ordered on Margarot's Motion that 1000 Copies of Extracts from Frends address to Republicans & Anti Republicans with remarks shod. be printed & that the Witness Margarot Baxter Junr. Bror. to the Prisr ffield Smith Turner & Stiff should form a Commee for this purpose wch should meet at Stiff's House – Hardy was ordered to give Carter's (the Bill sticker's) wife 10/6d. to inquire into the truth of a Complaint of Embezzlement she had made against Martin' ('Evidence of George Lynam', TS 11/954/3498).

62. Journal: LCS General Committee, 28 March 1793

Source: Add MSS 27812, fo. 39 (later copy in Add MSS 27814, fo. 110, dated 4 April)

[The previous part of the Report is cut out.]

A Motion was made, seconded, put and agreed to, That no Member of the Society calling itself "British Citizens" shall be admitted a Member of this Society without having first entirely seceded from the British Citizens.

A Special Committee of Delegates Margarot, Lynam Turner, Baxter and Field was appointed to revise, and consider the Constitution of this Society; and present their Improvements, Alterations &c to the General Committee; provided that nothing done by them be decisive till approved by the General Committee, and sanctioned by the Divisions individually.

This Special Committee was determined to be left open to any Delegate who might chuse to attend, such Delegate to be allowed an Opinion, but no Vote in the Committee.

63. Report from spy Lynam: LCS General Committee, 28 March 1793 [72]

Source: TS 11/958/3503

Sir

March 28, 93 No 31 Compton Street

The Patriotic Society of Holborn have been joining Division No 29 [73] – Venable Haberdasher – I am not clear if this is the person, he his a democrat
Division's No 10 & 14 cant get a Deligate for this quarter

No. of Division's.	29	10 & 14	5	23	13	16	7
Member's made	5	4	1	1	4	5	2
		Made this week	22				

Deligates	Field	Turner	Copley	Smith
No of Division	18	5	10	29
Sign'd yd Petition	73	65	50	40

72 Address: 'E. Nepean Esqr/ Whitehall'. Government description: '1st April 1793/ Mr Lynam./ (Secret)'.

73 'It was agreed to bring all the quarterage next Thursday, the Patriotic Society, in Holborn, joining the Division No. 29' (Lynam's testimony, ST vol. 24, col. 789).

Deligates	Hatton	Bell	Walne	
No of Division	25	1	4	23
Sign'd yd Petition	40	17	13,	20

Deligates	Stiff	Hardy	Margarot
No of Division	13	2	7
Signd y Petition	35	75	97

Deligates	Finly	Jno. Baxter	Dawe
No of Division	14	16	11
Signd y Petition	30	109	12

at Procter's Covent garden	30
at Ridgway's	12
In all to this time	718

No report from 5 Skin's that are out
A Select Committee chose to make extracts from Friends, address to Republicans and Antirepublicans, meet at Stiffs Paternoster Row, on Sunday evening next
A Committee chose to make new Law's for yd Society, and to submit them to each division, to meet every Thursday at 5 OClock
Vizt. Field, Jno. Baxter, C Turner, Lynam, Margarot [74]
Baxter's Skin & Petition to be taken in by Eaton a bookseller No 81 Bishopgate Street, He is under prosecution at this time – [75]

Division 5 meets at a School Tottenham court road near to Messrs Longman & Broderik Manufactory
5 Divisions meet at Robins Shire Lane
14 Deligates met [76]

64. Journal: LCS General Committee, 4 April 1793

Source: Add MSS 27812, fos. 39–9v (later copy in Add MSS 27814, fo. 110)

Thursday April 4th.
1793.

From the Reports it appeared that our Encrease was the last Week 7 – and that as far as the Delegates could account the total Number of Signatures upon the Petition Rolls was 1328.

Several additional Skins were granted, and the Petition ordered to be advertised for public Signature.

The Report of the Committee appointed to examine Mr. Frend's Pamphlet was recieved.

74 'any three to proceed to business, other delegates being allowed to visit' (Lynam's testimony).
75 For publishing The Rights of Man, part 2.
76 TS 11/966/3510B.

It stated that the Committee could not recommend the Whole of that Publication, but as there were Passages which might be serviceable as Extracts they beg'd Leave to sit again. Granted.

They recommended to the Committee to publish a small Appendix in Justification of the Death of Louis Capet. This the Committee negatived from the Consideration that our Enemies might infer from our vindicating the Death of Louis Capet in France, that we wish'd for a similar Event taking Place in this Country.

A Motion was brought from No. 5 respecting the supposed Ill-conduct of Richard Gay. The Committee pass'd to the Order of the Day.

A Motion was then made, and carried that the Thanks of this Society be given to Richard Gay for his Care and Attention in hiring, and providing for the Society's Use the Room in Compton Street.

65. Report from spy Lynam: LCS General Committee, 4 April 1793[77]

Source: TS 11/958/3503

Sir

April 4,   31 Compton Street   1793

Spence Rult & Co Mathmaticians Wapping, Spence a great friend & wishes for a Skin; Stiff whent with him to one of yd Church-wardens & Propose's that both shall go round

77 Address: 'E. Nepean Esqr / Whitehall'. Government description: '6: April 1793. / Mr Lynam / Secret'.
   At Hardy's trial, Lynam's account of this meeting did not include any of the material of this report. His account dealt with the meeting of a subcommittee: 'fourteen delegates met on the 4th of April, in Compton-street – the select committee to consider of their future regulations, first of all for the society at large – the general rules and private regulations for the admission of members – the week's payment – admission of strangers – vote of exclusion – the number of constituents before you branch off – the summonses sent to each night's meeting – that is one part of that committee's consideration to regulate – the next is, the constitution of general principles – committee's laws relative to themselves – the said delegates private regulations – laws relating to the society [–] election of chairmen and of door keepers.' At this point Lynam was told to go on to the next meeting (*ST* vol. 24, cols. 789–90).

yd Parish with him for signatures – Spence & Stiff got 23, Spence will get 40 to 50 certain Wm. Cleaver formerly of Holborn Division chose Sub Deligate for Division 29, reports most of them have joing L. C. Society
G Moor admitted to report signatures from Proctor's Covent garden
Lambert No 3 St. George's Mall Dog & Duck chose Deligate for 28

Divisions	25	23	5	28	1	No 5 Recovered
						5 old members
Made New Members	2	1	1	1	2	Encreased 7

Signatures to Petition to this time

Divisions No	2,	16,	6,	25,	13,	23,
	110	140	48	80	80	45

Divisions No	5,	28,	4,	7,	1	11,
	100	71	31	133	30	20

Divisions No	10,	14,	18,	29
	20	60	80	40

Proctor's   110
Williams   30
Gerrald Morning Post   20   In all 1,328

Division 25 to have another Skin – Ashley Holborn Society to have a Skin
Division No 1 (Bells) Skin lays at Owen's shoemaker Blackfryars road for signatures – Bell left us to go to House of Common's – Reported by Hardy that Osborn altho' a friend will not at this time receive a Skin for a thousand guinea's
The Petition to be advertized as laying for signatures at ye following places Vizt Eaton Bishopgate Street, Rigway, Morning Post, Courier, Proctors   Hardy No 9 Piccadilly
The Petition to be advertized for an equal representation upon the Duke of Richmonds Plan, and that it is already signd by two thousand
Hardy wrote to Birmingham, no answer received nor any correspondence
Hardy & Margarot brought Tickets to dine on yd 29 April with the Society for Constitutional information   Lord Sempill Chairman which were taken by most of the Deligate's
15 Deligates met
I have not yet made out Edwards, nor can I make out any other Venable
There are two other Societys about Spittle-fields, but have not particular's yet

66. Journal: LCS General Committee, 11 April 1793

Source: Add MSS 27812, fos. 39v–40 (later copy in Add MSS 27814, fo. 111)

April 11th. 1793.

The Signatures to the Petition were upwards of 2000 as far as the Delegates could account.

Some additional Places for public Signatures were appointed and ordered to be inserted in the Advertisements.

200 large posting Bills, and 1000 smaller Bills were ordered to be printed to inform the Public of the Petition.[78]

A Motion was brought from No. 4 That the Thanks of this Society be given to the Society of Friends of the People in a public Manner for their masterly Report on the State of the Representation: but the Committee understanding from their Secretary that the Friends of the People did not wish public Thanks, the Secretary was ordered to write to them a Letter expressive of the Purport of the Motion.

A Motion was put and carried that the Thanks of this Society be given to Philip Francis M. P. for his Speech on the 10th. Inn. in Favor of a radical Reform:[79]

The Secretary was ordered to draw up a Letter to that Purport and present it before the Committee for their Approbation.

A Circular Letter was produced by the Assist. Secretary read and agreed to – as also another addressed to the Friends of the People, containing the above Resolution which was also adopted, and ordered to be sent.

67. Report from spy Lynam: LCS General Committee, 11 April 1793[80]

Source: TS 11/958/3503

April 11   Compton Street

Division's No 8 – 9, 10, 11 & 14 can't get Deligates
Divisions No 18 – 5 – 16
made   1   1   2 Encreased 4 this week

Petition signd Vizt.

No	$\frac{4}{41}$	$\frac{18}{121}$	$\frac{5}{218}$	$\frac{9}{50}$	$\frac{16}{137}$	$\frac{10}{30}$	$\frac{14}{70}$

No	$\frac{75}{170}$	$\frac{23}{86}$	$\frac{29}{60}$	$\frac{13}{134}$	$\frac{1}{30}$	$\frac{2}{134}$	$\frac{7}{166}$	$\frac{28}{80}$

Hatton a Private Skin – 100   Stiff yd same   23
A Proctor's 143, Ridgway 100, Courier 2, Williams 80   Gerold 25 – In all 2000
Advertize a Skin lays at Spence's little turn stile Holborn
Recommend to get all signatures possible this week, very fearfull have try'd all their strength, and that the number will not make it respectable
Resolved to thank Friends of People for their impartial state of the representation
Constitutional Society of Sheffield have done it, and request they will publish it in a cheaper way – In their letter they say the enemies of the People are sleeping too long,[81] ingnorance

78 Headed 'REFORM IN PARLIAMENT. / LONDON CORRESPONDING *Society*, April 11, 1793', the bills announce that the petition 'praying for a Radical Reform in the Representation of the PEOPLE' can be signed at Ridgeway's Bookseller, York St, St James's Sq.; Hardy's, No. 9 Piccadilly; Lambert's Bookseller, No 3 St George's Mall, nr the Dog-and-Duck; Eaton's Bookseller, No 81 Bishopsgate-without; Spence's Bookseller, No 8 Little Turnstile, Holborn; the offices of the *Morning Post* and the *Courier* (handbill and posting bill in TS 11/965/3510A). A similar handbill has a postscript: 'N.B. Above 2000 Signatures have already been received. – No Expence attends signing' (Place Collection, vol. 36, fo. 45). James Davidson printed the bills at a cost of 7s and 7s 6d respectively. On four later occasions during April he printed a total of 6000 handbills for 15s and 1300 posting bills for £1 15s 6d (bill, TS 11/965/3510A).
79 Francis spoke against a bill to disenfranchise certain Stockbridge electors guilty of bribery. He argued that the bill was merely a pretended remedy, an occasional palliative, when what was needed was 'a complete alteration in the construction of the House of Commons'. The LCS soon published this speech under the title *Mr Francis's Speech on the Order of the Day for the Second Reading of the Bill for preventing Bribery at Stockbridge Election*. The LCS also published 1000 copies of their letter of thanks to Francis, dated 21 April, and his brief response, dated 22 April. When Francis learned that the

Society wanted to print these letters, he went to Hardy's house 'to tell him I was satisfied with their thanks, and wished them to decline printing'. Only at the trial of Hardy in 1794 did Francis learn that his wish had been ignored (Francis's speech in Add MSS 27814, fo. 33; printer's bill, TS 11/965/3510A; printed letters in BL; Francis's testimony, *ST* vol. 24, col. 1104).
80 Address: 'E Nepean Esqr / Whitehall'. Government description: '15 April 1793 / Mr Lynam / (Secret)'.
81 In Lynam's testimony, it was the people who were sleeping (*ST* vol. 24, col. 790).

in the People is the cause of the corruption in the Senate.

Resolved to send circular letter's to all Societys and request them to send Petition's directly Small Bill's to be stuck up in the night inform- ing the Public where the Petition lay's

Mr. Francis to be requested to present the Petition

14 Deligates met

Some of the Skin's very dirty, blotted, and marks of a X for a signature

68. Journal: LCS General Committee, 18 April 1793

Source: add MSS 27812, fos. 40–40v (later copy in Add MSS 27814, fo. 111)

April 18th. 1793.

It being observed by the Committee that Joseph Gerald had not properly attended in his Place as Delegate of No. 2. the Committee thought proper to appoint their Assist. Secre- tary to wait upon Division No. 2 on their next Night of Meeting, to inform them of their Delegate's Desertion of Duty, and to induce them to proceed to a fresh Election.

A Letter was produc'd by the Assist. Secre- tary, read and approved to be sent to Mr. Francis.

The total Number of Signatures as far as the Delegates could account was near 3000.

69. Report from spy Lynam: LCS General Committee, 18 April 1793[82]

Source: TS 11/965/3510

Sir

April 18. Compton Street

New Member's made

Division's No	25,	23,	7,	13
	1,	2,	2,	2

Encreased 7

Recommended by No 2 to advertize a general meeting of all the Divisions at some Tavern, and may get signatures by it

Division's No	4 —	18 —	16 —	28 —	29 —	23
signd	100,	131,	173,	106,	66,	100,

82 Address: 'E. Nepean Esqr./ Whitehall'. Govern- ment description: '18 April 1793./ Mr Lynam / Secret'. With this report Lynam sent a copy of the large posting bill advertising the petition and another smaller copy (paraphrase in TS 11/966/ 3510).

Division's No	1 —	2 —	7 —	25 —	13 —	9
signd	31,	177,	241,	170,	150,	80,

Division's No	5 —	10 —	14 —	11
signd	250,	40,	80,	20

Hatton 120, Spence 20, Williams 80, Proctor 170, Ridgway 120 Morning Post 14 Courier 10, Gerald 30 & Stiff 30

in all 2519

Ridgway to Publish a speach of Sherridan's, corrected by Mr. S——This not to be made Public

A Letter wrote to Mr Frances with our thanks for his speach on a reform in Parliament – signd M. M. & T. Hardy with Hardy's address – to be taken privately, and wrote at the corner 'from London Corresponding Society' - to be deliverd on saturday morning before he go's to Crown & Anchor Tavern

Reported that Ridgways tryal comes on next week, but dont know the day, he is quite in the dark

The business of the Deligates is falling away

Eleven Deligates met

Field continues secretary yet; I do not give up my hopes

70. Journal: LCS General Committee, 25 April 1793

Source: Add MSS 27812, fos. 40v–1 (later copy in Add MSS 27814, fo. 112)

April 25th. 1793.

Matthew Moore produced his Voucher as Delegate of No. 2 Vice Joseph Gerald super- seded by the Division upon the Representa- tion made from the Committee by their Assist. Secretary.

1000 Large Posting Bills, and 2000 Small Do. were ordered to be printed to advertize the Public of our Petition.

A Letter from Philip Francis M. P. in Ans- wer to the Thanks of the Committee was read; and 1000 Copies of our Letter and that Answer ordered to be printed for the Use of the Society – but as our Finances were low the Committee were under the obligation of ordering it to be sold.

An Address intended to be prefix'd to our Bills was presented from a Mr. Spence evinc- ing the Necessity of petitioning for a Reform in Parliament. Ordered to lie on the Table.

A Letter was recieved from Sheffield con- taining a Copy of the Sheffield Petition and the Address of the Sheffield Society to the Inhabitants of that Town and Neighbourhood.[83]

The Committee took next into Consideration which Member of Parliament was most eligible to present the Petition. Several were named by different Delegates – till the Delegate of Division 18 moved the Question whether the Committee ought or ought not to pay any Attention to local Propriety in offering it first to the supposed Representatives of Westminster, London, and Middlesex. This Question was maturely discussed, and the Committee agreing that some Regard should be paid to a supposed Decorum, determined that the Secretary should be authorized to write to Charles James Fox, to request of him to present the Petition: and in Case of his Compliance to George Byng Member for Middlesex, and Alderman Sawbridge, Member for the City, to support the same in Parliament.

A Deputation was also appointed to present the Petition to the presenting Member, consisting of four Delegates   Viz.

> Maurice Margarot
> Thomas Hardy
> George Walne
> Joseph Field.

71. Report from spy Lynam: LCS General Committee, 29 April 1793[84]

Source: TS 11/958/3503

[Lynam first gives an account of the anniversary dinner of the Society for Constitutional Information.]

The business of Deligates last night only collecting number of signatures 3500,[85] a deputation to request Mr. Fox to present yd Petition, Field, Gerald & Margarot. They have been several times and cant see him   Gerald took his skin to the Kings bench prison and got 200 signatures there –

83 Letter, Wm Camage to Hardy, 17 April 1793, TS 11/956/3501.
84 Address: 'E. Nepean Esqr. / Whitehall'. Government description: '30 April 1793 / Mr Lynam / Secret'.
85 The government summary of Lynam's reports indicates that another report of this meeting gives the number of signatures as 3420 and the meeting-place as 31 Compton St (TS 11/954/3498).

72. Journal: LCS General Committee, 2 May 1793

Source: Add MSS 27812, fos. 41v–2v (later copy in Add MSS 27814, fos. 113–14)

Thursday May 2nd.
1793

The Committee was this Evening visited by two Gentlemen of Sheffield Mr. Warburton and Son, who had been deputed to bring the Sheffield Petition to London. They gave the Committee an Account of it's Rejection that Evening in the House of Commons. They spoke of the firm Spirit of their Part of the Country, and the Determination of the Sheffield Society to persevere in their Exertions for a Reform.

Upon the Motion of Thomas Hardy, Treasuerer to the Society, seconded by the Delegate of Division No   the Committee declared Mr. Warburton and his Son Honorary Members of the London Corresponding Society. – [86]

50 Copies of the Society's Correspondence with Mr. Francis were ordered to be sent to the Sheffield, Norwich,[87] Birmingham, and Constitutional Societies.

From the Report of the Assistant Secty. it appeared that on Saturday last he had called upon Charles James Fox, but could not see him – that on Monday he had called and left a Letter requesting Mr. Fox's speedy Answer – That no Answer having arrived on Thursday at Noon the Chairman had written a Letter and left it at his House, which Letter the Chairman produced and read; and which desired an Answer previous to the Meeting of the Committee at 6 O'Clock that Evening. No Answer having been recieved the Committee were left to determine what Steps they would pursue: after considerable Deliberation it was unanimously determined that if no Answer was recieved by 12 O'Clock on the Morrow, it was the unanimous Opinion of the Committee that Charles James Fox had refused the Petition.

It was also resolved that in Case of no Answer or an unfavourable one, Application by Letter should be immediately made to Philip Francis M. P. by the Secretary to present the Petition on Monday next the 6th. Instant.

A discretionary Power was vested in the

86 The next day Hardy gave Warburton a note introducing him to the SCI, 'if it is not contrary to the rules' (Hardy to Adams [3 May 1793], TS 11/952/3496).
87 Later copy adds 'Manchester'.

Secretary either to get the Petition written or engrossed.

Some Discourse took Place respecting the 5 Seats vacant at the Constitutional Society, and the best Method of their being filled up: but the final Determination was defer'd from the Pressure of more important Business.

An Extraordinary General Committee was appointed to meet on Sunday Night, to examine the Skins of Parchment, and prepare them for the Reception of Mr. Francis on Monday.

Every Delegate was desired to state the principal Objections and Obstructions he had met with in his Exertions to obtain Signatures, when it appeared, Ignorance, Interest and Timidity had prevented many from Signing the Petition.

That the Threats and Inuendos of Parish Officers, Tax-gatherers, Placemen, and Pensioners had been universally employed to resist our Attempts.

That many Well-wishers to our Cause in the sub-ordinate Situations of Life had been obliged to sign the Parish Association papers by aristocratic Masters, and therefore dare not sign, as they term'd it, on *both Sides* of the Question.

That Publicans were fearful of losing their Licences, if they encouraged it, and Manufacturers of losing their Employ.

These and various other Causes operated against the Exertions of the Delegates, who had however by unwearied Diligence obtained between five and six Thousand Signatures.

The Committee were informed of the Loss of one Skin of Parchment from the Morning-post Office, supposed to be stolen.[88]

73. Report from spy Lynam: LCS General Committee, 2 May 1793[89]

Source: TS 11/966/3510B

Sir
                    31 Compton Street   May 2

11 Deligates met
Signatures in all 5030
Mr Fox wrote to Hardy that our saying a radical reform wo'd be understood universal sufferage which he was not a friend to, but wo'd

present the petition if we desired it, – in consequence Mr Francis is to be requested to do it

Enclosed is our former letter & his reply Several Gentlemen in their carriages have calld at Hardy's & signd yd Petition, some clergymen. Agreed to meet on Sunday evening and to collect all the Skins, and Present them to Mr Francis on Monday

Joel Barlow yd chief author of the Jocky Club & 2 other's – (from Hardy)

74. Journal: LCS General Committee, 9 May 1793

Source: Add MSS 27812, fos. 42v-4 (later copy in Add MSS 27814, fos. 115-16)

Thursday May 9th. 1793.

The Chairman informed the Committee that late on the last Thursday Evening a Letter had been sent by Charles James Fox to the Secretary, expressing his Readiness to present the Petition, but at the same time confessing that he thought it might with more Propriety be presented by some other Member, as it was understood the radical Reform for which we contended was Universal Suffrage to which he had always been an avowed Enemy.[90] The Letter was read.

The Secretary then informed the Committee that concieving this Letter to amount to a Refusal, he had written a Letter to Mr. Francis agreeable to the Will of the Committee, which he read, that Mr. Francis had returned a polite and compliant Answer. accordingly on Monday at 11 O'Clock the Deputation which was appointed had waited on him, they were recieved with Respect, and delivered to him their Petition;[91] the Event of which in the

88 'Also another skin of parchment which was not forthcoming by a Delegate' – later copy.
89 Address: 'E. Nepean Esqr. / Whitehall'. Government description: '2d May 1793/ Mr. Lynam / (one inclosure)'.

90 Fox wrote that he would present the petition as he would that of any of his constituents (2 May 1793, TS 11/956/3501).
91 The letter to Francis explained that the LCS had first asked Fox 'not from any implicit confidence in his patriotism' but because, as the Member for Westminster, he was the representative for the men petitioning. In reply, Francis set the meeting (draft in Margarot's hand, 3 May 1793; Francis to Hardy, 4 May 1793; both in TS 11/956/3501). He later recalled that after he agreed to present the petition he told the delegation that he was averse to the 'prayer' of it, that is, to the request for universal suffrage. According to strict parliamentary propriety, he pointed out, the LCS should have left the remedy of their grievances to the wisdom of the House of Commons. Hardy replied that he was sorry they did not know this earlier, for they could have left the prayer open; but it was now too late to alter it, as 9000 had

House of Commons is well known. Viz that it was recieved read and ordered to lay on the Table.

A Motion was then made, put and carried, that the Thanks of this Society should be given to Mr. Grey, Mr. Erskine, and the forty one Members of the House who supported the Cause of Reform on the 6th. Instant.[92]

Two Resolutions were accordingly drawn up, put carried and ordered to be inserted in three public Papers.

Resolved. That the Thanks of this Society be given to Mr. Grey for his Motion for a Reform in the House of Commons on the 6th. Instant; to Mr Erskine for seconding the same; and to the forty one patriotic Members of the House who so ably supported the Cause of the People.

Resolved   That this Society do request of those Gentlemen to perservere in their Exertions, by taking every favourable Opportunity of agitating the Question of reform, in Parliament; fully assured that had the Measure been adopted the Joy which would have been diffused thro' the Nation, would have contradicted the false and unfounded Assertion that the Wishes of the People were not with them.

It appeared our Encrease the last Week was 20.

It was proposed that Robert Lyttlejohn should be reeligible into the Society, from the Report of Delegate Smith of Division 29, and Delegate Baxter of Division 16; after some

Conversation, which turned upon his private Situation, no Person doubting his public Spirit, the Proposition was agreed to upon Conditions he clears up his Conduct, and when able pays the Secretary his Deficiencies.

A Letter from Sheffield was read, containing some energetic Resolutions against the present calamitous and impolitic War.[93]

Some Discourse took place respecting the Propriety of our entering into similar Resolutions, but no Determination ensued; it being thought most propert to consult the Sense of the various Divisions.

75. Journal: LCS General Committee, 16 May 1793

Source: Add Mss 27812, fos. 44–4v (later copy in Add MSS 27814, fos. 116–17)

Thursday May 16th.

Our Encrease of Members this Week was 4.
The Treasurers Accounts were audited . .
and were as follows

	£	s.	d
Ballance in Hand from last accounted Quarter and Receipts of the present up to this Day	32	5	9
Expended in Printing, Advertising, Parchment and sundry incidental Expences	23	3	5
Consequently there remains in Hand	9	2	4

Henry Lanseer produced his Voucher as Sub-delegate of Division No. 5, in the Place and during the Absence of Charles Turner Delegate of that Division.[94]

From the Reports of the Delegates it appeared to be the unanimous Wish of the Divisions that the Committee should adopt some measure to express their Detestation of the present War, and prevent it's Continuance.[95]

After considerable Debate, during which every Delegate delivered his Sentiments twice in Rotation, the Committee resolved that an Address pointing out the Impolicy and evil

signed it and it must be presented on 6 May, the day of Grey's motion for a reform of Parliament. Francis was favourably impressed by Hardy: 'I took notice of the quietness, moderation, and simplicity of the man, as well as his good sense.' Margarot, Walne and Field defended the concept of universal suffrage. Francis was surprised 'that men of their rank of life should have the command of such arguments' (testimony at Hardy's trial, *ST* vol. 24, cols. 1104–5).

92 After fourteen Members (including Francis) had presented petitions for parliamentary reform, Grey read a long petition from the Friends of the People and moved that this petition should be referred to a committee. After a long debate, which extended to the next day, the motion was defeated 282 to 41. The LCS petition was mentioned in debate by Lord Mornington: 'At the head of the signatures stands the name of Thomas Hardy, a name obscure in this country but not unknown in the National Convention of France.' Hardy's name on the list convinced Mornington that the petition came from the LCS. 'Can any man, who has observed the proceedings of that society, believe that the deluded persons who compose it will rest satisfied with any temperate reform?' (*Parliamentary History*, vol. 30, p. 864).

93 They urged the recall of British troops and the renewal of an alliance with France. Prefaced to the resolutions is the suggestion that all reform societies adopt similar resolutions. The accompanying letter reports that nearly 10,000 people signed their petition for reform (Camage to Hardy, 3 May 1793, TS 11/956/3501).

94 Voucher, 13 May 1793, TS 11/956/3501.

95 According to Lynam, Div. 7 introduced the motion (*ST* vol. 24, col. 791).

Consequences of the War, and followed by some Resolutions declaring the fix'd Abhorrence of it's Principles should be drawn up; and that M. Margarot, Thos. Hardy, and Joseph Field be ordered to draw up the same, and present it to the General Committee for their Approbation or Rejection.

Charles Turner appointed upon the Constitutional Committee being unable to attend, J. Smith was elected in his Room, and that Committee resolved to meet at 7 O'Clock on Thursday Evening next.

76. Report from spy Lynam: LCS General Committee, 16 May 1793[96]

Source: TS 11/966/3510

Sir

May 16 Compton Street

Division 25 made 3 encreased this week – 4 An annonimous letter recd. by Hardy, saying he is a friend to man & salutary rights, altho' unknown, very much approves the Petition & the thanks to the minority; and submits his opinion, of another Petition against the Present war, it will refute its being a Popular War[97]

Treasurers Acct

Advertizments since feby	9	14	6
Pamphlets & Cards	1	11	
Room	1	19	
Bill Sticking	1	1	
Davidson			
1000 Summonsing letters	1	1	
Parcel Sheffield		3	6
20 Skins Parchment	2		
Printing	5	13	5
	£23	3	5

Recd. sundry times £32 5 9   Ball: £9 3 4

Henry Lanceir chose Sub Deligate for No 5 Agreed that M. Margarot, Field & Hardy sho'd

96 Address: 'E. Nepean Esqr. / Whitehall'. Government description: '16 May 1793 / Mr. Lynam'.
97 He also suggested that the petition would have received more names if it had been 'carried round' as the loyalty resolutions were (13 May 1793, TS 11/956/3501). Presumably the delegates, who were 'to go round for signatures' (see no. 61), had not solicited extensively. The LCS tried 'perambulating' the next petition (see no. 96).

draw up an address & resolutions to the Public in handbills upon the state of the war Sheffield resolutions signd H. York Presdt
                                W. Carmage Secrety
12 Deligates met

77. Journal: LCS General Committee, 23 May 1793

Source: Add MSS 27812, fos. 44v–5v (later copy in Add MSS 27814, fos. 117–19)

Thursday May 23rd. 1793.

Our Encrease this Week was only 2.

The following Motion was presented from Division No. 2 as the Groundwork of a Measure recommended to the Attention of the Committee.

Resolved   That it is the Opinion of this Division, as well from local Knowledge as General Observation that a public Meeting of the Society ought to be held for the Purpose of invalidating the universal Slander so unjustly yet so industriously insinuated with a View to prejudice the public Mind against every Body of Men in the Kingdom united for the Purpose of obtaining a Parliamentary Reform.

That the Public in general are not fully satisfied respecting the Legality of our present Meetings, and consequently consider us as amenable to Law . . while that Idea is suffered to remain, instead of joining our Society they will avoid the supposed Danger by observing a shameful Neutrality.

That the Petition to Parliament as a public Act of this Society has in some Degree counteracted these invidious Reproaches so industriously circulated, and have in some Measure dispelled the groundless Fears of the People.

That as Fear is one of the principle Obstacles in our present Undertaking, a general Meeting convened by public Advertisement, would be an irrefragable Proof to the great Body of the People, who have been thus led astray, and whom it is necessary to convince, that our Meetings and Principles are agreable to the Constitution, and sanctioned by Law.

Upon this Motion, the Committee determined that the Substance of it should be carried to the different Divisions and their Opinions reported on the next Evening.

The Delegate of No. 1 Informed the Committee of his Intention to bring forward a Motion for lowering the Quarterly Payments of the Society, and for cancelling all Arrears due by the absenting Members.

A Letter was read by the Secretary, addressed to him by Robert Lyttlejohn, expressing his Attachment to the Common Cause, and his Astonishment at his Expulsion.

The Committee determined that as Robert Lyttlejohn was now fully in Possession of the Reasons of the Committee for his Expulsion, and had moreover been declared readmissible into the Society by a Vote of the Committee, no Notice could be taken of that Letter.[98]

The Chairman of the Committee appointed to draw up Resolutions and an Address respecting the present War, reported that that Committee had not proceeded in the Business in Consequence of the Publication of two Letters in the public Papers, by which it appeared that Offers of Peace had been made on the Part of the French Republic to the Secretary of State of Great Britain,[99] and as the Committee did not know whether such Offers were or were not the Foundation and Preliminaries to a pending Negociation, they had not thought it proper to proceed till the Data on which they were to establish their Address were fixed and ascertained.

The General Committee decreed that they had acted with Propriety, and desired them to produce their Address by the next Evening.

Some Conversation took Place respecting the Propriety of providing Rooms for the Society as a public Act[100] – but nothing decisive was agreed upon respecting the Proposal.

---

98 Lyttlejohn reproached the Society for not notifying him of his exclusion, which he discovered when he visited one of the divisions: 'You never sent a letter to Doctor Garthshore's, which you ought to have done; and to which I would have replied.' His explanation of his situation suggests financial difficulties: 'When I was deserted by my nearest friends and those most closely connected with me in business, I chose rather to run the risk myself than to apply to any person or men concerned in public principles.' Although he stated that he 'never meant or expressed a desire to secede from the worthy body of men', he evidently did leave the Society, for he is not mentioned in later documents (Lyttlejohn to Hardy, 18 May 1793, TS 11/956/3501).

99 The *Morning Chronicle* of this day (p. 4) printed two letters from Le Brun to Lord Grenville, both dated 2 April and delivered 26 April. The first said that the French Republic wished to 'terminate all its differences with Great Britain' and asked for a safe conduct for a representative who would come to London to negotiate. The second letter named Marat as the representative.

100 'instead of each Dvn providing rooms for themselves' – later copy.

78. Report from spy Lynam: LCS General Committee, 23 May 1793[101]

Source: TS 11/958/3503

Sir

      May 23 Compton Street

Lancur No 51 Upper Marylebone Street sub Deligate for Division No 5
Divisions No 1 & 7 made one each
Division 5 have taken a very good room at No 3 new Compton street for a Year @ 2/ per night; The Person will take in 3 other Divisions

[Next comes the proposal for a general meeting and the letter from Lyttlejohn.]

In consequence of Le Brun's letter's to Lord Grenville, agreed not to address the Public at Present, as it wo'd have the appearance of Our having some communication with France

2 or 3 of the Divisions dwindled away. 12 Deligates met

79. Journal: LCS General Committee, 30 May 1793

Source: Add MSS 27812, fos. 46–6v (later copy in Add MSS 27814, fos. 119–20)

Thursday May 30th. 1793.

The Encrease of the Society this Week was 5, but the Attendance of the Delegates not being very numerous every Division's Report was not exactly ascertained.

It appeared from the Reports that 8 Divisions viz 1, 2, 4, 7, 13, 18, 23, and 28 were in Favor of a public Meeting and 3 Divisions viz 25, 16, 29 were decidedly against it. –

A discussion immediately took Place respecting the Time, Manner, Place, Expence, and Business of such public Meeting; when after various Plans had been proposed, and various Arguments considered, the Committee determined to submit the following Outlines of the Plan to the various Divisions.

That the Day should be on a Monday.

That the Majority in the Divisions should decide whether 3 O'Clock or 6 O'Clock should be the Hour of Meeting.

---

101 Address: 'E. Nepean Esqr. / Whitehall'. Government description: '23 May 1793. / Mr Lynam'.

That the Place should be optional to the Committee, but in Town.

That the Expence should not exceed Sixpence each Member.

That Tickets of Admission should be issued, for the Accommadation of Members and their Friends.

That the Business should be to agree to certain Resolutions respecting the present War, and the Rejection of our Petition: and to publicly discuss our new Constitution.

A Circular Letter from Birmingham was read containing some printed Resolutions against the Rejection of Mr. Grey's Motion.[102]

The Secretary informed the Committee of his having taken the Opportunity of Mr. Urquhart's being in Town to write to the Society at Edinburgh, requesting a renewal of our Correspondence.[103]

102 The accompanying circular letter stated that to achieve 'the long lost rights of representation . . . there is only one thing necessary, *i. e.* the people to form one collective mass' (John Kilmister to Hardy, 13 May 1793 – endorsed by LCS as received 6 June and answered 10 June – TS 11/956/3501).

103 And saying that since the petitions were unsuccessful, 'our attention must now therefore

A Motion was made and carried that a patriotic Song composed by William Hamilton Reid should be printed for Distribution to the Members of the Society.[104] –

The Secretary received Orders for the Printing of 1000 Copies

80. Report from spy Lynam: LCS General Committee, 30 May 1793 (government paraphrase)

Source: TS 11/954/3498

30th May.   Meeting of Delegates at No 31 Compton Street

It was reported that all the other Societies were about to adjourn & Hardy gave Notice that he meant to make a Motion that the Corr. Society shod adjourn for 3 mos., but this was overruled

be turned to some more effectual means   From your Society we would willingly learn them' (draft in Hardy's hand, to William Skirving, 17 May 1793, TS 11/956/3501).

104 Reid later denounced the LCS in *The Rise and Dissolution of the Infidel Societies* (1800).

PART THREE

1793B

(June–December)

81. Journal: LCS General Committee, 6 June 1793

Source: Add MSS 27812, fos. 46-7 (later copy in Add MSS 27814, fos. 120-120 bis)

Thursday June 6th. 1793.

A Pamphlet in Manuscript, entitled "The Loyal Citizen or Republican Principles defended and Monarchy exploded by the Word of God" was presented for the Perusal and Approbation of the Committee – but objecting to the title of the Work,[1] the Committee passed to the Order of the Day.

on the Question, "how many Friends each Member should be allowed to bring with him to the General meeting" it was determined that every Member might be allowed tickets for as many as he might chuse to introduce

Thanks were voted to Mr. Wharton for his motion on the Constitution & ordered to be inserted on 4 different days in as many different papers

One Thousand Copies of sd. speech & motion were likewise ordered to be printed for the use of the Society[2]

Willm. Baxter Delegate of Div. No 16 gave notice that he meant on the ensuing night to bring an accusation against George Lynam Delegate of Division No. 23.

by the Delegates report concerning the place & time of our General meeting it was determined that it should be if possible at the Crown & Anchor that the most convenient hour would be 6 p. m.[3]

1 Originally: 'but as Republicanism forms no part of the Society's principles'.
2 'Extracted from the Morning Chronicle, / June, 1st. 1793 / THE SPEECH OF JOHN WHARTON, ESQ. M. P. IN THE HOUSE OF COMMONS, ON HIS MOTION ON THE CONSTITUTION; Printed by Order of the LONDON CORRESPONDING SOCIETY. (And distributed Gratis)'. Wharton's speech, extolling the provisions of the constitution as established by the revolution of 1688 and declaring that the most valuable of them had been taken away, ended with his motion to establish a committee to determine which of these invalidated provisions should be restored. The motion was defeated by 71 to 11.
3 Heavily written over to obliterate: 'A Callander J. Field M Margarot (were) appointed to (engage) Room at the Crown & Anchor'

82. Report from spy Lynam: LCS General Committee, 6 June 1793[4]

Source: TS 11/966/3510B

31 Compton Street   June 6

Resolved to have a meeting of all the Division's at a Public Tavern some afternoon, & to advertize it 5 for 6 OClock and admit all friends[5]

Division No 7 made 3 members, two of them going into the country and will take our resolutions &c. and will be very active in gaining Friends

Division No 5 made 2 member's encrease   5

Division No 3 & 28 Motion that our thanks be given to Mr Wharton for his motion & speach, agreed, and that comments sho'd be made thereon by a special committee of five, to be Publish'd 4 different days in yd following Paper's Vizt Courier, Chronocle, Gazzetteer & Ledger.[6]

A Letter from Leeds signd Charles Handley Secretary, saying altho a Society lately sprung up (27 Novr. 1792)   They are determined to instruct all their neighbour's, and to raise a subscription to support a Parliamentiary reform & recommend's it to all Societys, They are only 200 at Present but will Persevere, had a meeting 30 May, I. Forth Prist – By the desire of Sheffield wrote to Us, beging a correspondence & that they mean to correspond with all Societys

Secretary to answer this imediately[7]

A Letter recd from Birmingham which will get Most of the different Society's ajourn'd for the summer

Hardy means to move we shall likewise

Twelve Deligates

4 Address: 'E Nepean Esqr / Whitehall'.
5 The meeting was to be advertised for five o'clock, 'but the intention was to meet and begin upon business at six' (Lynam's testimony, ST vol. 24, col. 792).
6 Three divisions proposed that Wharton's motion in the House of Commons be printed. Then came the motion to thank Wharton, and last, the decision to have a special committee of five, 'an open committee', meet at six o'clock on Monday to draw up comments on Wharton's motion. The advertisement was to be published once in each of the four papers (Lynam's testimony).
7 Handley to Hardy, 30 May 1793, TS 11/956/3501. The LCS did not answer until 30 July.

83. Journal: LCS General Committee, 13 June 1793

Source: Add MSS 27812, fo. 47v (later copy in Add MSS 27814, fo. 120)

Committee 13th. June

The Order of the Day, being Lynam's tryal W. Baxter opened his Charge against him & informed the Committee that the Evidence he should bring forth would Satisfy them that Lynam was a Spy – the Committee after hearing his accusation, examining five Witnesses and attending to Lynams defence the latter was found innocent by a great majority – this tryal having taken up much of the Committees time nothing farther could be done that day – therefore an extraordinary Committee was appointed to meet on Saturday.

84. Report from spy Lynam: LCS General Committee (government paraphrase), 13 June 1793[8]

Source: TS 11/954/3498

13th. June – Meeting of Delegates at No. 31 Compton Street.

At this Meeting the Witns. [Lynam] was tried by the Genl. Commee of Delegates on a charge preferred agt. him by Baxter –

1st. As having been irregularly admitted into the Society – not having been proposed by a Member but introduced by himself

2dly. As being inimical to the Cause.

3d. As a Spy

But on hearing Evidence on both sides the General Commee were of opinion by a large Majority that he was not guilty

85. The trial of Lynam, 13 June 1793[9]

Source: TS 11/956/3501

Report of the Committee   13 June Tryal of Lynam

Baxter opened the Charge – stated the danger of our having a spy among us – the heinousness of the Crime – his wish Lynam might exculpate himself – his duty to accuse him – the nature of his Evidence – the impossibility to prove anything positively and concluded that in consequence presumptive proof ought to be admitted

His charges were

That Lynam previous to his admission was in company with two officers & that one of them was said to be Ld. Hood

that Lynam going from the Committee with the two Brothers Baxter asked of one of them the Del. of No. 9 where his division met that said Delegate suspecting Lynam, answered at a private House in Greys Inn Lane & that soon after a Book was published by Debrett containing among other things the different places of Meeting of our Divisions & therein mentioning Div. No. 9 as meeting at a private House &c

That a Mr. Turton in a Conversation betwixt Lynam & his Brother understanding that Lynam professed a disbelief of the avowed motives of our Society (a P. Reform) asked him whether he had seen our Declarations being answered in the Affirmative he again asked Lynam whether he belonged to the Society which the latter positively denied That Mr. Turton in Company with Lynams brother being met by a Mr. Salter the conversation turned upon Lynam when Mr. Turton positively affirmed Lynam to be a Spy and that he was seeking a place under Government neither of which Lynams brother denied but rather assented to

to prove these assertions he called as witnesses

Mess   Salter
Smith
Deacon[10]
Baxter Senior[11]
& Dawes
& Turton

---

8 At Hardy's trial Lynam said he had no minutes of this meeting and no recollection of it (*ST* vol. 24, col. 793).

9 This is an unfinished narrative of the trial, in the hand of Margarot. The notes taken at the time on scraps of paper are abbreviated almost to incomprehensibility.

10 On 11 June Joseph Field, assistant secretary, wrote Deacon, asking him to attend the meeting at 9.00 precisely, to communicate his information relative to an accusation against Lynam (TS 11/956/3501). Probably the other witnesses received a similar summons.

11 On the day of the trial John Baxter sent the general committee a note saying 'that he has a piece of work in hand which must be finished to night at all events, therefore hopes they will not judge unfavorably of him on account of his absence if that should happen but proceed with their enquiries' (TS 11/956/3501).

[The charge that Lynam was admitted to the LCS without following the proper procedure started with the accusation that he and two naval officers (one of whom was Lord Hood) were in the public house where Division 12 was meeting. The three men were making illiberal remarks, which were noticed by some LCS members. Then the three men, or at least Lynam, tried to gain admission to the area where the LCS meeting was in progress by enquiring for some unknown person. Watson, the president of the division, refused to admit him (or them). In his defence Lynam asserted that he did not know the two men, had never seen them before nor since. The witnesses disagreed on whether one of the officers called Lynam by name.

As for Lynam's being admitted without a sponsor, Peter Davy testified that during the following week he enquired about Lynam from a Mr Crab and learned that Lynam was of good character. Davy reported this at the next meeting of Division 12 and proposed Lynam as a Member.[12]

Shortly after Lynam's admission, Division 12 divided, Division 23 was formed, and Lynam campaigned successfully to be elected delegate. One night after the meeting of the committee of delegates, he allegedly asked either William Baxter or Robert Dawes the meeting place of Division 9. One of the two men told him that the division met at a private house in Gray's Inn Lane. Apparently Lynam asked the number of the house but was not told. Later Division 11 (not 9) was listed as meeting at a private house in Gray's Inn Lane in a 'List of Clubs' published at the end of an anti-reform pamphlet.[13] Lynam was alleged to be the only one who could have provided this address (probably it was false). In his defence Lynam asserted that he had asked the question in the committee room where all could hear the answer.[14]

12 See no. 14. n. 67 for Lynam's account of his first encounter with the LCS.
13 *A Collection of Addresses Transmitted by Certain English Clubs and Societies to the National Convention of France. . . . To which are added Extracts from the Seditious Resolutions of the English Societies; with a List of Those Societies*, 1793.
14 The testimony on this point, which is so confusing that no conclusion could be drawn, includes conflicting evidence about a private house in Laystall St.

Finally, after he had joined the LCS Lynam, allegedly in conversations with a Mr Turton, denied belonging to the LCS, reprobated the Friends of the People, said that the LCS went beyond reform, and ridiculed his brother as a republican. Moreover, according to Turton, Lynam had long wanted a place in government. Smith, Deacon and Salter testified that Turton had told them of these comments by Lynam. In reply, Lynam denied knowing Turton or Deacon and asserted that his arguments against reform had been intended merely to prevent his brother from being too forward in speech.

One delegate found Lynam guilty of the last charge; one felt the matter was 'dubious'; and nine voted that Lynam was not guilty.

On another vote, probably taken on 20 June, after William Baxter renewed the accusations against Lynam, three delegates voted Lynam guilty and ten not guilty.]

86. Journal: LCS General Committee, 15 June 1793

Source: Add MSS 27812, fos. 47v–8 (later copy in Add MSS 27814, fos. 120–1)

Extraordinary Committee 15th. June
The Admissions of the preceeding Week were Nine
The Vote of Thanks to Mr. Wharton was refused admittance into the Morning Chronicle under the pretence that it was libellous – the Committee therefore altered a few expressions, divided it into 4 Resolutions & ordered them to be published in the manner following

[Headed *Reform in Parliament / London Corresponding Society Thursday 6 June 1793*, the resolutions thank Wharton and the twelve men who voted with him, urge Wharton to persevere, and promise to support every measure which renovates the constitution and restores provisions for liberty established in 1688. Signed by Margarot and Hardy.]

At the instigation of Wm. Baxter, the Committee rescinded the judgment given the preceeding night in favor of Lynam & submitted to hear sd. Baxter further theron on the next night

87. Report from spy Lynam: LCS General Committee (government paraphrase), 15 June 1793

Source: TS 11/954/3498

15th. June – The Witness [Lynam] was present at an adjourned meeting of the Delegates held at No. 31 Compton Street

Margarot reported that the Constl.Society had determined to print 10,000 Copies of Mr. Wharton's Speech in a correct form & he woud. procure 1000 of them for the Corr. Society.

Notwithstg. the Acquittall. of the Witns. as above mentd. so much suspicion hung about him that he was not re-elected a Delegate at Midsummer – But Jno. Pickard (the person Elected for division 23 in his Room) not being able conveniently to attend on Accot. of the late hours to which the Society sat in an Evening he resigned & the Witns. was reelected a Delegate in the mo. of December.

88. Journal: LCS General Committee, 20 June–8 July 1793

Source: Add MSS 27812, fos. 48v–55 (later copy in Add MSS 27814, fos. 121–3)

Thursday 20th. June

The Committee after hearing what Willm. Baxter had farther to urge against G. Lynam, confirmed their former acquital

A Motion was made & carried

"That all Arrears due by the Members of the Respective Divisions of this Society be this day cancelled"

The General Meeting was fixed for Monday the 8th. July and a Committee of the following Delegates was appointed to find a place to receive the Society. Vizt.

A. Callander
J. Field
M. Margarot

The Society admitted only five Members this Week

Thursday 27th. June

The Committee which had been formerly appointed to draw up an Address to the Public brought forward three different ones– The General Committee after hearing them all read referred them to a Committee of the six following

Hodgson	Margarot
Moore	Field
& Smith	& Hardy

A Motion from Division No. 28 was brought forward

"That 1000 Tickets might be issued for the General meeting, & that it should not be advertized untill at the least 600 Tickets had been disposed of" – the Committee however thought fit to limit the number of Tickets to 600 –

This being the first Committee night of the Quarter the Delegates produced their Vouchers as follows[15]

For Division No.	
1	John Young
2	Mahew Moore
4	George Walne
5	Charles Turner
6	
7	Maurice Margarot
8	
9	
10	
11	
12	John Philip Francklow
13	Thomas Stiff
14	
15	
16	John Pearce
17	
18	
19	
20	
21	
22	
23	John Piccard
24	
25	Daniel Isaac Eaton
26	
27	
28	Richard Hodgson
& 29	John Smith

The Committee proceeded by Ballot to elect their Officers for the Quarter when

Maurice Margarot as Chairman
& Thomas Hardy as Secretary

were rechosen. Joseph Field was likewise reelected as Assistant Secretary but he wished to decline the Office & no other was chosen in his stead.

15 Vouchers for Divs. 1, 2, 5, 7, 16, 25, 28 and 29 antedate this meeting. The re-established Div. 12 elected their delegate on 31 July. Div. 23 elected their delegate on 16 July after appointing a delegate for one night on 2 July (John Low) and again on 9 July (Peter Davey). John Shelmerdine, James Lambeth and William Cleaver were elected subdelegates for Divs. 12, 28 and 29 (vouchers, TS 11/956/3501).

The Sub Committee who had been appointed for that purpose reported that they had aggreed with the Master of the Crown and Anchor for the use of his Great Room on the 8th. July at the price of five Guineas. – which sum the Committee ordered to be paid forthwith in order to prevent any underhand maneuvres of the Enemies to Reform from taking place.

Only one new Member was admitted this Week.

Thursday 4th. July

The Attention & time of the Committee were entirely taken up in revising & correcting so much of the Address to the Public as the Sub Committee had been able to prepare the Committee after appointing Maurice Margarot Chairman for the General meeting entrusted him [16] with drawing up the conclusion to the Address & the set of Resolutions which were to follow it

Three new Members were admitted this Week.

The General Meeting
Monday 8th. July

The Society having met to the amount of between Six and Seven Hundred, at 6 o Clock the Chairman opened the Business by giving a succinct statement of the Origin & progress of the Society together with the object they had in view & the Advantages that would most probably accrue from their success – he recapitulated the numerous Obstacles & persecutions they had experienced from Ministerial Adherents but expressed his hope that success would daily become more probable – he next acquainted the Meeting that an Address to the Nation had been drawn up by the Committee & would together with a set of Resolutions adapted to the Circumstance be submitted to their Consideration – and lastly he reminded them that Tranquility & Order had hitherto proved highly serviceable & he exhorted them to convince the Public by their behaviour at this Meeting that the Order & Decorum so strictly adhered to in their several Divisions was neither forgotten when out of them nor intended to be laid aside when the whole Society was convened together.[17]

The Secretary then proceeded to read the following [no. 89].

16 Later copy: 'him and the secretary'.
17 Later copy adds, 'after making a variety of pertinent observations he concluded a speech about a quarter of an hour long'.

89. *Address to the Nation from the LCS* (extracts), 8 July 1793[18]

Source: Add MSS 27814, fos. 51–4v

Friends and Fellow Countrymen,

Gloomy as is the prospect now before us, and unpleasing as is the task to bring forth into open day the calamitous situation of our Country: We conceive it necessary to direct the public eye, to the cause of our misfortunes, and to awaken the sleeping reason of our Countrymen, to the pursuit of the only remedy which can ever prove effectual, namely; – A thorough Reform in Parliament, by the adoption of an equal Representation obtained by Annual Elections and Universal Suffrage.

[When the present evils were still at a distance the LCS called on their fellow citizens to reclaim their rights; they laboured to destroy ignorance; and they proved that the restoration of their rights was the only remedy for then existing grievances. Since last November false and calumnious aspersions have been circulated, and those who would restore the House of Commons to a state of independence have been labelled levellers. Despite these alarms we pursued the course prescibed by the constitution for obtaining redress of grievances. The credit rashly given to false reports of riots and insurrections has not only delayed reform but also produced this 'Ruinous and Disgraceful War'. British troops have been sent to cooperate with the most detestable of despots; British gold subsidizes continental slaves. Provisions have risen in price; artisans are starving. Offers of peace have been spurned. France is reproached with anarchy while despots boast their skill in promoting it.]

Conscious as we are, that the trading and commercial interests of this Country, are neither *satisfied* of the policy of the War, nor

18 *Address to the Nation, From the London Corresponding Society. On the Subject of a Thorough Parliamentary Reform; Together with the Resolutions which were passed at a General Meeting of the Society; Held on Monday, the 8th of July, 1793. At the Crown and Anchor Tavern Strand, Printed by Order of the Society, and distributed (Gratis.)* The copy cited is annotated in Hardy's hand: 'The above Address was written by Mr. Maurice Margarot'.

75

duped by any delusive prospect of success, we cannot attribute the little resistance which has hitherto been made to it, to any thing else than the depraved state of the Representation; for had they that weight in Parliament, which the spirit of the Constitution evidently intended, and which was confirmed by the Revolution of 1688, We doubt not their open declarations against a War so hostile to their interests, and to the cause of Humanity, would ere now have refuted the fictitious idea of its being popular, necessary or just.

[Our only aim is a complete representation. We conjure you to] pursue with union and firmness the track we have pointed out.

[Resolutions 1–3 stress the importance of parliamentary reform; 4–9 express opposition to the war; 10 exhorts 'every well wisher to his country, not to delay in improving himself in constitutional knowledge'; 11–12 revert to the war; 13 asserts the LCS's endeavour to unite more closely with every political society in the nation which shares their principles; 14 sets the date of the next general meeting for the first Monday in September unless the general committee 'shall find it necessary to call such a meeting sooner'; 15 states that 20,000 copies of this address and these resolutions be printed and distributed gratis. Signed by Margarot and Hardy.[19]]

90. Journal: LCS General Committee, 11 July–22 August 1793

Source: Add MSS 27812, fos. 55v–61v (later copies in Add MSS 27814, fos. 124–30

Thursday 11th. July

The settling with the Treasurer for the Tickets delivered to the different Delegates took up the greatest part of the evening – it appeared that 614 Tickets had been issued &

that near a score persons had been admitted without tickets[20]

Delegate Walne Reported that having accidently found a number of Copies of a Book entitled the *Rights of Englishmen*, being a Dialogue between a Barrister & a Juryman, he had purchased the whole bundle[21] & would if required cede them to the Society for the same money they cost him namely 3 farthings each copy – the Committee joyfully accepted his offer & gave the Treasurer directions to pay him – Encrease of Members this Week   6 –

Thursday 18th. July

The Delegates were called upon to settle with the Treasurer[22] & most of them did so – the Secretary was instructed to call in all the Books of those Divisions which have joined others

Three Motions were brought forward this Evening

the 1st. from Division No. 28 'desiring the Committee to print a fresh Edition of the work entitled the "Rights of Englishmen.'[23] The Committee aggreed to make this Motion the Order of the day for the ensuing Committee & meantime the Delegates were to enquire in their respective Divisions how many Copies of the Work would be taken by the Members.

The 2d. Motion was from Division No. 5

19 After the Address and fifteen resolutions had been read and Margarot had left the chair, the thanks of the Society were given to him 'for the great attention which he has given to the interests of this Society, and particularly, for his impartiality and proper conduct at this meeting'. Thanks were also voted to Hardy 'for his unremitting perseverance and exertions in the Cause of Freedom' (printed copy of Address).

20 Later copy: 'and many had been admitted without tickets who were known to the doorkeepers and who had not an oppertunity of providing themselves with a ticket'.
21 Later copy adds: 'at a cheesemongers which had been doom'd to be torn up and destroyed'.
22 Later copy adds: 'for the tickets for the general Meeting'.
23 Sir John Hawles, *The Englishman's Right: A Dialogue between a Barrister at Law and a Juryman; Plainly setting forth*, I: *The Antiquity*, II: *The Excellently Designed Use*, III: *The Office, and Just Privileges, of Juries*, 8th edn, 1771). Originally published in 1680; the LCS reprinted this 8th edn.

The content of the pamphlet is well indicated by the full title, particularly the last part, *The Office, and Just Privileges, of Juries*. The revisions in the footnotes, which the general committee reviewed on two evenings, are minimal: two footnotes are omitted and two added, as well as the Latin in the text being translated. The six-page appendix deals with the methods of impannelling juries, a topic not 'elucidated' by Hawles.

According to LCS receipts for the pamphlet between 30 Sept. and 28 Dec. 1907 copies were taken and £11 10s 10½d received (TS 11/959/3505).

recommending likewise the printing of a Paper from Nottingham The Committee adjourned the consideration of this Motion untill the 1st. of August.

The 3d Motion was likewise from Division No. 5 praying the amendment of an Error which had obtained in the printing the Address to the Nation & recommending a Censure on him or those who had suffered that Error to remain. The Committee ordered the Correction of the Error but convinced that the fault lay not in any of the Delegates discarded the Idea of Censure.

In this Committee Six letters were read vizt.
    One from Tewkesbury
    One from Sheffield
    One from Norwich
    One from Birmingham
    One from Edinburgh
    & One from Hertford[24]
They were all ordered to be answered without delay

One of the Delegates reported that a convenient place of meeting had been found in the Borough & that a Division from No. 16 would in future meet there

The Secretary was ordered to pay Delegate Moore 12/ for Arrears of Room rent due by Division No. 26.

Encrease of Members this week   15.

Thursday 25th. July

The Committee postponed the publication of a new Edition of the Englishmens Rights untill all the Delegates can give in a Report of how many Copies will be taken by their Divisions

Those Members who as stated in the minutes of the preceeding week acquainted the Committee that they had instructed Josias Reed to bring them an account of what might be decided upon in the Committee relative to them   Accordingly the Committee proceeded to give the Delegate of Division No. 16 an Order to divide & as the No. 12 has not been refilled since the Seccession of that Division the new parted Members from No. 16 were empowered to take the Name of Division No. 12.

No letters had been this week received from the Country but the following answers to three of those which had been received the foregoing week, were read. vizt.
    An Answer to Edinburgh

    a Ditto to Hertford
    & a Ditto to Norwich[25]
all of them were approved & ordered to be sent immediately together with some of our Addresses

A Motion was presented from Division No. 28[26] "requesting of the Committee that their Meetings should in future be free from all extra expence to the Delegates

The Committee referred this motion to the consideration of a future Committee of Revisal of the Constitution

They then proceeded to elect by ballot a Committee of five to finish the already begun Revisal of the Constitution when the following Members were elected

   Smith Hodgson ⎱ N B this Committee
   Moore Margarot ⎰ appointed their first
      & Hardy   Meeting 1st. Aug. 6 o Cl.

Thursday 1st August

The Delegate of Division No. 7 prefaced the business of this Committee by proposing the Adoption of the word *Citizen* but owing to a diversity of opinions thereon in the Committee he declined pressing it any farther & withdrew his Motion.[27] The Division lately parted off from Division No. 16 & which had been authorized to take the name of Div. No. 12 sent as Delegate for the remainder of the

---

24 Some of these letters had been in the Society's possession for weeks, e.g. Edinburgh letter was received 10 June; Birmingham letter, 21 June; Norwich letter, 25 June.

25 Letter to Edinburgh lost. Letter to Hertford asks what reform they do favour if not annual parliaments and universal suffrage; it then defends these two LCS goals (to Richard Flower, 31 July 1793, TS 11/956/3501). Letter to Norwich urges them 'to throw aside unavailing complaint' and occupy themselves 'in instructing the People, in introducing & maintaining order & regularity in Your own Society & in forming a junction with all others . . . by keeping up a constant Correspondence with them. . . . Union & encrease being then our only ressources let us diligently exert ourselves therein' (to Buckle, 25 July 1793, TS 11/953/3497).

26 Div. 28 sent the same motion again a month later. Div. 16 sent a similar motion (TS 11/956/3501).

27 The use of *Citizen*, here proposed by Margarot, became an issue at his trial in Jan. 1794, when the prosecutor argued that it signified a desire for a (French) revolution in Great Britain. Opposition to titles was developing in the LCS: On some of the vouchers for delegates *Mr* has been crossed out, and on the draft of the letter to Leeds, approved at this meeting, *Sir* has been cancelled and replaced by *fellow Citizen*. Later, at a general meeting in 1795 there was discussion of addressing Earl Stanhope as Citizen Stanhope. The Society's magazine, in 1797, carried four articles designated 'On Titles'.

Quarter John Philip Franklow & John
Shelmardine as Sub Delegate.

By the Reports of the several Delegates it
appeared that about 700 Copies of the Rights
of Englishmen were subscribed for by the
Members of the several Divisions – the Committee therefore proceeded to settle every
thing relating to the printing an Edition of that
valuable work and by the Estimate given in by
the Printer the Committee being of opinion
that they would not cost 2d. each Copy they
resolved

1st.	that to the Members the price should be	2d
2	that to Strangers of all descriptions	3d
&	that on the Book the price be marked	4d

They then ordered

That 2000 be printed & the press kept
standing
That Circular letters be sent to all the
Country Societies to inform them that such
book is printing by us & to enquire whether
they will purchase any of them
That the Work be advertized by Posting
Bills & by Hand Bills
& That a Committee be appointed to
regulate the Advertising & to prepare an
Appendix
Consequently a Committee being balloted
for the following five were elected   vizt

Richd. Hodgson	Joseph Field
George Walne	Mathew Moore
	& John Smith

The Secretary produced & the Chairman
read the Answer which had been made to the
Leeds Society – the Committee approved of it
& particularly of the invitation therein made
to that Society of uniting their Society[28] to
our Own & adopting the title of Corresp.
Society – and the Committee were farther of
opinion that a similar offer should be made to
other Societies

John Harrison President of the Society for
Constitutional Information at Birmingham
sent his case accompanied by a letter – it
appeared therin that he had been extreamly ill
used by a band of Ruffians – but the Committee did not come to any determination
about him.[29]

Encrease of Members this week   22.

28 The letter also apologized for not answering the
   30 May letter sooner (it was mislaid), gave hints
   on conducting the society, and described the
   general meeting of 8 July, held in a room above
   that in which Reeves's Association was meeting
   (to Handley, 30 July 1793, TS 11/956/3501).
29 Later copy adds, 'not to make it public by any

Thursday 8th. August

Before the Sub Committee appointed on
the preceeding Committee Night for composing an Appendix &a to the purposed
Edition of the Rights of Englishmen, gave in
their report it became a matter of serious
Consideration with the Committee whether in
appointing that Sub Committee they had not
exceeded their Delegated powers in appointing
a Stranger, Joseph Field, to act in it[30] – the
Sub Committee having likewise overstepped
their Boundaries by sending a part of their
work to the Press before it had obtained the
Sanction of the General Committee   after
much debate the two following *Resolutions*
were passed vizt.

1st. That no Sub Committee shall ever be
empowered to print or publish anything committed to their care, without the written consent of the General Committee.

2d. That none but Members of the Committee shall be chosen to act on a Sub
Committee in future.

The Sub Committee then proceeded in their
Report unto the 20th. Page   the Report was
approved of & the printing Ordered to go on –
the Sub Committee were also recommended
to use all possible dispatch

The Secretary read the Copy of an Answer
he had sent to the Leeds Society[31]

public act of ours untill he came to London
which he gave us to understand would be soon'.
Harrison had asked to have his case laid before
the Society (letter to Hardy, 22 July 1793, TS
11/956/3501). In March Harrison had been
assaulted by a drunken jailor and other bullies
and had been dragged off to jail. Harrison sued
these men for assault; at trials in July and Oct.
they were acquitted (*A Letter to the Right Hon.
Henry Dundas, M. P. Secretary of State, &c. &c.,
or, An Appeal to the People of Great-Britain,
Being an Answer to some Reflections Cast upon
"A Citizen, whose Loyalty (it was said) was only
confined to his Razor!" In a Debate in the House
of Commons, February 21st, 1794, Occasioned by
an intercepted Letter, Signed J. Harrison, a Sans
Culotte, to Which is Added, An Abstract of A
Trial for Assault committed on the Author in the
Name of "Church and King for Ever,"* 1794).
30 Field was no longer a delegate; he wrote the
   appendix (Add MSS 27814, fo. 50).
31 Since the letter to Leeds was read at the previous
   meeting this was probably the letter to Tewkesbury, which urged the new society to 'pay great
   attention to the instruction of your Neighbours
   in their political rights' and suggested they
   incorporate with the LCS under the title of the
   Corresponding Society of Tewkesbury (3 Aug.
   1793, TS 11/956/3501).

John Lovatt produced his Voucher[32] as Subdelegate for Division No. 7.

Arthur Seale produced also his Voucher as Subdelegate for Division No. 5 in the room of Henry Landseer who has been appointed Delegate instead of Charles Turner who has resigned

A Motion from Division No. 2 *C. Calender. Pres.* "That every Member of the Society be furnished with a list of all the different places where the Divisions meet & also an account of the Nights of meeting" was negatived.

A Motion from the United Divisions No. 1. 13. & 29 *John Hewitt Pres.* "That John Harrison's case be not made public untill his arrival in London." was unanimously aggreed to.

In consequence of some of the Delegates not attending the Committee the Report of the week could not be thoroughly ascertained 15 New Members were however reported –

Thursday 15th. August

The Order of the day being to attend further to the Report of the Sub Committee appointed to revise the Pamphlet called the Rights of Englishmen the Chairman of sd Sub Committee in his Report went through the work & the ammendments being approved of by the General Committee Orders were given for the printing it immediatly – the Appendix is to be considered at the next meeting of the Delegates

A Motion was produced from Division No. 28 desiring "that at the next General Meeting whatever may be brought forward for the Adoption of the Society may be discussed, amended or altered, Article by article by the Company then present."

This Motion was Negatived in consequence of the very great inconveniencies which the Committee foresaw would attend its being adopted.

A Motion was made by Delegate Smith "that the Committee do postpone the General meeting of the Society untill the first Monday in November."

This Motion was also negatived & the Committee then Proceeded to nominate (by Ballot) a SubCommittee for the purpose of arranging the business of that Meeting which it was determined should take place on the 2d. of September according to the Resolution of the last General Meeting

The Members elected by Ballot were the following

32 TS 11/956/3501.

Delegates   Smith   Moore
              Walne   Hodgson
     & Margarot

It was likewise left to them to select the place of Meeting & they were empowered to expend for a Room the Sum of 7 Guineas – but the Hour on which the business of the Meeting should commence, the Committee aggreed to be 2 P. M. the price of admission the same as before & the number of Tickets to be 1000.

The Secretary produced a Circular letter which was approved of & ordered to be sent to the different Country Societies[33]

The Treasurers demand upon the Division No. 5 was not paid by their Delegate

With the Addition of two Members not reported last week the encrease of the Society was only 15.

Thursday 22d. August.

The Order of the Day being to receive the report of the Sub Committee appointed for the regulation of the next General meeting, the Chairman of that Sub Committee reported as follows. Vizt.

1st.   That it would be advantageous to the Society to chuse some other Chairman for the ensuing General meeting.

2dly.   That Mr. Lindley be desired to officiate as Reader

3dly.   That the Business of the Meeting be to consider of the propriety of Addressing the King. &a

4thly.   That Richard Hodgson be instructed to draw up an Address for that Purpose.

5thly.   That George Moore be instructed to prepare a proposal for relieving the British Manufacturers now unemployed

& 6thly.   That The Globe Tavern in Fleet Street be the place of Meeting

The Committee having heard the above Report acceded to it & to that purpose the following resolution was passed Unanimously Vizt.

That every Division do recommend on Thursday Next a proper person, a Member of this Society, willing to act as Chairman at the ensuing General Meeting & also another Person to Officiate as Reader. and that the Meeting be Advertised in 6 papers.

33 The letter solicited orders for *The Englishman's Right* at 25s per 100 (to Eyre at Derby; Keamer, Frost and Hibbert at Stockport; Stacey, Jackson and Walker at Manchester; Martin, Horsfield and Brown at Sheffield; Shipley at Nottingham, 15 Aug. 1793, TS 11/956/3501).

A Motion was next brought forward from the joint Divisions No. 1. 13. & 29.

"That a writer be employed for the purpose of Copying the letters received from the Country"

The Committee Ordered that the sd. Motion should stand as the Order of the Day for the 5th. Septr.

Two Motions were presented from Division No. 12. the

1st. "Recommending to the Committee not to postpone the day of General meeting" which was aggreed to.

2d. Recommending the establishment of a female Society of Patriots &a

The Committee thereupon came to the following Resolution "That the Motion from Division No. 12 is approved & that this Society will give every assistance to all who wish to promote the cause of Reform."

The Committee postponed the consideration of the Appendix to the rights of Englishmen & gave orders to the Secretary to purchase a new Publication entitled an Historical account of the Moral & Political Acts of the Kings & Queens of England from W. the Conqueror to the Revolution in 1688.[34]

The Report from the several Divisions for the preceeding week was extreamly favourable. New Members 41:

The Secretary reported that he had written to Derby to Stockport & to Sheffield.

Much business being before the Committee they aggreed to meet next at 7 o Clock

91. Report from spy Lynam, c. 23 August 1793[35]

Source: TS 11/966/3510B

Sir

I have not noticed any thing perticular of some time –

They have encreased within a few weeks in one made 50 new, but yet dont meet strong –

A New Division No 10 Bandy leg walk Southwark

Two Societys at Aldgate about to unite with L. C. S.

I had some conversation the other day with

M. M. who said something must be done soon, I can't learn yet.

I have been try'd as a spy – some time back, since which have been at Sheffield and as I have some reason to think may go again, am to act as an ajent[36] –

An address to his Majesty bringing forward –

92. Journal: LCS General Committee, 29 August –19 September 1793

Source: Add MSS 27812, fos. 61v–72v (later copies in Add MSS 27814, fos. 130–43)

Thursday 29th. August

The Order of the day being to take the Address to the King into consideration in order to finish it for the General meeting the subcommittee made their report of it & requested leave to sit again in order to perfect it sufficiently to be finally submitted to the General Committee immediately before the opening of the business on Monday – leave was granted

A Chairman for the occasion was balloted for from among the names returned to the Committee as proper persons to fill that Station, when Citizen Parkinson was elected – Citizen Field was appointed Reader & Citizen Lovatt inner Doorkeeper – the nomination of the two outer Door keepers was left to the Secretary.

A Motion was brought forward from Division No. 4 Vizt. "That 1000. Copies of Mr. Whartons Speech be printed & distributed at the General meeting." whereon The Committee ordered two thousands of the above Speech to be printed & 1000 of them to be distributed on monday

A Motion from Division No. 28. "That the Office of Delegate shall not in future be attended with expence." was referred to the Constitutional Committee

James Lambeth was chosen Delegate for the Division No. 28 instead of Richd. Hodgson who had declined serving any longer – the new Delegate produced his voucher –

as did John Baxter as Delegate for No. 16 in lieu of John Pierce who has emigrated to America[37]

34 'written by Richd. Dinmore junr.' – later copy.
35 Address: 'E. Nepean Esqr. / Whitehall'. Government description: 'Seditious Societies 1793'. Date conjectured: Journal of 22 Aug. contains the first mention of the proposed address to the king and the first record, in a long time, of substantial gains in membership, both noted in Lynam's report.
36 'I went down into Staffordshire, and into Yorkshire, upon business, upon an order that I had from America' (Lynam's testimony at Hardy's trial, *ST* vol. 24, col. 807).
37 TS 11/956/3501. Endorsement of voucher for Div. 16 gives name as Pearce.

A letter was read from John Harrison at Coventry informing the Committee that he had formed a Society in that place & requesting of our Society to Correspond with them – The Secretary was instructed to answer him[38]   a Letter from Tewkesbury was also read but suspicions being entertained about it the Committee passed to the Order of the day
Encrease this Week   28 New Members.

Monday 2d. Septr.
General Meeting

This Meeting appointed to be held at the Globe Tavern Fleet Street was prevented from meeting there by the illegal interference of Sir James Saunderson – the Committee therefore in order that the Society might not be disappointed aggreed with Lewis the Auctioneer at No. 314 Oxford Street for the Use of his Room, ordered the printing of 700 Hand bills & posted two men at the Globe tavern to distribute them[39]

At half past three the Society being nearly all assembled & Citizen Martin being called to the Chair[40]   the business after an introductory Speech from the Chairman began by reading the destined Address to the King for the obtainment of a Speedy peace & a Reform in Parliamt.

Joseph Gerald Having been appointed Reader began to read the following Address

[The 3000 word address 'To the Kings most Excellent Majesty' deals with abuses in the jury system, excessive taxation, pressing of soldiers and sailors, non-payment of Members of Parliament, political faction, courtiers, despotism, powers of a king, war with France, inability of soldiers and sailors to obtain redress for just complaints and tyrannical treatment of the Irish.]

38 Harrison wrote that he hoped to visit the LCS as soon as he could leave the Coventry society 'in safety'. That time must have come soon, for Margarot endorsed his letter, 'Answd. verbally', which, then as now, meant 'orally'.
39 On the morning of the meeting Saunderson threatened the landlord with loss of his licence and prosecution. The committee immediately rented the auction room (for five guineas) and composed the handbill announcing the new meeting place and the reason for the change (later copy Add MSS 27814, fo. 51). Tickets, purchased before the meeting, cost 6d.
40 'in consequence of Citizen Parkinson having declined the Office' – note in Journal.

This Address[41] having met the unanimous approbation of the Society was recommitted to the care of the Committee to make such Corrections as were indispensably necessary & take advice[42] & the Society after having heard several of their Members on the subject of Abuses, & their remedy vizt. a Parliamentary Reform Resolved

1st.   That the interruption they had met with on the Part of The Lord Mayor of London was unconstitutional but that the public Character of Sir James Sanderson was so despicable as to render him unworthy of the attention of the London Corresponding Society so far as even to Censure him

2d.   that a Certain Number[43] of Members of the Society would adjourn to Supper at the Globe Tavern in Fleet Street purposely to indemnyfy the Landlord from the effects of the unconstitutional prohibition of the Lord Mayor

3dly.   That the Address be printed & Signatures obtained to the Same in order that it may be presented to the King as soon as possible.

And 4thly.   That the next General Meeting of the Society shall take place on the 1st. Monday after the meeting of Parliament – liable to be convoqued sooner if the General Committee think it necessary

The meeting then was adjourned after the reading a Threatening letter which had been sent to the Secretary – but on which the Society looked with a Contemptuous indifference.

Thursday 5th. Septr.

The Order of the day being for the revisal of the Address the same was proceeded on & when finished the Motions of the Several Divisions hereafter named were taken into consideration

No. 5 – "Recommended to the Committee to expedite the Business of Revising the Constitution of the Society" The Committee referred the above to the Sub Committee appointed for revising the Constitution

No. 23. – "Recommended to the Committee to send Copies of the Address to the King to all our Corresponding Country Societies." Decreed –

No. 12 "Sent in a Motion improperly worded & replete with danger to the Society *relative to the Bank*"

41 'said to have been written by Richard Hodson' is added above the line.
42 'take advice of council' – later copy.
43 'That as many as can make it' – later copy.

Passed to the order of the day.

The Committee, granted leave to the Delegate of No. 16 to open a Correspondence with about 60 or 70 Persons at Godalmin in Surrey who intend to form themselves into a Society

Ordered 1000 of our first Addresses to be printed to serve untill the new Constitution was finished

A Report was given in that at Bath 5000 of our Addresses to the Nation had been printed there by a Patriotic Society

A letter from Norwich was Read.

Encrease of Members this Week only 11.

A petition was presented from William Carter

passed to the Order of the Day

Monday 9th Septr.

A Special Committee was called to take into consideration the Appendix to the Rights of Englishmen when in perusing it a false statement was discovered relative to Special Juries – it was therefore sent back to the Sub Committee to amend the same and Citizen Martin was desired to lend his assistance to the Sub Committee.

Thursday 12th. Septr.

The Order of the day being for to take into Consideration the Motion sent in on the 22d. August from the Divisions No. 1. 13. & 29 recommending to the Committee "to employ a hired Writer to Copy all the letters received from the Country" and a motion to the same effect being this day delivered in from Division No. 29. The Committee after much discussion aggreed to postpone their final determination thereon untill the 19th. Instant

A Motion was brought likewise from Divisions 13. & 29 Vizt. "That circular letters be written to all the Country Societies inviting them to adopt our Title & by incorporating themselves with us form in time a Universal Society"

But the Delegates of those Divisions aggreed to withdraw their Motion in consequence of hearing a letter read which the Secretary had just received from Tewkesbury from a Society to whom the offer had been made but was not accepted

A Letter from Birmingham was also read, as was a private letter from Paisley.[44]

The Proof Copy of the Address to the King being ready, the Secretary was empowered to take advice of Counsel thereon & when that

was obtained, to order the printing of Copies of it & to deliver one together with a Skin of Parchment to every Delegate in order that on the next meeting night of their Divisions they may take the Signatures of their Members.

The report of the week was very favourable & the encrease amounts to 42 New Members

[Two trials in Scotland on 30 August and 12 September[45] were portentous for the LCS. On 30 August William Muir was tried at Edinburgh for sedition, before a jury all the members of which belonged to a loyalist club. Muir was accused (1) of addressing reform societies in Kirkintilloch and Miltoun ten months earlier, saying that government was oppressive, tyrannical and corrupt; and (2) of helping to circulate seditious works and urging people to read them, especially Paine's *Rights of Man*. On 31 August he received a sentence of fourteen years' transportation.

Two weeks later, on 12 September, Thomas Fyshe Palmer, a Unitarian minister, was tried at Perth for seditious practices. He was accused of distributing, and possibly writing, an address delivered in July at a meeting of the Society of the Friends of Liberty in Dundee. This address is comparatively tame, and Crown witnesses admitted that Palmer had urged others to moderate it. It complains that the people are being reduced from prosperity to misery and that there are more bankruptcies than ever before – all because people have lost the rights and privileges their fathers enjoyed. On 13 September Palmer was convicted and sentenced to seven years' transportation. Like all other sentences handed down by the Scottish court of justiciary, there was no appeal.

The severity of these sentences marked a new phase in government's repression of reform activities. Earlier convictions for dealing with seditious works usually brought a sentence of no more than two years' imprisonment. And transportation was a sentence reserved for thieves. With these two sentences of transportation as a precedent, the Scottish court could, in January and March 1794, condemn LCS members to fourteen years' transportation and boast that these were mild sentences. The government success in imposing these sentences (no one rioted and no more than forty MPs opposed them) encouraged

44 Later copy adds: 'the name concealed'.

45 Both in *ST* vol. 23.

government, in May 1794, to try Hardy and other reformers for the ultimate crime, treason, with the ultimate punishment.]

93. Journal: LCS General Committee, 19 September 1793

Source: Add MSS 27812, fos. 71-2v (later copy in Add MSS 27814, fos. 142-3)

Thursday 19th. Septr.

The Order of the day being for the taking into consideration an adjourned motion from Division No. 29 praying "that all the letters received by the Committee be copyed by a Writer employed for that purpose alone in order that they might be read in every Division on the same night, &a."

This Motion being seconded by another to the same purpose from Division No. 13 the Committee after mature consideration resolved "That such parts of the letters received as were proper to be communicated, should be trans-cribed by an Assistant Secretary & unani-mously appointed Philip Franklow to that Office".

The Delegate of No. 12 gave the pleasing information that a Member of his Division entertained great hopes of forming a Patriotic Society at Hemel Hempstead the same Del-egate requested the Committee to grant a Number to & receive a Delegate from the Div-ision which had struck off from No. 12 a few Weeks back – the Committee granted his request & directed that they should take No. 14 which was then vacant

The Committee next proceeded to examine the proposed Appendix to the *Englishmens Right* & having approved of it gave directions for having it printed

The Address to the King was next taken into consideration[46] when the following Members were nominated as a SubCommittee for revising the same or drawing up another Vizt.

Parkinson	Walne
Baxter	Moore
& Margarot	

By the Reports of the Delegates it appeared that 31 New Members had been admitted during the Week

Visitors   Citizens Reynolds & Pearce

46 'and heard the report of the Secretary – of the opinion of Council thereon' – later copy.

94. Report from spy Lynam: LCS Division 23, 25 September 1793[47]

Source: TS 11/966/3510B

Sir
    I have now sent Six Patriots, they dont come out regularly
A new Society form'd at Coventry, they write of encreasing much within the last month
A new division of L. C. S meet in the Grove No. 10 Great bandyleg walk Boro' and are violent[48]
A Mr. Cruden lives at Walworth (keeps a Phaeton) going to belong to them, he wrote the offensive Play bill[49] some time back – my information says he his employd by National Convention
Div: No. 14 dropt, now revived fridays at No 3 New Lane Gainsford street Horsley down
A Society of Women at yd same house Saturdays   two Deligates sent to instruct them
Petition to his Majesty declared treasonable by Mr. Vaughan – to draw up another
28 New Member's made last week and meet strong

[The minutes of the meeting of the general committee on 26 September were ripped out of the Journal as were most of those

47 Government description: 'Information respecting the Seditious Societies / 25 September / November 1793'. Government paraphrase of Lynam's reports indentifies this as a report of a meeting of Div. 23 near Bunhill Row, Moorfields.
48 They branched off from another division and took the number 10, a previous division of that number having ceased to meet. One of the delegates reported that the members were very violent (Lynam's testimony, *ST* vol. 24, col. 794).
49 *The Guillotine*, according to Lynam's testimony. This mock play bill advertises 'A new and Enter-taining Farce, called LA GUILLOTINE; or, GEORGE'S HEAD IN THE BASKET!' This play bill alarmed the Privy Council, for in 1794 they asked LCS members if they had seen it and what they thought of it. John Bone had heard of it at a meeting of the 16th and 25th Divs. (PC 1/22/A37). Bailey was said to have printed some at the request of Thomas Williams. When Williams brought them to the meeting of his division at the home of Robert Hawes, 'Hawes disapproved of them highly and would not suffer them to remain in the House' ('The Information of John Thomas Slack', TS 11/966/3510B). Bailey how-ever said he had refused to print any for Joseph Walker (PC 1/22/A37). At Hardy's trial John Edwards testified that John Baxter had given him a copy in Oct. or Nov. 1793.

for the 3 October meeting. What remain of the latter set of minutes are the substitute address to the king – a 400 word petition for peace[50] – and the report of 31 new members. These two meetings must have dealt primarily with arguments over the substitution of a new petition to the king for the one agreed upon at the general meeting.

At one of these two weekly meetings the delegates produced vouchers for the fourth quarter. Only one voucher survives, that certifying James Harris and David David as delegate and subdelegate of Division 28.[51] As later reports indicate, Richard Hodgson was chosen chairman and Thomas Hardy secretary. Divisions 4 and 29 each introduced on 3 October a motion which the divisions voted on during the following week.]

50 The petition is annotated by Hardy: 'This petition is said to have been written by Matthew More.' The change from the first to the second version caused friction in the Society, as Hardy recalled: The 'very long address to the King against the war was read and agreed to [at the general meeting] but being rather hastily drawn up, the Society gave the committee leave to correct it and after a great deal of discussion in the committee it was set aside altogether and another substituted in its room – that conduct of the committee in that respect was very much reprobated by a great number of the society – they said that it was assuming to themselves more authority than their delegated power warranted The committee on the other hand had taken advice of council upon the first Address and joined with their own opinion pronounced it more spirited than Judicious not calculated to effect any possible good but endangered some of the individuals to a prosecution – The debates ran so high in the Society that it had nearly created a schism among them' (Add MSS 27814, fo. 5).

The debate was still going on when Hardy was arrested: 'There was also taken from Citizen Hardy's house, a petition solely relating to the present war, intended to have been presented to the king, but which had been delayed by the attachment which many of the members had to another petition, which included a wish for reform; and from the belief that the trouble of reconciling these two opinions would outweigh the success which was to be hoped from either' (*Account of the Seizure of Citizen Thomas Hardy*, 1794, p. 5).

51 TS 11/956/3501.

95. Report from spy Lynam: LCS Division 23 (government paraphrase), 7 October 1793[52]

Source: TS 11/954/3498

7th. Octr. A Meeting of the Divisn. 23 Pickard the Delegate reported that Richd. Hodgson was chosen president of the Society for the ensuing Quarter & Hardy continued as Secretary. –

96. Journal: LCS General Committee, 10–24 October 1793

Source: Add MSS 27812, fos. 73–7v (later copies in Add MSS 27814, fos. 143-9)

Thursday, 10th. Octr. 1793.

Report new Members, No. 2 – 4: – No. 29 – 3: – No. 7 – 4: No. 23 – 7: – No. 12:1: – No. 13: – 3. – No. 25 – 2: – No. 4: – 1. – Total 25. –

No. 7 admitted a Subscriber under Initials, not desirous of a Ticket: The Committee approved such admission but He was not included in the Number of new members reported, nor is to be considered as one.

Report of the Opinions of the Divisions on the Motns. referred on the 3d. Instant.

[The unit votes of Divisions 1, 4&c, 5, 7, 12, 13, 16, 23, 25, 28 and 29 are tallied. Divisions 2 and 6 are listed as sending 'No Report'. The motion from Division 29 and that from Division 4&c each received 6 negative and 5 affirmative votes. (Since the Journal entry for 3 October is missing, the subjects of these motions are not known.)]

Thus both those motions were negatived; but it was objected that the Delegates ought to have reported the Number of Voters on each side: This Objection was admitted but no Order made in Consequence.

Ordered that the Constitution be taken into Consideration on Thursday next. –

52 At Hardy's trial Lynam related other details of this meeting: 'The report of the delegate was, that there were eighteen new members made that week .... that a Mr. Bell, who was at Brighton, was going to Ireland, and would introduce a correspondence with the societies there, from the London Corresponding Society. At the last meeting of delegates a petition was brought forward, discussed, I suppose, against the war, nothing more is said of that' (*ST* vol. 24, col. 795).

Audited & approved the Treasurer's Account. –

Letter from Tompkins, Tewksbury, was committed to Citizen Margarot, in order to his preparing an Answer by Thursday next.

Letter from Citizen Callender, dated Edinburgh, 5 Octr./93 was referred to the Divisions for their Consideration of the propriety of our sending a Delegate to Edinburgh,[53] & recommendations of a proper Person. –

Ordered that the Delegates do enquire where skins for reception of Signatures to the Petition to the King may lay; who will take an active part in perambulating the Town for the Purpose of collecting Signatures & how many Signatures have already been received.[54] –

A motion from Divn. 28 recommending the Expulsion of Persons who shall be found guilty of propagating levelling Principles was referred to future Committee of Constitution. –

A motion from No. 7 tending to lessen the Number of Motions sent from the Divisions to the Committee was also referred to future Comee. of Constitn. –

The following was presented by Citn. John Baxter. Protest against the proceedings of the Committee of the London Corresponding Society, in their Sittings on Septr. 26 and Octr. 3 1793 When they adopted a certain Address to the King.

First, Because. At a general Meeting of the Society, convened on Septr. 2nd an Address to the King containing a Statement of Public Grievances, and requesting that He would put a speedy termination to the War; was unanimously adopted; but recommitted for the Purpose of "taking Advice of Council and making such Alterations as were indispensibly necessary."

Notwithstanding such Resolution the Committee, by their own Authority suppressed this Address entirely, and forced upon the Society a new one relating only to War. –

Second, Because. Many Persons were present who were not Members of the Society, and it is our Duty to hold Faith with the Public, or else we shall sink into Contempt. –

Third, Because. Such Conduct cannot be justified by the Plea of Necessity, is Unconstitutional, may be productive of a Schism, and thereby weaken, or perhaps totally Annihillate the Society. –

Signed for the 16th. Division J Baxter, Delegate. –
Signed for the 25 Daniel Isaac Eaton, Delegate. Octr. 7th. 1793. –

After reading the foregoing the Chairman made enquiry whether a Protest must, as such, be necessarily entered on the Journal? And No Objection was made to that Opinion.

Ordered that the Treasurer purchase[55] 18 Stars of Peace for the Use of the Divisions

Thursday, 17th: Octr. 1793.

Report of new Members. –
No. 29, 1: – No. 16:2: – No. 4 – 2: – No. 7 – 3: – No. 23 – 3: No. 12 – 3: No. 2 – 6: – No. 1: 1: No. 13: 1: Total 22. –

The Report of the Divisions on the Referd Letter of Citizen Callender[56] was as under

53 For a convention of delegates of reform societies. The Scottish reform societies held conventions in Dec. 1792 and May 1793, when they adjourned to 29 Oct. Callender's letter asked the LCS to send one delegate and offered to act as the second LCS delegate (to Hardy, TS 11/953/3497). His letter is written on the verso of a printed letter from Skirving, dated 30 Sept., notifying the reform societies of the convention. The endorsement indicates that Francklow, asst. sec. of the LCS, made copies for the divisions. Apparently the document was then loaned to the SCI (with the note on the outside, 'To be return'd to the Committee on Thursday next'), for it was found among the papers of the SCI secretary, Adams.

The LCS involvement with the Edinburgh convention is not as straightforward as these letters indicate. On 2 Oct. Skirving had sent Hardy a private letter (now lost) mentioning the convention. On the 5th Hardy replied, also privately, and asked Skirving not to mention their correspondence: 'the General Convention which you mention appears to Mr. Margarot (to whom alone I have communicated your letter) & myself to be a very excellent measure & as such I could wish You without delay to communicate it Officially to our Society without anyways mentioning that you had written to me privately'. This desire for secrecy was so strong that Hardy, in a paragraph later cancelled, repeated the request not to mention the exchange of letters (draft in hand of Margarot, TS 11/956/3501). Skirving's official invitation, dated 10 Oct., is a brief request for other reform societies to cooperate with the Friends of the People in Scotland by sending delegates to the convention. Only the last sentence refers to the LCS specifically (to Hardy, TS 11/953/3497).

54 'An Account of the Skins of Parchment' lists the men who took skins and the number taken: Field – 6; Barnes, Buller, Margarot, Spence – 3 each; Dawson, Piccard, Stiff – 2 each; Ashley, Child, Franklow, Hardy, Hartley, Hodgson, Pearce, Smith, Walne – 1 each (TS 11/959/3505).

55 'from Mr Hawes the printer' – later copy.
56 'to the Society about sending one or two Delegates to the Convention held at Edinburgh' – later copy.

[The votes of the members of Divisions 1&13, 2&6, 4, 5, 12, 28 and 29 are tallied. On the question of sending a delegation to Edinburgh, the vote was affirmative, 64 to 13. On the question of which person or persons to send, affirmative votes are recorded for 'Citn. Gerrald' (88:20), 'Citn. Margarot' (69:23), 'Citn. Sinclair' (39:0), 'Citn. Callendar' (66:2), and 'Citn. Field' (6:0). Divisions 7, 16 and 23 are reported as sending no recommendations on these questions.]

The Question was then put whether a general Meeting shall be called to decide on this Business; – and the Votes were,

Affirmative – 9 } Majty. Aff: 7.
Negative   – 2 }

Resolved that it should be held on Thursday, the 24th Instt. at Citizen Briellat's, Pumpmaker, Hackney Road: – at one O Clock in the Afternoon; – Delegates to attend with their Books at 12. –
Jno. Morton, Bookseller, New Brentford, & Citn. Stiff reqd a Skin for Reception of Signatures to the petition. –
Ordered that a Skin be given to Citn. Stiff for Him. –
On the Ballott for a special Committee to prepare Instructions for the Delegates which are to be sent to Edinburgh & other Matters relative to the General Meeting on Thursday next the Numbers were,

For	Margarot	10	Elected and agreed
	Baxter	6	to meet in Comee.
	Moore	9	Room on Saturday
	Francklow	6	the 19 at 7 in
	Hodgson	7	the Evening. –
	Walne	4	
	Ashley	4	
	Stiff	3	
	Davidson	2	
	Piccard	1	
	Walker	2	

Read and approved the Answer prepared by Citn. Margarot to Tewksbury, junior.[57] –
Read a Letter of Citn. Baxter to a Friend at Godalmin
Read two Letters from Carshalton & ordered Citn. Margarot to prepare Answers to them. –

Report of the special Committee held 19th. Octr. 1793.

57 Letter lost. Another letter written on the 17th was to Norwich, enclosing notice of the Edinburgh convention and offering *The Englishman's Right* at 3s per dozen (TS 11/953/3497).

That they had agreed to the following form of a Certificate. –
"At a General Meeting of the London Corresponding Society held at Citn. Breillat's, Hackney Road, 24 Octr. 1793
"This is to certify that A. A. was this day duly elected a Delegate to represent this Society at the ensuing Convention to be held in Edinburgh for the purpose of obtaining a thorough Reform in the parliamentary Representation of Great Britain

Signed   B. B. Chairman
To Mr. Wm. Skirving   T. H. Secretary
  Secretary to the Friends of the People
                    Edinburgh. –

That they had resolved as under
1st. That a Set of Instructions be given to the Delegate signed by the Chairman of General Meeting & The Secretary of this Society & that a Counterpart signed by the Delegate shall be kept by the General Committee.
2d. That if an Absentee should be chosen, in addition to one of the Candidates present; the Delegate present shall be furnished with two additional Copies of the Instructions; one of them signed by the Chairman & Secretary – the other to be signed by the absent Delegate previous to receiving his Credentials, and to be remitted to the Secretary of this Society
3 That the Instructions & Qualifications be discussed & finally arranged before any Candidate be nominated

ARTICLES OF INSTRUCTION,
To Citizen A. A.

Delegate from the London Corresponding Society to the ensuing Convention at Edinburgh for the purpose of obtaining a thorough Parliamentary Reform. –

1st He shall on no Account whatever, depart from the original Object & Principles namely the obtaining annual Parliaments & universal Suffrage by rational & lawful means. –
2d. He is directed to support the Opinion that Representatives in parliament ought to be paid by their Constituents.
3 That the Election of Sheriffs ought to be restored to the people.
4 That Juries ought to be chosen by Lot. –
5 That active means ought to be used to render every man acquainted with the Duty & Rights of a Juryman. –
6 That the Liberty of the Press must at all

Events be supported and that the publication of political Truths can never be criminal.

7 That it is the Duty of the People to resist any Act of Parliament repugnant to the original principles of the Constitution; as would be every attempt to prohibit Associations for the Purpose of Reform.

8th. That this Society considering all Party names & Distinctions as hostile to the General Welfare, do absolutely, restrict their Delegate from assuming or accepting of that Nature.

9 This Society farther require their Delegate to be punctual and trequent in his Correspondence with this Society.

> We do hereby promise to comply with the foregoing Instructions

QUALIFICATIONS

That no Person shall be eligible who has not been a Member Three Months and is at this Time a regular Member. –

Thursday, 24th. Octr. 1793.

In a General Committee previous to the General Meeting received the foregoing Report of the Special Committee, which was approved unanimously; except the Article of Qualification which was divided as under into two Articles; –

1st. That no Person shall be eligible who is not a regular Member. –

2d. That no person shall be eligible who has not been a Member three Months. –
On the first the Committee were unanimous in the Affve.
On the Second the Numbers were

> 6 Affirmative
> 6 Negative

The Chairman gave his Vote in the Affirmative.

Received Information that a considerable Number of Constables were assembled in the Neighbourhood and that two or three Magistrates were at the Nag's Head, a Public House close by: – Deputed Citizens Margarot, Sinclair, & Thelwall to wait on the Magistrates & Citizen Martin on being informed of the Circumstance went as a Volunteer.[58]

Resolved to recommend Citizen Hodgson as Chairman of the General Meeting.

GENERAL MEETING,

The Members being made acquainted with the Recommendation of the Committee and no other Candidate being proposed Citizen Hodgson was unanimously called to the Chair.

Many Members wishing to begin Business immediately, The Question was put whether a

curiosity others from a different motive to disturb the order of the Society' (Add MSS 27814, fo. 58). Government had stationed 'about one hundred Parish Constables' supposedly out of view and a dozen extra constables – Spitalfields weavers who were not known to be officers – in the field with orders to act as messengers and to bring an account of the proceedings every fifteen minutes. Thus the number of constables and magistrates was almost equal to the number of LCS members present. Patrick Colquhoun, who organized these forces, had two motives: to prevent unemployed Spitalfields weavers from rioting; and to arrest Thomas Briellat, whom he described as 'the ring leader and the most Criminal of the whole ' (letter, Colquhoun to Evan Nepean, 25 Oct. 1793, HO 42/26, fos. 806–7).

Briellat was certainly not a ring-leader. He was a pump-maker with a field in Spitalfields, which he offered at the previous general meeting after the Society had been forced to find a new meeting place on the day of the meeting. Hardy described the spectators gathering around the field: 'That being the first General Meeting of the Society that was held in the *open air* it caused a great stir in London (being announced in the Newspapers for about a fortnight previous to their meeting) especialy at that quarter of the Town all the streets and avenues leading to the place where the society assembled were crouded with people it being also on the publick road side to Hackney consequently many passangers were induced to stop to enquire what was the cause of such a Multitude of people being collected together in that spot – many curious and laughable observations were made by the bystanders some saying that "Tom Paine was come to plant the tree of liberty" and others that the French Jacobines were come – and others that the London Corresponding Society were met to lower the price of provisions – God bless them says some of the women and poor working people – success to them said others' (Add MSS 27814, fo. 57).

After seeing the size of the crowd, the LCS must have realized the power of open-air meetings to attract new members and supporters. 'Many who came there to ridicule and abuse', continued Hardy, 'went away converted and afterwards joined the society and became zealous promoters of the cause' (fo. 59).

---

58 'and he being a professional Man [i.e. a solicitor] it was thought he might be usefull' – later copy. Hardy explained that they went to the magistrates to ask for protection from the spectators: 'The people at the outside of the railing which incircled the field behind the house had attempted to break in upon the Society some perhaps from

Delay of ¼ of an Hour ought to be made, for the Return of the Deputation sent to the Magistrates? – Card. in the Affirmative by a large Majority.

The Deputation returning in a few Minutes reported That they found the Magistrates at the Nag's Head; That some of the Constables were riotous & forced into the House; The Magistrates polite; – The Deputies gave them their Addresses; – also the original Address of our Society; mentioned that about 200 were present and not more than 400[59] expected. That we were met for the purpose of chusing Delegates to be sent to a Convention in Edinburgh; – invited them to be present, which they declined: – That Citizen Margarot had given the High Constable[60] an especial Charge to keep the Peace; with a promise that we would assist Him & his Posse in the Discharge of their Duty but that we would see they did their Duty.

The Articles of Instruction & Qualification were then read and unanimously agreed to: – except the second Article of Qualification, which occasioned some Debate but was carried in the Affirmative by a large Majority.

Some Objections being then made to Citizen Callender, particularly his being absent & understood as offering to serve without Reward, contrary to the Principles of our Society; it was explained that he had not made any such Offer & on the Qn. of his Eligibility being put, it was carried in the affirmative by a large Majority.

On the Qn. of how many Dels. we should send; two were resolv'd on.

The Candidates then nominated as recommended to the Committee were

  Callender
  Gerrald
  Margarot
  Sinclair——
    Disqualified. by 2d. Article[61] –
  Field——Declined

In Addition to which the following were proposed.

  Wilson
  Jones[62]
  Jno. Baxter——Declined
  Thelwall——
    Disqualified. by 2d. Article[63]

On the Shew of Hands the Chairman declared the Majority to be in Favor of Citns. Margarot & Gerrald: – But Sundry Members objecting that the shew in favor of Callender was greater than that in Favor of Gerrald & doubts being likewise intimated respectg the Return of Margarot; The Chairman declared that he had no doubt of the propriety of the Return of Margarot but would take the Sense of the Meeting on that Question; which being put to the Vote was affirmed almost unanimously: – The Chairman then acknowledging that He had not an equal Confidence as to the difference of Votes for Gerrald & Callender, they were renominated & on being put to the Vote, the Majority in favor of the former was Satisfactory.[64]

During the latter part of this Business a Message was received from the Magistrs. requesting that we would expedite our Business as much as possible, on Acct. of the encreasing Concourse of the Populace round the Garden in which we were: – This Message being communicated to the Meeting They voted Thanks to the Magistrates

  Do. in particular to the High Constable

  Do. to our Fellow Citizens the Spectators (in Number about 4000)[65]

Resolved that a Subscription for Defraying the Expence of Delegation be opened immediately.

Collected £6,2s, – but it being found that the Subscriptn occasioned Delay & the Con-

59 Newspaper accounts of the meeting in the pro-government *Sun* and *True Briton* report 150 present (*Sun*, 26 Oct. 1793, p. 4; *True Briton*, 26 Oct. 1793, p. 4). This is the first mention of the LCS in either paper. The account of the meeting is included in the paper because it formed part of the story of the arrest of Thomas Briellat, which took place as soon as the LCS members had left Briellat's field.

60 Later copy indicates that Margarot was acting as chairman of the deputation and that the high constable, Mr Wright, became 'a good Member of the Society'.

61 Charles Sinclair soon became the SCI's delegate to the convention.

62 Charles Wilson and Daniel Jones (later copy).

63 John Thelwall, an author, editor and well-known political speaker at debating societies, joined the LCS a week before this meeting (i.e. about 17 Oct.) and was elected delegate of Div. 25 on 21 Oct. (voucher, TS 11/956/3501). His application for membership was sponsored by Joseph Gerrald (Mrs Thelwall, *Life of John Thelwall*, p. 115).

64 Joseph Gerrald may have been recommended as a delegate to the convention because he had just published a pamphlet urging that the House of Commons be replaced by a convention of 375 delegates, chosen from primary and secondary assemblies, at the ratio of one deputy for every 5000 primary voters (*A Convention the Only Means of Saving Us from Ruin. In a Letter Addressed to the People of England*, 1793).

65 Like many contemporary estimates of spectators at LCS outdoor meetings, this one is probably exaggerated.

course of People still continuing it was not compleated.

[The meeting ended at 3.30, and the members and spectators began to leave peaceably. When most of them had departed, a magistrate arrested Briellat ' in such a manner as to occasion no alarm among the people at large'. John Martin, apprised of the arrest, attended Briellat at the judicial examination that night, where Treasury Solicitor Joseph White was also present.

On 6 December Briellat was tried and convicted of having used seditious language a year earlier. The alleged seditious language included such expressions as 'a reformation cannot be effected without a revolution', 'we have no occasion for kings', I 'wish the French would land one hundred thousand men in England to fight against the government party'. The information on which these charges were based was given by a publican, William Goodwin, who said nothing about Briellat's expressions until he learned that Briellat's fields were to be used for a large meeting. Fearing a repetition of the Gordon riots, he went to the magistrates.

Briellat's counsel were Vaughan and Gurney; his solicitor, Martin (whose request for his fee led to a special meeting of the general committee in 1796).[66] Briellat was sentenced to twelve months' imprisonment, a fine of £100, security for his good behaviour for three yearsof £500 for himself, and two sureties of £250 each.

After his release he emigrated to America.[67]

97. Journal: LCS General Committee, 25 October 1793

Source: Add MSS 27812, fo. 78 (later copy in Add MSS 27814, fo. 149)

General Committee, 25th. Octr. 1793. –

Report of new Members No. 2 – 7: – No. 29 – 12 – No. 25 – 3: No. 16 – 8: – No. 4 – 3: – No. 12 – 1: – No. 13 – 1 Total 43. – Leave given to 29 to divide – The New Division to be Numbd. 3.

66 Details about the arrest of Briellat are in the minutes of this later meeting. See no. 337.
67 Colquhoun's letter; *ST* vol 22; Add MSS 27814, fo. 59.

NO MOTION FROM ANY DIVISION. – Recd. Information from Citizens Eaton & Hardy had voluntarily open'd Subscriptions for defraying Expences of Delegation. Resolved to allow the Delegates

		£.	S.	D.
For Fare up & down,	each	10:		
Expence up & down	do.	4:		
		£14	-	-

Weekly payment to commence from their Arrival at Edinburgh & continue to their setting out for London, at the Rate of 9s/ per day

Citizen Margarot reported from the Constitutional Society. – Their Resolution to call a general meeting next Monday. –

	£	S	D
Secretary reported total Collected	10:	7:	-
In Hand of Treasurer	4:	-:	-
	14:	7:	-

Ordered that the Delegates set off tomorrow Night.[68] –

98. Report from spy Lynam, 26 October 1793[69]

Source: TS 11/958/3503

Sir

I hope You will excuse the liberty I purpose takeing of waiting upon You on monday evening next at 8 OClock, and if not convenient to see me, to request the favor of Your own time

J. H. Tooke going a Deligate from the Friends of yd People[70]

68 On this day Hardy wrote to Skirving and to Adams announcing the choice of delegates. He asked Adams whether the SCI wanted copies of *The Englishman's Right* (ST vol. 24, cols. 422–3; TS 11/953/3497).
69 Address: 'E. Nepean / Esqr'. Government description: '26th Octo 1793. / Mr Ln. Rx'.
70 Tooke, who disapproved of the convention, had no intention of going. Other delegates from England were Charles Sinclair of the SCI and Matthew Campbell Browne of the Sheffield SCI. Henry Redhead Yorke, though elected delegate by the SCI, did not go to Edinburgh. Margarot acted as delegate for the Norwich societies, and Browne for the Leeds Constitutional Society. Two members of the United Irishmen left Edinburgh without attending the Convention (Goodwin, *The Friends of Liberty*, pp. 293, 295). The LCS, with their two delegates, provided half the English representation.

Several other Delegates are going from here, and Ireland
Callender – lives in John Street Tottenham Court road, either an Officer on half Pay, or some situation under government.
A great many of L. C. S. went from the meeting in Hackney road to Capel Court society,[71] determined to make a riot, Thelwall one of them very violent, they are determined to have Political Clubs

99. Journal: LCS General Committee, 31 October 1793

Source: Add MSS 27812, fo. 78v (later copy in Add MSS 27814, fo. 150)

General Committee   October the 31st. 1793

Citizen R: Hodgson having resigned the Office of Chairman of the Committee of this Society the 24th. instant. the ballot for the election of Another took place this evening when on casting up the number of votes Citizen John Baxter was declared duly elected for the remainder of this Quarter
Report from the Delegates respecting New Members when it was found that there was an increase of 19 this Week
No Motion from any Division
Citizen John Lovett returned as Delegate of Division 7 in the place of Citizen Maurice Margarot having been sent to Scotland by Delegation.
This Committee came to a resolution that a Committee be chosen by the Society at large to draw up a New Constitution for their good Government. That any Member is eligible, and that every Division send one Delegate to that Committee[72] which is to meet on Friday Novr. 8th. 1793 –

Correspondence

Read Letters from Bristol. Coventry. Norwich. and Sheffield

100. Court Testimony of spy Alexander: LCS Division 29, 5 November 1793

Source: *ST* vol. 24, cols. 639–41

[At the trial of Hardy, Henry Alexander, a spy, testified that on 5 November 1793

71 A debating society where Thelwall spoke.
72 Elected members included John Richter, Div. 2; Alexander Lee, 5; Anthony Beck, 7; William Arnold, 12; George Gimber, 13; Morris, 16;

Henry Yorke, who had recently become a member of Division 29, took leave of the Society at a meeting of the division at Robinson's Coffee House in Shire Lane. There were between sixty and a hundred people in the room. Alexander reported:
'On the last night that he [Yorke] was at the society, he took leave of them by a long speech – he said he was going to bel-gi-um – Bel-gi-na . . . [Yorke said] that he was going to head the French army, and should be back by Christmas; that he had received a letter from a friend of his in Bel-gi-um, where they were going; that they would be ripe [for revolution] by Christmas – he was going at the head of them. . . . He said he was in hopes he should come at the head of them to England [to London] . . . .
[Asked the substance of Yorke's speech, Alexander explained:] The substance of it was as I informed you before – that he had received a letter to go over; that he had an offer of being a member of the National Convention in France; and that he was in hopes he should have the pleasure of coming here either by Christmas, or the beginning of the year, at the head of them; and that he sould see them all ready to join him; and that he was in hopes that Mr Pitt, with the different ministers he mentioned, and the king's head, would be upon Temple-bar[73] . . . . he made some observations upon them [the king and queen of France], but I cannot recollect the words now . . . . The substance of it was, that it was what they had deserved – that they had met with their desert . . . . He did make mention of the Sans Culottes; that they were a set of brave fellows – He said a deal about them, that they were a set of brave fellows . . . . He said that he was in hopes when he came, he should find them [the members of the London Corresponding Society] all ready to join him, and that when the point came that he hoped they would not be afraid, and spring or shrink from what they pretended to be; he said, it was impossible to do any thing without some bloodshed. . . . He said, that there would be no good done without some

George Bowden, 25; Richard Hodgson, 28 (vouchers, TS 11/953/3497 and TS 11/956/3501).
73 According to Samuel Williams, Yorke never used these expressions about Pitt or the king. Yorke "said he was going to Belgium to his friend Vandvoot to fight for Gods not Men" ('Minutes of James Powel's Informn.', TS 11/958/3503).

bloodshed . . . . He said, that there was a set of brave men there [in Sheffield] . . . . when he got up we all got up and shook hands with him; all rose and shook hands with him when he got up and left the room.']

101. Report from spy Lynam: LCS Division 23, 5 November 1793[74]

Source: TS 11/958/3503

Sir

Hodgson has resignd & Baxter chose Chairman

Margarott & Gerrold went to Scotland 30 Octr.

Subscriptions not equal to the expence's are in debt.

A Second deligate chose from each division to form a subcommittee to revise the laws, and to meet No. 31 Compton Street every friday

A new Society from'd at Bristol

Harrison a Razor maker of Sheffield formd several Societys – if any one speaks seditiously, he must retract or be turnd out

I beg leave to take the liberty of waiting upon You this evening at 8 O Clock if agreable to see me

Thursday[75]

74 Address: 'E Nepean Esqr / Whitehall'. Government description: 'Delegates to the Scotch Convention / 5 Nov. 1793. (Int.)'. At Hardy's trial Lynam described this as a report from Div. 23.
75 Nov. 7. Div. 23 met two days before Lynam wrote this report.
   Government paraphrase of Lynam's reports adds: 'the Delegate reported that ffrancklow had stated that an Association was forming in Lambeth to learn the use of Arms, but that no person was to belong to it who was not a Member of the London Corr. Society that the Plan was not compleated but wod. come out in a short time' ('Evidence of George Lynam', TS 11/954/3498). In the paraphrase in TS 11/956/3501 this material is a marginal addition. At the trial Lynam did not mention the arming associations until the prosecuting council asked him if he recollected anything said by Franklow.
   Questioned by Hardy's counsel, Lynam admitted that he had no memorandum of this material. His testimony at the trial: 'I recollect it being said, that there was going to be an association formed at Lambeth, for the purpose of learning their exercise. . . . I understood that they were going to form themselves into different societies . . . a plan was forming for those

102. Journal: LCS General Committee, 7 November 1793

Source: Add MSS 27812, fos. 78v-9 (later copy in Add MSS 27814, fo. 150)

General Committee Novr: 7th. 1793

On Report from the Delegates of the new members made this Week it was found there was an increas of 18. –

No Motion from any Division –

The Committee Resolved that the petition to the King be Advertized in the Morning Chronicle, Courier, and Ayres's Gazette, and that a Subscription be Solicited from the Public for promoting Constitutional knowledge and prosecuting the Object of this Society Namely a Parliamentary Reform[76]

The Delegate of Division 1 requested leave to divide and meet at the Horse Shoe and Magpie Worcester Street Borough and take the Vacant No. 9. —granted by the Committee –

Correspondence

Read a Letter from our Delegates in Scotland in which they desire they may be at

societies to learn their exercise at different places all over London, and that it was to be confined to the London Corresponding Society . . . the forming of the society, and how they were to meet, to carry it on, was not at that time mature to the best of my recollection, but this was said, that there was a variety of people that did intend to learn their exercise, but this at Lambeth was the only one that was mentioned . . . it came out afterwards, and probably, it will not be improper to mention it here, that there were members of the London Corresponding Society, that had a desire of introducing the exercise among the London Corresponding Societies divisions on different nights, from the night that the division met on different evenings . . . . It was rejected at No. 23, but this is only anticipating it.'

Asked where the meeting took place, Lynam said, 'At the same place near Bunhill-row.' He also added one item not included in his written report: 'colonel Macleod, and Mr. Sinclair, were gone as delegates to Edinburgh, from the Constitutional Society' (*ST* vol. 24, col. 796).

76 Advertisement, dated 15 Nov. 1793, lists places where subscriptions might be received and the petition signed: Hodgson, 4 Broadway, Westminster; Lambeth, 3 St George's Mall, St George's Fields; Lovett, 4 Shepherd's Market, May Fair; Hardy, 9 Piccadilly; Peacock (Stationer), Globe Stairs, Rotherhithe; Spence, 8 Little Turnstile, Holborn; Ashley, 12 Fisher St, Red Lion Sq; Francklow, 1 China Walk, Lambeth; Thelwall, 2 Maze Pond, Borough; Stiff, Paternoster Row, Cheapside; Powell, 8 Goodge St. Tottenham Ct Rd (Add MSS 27814, fo. 5).

liberty to visit the different Societies in Scotland. —The Committee that it be referred to the Different Divisions.[77]

[The Edinburgh Convention, convened on 29 October, had passed some resolutions and adjourned by the time that Margarot and Gerrald arrived. On 7 November Skirving sent the delegates of the Scottish reform societies a printed letter announcing the arrival of the delegates from London and recalling the Scottish delegates to a continuation of the convention on 19 November.

On the verso of a copy of this letter, Margarot wrote to Thomas Buckle suggesting that the Norwich societies send delegates or authorize one of the London delegates to act in their name.[78] They asked Margarot to represent them; and they contributed to his support, even up to the time when he was on the ship awaiting transportation to New South Wales.]

103. Report from spy Lynam: LCS Division 23, 12 November 1793[79]

Source: TS 11/958/3503

November 12th

a Letter read from W Cole Secretary to all the Societys at Norwich approving of the convention & requesting a regular correspondence and doubt not of encreasing & succeeding Subscriptions very low £23 only received, requested each Member to subscribe again for support of Deligates, who are invited to visit all Societys in Scotland; Another General meeting to be held in Edingboro' for yd 19th alterd to be held at Glasgow Society Crown & Anchor request 12 Doz of

77 Hardy answered the letter the next day, explaining that the committee 'were pleased with the idea, but they thought that it could not be put in practice on account of the necessary supplies, which come in but very slowly. It is to be mentioned in the different divisions.' He also reported that the LCS had begun a correspondence with a new society at Bristol (to Margarot and Gerrald, *ST* vol. 24, col. 425).
78 TS 11/953/3497.
79 Government description: 'Constitutional Societies in and near London. 12 Nov. 1793'. At Hardy's trial Lynam identified this as a meeting of Div. 23.

Rights of Jewrys & can dispose of many, think them good things
Petition to yd King to be advertized in Eyres Sunday Paper Morning Chronocle and another that the same lays for signatures at Hogsons Spencer's & 4 or 5 other Places
York of Derby went to Shire lane Tuesday and spoke for 2 hour's, wo'd not stay in England for £20000 going this week to Holland or Switzerland both Places ripe for a revolt he was chose Deligate to go to Edinboro' by Constitutional Society but declined it

Meeting of Division's

No.	1	at the Horseshoe Boro' – just removed
	14	New lane at No 3 Gainsford Street Horsley Down
	10	In the grove bandy leg walk Southwark violent
	13	Coffee house Shire lane Temple Barr
	12	Spencer's Little turnstile Holborn
	16 & 25	Haw's Printer No 12. White Row Spittlefields
	28	No 4 St. George's Mills near Dog & Duck
	29	Coffee house Shire lane

At No 31 Compton Street Mondays, Tuesdays, Wednesdays & Fridays
Number's 7 – 15 – 4.   5 Divisions

At the Coffee house Shire Lane Monday, Tuesday, Wednesday Friday
Number's 13 – 26.   4 Division's

At No 8 Queen Street 7 Dials M. T. W. & F 5 Division's
Number's 2 – 5.

Friends of yd People Circus Coffee house Algate Society Jewen Street Aldgate

Continued Delegates
Margarot, Piccard, Lambert, Stiff, Hodgson
No 7   23   28   13   4
Moor, Baxter, Eaton
26   16   25
Baxter never withdrew his recognizance as desired by Martin, which he might have done, it not being enterd at Hicks's hall and therefore liable

104. Journal: LCS General Committee, 14–28 November 1793

Source: Add MSS 27812, fos. 79–80v (later copy in Add MSS 27814, fos. 150-2)

General Committee Novr. 14th: 1793

On the Report from the Delegates of the new members made this Week – there was an increase of 31 –

No Motion from any Division –

On the Report from the Divisions of this Society on the Letter referred to them last Committee – They were all of Opinion that our Delegates in Scotland should remain there as long as they could be of any service to the cause of Freedom and Reform – and they by their exertions would endeavour to make the finances of the Society Support them –

The Committee Resolved that a Circular Letter be addressed to such persons as are known to be friendly to the Objects of this Society – requesting them to favour the Society with their pecunary Assistance[80]

Resolved that a Committee of 5. be Appointed to draw up the said Letter – and Citizens Thelwall, Baxter, Moore, Walne, and Franklow, were chosen by Ballot for that purpose –

Citizen John Thelwall made An Offer to read political Lectures[81] on every Wednesdays and Fridays the terms of Admission for Members 3d. Strangers 6d. and the profits arising therefrom to be Applied to Support the Representation of this Society at the British Convention in Edinburgh

The Committee Resolved that 12£: 12s: – be sent to Our Delegates in Scotland – .

On Reading a Note from the Constitutional Committee in which they Observe, that while they are transacting the Business of the Society in that particular, they ought not to be at any expence. The Committee General Resolved that they bear their own expence as well as the General Committee.[82]

General Committee Novr. 21st. 1793

On the Report of the new Members made this week it was found there had been an increase of 33 –

No Motion from any Division –

Correspondence

A Letter was read from our Delegates, in which they recommend to us to Consider of the Propriety of adopting One General Name and Plan for the different Societies. – After mature discussion in the Society it was Negatived.[83] –

They also desired to know when their Commission was to end. Whether they were at liberty to Visit the Different Societes in Scotland, And whether one shod. remain after the Other was recalled. These Questions was appointed on the Order of the Day for Next Thursday.

Resolved that a Circular letter be sent to the Other Patriotic Societies, recommending to them without delay either to send delegates to the Convention, or Authorize ours to represent them.[84] –

Resolved that a Standing Committee of 5 Members be Appointed to receive and answer any Correspondence from our delegates with Power to Call a full Committee if Necessary – When Citizens Stiff, Davidson, Moore, Pearce, and Lovett were Chosen by Ballot.

General Committee Novr: 28th. 1793

On the Report of New Members made this Week it was found there had been an increase of 24. –

Motions

No. 1. That the thanks of this Society be given to Citizen Thelwall for his Patriotic exertions in the Cause of Freedom by the diffusion of Knowledge, and the Appropriation of the Pecuniary Advantages arising from his Lectures towards its Support – which Motion the Committee approving of they made a Resolution Accdgly. –

---

80 Printed letter, dated 15 Nov. 1793, stressed the expence of maintaining two delegates at the Edinburgh convention and listed the men who would receive subscriptions (TS 11/966/3510B). Government paraphrase of Lynam's reports named Baxter and Hardy as the authors.

81 Later copy adds: 'from Godwins Political Justice'. Thelwall was soon delivering original lectures, to which government sent spies.

82 Later copy clearer: 'Resolved that the Constitutional Come be on the same footing as the General Come in that respect.' The expenses at issue would be rent for the room at 31 Compton St (where both the committee and the sub-committee met), coals, candles, stationery and ink.

83 Hardy's reply, written the next day, did not mention this decision. Hardy enclosed a draught for £21 12s on Sir William Forbes & Co. He also noted that the new constitution of the LCS probably would not be adopted before the delegates' return (*ST* vol. 24, cols. 426–7). Debate on the adoption of a new constitution went on for another fifteen months.

84 Draft, 23 Nov. 1793, TS 11/953/3497.

No. 2 & 6.   Seeing the truth of the Principle that Persons Called upon to devote their time and abilities to the benefit of the Society ought to be put to no expence on that Account: declare it to be their Opinion that the Delegates Appointed by the various divisions of this Society ought to be provided with such articles as are Necessary for their use in the – execution of their Commission at the expence of this Society. Which Motion was after mature discussion referred back to the Committee for the revision of the Constitution

On the Report from the divisions respecting our delegates they were all of Opinion that the Delegates should not return to London till the Convention had finished their Business. –

Citizen Walne was added to the Standing Committee of the 21st. instant

The Order of the Day –

1st. When Mission of our Delegates terminates

Resolved – When the Convention Shall have finished their Sittings

2d. Whether they are at liberty to visit the Different Societes in Scotland. –

Resolved that their Original Commission was only to the Convention the discharge of their duty at that Place would fulfil the Object of the Society they are therefore to return without visiting the Other Societies. –

3d. Whether One should remain after the Other was recalled –

Resolved that they shall return together. – [85]

105. Government Examination: Joseph Goulding, LCS Division 25 (excerpt), 29 November 1793 [86]

Source: TS 11/965/3510A

Joseph Goulding. - I belonged to a Society at the corner house in Sandwich Street. Bishopgate Street. I was a member about

three months, I have Dropped it about the same time, the mans name who kept the house was *Euston* – he was a Weaver, an acquaintance of mine was the first person that asked me to go there, his name is lap he is a weaver – he lives No __ the corner of Silver Street, we paid a *penny a week* towards the use of the room – and a penny more for Letters & paper & printed books – I left it, because I thought it was better to follow my duty than loose my time there – The room was generally pretty full – there were forms all round generally *thirty* persons present – more or less. There were Delegates from every division – London is divided into about one hundred Divisions. I belonged to the twenty fifth Division – as this card [87] will shew you. Mr Eaton the bookseller is Delegate of the twenty fifth Division – the Delegates meet I believe very often – but the Division only once a week vizt on mondays there is only one Secretary & one Delegate for Each Division we meet two Divisions together at Mr Eustons – the twenty fifth and Sixteenth. the Divisions to which we belong are appointed by the Secretary and when he gives the ticket we are free of admission to all the Societies in London – I never went to any but my own because I was a watchman and generally on duty –
The Secretary was one Tubb he lives near Bethnal green he is also a Weaver, a youngish man –
The Division left that place in Sandwich Street and meet now at Mr Hawes's the printers No 12 near Red Lion Street Spital Fields – Mr Breilatt entered the very night after I did, There is nobody that I know of hereabouts – they come mostly from Spittal fields Bethnal green and from over the water . . . The Secretary always takes the books home with him – we meet at Eight and break up about ten –
Almost every body Speaks, and there is allways a very great noise, till the Delegate gets up – People generally grow very outrageous and won't wait, then the Delegate gets up and trys to soften them, There were no Soldiers in the meeting to my knowledge –

85 The next day this decision was conveyed to them in a letter signed by Hardy but written by someone else (*ST* vol. 24, cols. 427-8). Margarot replied urging the importance of their staying on 'to cement the Union' of the LCS with Scottish reform societies (to Hardy, 2 Dec. 1793, TS 11/956/3501).

86 Heading: 'Middlesex. The voluntary examination of Joseph Goulding of the Parish of St. Mary White-Chapel in the said County Watchman taken the 29. Novr. 1793'. Government description: 'Information of Goulding as to the Division No 25 of the Corr Society / In Mr Wickham's 31 Jany. 1794'. Goulding was taken up by police

officers after a fellow watchman, Murphy, charged him with using seditious language and with reading articles from the *Morning Chronicle* to his colleagues.

87 'A ticket of admission to the 25th. Division' – marginal note.

106. Journal: LCS General Committee, 5 December 1793

Source: Add MSS 27812, fo. 80v (later copy in Add MSS 27814, fo 152)

General Committee Decr. 5th. 1793

On the Report from the Divisions it was found there had been an increase of 17 New Members. –

No Motion from any Division

Robt. Chassereau sent as Delegate of No. 3. –
No 16 desired leave to divide again and form 2 New divisions and to take the vacant Nos. of 10. & 11 –
Resolved that 1000 of the Original Address and Resolutions of this Society be printd

Correspondence

Read a Letter from the Committee of Constitution relative to the defraying their expences. – which was referred to the divisions for their Instructions thereon. –
Resolved that £12.12.0 be sent to the Delegates. –

[When the convention in Edinburgh reconvened on 19 November, Margarot and Gerrald became the most active and articulate members (Margarot claimed that it was he who persuaded Skirving to summon the delegates back).[88] The convention sat for fifteen days, much of their time being occupied with setting up rules and committees for future meetings of the united societies of Scotland and England.

On 28 November (the ninth day) Margarot proposed that a secret committee of three and the secretary (Skirving) be appointed to determine a place where a convention of emergency could meet. At the end of this session, each delegate would be given a sealed letter with the name of the place. The delegate would deliver the letter to his constituents, who would keep it until a convention of emergency had been summoned. On 4 December (the thirteenth day) Margarot introduced a further motion about the secret committee, namely, 'that the moment of the illegal dispersion of the present convention be considered as our summons to repair to the place of meeting appointed for the convention of emergency by the secret committee.' That evening the motion passed unanimously.

Less than twelve hours later, at 7.00 a.m. on 5 December, Margarot and Gerrald were arrested in their room, confined all day, examined at night and then bailed, each for 2000 merks (about £1333).[89] The next day the meeting of the convention was broken up by the sheriff, and on the following day the Lord Provost issued a proclamation forbidding all assembling within his jurisdiction. A few days later Skirving was arrested, as were six other delegates to the convention.

Skirving, Margarot and Gerrald were tried, convicted and transported to New South Wales.]

107. Journal: LCS General Committee, 12–26 December 1793

Source: Add MSS 27812, fos. 81v–82v (later copies in Add MSS 27814, fos. 153–4)

General Committee Decr. 12th. 1793

On the Report from the Divisions of New Members it was found there had been an Increas of 24. –
Wm. Harrison Senr. elected Delegate for No. 3 in the Room of Cit Robt Chassereau having resigned.
Stephn. Wright elected Delegate for No: 11 –

Motions

The following Resolution was received from the Committee of Constitution Dated 11th. Decr. 1793 –
Resolved that it is so perfectly repugnant to the Principles of Liberty that Delegates should incur Expence in the performance of their; duty that they will not submit to the Practice, they have therefore adjourned to the 20th. day of this Month to give the General Committee an Opportunity of determining in what manner their expences should be Paid.
A. Beck. Chairman
The Committee then took the Report from the Divisions on this Subject, when it Appeared they were unanimously of Opinion, that their Expences should be paid. – when the Committee came to the following Resolution That the Members of the Committee of Constitution shall be paid their unavoidable

<hr>

88 The minutes of the convention are prefixed to the report of Skirving's trial in *ST* vol. 23, cols. 391–471.

89 Letters, Margarot to Hardy, 8 and 12 Dec. 1793, both in TS 11/956/3501.

expences, as soon as they can be audited by the General Committee

Resolved that it be recommended to the Society by the Committe of Delegates; to request the Constitutional Committee to Report Progress, each member in his respective division every Week.

No. 2. &. 6. United for the Purposes of Obtaining Universal Suffrage and Anual Parliaments by Constitutional Means.
We think it our duty and are determined to Support every – Member who in the peaceful Prosecution of such Our Object may be Prosecuted or any way Illegally put to trouble and that a Box be kept in every division into which each Member shall be requested to deposit weekly what he can conveniently spare for that Purpose – Referred to the different divisions with the Request of the General Committe to adopt the same Plan.

On a Motion made in the Committee the came to the following

Resolution that during the Continuance of Our delegates in Scotland no Subscription be opened in any division till that for the Delegates shall first have been brought forward and finally closed for the Particular evening.

Resolved that the thanks of this Society be given to Counsellor Vaughan for his able and Spirited defence of Citizen Briellat.

Likewise to Counsellor Erskine for his able defence of the Liberty of the Press, and the Printers and Publishers of the Morning Chronicle.[90]

Likewise to the twelve Honest Jurymen who tried that Cause.

Resolved that the above votes of thanks be published in the Morning Post, Morning Chronicle, and the Courier.

Resolved that £10. be sent immediately to the Delegates.

General Committee Decr. 19th. 1793

On the Report from the Divisions it was found there had been an Increase of 21 New Members

Motions

Nos. 11.16.25. that it be recommended to those members of this Society who have cards or Shopbills to have the hand in hand upon them. that they may be known to each Other.

It was by a Delegate suggested that very probably that this Committee or some of the Divisions of this Society might be by the arbitary and unconstitutional interference of the Majistrates disturbed[91] the following Members were therefore Appointed to Enquire and make a Report next Thursday in what manner we should conduct Ourselves on such an Occasion. Vizt. Citizens Thelwall, Stiff, Moore, Baxter, and Lovett. Citizen Isaac Purdie was sent as Delegate from Division No. 10

General Committee Decr. 26. 1793

On the Report from the Divisions it was found there had been an Increase of 15 – New Members

Citizen Thomas Raine was sent as Delegate from Division 23

Motions

That no member be qualified to be Elected a Delegate of this Society unless he has been a Member for the Space of Three Months referred to the Divisions.

90 On 25 Dec. 1792 the *Morning Chronicle* published as an advertisement a tame reform address from the Derby Society for Political Information. On 10 Dec. 1793 a jury decided that the printer and publisher of the *MC* were not guilty of political libel (*New Annual Register*, 1793, 'Occurrences'; *MC*, 10 and 12 Dec. 1793).
    LCS advertisement, dated 12 Dec., thanks both Vaughan and Erskine (*MC* 16 Dec. 1793, p. 1). Letters from Thelwall to each man personally convey the thanks of the Society (13 Dec. 1793, TS 11/956/3501). Erskine sent a polite reply (to Thelwall, 18 Dec. 1793, ibid).

91 'In the latter end of the year 1793 ... at one [public] house in the eastern part of the town, where a Division continued to meet, it was resolved to employ force for the purpose of dispersing them. This was accordingly done. Two PEACE Officers introduced themselves into their company, and after various endeavours to create a tumult by using provoking language, and repeatedly attempting to make false minutes, they seized on a respectable Housekeeper of the City of London, and a young Man who was a visitor at the Division, and dragged them to the watch-house: both of them were totally secluded from their friends, until the next day, when the former was discharged by the Magistrates, and the latter, although no accusation was made against either, was sent on board a Tender.
    'Threats were circulated that another Division, though meeting in a private house, was to be attacked in a similar manner. The Members therefore resolved to resist such illegal and unwarrantable proceedings, and agreed that at the next Meeting each of them should come prepared for his defence. One of them brought a Pike, with which he proposed to defend the Head of the Stairs; the other members contented themselves with Cudgels – but after waiting sometime the press-gang never appeared, and the pike and cudgels were never employed' (*A Vindication of the London Corresponding Society*, 1794, pp. 6-7).

Received the Report from the Special Committee Appointed the 19th. Instant respecting our Conduct in case of the Arbitary and *Illegal* Interference of the Magistrates.

Correspondence

Read Letters from Bristol, Wales, and two from the Delegates.[92]

[During the last week of December the correspondence from and about Edinburgh was more extensive than is indicated by the Journal for this week and the next. Skirving wrote to Hardy (24 Dec.) enclosing copies of his indictment and reporting the whereabouts of Margarot (East Lothian) and Gerrald (Perth). Alexander Scott, publisher of the reform paper, *Edinburgh Gazetteer*, wrote (24 Dec.) enclosing extra copies of his paper and offering the gloomy prophecy that both delegates would be found guilty, for – given the servility of juries – indictment has become synonymous with conviction.

Gerrald wrote to Hardy (n.d.) explaining why he had deviated from instructions by borrowing £15 from his friend George Mellis of Perth: he and Margarot believed

that one of them should return to London 'in order that a public and spirited attack should be made upon Dundas to give an account of the infamous and unconstitutional proceedings which have, of late, taken place at Edingburgh', but they lacked money for the journey.

Margarot wrote three letters during this week. In the first (27 Dec.) he expressed his belief that the proceedings against them would 'accomplish a reform or at least work up the minds of the people to the pitch necessary for effectuating it'. He dismissed the LCS request for an accounting of their expenditures: 'upon my word fellow citizens we have already more upon our hands than we can well manage without wasting time employed in business of much greater importance'. His second letter (29 Dec., a continuation of the previous one) asked the Society to deliver a letter to Lord Stormont in a public manner ('perhaps a procession of Members of the Society') and to have 500 copies made to be posted up about the town and sent to the newspapers. (The letter to Stormont protested the illegality of the impending trial.) Margarot also reported that indictments had been received for himself, Gerrald, Skirving, Scott and Callender and that Sinclair and Browne might also be indicted. The third letter (30 Dec.) enclosed his indictment, suggested that the Society have it printed (as they did), and asked Hardy to arrange the serving of subpoenas on the Duke of Richmond, Pitt and Dundas. Finally, Thomas Buckle wrote (30 Dec.) asking the fate of the £10 note which the Norwich societies had sent for Margarot.[93]

92 Bristol and Wales letters lost. Margarot's letters of 19 and 22 Dec. dealt with the receipt of a draft for 12 guineas and a £10 note (from Norwich), with Gerrald's impending return to London, with the request for more money, and with the need for action by the LCS: 'for God sake send forth some very strong Resolutions & above all talk of Impeachments & of Petitioning the King to remove from their Offices those persons who have thus violated the laws of the Realm.' The second letter was accompanied by a note introducing the bearer, William Moffat, an Edinburgh solicitor (to Hardy, both in TS 11/956/3501).

93 All addressed to Hardy; Gerrald's letter in TS 11/966/3510B, others in TS 11/956/3501.

1794A
(January-April)

Chronology

Oct.	16	Indictment of Franklow for treason	Dec.		Holcroft discharged
	21	Indictment of Spence for treason		1–5	Thelwall tried and acquitted of treason
Oct. 25–Nov. 5		Hardy tried and acquitted of treason		12	Hayward bailed
Nov.	4	Ashley discharged		13	*Politician* No. 1 issued
	16–25	Tooke tried and acquitted of treason		15	Baxter, Richter, Edwards and Williams released
Dec.	1	Bonney, Joyce, Kyd and		18	Franklow, Spence and Hillier released
				30	Parliament meets

108. Report from spy Lynam (government summary, extract), 1 January 1794

Source: TS 11/966/3510B

Thelwall's . . . Division has branched off into 2 others – one in Wapping damned the King – 2 or 3 going to recomend to them to be more guarded in their Expressions – The Delegates in Scotland are recalled – as they will have no Security afterwards for personal safety.

109. Journal: LCS General Committee, 2 January 1794[1]

Source: Add MSS 27812, fos. 82v–3v (later copy in Add MSS 27814, fos. 154–5)

General Committee Janry. 2d. 1794

The Production of the Delegates and Sub-delegates vouchers being the first Business they were given in as follows[2]

Division		Delegates	Sub Delegates
2	Citizen	Francis Dowling. –	
5	–	Davison –	
6	–	John Pearce –	
7			Richd. Chalk –
8	–	Harris –	Peacock –
12	–	J. P. Franklow –	Stephn. Bacon –
13	–	Thos. Harris Junr.	Richd. Stiff
16	–	John Baxter –	
25	–	John Thelwall –	
23		George Linam –	Oliphant
29		John Ashley. –	

The Committee being formed Reelected Thos. Hardy Treasurer and Secretary and John Pearce Sub Secty:

On the Report from the Divisions it was found there had been an Increase of 14 New Members –

Motions

It was moved and Carried unanimously to remove the Committee[3] as soon as the engagements of the Society would permit. –

It was moved and seconded that at the present crisis it is thought requsite to draw up on Thursday next and cause immediately to be advertized such Resolutions *as may best and most Constitutionally* express the Societies approbation of the proceedings of Citizens Margarott and Gerrald the Delegates of this Society and their disapprobation of the Interference of the Magistrates and their Steady Resolution to Support their Representatives.[4] this was unanimously Agreed to and

1 This is the last entry in the Journal. Before his arrest Hardy gave the Journal to John Pearce, who was to bring it up to date. When government began seizing the LCS papers Pearce handed it to Felix Vaughan for safekeeping. Hardy told the Privy Council that since Margarot's departure for Edinburgh the Journal had been 'very much neglected', that although he (Hardy) was nominally the secretary of the Society, Margarot 'did the greatest part of the business' (TS 11/963/3509, fo. 19v).

2 A government list of delegates for this quarter contains some differences: Div. 2: 'Wright aftds. Moore'; Div. 3 (listed twice): 'Jauncey – Richardson 30 Jan' and 'Jones Sub 6 Feb'; Div. 5: 'Davison – Belcher Sub'; Div. 7: 'J Williams 6 Feb. Chalk eld Del – & White Sub'; Div. 8: 'Dowling – John Harris 30 Jan; Div. 10: 'Purdy'; Div. 11: 'Wright – Gallant Sub / G. William Sub 6 Feb'; Div. 16: 'Baxter – 6 Feb. Blackburn – on B being elected of the Secret Commee'; Div 18: 'Lovett'; Div. 23: 'Lynam – Oliphant Sub / Picard'; Div. 27: 'Richardson 20 Feb'; Div 28: 'Dixon' (TS 11/966/3510B).

3 From 31 Old Compton St to 3 New Compton St. Thelwall had just moved his lectures to this address. When the lectures were disrupted in April, some wealthy supporters hired rooms for Thelwall in Beaufort Buildings in the Strand; and the LCS general committee began meeting there. Although the committee moved to New Compton St on 9 Jan. Hardy paid rent for 31 Old Compton St up to at least 12 Feb. when he paid £1 19s as rent from Christmas (Mrs Thelwall, *Life of John Thelwall*, p. 136; 'Information of George Williams', TS 11/957/3502; receipted bill, Add MSS 27814, fo. 162; see also p. 145 n. 131).

4 *MP* 6 Jan. 1794, p. 1. The plan to publish these resolutions antedated this meeting, for a draft of an advertisement expressing astonishment at the arrest and approbation of the delegates' conduct was dated 26 Dec. 1793 (TS 11/957/3502). Neither the draft nor the published document lived up to Margarot's demand for spirited resolutions and a petition for the removal of the magistrates involved in the arrest. The strongest resolution was the second: 'That the Proceedings of the Magistrates . . . *appear* to this Society highly illegal, and to demand the severest Investigation from every Lover of Freedom, and the British

Ordered to be printed in the Edinburgh Gazetteer, Chronile, Courier, and that 1000 of such resolutions be printed and distributed in Edinburgh.

On the Report from the Divisions on the Question of last Thursday which was to them referred. There Opinion was that no Member ought to be elected a delegate unless he has been a Member for the Space of 3 Months

The Committee Considering it necessary to have a General Meeting it was referred to the Divisions for their Approbation

Respecting a Public Dinner on That day[5] if so requesting them to nominate the Stewards and Report next Thursday –

Correspondence

Reced a Letter from Sheffield which was Ordered to be Answered immediately

Paid a draft to Mr. Miller [Mellis] of perth which he had advanced to Gerrald when there £15-0-0

110. Report from spy Lynam: LCS General Committee (government paraphrase, excerpt), 2 January 1794[6]

Source: TS 11/954/3498

14 Attended . . .

It was agreed to draw up a hand Bill approving of the Conduct of the Scotch Delegates & a Censure on the Magestrates & to distribute 1000 in Edinburgh   they were ordered to be printed immediately so as to be sent off if possible the followg. Night[7]

Constitution.' Margarot protested as soon as he received these resolutions: 'do you mean to stop there? You surely will not? – I recommended a Petition to the King for the removal of all these Magistrates previous to their impeachment' (letter to Hardy, 7 Jan. 1794, TS 11/966/3510B).

5 'The Committee considered it necessary to have a general Meeting of the society to consider of the Situation of their Representatives in Edinburgh and other important Matters and whether it would be proper to have a publick dinner on that day it being the Anniversary of the Society also' – later copy.

6 At Hardy's trial Lynam added that a letter from Sheffield was read describing a meeting attended by 2000 and 'recommending some spirited resolutions to be adopted to support the delegates immediately' (*ST* vol. 24, cols. 798-9).

7 This document did not appear until 20 Jan. when it took the form of an address to the people of Great Britain and Ireland. Lynam did not recall its

111. Trials of Skirving and Margarot, 6–14 January 1794

Sources: trials: *ST* vol. 23; letters: Ramsey to Hardy, 9 Jan. 1794, TS 11/966/3510B; Margarot to Hardy, 10 and 14 Jan. 1794, ibid; Hardy to Adams, 10 Jan. 1794, TS 11/951/3494; Hardy to Charles Cordrel (Norwich), 11 Jan. 1794, TS 11/953/3497

[The first two of the trials of the participants of the British Convention in Edinburgh took place in January 1794 and confirmed Alexander Scott's prediction that indictment was synonymous with conviction.

Skirving, tried on 6 and 7 January, was indicted for two offences, one of which was certain to bring a conviction if his participation in the British Convention did not: he was charged with circulating an address which had already been judged seditious – the July 1793 address of the Dundee Friends of Liberty, which stated the political evils of the times. Thomas Fyshe Palmer had been convicted of sedition for writing this address. The second prong of the indictment against Skirving was his participation in the British Convention as secretary. The government position was 'that the meeting itself, – that the whole proceedings of that meeting were, from first to last, illegal, seditious, and such as cannot be tolerated in any established government'. After his sentence of fourteen years' transportation was read, Skirving – often called 'Worthy Skirving' – reiterated his innocence and added, 'It is long since I laid aside the fear of man as my rule. I shall never walk by it.'

Margarot was to be tried two days later, on 9 January, but when he arrived in court, having been pulled in a chariot by crowds of well-wishers, he learned that the trial was postponed until the following Monday. The trial took place on the 13th, and on the 14th the jury returned a verdict of guilty and the judges sentenced Margarot to be transported for fourteen years.

Margarot was tried solely for his part in the British Convention and was convicted for an action - participating in a reform meeting - that was not considered an offence in England. Scottish law was different from and harsher than English law.

being read in the general committee (marginal note to paraphrase in TS 11/956/3501).

104

Margarot was not allowed to challenge jurors; his defence argument was labelled by a judge – in the presence of the jury – as 'sedition from beginning to end'; and a judge's known prejudice against him was dismissed as irrelevant (at a party a week before the trial the judge said of Margarot, 'what should you think of giving him an hundred lashes, together with Botany Bay'). Margarot's attempt to call as witnesses Pitt, Dundas and the Duke of Richmond was unsuccessful; according to the judges, Scottish law could not compel witnesses to come from England.

The prosecution stressed three points: (1) that the convention itself was illegal; (2) that the use of French words, the singing of French songs, the organization of the members into sections (as the French National Convention was organized) showed that the members of the British Convention were prepared to take all the measures of French revolutionaries; (3) that the resolution to appoint a secret committee which would call a convention of emergency under certain circumstances demonstrated that the convention had more sinister intentions than the proclaimed ones of obtaining annual Parliaments and universal suffrage.[8]

The LCS figured only briefly in the trial: in his defence speech, Margarot denied the identification of the LCS in the indictment as 'an association of seditious people'. He explained briefly (c. 100 words) the aims and organization of the Society. (It was not until the trial of Watt in September that Government developed the argument that the LCS directed the subversive activities throughout the kingdom.)

In London the Society printed Margarot's indictment and sent copies to (at least) the SCI and the Norwich societies. They agreed to pay William Ramsay to take a shorthand copy of the trial for publication. Little ineffective gestures, but all that the Society could legally and financially do when acting alone.]

8 The word *convention*, though common in the English language, had become fearsome to government after its use during the American War and the French Revolution. In both insurrections a convention replaced the established government. For a discussion of conventions as replacements for Parliament, see Terence Parsinnen, 'Association, convention, and anti-Parliament in British radical politics 1771–1848', *English Historical Review*, vol. 88 (1973), pp. 504–33.

112. Report from spy Lynam: LCS General Committee (government paraphrase), 9 January 1794

Source: TS 11/954/3498

9th. Janry – The Witns. [Lynam] was present at a Meeting of the Delegs. at No. 3 New Compton Street.

It was agreed there shod. be a Genl. Meetg. on the 20th. at the Globe Tavern in the Strand at 1 o clock to meet Gerald & to have a Dinner at 5 oClock – A Sub-Committee was appod. to arrange the Buss. for the Meeting consistg. of Thelwall, ffranklow & Stiff the Stewards were nominated namely Thelwall, James Agar the Counsel, Stuart Kyd, John Lovett, H. T. Harrison, Thos. Stiff, Barthw. Peacock J. P. Francklow, Thos. Harris, C. Sinclair J. P. Powell, Jno. Williams Thos. Mitchell, John Pearce Mattw. Moore, Williams Moffatt Delegate of the Scotch Convention and John Martin.[9]

Tickets to be 5/6 each for the Meeting & dinner – those who chose to be present at the Meeting only were to pay 6d. each for their tickets.

A Sub-Commee was also appod. on the Motion of Mr. Thelwall to draw up a Lre & send it to all the Societies to unite them all in one General plan of an Address to the public on the Subject of the invasion of their rights by the proceedings of the Magists. at Edinburgh & to discuss at the General Meeting the Conduct of Mr. Dundas.

The Witness thinks the Sub Commee named for this purpose are Thelwall, Baxter & ffrancklow.

Thelwall said it wod. be right in case any foreign troops shod. be landed or a Bill brought into parliament for suspending the Hab. Corpus Act proclaimg. Martial Law or preventing the people from meeting in Societies for Constitl. Informatn. to call a General Convention & the Witns. apprehends the resolutn. to that effect aftwds stated to have been passed on the 20th. Janry. to be the production of this Commee.

9 Advertisements and tickets for the dinner do not list as stewards Kyd, Mitchell or Peacock. Martin is listed on the ticket, but not in the advertisement (advertisement, *MC* 14 Jan. 1794, p. 1 and 18 Jan. p. 1; *MP* 14 Jan. 1794, p. 1 and 18 Jan., p. 1; ticket, TS 11/966/3510B).

113. LCS General Meeting, 20 January 1794: *Address to the People of Great Britain and Ireland* (summary and excerpts)[10]

Source: BL 8135.b.8

[The 1500 word address deplores the war with its loss of lives, its damage to commerce, and the increase in taxes. The situation at home is no less deplorable. The provisions of the Magna Charta and the 1689 Bill of Rights have been eroded by the practice of letting judges assess fines, by basing trials on a charge made by the Attorney General or an informer, by annulling verdicts of juries, by demanding exorbitant bail.

In Ireland and Scotland the right of the people to meet is threatened and attacked.]

Consider, it is one and the same corrupt and corrupting influence which at this time domineers in Ireland, Scotland, and England. Can you believe that those who send virtuous Irishmen and Scotchmen fettered with felons to Botany-Bay, do not meditate and will not attempt to seize the first moment to send us after them? Or if we had not just cause to apprehend the same inhuman treatment . . . should we not disdain to enjoy any liberty or privilege whatever, in which our honest Irish and Scotch brethren did not equally and as fully participate with us? Their cause then and ours is the same. And it is both our duty and our interest to stand or fall together. The Irish Parliament and the Scotch judges, actuated by the same English influence, have brought us directly to the point. There is no farther step beyond that which they have taken. We are at issue. We must now chuse at once either liberty or slavery for ourselves and our posterity. Will you wait till BARRACKS are erected in every village and till *subsidized* Hessians and Hanoverians are upon us?

You may ask perhaps, by what means shall we seek redress? . . . . THERE IS NO REDRESS FOR A NATION CIRCUMSTANCED AS WE ARE, BUT IN A FAIR, FREE, AND FULL REPRESENTATION OF THE PEOPLE.

J. Martin, Chairman.
T. Hardy, Secretary.

RESOLVED, that during the ensuing session of parliament, the General committee of this Society do meet daily, for the purpose of watching the proceedings of the parliament and of the administration of the government of this country. And that upon the first introduction of any bill, or motion inimical to the liberties of the people, such as, for LANDING FOREIGN TROOPS IN GREAT-BRITAIN or IRELAND,[11] for suspending the HABEAS CORPUS ACT, for proclaiming MARTIAL LAW OR FOR PREVENTING THE PEOPLE from MEETING IN SOCIETIES for CONSTITUTIONAL INFORMATION, or any OTHER INNOVATION of a similar nature, that, on any of these emergencies, the General committee shall issue summonses to the Delegates of each Division, and also to the Secretaries of the different Societies affiliated and corresponding with this society, forthwith to call a GENERAL CONVENTION of the PEOPLE, to be held at such place and in such a manner as shall be specified in the summons, for the purpose of taking such measures into their consideration.

Resolved, that the preceding Address and Resolution be signed by the Chairman, and printed and published.

[In addition to the *Address to the People of Great Britain and Ireland* and the resolutions, there may have been delivered a brief address 'to the various Patriotic Societies of Great Britain', written by Thelwall.[12] This speech attacked 'the conduct and principles of the present Administration', particularly 'the treatment

---

10 *At a General Meeting of the London Corresponding Society, Held at the Globe Tavern Strand: On Monday the 20th Day of January, 1794 Citizen John Martin, in the Chair. The Following Address to the People of Great Britain and Ireland, was Read and Agreed to*, 1794. According to Hardy, this was called Martin's Address (examination before the Privy Council, TS 11/963/3509, fo. 21). Thelwall reported that it was 'partly the Work of Horne Tooke & partly of the Citizen who has signed it as Chairman' ('Index to Thelwall's Papers', item 18, TS 11/950/3501). Hardy told the Privy Council that he paid Bailey £4 to print this address.

11 According to one member, this part of the resolution was founded on the apprehension of the LCS members that the Hessians and Hanoverians were to be brought up to suppress their meetings (examination of John Edwards before the Privy Council, TS 11/963/3509, fo. 202).

12 *Address of the London Corresponding Society, united for the Purpose of obtaining Universal Suffrage and Annual Parliaments, to the various Patriotic Societies of Great Britain*. Thelwall's authorship is indicated by such Thelwallian

of the several Delegates of the British Convention' in Edinburgh, and urged that the reform societies 'act with unanimity and concert' to investigate 'these circumstances'. The way to do this was to hold a convention: 'we have yet the *power*, in this or any other part of England to assemble, by a still more general delegation (and we recommend it to you to hold yourselves in preparation for such a measure, should it be found necessary) to co-operate in the constitutional measures of our Committee of Convention yet assembled. Exigencies may arise in which we ought not to trust to the slow, the precarious, and imperfect intercourse of epistolary correspondence.' The other societies were also recommended to send 'a *Remonstrance* to each of the three branches of the Legislature against the dangerous innovations which prerogative and ministerial artifices are making upon the *valuable parts* of our Laws and Constitution – the system of spies and persecutions – the usurpations of inferior magistrates -- and particularly the alarming transactions of the police and courts of law in Scotland.'

At the end of the printed copy of the speech is a resolution that 'a printed Copy of the above Letter be sent, without Delay, to the Secretaries and Chairmen of the respective patriotic Societies in Great Britain and Ireland'.

Whether this speech was delivered is uncertain. The spies did not report such a speech; nor was it mentioned at the trial of Hardy, where the LCS plans for a convention were detailed and where all the other addresses of the Society were read. On the other hand, the *Morning Post* reported that 'Thelwall moved an Address to the various Societies in Great Britain, which, after some trifling objection to some expressions, was carried'.[13]]

phrases as 'an infamous *inquisitorial system* of SPIES and INFORMERS' and by a letter of 23 January in which he avows his authorship ('Index to Thelwall's Papers', item 18, TS 11/956/3501; see also 'Index to Thelwall's Papers from No. 41 to the End', item 54, TS 11/951/3495).

13 21 Jan. 1794, p. 2. It is possible that the address was not read at the meeting but that Thelwall, expecting to read it, sent the newspaper an account of the meeting in advance of the event. Evidence of its not being read and approved is its absence from Place's extensive collection of reform publications, the list of which includes titles of all other LCS documents. The only copy I know of is at the John Rylands Library.

114. Report from spy Lynam: LCS General Meeting (government paraphrase), 20 January 1794

Source: TS 11/954/3498

20th. Janry – The Witns. was present at the Meeting at the Globe Tavern   he went there between 1 & 2 oclock into a Room up one pair of Stairs – the floor of which from the Number of people assembled gave way & the Meeting was adjourned to the great room above[14] – this occasioned a delay of ¾ of an hour & about 3 o Clock Martin Thelwall Richter Hardy & two other persons went into the Balcony which over looks the Room – The Shorthand writer who had taken down Margarots trial (Mr. Ramsey) read the Accot. of that trial – there was a general Conversation about an insurrection here, & Gerald say'd in Scotland they wod. soon break out.

Martin stood in the Centre of them who were in the Balcony & was considered as the Chairman.

The Witns. was not in the Room when he was called to the Chair being unwell & sometimes down stairs.

He heard Thelwall read the address to the Nation . . .

Martin put the Question on this address & almost the whole of the Meeting held up their hands for adopting it – there was no hand held up agt. it – . . . Richter, Thelwall & Gerald spoke

About 4 or 500 were at the Meeting & 170 stayed Dinner – Thelwall being in the Chair. . . .

115. Report from spy Taylor: LCS General Meeting, 20 January 1794[15]

Source: TS 11/955/3499

January 20th. 1794
Meeting of the London Corrg. Society at the Globe Tavern Craven Street Strand.

Mr. Martin by the appellation of Citizen was called to the Chair – He address'd the meeting in a short speech signifying the intention of calling them together for the purpose

14 According to Hardy, one of the principal beams in the floor broke and gave way about a foot; everyone fled the room; carpenters immediately put up temporary supports in the coffee room underneath; and the Society resumed the meeting (Add MSS 27814, fo. 69).

15 Taylor's reports, assembled by government and copied consecutively, are headed, 'State of John

of entring into several Resolutions that had been prepared and that then would be submitted to their Consideration[16] – these Resolutions were read by a young Man (whose

Name was Richter) standing next the Chair some Observations were made upon them by some persons whom I learnt were members of the London Corresponding Society and the Resolutions were loudly called to be repeated in consequence Thelwall arose read them again commented upon each and in very bold and strong Language recommended their Adoption adding that if Ministry attempted to land any Foreign Mercenaries or subsidized Troops then to repel by Force such innovation of the Constitution   These Resolutions were then put by the Chairman each singly and carried in the usual manner by a shew of Hands and most of them unanimous – there was computed to be 1000 persons present – five hundred of which partook of a Dinner provided for the occasion,[17] soon after the Cloth was drawn Thelwall took the Chair gave several republican Toasts one of which was the Rights of Man[18]   He also drank to the Scotch Delegates – Sung most of the Songs which he has since published and sold in the different Divisions and at his Lectures[19] – During the time of reading the Resolutions and conducting the Business of the day the Chair was placed in the Music Gallery in the large Room, and from whence Richter and Thelwall read the resolutions – Thelwall also threw several printed papers among the Assembly (I saw one in the hands of a Person next to me which I suffictly. noticed to be the same, as is intitled

Taylor's Account of the Proceedings of the London Corresponding Society and of Thelwalls Lectures from the 20th. Jany. to the 2d. May 1794'. At the end of the document are four pages of notes made during Hardy's trial, intended to refute doubts which the defence counsel cast on Taylor's evidence. Some of these notes assert the accuracy of his reports: 'These are Minutes he has been speaking from. . . . Minutes made next night or follg Morning   These are Copies from the origl. Minutes – exact Copies. Copies from Original Minutes – made immly   First made rough Minutes & then Copied from Rough Minutes in the Course of the day   In sense & substance & in words they were.' Taylor's veracity had been challenged by the defence who revealed, on cross-examination, that Taylor had used another name and that he was a bigamist.

Taylor was revealed as a spy when he testified at the trial of Robert Watt in Edinburgh on 3 Sept. Asked about his notes, Taylor testified he did not take the notes during the meetings (that was not allowed), but he sometimes went from a meeting to a coffee-house to do so (ST vol. 23, col. 1238). At the trial of David Downie two days later, Taylor said he made his notes regularly after he came home (ST vol. 24, col. 24).

At Downie's trial Taylor said that Samuel Webb had urged him to attend this meeting (on 20 Jan.) and to become a member. 'I became a member of the London Corresponding Society for no other purpose but amusement. I had no other view; no view to give information of what passed there' (cols. 24–5). Taylor was soon spending four nights a week at his spying – two at division meetings and two at Thelwall's lectures.

16 Martin also read them a letter from Margarot (as he reported to Margarot): 'When I read your Letter to the General meeting I could see the Tear starting in the Eyes of the honest men to whom it was addressed and the succeeding groans helped to relieve their swoln hearts' (letter, 22 Jan. 1794, TS 11/966/3510B). The letter read was probably that of 14 Jan. in which Margarot reported the outcome of his trial and exhorted the Society: 'Fellow Citizens, with fidelity I have fulfilled the trust You reposed in me   with undaunted firmness I have encountered every Danger   I am willing to encounter every hazard in the service of Mankind – chearfully have I done this and will continue – but I must now call upon You for the performance of Your duty – I do not point it out to You – Your hearts will instruct You sufficiently how to act – adieu remain assured that I am & will be always the same.' A letter from Margarot on 17 Jan. was less likely to evoke tears and groans, for it dealt with Ramsay's copy of the trial and with the popularity of Margarot and Skirving ('even the Ladies condescend to visit us') (to Hardy, ibid.).

17 Between Lynam's estimate of 170 at the dinner and Taylor's of 500 are James Davidson's of 300 and Hardy's of 400. The dinner tickets cost 5s 6d including wine at 2s 6d per bottle, and the dinner lasted from about 6 to 10 p.m. (Davidson's testimony at Hardy's trial, ST vol. 24, col. 440; Add MSS 27814, fo. 73). LCS records do not show receipt of more than £15 for tickets – perhaps a deficiency in Hardy's book-keeping rather than in the members' payment. The room rental and dinner cost the Society £71 4s 6d (records of tickets, TS 11/959/3505; receipted bills, Add MSS 27814, fos. 157–8).

18 The seventeen toasts included ones to the British Convention, the LCS, Margarot, Gerrald, Hamilton Rowan, Muir, Palmer, Paine and John Frost; to the apostates from liberty: Lord Loughborough, the Earl of Moira, and Sir Gilbert Elliot; to the transactions at Toulon; to the arms of freedom; to all that is good in every constitution; to peace with France; to the starving manufacturers and neglected peasantry of Great Britain and Ireland; and to citizens now in prison for matters of opinion.

19 Three of the songs are printed in Thelwall's Life (pp. 445–51): 'News from Toulon; or, the Men of Gotham's Expedition', 'A Sheep-shearing Song', 'Britain's Glory; or, the Blessings of a Good Constitution'.

the address and Resolutions of the London Corrg. Society one of which I obtained on the 23d. Instant from the House of Mr. T. Hardy Secretary to the Society.

116. Report from spy Lynam (excerpt): 23 January 1794 [20]

Source: TS 11/958/3503

Sir –

. . . . Gerald & Sinclair say that an insurrection will take place very soon in Scotland –

It is very doubtful whether Gerald returns to Scotland or not [21] –

Many of the Company are sure violence will [be u] sed very soon – . . . .

20 Address: 'E. Nepean Esqre / Whitehall'. Government description: '23 Jany. 1794. / Mr. Lynum'.
21 An undated and unsigned remonstrance to Gerrald expressed the fear that he might jump bail: 'The undersigned Members of the London Corresponding Society alarmed at the Appearance of Citn. Gerald's Reluctance to return to Edinburgh have convened for the purpose of taking that Circumstance into Consideration: – They are decidedly of Opinion that if He should avoid his Trial in Edinburgh it would materially injure the Cause of Liberty tend directly to encourage future Prosecutions & set an Example of timidity. . . . He could be of no service to the Society . . . . the unwillingness of many persons at the general meeting for his return is a strong argument for his going since it shews that if he goes with manly resolution to brave his fortune that there is an enthusiasm of attachment . . . which . . . might be productive of the most fortunate consequences' (ms marked by government, 'apparently in Thelwall's hand'; written between general meeting of 20 Jan., to which it refers, and Gerrald's departure on 26 Jan.; TS 11/956/3501).

Among the friends urging escape was his former schoolmaster, Dr Parr, who recommended this course as late as the night Gerrald set off for Edinburgh (*Memoirs and Trials of the Political Martyrs of Scotland; Persecuted during the Years 1793 and 1794*, 1837, p. 30). According to Thelwall (or Mrs Thelwall) when several friends offered to pay the amount of the bail if he would escape, Gerrald 'resolutely refused' (Mrs Thelwall, *Life of John Thelwall*, p. 124n). The pressure to return came not only from the LCS but from his friend William Godwin, who wrote: 'Your trial, if you so please, may be a day such as England, and I believe the world, never saw. It may be the means of converting thousands, and progressively, millions, to the cause of reason and public justice' (letter, 23 Jan. 1794, quoted by Charles Kegan Paul, *William Godwin: His Friends and Contemporaries*, 1876, vol. 1, p. 126).

117. Report from spy Lynam: LCS General Committee (government paraphrase), 23 January 1794 [22]

Source: TS 11/954/3498

23d. Janry – The Witness was present at the Meeting of Delegates at No. 3 New Compton Street – It was reported that Gerald & Sinclair were to set off for Scotland the next Evening

There had been a Box at the Meeting on the 20th. Janry for Subscriptions for the Scotch Delegates which it was proposed to open at this Meeting – It was opened accordingly & £13 . . 4 . . 5 found in it [23]

It was proposed to publish the Names of those who had given Evidence agst. the Patriots but opposed by Thelwall as it might lead to Massacres

It was ordered that each Division shod. chuse 2 Sub Delegates to constitute with the Delegates a perpetual Commee to watch Parliament every night & all to meet every Thursday – but the proposal for Sub Delegates was not carried [24]

Thelwall proposed that 100.000 Copies of the address to the nation voted on the 20th. Janry shod. be printed & distributed by the society which was carried

Thelwall also proposed that the Toasts Drank at the Meeting should be printed at the end of the Address which was also carried

[According to an advertisement in the newspapers, the general committee met this day (Friday) in pursuance of their resolution at the general meeting to meet every day during the present session of Parliament. They resolved to publish Stanhope's

22 In his testimony at Hardy's trial, Lynam added one item not found in this paraphrase: 'It was recommended that hand-bills be stuck up in all parts of London, saying what grievances we wish to redress' (*ST* vol. 24, col. 802).
23 'and there were nine bad shillings in it' (Lynam's testimony). Martin, in his letter to Margarot, indicated that their financial troubles were ended: 'though I at one time dreaded the want of money, yet that is now over – Those who opposed the Subscription at first are now putting their hands to the very bottom of their pockets and swear by God you shall be supported with the last Guinea – We must have another General Meeting in a Chapel or some large place and declare the purpose of a Subscription & I think we shall get plenty of the needful for that & other purposes.'
24 However a committee of delegates was chosen. Lynam did not recall whether the motion that the committee be perpetual was carried.

speech in the House of Lords on 23 January and to advertise their approbation of him.[25] They also voted to sent the SCI copies of 'their Late publications', presumably the address(es) and toasts given at the general meeting and dinner.[26]]

118. Report from spy Taylor: LCS Division 2, 27 January 1794

Source: TS 11/955/3499

January 27th. 1794.
Meeting of the London Corrg. Society
No. 3 New Compton Street
Second Division

I was introduced by a Member proposed and seconded went thro' the usual Ceremony and was admitted as a member of the L. C. Society – the Resolutions that had been put and carried at the General Meeting the Monday preceeding being the 20th Inst. were printed and delivered to the Members by the Secretary T. Hardy.

119. Report from spy Lynam: LCS General Committee (government paraphrase), 30 January 1794[27]

Source: TS 11/954/3498

30th. Janry – The Witness was present at a Meeting of the Delegates, at No. 3 New Compton Street

Wright Delegate of Division 11 proposed to arrange the Divisions according to their situations in the Metropolis that a Communication might be kept up with all parts of the Town[28] & this wod. be particularly useful in soliciting subscriptions for the Delegates as many might be inclined to subscribe who wod. not put down their Names as Members

This was referred to the Constitutional Committee

It was recommended that all the Members shod. subscribe a penny per Week for the Delegates

Thelwall proposed that there shod. be a permanent Committee of Delegates to consider of Measures to be pursued during the present posture of Affairs & to be a secret one – the places of those of the General Committee who shod. be chosen to compleat it to be filled up by other Delegates & the special Committee to have a Discretionary power either to report to the General Committee or not but the General Committee to have a power to dissolve them if they thought proper, The Secret Committee to consist of Martin Baxter John Williams Thelwall & Moore[29]

25 Advertisement, *MC* 29 Jan. 1794, p. 1; *MP* 29 Jan. 1794, p. 1. (The SCI also published thanks to Stanhope on 29 Jan..) Stanhope argued that British predictions about the military impotence of the French had not been fulfilled. He extolled the French constitution and ended with a motion that the king order·his ministers to acknowledge the French republic. *The Speech of Earl Stanhope, in the House of Peers, On His Motion to Acknowledge the French Republic. January the Twenty-Third, 1794. London: Printed By Order of the London Corresponding Society. 1794 (Price One Penny)*.

26 Letter, Hardy to Adams, 24 Jan. 1794, TS 11/951/3494.

27 At the trial of Hardy, Lynam gave further details of this meeting: 'the division No. 13 recommended that the delegates be instructed to advertise, and request a [sic] many spirited friends that do not belong to us to come forward and subscribe to the support of the delegates. . . . Division No. 8 in Rotherhithe, wished to know if they should remove into the Borough, having had a constable with them, many have lost their business, and are afraid of press-gangs. The next was the call of the house. . . . The delegates attended the call of the

house. . . . There was a letter from Margarot, but I have no memorandum whether it was read or not' (*ST* vol. 24, col. 803). Margarot's letter of 24 Jan. reproached the LCS for being less generous than Sheffield, discussed the proposed edition of his trial, and urged them to action: 'Armed Associations are I perceive now set on foot by the Rich – wherefore should not the poor do the same are you to wait patiently untill 20000 Hessians & Hanoverians come to cut Your throats? and will You stretch forth Your necks like lambs to the Butchers knife & like lambs content yourselves with bleating' (to Hardy, TS 11/966/3510B).

28 'The opening of those divisions was, to endeavour to have meeting houses all over London, of different divisions of the society, those that lived nearest to a place of meeting, it was recommended to them to attend at the meeting nearest to them, for the purpose of collecting friends round about near that place where that division met, and so all round London' (Lynam's testimony, *ST* vol. 24, col. 802).

29 'The secret committee was to consider of what measures were necessary to be adopted at that time, and so long as they should sit, according to the measures that were adopted in the House of Commons' (Lynam's testimony, *ST* vol. 24, col. 803). Between 27 January. and 15 April measures which might help Margarot and Gerrald (for his conviction was inevitable) were introduced and rejected in both Houses of Parliament. Robert Adam (on behalf of Muir and Palmer) tried to introduce first a bill to allow appeals from the sentence of the Scottish court of justiciary, then

This was carried unanimously

The Secret Committee was to have power to call the General Committee together whenever they thought it necessary at any time or place

This was also agreed to[30]

He then proposed that a Sub Committee of 3 should be appointed to consider of the best mode to increase the subscription for the Delegates in Scotland

This was referred to the secret Committee for them to act as they thought proper

The Letter from Bristol . . . was laid before the Meeting[31]

It was proposed by Thelwall That a Committee of Exigence shod. be formed of 2 Members from each Division who might consider what Measures were necessary & to Report to the General Committee but not to publish any thing – This Motion was withdrawn

120. Report from spy Taylor: LCS Division 2, 3 February 1794

Source: TS 11/955/3499

February 3d. 1794
Meeting of the London Corresponding Society
No. 3 New Compton Street.
2d. Division

Two Letters were read by the Secretary Hardy from the Corresponding Societies at Birmingham and Bristol thanking the London Corresponding Society for their Information and requesting their future Assistance adding that the Societies in Birmingham and Bristol increased rapidly.

121. Report from spy Taylor (government summary): 5 February 1794[32]

Source: TS 11/953/3497

5 Feb. – Taylor was present at a Meeting of the London Corr Society when Thelwall & others said they intended to rescue Gerald & Margarot[33]

122. Report from spy Lynam: LCS General Committee (government paraphrase), 6 February 1794[34]

Source: TS 11/954/3498

6th. Febry – The Witness [Lynam] was present at a Meeting of the Committee of Delegates at No. 3 New Compton Street

a bill to regulate this court; he and Stanhope and Lauderdale introduced bills to review the trials of Muir and Palmer. All were rejected. Sheridan was able to introduce a petition from Palmer, protesting the severity of his sentence, but that too changed nothing.

30 Lynam omitted that he made a motion to appoint two messengers to report the proceedings of the secret committee to the general committee. At Thelwall's trial, his counsel, Erskine, made Lynam admit not only that he introduced this motion but that he had brought two prospective messengers with him. With effort Lynam recalled that the motion was rejected because Thelwall said that it would be productive of much mischief ('Trial of John Thelwall', p. 34, in *State Trials for High Treason, Embellished with Portraits*, 1794).

31 On receiving a 'second epistle' from the LCS (now lost), the reformers at Bristol determined to reassemble the Bristol Society for Constitutional Information and to publish an address declaring their sentiments. The LCS letter quickened their courage, vivified their patriotism and roused them to resolution. Their numbers increased, and they anticipated that a 'third epistle' from the LCS might do great things. They ordered a dozen copies of the *Englishman's Right*, mentioned in the LCS letter (J. Lawrence to Hardy, 28 Jan. 1794, TS 11/966/3510B).

32 The TS papers are headed 'Index to Bundle J being General Papers of the London Corr. Society & the Society for Constitutional Information of 1794'. The transcript of Taylor's reports does not contain one for this date. This item is probably an account of a Thelwall lecture rather than an LCS meeting. The government compilation titled 'Persons agt. whom Taylor's Reports furnish Evidence' so presents it: '5 Febry/ Thelwall after his Lecture gave Wine to about 40 who stayed – it was discussed how to rescue Muir Palmer Margarot & Skirving on their Way from Newgate to the Transport' (TS 11/954/3498). This subject allegedly occupied Thelwall on 9 April when Taylor attended his lecture: 'One of the principal topics intended for Discussion that Day was a Plan to rescue the Scotch Delegates' (ibid).

33 Margarot and Skirving had been moved from the Tolbooth in Edinburgh to the *Surprise* at Woolwich. Gerrald was in Edinburgh awaiting trial, but it was certain he would travel south to a transport ship.

34 At Hardy's trial, Lynam reported some further details of this meeting: 'The first thing that was mentioned there was, that a letter was received from citizen Stiff with respect to his going down to Rotherhithe, on account of the society established there being disturbed. . . . Division No. 11, recommended the committee to consider of the situation of Hodson and his wife, he was put among the felons, and deprived of seeing his friends: this was sent back on account of the

It was Ordered that addresses &c. should be sent to Hereford Baxter & Thelwall proposed that the secret Committee nominated at the last Meeting shod. be dissolved as their Names were known to all the Delegates & might get abroad and that they shod. have a power of nominating a New Secret Committee whose Names by that means wod. not be known, the rest of the secret Committee were present & the General Commee adopted the proposal[35]

Hodgson produced sevl. printed Copies of the Report of the Committee of Constitution & sold them[36]

Hardy was directed to provide a short hand Writer to take down Gerrald's Approaching Trial[37]

123. Report from spy Taylor: LCS Division 2, 10 February 1794

Source: TS 11/955/3499

February 10th. 1794
Meeting of the London Correspondg Society
No. 3 New Compton Street
Second Division

The Report from the General Committee was read by the Delegate vizt. that 37 Members had been added to the Society in the Course of the Week that two Letters had been received by the Secretary Hardy one from Gerald[38] in Scotland and one from Hodson a prisoner in Newgate[39] from the first stating that his Trial was to come on the 17th. Instant (ffebruary) and requesting a short Hand writer to be sent to him and informing the Society that he had a fresh Bill of Indictmt. found against him, but that it differed only in the former one by an increase of its Stupidity, Hudsons Letter was a very seditious one, concluded with requesting from the Society assistance to Support himself and ffamily – Report was brought from the Committee of Constitution for the approbatn. of the Division consisting of the following proposal that the Secretary be ordered to issue new Books to the several Divisions for the purpose of entering the names & places of abode of the several Members, that on any Emergency they might easily be collected togr. Barnes the Keeper of the House in Compton Street Dowling in New Street Covent Garden & Eight other Members accompanied by Hardy the Secretary went

lowness of our funds, being obliged to support our delegates [in Scotland]. Motion from division No. 29, that the names of those who have subscribed for the distressed weavers be printed, and posted up; that was not carried. A letter was received in a parcel from Sheffield from Margarot to Hardy, dated the 7th of January. A letter from Sheffield, dated the 30th of January, Joseph Scofield the bearer, recommended to spend all his time in the societies' (*ST* vol. 24, col. 804).

35 Government was understandably interested in this secret committee. When questions about it were raised at Hardy's trial, John Williams was angry with Erskine (Hardy's counsel) for not letting him testify that the committee adjourned without doing any business ('Minutes of James Powel's Informn.', TS 11/958/3503).

36 See Introduction, p. xxvii.

37 'A letter was received from Gerrald, recommending them to send down a short-hand writer to take his trial. . . . It was mentioned that Mr. Ramsey charged forty pounds for taking Margarot's trial; Jenmins who was recommended cannot go. Sibley, in Goswell-street, to be applied to, to go down, and if he was not prevailed upon to go, Hardy should appoint somebody to go down' (Lynam's testimony, *ST* vol. 24, col. 804).

38 Letter lost. Two previous letters notified the LCS that Gerrald (with Charles Sinclair) arrived in Edinburgh on 29 Jan., two days late (as a result of the heaviest snowfall in many years) and narrowly escaped having the sentence of outlawry passed upon him. Since Sinclair did not receive money he expected, Gerrald paid all the expenses of the trip. In addition to being penniless, he faced a bill of £14 for his and Margarot's stay at the Black Bull. He concluded by wishing that each division would buy his book: 'they sell here like wildfire' (to Hardy, 27 and 31 Jan. 1794, both in TS 11/966/3510B. A letter from Sinclair to Hardy is on same sheet as first letter).

39 On 9 Dec. 1793, William Hodgson (Hudson, Hodson), a member of Div. 2, was sentenced to two years' imprisonment and a fine of £200 for seditious words uttered on 30 Sept. when he and Charles Pigott (of Div. 25) were in the New London Coffee House reading the newspapers and commenting on the news. Hodgson spoke of the king as a German hog-butcher who sold his Hanoverian subjects to his British subjects for £30 apieece; he also drank toasts to the French Republic and added, 'may it triumph over all the governments in Europe'. After the expiration of his sentence in Dec. 1795 he was detained in Newgate because he could not pay his fine (*ST* vol. 22, cols. 1019–32; Charles Pigott, *Persecution. The Case of Charles Pigott: Contained in the Defense He Had Prepared, and Which Would Have Been Delivered by Him on His Trial, If the Grand Jury Had Not Thrown Out the Bill Preferred Against Him*, 1793; William Hodgson, *The Case of William Hodgson, Now Confined in Newgate for the Payment of Two Hundred Pounds, after . . . Two Years Imprisonment on a Charge of Sedition, Considered and Compared with the Existing Laws of the Country*, 1796).

down to Woolwich to See Messrs. Palmer Muir Margarot and Skirving some of them with difficulty got on Board, Barnes reported to the Division that their Accommdns. were better than could be expected, & that he had reason to believe from some conversatn. that arose that the mate & all the Crew were Democrats a whisper went round to attempt some mode of rescuing them the Delegates from on Board the Transport, but no specific plan was adopted and it was in general thought impracticable, an observatn. was made by one member that Mr. Williams's plan was the best but on that subject no more was said –

124. Report from spy Groves: 13 February 1794[40]

Source: TS 11/954/3498

13th. Feby 1794

Sir

When I had the honour of writing you last I acquainted you that I had introduced myself to a person of the name of Jones, a White-Smith in St. Martins Lane near the Church – that he was a Clerk to a presbyterian Meeting in the Court in which I live & a Member of the London Corresponding Society – That I should through his means endeavour to become a Member of the Society held in Compton Street, & would inform further –

I have now, Sir, to inform you that Jones has fixed on next Monday Evening to introduce me there, & that he is to call on me at 7 oClock for that purpose –

The Steps, Sir, I have taken to bring this about are too circuituous to be communicated

by Letter, nor are they of importance enough, I shall only add that had I pressed it, or seemed anxious I should most likely have been disappointed.

But, Sir, his conversation of this day occasions my immediate address to you, as it seems sufficiently important to trouble you about

He told me that he is related to Mr Brellat, the pump Maker now in Newgate with whom, and the Revd. Mr Winterbotham,[41] he was the other day – He added that Orders were given in this Country for many thousand Daggers – & he pulld out his Rule to shew me the Size wch. was nine inches – that the intention of them was to be carried under the Coat, and that it was determined to put an end to Mr Pitt & all the leading Men on that side, but that it would not happen to day nor to morrow, but, in all probability in *Six Months time* – That there was a communication & a Correspondence carried on between some of the Members of the French National Convention, & the leading Members of the Conventions in England Scotland & Ireland – that Brellat had told him that "As to the *Girls*, poor Creatures, there would be no harm done to them, but as to the *Boys*, they must shift for themselves" – He laughed, I knew his meaning, & said directly in order to be sure I was right "It is very hard upon them indeed, for they go nowhere but from Kew to Windsor from Windsor to London & back again" – "That is what Mr Winterbotham said the other day," he replied, "they are denied the first Rights of Nature, Winterbotham loves a fine girl" –

He added also that Mr Winterbothams opinion was "that the people had began at the wrong end – that violent & *noisy* people wod. do no good but great harm to the cause – & that cool determined *acting* Men were the Men that were wanted, & that it was his (Winterbothams) Advice for the people to begin afresh –

He repeated his Assertion of the Daggers, & that I might depend upon it they were now making –

His conversation, which I turned occasionally, went to the proceedings in Scotland agt. Muir &c &c &c on which he inveighed with

40 Government description: '13 Feby. 1794. / Mr. Groves'.
    John Groves, of Crown Court, Russel Street, Covent Garden, was a conveyancer and a solicitor at the Old Bailey. A government summary of his evidence, titled 'John Groves will prove', gives his motive for spying on the LCS: 'conceiving it to be a dangerous Society he resolved to become a Member of that Society in order that he might watch their proceedings & report them to His Majestys Ministers' (TS 11/953/3497). At Hardy's trial Groves reluctantly testified that he attended the LCS, first at the general meeting on 20 Jan. 1794, at the request of 'a person high in office under his majesty', a 'gentleman' to whom he had been 'personally known' for ten years (*ST* vol. 24, col. 753). Hardy's counsel was not allowed to make Groves name this government official, but presumably it was Undersecretary of State Evan Nepean to whom Groves sent his reports.

41 William Winterbotham had been sentenced to four year's imprisonment for seditious statements in his sermons, e.g. the laws made in 1688 have since been abused; the English believe they live under a mild government, but they do not; the English have as much right to stand up for their liberty as the French did (*ST* vol. 22, cols. 823–908).

great acrimony – but his general abuse was too extensive to be minuted

His Brother was present all this time, who is a young man of about 20 yrs. of age & who said he was last Monday at the Society in Compton Street

Jones is to call on Me this Evening for another Job, but I thought his Conversation this Morning demanded my giving you an immediate account of –

I have no doubt Sir of finding out the true secrets of this horrid set by application & time, at which I must confess myself truly astonished – If you wish to see me be pleased to send me a line   I am Sir
                Yr most Obedt Servt
                J Groves

125. Report from spy Taylor: LCS Division 2, 17 February 1794

Source: TS 11/955/3499

Febry 17th. 1794,
Meeting of the London Corresponding Society
No. 3 New Compton street
2d. Division

Brooks in the Chair – The Sub-Delegate Pearse read the report from the General Committee namely, that 41 Members had been added to the Society in the Course of the week a Letter had been received from the Society at Sheffield thanking the London Corresponding Society for their informn. & for the several publicatns sent to them –

Richter rose to read a Motion from the Constitutional Committee appointed to form a New Constitution as follows, That the Secretary Hardy be directed to issue new Books to the sevl. Divisions for the purpose of entering the name & place of abode of each Member in order that an arrangemt. might be adopted for placing all those Members living in one Neighbourhood or District in one Book – so that by a reference being made to that Book they would easily be collected together on any Emergency   the emergency I understand to mean in case the Society met with any opposition from legal authority & that there should be Thirty Members to each Division the overplus when amountg to Sixteen to form a New Division the Question was put by the Chairman and by a shew of Hands carried unanimous – A Member of another Division attended to report that he had been informed that the

Habeus Corpus Act wod be suspended in the Course of this or the ensuing week, This gave Richter an opportunity in a violent speech to reprobate the Constitution & Laws of this Country & the administration thereof, advised each-Member to provide himself with arms & ammunition in order to defend himself against whomsoever he should be attacked whether of this Country, or that of Prussians, Hessians, or Hanoverians – Richter also distributed some Hand Bills containing some indirect reflections on their Majesty's – Similar ones of which he said had been distributed to the Public on their entering the Theatre this Night their Majestys being there. –

126. Report from spy Taylor: LCS Division 29, 18 February 1794

Source: TS 11/955/3499

Febry 18th. 1794 –
Meeting of the London Corresponding Society
Robins Coffeehouse   Shire lane
29th, Division, –

The Chair being taken Ashley the Delegate read the report from the General Commee which was the same as that given in the second Division the precedg. Evening   the Motion from the Constitutional Committee for issuing New Books was also the same & on the question being put was carried in the affirmative a debate took place between Thelwall and Hodson on the present existing form of Government in this Country which was violently Condemned by both, Hodson argued in favor of some System being requisite Thelwall against the necessity of any and his opinion was most applauded –

127. Report from spy Lynam: LCS General Committee (government paraphrase) 20 February 1794[42]

Source: TS 11/954/3498

20 Febry – The Witness [Lynam] was present at a Meeting of the Delegates at No. 3 New Compton Street

42 This is the last report from Lynam. The paraphrases which constitute 'The Evidence of George Lynam' end with an explanation:
    The Witness on Account of Indisposition was

The Delegate of Division 13 proposed that the reference of the Motion for a new Arrangement of the Divisions to the Constl. Committee shod. be rescinded & that the General Committee of Delegates should discuss it themselves

It was Ordered that Pearce shod. get the "Rights of Swine"[43] reprinted

Pearce proposed that a Committee shod. be appointed to revise & shorten the Society's Addresses & Resolutions as published in 1792

A Committee was also appointed to revise the Report of the Constitl. Committee to consist of Baxter, Moore Thelwall Pearce & Lovett

It was Resolved on Thelwall's Motion to print 50,000 hand Bills of Lord Stanhope's Speech respecting fforeign Troops & to return thanks to his Lordship for it[44]

not able to attend the next Week or the Week after – & still being under some suspicion notwithstanding his acquittal – as before mentioned – the Division No. 23 chose another Delegate in his Room & from that time he ceased to have any connection with the Society

A cancelled sentence in the version of this passage in TS 11/956/3501 shows his usefulness as a spy was over: 'the Delegates refused to admit him to one of the Meetings in March'.

43 'Rights of Swine; An Address to the Poor', by the Stockport reform society. Groves heard the address read at a meeting of Div. 2, probably on 25 Feb. (ST vol. 24, cols. 745–8).

44 On 27 Jan, the king announced that he had ordered a corps of hired Hessians, who were anchored off the Isle of Wight, to disembark (in order to prevent illness) and to be stationed at Portsmouth, the Isle of Wight and adjacent places. On 10 Feb. Gray brought to the Commons a motion that it was illegal to bring foreign troops to England without consulting Parliament (motion defeated 184–35). On the 19th Stanhope in the Lords also condemned the introduction of foreign troops without the consent of Parliament and recommended that if they were marched to any part of the kingdom the people should resist in the manner which the constitution provided, 'by forcibly seizing and arresting as the Law directs, the Traitor who should be guilty of such High Treason against them'. *The Speech of Earl Stanhope, in the House of Peers, on February the 19th. 1794. With the Resolutions of the London Corresponding Society theron. London: Printed by Order of the Society. And Distributed Gratis; MDCCXCIV.* The three resolutions approve Stanhope's conduct, urge LCS members to 'diffuse' the sentiment of the speech, and order the publication of 50,000 copies of it.

128. Minutes: LCS Committee of Constitution, 21 February 1794[45]

Source: TS 11/951/3494

Comee. of Constitution 21 Feby. 1794.
John Powell in the Chair
Pearce from the General Committee brought the following proposal verbally "That the Genl. Comee. had resolved that the plan of Constitution for the Society be revised by a Comee. of Seven formed in the following manner, – two to be elected by the General Comee. two by the Constitutional Commee. each out of their own body & three Members from the body of the Society to be appointed by the General Committee"

He said this motion had been Recommended by two of the Divisions. – He was then asked what number of Divisions had sent reports of their agreement to the organising the Society into Divisions of 30 each. – He could not tell. – The several delegates then present declared that No. 2 & 6, 4 & 5, 7, 13 & 30 had agreed to it. – That 12 had not decided & that the determination of 28 had been interrupted by a Riot made by Magistrates Runners &ca.

After complete discussion Richter proposed & Hodgson seconded the following motion

"That the proposal of the General Committee is without sufficient authority Unfair & altogether Useless & cannot be acceded to by the Constitutional Committee"

Which was passed unanimously, & was Signed & delivered to – Pearce as our answer. – Hodgson Moved & Arnold Seconded the following motion

"That the Organisation of the Society undertaken without authority by the Committee of Secrecy is a Gross usurpation & entirely foreign to the purposes for which they were instituted"

45 Government description: '21 Feb. 1794 / [at bottom of page] Walne'. The government index to Richter's papers (TS 11/951/3494) gives a précis of Richter's account of the committee of constitution and notes that a similar account was found in Walne's custody. Presumably this is Walne's version. Another (similar) précis of Richter's account is in 'Index to Bundle J being General Papers of the London Corr Society & the Society for Constitutional Information of 1794' (TS 11/953/3497). According to the précis of Richter's account, the committee of constitution made a Report which was published in Richter's divisions (2 and 6) on 10 Feb. 1794. The Committee discontinued their meetings, but on 21 Feb. they were called together again to hear Pearce's proposal for a new committee.

Resolved on the motion of Richter

"That we were appointed to frame a plan of a constitution for this Society to be laid before our respective divisions for their consideration"

Resolved therefore

"That any discussion or resolutions of any constituted body relative to this object are Factious & can only tend to *over awe* the opinion of our Constituents."

"Resolved that Divisions No. 1, 3, 8, 9, 10, 14, 15, 17, 19, 20, 21, 22, 24 & 26, if they exist (as has been reported) are unknown to this Comee."

Resolved therefore

"That Citizens Beck, Richter & Hodgson demand from the principal Secretary of the Society the places of Meeting of such divisions that this Committee may have *free Communication* with the whole body of this Society"

Resolved

"That if there are any divisions of this Society who have no delegates in this Committee it be recommended to such Divisions to appoint one to meet us for the purpose of Collecting the individual votes of the members of the whole Society upon each article of our Report & *that* the Discussion of it in that way do commence immediately in every division." –

Resolved

"That Such delegates be desired to call on Citizen Spence No. 8 Little Turnstile Holborn on or before Friday next at ¼ before 8 OClock & he will inform them of the place of Meeting of this Committee"[46]
Adjourned

Saturday[47] ½ Past Three oClock
Beck Richter & Hodgson called upon & saw Citizen Hardy the Secy. of the Socy. in consequence of the above 6th Resolution & demanded the information there stated. –
This he refused to give having as he said no orders on that Subject, altho he acknowledged that if any of us individually had asked him he would not have hesitated to inform us. –

46 Précis of Richter's account: 'Beck Richter & Hodgson were deputed to demand from Hardy the Places of Meeting of those Divisions that proposed a *new* Committee – *their* Delegates were to be desired to call on Spence – who would inform them of the Places of Meeting of *this* Committee.'
47 The next day, 22 Feb.

129. Report from spy Taylor: LCS Division 2, 24 February 1794

Source: TS 11/955/3499

February 24th. 1794.
Meeting of the London Correspondg Society
No. 3 New Compton street
2d. Division

The Chair being taken the Sub. Delegate Pearse, read the report from the General Commee vizt, that this Commee had recieved the report of the Commee of Constitution appointed to Organize the Society which in many Parts they disapproved & sent the following Motion to be put to the sevl. Divisions that two out of seven of the Committee of Constitution and a Delagate of each Division be appointed to revise & correct this New Constitution, the Chairman put the Question & it was carried by a shew of Hands in the affirmative – a Debate took place between Pearse and Richter the latter opposing the Motion avowing himself the framer of his new code of Laws and calling of [i.e. calling it] his legitimate darling child –

130. Report from spy Taylor: LCS Division 29, 25 February 1794

Source: TS 11/955/3499

Febry 25th. 1794
Meeting of the London Corresponding Society
at Robins Coffeehouse   Shire Lane
29th. Division

The Chair being taken Ashley the Delegate read the Report from the Genl. Commee verbatum as in the second Division of last night and the Motion for appointing two out of seven of the Commee of Constitution and a Delegate of each Division to revise & correct the New Constitution was put & carried in the affirmative without a Division   Saml. Webb was appointed Delegate.

131. Report from spy Groves: 26 February 1794[48]

Source: TS 11/954/3498

26th. Feby 94
Dear Sir
I am much concerned to learn that you are

48 Address: 'Evan Nepean Esqr / &c &c &c / Whitehall'. Government description: '26 Feby. 1794 /

confined through indisposition which I sincerely hope will be speedily removed

Since I had the honour to see you I have been at No. 4 Checquer Alley Bunhill Row, Moorfields, & I have also studiously & diligently applied myself to make myself acquainted with, & gain the good opinion of, Secretary Hardy which I shall, I doubt not, acquire.

I conceive it a proper mode of effecting what you wished – but I must submit that to you.

Last Night I was again in Compton Street – I have inclosed several papers for your convenient perusal.[49] – You need not return them as I have Duplicates –

The business of the Night was solely taken up upon the paper intituled the Report of the Committee of Constitution. I will not trouble you *now*, Sir, with the details – it would be tedious – I have made proper Memorandums of it – But there are certainly Cabals & Intrigues among them which seem likely to effect a good purpose.

As I am sure, Sir, it would not be perfectly right to frequently call on you, and as you told me that I should be supplied with what money I wanted I request the favour of Your Sending me by the Bearer a Draft for Thirty Guineas – I remain, Sir,

Yr. much obliged & Obedt Sert
J G

[At the meeting of the general committee on 27 February it was unanimously agreed to strike a medal commemorating the acquittal on 24 February of Daniel Isaac Eaton on charges of seditious libel for publishing an allegory by Thelwall in *Hog's Wash*.[50]

Mr. J. G. / Rx 25 / London Corresponding Society, / Meeting Checque Alley / Bunhill Row, Moor fields / (With four Enclosures)'.

49 One of these papers was the Stockport address, 'Rights of Swine'. Another was Stanhope's Speech of 23 Jan. 1794; a copy is marked 'In Mr J. G's of the 26 Feb 1794' (TS 11/954/3498). See p. 110.
50 Thewall's allegory deals with a despotic cock which was 'fond of foreign wars and domestic rebellions', which ate the greatest share of the grain and then kicked and cuffed the poor doves and pullets so that they could not eat the scanty remains his taxation had left. The speaker cut off his head and, when his trappings were removed, found him 'no better than a common scratch dunghill pullet' (*ST* vol. 23. cols. 1014–16). The

It was also resolved to publish resolutions expressing the LCS's approbation of Eaton's jury, the Society's belief that adherence to principles of reason and justice by juries does more to secure attachment to the laws than armies of Hessians and Hanoverians, and the intention to have the medal struck.[51]]

132. Minutes: LCS Committee of Constitution, 28 February 1794[52]

Source: TS 11/951/3494

Friday 28 Feby. 1794

Admitted	Citn. Higgins in place of Gimber from Divn. 13	
do	Citn. Webb from	29
d	Ward from	18
d	Jno Norman from	27

Reports

No. 2 & 6 Resolved that Comee. of Constitution ought to be dissolved & a new Committe appointed to revise their Report & both the Report & the revision to be laid before the Divisions—17 to 10—The New Comee. proposed by this Division ought to consist of one Delegate from every Division.—unanis: i.e = 27 —That the above proposals be Referred to the Divisions—unans: i: e = 27

No. 4 Agreed unanimously to *discuss our Report Themselves*

5 Voted for dissolution of the Constl. Comee. - but several Members afterward declared they had understood the question to go no further than superceeding their own Delegate for Neglect & appointing another - the erasement

LCS medal has the names of the jurors on one side and a figure of a gamecock on the other. Three silver medals were about to be sent to Eaton's counsel, John Gurney and Felix Vaughan, and to the foreman of the jury, Joseph Stafford, when Hardy was arrested and the undated drafts of letters to these men were seized by government (TS 11/966/3510B). The medals and commendatory letters were finally sent in mid-1795 (see nos. 274, 279, 284).
51 Advertisement, *MC* 8 March 1794, p. 1; *MP* 10 March 1794, p. 1.
52 Probably this is also Walne's account of the committee of constitution. See above p. 115 n. 45.

of their names was however refused by Chairman & Delegate.

No. 7 – Approved the Septemviri
11 & 12 – No Report
13 – Same as No. 4
16 – Same as No. 7
18 – Same as No. 4   25 agt. 1
23 – No Report
25 – Same as No. 7
27 – Same as No. 4   28 29 & 30 the same as

No. 4 – the last discuss[tear in paper] [a]rticles.

Citn. Spence informed that the following Question was referrd to the Divisions by the Genl. Comee. Viz "Whether the General Comee. shall be allowed to appoint Comee. of Revision"

Resolved that it be recommended to Dn. No. 30 to consider the Situation of Cn. Spence & Separate their Representation in this & in the Genl. Comee.

Resolved
1st That when this Comee. was instituted it was on the followg. principle, "That the actual Governmt. of any Society ought to have no Share in regulating or defining its own powers"
2d That the proposed Cee. of 7 or any other institution to be appointed by the Genl. Cee. would be directly Repugnant to the foregoing principle. –
3 – That the following Question be put to the Divisions. – "Shall the individual opinions of our Constituents on every article of our Report be collected by this Comee. or shall another Comee. of one delegate from each Division be appointed for that purpose agreeable to the proposal of No. 2 & 6?
4. That each Delegate Shall report the No. of votes on the foregoing Question both affirmative & Negative.[53]

133. Report from spy Taylor: LCS special meeting, 28 February 1794

Source: TS 11/955/3499

28th. February 1794
Meeting of a Select party of the London Corrg. Society at No. 3 New Compton Street at a Dinner provided for the purpose of turning to Redicule the fast appointed to be Observed by Order of Government[54]

About 20, persons present – John Williams of Leicester Square in the Chair, Eton and the foreman on the Jury on his Trial was present – John Williams read a private Letter he had received from Sinclair in Scotland Stating that he had demanded of the Court of Justiciary an Agent to plead for him on his trial – The Lord chief Justice Clerk ask't him if he could not find one in Edenburgh that would do   He replied that no one would Undertake his Cause knowing that if any Counsel there pleaded for a reformer he lost his employ – The Court desired him to try and let the Court know, he did and delivered several Letters in Answer to his Applications to persons to undertake his Cause – The Court then Ordered his trial to be deferr'd for a Fortnight in which time the Court would appoint one, which he (Sinclair) intended to reject[55] – Complained that he could not obtain Credit or Cash for any bill sent from London to him or that he drew upon London – John Williams said he went to Sir Robert Herries and deposited the Cash for a bill on a house in Edenburgh, but when it was known to Sir Robert Herries who it was for he refused it – George Williams of Smithfield who was present read a printed paper Intitled "For the benefit of the Tythe and Tax Club" which gained great applause – I understood it was the production of the constitutional Committee[56]   George Williams

53 Précis of Richter's account ends: 'Hodgson or Powell agreed to attend Divisions 2 & 6 – Richter Div. 5'.

54 In hopes of persuading God to reverse the trend of French military successes, the English were to spend the day in fasting, prayer, penance, dedication and solemn resolve.

55 With Henry Erskine and Archibald Fletcher as counsel, Sinclair went to trial on 17 Feb. Erskine advanced arguments about the relevancy of the indictment. The judges rejected the arguments (as they did at the trials of Margarot and Gerrald), but the court adjourned and the case was never resumed. Erskine attributed this satisfactory outcome to his insistence that Sinclair leave the defence entirely in his hands (Margarot had conducted his own defence) (*ST* vol. 23, cols. 777–802). Rumour attributed the outcome to Sinclair's agreeing to become a government spy (Lord Cockburn, *An Examination of the Trials for Sedition which have hitherto occurred in Scotland*, 1888, vol. 2, p. 4; *MP* 22 March, 1794, p. 3). This is unlikely as is the *Annual Register's* assertion that Sinclair's case was dropped 'on account of the imbecility of his mind' (1794 'Chronicle', p. 9). More probably, as the *Morning Post* maintained, a relative, Sir John Sinclair, 'made interest with the Government' in behalf of Sinclair.

56 A large handbill headed 'Amusement for starving Mechanics' and pretending to advertise a play, 'The Comical Tragedy of Long Faces', for the 'Benefit of the Tax and Tythe Club', it contrasts the 'Plunderers and Assassins' who call upon their Babylonian god 'to bless their Arms and sanctify their crimes' with the friends of mankind who

also read an extract from the Resolutions of the Society for Constitutional Information where they resolve speaking of the parliament to call it His Parliament meaning his Majesty the Chief Subject of Conversation was on the acquittal of Eaton, in which they greatly exulted the same Toasts were given and Songs Sung as has been related in former meetings – Thelwall acknowledged himself the Author of the libel of the Bantum Cock –

134. Circular letter: LCS to other reform societies, c. 1 March 1794[57]

Source: TS 11/953/3497; TS 11/954/3498 (printed copies)

CITIZENS!

THE critical moment is arrived, and Britons must either assert with zeal and firmness their claims to liberty, or yield without

resistance to the chains that ministerial usurpation is forging for them. Will you co-operate with us in the only peaceable measure that now presents itself with any prospect of success? We need not intimate to you that, notwithstanding the unparalleled audacity of a corrupt and overbearing Faction, which at present tramples on the rights and liberties of the people, our meetings cannot in England be interrupted without the previous adoption of a Convention Bill: a measure it is our duty to anticipate, that the ties of union may be more firmly drawn, and the sentiments and views of the different Societies throughout the nation be compared, while it is yet in our power, so as to guide and direct the future operations of

are desired to pray to the God of Elijah. At the bottom the the sheet is a poem ('Ye tyrants bend to Molloch's shrine', etc.) by Richard Lee, who printed it. George Williams, a member of Div. 2, saw copies of it at a division meeting a day or two before this dinner (examination before Privy Council, TS 11/963/3509, fo. 320). A month later, at the York assizes, a Mr Hardley was sentenced to two years in jail for publishing and dispersing the handbill (*Oracle*, 5 April 1794, p. 3).

57 The date of this important letter is uncertain. It must have been written after mid-Feb. when the secret committee was formed, for that committee wrote it. According to Hardy, it was printed by Bailey, copies were delivered to his house when he was out, and he did not know of their arrival until a fortnight later when the secret committee asked if he had sent them. His recollection (in May 1794) was that he sent them in Feb. or March (testimony to the Privy Council, TS 11/963/3509, fos. 34–5v, 54v, 214, 216). A correspondent in Strathaven wrote that the societies in his vicinity met on 1 April to act on the letter (Alexander Mitchell to Hardy, 9 April 1794, TS 11/966/3510B). This suggests March as the date of dispatch; so does Broomhead's testimony to the Privy Council that copies had come to Joseph Gales at Sheffield eight or ten weeks earlier than 29 May (TS 11/963/3509). Government was probably wrong in assigning early May as the date and a joint LCS–SCI committee as the author ('The King agst. John Horne Tooke for High Treason', TS 11/958/3504).

Hardy told the Privy Council that he sent copies to most of the reform societies (including a parcel of them to Sheffield and a single one to Norwich) and received replies from many. Only two answers exist. The reply from Strathaven

stated that reformers of Kilmarnock, Galston, Newmills and Dowill united with them to elect a delegate to the convention and a secret committee. The Bristol Constitutional Society asked for more details about the convention (John Cockburn to Hardy, 24 April 1794, TS 11/966/3510B. This may be a response to the mention of a convention in the printed proceedings of the 14 April general meeting; but, if these proceedings were not printed until the 21st, it is unlikely that the Bristol society were responding to them on the 24th).

The routes of this circular letter are indicated by George Ross of the Friends of the People in Edinburgh. He testified that he received six copies of this letter from a Mr Stock, a member of another reform society in Edinburgh. Ross sent one copy to Walter Miller at Perth, one copy to Strathaven, one to Paisley, and copies to other towns in the country (*ST* vol.24 cols. 840–1).

The failure of the spies to inform government of this letter suggests that it was not read at the division meetings. Two LCS members testified before the Privy Council that they had never seen the letter or heard of it (examinations of John Smith and George Higgins, PC1 22/A37). If the LCS members were not being canvassed about the possibility of a convention, the other reform societies certainly were, as the dissemination of this letter indicates. And Hardy closed a letter to Buckle of Norwich with the question, 'What think you of a convention?' (12 March 1794, TS 11/953/3497).

This circular letter is of considerable importance in showing the LCS acting as leader of the reform societies in England and Scotland. The convention proposed in this letter would have more urgency than the British Convention in Edinburgh in November and December. Since then the harsh sentences passed on the parliamentary reformers Muir, Palmer, Skirving and Margarot made it clear that the reform societies must take stronger action or else disband. Perhaps this need for more effective action explains why the LCS never sent the king their petition, for which they so assiduously gathered signatures.

the Friends of Freedom. Rouse then to one exertion more; and let us shew our consciousness of this important truth – "If we are to be beaten down with threats, prosecutions, and illegal sentences, we are unworthy – we are incapable of Liberty." – We must, however, be expeditious. Hessians and Austrians are already among us; and, if we tamely submit, a cloud of these armed Barbarians may shortly be poured in upon us. Let us form, then, another British Convention, We have a central situation in our view, which we believe would be most convenient for the whole island; but which we forbear to mention, (entreating your confidence in this particular) till we have the answer of the Societies with which we are in correspondence. Let us have your answer, then, by the 20th, at farthest, earlier if possible, whether you approve of the measure, and how many Delegates you can send, with the number also, if possible, of your Societies.

We remain yours,
in Civic affection,
The London Corresponding Society.
T HARDY, Secretary.

For the management of this business we have appointed a Secret Committee; you will judge how far it is necessary for you to do the same.

135. Report from spy Taylor: LCS Division 2, 3 March 1794

Source: TS 11/955/3499

March 3d. 1794
Meeting of the London Correspondg Society
No. 3. New Compton Street
2d. Division

Moore in the Chair – The Report from the General Committee was read from the Chair[(] The Delegate not being present) vizt. that they had Ordered an Advertizement to be inserted in the Morning Post and every other paper that would   Admit it testifying the Societies Approbation of the Conduct of the Jury who so honorably acquitted D. I. Eaton, and that the Society had voted a Silver medal to be Struck and presented to each of them with their Names on one side and a Bantum Cock on the other – Hodson of Westminster one of the Committee of Constitution attended in Order to Support the Report of the new framed Constitution and to oppose the motion of a Committee of Revision being appointed a long debate took place between him and Moore, Hodson Argued that it was unfair to Condemn the work till each Section had been

read to the division And put several Motions to this Effect, but they were all negatived (In the Course of his Argument he observed that many of the Sections had the Approbation of Margarot and that they were suited to the Exigence of the times[)] the Original Motion therefore stood for a Committee of Revision –

136. Report from spy Groves: LCS Division 2, 3 March 1794[58]

Source: TS 11/954/3498

Reports of the proceedings of the Division of No. 2   Compton Street

Monday   March 3d. 1794.
Citizen Moore, Chairman

The Delegates (two) from the Division No. 6 attended in order to make known the Report of the Committee of Constitution & take the sense of the Division No. 2 on the Same.

The Report being made, vizt., that the Committee of Constitution had fulfilled their Mission by drawing up & distributing to the different Divisions the Laws and Regulations for the better government of the Society, the Delegates attended to know the Sense of the Division No. 2.

A Citizen moved first, that the Delegates having fulfilled their Mission, & drawn up their report, & distributed the same to the different Divisions the Committee of Constitution be *dissolved*.

This was violently opposed by One of the Delegates who insisted that their business was to know, first, whether the Division accepted or rejected the Constitution.

The Chairman replied that with regard to the Rejection or Acceptation of the Form of Laws proposed by the Commee it was a question of another Nature – that if the Committee wanted to *Cram a Constitution down their throats*, they were greatly mistaken – the Committee were charged to draw up Laws – they had done so – they had submitted those Laws to the different Divisions – and the Committee were dissolved & that they had nothing further to do –

After several spars between the two Delegates & the Chairman & others the Question was put, "Whether the Committee of Constitution having performed their Duty be discharged? this was carried by 26 to 4 –
NB.   The Mode of holding up hands pro & Con.

58 Government description: 'Groves's / Report of the London Corresponding Society / 3d. March 1794'.

Another Member proposed that as the Report consisted of 203 Articles, & it might be reduced to the first & last figures, omitting the 0 that there be a Commee of Revision to correct the Report & reduce it to the Standard of Common Understanding

It was urged by One, who was for the Standing Committee that the Report ought to be Revised by that Committee

To this it was answered that the plan would be fruitless as the Commee were too fond of their brat, & ought not to have the nursing it – NB – From the whole of what was said it plainly appeared that there was a Jealousy subsisting between the leading Members of that Division, & the Committee of Secrecy, who had planned the idea of a Constitution & a Committee of Constitution, consisting of a Delegate from each Division to form it.

The private grounds of that Jealousy I am still unacquainted with, & therefore, in order to get at it, & obtain confidence & as I thought it a good opportunity, I moved "That as the Committee of Constitution were, by the Vote of this Division, dissolved, That *two* Delegates from each Division be appointed to reduce the Report of the Committee of Constitution & bring it more to the Standard of our Common Understanding it being too voluminous & complex.

This Motion was seconded & then put by the Chairman, who, by winks & nods highly approved of it. It was carried 19 to 10 –

The Meeting then broke up & several of us adjourned to an Opposite Public House, where Citizen Moore joined me, and expressed his Satisfaction at the Motion, which he said, went to let the Committee know that the Divisions, who created them, were a power superior to them, & that if a delegated authority wd. perpetuate itself, there was an end to the great body of the Society –

Citizen Jefferies, a Journey Coach, maker, upwards of 50, whom I have known many years, told me, that he should propose me as one of the new Delegates of Revision, & said somethings to me, of what he had informed several of the Divisions about my Abilities, which I wish not to repeat – Jefferies is a Milk & Water Character & one on whom I can easily play –

The principal leaders in this Division are
T. Hardy   the Secretary – Shoemaker
    No. 9 Piccadilly
_____Pearce   an Attorney
Wm. Moore   Taylor   Princes Street
    Leicr. fields
_____Jones   Whitesmith   St. Martins
    Lane   near the Church

_____Green   perfumer   Orange Street
    Leicr. fields
All Housekeepers

The Character of Mr Moore seems to me to be of a very dangerous cast – He has abilities. He is a close Reasoner, he is perfectly cool, & his manner conciliating – He seems to be a Man whom no harsh Language or indecent appellation can irritate, as he always parries it with a smile – And, I am greatly deceived if he is not as determined as he is cool – But there is a shrewdness, a subtlety & craft about him, that renders him a character only to be got at by Sass

There is more peril in this Man than in any promiscuous Hundred

Hardy is a very reserved character – seldom speaks but to business points, & that concisely –

I made an observation of this to Jones who told me there was a reason for it – He is a public marked Character by Government, & has recd. particular advice to say little

Mr. Pearce is without abilities – He is an affable man – He had Blackstone's Commentaries under his arm, & told me he thought he should have had an occasion to make a quotation or two for the instruction of the Citizens, respecting the power's of Bodies who *create* & the Subordination of the *Created*, but that my Motion had prevented him –

Hardy is just returned from Portsmouth where he has been on a *Delegation* to Citizens Muir &c &c. on board the Transport

I will endeavour to know his errand   All I can at present learn is that the prisoners, except Muir who is very dull & pensive, are exceedingly merry, & well treated by the Captain

I had this from Green Yesterday – I endeavoured to sound Green to know if he was acquainted with the purpose of Hardys Visit, – by saying "I hope for the Honour of all the Societies they (the prisoners) will not Petition for Mercy"

It struck me that that might have been the Errand – Green only said

"I dare say that that will not be the Case"

137. The trial of Gerrald, 3–14 March 1794

Source: ST vol. 23, cols. 803–1012

[Gerrald was tried for sedition in Edinburgh on the 3rd, 10th, 13th and 14th of March, 1794. Like Sinclair he had difficulty finding in Edinburgh counsel willing to represent him. On the 3rd he asked the court to appoint counsel for him. On the 10th he and his counsel protested against the partiality of the Lord Justice clerk (who favoured public whipping of reformers and who stated that 'the mob would be the better for the spilling of a little blood') and the relevancy of the indictment. Their arguments were rejected.

On the 13th the jury was selected (as in Margarot's trial, and all Scottish trials, the defendant was not allowed to challenge jurors). The arguments of the prosecution were the same as those advanced against Margarot – the illegality of the speeches at the convention, the seditious implications of organizing the convention the same way the French did, and the revolutionary conclusion to be drawn from the appointment of a secret committee. As at Margarot's trial, the reformers' aims of annual parliaments and universal suffrage were dismissed with contempt.

In his excellent defence speech, Gerrald argued that the constitution had frequently been changed and that the most important changes in history were innovations – the revolution of 1688, the Reformation, even Christianity. Here the Lord Justice clerk interrupted: 'You would have been stopped long before this, if you had not been a stranger. All that you have been saying is sedition; and now, my lords, he is attacking christianity.'

The jury returned its verdict of guilty the next morning, 14 March, and the judges (who had also presided at Margarot's trial) passed the expected sentence of fourteen years' transportation.]

138. Report from spy Taylor: LCS Division 29, 4 March 1794

Source: TS 11/955/3499

March 4th. 1794.
Meeting of the London Correspondg. Society at Robins's Coffeehouse Shire Lane – 29th. Division

Palmer in the Chair Ashley the Delegate – Read the Report from the General Committee which was the same as that read in the Second Division the preceeding night – A Motion was made by the Delegate that only seven should sit at one time in the Committee of Revision

which on the Question being put was carried by a shew of hands unanimous.

139. Report from spy Taylor: LCS Division 2, 10 March 1794

Source: TS 11/955/3499

March 10th. 1794
Meeting of the London Correspg. Society at No. 3 New Compton Street

Le Maitre in the Chair – Pearse the Sub-Delegate read the Report from the general Committee vizt. That 27. New Members had been added to the Society in the course of the week, the Resolutions past at the last general Meeting had been reprinted with the Addition of some of the Resolutions past at the Society for Constitutional Information and His Majesty's speech on the Opening the Sessions of Parliament the Secretary (Hardy) destributed them also a paper Containing Lord Stanhope's speech and the London Corresponding Society's resolutions upon it (they are here inclosed) the appointment of a Delegate to the Commee of Revision was confirmed and Moore was chose for this Division –

140. Report from spy Taylor: LCS Division 29, 11 March 1794

Source: TS 11/955/3499

March 11th. 1794.
Meeting of the London Corresponding Society at Robins Coffee House, Shire Lane

The Chair being taken Ashley the Delegate read the Report from the General Commee the same as in the Second Division of the Preceeding Night – Some very violent Persons present who gave toasts and sung Songs of a very treasonable tendency – One person drank a Speedy Guillotine to the King meaning his Majesty but I could not learn his name –

141. Report from spy Taylor: LCS Division 2, 17 March 1794

Source: TS 11/955/3499

March 17th. 1794.
Meetg of the London Correspondg Society No. 3 New Compton Stt

Dark in the Chair – The sub-Delegate Pearse read the Report from the General Committee Vizt that 34 Members had been added to the Society in the course of the last Week some Motion had passed in the General Commee relative to the new form of Constitution as framing in the Committee of Constitution   a Motion was also made and carried that two additional silver Medals should be made (making in all fourteen) and presented to Messrs Vaughan and Gurney   D.I. Eatons Counsel as a Mark of the L. C. Societys approbation of their abilities the Committee of Secrecrecy was ordered to draw up an address to Margarot to express the Londn Corresponding Societys sentiments of his virtue and patriotism and to condoul with him in his unhappy situation[59] which was done and signed by Thelwall as Chairman of that secret Commee and ordered to be inserted in five papers Vizt. Morning Post Morning Chronl. Evening Courier, Star, & any one other paper that would admit it which also had been done The Secretary (Hardy) read it from the Morning Post to the Division and it met with great applause   He also read an Advertizement or Address to Mr Whitbread Junr for his motion on Thursday last in the House of Commons on the subject of foreign Treaties[60] which had

been ordered to be done by the General Committee and inserted in the above named papers a Letter had been received from Gerald in Edinburgh by the Secretary (Hardy) addrest to the London Correspondg Society informing them of his Conviction and Sentence by the Court of Justiciary the court he observes was much crouded, He will not say a Court of Justice but an Assembly of Men met to pervert all Justice   He continues that the Court was severe upon him of course he retorted and told the Court he rejoiced in his Sentence to go and Join his Patriotic Colleagues that Botany Bay was better than England or Scotland where all liberty and Justice was fled, He remarks that his good Conduct had gained him the favourable opinion of all Scotland and that since his Conviction he had been visited by the most respectable people there and had had the most generous offers made him even from Men of different political sentiments   the Secretary (Hardy) had received him from the Corresponding Society at Sheffield a Letter with a Pamphlet inclosed intitled "If the Cap fits you wear it, or a Lecture on the ffast Day Febry 28th Ultimo", with several Resolutions of the Society there annext to it[61] The Letter mentions that this Lecture was delivered to 5000 persons in an open ffield   The Secretary (Hardy) read the Resolutions annext to this Lecture, the Lecture was also read met great applause & was desired to be printed for the Use of the London Corresponding Society.

142. Report from spy Taylor: LCS Division 29, 18 March 1794

Source: TS 11/955/3499

March 18th. 1794
Meeting of the London Corrg. Society at
Robins Coffee house   Shire Lane
29th. Division

59 The 'Address from the London Corresponding Society, to their Delegate Maurice Margarot' is an extravagant paean: 'our hearts are still glowing with all the love and veneration of filial remembrance, for one whom we cannot but consider as a generous and affectionate Parent . . . who in this last instance of personal sacrifice, like the Pelican in its nest, seems to be so cheerfully nurturing his beloved Progeny with the Blood from his own Bosom. If Patriot virtue ever in this degenerate age made its appearance upon earth, it was surely in thy person', etc. (*MP* 17 March 1794, p. 3). Margarot replied in a vein almost equally lofty: 'You do me justice dear Friends, it was for you that I combatted; it was for you that I fell; but in falling I have opened to you the road to victory. Pursue then, dear associates, continue the conflict with redoubled energy, and be assured of success' (letter, to the LCS, 27 March 1794, *MP* 7 April 1794, p. 3, *MC* 7 April, p. 3).

60 *MP* 17 March 1794, p. 1. Whitbread's 'motion to petition the king to endeavour to extricate himself from the different engagements entered into with foreign powers so detrimental to the interests of this Country' (as the *Senator* summed up the seven-paragraph motion) was defeated 26 to 138 on 6 March (no. 9, p. vii). The LCS resolutions thanked Whitbread for his motion, which exhibits 'one of those rare specimens of Integrity and Independence' in the House of Commons; called attention to his sentiments (a) that the abuse bestowed on the French is like that used to 'the best men in all Ages when their conduct was displeasing to those against whom they acted', and (b) that 'the Tyranny in France . . . was the consequence of the Combination formed

by the Oppressors'; and stated their belief that the people of England should 'reflect upon the best Methods for procuring a speedy and honourable Peace'.

61 *A Serious Lecture delivered at Sheffield. Feb. 28th, 1794, being the Day appointed for a General Fast* states that truth has always met opposition when it clashed with the interests of kings, courtiers and priests. The speaker believes there is now a combination of kings apparently leagued against the cause of freedom, 'a combination which I believe is Odious in the sight of Heaven'. The ten resolutions deplore war and fasts to further war and give thanks to Stanhope and Sheridan (*ST* vol. 24, cols. 636–8).

The Chair being taken Ashley the Delegate read the Report verbatim from the General Committee as was read in the Second division the preceding night, the Letter & Lecture from Sheffield together with the L: C: Societies Address to Mr. Whitbread was also read & met great Applause, the Delegate (Ashley) read a Report from the Secret Commee which had met on the Saturday preceding on special matters partarly to take it into considn. to call a general Meeting for the purpose of arranging some plan to rescue Margarot and the other Scotch Delegates from their abominable Sentence a Motion was made by a Member that a Commee consisting of five Delegates be appointed from the General Committee to draw up & present a petition to his Majesty in behalf of Messrs Muir Palmer Margarot & Skirving on some on Levee day that should hereafter be named on this Motion a debate ensued several Members spoke upon it & tho' they all agreed that they despaired of its obtaining the desired end yet they were unanimous in opinion that it would shew to his Majesty the determined spirit of the London Corresponding Society on the original Motion being put for calling a General Meeting this motion dropt and it was carried unanimously by a Shew of hands that it was necessary on many special matters to call a General Meeting as early as possible – A Member entered and addressing the Chair informed him that he had had intelligence that a disturbance was meditated against the Political Lecture intended to be given by Thelwall the following Evening in Compton Street by a number of persons hired for that purpose and whom he called Bludgeon Men, He further learnt they were to rendevous at a public house in Windmill Street were employed by Ministry and to be headed by a young Gentleman supposed to be Son to Lord Hawkesbury and the same person who was detected in taking notes at the Lecture the preceding Wednesday, Thelwall came in and confirmed this Information and requested of the Members to attend as numerous as possible, they promised to do so, and to arm themselves with Weapons of Defence and if any attempt was made to disturb him or them they would defend him and themselves at the hazard of their lives – Thelwall drew from a Case of Leather formed like a Stick a small Sword which he declared with an Oath if he was attacked, He would not scruple to run it into the heart of any Man that should so attack him. –

[On 20 March the general committee voted

to publish a set of resolutions about the debate in the House of Commons on the detention of Lafayette in Prussia[62] and a resolution commending the Society of United Irishmen at Dublin for their address to the people of Ireland on parliamentary reform.[63]]

143. Report from spy Taylor: LCS Division 2, 24 March 1794

Source: TS 11/955/3499

March 24. 1794
Meeting of the London Correspondg. Society
No. 3 New Compton Street
2d. Division

Brooks in the Chair – The two Delegates present Dowling and Pearce Dowling read the Report from the General Committee Vizt. that forty Members had been added to the Society in the course of last Week – some little remark made upon some Section of the intended new Constitution but of no import the General Meeting was fixt for Monday April the 7th. next ensuing the place where to be held to be determined on in the general Committee on Thursday next by a Report from the Secret Committee appointed to chuse a proper situation a Committee had also been appointed consistg. of the following four persons Thelwall, Ashley Moore and Baxter to arrange the Business to be brought before the Society on the General Meeting[64] Dowling resigned

62 Speaking against a motion asking the king to intercede with the King of Prussia, Pitt said that such interference would violate customs observed by independent states. One LCS resolution stated that it was a 'barefaced violation of Principle' to affect tenderness for the internal regulations of a despotic country (Prussia) while attempting to control the government of an independent republic (France). Another resolution thanked Mr Courtenay for observing that while there was much declamation over atrocities at Paris, no one mentioned the cruelties committed by 'royal aristocrats' (advertisement, *MC* 23 March 1794, p. 1; *MP* 22 March 1794, p. 1).

63 This address was a reasoned defence of their proposal to let every adult male vote. It refuted such familiar arguments as those that the people are too ignorant to choose wise legislators, that they have no stake in the country if they do not own or lease property, that if they pay no taxes they have no right to vote (*MP* 19 March 1794, pp. 3 and 4).

64 Taylor heard the same report by delegate Ashley the next night at Div. 29 at Robins Coffee House. Harrison was chairman.

his situation as Delegate and Pearse as sub Delegate Le Maitre was chose Delegate, Richter a Sub Dublegate for the Quarter ensuing –

144. Letter: Hardy to Daniel Adams, Secretary of the Society for Constitutional Information, 27 March 1794[65]

Source: TS 11/952/3496

March 27/ 1794

To the Secretary of the Society for Constitutional Information

Citizen –

I am directed by the London Corresponding Society to transmit the following Resolutions to the Society for Constitutional Information and to request the Sentiments of that Society respecting the important measures which the present juncture of affairs seems to require

The London Corresponding Society conceives that the moment is arrived when a full and explicit declaration is necessary from all the friends of freedom – Whether the late illegal and unheard of prosecutions and sentences shall determine us to abandon our Cause or shall exite us to pursue a Radical Reform with an ardor proportioned to the Magnitude of the object and with a Zeal as *distinguished* on *our* parts as the *treachery* of *others* in the Same glorious Cause is *Notorious*—The Society for Constitutional Information is therefore required to determine whether or no they will be ready when called upon to act in Conjunction with *this* and *other societies* to obtain a fair Representation of the PEOPLE—Whether they concur with us in seeing the necessity of a *Speedy Convention* for the purpose of obtaining in a Constitutional and Legal method a redress of those grievances under which we at present labour and which can only be effectually removed by a full and fair Representation of the *People* of

Great Britain—The L. Corresponding Society cannot but remind thir friends that the present Crisis demands all the prudence, Unanimity and Vigor, that ever were or can be exerted by *Men and Britons* nor do they doubt but that Manly firmness and consistency will finally, and they believe *shortly* terminate in the full accomplishment of all their wishes

I am fellow Citizen
(in my humble measure)
a friend to the Rights of Man
Thos. Hardy   Secty.

Resolved Unanimously

[The first and second resolutions state that the continuance of justice and liberty depends on equal laws, which in turn require a full and fair representation of the people; and that obtaining this has been the sole object of the LCS.]

3d. That it is the decided opinion of this Society that to Secure ourselves from future illegal and Scandalous prosicutions, to prevent a repetition of wicked and unjust sentences, and to recal those wise and wholesom Laws that have been wrested from us and of which scarcely a Vestage remains – There ought to be *immediately* a *Convention* of the *People* by Delegates deputed for that purpose from the different Societies of the *Friends* of *Freedom* assembled in the various parts of this Nation— And we pledge ourselves to the Public to pursue every Legal Method Speedily to accomplish so desirable a purpose

P. S. I have to inform you that a General Meeting of the Society will be holden on Monday the 14th. of April the place to be Anounced, by Publick Advertisement.

145. Report from spy Taylor: LCS Division 2, 31 March 1794

Source: TS 11/955/3499

March 31. 1794
Meetg. of London Correspg. Socy.
No. 3 New Compton Stt.
2nd. Division

Pearce in the Chair – Le Maitre the Delegate read the Report from the General Committee vizt. that 53 New Members had been added to the Society in the course of the last week – a Motion was made in the Genl. Committee and carried unanimous that a protest against Mr. Dundas's Speech in the House of

65 At the end of the letter, in another hand, is the response of the SCI: 'It was resolved by the *Society for Constitutional Information* that their Secretary should assure the *"London Corresponding Society"* that they heartily approved of their intentions, and would co-operate with them in obtaining an object of so much importance to the peace & happiness of Society. And that He [sic] also request the London Corresponding Society to send a delegation of its members, to confer upon the Subject with an equal number of the Society for Constitutional Information.'

Commons on the 25th. inst be advertized in several of the Newspapers (vide Morng. Chronicle of this day)[66] a Motion was also made & carried unanimous that Letters be sent from this the London C. Society to the Society for Constitl. Information to consult with them for the purpose of calling a General Convention of the people – another motion was made & carried unanimous that the Genl. Meetg. be appd. for the 14th. of April next ensuing an earlier day being found incompetent to the purpose of making it generally known   the place appointed for it to be held at is at a Room in Store Street Tottenham Cot. Road occupied by a person who usually lets it as a Ball Room   Pearce was appointed Sub: Secrety. – a New made Member of the name of Jones rose and in a speech of some length with a Degree of Oratorical abilities or at least comparatively with the Speakers in general in the Division lamented in forcible language the supineness of the London Correspg. Socy. in not exerting themselves in a more open manner to obtain redress for the unprecedented & infamous treatment of their Scotch Delegates Margarot &c. He advised the L. C. Socy. to go in a Body to the Senate or as it was called the Parlt. House & their assert their rights & demand redress. He then proposed the followg. Motion that Letters be sent from the L. C. Society to the Society for Constl. Informn. & the Friends of the people requesting them to join the L. C. Society and in a Body to go before the House of Commons there claim their Rights – Richter replied & opposed the Motn. not in its substance, but on the Grod. that the Committee for arranging the Business for the Genl. Meetg. had this subject in contemplatn. & it would be brot. forward at the Genl. Meeting[67]   Moore also

66   p. 1. On 25 March Adam moved that a committee be established to take into consideration certain aspects of the criminal law in Scotland. Speaking against the motion, Dundas said that 'when he saw the numberless seditious writings which were daily circulated at a great expense, not by any individual, in a sudden fit of political phrenzy, but by a large body called the London Corresponding Society' he became convinced that the present laws of England were inadequate. The LCS advertisement quoted his statement about the insufficiency of the laws and the need for new legislation, resolved that any attempt to substitute the practices of Scottish courts for English laws would be treason, and announced a general meeting for 14 April.
67   Slightly different version in government compilation of Taylor's information: 'he [Richter] said the Committee (for arranging the Business of the General Meeting) had it in Contemplation to

spoke on the same side the question with Richter. – He admitted the principle of the Motion to be good, but objected to the question being put for the same reason that Richter had advanced that the Commee was at that time sitting & deliberating to form some plan of immediate & effectual redress – Jones withdrew his Motion.

146. Report from spy Groves: LCS Division 2 (excerpt), 31 March 1794[68]

Source: TS 11/954/3498

2d. Division . . . little was done but the Chairmans informing the Citizens that there would be a General Meeting called soon and the delivering out a printed Lecture as delivered at Sheffield . . . on the Fast Day. . . . It was read by a *Citizen* of the name of Taylor.

147. Report from spy Metcalfe: LCS Division 11, 1 April 1794[69]

Source: TS 11/956/3501

Meeting of the 11th. Division of the London Corresponding Society at the Hope in Woods Close Clerkenwell Tuesday Evening 1st. April 1794

Three New Members were this Night admitted. After which   Wright of Shadwell   Delegate

propose something relative to delivering Margarot & Gerald' ('Persons agt whom Taylor's Reports furnish Evidence', TS 11/954/3498).
68   Government description: 'Report London Corresponding / Society / Recd. 9th April 1794.'
69   Government description: 'Minutes of London Corresponding Society. 11th. Division, 1st April 1794'.
William Metcalf of No. 6 Dowgate Hill was an attorney and sometime clerk to the Tallow Chandlers Company. From 1784 or 1785 he had been employed by government several times 'in conducting Criminal prosecutions'. About 1793 Evan Nepean sent him to Shropshire 'upon a business of Confidence and Secrecy', then to Worcestershire 'upon another business of considerable consequence to Government', and after that to Liverpool 'to enquire into the Riots'. At the beginning of 1794 Nepean asked him to spy on the 'disaffected Societies' in London (letter, Metcalfe to the Duke of Portland, 5 Jan. 1795, HO 42/34, fos. 11–12v). He began attending Thelwall's lectures, often twice a week, and became a member of the LCS. The government copy of his reports, titled 'Abstract of the Account of the Proceedings of the London Corresponding Society and of Thelwall's Lectures

from this Division reported, that it had been resolved in the Committee of Delegates that the General Meeting of the Society should be postponed until Monday the 14th. Inst. that the place of Meeting was not yet determined upon, but that when a fit place was provided, each Delegate would give timely Notice to his respective Division. He also reported that the Committee had passed a Resolution expressing the Sentiments of the Society upon the infamous Speech of Secretary Dundas upon the Subject of the Scots Criminal Law and which were Ordered to be incerted in the News Papers.

The Delegate then informed us that on the present Evening the Term of his Delegation expired and that it would be necessary to choose a Delegate and other Officers for the ensuing Three Months, and he said that it gave him great pleasure that he was able to announce to us that the Society was rapidly encreasing and that in the last three Months 354 New Members had been admitted.

A Motion was then made that Mr. Wright should be re-elected Delegate for this Division for the ensuing three Months, which was carried,

from the 21st. Feby to the 2d. May 1794', contains 32 pages, 26 of which are accounts of Thelwall's lectures (TS 11/966/3510B). Although this is the earliest extant LCS report from Metcalf, it may not have been his first, for he later wrote that 'a great many, of the reports he sent government were 'wanting' (letter to Treasury Solicitor Joseph White, 5 Nov. 1794, TS 11/956/3501). And on 7 March he had sent government a copy of 'Rights of Swine', which he might have acquired at a division meeting (copy marked 'W. M/ 7th. March 1794' in TS 11/954/3498). However, the last sentence of this report (revealing that Metcalfe has just learned that the general committee meets on Thursdays) suggests that he has not been a member long.

Metcalfe was revealed as a spy at the end of Sept. 1794 when 'at the pressing request of Mr. Ford and in compliance with the wishes of the Privy Council', he was 'present at and contributing to' the arrest of Le Maitre and the others accused of the pop-gun plot. Nepean, with the consent of Dundas, had been paying him £300 per year, but after the state trials when his utility as a spy was ended (he was listed as a government witness although he did not testify), government proposed discontinuing his pay. Metcalfe protested that he had lost his professional business because he had spent all his time in the service of government – 'during the whole of the time I was a Member of the Society I had a constant attendance and that the most unpleasant among persons of the very lowest Orders of Society four Days in the Week' (letter to Portland).

Mr. Harrison was Elected Sub Delegate
&
Gordon (the late Secretary) Secretary

Mr Wright then informed the Division that the Numbers of Members had increased sufficiently to enable them to branch off a sufficient Number to fform a New Division, that he had provided a House to receive them and that it would be expected there should be as full a Meeting on the Morrow Evening at the Parrott in Green Harbour Court in the Old Bailey as would give encouragement to the Mistress of the House to attend to the New Division, and permanently to establish them in that Situation which being central was a very desirable one./.

The Evening concluded with the Singing of several most Seditious Songs. &c.[70]

The Committee of Delegates meet at Robins Coffee house Shire Lane Temple Bar. every Thursday Evening./

148. Report from spy Taylor: LCS Division 29, 1 April 1794

Source: TS 11/955/3499

April 1st. 1794.
Meetg. of the London Correspg. Socy.
Robin's Coffee house   Shire Lane
29th. Division

Watson in the Chair   Ashley the Delegate Read the Report from the General Committee which was the same in substance as that read in the 2d. Divisn. last Night but with some variation in the wording   Citizen Thelwall as one of the special Committee for arranging the Business to be brought forward at the General Meeting finding it a matter that requires the utmost exertion of Mental powers to simplify & at the same time to make the Sentiments of the Socy. known in bold & Nervous Resolutions requests of the Genl. Committee a further time for Deliberatn. on the several points the General Meeting was therefore to be postponed till the 14th. of April next ensuing   Thelwall also observes that the special Commee have determined that the Business to be brought before the Society at the Genl. Meeting is of so important a nature

70 Metcalf enclosed one of them, 'A New Song by J—— M——', which starts, 'Come my Sons of true Liberty, let us agree/ To form an Alliance firm honest and free/ Lets join hand in hand, as Reason upholds/ Her bright Torch to Friendship. Ah! let us be bold.' The author may be Mathews, a bookseller who published a volume of songs.

to the Society & the Cause in which they are engaged that Secresy is absolutely necessary, therefore it will not be made public in the several divisions till the day of the Genl. Meeting the special Committee also moved that 3 more Members be added to their Committee Richter & Beck were 2 that were appointed.

149. Report from spy Metcalfe: LCS Division 11, 2 April 1794[71]

Source: TS 11/956/3501

Meeting of the 11th. Division of the London Corresponding Society at the Parrot in Green Harbour Court in the Old Bailey Wednesday Evening 2nd. April 1794./.

Thirty three attended when Thirteen gave their Names to be branch'd off to form a new Division at this House.

Mr. Worship of Ball Court Lombard Street Engraver was chosen Secretary,

Mr. Wright the Delegate of the 11th. Division having signifyed that no Delegate could be appointed by a less Number than 16, the choice of a Delegate for the New Division was postponed until Wednesday next and Mr. Wright was requested to report to the Committee of Delegates that a part of his Division had branch'd off, and to procure a Number for the New Division &c. which he undertook to do. he mentioned that several places had been proposed for the General Meeting, among the rest, Lords Cricket Ground, The Boot Bowling Green behind the Foundling Hospital and the Adam and Eve at Pancras, but that the place was not yet determined upon./.

Among other Conversation on this Evening, *Wright said he thought it would an adviseable measure for the Society to learn the use of a Musket and how to form themselves into Ranks, and that he meant to move in the Committee of Delegates, that each Delegate be directed to recommend such Measure to his respective Division, and also that the Members of the Society should have engraven on his Card of address or Shop Bill some Emblem* to denote him of the Society, and he thought there could not be a better than The Hand in Hand./.

A Subscription was then made for Citizen

71 Metcalfe's description: 'Minutes London Corresponding Society/ Branch from 11th. Division 2nd April/ 1794'; in another hand: 'Wright recommends learning/ the Use of a Musket'.

Hudson, & half a Guinea was collected, which Citizen Eaton was desired to convey to him in Newgate.

150. Hardy's Minutes of first conference between SCI and LCS: 4 April 1794[72]

Source: TS 11/966/3510B

Friday April 4/ 1794 a Conference with the Society for Consl. Information present Adams Secty. Kid Holcroft Joyce Wardle Sharp from the Correspg Society Moore in the Chair Baxter Lovett Hodgson Thelwell Hardy Secty.

a Motion for Comtg. to the Commitee the Letters of Communication from the Societies in the Country to the London C. Society – Carried

Resolvd. the delegates be requested to Communicate all the information they Can at next meeting relative to the State of the different Societies associatd for obtaining a fair Representation of the People

72 In Hardy's hand. This meeting of the two societies was the subject of much questioning in examinations before the Privy Council after the arrests of Hardy and other reformers in May. Government saw this meeting as the first step toward unifying all the reform societies in the country. The initiative came from the LCS, who wrote to the SCI suggesting the meeting. After the SCI agreed, the general committee of the LCS on 3 April appointed or elected five men to confer on 4 April with 'such Members of the society for Constitutional Inforn as they shall think fit to appoint' (letter, Hardy to Adams, n.d., TS 11/951/3494). At the weekly meeting of the SCI the next day five of their members were appointed to this committee ('Resolutions of the Society for Constitutional Information in the custody of Daniel Adams', TS 11/953/3497). After the regular SCI meeting, the ten delegates, five from each society, remained. According to William Sharp, 'one of the Delegates from the Corresponding Society took the Chair – he was a tall Man, the most Gentlemanly of the Delegates, but does not know his Name – This Chairman talked about an equal Representation of the People and putting an End to War. – Holcroft introduced a Conversation on the Powers of the Human Mind which lasted an Hour and a half and the Meeting broke up without any Business being done' ('Information of William Sharp', TS 11/963/3509, fo. 304). Sharp's statment that no business was done appears inconsistent with Hardy's notes, but the two matters of agreement in the notes may have slipped Sharp's mind as he listened to Holcroft.

adjourned to Monday Evening
No[73] 2 Beaufort Buildings Strand

151. Report from spy Groves: LCS Division 2, 7 April 1794

Source: TS 11/954/3498

[2d. Division – No. 3 Compton Street]

Monday April 7th. Mr Richter proposed Reading the Trial of Mr Walker at Manchester,[74] which he did from the Courier, copied from the Morning Chronicle & with great energy – The commitment of Dunn, the Witness, for perjury, was received with great applause, as was Mr Walker's answer to Mr Justice Heath who told Mr Walker that he hoped it would be an *Admonition* to him what Company he kept in future

Walker's answer was in substance that he never kept worse company than the wretch who stood by him – that there was not an Action or a word of his life that he should be ashamed or afraid of either before God or Man"

Richter then begged leave to read Lord Stanhope's Speech & Motion which he did, with Lord Grenville's reply, & the Lord Chancellors putting the Motion,[75] & concluded

with adding that he thought the Lord Chancellor and the House of the Lords ought to have the Thanks of the London Corresponding Society voted them, for the part they had taken & the disposition they had manifested on the Subject

The business of the Evening concluded with a Collection for the *Condemned* Delegate Gerald which amounted to Nine Shillings – there were certainly 30 Members present, & out of that 9s. I contributed Two Shillings, so that the actual Citizens Subscription was 7s. –

These Subscriptions are carried on every Meeting Night, & are in proportion – they are collected for the purposes of *buying Stock* – i.e. Sea Stock for the Journey to Botany Bay

At ¼ past 10 the Meeting broke up & adjourned to the next Monday –

Richter, Pearce & Jones, (who went with me) & myself went into the Front Room called the Coffee Room, where were Hardy the Secretary, & Mr Moore of Princes Street

The Conversation turned upon the advertized Meeting on the 14th. instant

I asked Richter if he knew the purpose of the Meeting – He informed me it was to propose an Address to the Nation at large with some strong spirited resolutions thereon   And also to propose an *Address* to the King on the Subject of a Reform in Parliament   a *Remonstrance* on the Corrupt State of it and a *Petition* to dissolve the present one – The Address Remonstrance & Petition to be couched in One

Another Reason was also assigned by Pearce – it was to try their strength, & to see how far their Union with the Constitutional Society would carry them in point of Numbers –

There is also in agitation a proposed Union of all the Societies in England Scotland & Wales – The language of some is "Legal & peaceable means" – of others "We are too slow in our measures" and I believe they depend much on the Meeting of the 14th. with regard to Numbers in order to evince the Sence of the *Nation*, vizt. the Sence of those who have none at all, & the designs of those who have too much. – for I am certain nine tenths of them have not common understandings, & the other odd one, who do possess it, strive to apply it to the most mischievous of all purposes

Richter informed me that the Room in

73 Crossed out before this address: 'Robins Coffee House half past 7 O Clock'. This notation must be a reference to the next meeting, for the SCI did not hold its weekly meetings at Beaufort Buildings.

74 On 2 April Thomas Walker and six other men were acquitted of a charge of conspiracy to overthrow the constitution and assist the French if they invaded England. It was shown that the government's chief witness, Thomas Dunn, had been bribed to make false statements (*ST* vol. 22, cols. 1055–1166).

75 Stanhope spoke against the notion of restoring the monarchy in France by encouraging a civil war. His resolution (not motion) was to the effect that government ministers would incur the displeasure of the House of Lords if they attempted to excite such a civil war (*The Speech of Earl Stanhope in the House of Peers on his Motion to prevent His Majesty's Ministers from interfering with the Internal Government of France. April the Fourth, 1794*. Printed by Order of the London Corresponding Society, 1794). Grenville replied, 'I never heard with such resentment any speech as that which has just been delivered.' He said he was sorry that Stanhope's passions had got the better of his reason. The Lord Chancellor, concurring with Grenville, announced that he would read (into the parliamentary record) only the words of the resolution (i.e. not the preliminary speech). Grenville went

one better and moved that even the words of the resolution be 'expunged from the Journals'. Only Stanhope voted against this (*Parliamentary Register*, vol. 39 (1794), pp. 208–10).

129

Store Street in which the Meeting was to be held, contained 1600 square feet, & that it wod. of course hold 1600 people – that it was well understood by those who had as much understanding & who were as *deep* as anybody that none of those convicted at Edinburgh would be sent to Botany bay & that it was the opinion of Horne Tooke who he said, would have a share in preparing the Address Remonstrance & petition.

Friday Noon 8th. April 1794

152. Report from spy Taylor: LCS Division 2, 7 April 1794

Source: TS 11/955/3499

April 7, 1794
Meeting of London Correspondg. Society
No. 3. New Compton Street
2d. Division

The Chair being taken Le Maitre the Delegate read the Report from the general Comittee vizt. that 23 Members had been added to the Society in the course of the Week, a Letter had been received by the Secretary (Hardy) from the Secretary (Adams) of the Society for Constitutional Information in reply to the Letter sent by the L. C. Society, inviting them to join this Society – this answer express'd their desire of co-operating with the L. C. Society in all things to obtain their great end and for which purpose the Society for C. I. requests a Deputation of Members may be sent to consult & deliberate with them in consequence the following Members of the Committees were appointed Thelwall, Baxter, Hodson, Moore, and Lovett – A Letter from Margarot addressed to Mr. Secretary Dundas[76] inserted in the Morning Post, was read, also the Toasts that had been given at the Anniversary Dinner of the Friends of the People at Freemasons Tavern on Saturday last[77] together with their answer to the L. C. Society declining to co operate with

76 Margarot wanted Dundas to tell the captain of the *Surprise* how Mrs Margarot was to be treated on board. He also wanted to know if on arrival Mrs Margarot would be entitled to the advantages of a free settler and he would be restored to liberty (27 March 1794, in *Cambridge Intelligencer*, 19 April 1794, p. 2).

77 In addition to pious toasts to reform in Parliament, to Sheridan, Grey, Fox, Muir and Palmer, there were some witty ones at the 5 April dinner; e.g. 'Lord Justice Clerk and the Duke of Richmond; may the one forget his principles and the other recollect them' *MP* 7 April 1794, p. 3).

them[78] – Richter rose and read the speech of Earl Stanhope in the House of Lords on Friday last. He made some comments upon it tending to prove that the conduct of the Lords in that days debate would the sooner facilitate the cause of the Society, by opening the Eyes of the People to see their injuries – the Speech of Earl Stanhope gained great applause and a Motion was made that it should be printed by the Society, but on Richter's stating it was the intention of the Committee to order it to be printed from the correct Notes of a short hand writer that was present in the House of Lords at the time with the addition of the string of Resolutions moved by the Noble Earl the Motion was withdrawn – Richter read the Tryal of Walker of Manchester, took the opportunity of reviling the Instruments of such prosecutions which he called arbitrary and illegal. Jones in a very flaming and seditious Speech, recommended the Citizens not to set tamely silent and inactive but to rouse themselves and not only with words but arms assert their Rights   He alluded to the sufferings of the Scotch Delegates Messrs. Muir Palmer Margarot Skirving & Gerald – Said the L. C. Society was on the Eve of a general Meeting the Members should go with their Minds prepared to adopt a System that may be reduced to speedy practice and rescue those Fellow Citizens from their degrading Situation[79]

78 On 7 April the LCS sent a letter soliciting 'the concurrence and assistance of the Society of the Friends of the People, in assembling, as speedily as the nature of the business will admit, a Convention of the Friends of Freedom, for the purpose of obtaining in a legal and constitutional method, a full and effectual representation' (signed by Hardy, but written by Jeremiah Joyce, according to a note by Hardy in Add MSS 27814, fo. 71) In a reply dated 11 April, the FoP declined sending delegates to a convention. 'They fear it will furnish the Enemies of Reform with the means of calumniating its Advocates, and so far from forwarding the cause, will deter many from countenancing that which they approve' (signed W. Breton; both letters printed in *At a General Meeting of the London Corresponding Society, Held on the Green, at Chalk Farm, on Monday the 14th of April, 1794, J. Lovett in the Chair . . .*). Presumably the refusal to cooperate was first delivered orally at the FoP dinner on 5 April.

79 Slightly different emphasis in government compilation of Taylor's reports: Jones 'recommended a Rescue of Margarot &c by the L C Society' ('Persons agt whom Taylor's Reports furnish Evidence', TS 11/954/3498). Richter asserted that he publicly reprobated this speech

153. Report from spy Nodder: Exercise Society and LCS Division meeting (summary and excerpt), 7 April 1794[80]

Source: PC 1/21/A35

Mond: Evg. (—Apl. 7) – 1794

[Nodder, accompanied by Long, a copper-plate printer, and Cumming, Long's journeyman, went to the house of the bookseller Spence, who is the 'depot for the Holbn. division'. In an upstairs room, behind closed curtains, they exercised with mop-handles, under the direction of a gun-smith. In addition to these five men, there was a man who entered with the gunsmith

by Jones (Richter's notes for his trial in Add MSS 27816, fo. 525).

80 Nodder's description: 'No. 2/ Mr. N - d - - - r's - Mins./J: P - - n'. Government description: 'In Mr Grettans' 11 April/ 1794'.
Frederick Polydore Nodder of Brewer Street, Golden Square, was the botanic painter to the Queen (TS 11/963/3509, fo. 156) and an exhibitor at the Royal Academy in 1786, 1787 and 1788. Some of his numbered reports, including no. 1, do not survive. His reports are mostly about a military society in which John Williamson, a shoemaker, and John Philip Franklow, a tailor, were active. At a meeting on 30 April – when the only recruits were Nodder and another spy – Franklow explained that he and Williamson were attracted to arming because Margarot, on the night before his removal from prison to the transport ship, 'most earnestly desired them never to abandon that thought advising them never to have more than Ten at any one meeting' (PC 1/21/A35). Margarot's advice was superfluous, for Nodder's reports show at most eight men at a meeting, including himself and at least one other spy. An unidentified spy who attended the arming society regularly (probably Nodder's companion Sanderson) informed his government employer on 26 May that the society was not increasing and that he would not attend in future unless ordered to do so. He described the society as organized by 'a few of the most desperate' of the LCS, meeting at the house of Shelmerdine in the Borough; they were to be supplied with guns by Williams, a gun engraver, and to be drilled by Orr, a Camberwell tailor. When it became necessary to leave Shelmerdine's house, the society split in two, one section meeting at Spence's house and one at Smith's shed near the prison in Tothill Fields (HO 42/30, fos. 283-4). Both were also meeting places of LCS divisions.

and a man who had been chairman of the meeting at Worcester St in the Borough.]

this meeting was . . . adjourned to friday night – two of the members having signified their intentions of going to a corresponding Soc: held at the Robin hood – Nr. went with them – they produced their 1/4ly. tickets (Liby. to those who dare defend it) and on paying 2d. they were admitted into the Room where he saw between 40 and 50 people – N: was asked no questions – but soon after seeing two of the Members of the Holb: division who were at the *Worcester Street Club* the night he was admitted a Member he entd. into conversation with them and they informed him that the Secy had just finished reading the weeks *transactions* of the difft. divisions – while there Nr saw 3 New Members enrolled – the Articles that were read to them are 3 in numbers which specified and contained the necessity of a *speedy – annual & reformed Parliamt* to these Articles they assented. the Chairman & Secy then informed the meeting – calling them Citizens that he had tickets to dispose of per 6d each for the general meeting to be held in *Store Street* Totdneham Court on Monday next[81] – that every Citizen had liberty to bring with him a friend – this meeting to be at 2 o'Clock the Chair to be taken at 3 o'Clock and that it was expected this meeting would be very numerous – that Mr. Sherridan had in the *Soc:* of *the friends* of the *People* proposed a meeting of *that Soc:* to be convened for the Wednesdy after in order that the resoluts: of the aforesaid Monday meeting in Store Street might be reported to the *Soc:* of the friends of the *People* – Nr. was further informed by those men that one *Stiff* a hair dresser of Pater-noster – Row had been at the expence of procuring a drawings and getting those drawings engraved of the different positions and evolutions of the manual and ⟨dn.⟩ exerciscе of the Soldiery for the use of the *Citizens* of these divisions – and these

81 The meeting was advertised on 3 April in the *Publican's Morning Advertiser* (TS 11/965/3510A), on 4 April in the *MP* (p. 1), and on 7 April in the *MC* (p. 1). The advertised purpose of the meeting was to express the concurrence of the LCS with the sentiments of the parliamentary reformers under sentence of transportation and the LCS's 'sense' of the court proceedings in Edinburgh, as well as to consider a method of testifying their attachment to the reformers. Tickets were to be had from Hardy, 9 Piccadilly; D. I. Eaton, Little Turnstile, Holborn; Smith, Portsmouth St, Lincoln's Inn Fields; Thelwall, 2 Maze Pond, Borough.

prints will be ready *next week* – this is the *same Man* mentioned *by Mr. G——n to Lord Sydney.* –

F.P.N.

154. Report from spy Taylor: LCS Division 29, 8 April 1794

Source: TS 11/955/3499

April 8 1794
Meeting of the London Corresponding Society
Robins Coffee House   Shire Lane
29th Division

The Chair being taken Ashley the Delegate read the Report from the General Committee verbatim as that read in the second Division of last Night, also was read the Letter from Margarot to Mr. Dundas and the Speech of Earl Stanhope, a person of the Name of John Harrison was present and read a Manuscript Letter or pamphlett, intitled an Appeal to the people in an Address to Mr. Secretary Dundas[82] (this pamphlett being since published and delivered with other papers I omit making my own observations upon it) in a Conversation I had with a Young Man present of the Name of Oxley a Member of the Society and belonging to the 13th Division arising from his appearing in a Blue Coat and Red Collar which a Member observed was very Aristocratical, Oxley excused himself by saying it was a Military Dress & observed there were Military Institutions in the L. C. Society and one of which he was a Member having formerly been an officer in the Militia   He furr. informed me there was one of these Military Divisions met in Saint Georges Fields but he declined saying where as he asserted he had taken an oath of Secrecy. He said some persons attended who had been in the Army to learn any persons who chose to attend the use of Fire Arms and other Military Exercises I enquired of him how to obtain Admission he referred me to Spence of Little Turnstile who had the Management of this particular Division and was Delegate to the 30th Division   Meeting at the Hole in the Wall   Gate Street   Lincolns Inn Fields

82 For full title see 90, 1 Aug. 1793. In the 45 pp. pamphlet Harrison complained about the taxes, war, state of the poor and representation in Parliament. Dundas sarcastically alluded in Parliament to a letter signed 'John Harrison, a Sans Culottes', and he described Harrison as 'a Citizen whose loyalty was confined to his razor' (*Senator*, vol. 9, pp. 435–7).

155. Official Minutes: Conference of SCI and LCS, c. 9 April 1794[83]

Source: BL 8135. b. 8

I. That it appears to this Company very desireable, that a Convention or General Meeting[84] of the Friends of Liberty should be called, for the purpose of taking into consideration the proper methods of obtaining a full and fair representation of the People.

II. That it be recommended to the Society for Constitutional Information, and London Corresponding Society to institute a regular and pressing correspondence with all those parts of the country, where such measures may be likely to be promoted; not only to instigate the Societies already formed, but to endeavour also to produce such other Associations as may farther the General Object.

III. That it appears to this Committee, that the General Object would be promoted, if a standing Committee of Co-operation between the two Societies were established for the purpose of holding personal communication with such members of similar Societies in other parts of the country as may occasionally be in London, and who may be authorized by their respective Societies to act with such Committee.[85]

83 In *Proceedings, &c. of the Society for Constitutional Information*, 1794. The committee was scheduled to have its second meeting on 7 April, but the SCI members, who had not been notified, did not attend. By 10 April the committee had met and passed these resolutions.

84 At the meeting Thelwall produced a sketch of a plan for a convention. The delegates from the SCI objected to the word *convention* and wished to substitute *meeting*. The delegates from the LCS insisted on the word *convention*. Thelwall said it would be cowardice to be afraid of a name when the intention was to convene the people for the purpose of a fair representation. It was then agreed to use the expression *convention or meeting* ('Index to London Corresponding Society papers mentioned in the Report from the Committee of Secrecy of the House of Commons', TS 11/956/3501). According to William Sharp, most of the meeting was devoted to this discussion of words (Sharp's examination before the Privy Council, TS 11/963/3509, fo. 296).

In his biography, however, Thelwall is said to have opposed the proposal of a convention and to have decided 'to withdraw himself, in the least offensive way he could, from the Society' (Mrs Thelwall, *Life of John Thelwall*, p. 151).

85 On 10 April Hardy wrote Adams that the general committee had approved these resolutions of the 'Committee of Conference' and had appointed Baxter, Hodgson, Lovett, Moore and Thelwall to

156. Resolutions and Address to Gerrald: LCS General Meeting, 14 April 1794[86]

Source: Add MSS 27814, fos. 70-3v

Resolved Unanimously,

I. That this Society have beheld with rising indignation, proportioned to the enormity of the evil, the late rapid advances of despotism in Britain; the invasion of public security; the contempt of popular opinion; and the violation of all those provisions of the Constitution intended to protect the People against the encroachments of Power and Prerogative.

II. That our abhorrence and detestation have been particularly called forth by the late arbitrary and flagitious proceedings of the Court of Justiciary in Scotland, where all the doctrines and practices of the *Star Chamber*, in the times of Charles the First, have been *revived* and *aggravated*; and where sentences have been pronounced in open violation of all Law and Justice, which must strike deep into the heart of every man, the melancholy conviction that BRITONS ARE NO LONGER FREE.

[III and IV approve the proceedings of the British Convention in Edinburgh and the conduct of Margarot and Gerrald in particular.]

V. That any attempt to violate those yet remaining Laws, which were intended for the Security of Englishmen against the Tyranny of Courts and Ministers, and the Corruption of dependent Judges, by vesting in such Judges a legislative or arbitrary Power, (such as has lately been exercised by the Court of Justiciary in Scotland) ought to be considered as disolving entirely the social compact between the English Nation and their Governors; and driving them to an immediate appeal to that incontrovertible maxim of eternal Justice, *that the safety of the People is the SUPREME, and in cases of necessity, the ONLY Law.*

VI. That the arming and disciplining in this Country, either with or without the consent of Parliament, any Bands of *Emigrants and Foreigners, driven from their own Country for their known attachment to an* INFAMOUS DESPOTISM, is an outrageous attempt to *overawe* and *intimidate* the *free* spirit of Britons; to subjugate them to an army of *mercenary* Cut-throats, whose *views and interest* must of necessity be in direct opposition to those of the Nation, and that *no pretence whatever* OUGHT to induce the people to *submit* to so *unconstitutional* a measure.

VII. That the unconstitutional project of raising money and troops by forced benevolences (and no benevolences collected upon requisition from the King or his Ministers can ever in reality be voluntary) and the equally unjustifiable measure of arming one-part of the People against the other, brought Charles the First to the block, and drove James the Second and his posterity from the Throne; and that consequently Ministers in advising such Measures, ought to consider whether they are not guilty of High Treason.

[VIII facetiously refers to the treatment in the House of Lords of Stanhope's motion of 4 April; and IX thanks Stanhope for his conduct in Parliament.[87]]

X. That it is the firm conviction of this Society, that a steady perseverance in the same bold and energetic sentiments which have lately been avowed by the Friends of Freedom cannot fail of crowning with ultimate triumph,

---

put into practice resolutions 2 and 3 (TS 11/966/3510B). According to John Pearson, dealing with the country correspondence was the only intended function of this joint LCS-SCI committee (examination before the Privy Council, TS 11/963/3509, fo. 173v). The next day, 11 April, the SCI voted to call this a committee of cooperation. According to Sharp, there was no further meeting with the LCS delegates (examination, TS 11/963/3509, fo. 297). But in May Hardy informed a country correspondent that the 'Committee of Correspondence and Co-operation ... meets regularly twice a week at No. 2 Beaufort-Buildings, Strand' (letter to P. Smith of Newcastle-upon-Tyne, 1 May 1794, TS 11/966/3510B).

86 *At a General Meeting ... 14th April, 1794.* This document first gives the 7 April letter to the Friends of the People and their 11 April reply, then the ten resolutions, the address to Gerrald, and finally the resolutions of approbation and felicitation.

87 See p. 129 n. 75. These two resolutions were sent to Stanhope with a letter (written by John Richter) expressing the approbation of the LCS. This letter, dated 28 April, and Stanhope's brief acknowledgment, dated 1 May, were printed in the *MP* (7 May 1794, p.3).

the virtuous Cause in which we are engaged, since whatever may be the interested Opinion of *Hereditary* Senators, or *packed* Majorities of *pretended* Representatives; Truth and Liberty in an age so enlightened as the present, must be Invincible and Omnipotent.[88]

This Society having already addressed M. Margarot, *their Delegate, an* ADDRESS *to* JOSEPH GERALD *was read as follows, and carried unanimously.*[89]

To JOSEPH GERALD, *a prisoner sentenced by the* High Court *of Justiciary of* Scotland, *to* Transportation *beyond the Seas for* FOURTEEN YEARS!

We behold in you our beloved and res-

pected friend and fellow-citizen, a Martyr to the Glorious Cause of Equal Representation.

[Paraphrase: We cannot permit you to leave this degraded country without expressing the obligations owed you for your exertions in the cause on all occasions, but especially during the British Convention in Edinburgh and the consequent proceeding (we will not call it a trial).

We know not which most deserves our admiration: your splendid talents, your exalted virtues, your perseverance and firmness, or your manly and philosophical suffering under the cruel and vindictive sentence. We are indebted to you and your associates: for us you are suffering transportation to New Holland, where your sufferings may be alleviated by remembrance of your virtuous conduct and by the esteem of your fellow citizens.

Unpunished, we are daily repeating the same words and committing the same actions for which your are sentenced. Either the law was unjust to you or it ought not to deprive us of the glory of martyrdom.

We will continue to demand our rights until we have obtained equal representation of the people. We shall never forget your name, your virtues, nor your great example. Signed John Lovett, chairman, and Thomas Hardy, secretary.]

[The address to Gerrald is followed by resolutions to convey the approbation of the Society to Archibald Hamilton Rowan, then a prisoner in Dublin;[90] to John Philpot Curran, defender of Rowan; to the Society of United Irishmen; to Skirving, Palmer and Muir; John Clark and Alexander Reid, who gave bail for the LCS delegates; to Adam Gillies, Malcolm Laing and James Gibson, who assisted Gerrald in his trial; and to felicitate Thomas Walker and Sir Joseph Mawbey.[91]]

88 John Martin wrote a set of resolutions which were not read at the meeting (one copy was found among his papers and two copies among Thelwall's: TS 11/957/3502; TS 11/959/3505; *Second Report from the Committee of Secrecy*, 1794, pp. 24–5). These resolutions call for a convention to be held at a place to be named by the secret committee of the LCS, and they exclude from the oath of allegiance the words, 'it is not lawful, upon any pretence whatever, to take arms against the King'. Understandably government found these resolutions alarming, and the Privy Council asked many questions about them. Richter and Ashley said they had never seen them. Lovett explained that 'before the meeting many people were proposing resolutions according to their different sentiments' (Add MSS 27816, fo. 526; TS 11/963/3509, fos. 71v-2, 189). Thelwall told the Privy Council that 'it was a paper rejected by myself and all the Committee to whom it was referred' (*Tribune*, no. 4, 4 April 1795). He later said that these resolutions were unanimously rejected by the committee (*The Natural and Constitutional Right of Britons to Annual Parliaments, Universal Suffrage, and the Freedom of Popular Associations: Being a Vindication of the Motives and Political Conduct of John Thelwall, and of the London Corresponding Society, in General. Intended to have been delivered at the Bar of Old Bailey in Confutation of the late charges of High Treason*, 1795).

89 The address was written by John Richter (Add MSS 27816, fo. 523). An address from the LCS to Muir and Palmer (dated 30 April) must be by a different man, for it contains religious sentiments: 'You know that life is the gift of God, for the purpose of human happiness and can only be employed acceptably to him, when expended in acts of Benevolence to his Creatures. - You, therefore, rank among the most highly .favoured of your Species in being thus called to testify your Devotion to the Will of the Almighty' (*MP* 8 May 1794, p. 2).

90 On 7 Feb. 1794, Hamilton Rowan was sentenced to two years' imprisonment and a fine of £500 for publishing a seditious libel, an address from the United Irishmen to the volunteers of Ireland. On 1 May he escaped (*ST* vol. 22, col. 1189).

91 At a meeting intended to raise money for additional military companies, Mawbey spoke out, asserting the illegality of such subscriptions and accusing the potential contributors of expecting to profit by subscribing (*MC* 11 Apr. 1794, p. 4).

157. Report from spy Groves: LCS General Meeting, 14 April 1794[92]

Source: TS 11/954/3498

Minutes of the Meeting of the
London Corresponding Society
Monday April 14th. 1794
at Chalk Farm near Hampstead

This Meeting, which was advertized to be at the Dancing Room in Store Street, Tottenham Court Road, was only a feint in order to deceive Government, for it was determined that it should not be held here, and Mr. —— whose name I have forgot, had been up to the Landlord at Chalk farm, the Sunday week before the Meeting was held, in order to get the Landlords Consent – The Landlords Answer was that they might meet there if they would – he did not know their business nor did he wish to know it –

The Man who applied for the Use of Chalk Farm lives near Red Lion Square – his name I can get if necessary[93] –

For the future, the publick Meetings will be Advertized in Beauforts Buildings, where Thelwal lives, & no one will know of the Real place determined on till the hour of Meeting, which was the Case at this Meeting, a paper having been Stuck up at the Room door in Store Street for that purpose

Mr. Addington also had written to the Man who keeps the Dancing Room advising him of his danger, as his Dancings were illegal, if He suffered the Meeting to be held there – that he should be prosecuted if he did, – the parish officer had also interfered on the occasion & held out the same threats –

All this Thelwal told me –

The great intention of this Meeting was to

92 Government description: 'Report 14th April 1794/Mr. Groves./Meeting at Chalk Farm'. Reports of the meeting were also sent by Metcalfe (PC 1/21/A35), Taylor (TS 11/955/3499). Nodder (PC 1/21/A35), and James Walsh of the Bow Street Police Office ('Index to Bundle J', TS 11/953/3497).

This was the first LCS meeting attended by Edward Gosling, a spy employed by William Wickham. At the end of March or beginning of April Wickham (officially, the superintendent of aliens) told Gosling to verify information that an LCS member named Phillips was seditious. Having seen LCS publications in Hillier's shop window, Gosling thought Hillier might be an LCS member and might know about Phillips. Hillier he found was a member but gave no information about Phillips (whom Gosling later met and found harmless). Hillier gave 'general and evasive answers' to Gosling's questions about the LCS; but he did sell Gosling a ticket to the general meeting. With Wickham's approval Gosling attended and later became a member of the Society. On 18 May he gave a statement of his activities to Wickham; it is headed, 'The Voluntary Examination of Edward Gosling . . . ' (TS 11/963/3509, fos. 93–100). The next day, 19 May, he was examined by the Privy Council (ibid., fos. 101–6v). Shortly afterwards Gosling wrote a lengthy account of his LCS activities: 'The Information of Edward Gosling stating upon what occasion he first introduced himself to Hillier – the proceedings at Chalk Farm on the 14th Day of April 1794 – and the proceedings of the London Corresponding Society as far as consists with his Knowledge, and appears to him of an interesting Nature' (TS 11/954/3498). In it he indicates that his account of the 14 April general meeting is from 'recollection'. The reports of other events are based on notes he made at the time of the event (see his testimony in *ST* vol. 24, col. 713). Government may have used these notes in preparing 'General State of the Evidence as to Arming' (TS 11/956/3510), for it contains details attributed marginally to Gosling which are not in the 'Information'. Only one of Gosling's original reports exists, that for 13 May.

On 4 Aug. Gosling was denounced as a spy in Div. 2. His role became completely open in September when he testified for government in the Edinburgh trial of Watt.

The Corresponding Society accused Gosling of being an agent provocateur (see *A Vindication of the London Corresponding Society*; also, cross-examination of Gosling at Hardy's trial, *ST* vol. 24, cols. 722–3).

At the trials of Watt (3 Sept.) and Hardy (30 Oct.) Gosling testified that he was employed by W. Wickham. Before that he had worked occasionally as a writer for Patrick Colquhoun, the magistrate in Worship Street. This employment, he testified, started 'about September last' and included writing on Colquhoun's private as well as his public business. Prior to that he kept a broker's shop.

Under cross-examination Gosling did admit that for seven years, while working as a hairdresser, he lived under the name George Douglas; that during this period he drew up a widow's will, by which her property was left to his stepson; that when he reverted to the name Gosling he left an undischarged debt; and that when he and his wife kept a shop they sold fraudulently heavy hams, stuffed with mortar and stones (*ST* vol. 24, cols. 719–27). Gosling, of course, denied any evil intent in these actions (but he did provide government with a 3 pp. explanation of the will, 'A narrative of my Conduct as far as relates to the Will of Mrs Coleman', TS 11/966/3510B).

93 Probably John Ashley, who lived at no. 12 Fisher Street, near Red Lion Square.

have proposed a spirited Address Remonstrance & petition to the Throne on the Subject of a parliamentary reform, & a Dissolution of the present parliament – praying Annual parliaments & Universal Suffrage   This, Mr Richter told me on Friday Evening last.

Another intention of the Meeting was to Communicate to the Members what had passed between their Society, the Society of the Friends of the people, & the Constitutional Society on the Subjects of a Reform in parliament & the Necessity of an Union among them for that purpose & in order to effect it. – (Richter)

I was in Store Street at One oClock, – there were then but Seven or Eight *Citizens* before the door – they were in deep discourse, & Mr Reeves's relation standing close by, who left them as soon as he saw me – He walked up & down the Street & placed himself at the Corner of Tottenham Court Road –

In a few Minutes Thelwal appeared & stuck up the paper giving Notice of the Adjournment to Chalk farm.[94]

I joined him & it was then & on our way to the Farm he informed me what I have already stated –

The Crowds that Packed there were inconceivable & beyond all my ideas[95] – Every

person delivered his Ticket at the Garden Gate[96] which was torn & one part returned to be placed in the hat in order to prevent any person getting in, or remaining there without a Ticket – The Example was set by Thelwal.

By 3 oClock I am sure there were upwards of 2000 persons – I saw Mr Walsh come in – there was with him a Young fellow whose name I was told by a Mr Davis of the Morning Post Office was Catmore & the Son of a Mr. Catmore in some public office – Davis pointed them out to Thelwal – Thelwal accosted Walsh with a "How do you do Sir, – I hope your late Irish Journey agreed with you – I suppose you will give a very good Account to morrow of our proceedings to day, & let Government know all about it? – Walsh no? not understand him – as Thelwal is volatile he did not stay for an Answer –

Davis also accosted him & asked him about his Journey to Ireland & if he had made a good thing of it – Walsh said he went over about a d – d Chancery suit –

In short he was badgered about by half dozens & dozens till he was obliged to retreat – at last he came in again – Some were for shoving him out – others for hissing & hooting him, but Hardy & Thelwal desired he might be let alone as their Meeting was legal peaceable & Constitutional & would shake his employers with terror –

At last at about ½ past 3 the Chair was called for[97] Thelwal proposed Citizen

94 Taylor reported that when he reached Store St he found that the committee had stationed Ashley 'at the Door of the House with a Number of slips of paper in his Hand with these words printed on them   Chalk Farm Hampstead Road which on each Members approach he put into his Hand. I received one and with many others proceeded to the place agreeable to that Direction.' According to the LCS, on his way to Chalk Farm 'Taylor used every artifice to rouse the passions of the party which accompanied him, and induce them to favor the most violent proposals' (*A Vindication of the London Corresponding Society*, p. 9).

95 All the spies reported that about 2000 attended, and the *Morning Post* claimed 'upwards of THREE THOUSAND members assembled' (19 April 1794, p. 3). But John Pearce told John Martin, detained in Newgate, that there were not as many people as expected (TS 11/955/3499). These figures probably represent the number of people present, not the number of members. At Hardy's trial Groves testified that 'there were not above eight or nine hundred of the London Corresponding Society there' (*ST* vol. 24, col. 759). The LCS records of tickets (6d each) taken and paid for by members show that 443 tickets were taken between 1 and 14 April and 398 were paid for by 25 April (government copy of Hardy's account book, TS 11/959/3505). The largest number, 200, were taken by Ashley on the 14th, and on the 17th 189 were paid for by 'Eaton for

Ashley'. Since Ashley and Henry Eaton (son of Daniel Isaac Eaton, employee of Thelwall) were at the entrance of the advertised meeting place, these were tickets sold at the door. The sums paid in for tickets amount to £7 8s, Eaton for Ashley paying £2 3s 6d instead of £4 14s 6d. The other members paying for tickets are Cooper (30), Hillier (30), Jones (28), Robertson (27), Seal (19), Wright (17), Edwards (12), Bone (11), Hodgson (10), Lovett (7) and Wormsley (6). The advertisements for the meeting do not list any of these men as selling tickets.

96 The tickets were taken by Anthony Beck and Richard Hodgson (TS 11/963/3509, fo. 203).

97 The meeting place was a trap-ball green in front of steps leading up to a long refreshment room on a bowling green. When the meeting started, Thelwall and ten or fifteen others mounted the steps (Taylor's report; examination of Henry Eaton before the Privy Council, TS 11/963/3509, fo. 58v; testimony of John Edwards at Hardy's trial, *ST* vol. 24, cols. 679–80). In an addendum written about 22 April, Groves noted that the persons who assembled on the stairs included Lovett, Hodgson, Hardy, Richter, Moore and Pearce, all from Div. 2. He concluded that the leading men of Div. 2 were the leaders of the LCS. Thelwall, whose division Groves did not

Lovatt wch. was seconded by Richter & agreed to.

Lovatt in a short Exordium opened the business first recommending peace and good order as the sure means of obtaining their Ends – He proceeded to state that a general union of the Societies for promoting parliamentary Reform was greatly to be wished for, & had been earnestly sought.[98] The Address of their Society to the Chairman of the Society of the Friends of the people would be read to them, as would their Answer – The Letter also to the Society for promoting Constitutional Information & Answer, all which he begged their patient attention to – That several spirited Resolutions would be read to them & the question put upon each Resolution He talked of Spies & Informers, but said the Society need not fear any such Creatures as their Meeting was legal & Constitutional – they were only to shew their firmness in the Cause of Universal liberty by their peaceable conduct & they were sure to obtain it – to promote riot and disorder was the employment of Spies who he did not doubt would be disappointed

This man is cool & steady – no education – seems much in the habit of thinking, dull & obstinate, & very reserved – about 30 yrs. of age –

Richter in a short preface[99] stated that the Society of the Friends of the people had been written to for the purpose of joining the L. C. Society, & "I think" added he – Hardy interrupted him, saying

Make no Comment but read it

He read it – Addressed to R. B. Sheridan Esqe. & dated 5th April –

Great Applauses

The Answer read – Signed Wm. Breton Chairman – It was short – It approved of the necessity of a Reform in parliament, but differed with the L. C. Sy. as to the means, & therefore declined an Union.

A few groans

Letter and Answer to & from the Society for Constitutional Information read

Answer – agreed to an Union –

Great applauses

Thelwal made a speech on this desiring the Spies & Informers to be sure to inform Harry Dundas of this – said that he & Billy Pit must shake at the Information of such a respectable number of Citizens joined in so glorious a Cause –

Lovatt informed the Meeting that the Landlord had been with him, desiring him to persuade the people to disperse or go to anor. place & that he had expressed his fears about his Licence being taken from him

Lovatt desired them to remain & be peaceable – The Landlady then appeared at the Window in great distress & begged them to disperse – She was assured by several that no harm should be done either to her or her property –

Richter then read 6 or 7 Resolutions As the Letters Answers & Resolutions, &c &c were ordered to be printed I conceive it is unnecessary to state them

[Taylor differed in his account of the reading of the resolutions and the interruption by the landlord or landlady:

'the Chairman then proposed the Resolutions to be read, but first wished to take the Sense of the Meeting whether they should be all read together and the Question put upon the whole or whether they should be read one by one and the Question upon each, the latter was adopted. Thelwall rose and addressed the chairman by observing that to have read the whole of the Resolutions together would have had the Appearance of following the Example of a certain House and he begged this Society might not be stigmatized with do[ing] any thing dirty particularly as he observed several Spies present naming a Mr. Walsh and a Mr. Lavender . . . Richter was then proceeding to read the Resolutions when he was interrupted by the Master of the House addressing the Chairman telling him he had received instructions from the Magistrates to desire them to disperse and on their refusal he should be liable to loose his Licence and his future Bread and indeed he was alarmed for other Consequences as he was told the Military would shortly be there,[100] the Chairman told him they

know, spoke from two different places (TS 11/954/3498).
98 Nodder thought that Lovett recommended reform of both Parliament and the church. Nodder also believed that the resolutions 'hinted strongly at' church reform.
99 According to Walsh, 'Richter said that the Exertions which had been made to obtain a fair & equal Representation of the People in the Room of the present corrupt & venal Parlt. having failed – it had been determined to call a Convention of the People of Great Britain to elect Deputies for the Purpose of obtaining a parliamentary Reform.'

100 According to Hardy, the magistrates, who were at an upper window in the public house,

could by no means depart as that would be more likely to creat Tumult than their continuing in the Quiet peaceable manner they intended and desired him to inform those that sent him that they should remain and proceed on their Business what ever might be the Consequence the Landlord then departed and the resolutions was read in part by Richter and in part by Hodgson[101] some little debate arose upon some of them in which the principal Speakers were Thelwall Hodgson Moore Richter Pearse and Duckett, the Chairman put each Resolution singly and the question being put they were carried in the Affirmative Unanimous by a shew of Hands Thelwall on the reading the second Resolution paid his usual tribute of praise to Margarot and Gerald and his abuse of the Justiciary Court of Scotland he introduced Mr Dundas's Speech in the House of Commons on the subject of similar Laws in England, which he called the impudence, the audacity of Mr. Dundas[102] a Motion was made by Thelwall in a Speech of some length for a subscription being collected at the Meeting for the Service of Margarot[103] it was seconded put and carried, and Citizen Stiff was desired to take the Box and collect it at the Door on the Members retiring which he did']

Address to Citizen Jos: Gerald proposed & seconded[104]

ordered the landlord, Mr Rutherford, 'to lock his cellar door and would not suffer him to draw a drop of Beer or liquer of any kind to any that were there except themselves and their creatures that were in the house – although it being a remarkably hot day and the people parched with thirst'. Many of the people who were accustomed to dining at one or two o'clock went without food and drink from twelve until after five o'clock (Add MSS 27814, fos. 75-6).

101 Nodder reported that the resolutions were first read by Richter 'in a very forcible and impressive manner . . . he then gave them to another who again repeated them Article by Article'.

102 Thelwall allegedly said that if Dundas attempted to bring Scotch Laws to England (as he advocated), 'they must repel force by Force . . . [and] he would fight Life for Life Limb for Limb and that if he had not Numbers on his side he had Truth and Enthusiasm' (Gosling).

103 The subscription was for 'the funds of the Society', according to Metcalf, and 'for their Suffering Brother Gerrald', according to Walsh.

104 According to Nodder, the meeting 'vehemently approved it' and it was ordered to be delivered

An Address of Thanks to Earl Stanhope for his speech & Conduct in parliament

Earl was objected to, & *Citizen* proposed[105] Agreed after a trifling cabal to stand Earl, Hobson, who is just such anor. character as Lovett having explained the derivation of *Earl* – 1st. from the intrusting of old & wise Men to consult on and direct public affairs

2d. from the word Ealderman

One of the Resolutions, making use of the Words "British Senate" Thelwal objected stating the word Senate to mean "Respectful & Wise Men", & proposed the Words "His Majestys Parliament"

Some were for the Words "His Majestys Faithful Commons" – "His Majestys Parliament" stood[106]

In a Resolution implying that "from what has been done in Scotland, what might be expected to be done here["] the Word *Englishmen* objected to by Mr. Moore & the Word *Briton* proposed –

Mr Moore contended that the least distinction ought not to be made use of –

A great many adopted his idea Lovatt – Hobson & others explained that the Resolution related to innovations made in the English laws, – as the Scotch laws were different and therefore the Word Scotland only used comparatively – Agreed to stand "Englishmen"

Thelwall again spoke – He attacked Mr Walsh by name – & also Lavender the Clerk at Bow Street – he touched upon a journey of Mr Walsh's to Ireland – called him a Government Informer – He was also witty on the name of Lavender, as a perfume employed by Ministers to scatter the Essence of Despotism over Mankind, & informed the Meeting who &

to Gerrald in Newgate and to be published in all the newspapers that would take it and in every other manner possible.

105 Proposed by Duccat. Opposed by Richter and Hodgson. Rejected unanimously, except for dissent of Duccat (Richter's annotation of resolutions as printed in *First Report from the Committee of Secrecy of the House of Commons*, 1794, p. 33).

106 Duccat proposed adding 'and His only' to 'His Majesty's Parliament'. Richter opposed this, contending that it was 'absurd' and that the words in the resolution were proper as the ones by which the king styled Parliament (ibid). Gosling thought that at this point Thelwall 'observed that "His Majesty's Parliament was sufficiently expressive and that it was necessary to use Caution as well as Courage" or words to that Effect'. The substitution was carried 'with every mark of approbation hazzaing! &c! &c!' (Nodder).

what he was & then drew an inference of the weakness of the Societys Enemies by the employmt. of such insignificant tools He concluded with desiring the Citizens, not to hurt a hair of the poor creatures heads, as the proceedings of that [day] [107] would make their Masters hairs stand on end [108]

Richter read a Letter from a Gentn. at Manchester respecting a Mr Yorke & a Meeting at Sheffield – upwards of 7000 met – Yorkes horses taken from his Carriage & drawn home by Citizens [109] – 200,000 Copies of Resolutions ordered to be printed [110]

A General Meeting was mentioned by Richter to be called in about Six Weeks [111] –

Meeting Dissolved.

The principal persons who seemed to be the leaders were – Thelwal Lovatt Richter Moore Hardy Hobson Green Pearce & anor. or two whose names I know not. –

I was much surprized to see there an Old acquaintance of mine a Mr Metcalfe, an Attorney in the City whom I always considered a respectable – He told me that Governmt. had employed him – that he was above an 100£ out of pocket by them & that they had used him very ill

I thought proper to add "They use nobody well" – Thelwall desired all the parts of Tickets Stuck in the Hats to be taken out – it was done directly

Before the business began there was some Bread & Beer called for [112] – Pearce & two or three others pulled out large Knives with White Ivory or bone handles & long blades (pointed) evidently made at One Manufactory, & they said almost all the Citizens had them – I enquired of Pearce where I could get One – he reply'd Green sold them & laughed saying, they will not fly back when you strike

They are what the French call Couteau Secrêt – you cannot shut them without being acquainted with the Secret Spring.

Every Division had a Supper in the Evening – I went to Compton Street – Thelwall was Chairman [113] –

---

107 'Day' added in government copy of Groves's report (TS 11/955/3499).
108 'Thelwall then read a letter from a person who signed himself a Scotchman assuring the meeting of the affections of that Country and how much it execrated and detested Mr. Dundas and Mr. Pitt' (Nodder).
109 Just before the meeting broke up (at 6.00 p.m.) a member handed Richter this letter, about which there are some differences in the reports: Taylor said the letter was from Yorke, then at Sheffield; Nodder said the letter described a meeting at Manchester. All agreed that the letter was loudly 'huzzaed'. It stated that they had resolved to petition Parliament no longer (Gosling).
110 Richter explained that 200,000 copies were needed because 100,000 of their last resolutions and of Stanhope's speech had been insufficient (Walsh). No such quantities of any of these documents were printed. Also according to Walsh, Richter said that those who proposed increasing the internal military forces should recollect that arming one part of the nation against the other had cost Charles I his head and James II his throne. 'A Man reported to be a Delegate from Ireland said in alluding to some Remarks on the inordinate Power of the Monarch in this Country – that he was in that enlightened Assembly the National Convention of France at the Time Roberspierre made the Motion for the Abolition of Monarchy & he had but 7 good Republicans to support him – but within 12 Months Monarchy was abolished & Tyranny punished – This was a Lesson the People should never lose Sight of.'
  At the statement about Charles I's head and James II's throne, 'the Persons present shouted and waved their Hats upon a signal from Burk – some Person called Burk to order for promoting this Shouting Burk replied that Zeal ought not to be checked and added he wished to be heard at St. James's' (Gosling).
111 'It was then recommended to the persons forming this meeting to hold themselves in readiness for another call in order to chuse delegates to appear at a Convention which it was hoped and

expected was to be held in about 6 weeks or perhaps sooner at a proper distance from London' (Nodder).
  Gosling understood (perhaps from later conversations) that the convention was to exercise 'the supreme authority' until the election, on the principle of universal suffrage, of a 'Convention of the People'.
  Richter later asserted that the plan for a convention was less definite: at the request of Thelwall, Richter announced that it *might possibly* be necessary to call another general meeting in about six weeks to consider the propriety of calling a convention of delegates of various reform societies in order to discuss the best legal and constitutional means of obtaining a reform in the representation of the people. But, stressed Richter, this was only a matter of possibility (Richter's annotation of the resolutions of the 14 April General Meeting, in BL copy of *First Report . . . Secrecy*, 1794).
112 'There was a kind of shed in which we were all sitting previous to the commencement of the business, and there was a bit of bread and cheese and some porter brought' (Groves's testimony at Hardy's trial, *ST* vol. 24, col. 743).
113 Taylor reported that there were about eighty present, but before the Privy Council he lowered the numbers to fifty or sixty (TS

139

Except a great number of jokes about Sans Coullottes & Swinish Multitude, there was nothing worth notice but the two following circumstances

1st. Mr Thelwall took a pot of porter & blowing off the head, said – "This is the Way I would serve Kings"[114]

2d. He gave a Toast as follows

"The Lamp Iron at the End of Parliamt Street & called for some person to cover it to which some one at the or. end of the Room said "The Treasury Bench"

Green told me that Universal Suffrage & Annual Parliaments were only intended as Ladders to obtain their Ends, & that no Parliaments could do the Country any good at 12 oClock it broke up –

158. Spy Gosling's 'Information':[115] LCS Division 11, 15 April 1794

Source: TS 11/954/3498

On the 15th of April I called at Hillier's to learn from him the names of those Persons

11/963/3509, fo. 89v). Lovett, Richter, Hodgson, Moore, Pearce – all the leading men – dined there. With a hint of weariness Taylor concluded his account: 'the Rights of Man with the same list of Democratical Toasts were given as I have usually heard at the Meetings of the London Correspondg Society all the Songs published by Thelwall was also sung mostly by himself'.

114 'This is the way I would serve all tyrants,' according to LCS members Thomas Bedda [Bedder?], John Powell, Florimand Goddard, Stroad and Ashley ('Minutes of James Powel's Informn', TS 11/958/3503). Stroad is not mentioned elsewhere in LCS papers. Thomas Bedder Jr twice contributed to the subscription for the families of the 1794 state prisoners.

115 All accounts by Gosling are from this document, except his report of 13 May. On 16 April when Gosling informed Wickham that he had become a member, Wickham 'desired me if I should hear any further conversation about Arms to direct my attention particularly to discover whether they were serious in their conversation and really intend to procure Arms or had any secreted'. It is not surprising, then, that Gosling reports numerous conversations about arming. His reports are the basis of a document, drawn up by Wickham on 6 May, about the dangerous tendencies of the LCS: 'Substance of several Informations on the Views and proceedings of the different Republican Meetings known by the Name of Corresponding Societies – particularly those at the Eastern end of the Town and in the City' (TS 11/965/3510A).

who appeared most active at Chalk Farm, as I then knew no other Person who was there excepting him: Hillier then invited me to attend the Division to which he belonged telling me he could introduce me as a Stranger for one night and that if I approved of it he would propose me for a Member and get some other Member to second his Motion on the next meeting night – I went with Hillier;[116] and Gordon the Secretary of the Division asked if there were any new Members to be proposed? Hillier proposed me immediately, and unexpectedly on my part; but as the Meeting at Chalk Farm and at this Division appeared of an extraordinary nature to me, and as Mr. Wickham had before directed me to go with Phillips if he should ask me I consented and was admitted a Member without being seconded (which was usual) or even known by any person present Hillier excepted. The Conversation was that Evening carried on in small Parties some of whom talked about the Convention[117] which had been spoke of at Chalk Farm and about arming to protect that Convention as the Citizens of Paris had done in France. At that Time I considered this Conversation as the Effect of their Minds being heated by the proceedings at Chalk Farm rather than a Plan they really meant to adopt. A new Constitution for the Society was also talked about but it was agreed to defer the consideration thereof 'till a Report should be received from the Committee which Committee I understood was composed of Delegates from the different Divisions.

159. Report from spy Taylor: LCS Division 29, 15 April 1794

Source: TS 11/955/3499

April 15th. 1794.
Meeting of the Londn. Corr Society
Robins Coffee House Shire Lane

Upton in the Chair Ashley the Delegate read the Report from the General Committee

116 This was a meeting of Div. 11 at a public house kept by Mr Holt in Northampton Street, Clerkenwell. About thirty persons were at the meeting (Gosling's testimony at Hardy's trial, *ST* vol. 24, col. 711).

117 'It was said at a Meeting of the 11th. Division That the Convention (which was to supersede the powers of the present Parlt.) was delayed only till a Report could be made from the Committee of Correspondence & Co-operation to whom the whole was referred' ('General State of the Evidence as to Arming', TS 11/956/3501).

Vizt that thirty seven Members had been added to the Society in the course of the last Week   a short Report on some internal Regulations of the Society of no Consequence.

160. Report from spy Metcalfe: LCS Division 6, 16 April 1794 [118]

Source: TS 11/956/3501

Minutes of the 6th. Division of the London Corresponding Society at the Parrot in Green Harbour Court Old Bailey
Wednesday Eveng. 16th. April 1794./.

The Delegate of this Division reported that the Resolution returned to the Committee of Revision by the 11th. Division viz. "That Apprentices shall not be admitted Members of this Society," had been taken into consideration by the Committee and that after much Debate thereon, they had determined to take the Sence of the whole Society upon the Subject and that each Delegate was to report the Opinion of his respective Division to the Committee on their next Night of Meeting.

The Question was then put,[119] and the Majority was "for admitting Apprentices,["] and the Delegate was Ordered to report to the Committee this Opinion of the 6th. Division

I then moved, that in future all the proceedings and business of this Division should be regularly entered in a Book to be provided for that purpose, that the Delegate's Report should be entered in the Book previous to the Meeting of the Division and Read from such Entry, and that the Question should not be put upon any Motion to be made until such Motion was entered in the Book. This was carried unanimously, And the Delegate was desired to submit it to the Committee as a proper Measure for them to recommend to all the other Divisions for their Adoption./

It was observed by Citizen Worship, that the Night of this Division's Meeting being the Night on which Citizen Thelwall gave his Lectures it prevented many from attending those Lectures who very much Wish'd it, he there-

fore Moved that this Division in future meet upon a Monday Evening, instead of Wednesday, which after much debate was carried in the Affirmative.

The Delegate informed this Division, that the Committee had reced a Letter Signed with ten Names, requesting that they might be admitted Members of this Society, and that they might have a Number in Order to form a New Division at Chelsea, which the Committee had thought fit to accede to, and had sent them the Number 22. he did not he said know exactly at what house they met, but would give that information on our next Night. the Delegate of the New Division, was named – Wood.

161. Minutes: LCS General Committee, 17 April 1794 [120]

Source: TS 11/957/3502

London Corresponding Society
April
   17
          34 New Members
18s Collected
Motion that no apprentice be admitted as a delegate
Motion that each Division is at Liberty to chose their own officers with out restriction
Letter from the Constitutional Soccet
appointed a Committe of Cooperation
Cittizen Edward Hodgson to fill up the Committee
Letter from Hereford

162. Spy Goslings 'Information': 21–2 April 1794

Source: TS 11/954/3498

A short Time after this [i.e. after 15 April] I called at Hilliers and found him talking with an Acquaintance (one Davis a Cheesemonger in Tooley Street) in his back parlour – the Subject of their Conversation was a Reform in Parliament. Hillier said the Society were determined to have a Reform and if they could not obtain it by fair means they would by Force.[121] Davis asked Hillier if he had a

118 Metcalfe's description: 'London Corresponding Society / 6th. Division. 16th. April 1794'.
119 Metcalfe told the Privy Council that some argued against the admission of apprentices on the ground that it would make them unfit to be managed by their masters. For the same reason others favoured their admission. All agreed that it was shameful to continue 'the Bondage of an Apprenticeship beyond the 18th Year' (TS 11/963/3509, fo. 65v).

120 These rough minutes are on a scrap of paper 10cm x 16.5cm.
121 At the end of his 'Information', Gosling added a note headed, 'Information respecting Hillier of an exculpatory Nature', in which he explained that Hillier was indebted to LCS members for his livelihood and might have been expressing the opinions of the Society rather than views he wished to see executed. Hillier, a failed tallow

Musket Hillier replied that he had no musket but that he had a Pike[122] Davis said he had two or three Guns but that one of them was a very good Musket and had cost him 28 Shillings – he further said his Brother had also a Musket which he had given 2 Guineas for – I asked Hillier to let me see his Pike he told me he had lent it but that an old Bayonet fixed to a Stock 8 feet long would answer the same purpose as it would reach farther than the Soldier's Bayonets upon their Muskets. Davis talked of purchasing a neutral Bottom but I do not recollect that he said for what purpose.

April the 21st. I attended Divisions 16 & 25 at a Jack Makers in Brick Lane.[123] Charles Turner Williams an American was among others admitted a Member and Dr. Hodgson recommended to be relieved.

April 22d – I went with Hillier to Newgate to see what He called the imprisoned Patriots I was particularly introduced to Dr. Hodgson; but Lloyd and Cummings were also in the same Room. Lloyd was writing at a Table, with a Frenchman (Roselle) standing by him. C. T. Williams came in a short Time after to see Lloyd: He was called Captn. Williams. The conversation I had was more particularly with Dr. Hodgson, during part of which Lloyd was writing at one Table and Cummings was draw-

ing at another. Hodgson asked me some question about the new Constitution of the Society I answered that I was a very young Member and did not understand what the Constitution of the Society was. He said he had been told that the old Constitution was not much attended to but that a new one would be shortly adopted. He said he had not a Copy of it or he would shew it me but the Tything he said was the most material and best part of the plan. I asked him to explain what the Tythings meant which he did thus – He said the Society was to be divided into Sections and those Sections into subdivisions which were called Tythings because they were to consist of ten Persons each – who were to be classed according to their residence – and each Tything was to chuse one Person as a kind of Officer to be called a Tything Man, and who was to have a Duty assigned to him: He further said these Tythings would answer several good purposes as the Persons in each Tything would then know each other and Spies could not get among them.[124] he further said that as they lived near each other the different Tythings might learn the use of arms without suspicion[125] he further observed that in another way it might have a good effect he said the Members of the Corresponding Society were chiefly Labourers and Mechanics who received their Wages and paid their Scores weekly and that their Money enabled many Tradesmen to give Credit to more Opulent Customers and that if the Members of the Society came to a resolution to lay out no ready money with any one who did not belong to the Society many Aristocratic Tradesmen would be unable to serve their other Customers – that some from discontent would join the Society and others learn the value of Liberty in a Jail: If said he we unite the commercial policy of the Quakers to the Zeal diligence and Enthusiasm of other Sects

chandler, had been assisted to take over Eaton's shop with the assurance that Eaton would supply him with enough books for him to make a good living. All Eaton supplied were reform publications. LCS members, who were his principal customers, also assisted him in other ways.

122 According to Hillier, the pike was a defensive weapon he ordered from Mr Morris of Brick Lane. 'It was rumoured in the London Corresponding Society that the Foreign Troops were come up to London to prevent their Meetings and further Associations. It was mentioned several times at several different Meetings that the Members should arm themselves with Pikes' (Hillier's examination before the Privy Council, TS 11/963/3509, fo. 136).

123 One of these divisions meeting at the house of Morris in Spitalfields may have been newly reconstituted. On 6 May Wickham recorded that a new division numerously attended (twenty-five or twenty-six were at this meeting on 21 April) had been opened in Brick Lane and that there had been no regular meeting in that district since Christmas 1792. Another division in the East End was to be opened in Mile End as soon as a meeting place could be arranged; and still another was to be opened in Whitechapel High St in the house of Philips, a greengrocer ('Substance of several Informations'; *ST* vol. 24, cols. 713–14, 728).

124 When they were thus secured from spies, so the leaders allegedly told members, a great number would join the Society. Gosling, or his employer Wickham, recorded that the Society had increased greatly in 1794. For the first quarter of the year, dues of £280 had been paid. A note translates this to a membership of 5600 ('Substance of several Informations').

125 'The Individuals of each Tything are to be exercised at a Members House – the three Tythings form a Section of Thirty Persons and are to be exercised together also in private Houses – the Tything Men are to act as Door-Keepers and to relieve one another every Hour according to which arrangement no Stranger can be admitted to see or know what is passing' (ibid.).

our numbers will soon be to formidible to be resisted. I observed to Hodgson that this might be a very good Plan but that I did not think the Society had Money sufficient to effect anything of consequence: Rosselle (who had attended to this part of our Conversation) immediately said that when the Society should be organized and ready to act Money should not be wanting[126] I understood and I think he said Money might be had from France. We had some Porter and during the Conversation I have stated Lloyd gave the following Toast "The World a Republic or a Desart." Roselle now gave a Toast which was "May every Tyrant be really Toasted". Both these Toasts were drank by all present and Hodgson said I hope soon to see a Revolutionary Tribunal established; all other Tribunals I despise. Lloyd gave a Letter to Roselle who said he was going to Thelwall and should set off the next Day Lloyd said for the Continent Roselle answered "oui" Hillier said what to France Roselle answered "Yes"....

On the same Evening I went to a Meeting of the Division to which I belonged[127] – Gordon the Secretary resigned his Office saying he was sorry to quit the Society just as they they were going to act as well as think and to regenerate their Country. He said he was going to America that he should take with him some Copies of their spirited Resolutions, and circulate them among the popular Societies there. I understood that he was a Silversmith, and, I have since heard that he was known by or acquainted with Edwards. As the meeting was breaking up there was some Conversation about Arms &c Wright the Delegate said to me in the hearing of Hillier and others, I have got my Arms I have a Musket we ought all to have Arms as we may be soon compelled to use them. Hillier and some others accompanied me part of the Way home, they all appeared to understand that the Society intended to Arm

126 Roussel denied he had said this; and Hillier thought Roussel had nothing to do with this discussion of money (examinations before the Privy Council of Jean Baptiste Roussel and John Hillier, TS 11/963/3509, fos. 131v, 169). Richard Hayward, however, recalled that at some point Roussel had spoken of getting money from France.

127 On 22 April, Div. 11 met at the Hope in Northampton Street with about 38 members present, according to Gosling's court testimony. But on cross-examination he reduced his estimate of the number present to 25 or 26 (ST vol. 24, cols. 714, 728).

and to approve of their doing so. A subscription was opened for Hodgson and a Sum collected I gave a Shilling and Hillier was appointed to take the Money to him –

About this time I called at Hillier's one Evening to get a printed Copy of the new Constitution – I found Hillier talking with some Persons whom I do not know but understood to be Members of the Society – the Subject of their Conversation was the Arming of the Society – Hillier said Arms might be had without going to the Tower for them to which another Person answered that they might be easily had at the Artillery House.

163. Report from spy Taylor: LCS Division 2, 21 April 1794

Source: TS 11/955/3499

April 21st.
Meeting of the London Corr Society
No. 3 New Compton Street

The Chair being taken La Matre read the Report from the General Committee vizt. that 37. Members had been added to the Society in the course of the last Week that the five Delegates Thelwall Baxter Moore Hodgson & Lovett appointed by the London Corresponding Society and the same number Appointed by the Society for Constitutional Information had been mutually accepted and their mode of Correspondence adjusted and is to take effect in the General Committee on Thursday next Moore one of the Committee for revising the new Constitution Reported that the Committee had finished the Business and that the Plan of the new Code of Laws had been Ordered to be Printed for the use of the Members (the inclosed is one) in order for their Perusal after which it is proposed that the Chairman of each Division shall on some Subsequent Night read first the Declaration of the Principles and then each Clause or section singly, putting each to the vote by the usual way of a shew of hands & when this has past, the sevl. Divisns. the numbers on both sides the question are to go into the genl. Commee & the adoption of each & every Section to be regulated by the Majority of Numbers – Jones requested permission to read a Speech he had prepared to deliver at the Genl. Meeting but had been advised agt. it, it was very flamatory recommending the Society to pursue violent Measures, mostly a repetition of what he had before said –

164. Report from spy Taylor: LCS Division 29, 22 April 1794

Source: TS 11/955/3499

April 22d. 1794
Meeting of the London Corr. Society
Robins Coffee house   Shire Lane

Smith in the Chair – Ashley the Delegate read the report from the Genl. Commee which in part was the same as the Report in the 2d. Divn. of last night but with the follg. additions that the Treasurer had accod. for £18 wch had been collected at the Door on the Genl. Meeting   Monday Apl. 14th.[128] a short Letter had been reced by the Secretary (Hardy) from the Secy. (Adams) of the Society for C. I. to inform the L. C. Society that they had nominated 6 Delegates (the follg. are the names of four of them   Horn Tooke, Joyce, Lovett, Bonney & Wassel) to correspond & act with the same number of Delegates appd. by the London Corr. Society & that the Society for C. I. wod. act in conjunction & Co operation wth the L. C. Society, a 6th. Delegate was to be added to make the number equal – a Lre had also been reced by the Secretary from a pson of the name of Powell at Hereford desiring to have sent him the plan & rules of the L. C. Society for the ppose of establishing a Society upon the same principles in that City there being psons desirous of joining & to establish a regular correspondce., Hardy reced instructions from the Commee of Corre. to take the necessary steps to facilitate so desirable an event[129] – a Letter was put into the Hog trough at D. I. Eatons   i.e. the Letter Box containing an Accot. of the Herd of pensioners that lived on the luxuries of the Nation to the Ruin of the poor, with advice how to remedy these evils, this Letter was addressed to the L. C. Society with proposals to them to print it, it was sent to the Genl. Commee who ordd. a number to be printed & distributed – Smith stated a Report that was in circulation that Administratn. had it in contemplation to

128 The subscription for Margarot and Gerrald.
129 Joseph Powell revealed the efficacy of the LCS advertisements: he had 'repeatedly' seen Hardy's name in the newspaper as the secretary of the LCS (12 April 1794, TS 11/966/3510B). In reply, Hardy sent copies of the proceedings of the 14 April meeting and explained that the LCS aimed 'to procure Universal Suffrage and Annual Parliaments as the only likely means to annihilate the present most abominable System of Corruption' (n.d., ibid.; on 12 May Hardy told the Privy Council that this letter had been sent 'last Week', i.e. 4–10 May).

bring in a Convention Bill & if this Society did not pursue with much avidity the means of calling a Convention of the people it wod. be prevented by this Bill, then it was said from the Chair (& all joined) it will the sooner bring to issue our point & the word will be Arms, Arms, –

165. Report from spy Nodder (excerpt): 22 April 1794[130]

Source: PC1/21/A35(a)

Mr. N-dd-r's --(5th; Report)-- April --22d. 1794

April 21st: – [Nodder and Sanderson tried to find Williamson, a shoemaker of Charles St, Westminster. B]ut after a very fatiguing & fruitless search they gave it over and they went by Nddr's recommendation to the *Corresponding Soc:* in Shire Lane they enquired there for Orr – he was not there – soon after a person came down stairs who N-dd-r rememberd was at the Club in Worcester street the night he was initiated – he told them they could not be admitted into the Correspd. Soc: any more witht. being members of it and he offerd to propose them – they followed him into the Room where they were proposed and admitted – Among the members was a Man N-dd-r thinks of the name of *Smith* who was distributg. *certain publications* at 1d each one of which was bought by S-nd-rs-n – *Scofield* was *Chairman* of this nights Club he is a young man – is said to be a lawyer and is also of the arming Soc: – N-dd-r was informed by one of the Members that there had been armed meetings at the Grove since he had been there which are adjourned to another place Shelmerdine's wife being inimical to them through fear – while they were in the Room two publications (inclosed herewth) were given to them – About ½ after 10 o'Clock a loose conversation was held upon the prest. principles of Governmt. – the president of the night took from his pocket a little publication which (he said) he had just bought at Spence's in turnstile entitled *"How to Make a King*["] the story is of *Corsica!* and their making a wooden *king* – this he *read* to the *Club* and recd. great *applause*   mention was made of a Vol: of Songs published by a Man whose name N-dd-r thinks is Mathews and for which he absconded but 10 minutes before the Officers came to take him & to search his house – (his flight and escape was effected by means of a

130 Nodder's description: 'Mr. N-dd-r's 5th; Report / April 21st; 1794'. Government description: 'Nodder's Report'.

private informatn. sent him abt. 10 Mins: before the Offs. came as before stated) – At the time they entd. they found his wife just delivd, of a Child and in anor. Room a Man dying that under the bed of the latter it had been contrived to secrete a Number of these Vols. of Songs – A Member then addressed the Club and advised them to be upon their Guard for fear of *Spies* – adding *he was not suspicious of any one in that room* but he knew the man who had informed agt. the above Bookseller – All the Club immediately called for his *Name* – but was answd. *No he was sure that Man* would *never inform again* and it was then said this *Bookseller* was *now* fighting the *Duke* of *York* – upon which it was proposed that *Honourable* mention should be made:

From the complexion of this & the other parts of the Corresponding Socy. & as also of the Arming Socy. N-dd-r is free to say that the danger is great to any Man who is discover'd giving information to G-v-nm-t of their proceedings – he therefore again repeats and requests that neither *his name* or *any Accts.* or *even hint of him* be given in any *manner or form what soever* as to the prest. situation he is in relative to these Socs. and G-v-nmt.

F P. N..

[On 24 April the general committee moved to a room in Beaufort Buildings, Strand, which was leased by Thelwall.[131]

Among the many letters Hardy received in April was one from Richard Davison of Sheffield offering to sell pikes to patriots and begging for encouragement in the enterprise.[132] He asked Hardy to forward to the Norwich Patriotic Society a similar letter, which he enclosed.

Some time after Hardy received this letter, John Edwards, who was planning an arming society, asked Hardy to enquire, in his next letter to Sheffield, if there was any one who could forge some blades for pikes. Hardy read Davison's letter to Edwards and wrote the address on a small piece of paper. At the trial of Hardy, the prosecution presented this letter and Hardy's writing the address as evidence of a national conspiracy to arm. The defence pointed out that Hardy never opened or forwarded the letter to Norwich and never answered Davison's letter.[133]]

166. Spy Gosling's 'Information': 25 April 1794

Source: TS 11/954/3498

April the 25th   In a Conversation at Hillier's[134] with him Bennet[135] and three Persons whom I do not know. – One of these Persons[136] said he had received a Letter from Sheffield which contained a Drawing of some Knives which were making there of a particular construction for cutting the Reins[137] with this Observation   These are the Instruments we shall soon use" (One of of these three persons appeared to be intoxicated and did not join the Conversation)   It was

131 Thelwall, who had been lecturing at No. 3 New Compton St, opened his lecture room in Beaufort Buildings in the Strand on 23 April (*MP* 24 April, p. 1). The LCS general committee met in a room above the large lecture room. Place described it as 'fitted up with benches and desks in the manner of a school room. The presidents chair was in the middle of one of the ends, advanced a few feet from the wall   it was a sort of pulpit   the floor of which was raised about three feet above the room floor, there was a seat for the secretary in front of it raised about half that height, the treasurer and the members of the executive committee had seats at the sides of the President' (*Autobiography*, pp. 140–1). To pay for the use of the room, the delegates were assessed 2d per week, but between 10 May and 3 July 1794 only 10s was collected. This method of defraying the expense of the room must have been abandoned. On 13 June 1795 Thelwall was paid £1 11s 6d for the committee room. The records of sums paid for the various meeting rooms for the general committee indicate a weekly rent of about 2s 6d.

132 24 April 1794, TS 11/966/3510B.
133 *ST* vol. 24, cols. 672, 955. Well before the trial Hardy saw the potential danger of Davison's letter, for when the Privy Council questioned him about it, he commented, 'I had rather not have received it' (TS 11/963/3509, fo. 38v).
134 Changed to 'a Meeting at Hillier's' in 'General State of the Evidence as to Arming'.
135 Richard Bennet, a young mercer, acted as clerk to his brother. He is variously listed as living in Elder Street, Spitalfields, and in Edmunds Row, Mile End. Gosling identified him once as the president of Div. 16 and once as the secretary of the combined Divs. 5 and 16 (TS 11/963/3509, fo. 205; *ST* vol. 24, col. 714; 'General State of the Evidence as to Arming'.
136 'Wixley Westmoreland Bldgs. Falcon Square' – marginal note. Spelled Wicksley and Hicksley in *ST* vol. 24, col. 714.
137 The letter also 'informed him that they had a numerous meeting, and had determined to petition no more for a parliamentary reform' (Gosling's testimony, *ST* vol. 24, col. 715).

said either by the Person who had received the Letter or by Hillier that the principal dependance of the Society was in securing the Royal Family and both Houses of Parliament[138] and that when this was done if they[139] could resist the first Shock there would be no fear afterwards as the Army having no Head to look up to would accept of the additional Pay which would be then offered to them.[140] – Bennet and the others joined in and appeared to approve of it.[141] Bennet walked with me and still kept talking about this plan until I checked him upon Fish Street Hill and told him the Persons behind him were taking notice of him. It seemed to be the Opinion of the Persons present that the Society would soon be sufficiently strong to act, and that their principal Wants were Discipline and Arms.

167. Report from spy Taylor: LCS Division 2, 28 April 1794

Source: TS 11/955/3499

April 28th. 1794.
Meeting of the L. Correspondg, Society
No. 3 New Compton Street

Griffiths in the Chair – Le Maitre the Delegate read the Report from the general Committee but he had taken it so inaccurately that I defer giving it 'till I take it from the Report Tomorrow Evening in the 29th. Division – Pearse proposed reading the Report on the

Revision of the New Constitutn. it met with some opposition & on the question being put it was deferred till the next Meeting of the Division on the following Monday.

168. Report of spy Groves: LCS Division 2, 28 April 1794[142]

Source: TS 11/954/3498

Monday 28th. April 1794

I Called on Mr Green of Castle Street Liecester square perfumer and told him I called for what we had talked about – he brought me directly about a dozen Secrets, & said he should have in about a Week a fresh lot from Sheffield – I ask'd him if they were made there & he said yes – after some conversation I bid him look me out one of the best – he tried several, & gave me one which he charged 2s/6 for

He asked me at the same time if I had got the printed proceedings at Chalk Farm – I told him I had not, & he gave me two printed Copies, saying, There is one for your friend –

I asked him if he had sold many of the secrets – he told me about or near 300[143] I enquired if he could tell whether the time was fixed for the Meeting of the London Corresponding Society & the Society for Constitutional Information – he told me he did not but that it would soon be & that whenever it was, the real place would be kept a Secret, to prevent being interrupted by Magistrates, till the Morning of the day but that a *sham* place would be advertized, although he

138 At his examination Hillier said that he had heard members of the Society say that it would be 'proper' to seize the Royal Family and Members of both Houses. Hillier had heard this more than once or twice and admitted that he might have said it himself (TS 11/963/3509, fo. 139). In general, Hillier confirmed Gosling's account of conversations.
139 Gosling assumed that 'they' referred to the members of the different reform societies (testimony at Hardy's trial, ST vol. 24, col. 715).
140 Hillier had heard 'some thing said about the Army having 1s 6d per Day instead of 6d – it was said it would have an Influence on the Minds of the Soldiers – that they would not act agt their Countrymen' (examination of Hillier, fo. 139v). At Hardy's trial Gosling testified that 'there was something said, I believe it was eighteen-pence; that the men would not fight for sixpence a-day if they could have eighteen-pence' (ST vol. 24, col. 715).
141 At his examination Bennet denied participating in or even hearing the conversations Gosling reports in this document (TS 11/963/3509, fos. 204-9).

142 Government description: 'Monday 28 April 1794 / Mr. Groves's Report / Rx 29'.
143 At Hardy's trial Groves added a detail about this purchase of knives at Green's shop: 'Mr. Green told me to speak very low, for the parlour-door was open which was adjoining the shop, and he smiled and said, for my wife is a damned aristocrat . . . and we both of us laughed' (ST vol. 24, cols. 744, 759). Green, however, denied these allegations: 'I swear I said no such thing; these knives all lay open in my shop, so far from hiding them from my wife, or from any man in the parish, that they lay openly in the show-glass, and in the window for sale.' Green also denied saying that he had sold nearly 300 of them. Actually he had sold only 16, but when Groves asked him if the knives sold well, he said, 'yes'. 'No man in business would tell a person that that it was not a saleable article; they would not purchase it if he did.' Far from being of a new construction, these knives had been in cutlers' shops for the previous seven years (testimony at Hardy's trial, ibid., cols. 835-6).

thought it wod. be on Blackheath   In the Evening I attended the Division in Compton Street when the Report of the Commee appointed to revise and abridge a former report of the Commee of the Constitution of the London Corresponding Society was to be read & considered

Mr Jefferies voted in the Chair At this time ½ past 9 there were but 13 members present – Mr Le Maitre, a very young man & one of the Delgates, read a Recommendation from the General Commee of Constitution to the different Divisions for a Subscription for Dr. Hodson, (in Newgate) and the rest of the Suffering patriots.

Mr. Brooks opposed any Subscription for Dr Hodson, because it had been before voted that his conduct had not merited the compassion of the Society – he had been guilty of intemperate behaviour & his conduct had done an injury to the general cause

Two or three Citizens said That though they did not justify Citizen Hodson, yet they argued for him on the general ground of compassion, & on account of his wife & children who were nearly in a starving state

Mr. Pearce said that Citizen Hodson had been violent & such violence could do no good but that Dr. Hodson was a Member of that division almost ever since its institution he was one of the first to propose a subscription & did subscribe for others, when he could not have thought of ever wanting it himself – that tho' he had been wrong in the warmth of his expression, yet we should forget his failings & remember only his virtues

Mr Brooks again stated that he had no objection to give Charity, but if the Society had a Constitution it ought to be preserved pure – that that Division had already passed a vote on Dr. Hodsons former application & rejected it. – they could not, therefore, as a Society make a subscription for him, & that if they were daily altering & contradicting their own resolutions their Society would become ridiculous & that if they now voted a Subscription any desperate man might get himself into Dr. Hodsons situation merely to be provided for

This idea was generally scouted on the ground of improbability

Mr Moore said Citizen Brooks only meant consistency in the Division & not to oppose Charity

Mr. Pearce said the best way would be to move for the Chairman to quit the Chair & then they might consistently, as Individuals grant him a Benevolence

This occasioned some laughter. Le Maitre

said – It was no *direction* from the General Committee, but merely a Recommendation – that altho' he had inadvertently introduced the name of Dr Hodson yet the Recommendation was general, as it included the suffering patriots, & also that whatever subscription was raised it was to be disposed of as the General Committee should think fit

It was then stated there were but a few members present & it was proposed to adjourn the consideration of the recommendation to the next Monday Night. –

This was agreed to by show of hands   It was then proposed to take into Consideration the New Report of the Committee on the New Constitution

One or two objected to taking it into Consideration then as it was impossible to give an Opinion upon Laws to govern a Society, witht. those Laws had been properly & timely distributed – that hardly any Copies had been given out – that it was now late, near 11 oClock, & to consider it now would be taking up the whole of the Night

Mr Brooks said it would be like smuggling a Bill in another Society, & that they were going to determine on what had hardly been seen or read –

I proposed that we should take up only for that nights consideration "The Declaration of Principles" – that they should be first read, and afterwards each Declaration debated, if any debate was necessary & regularly put to the Vote, both on account of each Citizen thoroughly understanding the foundation & ground work of the Structure as well as lighten the business of the next Evening – but leave the Consideration of the Organizing part of the Constitution for the next Monday

This idea met approbation, & Citizen —— proposition was put & carried Nem Con.

Mr Le Maitre then read The Declaration of principles through & began with the first wch. passed Nem: Con:

The 2d. was read & passed the same

The 3d. which stated "that all Government abstractedly considered is considered being itself an evil" &c seemed likely to promote a debate[144] a motion was made to adjourn & seconded it being ½ past 11

A Conversation then began respecting a

144 'That all government abstractedly considered being in itself an evil, and no farther to be approved in practice, than as it may tend to prevent other evils of a more serious nature, the experiment in every country ought to be not how much the people will bear but with how little the grand object of general happiness can be secured.'

speech which some said had been made by Mr Mainwaring, the Chairman of the ⟨Quarter Sessions⟩ at Clerkenwell Green, Yesterday to the Grand Jury of the County in which Speech the London Corresponding Society were publicly alluded to –

It was recommended that the Citizens shod. attend Citizen Thelwalls Lecture on Wednesday Evg. in Beaufort Buildings who would address the Citizens on that Subject[145]

169. Report from spy Nodder: LCS Division 13, 28 April 1794[146]

Source: TS 11/953/3497

Mr: Nddr's - - - - - - *(7th: Report)* - - - - - - *April 30th: 1794*
Apl. 28th. – Called upon S-nd-son and at 8 the same Evening went with him to the Lond: *Correspd. Socy:* held in *Shire* lane – the Citizen delegate *Hooper* who is Sec: to this Soc: for the prest. quarter informed the division that the Comee. had not compleatly investigated the New Constitn. – he wished this divisn. would defer going into that business 'till the members had well considd. it by reading the printd. Paper (*sent pr. last Report*) but in this he was overruled and the *said new Constitn.* read Article by Article & several ammendmts. made thereto and also some of the Old Constitn. kept in – the whole of the eveg. was taken up on this business – *Two New Members were admitted* – Next Monday the remaining *Articles* of the new Constitn. not discussed are to be considd: and adjusted –

Between 9 & 10. o'Clock *Frankloe* came into the room – he was dressed in *a blue Coat & red Collr. - buff on white Cloth Waistct. & breeches, black Stiff Stock* and *a Military Cock'd Hat* with *a large Cockade*

145 In an attempt to suppress Thelwall's lectures, John Reeves presented one of them to the grand jury to see if it would furnish a foundation for a prosecution. Two grand juries at the Court Leet of the Duchy of Savoy refused to find his lecturing a nuisance (Mrs Thelwall, *Life of John Thelwall*, pp. 137-9). Mainwaring, addressing the grand jury, described the members of the corresponding societies as indolent, dissolute men of profligate manners and seditious hearts (newspaper cutting in Place Collection, vol. 36, fo. 107). Thelwall lectured on the subject of this prosecution for at least two nights, as both Taylor and Metcalfe reported (TS 11/966/3510B; "Persons agt. whom Taylor's Reports furnish Evidence", TS 11/954/3498).
146 Government description: 'In Mr Gretton's of 30th April 1794'.

Abt. 10 – o'Clock one of the Members informed the Club that News was just arrived that the Emperor of Germany had demanded of this Country 1½ Million to enable him to carry on the War – which information was recd. with a great apparent pleasure & joy by all prest. who were abt. 50 in Number – As it was said – "this would bring *Pitt* to his sences – for he would now be obliged to make a peace and other such like jibes and taunts were thrown out with great seeming satisfaction –

F.. P. N

170. Report from spy Taylor: LCS Division 29, 29 April 1794

Source: TS 11/955/3499

April 29th. 1794.
Meeting of the London Correspondg. Society Robin's Coffee house   Shire Lane

Bullock in the Chair – Ashley the Delegate read the Report from the general Committee vizt. that 18 Members had been made in the course of last Week & added to the Society, several Motions from various divisions to the General Committee for the purpose of introducing many regulations in the Divisions, the Committee objected to them because when the New Constitutn. was adopted it would answer every end proposed by those Motions – A Letter had been received by the Secretary (Hardy) from Hodson a prisoner in Newgate requesting the Society to relieve him from his extreme distress, four & six pence was only collected in this Division, the Delegates recommended the Members to attend constantly their own Divisions & to visit as often as possible the other Divisions in order to give energy to the Society, he added he had great satisfaction in informing this Divisn. that the Friends of Liberty & Freedom at Bristol & Newcastle upon Tyne had greatly increased in number & spirit.[147]

147 The Bristol Constitutional Society must have received the circular letter 'The Critical Moment is arrived', for they asked for a sketch of the LCS plan for a convention (John Cockburn to Hardy, 24 April 1794, TS 11/966/3510B). The newly formed reform societies of Newcastle-upon-Tyne informed the LCS of their surreptitious existence; they seem to have heard of the LCS from an advertisement testifying the Society's approval of Margarot and Gerrald; they request information about the LCS (to Hardy, 24 April 1794, ibid.). In reply to Bristol, Hardy did not speak of the convention, but he did announce that 'a printed circular letter, of which you may expect a copy in a few days, has

171. Spy Gosling's 'Information': LCS Divisions 6 and 11, 29–30 April 1794

Source: TS 11/954/3498

April 29th – I attended a Meeting of 2 Divisions No. 11 and No. 6.[148] – A print of the Manual and Platoon Exercise was produced by Worship Secretary to the 6th. Division and recommended for the use of the Society.[149] The Figures were in Caps and Pantaloons and Worship said the Caps were to be coloured Red. Dalton was appointed Secretary in the Room of Gordon, and much was said about Arms. April 30th I called at Hillier's and told him of the Print which Worship had brought to the Society and said I did not think I could learn the Exercise from it. Hillier answered that many of the Members already knew their Exercise and would teach it to others after the Tythings were adopted. He particularly mentioned that Stiff a Hair Dresser in Paternoster Row who belonged to a Division that met at Robin's Coffee House and Fletcher who inlisted Soldiers for the East India Company could teach it. Hillier afterwards informed me that the Print produced by Worship was drawn by Stiff.

172. Spy information about new LCS Division: 30 April 1794[150]

Source: TS 11/965/3510A

On Wednesday April 30th. it was stated that 50 Persons in the neighbourhood of White Fryars principally Irish would join the Society on the following Week. It was observed on this occasion by the Man who proposed them, that as most of them were ignorant it would be better for them to have a Delegate from one of the old divisions "as a Man might be a good Soldier who would not do for an Officer." In consequence of this remark it was settled that six of them were to be made at Robin's Coffee House Shire Lane where one Higgins from another division was to meet them & be their Delegate and they were to agree upon a House in the neighbourhood of White Fryars for their future Meetings.

been determined upon' (draft in Thelwall's hand n.d., ibid.; on 12 May Hardy told the Privy Council that this letter had been sent 'last week'). Hardy testified that the circular letter, intended to be sent the week of his arrest, was to announce the union of the LCS and SCI (examination before Privy Council, TS 11/963/3509, fo. 41v). In reply to Newcastle-upon-Tyne, Hardy expressed a willingness to unite with other reform societies and instanced the LCS–SCI committee of correspondence and cooperation. 'If ever a crisis arrived that required the exertions of the People, . . . it is the present. In God's name then let us use these exertions; – we are called upon by every thing that is dear to us as men and as Christians' (to P. Smith, 1 May 1794, TS 11/966/3510B).

148 When the keeper of the Parrot was threatened with loss of licence, Div. 6 temporarily joined Div. 11 at the Hope in Northampton St. Forty or fifty people were present, several of them 'genteel well dressed People', and, for the first time, a gentleman's coachman and two shop-men. Wright, Eaton, Gordon, Laney, Skinner and Burks were also present (Substance of several Informations'; 'General State of the Evidence as to Arming'; *ST* vol. 24, col. 729; 'Voluntary Examination of Edward Gosling', fo. 97).

149 The large (33 x 33 cm) drawing showing positions for arming was professedly intended for pro-government arming associations (then under discussion) but really for these revolutionary arming clubs ('Substance of several Informations'). The drawing is advertised at the end of John Harrison's *Letter to Dundas*.

150 From 'Substance of several Informations'. When Wickham, the compiler of this document, was asked who proposed these men, he did not know. 'He had a strong Irish accent but his name was not known to the person I employed – I have cautioned him against being too curious in asking people's names.'

Besides this Irish influx, Wickham noted 'a new description of members, i.e. 'several persons from the Water Side Porters and Shopmen from Warehouses in the City and some Gentlemens Servants'. In a note he identified two of these new members: Hagen of Gravel Lane, a baker for the military forces at Plymouth, who was to distribute pamphlets there; and Aaron Booth, of Warwick Ct, Warwick Lane, who was to bring four of his fellow servants to be members.

PART FIVE

1794B
(May-June)

173. SCI Anniversary Dinner (report by Groves, excerpt): 2 May 1794

Source: TS 11/953/3497[1]

[On 2 May 1794 the Society for Constitutional Information held an anniversary dinner at the Crown and Anchor. Twenty or thirty LCS members were present, some of them having been given the tickets, which cost 7s 6d. Groves was one of the recipients of a free ticket.[2] A paraphrase of his report includes the following:]

Davis of the Morning Post told Groves that the Time of the General Meeting of the two Societies was not determin'd that they waited for News of the French getting a Victory over the Allied Army or some Part of it, & then to call the Meeting, by which they were in hopes of greatly increasing their Numbers.

Sevl of the Members of the Corr Society desired Groves to go with them to Thelwall's Lecture – a Riot being expected there – he went accordingly.

[On 2 May Margarot, with Muir, Palmer and Skirving, sailed for New South Wales, after being on board the *Surprise* for more than eleven weeks. On 7 March Hardy visited them, taking £20 which he had solicited from the Norwich Societies.[3] During April Margarot sent Hardy three letters, chiefly about his financial affairs and his failure to hear from other reformers.[4]]

1 i.e. 'Index to Bundle J'.
2 At 9.00 or 10.00 p.m. on the night before the dinner, Hardy went to Groves's house, gave him a ticket, and refused to take money for it. Francis Dowling, however, paid 7s 6d for his ticket. Other LCS members among the 350–400 diners were Hardy, Thelwall, Richter, Lovett, Moore, Pearce and Jones. Government saw the distribution of free tickets as a manifestation of the control of the LCS by the SCI (*ST* vol. 24, cols. 749, 760, 960; *MP* 2 May 1794, p. 3).
3 Letters, Hardy to Charles Cordrel, 14 Feb. 1794; Hardy to Henry Buckle, 12 March 1794; both in TS 11/953/3497.
4 12, 21 April, n.d. [28 April?], TS 11/966/3510B. For several years Margarot continued to write to

174. Report from spy Taylor: LCS Division 2, 5 May 1794

Source: TS 11/955/3499

May 15th. 1794 [May 5]
Meeting of the London Correspg. Society
No. 3 New Compton Street

Jones in the Chair – Le Maitre the Delegate read the Report from the General Committee

Hardy, each time mentioning that he had not heard from anyone in the LCS.

In 1810 he returned to England and attempted to refute accusations made in 1794 by his shipmates Muir, Palmer and Skirving. Even before the *Surprise* left England there were signs of friction between Margarot and the other three reformers. 'Some Grocery stores were received after we were put here,' wrote Skirving. 'At first they were called our Stores. Now, – Mr. Margarot speaks of them always in the singular number; and yet does not charge me for my share of the cost' (letter to Hardy, 12 April 1794, ibid.). After they sailed, Margarot allegedly sent Skirving a bill for 25 or 30 shillings for some fifty or sixty copies of the *Englishman's Right* which had been given to Skirving in Edinburgh ('Maurice Margarot's account current with the London Corresponding Society from November the 6th. 1793 . . . untill the 31st. day of January 1794 . . .', ibid.; Thomas Fyshe Palmer, *A Narrative of the Sufferings of T. F. Palmer, and W. Skirving, During a Voyage to New South Wales, 1794, on Board the Surprise Transport*, 1797, pp. 42–3; in Add MSS 27816, fos. 23v–24).

This bill is a minor incident in the dissension between Margarot and the others. Margarot became friendly with Captain Campbell and sided with him when he accused Palmer and Skirving of plotting a mutiny. After their arrival in New South Wales on 25 Oct. 1794, Muir, Palmer and Skirving sent letters to England, dissociating themselves from Margarot and accusing him of instigating the mutiny charge. This letter were published in the newspapers (*MC* 29 July 1795, p. 3; *Telegraph*, 13 July 1795, p. 3). Palmer's account of the journey to Botany Bay was published in London by his friend Jeremiah Joyce. These publications started a long-lasting quarrel between the supporters of each side. As late as 1836–7, there were objections to putting Margarot's name on a plaque with the names of Muir, Palmer and Skirving.

Besides defending his reputation after his return, Margarot tried unsuccessfully to claim family properties in France. To support him, former LCS members organized a subscription; Lord Byron gave ten guineas. Margarot died in Nov. 1815.

vizt. That 37 Members had been added to the Society in the course of the last Week, it also relates a dispute that had arose between the Committee & the Artist (Goddard of Rathbone Place) who made the Die from which the Medals was struck that was presented to the 12 Jury & 2 Counsel on D. I. Eaton's Trial, on the price of the Die & the Sale of the Copper Medals the G Committee ordered a Committee of 3 to wait on Mr Goddard & settle the Business, the Report on the Revision of the new Constitution was then Read (by Pearse S. Secretary) as far as the Declaration of Rights & on reading the third Article beginning with the words "All Government abstractedly considered is an Evil" a debate arose in which several Members spoke those who were against this Clause argued that it would give room to the Enemies of the Society & the Cause to declaim against their principles. Those who argued in favor of it asserted that it was strictly consistent with the principles of the Society, on the question being put it was carried three to one in favor of its Standing, the remaining Clauses was all carried without a division except the fifth position in the 6th. Article which was considered only as a Repitition of the preceeding one & ordered to be omitted.[5]

175. Report from spy Nodder: LCS Division 13, 5 May 1794[6]

Source: PC1/21/A35(a)

Mr; N-dd-r's - - - - (10th Report) - - - - May 6th: 1794

May 5th; Went with Saunderson to the London Corresponding Socy: The delegate to this Soc: (*Saml: Cooper* –) who is also Secrety. & treasurer (for the prest. quarter of the Year & who pays all the Money that comes into his hands in the course of this ¼ – at the expiration thereof into the hands of *Mr. Hardy* the principal Secy.) – called upon a Mr. *Evans* to take the Chair – the business was then open'd by reading the transactions of the past week by sd. *Cooper* who reported that *Thirty one new Members* had during the week been made by the difft. Socs; – that a silver *Medall* was striking by order of the Comee; thereof and that a Number of the same was to be

struck upon white mettal and sold to the Members at 6d / each which might be had of the *Delegates* of the difft *Sections* – he also reported that Dr; *Hudson* who is in *Newgate* at the suit of the Crown for sedition had wrote to some of the sections for relief – *ye Secy. said he wished a contribution should take place for the Dr.* and *others suffering in the like Cause* – which took place and the *Money subscribed* was given *to him* a member observed that the Dr. was inprisoned for words not half so bad as were spoke in that room and thought no sedition. –

The Secy: also informed the meeting that two of the divisions were removed – the one into *Bishop gate Street* and the other to *a private house* at the *West end of the Town* –

Five of the Members were of very respectable appearance – one of the name of *Francis a tall, genteel Man with a dimple* at the bottom *of his Chin of a placid easy countenance.* another of them is a *short thin Young Man* and is a *Fishhook maker* in or near *Billiter Land* –

The chief business of this night's meeting was to consider and adjust some of the remaining Articles of the *New Constitutn.* at 11 o'Clock N-dd-r & S-nd-n left the room –

F . . P. N . .

May 6th; 1794

176. Spy Gosling's 'Information': LCS Division 6, 5 May 1794

Source: TS 11/954/3498

May the 5th I attended a meeting of the 6th Division at Hillier's House.[7] A Mr. Metcalfe said to be Clerk to the Tallow Chandlers Company and on that account a suspected Member asked when the convention was to meet but received no particular Answer. Worship again produced the print but did not come 'till after some of the Members were gone – he sold two or three of them – he looked at me and said he should have some properly delineated with the Bonnet Rouge. His Reason for looking at me was that I had called at his House to buy a coloured one by desire of Mr. Wickham, he then told me they were not yet coloured but that they would be in a few Days – I called again and he told me

---

5 This article lists the civil rights of the individual; sub-points 4 and 5 deal with freedom of speech and worship.
6 Government description: 'In Mr Gretten's 6 May 1794'.

7 Div. 6 (and Div. 11) had to leave the Hope because Mr Holt, the keeper, received a 'cautionary letter' from his landlord ('Substance of several Informations'). Skinner, Burks and Holt were present.

if I would give him my Address he would send me one   this I declined.[8]

177. Report from spy Taylor: LCS Division 29, 6 May 1794

Source: TS 11/955/3499

May 6th.
Meeting of the 29th. Divn. of the London Correspg. Socy. at Robin's Coffee house Shire Lane

Maine in the Chair – Ashley the Delegate read the Reports from the General Committee & which was verbatim the same as given in the 2d. Division the preceeding Evening   with this addition that a Letter had been sent from the Committee of Correspondence to the Society of Manchester requesting to know their proceedings on their general Meeting – The Report on the Revisn. of the New Constitutn. was brot. forward – Read – and every Clause past without a Debate.

178. Richter's narrative: LCS General Committee, 8 May 1794[9]

Source: Add MSS 27816, fos. 459-9v

At the last regular meeting [i.e. 8 May] of this [General] Cee: it had been resolved that it was desirable that a full & complete Representation of one in ten of such as were deemed actual members of the Society should be convened to collect & arrange the opinions of the divisions respecting the two Reports of the Constitution of the Society & to determine finally thereon.

179. Resolution of LCS General Committee: 9 May 1794 [10]

Source: TS 11/966/3510B

London Corresponding Society
May 9th. 1794 –

Resolved
That Citizen Hardy take all the Medals out of the Hands of Citizen Goddard and Order

Others to be struck if necessary and that they be by him distributed at the following places Vizt:
Citn. J Thelwall
Smith
Hillier
Spence
Eaton and At Other places
which may be by the Secretary thought proper

John Ashley – Chairman
John Pearce Sub. Secty.

180. Spy Gosling's 'Information': 9 May 1794

Source: TS 11/954/3498

May the 9th – I called at Hillier's. several Members were there some of whom went away – there remained Hillier – Bennet – J. Hill[11] – Baxter who I understand was a Member of the Committee of Correspondence and Cooperation and myself. – Baxter said he had been with Mr. Joyce – with Gerald and also with an Officer who had lately kissed the Queens Hand upon his promotion. the latter person Baxter stated to have used a particularly indecent expression relative to the Queen and to have asked him Why they did not blow up the Family altogether. Baxter further stated that Mr. Joyce was Secretary to Earl Stanhope and that he had informed him that the last Speech of Earl Stanhope was to be published and that a number of Copies were to be printed with an addition   Baxter said those Copies which had the addition must be circulated with great Caution and only shewn to Persons in whom we could confide. Baxter further said that Mr. Joyce had told him that Stone had too much firmness to let them by intimidation get any thing out of him and that

the hand as Pearce's. Government observation: 'The distribution of these Medals which were struck on the Occasion of Eaton's Acquittal seems to have been the only Business submitted to the General Committee of Delegates since the Appointment of the Committee of Co-operation' (index to LCS papers mentioned in the Report from the Committee of Secrecy, TS 11/956/3501). Presumably this resolution was agreed upon at the meeting of the General Committee on the previous night.

8 Gosling had given a fictitious address when he joined (*A Vindication of the London Corresponding Society*, p. 8).
9 This is part of Richter's narrative of the meetings of the Society in May, of his arrest on 16 May, of his examination before the Privy Council, and of the first three weeks of his imprisonment. It may have been written as early as 6 June, a few days after he was allowed pens, paper and books.
10 Government copy in TS 11/959/3505 identifies

11 'Shoe Maker in Ferriers Buildgs Bishopsgte.' – marginal note. According to 'General State of the Evidence as to Arming' (which calls this 'a meeting'), Roussel and Harvey were also present, and those who remained included Reed, a shoemaker; and an unnamed weaver from Elder St, Spitalfields (Bennet?).

he had nothing to fear[12] – Hamilton Rowan's Person he said was so remarkable he feared he would be retaken but if ten thousand Pounds would effect his Escape it was ready. He now introduced the Subject of Thelwall's Lectures and the Conduct of Mr. Reeves; – the Jury he stated to have attended a Lecture and to have declared it no nuisance, he likewise spoke of one Richards – as having some Power and being friendly to Thelwall: Baxter then said that Hutchins had acted very wrong by endeavouring to check their Huzzaing at Chalk Farm – he said shouting inspired them with Enthusiasm and that was every thing he then recommended us to attend Thelwall's Lecture – and to shew our approbation by shouting – he said it had a good Effect – and Thelwall had no objection – but he further directed that when we met at Public Houses, no noise should be made for fear of hurting a Citizen Landlord. Baxter then stated that in a Conversation he had with one of the Guards he had been told that if the Society once shewed themselves in Force they would find more Friends in the Army than they expected; he said the Old Soldiers in Westminster were in general Friendly to their Cause but that we must expect some resistance from the Young Recruits on account of their Ignorance.[13] Baxter said one Moore had been successful in making converts of the Soldiers and was very active, and further that the Committe of Correspondence and Cooperation were then preparing an address to the Army; and that Men of abilities and prudence were wanted to circulate them among the Army.[14] I said this would be a dangerous Employment and that I thought the Fear of Imprisonment would

deter any Person from undertaking it: I further told Baxter that when I went to see Dr. Hodgson in Newgate I was shocked to see a Man bred to a liberal profession in such a wretched distressed Situation – Baxter replied that I should recollect that Dr. Hodgson was imprisoned thro' his own Imprudence and not from any thing he had done to serve the Society and that they had no other Reason for assisting him at all than that he wished well to the Cause: but said he Men like Gerald and others who suffer in the Cause of the Society we are bound to support and if the Expences of sending Persons to Scotland and the many calls we have at present for Money had not reduced our Funds we would support them better. I said the Society discriminated very justly. Baxter now said that before the Convention was called, it was necessary that we should have an Armed Force to protect it, and therefore could not meet so soon as was expected he then asked me If I knew any Friends who would purchase some Pikes.[15] – I answered that I should like to purchase one, but that it would not be of much use unless I knew how to use it – Baxter then directed me to go to the Parrot in Green Arbour Court in the Old Bailey that Day Week about 8 o Clock and to ask for a Young Man whose Name was Edwards who would be called out to me and to tell Edwards that Baxter had sent me – he said Edwards would then let me have a Pike and introduce me to some Persons with whom I might learn to use it he said Edwards could use the Pike very well and that the Woman who kept the Parrot had some empty Houses where we might learn without suspicion. He said Thousands of Pikes were making at Sheffield – that the Heads were to be sent from there and to be stocked in Town, and explained that they differed from Hillier's Pike as they had a Spear a Hook and a Cutter. he said they were so cheap that many would buy them who could not afford to buy a Musket and would be more useful as Persons might do mischief with Muskets if they did not know how to use them. He said he knew there were Spies in the Society and therefore nothing about Pikes must be talked

12 William Stone, a coal and coke merchant of Rutland Place, Upper Thames St, was arrested on 3 May for allegedly conspiring with his brother, John Hurford Stone, and William Jackson to provide France with information about the probable reaction of the English and Irish to a French invasion. Although Stone's assistance to Jackson (on behalf of Stone's brother in Paris) took place between February and April 1794, he was not tried until 28 Jan. 1796. He was acquitted (*ST* vol. 25, cols. 1155–1438; Goodwin, *Friends of Liberty*, pp. 322–4).

13 'but that if they could but gain one third of the Army, the remainder if they did not join them, would not act against them with any spirit' – 'The Voluntary Examination of Edward Gosling', fo. 99. Cf. *ST* vol. 24, col. 716.

14 Baxter said that the address would contain 'some strong resolutions [and] that prudent and determined men were wanted to propagate the opinions contained in those resolutions' (Gosling's testimony, *ST* vol. 24, col. 716).

15 Gosling attributed Baxter's new openness with him to a recent incident: Gosling routed from Hillier's bookshop a man who was questioning Mrs Hillier and trying 'to take advantage of her Answer'. Then, for over an hour while the stranger watched the shop from outside, Gosling remained with Mrs Hillier. Baxter, so Gosling speculated, heard of the incident and assumed it was safe to speak in front of Gosling.

of in the Divisions,[16] and directed that whenever we heard any talk about arming at any of the Divisions we should immediately dis-approve of it and put them in mind of the Caution which was usually read from the Chair. I told Baxter that I thought when Government found we were armed and determined we should have a Reform without coming to Blows   to this Baxter answered "Is there one Man in the Society who believes a Parliamentary Reform is all we want; no not one": he further said that many Men of Property who had hitherto kept back on account of the sanguinary Conduct of the French were willing to come forward as they were now convinced that a Revolution might be effected in a few Hours. He said if the French who were prisoners could be set at Liberty they would be useful but that the Emigrants if they resisted should share the Fate of the Swiss at Paris. Baxter farther said that it must be expected some Blood will be shed – that Mr. Pitt – Mr. Reeves and some others[17] had offered such Insults to the People that Human Nature could not overlook that the People must and would have Vengeance. He said the opinion of one Person was of little Consequence but that he did not wish the King or his Family to lose their Lives – he thought they might let him go to Hanover and take his Family with him. I walked towards home with Baxter who then informed me that the address of the Committee of Correspondence which was preparing for the army was calculated to excite a Jealousy between them and the French Emigrants and to make them dissatisfied with their pay and Treatment, and recommended me to mix with the Soldiers to treat them with Beer and to use Arguments to the Effect above stated but first to try their principles, if I found them favourable or moderate to go on by Degrees but if I found them Aristocrates not to proceed.[18] Bennet – Hillier and Hill were present and appeared to

16 'But recommended that nothing about Pikes should be talked of at the Divisions 'till the new Constitution was adopted and the principles of the Members tried' – 'The Voluntary Examination of Edward Gosling', fo. 99; cf. ST vol. 24, cols. 717–18.
17 Dundas was named in Gosling's testimony at Hardy's trial (ST vol. 24, col. 718).
18 'He [Baxter] stated the means that Moore had used to get over some of the army; that he had told them that by their oath they were to fight for their king and country, but when the king and country were at variance, they had a right to fight on which side they pleased' – Gosling's testimony.

approve of every thing Baxter said, but I have not noticed them much as I took the principal share in the Conversation with Baxter and directed my attention to him particularly because I had been before told that he was of the Committee with Thelwall – Horne Tooke &c and I therefore supposed that he had the best Information of the real Intentions of the Society.

181. Hardy's account of his arrest: 12 May 1794

Source: Letter, Hardy to Place, 7 July 1831, pasted into Richter–Place copy of Report from the Committee of Secrecy, 1794, in BL C.61.6.16.(1)

Dear Sir/   Agreeably to your request I have endeavoured to give you as near as I can recolect at this distance of time some of the particulars respecting that infamous seizure of my person and property which was effected on the 12th. of May 1794 at 6 O'Clock in the Morning at my house No. 9 Piccadilly. At that early hour there was an uncommon loud knocking at the street door which awakened me and I instantly got up hastily put on my breeches and slippers only, and went to see what it could mean. When I opened the door, in a moment E. Lawzun rushed in. At that time he was an assistant kings Messenger, a new hand, but very active in his new situation. He was followed by John Gurnel a kings Messenger – P. Macmanus and John Townshend constables of Bow St. Office, more generally known by the name of thief takers – John King Esqr. now Sir John, one of the Under secretaries of state and I think two or three more, they all followed me into the parlor. Lawzun then took a paper out of his pocket and said it was Warrant from the secretary of state to apprehend me on a charge of High Treason, and to search my house. He opened the paper and showed me Dundas's signature he immediately folded it up and put it into his pocket. I did not read it, he would not allow me time. He then asked me for my keys which I refused. He then took the pocker from the fire place and said, I shall soon open them. Mr. King said no no send for the smith, who was in waiting at the street door ready to be called in with a large basket of tools fit to open all sort of locks, which he effected in a few minutes. Then the plunder began. They ransacked trunks, boxes, drawers, and desk. Hundreds of letters and manuscript papers belonging to the London Corresponding Society, were seized which they carried away in four silk handkerchiefs. And many old and valuable private letters from kind friends in America and other places. They were not satisfied with letters and papers only, but they took books and pamphlets which nearly filled a corn sack. Not a single article did they *Mark*. Now figure to yourself if you can what a state of mind my dear Wife was in when she witnessed all that nefarious transaction, sitting up in her bed and could not get up to dress herself among so many strange men, untill the plunderers had left the *parlour*, which was our *bedroom* at that time. She was then in a very delicate state of health at that time being six months gone with child, three months after *she died in child bed.* The next Morning that Melancholy event I was informed of by one of the Warders, being then a close prisoner in the Tower. The state of mind I was then in is easier concieved than described. When they had ransacked every place in our bedroom that they thought fit they then went into the shop Expecting no doubt to find treason hatching among the Boots and shoes. In their absence my Wife got up and dressed herself, and when they returned to the parlour they searched the bed all over. Before the plunderers had left the parlour I was sent off in charge of Mr. *Gurnel* the kings Messenger in a Hackney coach with the silk handkerchiefs full of the letters and papers with *Townsend* to assist him to take care of his prisoner. I was taken to Mr. *Gurnels* house where I remained and was civily treated by him and his family untill the 29th of May the Anniversary of the Restoration which ought now *to be blotted out* as a day of rejoycing. The park and Tower Guns were firing when I was on my way to the Tower in a Hackney Coach. Mr. *Gurnel* sat beside me, and a sergeant of the Guards on the seat before me, with his drawn sword, and a pair of pistols lay beside him. When Mr. *Gurnel* arrived at the Tower he delivered me over to the *governour* of the Tower, and then went home very happy no doubt when he was relieved from his unpleasant charge.

I forgot to mention that a short time after, perhaps about half an hour, the legal plunderers had left my house with their booty, they returned having omitted to search the large drawer under the cutting board in front of the shop where the *Journal* of the L. C. S. was generally kept with letters and papers. There is not a doubt that they had met some *rascal* in their way back who was acquainted with me and knew of the drawer and told them of it which they had not observed. However they were too late for some of my friends

had been there before them and emptied it, and opened the shop. When they were entering at the shop door, my friends went out the street door in safety. It was a very fortunate circumstance that I had given the *Journal* the night before to Mr. *Pearce*, clerk to *Martin* the Atty to enter some papers in it, which I had no time to do myself.

182. Report from spy Nodder: LCS Division 13, 12 May 1794[19]

Source: PC1/21/A35(a)

Mr. N-dd-r's - - - - - (12th Report) - - - - - May 13th; 1794

May 12th: – Going down new *Compton Street* at ½ after 8 o'Clock saw some of the Bow Street runners go into No. 3 – if these Men went there on any business of importance they were *much too early* –

Got to Spence's abt; – 9 – found the Shop full of Men among them was *Frankloe* – who went up Stairs with N-dd-r – finding they were alone he addressed himself to N-dd-r saying that *Hardy was taken* and that *he* was very *allarmed for his own safety* N-dd-r then told him what he had *seen* in *New Compton Street* they then quitted Spence's and both went in Company to the Correspd; Socy: held in *Shire* lane (as before stated) in going there *Frankloe* informed N-dd-r that he had *a friend* who told him that an information was made against him in *the Office* – And he assured N-dd-r that Money had been offered to him *to change* his principles but that *he never would.* and so cautious was he that when they came to Shire lane he advised a sharp look out least any improper person's should trace them going into the house there – but seeing none they both went into the Room which was very full of Members – *Cooper* the *delegate* and Secy read a Report respecting *those* who are now *in Custody* – Three new members were made – Cooper then told this Section that the Grand Comee; of this Socy: recommended that every *Tenth* members of the different sections of the Soc: should be appointed to revise the new Constitution thereof, this produced great debates at last a Motion was made by Mr. *Oxley* that all the Sections do consider & determine in each Section the new Constitution when that is done a general public meeting be called and that the said New Constitutn. be then read Clause by

19 Nodder's description: 'Mr. N-dd-r's 12th; Report'; government description: 'In Mr. Gretton's 13th May 1794'.

Clause – this Motion was card. by a majority of *two*.

Smith the Bookseller the corner of a Court going from Lincoln's Inn Square to Clare markett – told the Socy: in what manner *Hardy* had been taken and that an Attorney had offerd his Service that the said Atty. would go to the Secy of State on the morrow morn (*this day*) to obtain an interview with *Hardy* – Smith added – "thank God the Paper *they* want was not at *Hardy's* that it was for that Paper he was sure they went *the second* time ! ! ! to Hardy's House – at the time the new Members *were charged to promote to the utmost of their power* a parliamenty. reform – A Voice called out by *drawing a trigger* – this was approved by some but reprobated by others – And it was recommended in general not to *express* such sentiments but to speak strictly constitutionl – N-dd-r has been informed of a Mr. *Britton* who is a Man of *Fortune* and living in *Sommesett Street* whose *conduct* he conceives (& recommends) ought to be narrowly watched –

N-dd-r has an appointmt; to meet *Frankloe* on Wednesday Evening next at the usual time –

As matters begin now to wear a very serious aspect and as N-dd-r will in no instance shrink from the great line of duty & service in which he is engaged which may be the means of involving him in situations highly dangerous and perplexing he requests *some mode* may be adopted with his friend Mr. Gretton to secure him from being taken into Custody exposed in the publick prints or otherwise held up to the Public –

Such situations would be not only highly disagreable to his own mind, but might tend to the loss of his business from the ill opinion the world would entertain of him as an Enemy to his King & Country whilst he is doing every thing in his power to ⟨serve⟩ the one & the other –

       F.. P.. N-

May 13th; 1794
 NB. Saunderson was not at *Spence's* or at the Soc: in Shire Lane last night – !! –

183. Report from spy Groves: 12 May 1794[20]

Source: TS 11/965/3510A

       Monday Evg ½ past 11
Sir
 I should have waited on you ⟨since⟩, but,

20 Government description: '13 May 1794 / Mr. Groves'.

under circumstances, I wish your directions – I am just come from Compton Street – The apprehension of Hardy has struck a panic – Jealous & M. Mann, had just left the Coffee Room when I went in, – They came, as I am informed, after Barnes who keeps it – They never went into the Division Room   Richter came in soon after, & said in a whisper to me, it was him that J' & Mc.M- came for.

Richter proposed Delegates to be sent next Thursday Evg. to meet a General Meeting of Delegates at Thelwalls – It was agreed to, & I am chosen one – The End of the Meeting is to consult about steps to take in their present Situation, & it is to be called the General Meeting of the Delegates on the present Emergency

Be so good, Sir, as to let me know when I shall wait on & where

         JG
  13 May '94[21]

184. Report from spy Taylor: LCS Division 2, 12 May 1794

Source: TS 11/944/3499

      May 12th. 1794
Meeting of the London Corrg. Society Society
   No. 3 New Compton Street
     Second Division

 The Chair being taken Le Maitre the Delegate read the Report from the General Committee namely that Seventeen Members had been added to the Society in the Course of the last Week, some immaterial Observations on the Revision of the new Constitution – Pearse the Sub Secretary having announced to the Division that their Secretary (Hardy) had been Arrested by Order of Government it was necessary that the Society should take some very effectual means to Counteract such Arbitrary steps[22] in Consequence he Submitted the following Motion that one Member out of Ten in each Division be Delegated to add to the General Committee in order to Strengthen and give energy to their Proceedings   after some debate in which Jones took the lead the question was put and carried unanaimous, twelve Members were then Nominated from this Devision it appearing by the Book in which the names of the Members are entered

21 Date in another hand.
22 The Privy Council asked Pearce if he had announced 'that it was necessary to take some Measures to counteract these Proceedings'. Pearce 'denied that he had used these latter Words' (TS 11/963/3509, fo. 335).

that there is at this time 120 effective Members (this Book is in the hands of Pearse)

185. Spy Gosling's 'Information': LCS Division 2, 12 May 1794

Source: TS 11/954/3498

May the 12th I got introduced to Young Edward's by Hillier and was shewn his Pike Magic Lanthern[23] Guillotine Bill &c as stated to the privy Council: He explained the Difference between his Pike and those that were to come to him from Sheffield the Direction where to send for them he said had been given him by Hardy – that we were to subscribe 1 Shilling each and that the overplus would be paid by a Printer at Sheffield[24] he said he was not to write to this Person for them but to another who was not at all suspected. Edwards being informed that Hardy was taken cleaned himself and I went with him in search of Hardy We first went to the New Compter where Edwards informed Burgh and Duffel that Hardy was taken and said something must be done immediately or words to that purport Duffel said he would give us two Nights and a Day to do the Business in Town.[25] Edwards also informed another Person a Prisoner for Debt that Hardy was taken but nothing passed of consequence – I went to other Places with Edwards as was before stated to the Council[26] – at Hardy's

it was said they had missed what they most wanted – At Compton Street we found the Bow Street Officers had been[27] – ½ past ten Richter came and after stating the apprehension of Hardy said If the Society suffered their valuable Servants to be taken away one by one there was an end of the Society and further that the Committee recommended that one Person out of every 10 should be chosen from the different Divisions and form a Committee of Emergency to consult what was proper to be done:[28] this was adopted

23 'he had a Magic Lanthorn which he said he had from Chauvelin with Shades of the King of France beheading and the Bastile &c . . . . some of the Shades were not yet painted, and the Witness [Gosling] understood they were to have on them Figures of People in this Country whenever the Guillotine was introduced here' (examination of Gosling by Privy Council, TS 11/963/3509, fos. 117v–18, 123–3v). Edwards, however, said he had the magic lantern from Wilson, the broker, who lived opposite his father (examination of John Edwards by the Privy Council, ibid., fo. 127).
24 Edwards denied saying that the Sheffield printer would pay the deficiency (examination by the Privy Council, TS 11/963/3509, fo. 127v).
25 'He understood *the Business* meant seizing the Members of both Houses and the Royal Family – he [Gosling] has heard this talked of at different places, particularly when in company with Baxter' (examination of Gosling, TS 11/963/3509, fos. 123v–4). Edwards, however, understood that 'the business' meant rescuing Hardy (examination of Edwards, ibid., fo. 127v).
26 'Then they went to Tothill Fields Bridewell – There they saw Hodson in Custody, who is employed in Drawing Beer there – Edwards had a

pot of Beer with Hodson. From thence they went to Hodson the Hatter, Broadway Westminster, who he said was called Hodson the Jacobin. Hodson was not at Home – from thence they went to Hardy's House' (examination of Gosling, TS 11/963/3509, fo. 102v).
27 'there was a Debate about a Spy owing to his [Gosling's] being seen to speak with Jealous the Officer' (examination of Gosling, TS 11/963/3509, fo. 103).
28 Richter's account: 'As to the Speech on Hardys arrest on ye. Monday it was in Substance To induce the members to remain firm in the cause & not to be at all disheartened by the circumstance. That if at this momentous crisis we should shrink from our principles & from the assertion of what we conceived to be our just & indisputable rights the cause of liberty would be lost phaps for ever & many individuals be sacrificed to the [undecipherable word] of our adversaries. For I had no doubt but they intended to carry us off one by one & by destroying those who appeared to be the most active they hoped effectually to crush & for ever that Spirit of Reform which they themselves had set on foot; But I desired them to consider that in that Socy. there were *no leaders & no parties* that all judged for themselves & that when one active mean was taken from the field ten others would rise to supply his place that now or never was the time to shew that were were not to be intimidated, but that every attempt against us would only serve to unite us more closely together in support of that cause which we had resolved never to forego but with our lives. *That the time was now come when the exertion of the whole wisdom & firmness of the Socy. was absolutely necessary* & I therefore recommended that the motion should be adopted not merely for the purpose for wch. it was originally intended but to act as an enlarged representation of the Society wherein might be collected its whole wisdom & firmness. And I hoped they would not elect any to this important station who did not possess their full & entire confidences as to wisdom firmness intregrity & patriotism' (Add MSS 27816, fos. 476–77v). After his arrest, Richter was asked by the Privy Council if he stated in this speech 'that the time was now arrived when force was necessary'. Richter said no (ibid., fo. 481).

and 12 Persons chosen for that Division – A Mr. Jones one of the 12 Persons so chosen said that when he first heard of the apprehension of Hardy he was nearly in a state of desperation but that when Reflection came to his Aid he thought the Society should patiently wait 'till they knew the Crime with which Hardy was charged – to see that he had a fair Tryal, and if they found that his only Crime was performing his Duty as Secretary to that Society they were bound to defend him to the last Extremity. Taylors accusation &c is not necessary to be repeated. *Pearce* the Sub Secretary walked part of the Way home with Edwards and me – and also *Said that all the Papers were not taken.* I after this heard at Hilliers that the *Country Correspondence* and *other important Papers were entrusted with Pearce.*[29] Returning home thro' Smithfield Edwards informed me that as he was returning with some Members from a Division which met on Snow Hill which I know nothing about one of the Members had measured the large Board which is there fixed up to know how many Heads could be taken off at a Time if it should be converted into a Guillotine. – My only Reason for going with Edwards was a desire to obtain a direction where these Pikes were that they might be seized. Edwards stated that a Society of 60 at Lambeth had Arms Accoutrements & a Uniform.[30]

29 Pearce had given the Journal of the LCS to Felix Vaughan for safekeeping. Government was supplied by informers with names of other men alleged to have LCS papers. Hartly, a grinder in Broad St, Carnaby market, was said to have the papers of Hardy and Thelwall under his bed in a leather case (letter, L. M. to Mr Bond at Bow St Police Office, 21 May 1794, HO 42/30, fo. 234). 'Papers of the greatest consequence' were said to be in the possession of James Cornfoot, coal merchant, Tottenham Ct Rd; James Lapworth, baker, Carnaby St; John Moody, shoemaker, Carnaby St; Samuel Moody, carpenter, Carnaby St; Phillip Willby, at Lapworth's; William Bunbow, watchmaker, at Lapworth's (letter, James Hartley to Henry Dundas, Rx 24 May 1794, ibid., fo. 255). There is no record of LCS members with names like Willby and Bunbow. Cornfoot (or Cornforth), Lapworth and Moody were members. Hartley (Thomas?) was an active member, taking a skin for the petition, 12 copies of the *Englishman's Right*, and 6 tickets to the 14 April meeting.
30 According to the LCS version of Gosling's activities, he encouraged the members to arm: after joining the Society, he 'immediately sought to recommend himself to the division by the most excessive violence of language; but soon finding himself curbed in this proceeding, he

186. Richter's narrative: Committee of Emergency, 13 May 1794

Source: Add MSS 27816, fos. 458–63v

[Hardy was arrested on Monday, 12 May.] Adams was seized in like manner at the same time. A Message from the King was received by the Commons informing them of these Circumstances pretending that their crime was imitating the manners of the french or something to that purpose. And purposting to call a Convention of the People.

The Society were no ways intimidated by these proceedings meeting as usual in their divisions that evening; but some individuals summoned an Extraordinary Meeting of the General Comee: for the Tuesday Evening. . . .

On the Tuesday the General Cee: met, to their honour be it said, much more numerously, even at that short notice, than had been known before. Their attention was called to the measures to be taken. . . . they therefore passed some spirited resolutions declaring their attachment to their Secy. & their firm determination to Support him to the last hour of their existence in every act which had been

adopted more artful methods: [he allied to himself a member with a pike and advanced] artful and guarded proposals for establishing a club, the members of which should be furnished with pikes like his, and learn military exercise. These proposals were extended to five or six persons, but strong objections were stated; which Gosling rebutted, by observing that there was no treason in a man's having a pike in his house, or learning the military exercise, both being allowed by the laws of the land. Having by these artifices gained the attachment of two or three zealots, he left it to them to urge the business in the Division; where, however, it was not only reprobated, but an accusation was sent to the General Committee against the most active of them (a youth under age) which accusation was pending at the time he was taken into custody on the accusation of his treacherous Counsellor. Previous to this, the cunning plotter procured a few individuals . . . to be furnished with pikes, which he proposed should be procured from Sheffield through the medium of the Youth already mentioned, whose father had a connection in trade there. The letter was accordingly written; and Gosling, under a plea of the danger of the post, prevailed on the Young Men to deliver it to Hardy, who was totally ignorant of the business, to be forwarded in his next parcel to Sheffield; – and no sooner was the Letter lodged in Hardy's house than he and his papers were seized' (*A Vindication of the London Corresponding Society*, pp. 8–9).

occasioned by the resolutions of the
Society.[31]

These Resolutions were then directed to be
communicated by the Cee. in a body to such
of the divisions as were then sitting; together
with a further recommendation of the former
Motion for obtaing a full representation of
the whole Wisdom & firmness of the Society.

The Cee. adjourned for this purpose &
Thelwall was of course the last who left his
own house;[32] The others had gone forward
when a body of men headed by Walsh who
had been pointed out by him as a Spy at
Chalk Farm seized him & another as he shut
his own door. The news of this event spread
like wild fire & reached those who were gone
forward, but it was determined that their
return could be of no avail & that it was now
doubly important that they should go to the
places of their destination.

Unfortunately there was but one copy of
the Resolutions & that was in possession of
Thelwall, Memory therefore but imperfectly
supplied this defect. They were however every
where approved.

187. Resolutions: Committee of Emergency, 13 May 1794[33]

Source: Mrs Thelwell: *Life of John Thelwall*, p. 157

1st. Resolved, that it appears to this Committee that no person can be legally apprehended, and his papers seized, in this country,
but upon a *specific* charge of High Treason.

2d. That, as far as this Committee is
acquainted with the conduct and deportment
of Citizen Hardy, there does not appear to be
the slightest foundation for charging him with
that crime.

3d. That, as far as the conduct of Citizen
Hardy shall be found, as this Committee believes it to have been, entirely legal and constitutional, we will support him to the utmost
of our ability.

31 At the meeting Thelwall read and expounded the
law of treason as laid down in Blackstone's
Commentaries and applied it to the case of
Hardy. Thelwall moved the resolutions which,
after some debate among Richter, Baxter and
himself, were adopted unanimously (Mrs
Thelwall, *Life of John Thelwall*, p. 156).
32 Thelwall had left the group to inform his family
of his intended absence (*Life of John Thelwall*,
p. 157).
33 Presumably Thelwall reconstructed these resolutions from memory when preparing his auto-
biographical materials.

4th. That this Committee proceed, in the
most solemn manner, to communicate to such
of the divisions of the London Corresponding
Society as are now sitting the preceding Resolutions, and conjure them not to be dis-
couraged or alarmed by the violent proceedings of the Government; but to pursue, with
unabated ardour, the objects of their Institution.

188. Spy Gosling's 'Information': 13 May 1794

Source: TS 11/954/3498

May 13th. I called at
Hilliers I saw Baxter with a Bundle – I called
him and asked him If he knew that Hardy had
been apprehended he said Yes and he expected to be sent for – he further said "I have got
a Bundle of Sedition here which I am going to
conceal at a Friends House but they are only
printed Papers I have burned all my Manuscripts – I told him what passed in Compton
Street which he approved of and said that the
Tythings ought to be adopted immediately
and the Society scrutinized that then the Firm
should be selected from the Timid and a
Power given to a few Persons to regulate the
Business of the Society and to call them into
Action – he said that it was absolutely necessary that only a few Persons should know the
Time to prevent a discovery – that Arms
should at the Time Fixed be offered to all and
then said he "If any refuse to act with us we
will take care they shall not act against us[34]
– I asked him if we were to go for the Pikes on
Fryday as he had told us or if we Should have
them sooner he said he would enquire and
let me know.

189. Report from spy Gosling: LCS Division 11, 13 May 1794[35]

Source: PC1/21/A35

Information obtained at a meeting of
the 11th Division of the Corresponding
Society Tuesday May 13 – 1794 at
Blackburn's No. 3 Craven Street –
City Road. –

Three new members were made –

34 'Baxter said our Number was not sufficient to
use open force and that it must therefore be
effected by surprise in the Night' (addendum at
the end of this 'Information').
35 Government description: 'Gosling – 14. May –
/ 94 / In Mr. Wickham's report / 15th. May
1794'.

The total Number of this Division being 65 – Six persons were chosen to meet the Committee of Emergency to meet on Thursday Evening — *I was the first Person chosen for this purpose.*[36] –

It was stated at this Division that Government were in possession of the comparative Numbers – by returns from all parts of the Kingdom and that according to those Returns Government had three to One in their favor. But said this Person they have reckoned all the Army their Clerks and Excisemen in this List – and when Strong Measures are used Government will find they have three to one against them.

Two Hand Bills were read from Sheffield[37] and given to Hillier to have printed & sold in Bishopsgate Street. – A Magistrate of the Name of Wilson was said to be "a good Patriot". The Person who produced these Hand-Bills was lately at Sheffield and is one of the six Persons chosen by this Division[38] for ye Commee of Emergency

It was recommended to the Members to be firm – united and constant in attending their Divisions –

It was recommended to the Members of this Division to encourage Hardy by *each* having a pair of Shoes of him and to circulate his Cards thro' all the Divisions and recommend the same   This Proposition came from Ebenezer Davis[39] a Jew Apothecary and one of the Six chosen by this Society—

The Advertizement from the Sheffield Society published in a News Paper was also communicated to this Division it related to arming to prevent any Disturbances that might arise from the "*War Whoop of Church and King*".—

The Apprehension of Hardy and Adams was said to be an artful Manoeuvre to make Parliament swallow a Convention Bill and that the Society instead of being intimidated ought to be more strongly united. –

36 Gosling attributed his election to his having urged the thirty members present to support this proposal (Gosling's 'Information'). Hillier, G. Williams, Young and Cuthbert were also elected (examination of Gosling, TS 11/963/3509, fos. 104v, 118).
37 George Williams, a leather seller of 60 Smithfield, brought these handbills and also the advertisement mentioned later in this report (examination of Gosling, TS 11/963/3509, fo. 104v; examination of Williams, TS 11/957/3502).
38 Remainder of sentence is in another hand.
39 Marginal note: 'The Man that I have employed W. W.'

190. Report from spy Taylor: LCS Division 29, 13 May 1794

Source: TS 11/955/3499

May 13th.
Meeting of the London Corr. Society
Robin's Coffee House
Shire lane – 29th. Division

Palmer in the Chair – the Delegate (Ashley) being at the Extra Committee at the Committee Room at Thelwalls house deliberating on what steps to take in order to effect the Speedy liberation of the Secretary (Hardy) Williams of Falcon Square was dispatched to know the result of their proceedings – Ashley returned with him and informed the Division that the Committee had not come to any definitive Determination but recommended in the general to each Division to meet numerous and act with firmness and resolution – the Report from the General Committee (as usual) was then read and was the same as in the second Division of last Night, the same Motion was also made for the appointing one Member out of ten as a Delegate to attend the general Committee and on the Question being put it was carried unanimously – after some little time had elapsed Richter entered and reported from the Committee (which had been sitting that Night) the result of their resolves which amounted to no more than what Ashley had before delivered. He added that with deep regret he must inform them that as Thelwall was attending them to the Door of his House from the Committee Room he had been seized put into a Coach and carried he knew not where, a general Cry went through the Room   let us go and rescue him (near a hundred was present) and most rose for the purpose – Ashley addressed them and said these arbitrary proceedings of Government will the sooner bring on the Crisis we have in view – have a little Patience – sometime after Baxter Pierce Hodson and Smith came in and said they had followed the Coach that had conveyed Thelwall to the Secretary of States Office where, on the Coach stopping, a Messenger that was on the Box called to the Centinel to disperse those Men   they refused to go and insisted they had a right to walk there as long as they thought proper – the Centinel in mild terms desired them to depart, but on their still refusing he let them pass – Baxter made this remark   the Soldiers are our Friends we want but a beginning.

191. Spy Gosling's 'Information': 14 May 1794

Source: TS 11/954/3498

May the 14th I call'd at Edwards's I asked him if we were to meet about the Pikes on Fryday or not. he said he did not know whether the Direction for them had not been taken upon Hardy and therefore could not say but if I would call on Fryday Morng. he would let me know. He said it was to be proposed that night in the Committee to swear all the Members and to expel those who would not swear to live Free or Die and that it had been agreed that the Convention Bill ought not to be submitted to by the People and that a motion to that Effect had been made in the Committee. Burk was present and said he had been at Thelwall's 'till 4 that Morning Burk and Edwards both told me that a Person had brought a Letter from Sheffield to the Committee – that it was addressed to Hardy – and that the purport of the Letter was to know their plan for the Convention and how they were to Cooperate. In the Evening I went to the Society at Cross Street Hatton Garden where I had been once before.[40] The Delegate apologized for not having brought the Resolutions of the Committee with him – he said he believed they were taken with Thelwall and were to the following purport –
Resolved. That the conduct of Citizen Hardy as far as concerns the Corresponding Society merits our approbation and Applause. Resolved That we will defend Citizen Hardy with our Lives
Resolved. That we will live free or Die. These Resolutions were put and carried with a degree of Enthusiasm I had never before witnessed in their Meetings and many of them declared that the Day any of the Members should be brought to Punishment for what they had done in their Cause they would die or save them. – After the meeting was thinned the Landlord asked us to remove into the Tap Room as it was late, which we did – he gave as a Reason that he had received a Caution from Mr. Bleamire the Magistrate but said he did not fear him for the Officers were his Friends and he had always something for them to eat and drink (As the Father of the Delegate was in Company I think it proper to mention one Circumstance which happened at the Time I attended this Division once before – The Delegate was objected to on account of his Youth and offered to resign but was confirm'd in his Situation upon Ashley's Observing that he understood the Duty of a Delegate and that Young Men were fittest for Delegates because they had more Enthusiasm and not so many prejudices to get rid of as older persons.) The Conversation of the Delegate and his Father was particularly Violent the Father wished to see Temple Bar covered with Heads – and the Son to see a head on every Lamp Iron about London Bridge. The Delegate shewed me a Hand Bill about In's and Out's threat'ning us with an Invasion &c as I before stated.[41] Much other Conversation passed about Arming and the Society, in which it was stated that many in the Army & Militia belonged to the Society but that their Names were never entered – The Delegate particularly told me this, and also confirmed what I had been before told that the Country Correspondence had not been taken saying I wish it had for it would have made them tremble. Previous to our coming down Stairs a Member handed a New Cutlass or Hanger across the Table to another who put it under his Coat saying "these are the Things but the Scabbard is hardly dry". –

192. Report from spy Groves: Committee of Emergency, 15 May 1794[42]

Source: TS 11/965/3510A

Thursday Evg. ½ past 11
I am just come from Thelwalls where the Committee of Emergency met –

41 '[It was] to this effect: "The Ins tell us We are in danger of Invasion from the French The Outs tell us, that we are in danger from the Hessians and Hanoverians In either case we should arm Ourselves – get Arms and learn how to use them." He [the delegate] said he had but that one Copy, and was going to get more printed' (examination of Gosling, fo. 105v).

42 Government description: 'Thursday night 15 May 1794 / Mr. Groves / Rx 16 at 1 a m'. At half past three that afternoon Groves had written to Nepean, explaining that he could not quiet the 'fears and apprehensions' of Mrs Groves. 'I need scarcely tell you, Sir, what distress I must feel in seeing a good and virtuous woman on her knees, at my feet, imploring me, with sighs and tears, to relinquish such an undertaking I have promised, on my honour, to comply with her intentions' (TS 11/965/3510). As Groves's presence at the meeting that night

40 About 40 or 50 were at this meeting in the Coach and Horses ph. Late in the evening songs were sung. Gosling, who stayed until midnight, described the delegate as 'quite a Lad' (examination, fo. 105; cf. *ST* vol. 24, col. 719).

At 8 oClock Horne Tooke & Frost came to the door just as I did –

They enquired for Mrs. Thelwall & went up Stairs to her. I saw them no more. –

I suppose they not being Members of the L C. Sy. they cod. not be admitted to the Commee of Emergency

By 9 oClock about 30 were met, & at ½ past 9 about 50 – when the business began.

The first thing done was reading the amount of the different subscriptions from the difft. divisions – it was about 40s. –

The Number of Members admitted during the Course of last Week – in all 23.

A resolution was then read from Division 23. recommending a Spirited Remonstrance upon the present proceedings, leaving it open to the discussion of the Delegates to whom to address it

Some were for the Ho of Coms.

Others to the House of Lords

Others to the King

I was of that Opinion as we cod. not expect to meet with any Redress from the two former but that His Majesty having been Misadvised by his Ministers it was proper to send our principles & resolutions to him that he might fully understand them

A great many agreed to it Others objected – Saying We ought from the Conduct of the whole legislative power show an equal Contempt to them all & address the people

In the midst of this, Pearce rose & said that he had to inform the Delegates that Justice Addington was in the House That his Runners were at the door, & the Military coming – he recommended to them quiet behaviour & submission – not to answer interrogatories, & to exculpate themselves, if they were charged with any thing, before a Jury of their Country – he recommended dispatch – So did Lovatt & an immediate Adjourmt. The minds of a great many grew warm. – It was agreed at last to draw up a Remonstrance to the people with a Narrative of their proceedings & a defence of their principles –

The Delegates adjourned to next Thursday – Re J: Addington – no Runners, no Military – a false alarm

A Committee is appointed to draw up the Remonstrance & Narrative & to report it next Thursday

15 May 94[43]

shows, government persuaded him to break that promise.

43 Date in another hand.

193. Spy Gosling's 'Information': Committee of Emergency and other matters, 15–17 May 1794

Source: TS 11/954/3498

May the 15th I attended the Committee of Emergency[44] – Ashley was in the Chair and the Delegate I above mention'd was his Supporter on one Side – Edwards kept the Door. Some money was paid to Ashley for the "imprisoned Patriots" – Ashley said they had not brought any Journals or Accounts of their former proceedings – and a Member proposed that No pen and Ink should be produced – or their proceedings that Night reduced to writing – this was overruled. Taylor again denounced by several &c &c. The principal Business was first a Recommendation from the 23d Division the purport of which was That a spirited Remonstrance should be drawn up and published against the illegal proceedings of Administration by seizing the papers of Citizen Hardy – this was put and carried[45] It was then debated to whom it should be addressed. Mr. Groves – wished it to be published in the Papers and circulated by Hand Bills thro' the Kingdom with a declaration of Principles that they were the same Mr. Pitt and the Duke of Richmond formerly professed that universal suffrage was the Object of the Society and that they would not abandon it but with their Lives – he said the Society had been calumniated that it had been reported they wanted to send the King to Hanover but he knew of no such intention.

Mr. Jones said "The House of Commons are our Accusers we cannot therefore expect that they will hear us with attention or that our grievances will be redressed by those who are interested in their continuance. In the House of Lords we have but one solitary Friend can we expect they will receive our Remonstrance with Temper or consider it with Candour. He then quoted a precedent in the Case of Wilkes and Said – I vote that it be presented to the King not that I think he has the Power if he had the Will to redress our wrongs for the Government of this Country is exercised by a Junto of about Twenty Persons and neither by King – Lords – or Commons or

44 'there appeared to be 100 people' (examination of Gosling, fo. 105v).

45 'it was proposed orally by the Secretary of the Division in Compton Stt. as well as Gosling can recollect – Ashley put the question upon it it was carried by holding up of hands' ('General State of Evidence as to *Arming*').

by them united but if we remonstrate to the King it will have this Effect it will convince the Country that we have done every thing in our Power to do and that if we resort to other measures we do it as our last our only Resource – Let us then said he present a spirited remonstrance to the king alone it will shew our Contempt for the two inferiour Branches of the Legislature and should he disdain to receive it let us shew him that we can also treat him with Contempt and appeal to the Majesty of the People.

Another Member observed that if we stated our Grievances to the King and remonstrated against them with Spirit he might (with the example of a neighbouring Kingdom before his Eyes) dismiss the Administration which misadvised him and redress our wrongs

This Language was objected to as threatening the King

Pearce now informed the Committee that Mr. Addington was below and that the Guards were coming to assist in apprehending them. It was now proposed to adjourn – this was opposed by Ashley and others who observed that this might be the last Time we might have it in our Power to do anything and that it ought not to be delayed –

It was said We are accused by the House of Commons – The Eyes of the Country nay the World are upon us – The Country waits our Decision –

Mr. Jones – withdrew his opinion that a remonstrance should be presented to the King saying What is right to be done tomorrow is right to be done tonight: Shall we remonstrate said he with those who hold a knife to our Throats who have the Axe already whetted and thirst for our Blood no Let us in contempt of Death make an appeal to the People and to the People only. – A Member now observed that the Society had already resolved at a General Meeting to Petition Parliament no more and that it must be from our own Laws and not the Laws of our Oppressors we must expect redress.

Ashley observed this was a Remonstrance not a Petition:

It was then carried Nem. con. that the Committee of Correspondence and Cooperation be authorized and directed to draw up a spirited remonstrance against the Conduct of Administration and that it be addressed to the People and the People only:

Baxter now observed that the Committee of Correspondence and Cooperation were deprived of a most valuable Member (Thelwall) Ashley said many others would come forward to supply his place – Mr. Jones was

then proposed to be added to the Committee (vice Thelwall) and appointed – A Motion of Adjournment was now put and carried.

May 16th – I went to Hilliers[46] and met Hayward there – Haywood said Rosselle had told him he was going to France upon private Business and should return again shortly he said the Captain of a Neutral Vessel had refused to take him because he had no passport. – he said Rosselle lived in George Street Blackfryers Road (from whence he was taken). Haywood said he was acquainted with Thelwall – Joyce &c that a Letter would be received that Day from Sheffield and that he hoped the Society would now throw off the Mask and boldly avow their Principles.[47] – I called at Edward's but his Father would not let me see him

May the 16 at the three Kings in the Minories – Phillips who I had been first directed to make enquiries concerning was here and shortly after introduced the Subject of Persons being Employed as Spies to watch the Conduct of the Society – To avoid suspicion I gave as a Toast – Citizens Hardy Thelwall and the other imprisoned Patriots – and joined them in their Songs – which had the Effect I desired. – Blackburn of Whitechapel mentioned his dining with the Constitutional Society and said he was of opinion that 6 Weeks was too short a Time to call a Convention in – he stated Horne Tooke to have given it as his Opinion that Parliament would not reform itself but that the Time was not far distant when it would be reformed with a vengeance from without – A song was sung which related to 30.000 Americans refusing to give or take Quarter the Person who sung it said this is what we Want Lloyd who was in the Chair said We must first Know our Strength and make the Blow sure both these observations were received with applause.

May 17 – At Hilliers in the Morning there was a Conversation between Hillier and Bennet about the best plan for an insurrection. Bennet said it would be best began at Sheffield as it would give them Time in Town – Hillier said it would be best to strike every where at once but that he thought it a good plan to dagger

46 At about 10.00 a.m. (examination of Gosling, fo. 106v).
47 On either this day or the next, according to Gosling's postscript, Stiff and Caney of Wood St, 'a very active Member', said that if £200,000 or £300,000 could be obtained from France, the LCS 'would be able to effect their Object'.

the private Committee of the House of Commons as an Example to the Rest.

In the afternoon[48] at Hilliers with Bennet – Haywood – Harvey – and Hillier Haywood said Rosselle had good Information and must be got over to France[49] – that if he could row he would assist him to get over in a Wherry – he said a Victory in Flanders by the French was as useful as if obtained in St. Georges Fields[50] – he said £300 had been offered for a Vessel not worth £150[51] to hover on the French Coast that Rosselle might be taken and the Captain escape being tried for Treason. &c &c &c as stated to the Privy council, respecting the House of Commons[52] – the Prisoners in Newgate &c &c.

[By the end of May government had arrested men throughout the nation on suspicion of treason. In London thirteen LCS members were arrested: Ashley, Edwards, Franklow, Hardy, Hayward, Hillier, Lovett, Pearce, Richter, Roussel, Spence, Thelwall, and Williams. In addition John Martin, already in prison for debt, was taken up on a king's warrant. Some six members of the SCI were also arrested: Daniel Adams, John Augustus Bonney, Jeremiah Joyce, Stewart Kyd, William Sharp and John Horne Tooke. Two of these men, Pearce and Sharp, were detained only a few days; the others were in prison for months. William Stone, unconnected with these societies, was also put under arrest in May. In addition to these men who were served warrants, there were several who managed to postpone or escape being served: Baxter (arrested 7 July), Thomas Holcroft (surrendered in October), Moore, Hodgson and Thomas Wardle (evaded the warrants). In Sheffield William Broomhead, William Camage and Robert Moody were arrested and brought to London. From Norwich Isaac Saint was taken to London for examination by the Privy Council. In other parts of the country reform leaders such as George Mealmaker of Dundee were arrested and detained in local prisons for long periods.

On 12 May, the same day that Hardy was arrested, the king sent the House of Commons a short address: 'His Majesty having received information that the seditious practices which have been for some time carried on by certain societies in London, in correspondence with societies in different parts of the country, have lately been pursued with increased activity and boldness, and have been avowedly directed to the object of assembling a pretended general convention of the people, in contempt and defiance of the authority of parliament, and on principles subversive of the existing laws and constitution, and directly tending to the introduction of that system of anarchy and confusion which has fatally prevailed in France' has ordered that the books and papers of these societies be seized and laid before the House of Commons to take measures to prevent 'further prosecution of these dangerous designs'.

The House immediately appointed a committee of secrecy to examine these papers, and four days later, on 16 May, Pitt submitted the report from the committee (their speedy performance would be more remarkable if government had not already possessed accounts of meetings since November 1792 as well as all the Society's printed documents). After the

48 At 3.00 or 4.00 p.m., according to Hayward (examination of Richard Hayward by the Privy Council, TS 11/963/3509, fo. 209).

49 According to Gosling, Hayward said that 'Russell must be got over to France at any Rate, as half a million of money depended on it.' According to Hayward, Roussel said that 'if I could get over there, I know where there is ½ Million of Money' (examinations of Gosling and Hayward, TS 11/963/3509, fos. 132v, 209).

50 Hayward asserted that he had been in liquor on 17 May and did not remember saying this; but he acknowledged that he might have said it. He admitted that he might have said many of the things Gosling attributed to him. In particular he repreatedly said he would not deny what Harvey – the fourth person in the conversation – testified to (examination, fo. 209). Gosling denied that Hayward was drunk, but Hayward's account of that Saturday does include a good amount of liquor (ibid., fos. 212-13).

51 Hayward maintained that 'he never said any thing about Money being offered for a Ship for Roussel'; that he told Hillier that Roussel could not get passage; and that Hillier then spoke of hiring a vessel, and Hayward said that would cost £300 (examination, fos. 166-6v). Hillier, however, confirmed Gosling's account of this conversation (examination of Hillier, TS 11/963/3509, fo. 168v).

52 They discussed ways of entering the House of Commons and spoke of which sides Pitt and Fox sat on. The Privy Council asked Richard Bennet 'why they held this conversation about getting into the House of Commons – he said, it was in order to know the Members. Being asked, why they wanted to know the members – he said it was to illegally asssassinate them' (TS 11/963/3509, fo. 279).

report was read, Pitt moved for a suspension of Habeas Corpus on the ground that when a conspiracy against government existed government ought to be empowered to proceed with vigour and speed. Fox, Courtenay, Sheridan and Grey spoke against the motion, but on first reading it passed by 201 to 39. The next day, 17 May, the bill passed its third reading. On 20 May the House of Lords elected a committee of secrecy, whose first report was read on 22 May. Grenville then introduced a bill to suspend the Habeas Corpus Act. It passed through its third reading that day, despite opposition from Stanhope, Lauderdale and Lansdowne. During all these debates, the LCS was the focus of attention, repeatedly named and reviled, its members and actions described in words such as *meanness, contemptibility, carnage, butchery, ruin, cunning, arrogant, wretches, disastrous, insurrection.*

The *First Report of the Committee of Secrecy*, 1794, consists chiefly of LCS and SCI documents printed complete. The conclusion of the committee is that the two societies intend to supersede the House of Commons and to assume 'all the Functions and Powers of a National Legislature'.

The *Second Report of the Committee of Secrecy*, read in the House of Commons on 13 June, brings together all the talk of arming, exercising, assassinating, as well as the alleged Francophilia of the LCS. It also traces the proceedings of the SCI and of the LCS, as derived from their documents. Its conclusions are that not only the LCS but all the principal reform societies have been regulated by the SCI; that the societies intended to accomplish their designs by force; and that their designs to reform the House of Commons 'led, if carried to their natural extent, to the extinction and destruction of the other two branches of the legislature'.]

194. Report from spy Metcalfe: LCS Division 6, 19 May 1794[53]

Source: TS 11/956/3501

Meeting of the 6th. Division of the London Corresponding Society at the par-

rott in Green Arbour Court Old Bailey, Monday Evening 19th. May. 1794 ./.

I early this Evening calld on Citn. Worship at his house and had a long Conversation with him, in the course of which he said he belonged to the City Artillery Company amongst whom there were a great Number of good Democrats and he was sure if occasion offerd one half of that Company would join us, (the Corresponding Society) and he mentioned the Name of a Mr Page an Attorney as a staunch Friend to the Cause, and recommendd me very much to belong to that Company by which means I should have a compleat opportunity of learning the Manual exercise./.

He then related what passed in the Committee of Emergency on the Evening that Thelwall was taken into Custody, and said that it had been determined not to address the King or the parliament which had been proposed but to draw up an Address and Remonstrance to the people and the people only /. That they approved the Conduct of their Secretary Hardy whose line of Conduct they would pursue and that they would continue to meet in spite of any Convention Bill, that it was determined to leave for the present any consideration of the Constitution and to go round in parties of two or three to the several Divisions who met on that Evening to Spirit them up, and to induce them to resolve to send One from every Ten as a Committee of Emergency &c.

I accompanied him to the parrot to which place we had been directed to go[54] in consequence of Hillier's having been taken into Custody that Morning ./

There were about 24 present the Delegate Burks had not brought his Minutes, fearing as he said that he might be laid hold on, upon the Road, but he reported from Memory the proceedings which agreed with Worship's Account, except only that Burks said the Committee of Emergency meant that the One in Ten to be chosen by each Division were to

53 Metcalfe's description: 'Meeting of 6th Division of / London Corresponding Society on / Monday Eveng. 19th. May 1794'. Government description: 'Metcalfe's report of / 6th. Division May 19. 1794'.

54 During the day Burks notified the members to attend this meeting 'on very Important Buisiness'. One of the members was a new spy, D, who reported to the constable William Wright. Unfortunately for us, 'D wishes his name might be Kept Secret has he thinks he Can get great Information by so Doing' (letter, William Wright to William Wickham, 19 May 1794, HO 42/32). Perhaps he is Ebenezer Davis, an apothecary whom Wickham identifies as the man he has employed (see 189). Davis figures in a report of Div. 11; this is a report on Div. 6; but Divs. 6 and 11 sometimes met together.

be The Committee of Emergency as well as to fill the Office of Tything Men, Worship contended they were to be different persons./

The Evening having been taken up by dispute upon the Subject, at a late Hour they proceeded to the Choice of Tything Men and Myself Smith and Gallant were appointed,[55]

Skinner said there was no time to be lost something should be done and that immediately, that most likely an Act of Parliament would be passed to prevent a Convention of the people and therefore there was not a Moment to be lost. and he recommended a Subscription to be set on foot for the purposes of defraying the expences of those Delegates whom the Divisions should send to such Convention and which he should recommend to be held in Yorkshire, where their *friends* were in great force &c. this measure I seconded and spoke upon wch I believe produced my Election to the Office of Tything Man &c.

At 12 the Division broke up, and I walked part of the way home with Burks and Worship, on going along Cheapside a Musical party were playing God save the King, We join'd them and Burks and Worship several times calld out God save the Rights of the People, God save the rights of Man, they Damn'd the Rights of Man and continued singing God save the King on which Burks and Worship accompanied them to the end of Cheapside singing Ca Ira, at which place we parted

Burks reported that from 24 to 30 had been admitted into the Society in the last Week

On our Way to the parrott, (Worship and myself) we calld in at Eaton's, in Newgate Street, Worship having made a drawing for a frontispiece to the first volume of Hogs wash, which represents Swine feeding out of *a trough*,[56] and a *Cock* upon some paling in the back Ground, on one Side an Oak tree on the other the Tree of Liberty, the Shop was full, and on Worship's producing the Drawing, it was handed about, many making comments upon it, One person having the appearance and dress of a Gentleman, observed that he should have represented King Chanticleer without a Head, or with a fools Cap on, we all remembered who (it had been said) the Cock represented.

I should also have observed that Worship has removed all political papers and such as have any reference to politics or the London Corresponding Society from his House

195. Resolutions: LCS Division 6, 19 May 1794[57]

Source: TS 11/953/3496

L. C. S. Division No 6[58]
Rd. That the Moved Constitution be discuss'd arranged and passd, as quick as possible and that the Tithing Men be properly arrang'd and their duty approvd
Rd. That it appears expedient the Tithing Mn. should meet and adopt a Regularity for their fellow Citizens under their Tithing
Rd. That the Tithing Mn. do meet to Mw and adopt the plan as shall be approvd amongst them for the rendering themselves useful in Case of Emergency

196. Report from spy Groves: LCS Division 2, 19 May 1794[59]

Source: TS 11/965/3510A

Monday May 19th. 1794
Report of Meeting of Division No. 2
Compton Street

At 8 oClock about 20 Members were met – Citizen Groves, proposed to the Chair by Pearce – seconded by Le Maitre, the Delegate of the Division No. 2.
Carried Nem: Con:
Pearce opened the business by informing the Citizens that as times were precarious, and as there was no certainty but that the Citizens might be taken into Custody, and the Runners from the Public Offices near at hand for that purpose, the Use of pen Ink & paper might be dispensed with, for the Citizens might very

55 Three days later Burks gave Metcalfe his tything list in a form letter with an explanation that the tythings were to meet as a division if the regular division could not assemble. The nine other men in Metcalfe's tything were Worship, 3 Ball Alley, Lombard St; Caney, 82 Wood St, Cheapside; Savage, 1 Maiden Lane, Wood St; Davis, 66 White Chapel; Philips, 55 Whitechapel; Salmon, 11 Montague St, Spitalfields; Noon; Burks, 1 Great Gardens, East Smithfield; Bonfield, Bath Buildings, Hard Walk, Hoxton (22 May 1794, TS 11/956/3501).
56 Burke's fear that 'learning will be cast into the mire, and trodden down under the hoofs of a swinish multitude' (*Reflections on the Revolution in France*, Penguin edn, p. 173), was popularly taken to mean that he regarded the common people as swine.
57 Government description: '(J. T——k) 19th May 94'.
58 '6' written above '5'.
59 Government description: 'Groves's Report / May 19'.

well carry in their pericraniums the business of that Evening.

He stated that strong grounds of suspicion were entertained of Citizen Taylor being a Spy – that he had been observed on a former Evening in a Whisper with Jealous of Bow Street – that on that Evening he had been seen giving motions to Jealous in the Street, previous to & just before the latter came in to search for Citizen Barnes – that Taylor had been appointed a Delegate on the Emergency & never attended his duty – that he had been seen with different Runners – that he did not attend his duty this Evening – that there were various strong reasons for believing him a Traitor to the Cause of the London Corresponding Society & therefore he moved that Citizen Taylors name be struck out of the Books –

Le Maitre said he had proofs, if necessary to produce, that would shew Citizen Taylor to be a Spy, & mentioned that proof of the correspondence between him and Jealous on the Night mentioned by Citizen Pearce & therefore he seconded the Motion

The Chairman said That he thought the Neglect of Citizen Taylor in not attending his duty when chosen to as honorable an Office as a Delegate upon the Emergency of Affairs highly reprehensible, but the neglect of Citizen Taylors attendance that Evening to apologize for such Neglect not only strengthened the Suspicion, but carried in themselves great criminality –

A general cry of "Expel him"

Citizen Jones (of Tottenham Court Road a Delegate) said "Nothing could induce him to oppose the general voice of the Citizens but a strong sense of Candour – He wished Citizen Taylor present – that he might combat the Charge, & therefore he wished that the expulsion might be postponed till the next Meeting, & Citizen Taylor have notice given him to attend –

Pearce undertook to give him Notice

The Chairman wished that Citizen Pearce would at the same time give Taylor an Account of what had passed this Evening & the Reason why he was required to attend, adding, if Taylor was innocent he would attend & justify himself – if guilty, his guilt would keep him away, & the Society would then be rid of so dangerous a Member –

This was agreed Nem: Con.

Le Maitre stated the Weekly report from the Committee, vizt. that 19 Citizens had been made that Week – that the Division No. 23 had submitted to the Committee of Delegates of Emergency the Necessity of a Spirited Remonstrance on the present Tyrannical Proceedings of the Ministry which was agreed to, but that three propositions had arisen from the Recommendation

1st. Whether to present it to the House of Commons

2dly. Whether to present it to the House of Lords &

3dly. Whether to Address it to the Throne

He said that all these propositions had been rejected as useless, as no Attention would be paid to it by either branch of the Legislature That it had at last been determined to draw up a Remonstrance & Narrative to the Majority of the People, in order to vindicate the Society from that Slander which the Ministry had cast upon them and their proceedings – That a Select Committee of Delegates had appointed to draw up the Remonstrance & Narrative which would be reported to the Committee of Delegates of Emergency the next Thursday Evening –

He concluded by presenting to the Chairman the following Motion, which he desired to be read

The Chairman read it, as follows

"That it be recommended to the Division to hold a General Meeting of the Friends of Peace and Reform, as soon as possible, in order to consider the most proper and legal steps to be taken on the present occasion"

The Chairman put the Question –

A Citizen (a Visitor) argued against it as it would give a pretence to the Ministers to act with more severity against the Society, and that it would be better to lay quiet till the Storm was over, and the Society saw what was the Result from the apprehension of those Citizens already in Custody –

Citizen Jones in a violent speech opposed the idea of waiting till the Storm was over – it would be considered as deserting those worthy patriots now in confinement on account of the great services they had done the Society – it would be considered as Cowardice – that the Cause would be lost – he did not advise a Meeting with Arms – but the sooner the Meeting was held the Country would be undeceived & Ministry convinced they (the Society[)] were determined to persevere with their lives to promote a Reform in Parliamt.

The Chairman put the Question   Ayes 31 – Noes——

Carried Nem: Con: the Citizen who opposed it being a Visitor having no Vote –

The Committee of Delegates of Emergency meet on Thursday Evening at Thelwals, if no Notice of another place given in the mean time

197. Oral report of George Sanderson: LCS Division 13, 19 May 1794[60]

Source: TS 11/963/3509, fos. 158–8v

On last Monday Night [19 May] at the 13th. Division at Robin's Coffee House, Shire Lane – a Member stood up and said that the House of Commons met at three, and Mr. Pitt will go over Putney Bridge at 12 o'Clock.

No Explanation was made[61] – but the Examinant understood it to mean that there would be an Opportunity for any one to dispatch him.

He does not know the Man, who said so – nor should he know him.

One observed he had a Piece of good News to tell his brother Citizens, that one of the Kings Messengers had been hanged at Sheffield by the Mob.

Citizen Higgins said he had an Uncle who was a Kings Messenger, he said if it had been his Fate he should have gloried to have seen his Blood run for undertaking the Work of Despots.

It was observed by the Chair – that as Mr. Dundas had his Spies always amongst them, they should be careful of what they said, and those who were most Violent were most liable to be suspected of Criticism, as was the Case in the National Convention of France.

A Motion was made by the Delegate that as there was a Difficulty in meeting in Public Houses where the Spies of government obtruded that they should meet in Tithings and that the Tithing Man could easily recieve the Nine into his own House.

This was put off to be considered by the general Committee, The Subdelegate said one of the general Committee would be denounced as a Spy – a Member asked whether no one was present who had Spirit to blow his Brains out   This Member of the general Committee he understood was Taylor.

198. Report from spy Metcalfe: Committee of Emergency, 22 May 1794[62]

Source: TS 11/956/3501

General Committee of Emergency held at Citn. Dowlings in New Street Covent Garden on Thursday Evening 22nd. May 1794./.

Citizen Ashley in the Chair./.

The Citizens betrayed much exultation at the Glorious News of the Duke of Yorks Defeat.[63] &c.

A Motion was made that the thanks of the Society be given to those Members of the House of Commons who had opposed, the Suspension of the Habeas Corpus Act, but which after much Argument was Negativ'd. It appearing to the Society that the Opposition had not arisen from any Motives of Good Will towards the Society, but was to be attributed to motives of self interest and to gain popularity at the eve of a General Election./.

A Motion was then made that the Society imediately print 10000 Copies of the Report of the Select Committee of the House of Commons," for that the Report contained at length many of most pointed and the best resolutions which that Society had ever passed, and which at this time they would not dare to publish, To which it was answer'd that however desirable it might be, the Circumstances of the Society were so much reduced as to prevent them from carrying such a Measure into Execution It was also observed that there was now in publication, An Address to the people,[64] which might answer the same

---

60 This is part of Sanderson's testimony before the Privy Council on 22 May 1794. At the trial of Hardy, Sanderson – who acknowledged he was a spy – may have given different dates for the events presented here. The edn of Hardy's trial by Manoah Sibley (2 vols., 1795) has Sanderson saying, 'It was in the month of May, I don't recollect the night' (vol. 1, p. 466). The *ST* edn has Sanderson saying that the announcement of Pitt crossing the bridge occurred on 3 May and that about the king's messenger on 21 April (vol. 24, cols. 707–16). A government MS, 'General State of the Evidence as to *Arming*', gives 19 May as the date of the Pitt story (TS 11/965/3501).

61 But 'there was a general clap upon the table, and some said it was very improper to make any comments upon it' (Sanderson's testimony at Hardy's trial, *ST* vol. 24, col. 707).

62 Metcalfe's description: 'Committee of Emergency of the / London Corresponding Society in / New St. Covent Garden 22nd. May 1794'. By the following day, 23 May, the Privy Council had read a report of this meeting and referred to details of it in the examination of John Ashley, arrested that morning (TS 11/963/3509, fos. 183 ff.).

63 On 18 May, in a battle for Flemish lands, the Duke of York was almost captured, and the military force under his command lost 1000 men and a considerable train of artillery (*Annual Register*, 1794).

64 '*An Account of the Seizure of Citizen Thomas Hardy, Secretary to the London Corresponding Society; with some remarks on the Suspension*

Good purpose On which the consideration of the subject was referred to the Committee of Co opperation. &c.

One Citizen observed that we were surrounded, that is that the Town was surrounded by certain persons (meaning Soldiers) among whom it would be very adviseable to distribute some of their pamphlets, that he had lately been much in the Company of many of them, and that he could inform the Society, that there was among them 3 to 1 in their favor. Referred.

Citizen Pearce observed that as the Secretary of State had by seizing their Secretary's papers, got possession of a vast Quantity of their blank Tickets, it would be proper in Order to prevent them from being made an improper use of, that the Color of those Tickets should be alter'd, and Citizen Worship offer'd to engrave a plate for the purpose and to make the Society a present of it Resolved that Citizen Worship's Offer be accepted and that every Member be required to produce at the next Meeting his present Ticket, that it may be exchanged for one of the New Ones.

It was reported by several Tything Men that their Delegates had taken alarm at the present violent Measures of Government and that without the Society took some imediate Measures, it was to be fear'd several of the Divisions might seperate and for want of Officers be so scatter'd as to be lost to the Society, upon which it was resolved that a Deputation

of the Habeas Corpus Act. Printed by Order of the London Corresponding Society. (And Distributed Gratis)'. The first page of this 8 pp. pamphlet describes Hardy's arrest; the rest is primarily a refutation of charges in the *Report from the Committee of Secrecy*: there never was any correspondence between the LCS and the Jacobins of France. The Address to the French National Convention has to be understood in the context of the period when it was sent; it expressed sentiments 'which the whole nation held at that time'; the LCS petition for parliamentary reform presented by Mr Francis is evidence that the Society did apply to the legislature for redress of its grievances; the LCS did intend to call a convention, but only to devise means of attaining a representative body of the whole nation on the principles of universal suffrage, equal personal representation, and annual Parliaments ('the people are the only legitimate source of authority'); as to arming, Alfred the Great 'encouraged all the nation to have arms': some LCS members have applied themselves to 'the knowledge of arms'; if their example were followed by the whole nation, we would not need to fear invasion (from Frenchmen, Hessians or Hanoverians), nor would we be alarmed by mock-discoveries of non-existent plots.

from the Committee of Emergency should attend the several Divisions who were so circumstanced in Order to rally them and to appoint new Officers &c. And that it be recommended to every Division imediately upon their Delegate or other Officer's non attendance, to suspend such Officers and appoint another in his Place,

It was recommended to the Delegates to promote in their several Divisions, as much as possible, Subscriptions to encrease the fund of the Society. After which Citizen Ashley was appointed Treasurer.

The place of Meeting on next Thursday, was not appointed but the Delegates were informed a place would be fixed upon & of which place they might inform themselves, by application to Citn. Hodson of the Broadway Way Westminster

Adjourned.

199. Report from spy Groves: Committee of Emergency, 22 May 1794[65]

Source: TS 11/965/3510A

Report of Meeting of Delegates
Thursday May 22d 1794 –

Notice was given to the Delegates who were to meet at Thelwalls that the place of Meeting was changed to Dowlings in New Street Covent Garden –

This is a place of Meeting for the Division No. 5 – Dowling is a Breeches Maker, but has turned half his Shop into a Constitutional Saloop Shop, upon the plan of Barnes's No. 3 Compton Street

Pearce I understand engaged the Room of Dowling for that Night only – At 9 oClock Ashley took the Chair – The first business was the taking into Consideration a Recommendation of One of the Divisions to Return the thanks of the Society to those Members of the House of Commons and House of Lords who opposed the suspension of the Habeas Corpus –

Pearce gave it in writing nearly as follows ["] That the thanks of the London Corresponding Society be given to Messrs. Fox Sheridan Grey and other Patriotic Members of the House of Commons who so strenuously opposed the Suspension of the Habeas Corpus Act, that Bulwark of the Rights and Liberties of Englishmen"

He also presented a similar Motion of

65 Government description: 'Groves's Report of Meeting of Commee of Delegates May 22. 1794'.

172

Thanks to Earl Stanhope Lord Lauderdale the Duke of Grafton &c &c

After a short debate, in which Mr Fox was censured by all the Speakers as being luke-warm, as having shifted his Opinions with the Times with regard to the London C: Sy, & as having in most of his Speeches thrown an undeserved odium and reproach on the L.C S.,[66] Citizen Hodson (of the Broad-way Westminster) moved "That the thanks of the L. C. Sy. shod. *not* be returned to any of those Members"

Ashley the Chairman gave his Opinion the same way and said that none of the Members of the Opposition deserved the thanks of the Society except Lord Stanhope, & it would be too singular to thank him at present.

Question of Thanks called for & Negatived Nem: Con.

Hodsons Motion called for & carried Nem: Con

The Question of Thanks to the Members of the House of Lords disposed of the same way –

Citizen Smith (Bookseller of Portsmouth Street Lincolns Inn Fields) proposed That as Citizen Hardy who was in Custody could not any longer carry on the business of the Society as its Secretary, or any ways perform his duty, another Secretary should be elected – And, therefore, he proposed Citizen Pearce –

Le Maitre seconded the Motion – Before the Question was put by the Chairman Pearce said That he wished to decline the honour intended him on Account of his Avocations – He added "That he was not yet his own Master & *that he was but a Clerk to Citizen Martin*, but that he did not doubt if it was the desire of the Delegates, he might be allowed to spare time –

The Question put & carried Nem: Con.

Citizen Smith then said that as the two offices of Secretary and Treasurer to the Society had been united in the person of their worthy Citizen Hardy, & as he was deprived of his liberty, he wished a Treasurer also should be chosen for the Society & proposed Citizen Ashley, as he *now* wished the two Offices of Secretary and Treasurer to be divided

A General approbation –

Hodson seconded the Motion which was carried Nem: Con: – Ashley returned thanks

66 Denying that the proposed convention was dangerous, Fox argued: 'the idea of these persons assuming the authority of Government, was so contemptible and ridiculous, that Bedlam was the only receptacle that was fit for them' (*Senator*, vol. 10, p. 1182).

for the honor & promised to act with *integrity*.

N. B. It appears by this that it was not thot. altogether so proper to intrust Citizen Martins Clerk with the Cash.

The Delegates were called on to make their reports from the different Divisions

The number of Members made last Week throughout the whole Divisions were but Eleven.

Some Delegates stated the total desertion of the Members of their Divisions

Others the desertion of the Delegates of the Divisions

Some stated the avowed fears and pusillanimity of Members & Delegates No. 3 7. 11 & 27 were particularly mentioned

No. 2 (Compton Street) to have had 31 Members present which was almost as great a number as they ever had had, & that four Members had been made –

A general defection was stated Hodson, Smith, Pearce Ashley Worship Le Maitre Groves & others were of Opinion that the Moment a Delegate was Coward enough either to express his apprehensions for personal safety or to desert his duty at a time when it was more than ever required, that Delegate should be instantly superseded, & another chosen in his room

The proposition was approved, – Ashley thought that the Complaint of either shrinking through Cowardice, or negligence, should originate in the Division to which each Delegate so culpable belonged, & afterwards be brought, with the approbation of the Division, to the Committee of Delegates for their determination.

This was unanimously agreed to

Le Maitre said That a Recommendation had passed in the Division No. 2 to call a General Meeting of the Society, as soon as possible, in order to consider what measures were most proper & legal to be taken on the present Emergency –

He added, that as Delegate of the said division, he had been guilty of a Neglect in not being able to produce the Original Motion as signed by the Chairman, Citizen Groves, when that Motion passed in the division, as he had locked it up at home, & unfortunately came out & forgot it –

To supply this Defect he begged to call on Citizen Groves to vouch for the Motion having passed the Division & being so signed, and also to produce a Motion he had then just drawn up, as near as possible to the Original, and in which Citizen Groves had assisted him, in order to supply the Chasm, & hoped that he should by those means be able to supply the want of the Original Motion & Recommendation

Mr Ashley objected to it, as contrary to the established regulations of the Society which positively said That every Recommendation from any division, or Motion, must be presented Signed by the Chairman of that Division – If the precedent was once allowed it might tend, perhaps, to imposition & confusion, and open a door to that timidity which had shewn itself too much already – He wished, therefore, Citizen Le Maitre to withdraw his Motion, & to produce at the next Meeting of Delegates the Recommendation signed by the Chairman.

It was withdrawn.

Pearce said that as the Tickets taken from Citizen Hardy were now in the possession of the Ministry & the Society thereby liable to have tricks of a very serious nature played off upon them, he moved That the old Tickets be called in & new ones delivered of a different sort in order to prevent any Ministerial trick by the Introduction of Spies or otherwise, as it was easy for them to forge a Number & Name & so impose on the Society –

This was much approved.

Worship offered his Service to engrave a plate gratis – It was accepted – He had the thanks of the Delegates voted him for his liberal offer –

Pearce wished two hands united to be engraven on the Top of the Ticket

A Delegate proposed that the Cap of Liberty be engraven on it, & said that he could see no objection to it, as the King had lately ordered the Cap of Liberty to be carried in triumph from St. James's to St. Pauls –

Citizen Groves thought the procession in which the Cap of Liberty was carried was not intended as a Compliment to that Cap, but a Compliment to the Lion & Unicorn –

Hodson said that French Insignias and devices had prevailed too much already & had done the Society no Service, as it had been Misunderstood – Worship was left to himself to execute it

The Committee broke up & Citizens Hodson & Smith ordered to provide another Room for the Delegates to meet in next Thursday, the present one being too small & close.

P. S. It appeared that the Finances of the Society were at so low an Ebb as not to be able to afford to pay for the Advertisements intended as Thanks to the Members in opposition even to those Papers which would insert them

200. Report from spy Groves: LCS Division 2, 26 May 1794[67]

Source: PC1/23/A38

Report of Proceedings of Division 2 Compton Street – Monday 26th. 1794.

About 9 oClock Pearce, Le Maitre, Jones Groves and about Ten others were assembled in the Coffee Room.

A Sheriffs Officer of the Name of Davelin an Attorney of the name of Willingham, and a Constable of the name of Humpage had taken possession of the Furniture in Barne'ss House, and were removing part of it in a Cart under a Distringas in consequence of a Clausum fregit which *Barnes* had been served with for a paltry debt of Three or four pounds[68] –

As no Appearance had been put in to the Writ, the first levy was for 40s. – this was the second for 4£ on account of Nonappearance, & the Goods were removed –

But it seems that the Goods are not the property of Barnes, but of his Mother in Law who purchased them, has the Inventory and who is the Landlady

In removing the Goods Humpage was said to have found 33 Gun Powder flasks, or Cannisters, in the Garret, and that he had sent to One of the Police Offices & also to the Treasury an Account of it – that there was no Gun Powder in them, but that some of them were painted on the Outside with that Word.

Barnes's people said That a painter who lived in the Garret had got them to paint for a person in the Neighbourhood

On the Report of these powder flasks or Cannisters being found, and also of the Message sent to the Treasury & the police office, it was soon Whispered round that detachments of Horse and foot were coming to Compton Street, & that it would not be safe to stay there any longer.

Pearce said that as a Division was that Night met in Winslow Street Oxford Street it would be best to adjourn there –

This was agreed to and they paired off two and two instantly.

At the Division in Winslow Street which is No. 13. & held at the Horse & Groom Public

67 Government description: 'Proceedings of division No. 2. / May 26. 1794'.
68 *Quare clausum fregit* is a process to compel the appearance of a person by summons and distress against his goods. A *distringas*, in this case, is a writ directing the sheriff to obtain payment of a debt by seizing the defendant's chattels (Jacob Giles and T. E. Tomlins, *The Law Dictionary*, 1797).

House Citizen *Thompson* was voted in the Chair

Pearce acquainted them with the Reason of the Visit – It was proposed to subscribe for Mr. *Barnes* to discharge the debt & Costs – but it was over-ruled by almost the whole body

It fully appeared that the Society were considerably in debt, and to One printer only in the Sum of 50£. – that there was no Stock at all in hand, not even to pay for necessary Advertisements, & more particularly that Gerald was without a Shilling at this present time

An Accusation was made by one Citizen on the score of an unfair appropriation of the Monies collected – that there was something dishonest in collecting Money for printing pamphlets &c for the use of the Citizens & for distribution, & making Citizens pay again for them when printed, which was paying twice, & he wished to know how they could be in debt with the printer

It was answered that the Expence of the Delegation to Scotland cost upwards of 240£. -- that Secretary Hardy, who was Treasurer also, had made up *his* Accounts,[69] – that

if the Delegates who had collected the Sub-scriptions had acted dishonestly, in withold-ing the Money, it was not his fault, but there was no Cause to suspect them & that all Accounts had been fairly Audited

It was said by One Citizen that a large Sum of Money must have been collected at Chalk farm by the Sale of the Tickets at 6d. each and must have amounted to near 80£. as there were full 3000 present.

Le Maitre said that Ministry wished to make it appear so, and he did not wish to un-deceive them, as the strength of their legal demands lay in their Numbers

Various propositions were made to increase their resources

Some were for calling a General Meeting at 1s. pr. Ticket – others for the payment of 2d. on every Citizens entering the Division Room, and others for increasing the price of Admis-sion

Nothing specific was resolved but left to the Consideration of the Meeting of the Dele-gates to be sent to the General Committee

It was recommended & agreed Nem: Con. that for the future, in order to destroy the effects of a Junto among them, that whenever there was a Vacancy in any Committee, whether in the General Committee, Com-mittee of Correspondence, or of Delegates, that it be supplied by the Division in which the Vacancy happens, and not filled up by either of those Committee From this resolu-tion it is apparent that there is a general dis-trust among the Divisions, of their Commit-tees – that they are suspected of betraying them – and that the Committees wish them-selves to consist only of their own choosing –

It is clear also that from the poverty of them they are incapable of carrying their views into practice, vizt. that of disseminating their principles by pernicious publications – and that from the general ideas of misapplica-tion of money and concealment also, there is a general want of Confidence throughout the Society

Citizen Groves was chosen Delegate in the Room of Richter

The Place of Meeting of Delegates is to be learnt at Smiths Portsmouth Street, who with Ashley (now in Custody) were to provide a place

69 A government copy of these accounts shows that up to 26 April the LCS paid £244 15s 5d in connection with the delegation, and up to 10 May they received subscriptions totalling £240 13s 4d ('Extracts from Hardy's Account Book as Treasurer of the London Corresponding Society', TS 11/959/3505). Most of the con-tributions were a shilling or half-crown. Larger sums came from Norwich (£30), from 'Sundries in the City by W. W.' (£10 10s), from T and R Walker (£5 5s each), from collections at the general meetings in October (£6 6s), January (£13 4s 5d) and April (£18). Thelwall's lectures, which he started as a means of supporting the delegates, produced £28 7s 3d between 21 Nov. and 4 April. (The lack of any entry for Thel-wall's lectures after 4 April lends credence to the charge (probably made in May) that lately none of the money from the lectures has gone to the LCS or to anyone except Thelwall. 'Infor-mation of George Williams', TS 11/957/3502.) The subscription in the divisions brought in £61 1s 1d. This total does not reflect accurately the generosity of the members, for many of them contributed directly rather than through their division subscription. Still, the record of the divisions does reveal the state of the Society between November and May. Almost half of the divisions (6, 9, 10, 14, 15, 17, 18, 19, 20, 21, 24 and 26) did not subscribe at all. Div. 1 sub-scribed only once; Divs. 8, 27 and 28 only twice each. At the other extreme Div. 29 subscribed twelve times and Div. 7 thirteen times. Here are the total sums from each division: 1 (5s 6d), 2 (£3 4s including £2 0s 2d from a 'private fund'), 3 (£1 14s 2d), 4 (£2 12s 6d), 5 (£2 3s), 7 (£8 3s 10d), 8 (£2 5s 6d), 11 (£3 11s 4d, plus a joint contribution with Div. 16), 12 (£1 13s 8d), 13 (£8 9s), 16 (19s 6d; £2 14s 6d with Div. 25; 6s 6d with Divs. 11 and 25), 23 (£5 2s 0d), 27 (£1 6s 5d), 28 (9s), 29 (£16 0s 8d).

201. Report from spy Metcalfe: LCS Division 6, 2 June 1794[70]

Source: TS 11/956/3501

Meeting of the 6th. Division of London Corresponding Society at the Parrot on Monday Evening 2nd. June 1794

Present 15.

Citizen Worship stated that Citn. Hudson a Prisoner in Newgate had complained of the neglect and inattention which the Society treated him with, that they had promised to support him, which had prevented his receiving any relief from his Relations, but that for the last 3 or 4 Weeks he had not seen or heard from the Society. He therefore moved that the Delegate be instructed to enquire of the Committee whence this neglect proceeded and to call their attention to the relief of Citn. Hudson

The Delegate was then instructed, to inforce in the Committee, the absolute necessity of calling a General Meeting, that the Society might be informed what had been done towards the end for which they had originally formed themselves into a Society, and to rally their Panic Struck Members,

Citizen Worship said he had been to see Citizen Gerald in Newgate[71] who was much dissatisfied with the Society for their want of Spirit, and said he had no doubt some of those in the Tower would be Hanged and he supposed the Society would stand by silent Spectators.

A proposition was then made to subscribe towards the Society's fund, in Order that they might be enabled to print 2000 of the annexed papers,[72] but no Money was subscribed on this Evening

It was observed that Citizen Ashley who had been appointed Treasurer at 12 o'Clock on the Thursday night, had been taken into Custody for being Treasurer early on Friday Morning. that therefore there must have been among them some Rascally Spy and there was every reason to believe Grove was the person that it would therefore be right at once to denounce and expell him, And that the Dele-

gate be instructed to inforce this in the Committee./.

On account of the Hollidays, this Division not to meet until Wednesday Evening in the next Week, instead of Monday

202. Report from spy Groves: LCS Division 2, 2 June 1794

Source: TS 11/954/3495

Report of the Meeting of the Division No. 2. Compton Street Monday June 2d. 1794

Very few met till near 10 oClock – There were fourteen in all – Le Maitre, Jones (of Tottenham Ct Road) Hastie and Groves were the principals

To make the above Number there were Five or Six Citizen Visitors –

Hastie was proposed by Le Maitre to the Chair, it was seconded & carried –

Le Maitre, One of the Delegates for Division No. 2. reported the proceedings of the Commee of Delegates held at Citizen Dowlings in New Street Covent Garden on Thursday Evg. May 29th. –

That Report consisted of

1st.   That there appeared to be a general deficiency in the Finances of the L. C. Society

2d.   That several Delegates had neglected to pay to the Treasurer the Subscriptions they had collected at their different Divisions

3dly. That the Expences of the Delegation to Scotland was very expensive & had cost the Society 250£., as the Society were obliged to *equip out* the Delegates, for that purpose that they might make a decent appearance

4thly.   That the Expences of the Society in printing had been so expensive as not only to exhaust the finances, but to run them upwards of 50£. in debt with the printer, who would not give any further credit

5thly.   That a Narrative of Citizen Hardy's Apprehension had been drawn up with some remarks on the Suspension of the Habeas Corpus Bill, with a justification of the Society's Conduct & that some few had been printed for the Use of the Delegates, but that owing to a want of fund, the Number voted by the Commee of Delegates, vizt., 10,000 – could not be compleated till a Subscription for that purpose had been raised – And

6thly.   That the Recommendation of that Division for calling a General Meeting of the Society to consider of proper & legal means to be adopted on the present Emergency, was rejected by a great Majority vizt. 24. to 4. And That another Division had recommended

---

70 Government description: 'Meeting 6 Division London C. Society / 2nd. June 1794'.

71 Gerrald had been in Newgate since 27 March. Groves met him there on 12 April and reported to government his 'humorous sarcasms' about his Scottish judges, his 'reverie', and his 'sneering' at John Bull (TS 11/954/3498).

72 The account of Hardy's seizure.

a Meeting also, & had proposed Whitsun Monday for the day – That he had enforced the idea of a General Meeting and had approved of that day – but that he was outvoted in both

He then stated the misfortune that had befel Citizen Pearce, another of their Delegates, who *that very Morning* had been apprehended, and lamented the thinness of the Meeting as indicating a timidity unworthy of good Citizens

He also said that Mr Powis, the Member, one of the Secret Committee,[73] had informed his friends that he was implicated in the Charge with the rest of his fellow Citizens, & added that his friends informed him that, on account of his Youth, if he would relinquich his Situation, & totally abandon the Society, the Warrant would not be executed – that he had refused repeatedly so to do, and should continue as long as the Society lasted

Mr Jones lamented the apparent Cowardice of the Citizens, and compared them to the Moderes of France – He expected, he said, every hour to be taken into Custody, but that should not deter him – that the Motion which had been rejected by so great a Majority of the Delegates had arisen with him – he, it was, who had made the Motion for the General Meeting – he then saw the great Necessity of it – he now saw it still greater – He was sorry he had not been present at the Meeting of Delegates, when he would have supported his Motion in opposition to that Majority – that the rejection of it would be fatal to the Society – it would cast a damp on & dispirit the Citizens, who were, he was sorry to observe, too much dispirited already by Ministerial Measures which now, more than ever, required the firmest perseverance of the Society, and that all that Ministers wanted was to drive them from that hold which their Union had so strongly fixed them in, & he concluded by saying that he would on the next Meeting produce a plan for the better Regulation and Organization of the Society

Le Maitre observed that Citizen Groves had been chosen Sub-Delegate for that Division for the preceding Meeting of Delegates in the Room of Citizen Richter but for that Night only – He begged to move that Citizen Groves be appointed Delegate for the ensuing Quarter

The Motion, seconded by Jones, was carried Nem: Con.[74]

73 The Committee of Secrecy of the House of Commons.
74 Groves then copied the voucher (signed by Robert Hastie, chairman) certifying him as subdelegate.

203. Report from spy Metcalfe: LCS Division 11, 3 June 1794[75]

Source: TS 11/956/3501

Meeting of the 11th. Division of the London Corresponding Society at Citn. Worship's in Ball Court Lombard St. on Tuesday Eveng. 3rd. June 1974.

Present 16 among them a person from Scotland a very violent Democrat. he said he had been 30 times apprehended in the last 15 Months and had quitted Scotland for a short time in Order to avoid being again taken into Custody, he reported the Scotch to be in great force, and resolved on obtaining a reform and redress of their Grievances, that they would long ago have proceeded to violent Measures but that they had been induced to wait from the favorable Reports they had heard of the London Corresponding Society, but that he was sorry to say they had been deceived, they had been much disappointed that a Convention of Delegates had not been appointed, their's were ready to set off, but that he was sure they would wait no longer, and we might shortly expect to hear of such measures in Scotland as the London Corresponding Society would be afraid to think of, he would not tell his Name, but said he should return to Scotland very shortly
Motions similar to those made last Night by the 6th. Division was then made and carried

One New Member made

A person of the Name of Latham is the Delegate
—— Jackson   Secretary

There was a great Deal of most seditious and Treasonable Conversation took place on this Evening, One Member remarked how very astonishing it was that the Mass of the people should submit to the Tyranny and oppression of so small a Number of Men as the Ministry were composed off, that a very few determined Men would be sufficient to rid the World of them and observed what a Glorious thing it would be to lug that Scoundrel Pitt from the Treasury Bench and put an End to his miserable existance   another said he should like to be the first to seize him by the Collar.

A person of the Name of Cook a Baker

75 Government description: 'Meeting of 11th Division of London Corrg Society   3d June 1794'.

who lately lived at Cambridge was there, a very violent Democrat, and who said he had been obliged to quit Cambridge on account of his political opinions. &c.

204. Report from spy Metcalfe: LCS General Committee, 5 June 1794[76]

Source: TS 11/956/3501

General Committee of the London
Corresponding Society
Thursday 5th. June 1794
in New St. Covent Garden

Citizen Burks in the Chair
34 present.

Ltre read from Sheffield, concerning the apprehension of three of their Members, stating their being taken away, without the means of support or a change of Linen, and requesting the Society to relief their necessity's &c. Referred to the Committee of Correspondence.

Citizen Smith, read a Letter he had received from Citizen Gerald, stating his great necessity, being in absolute want of the means of existance, and that he expected to be sent off for Botany Bay every Day and requesting the Society would furnish him with some few necessarys for his Voyage.

Resolved that the Delegates recommend to their respective Divisions the pressing necessitys of Citizen Gerald and to promote a Subscription in his favor, and that for the present all the Moneys subscribed be appropriated solely to the use of Citizen Gerald

Other applications from Citizens Hudson Ashley &c. were reced praying Relief, Referred to the Committee of Correspondence

Citizen Hodgson moved that the Committee of Correspondence be authorized to put an Advertizement in the papers, stating the wretched Situation of the Wives and Children of those Members of the Society who are now imprisoned, and to request the public to subscribe towards their Relief. Resolved that the Committee of Correspondence have the disposal of all monies subscribed. &c./

Citizen Jones, then addressed the Committee, stating the absolute necessity of the Societys taking some measures to remove the prejudices of the public against the Society, and which had been occasiond by the false statement of their wishes and intentions which the Minister and the Secret Committee, had hold out to the

Public, and to state in plain and forcible Language the objects which this Society had in view and of their determination to persevere until they should effect Universal Suffrage and Annual Parliaments taking place of the present Corrupt System and to assure their Fellow Citizens and the World, that the London Corresponding Society would never abandon their principles, but with their Lives. He then produced 7 or Eight Resolutions which he had drawn up and which he submitted to the Committee for their adoption, and that they should be forthwith incerted in the Morning Post and Morning Chronicle, as the Resolutions of the Society, which on the Question being put was carried unanimously

The Resolutions of the 6th. 11th and two other Divisions, "that it be recommended to the General Committee to call a general Meeting" was referred back to the several Divisions, to report their opinion thereon at the next General Committee.

Citizen Smith reported that he had received Subscriptions to the amount of £2.17.6 for the use of Citzn Gerald which he had paid into his hands./

The amount of the Subscriptions paid in by the several Delegates was £2..16. – which was paid to the Treasurer

Report by Citizen Smith that the Society were in Debt for printing &c. £31..16..6.

Citizen Burks appointed Secretary[77]
adjourned

205. Report from spy Groves: LCS General Committee, 5 June 1794[78]

Source: TS 11/965/3510A

Report of Committee of Delegates
Thursday 5th. June 1794
held at Dowlings New Street Covt Garden

Present

Jones	(Tottenham cot.)
Le Maitre	Denmark St.
Hodson	Broadway
Metcalf	Atty. (City)
Groves	Covt Garden
Smith	Portsmouth Street

77 Burks was the nominal secretary, but Smith was the real secretary, according to Thomas Upton (examination by the Privy Council, PC1/22/A36C).

78 Government description: 'Report of Committee of Delegates of the London Corresponding Society / 5 June 1794'.

76 Government description: 'General Committee London Corresg Society / 5th. June 1794'.

Burke
Bone
——————   Hardys Shopman
Becks

The names of the rest (about 14) unknown

Le Maitre was employed till ½ past 9 in reading Accounts of the various Successes of the French Naval force – Roberspierre's Address to the Convention, &c in the Courier.

Every Article of News that either gave a seeming serious account of French Success or an ironical statement of the disposition of Our Fleet, afforded the utmost pleasure

A Paragraph that stated the disposition of the whole French Armament into four Squadrons for the purpose of seizing the whole of English Merchant Ships; yet so divided as to be able to join in Case the English fleet should be seen, and give them battle infused the highest satisfaction among the Delegates –

At ¼ before 10 proceeded to business, & Citizen Burke voted to the Chair   Jones opened the business by lamenting the general falling off since the Suspension Bill took place, & the panic which had seized the Society – Even in the Commee of Delegates he could not help observing the obvious deficiency in the Attendance – He argued, that the principles wch. were the basis of the Society & at first cemented them together should be now more firmly than ever persisted in, & that the Society should manifest itself in proportion to that opposition & persecution wch. it met with from the Ministry.

After placing these arguments in those opposite points of view as either tending to annihilate the Society, or rivet it more firmly & also of increasing the Numbers of the Society – he read a paper consisting of 9 Resolutions

These Resolutions were an Explanation of the Cause of the institution of the Society – vizt. A Reform in the Representation in Parliament by Annual Parliaments and Universal Suffrage –

The General tendency of the Resolutions were the Necessity of such a form of Representation, accompanied with a determined perseverance till obtained, in order to shew the public at large, that the principles of the Society were not hostile to the Constitution of the Country, that the Society did not consist of a bandetti of depredators, who wanted to seize on all property & divide the plunder, as, he said, Ministers & their Tools had given it they were, And also that by thus publishing their views & principles, the Society might so increase the body of it as to convince Ministry,

notwithstanding the present persecutions that in the End the object must be obtained. He concluded with a Motion that they be printed in those papers that wod. insert them – The Resolutions were read by the Chairman and debated each seperately

Smith objected to them in toto, as the Society was not in a state to afford the Expence

Jones replied & said it was a humiliating reflection that all the Societies for parliamentary reform in the Country, which looked up to the London Corresponding Society for the adoption of measures on the present Emergency should find that this Society, wch. was the Spring & Fountain of the Rest, & from wch. Ministers had most to dread, should not be able to afford a small sum to print a few Resolutions, & therefore sooner than the Resolutions should be lost & the Society be so hurt he begged to be permitted to pay for the insertion himself – The proposition was Recd. with loud applause –

After a few immaterial objections by Hodson & Smith who withdrew them the Resolutions were agreed to   Nem: Con

Hodson made a Motion for thanks to Citizen Hardy to [be] inserted as the Conclusion of the Resolutions –

Jones begged that dispatch might be made or it wod. be too late to get them inserted that night

Groves proposed that the Delegates should by a Subscription among themselves defray the Expence of printing the Resolutions & if that was agreed to he was ready to contribute, as Delegate, his Mite

A Delegate, after the honorable offer of Citizen Jones it would be hurting him to collect a Subscription

Jones went away to get the Resolutions inserted in the Morning Chronicle   Morning Post & Courier

Hardys Shopman read a Letter from the Society at Sheffield, – it consisted of Complaints of the manner in which their Worthy Citizens had been dragged away – that they were not allowed even to change their linen, nor had they money or the means to procure necessaries & therefore intreated the assistance of the L C. Society

A Letter was read by Smith from Gerrald to him complaining of his being destitute, & requiring support –

Smith said that he went immedy to him & gave him half a Guinea – that his Division had collected 2£ 17s 6d for Gerrald wch. Smith had taken him, deducting his half Guinea out of that Collection & that Citizen Gerrald had made him his Treasurer, that he might neither spend it or be robbed of it, as the turnkeys & others about the prison were Thieves

Smith read a Letter from their worthy Citizen Ashley now in Custody – it was brought him by his Wife – it only stated a few deficiencies in the hands of different Delegates & prayed Relief for several of the Wives & Children of those Delegates, who were distressed & in a state of great poverty -- the Letter concluded with his Resolutions to be firm in the good Cause.

It was recommended by the Chairman to the Commee for each Member strongly to ⟨express⟩ the necessity of a speedy & liberal Subscription

It was stated that ever since the Suspension Bill not one of the Citizens of Division No. 11. had ever met except Delegate

Citizen Burke Elected Secretary – to sign no Resolutions – to be signed by Order of the L. C. Society – to be kept secret from the Divisions   Citizen Becks appointed Receiver – the Word *Treasurer* changed into it – to be kept a secret from the Divisions –

Delegates to bring a Voucher – of Monies Collected in the Divisions signed by the Chairman – The Receiver to give a Rect. for it & countersign it as Recd.

There were four Divisions sent a Written Requisition for a General Meeting, which after a short Debate, between Hodson Le Maitre & Smith, which last opposed it was negatived by a large Majority – as injurious to the Society – dangerous to its Citizens who had abilitiy & wod. stand forward & therefore highly impolitic – .

Adjourned at 1/2 past 12 oClock

206. Resolutions: LCS General Committee, 5 June 1794

Source: printed copy in Place Collection, vol. 36, fo. 126[79]

London Corresponding Society
General Committee, 5th. June, 1794
Resolved Unanimously.

1st.   That *The London Corresponding Society* was instituted solely for the purpose of obtaining UNIVERSAL SUFFRAGE, and ANNUAL PARLIAMENTS; and has never asserted any Principles which had not this for

79   Copy in TS 11/956/3501 annotated: 'Prepared by Jones, brot. to the Division by Barrow–Smith also gave Metcalfe 50   the former a Printer in Lin. Inn fields'.

their basis, nor adopted any measures which have not been openly and publicly avowed.

2dly.   That fully convinced of the Legality of its Proceedings, and firm in its Principles, it feels no Inclination, at the present *crisis*, to retract any of its former Assertions, nor depart from its original Purpose.

3dly.   That to wish for a Parliamentary Reform is neither *illegal, seditious,* nor *treasonable.*

4thly.   That peaceful assembling of Men in a *Meeting* or *Convention*, to deliberate upon Public Measures, and seek Redress of Grievances, is not YET declared by Law, to be illegal, seditious, or treasonable.

5thly.   That these two Circumstances, taken apart, being innocent, their Combination cannot infer Guilt; since the union of two proper and virtuous Actions can never produce either an Impropriety, or a Crime: and that, therefore, to wish for a Parliamentary Reform, and to assemble peacably, are in themselves *legal*; so to meet in a Convention, and there wish for a Parliamentary Reform, must be perfectly and strictly legal.

6thly.   If the foregoing Propositions be just, it follows that the *Imprisonment* of any *Individual*, ought not to affect the existence, or the continuation of this Society; since, as its object is legal, and its means honest, its best security, while law is practised, and Trial by Jury remains, is to resign itself peacably to the decision of its Country, convinced, that by such a conduct the ultimate event must be to this Society, a PILLAR OF GLORY, to its Enemies, a *Monument of Shame.*

7thly.   That it is not only the Right, but the Duty of every individual in possession of his Reason, to improve his faculties by investigation, and exercise his judgment on every subject, wherein he is essentially concerned; and that he who contributes to the support of that Form of Government, under which he consents to live, ought to be well instructed in the precise nature of its privileges and obligations.

8thly.   That to deprive Men of the *exercise* and enjoyment of their *Faculties*, is to take away the very Foundation upon which all Government stands; and for that which appeals not to *Reason*, but to *Force*; which seeks not to convince the *Judgment*, but coerce the *Will*, is not Government, but

TYRANNY and OPPRESSION; or if a Government is one fitted, not for MEN, but for BRUTES!

9thly. That the apprehension and imprisonment of many of its most valuable and useful members, though in so much as it concerns themselves individually, it affords considerable regret; to the Society in particular, and to the public in general, ought rather to be a matter of satisfaction, since while it proves that the enemies to *Peace* and *Reform*, have no other weapons to oppose to them than those of *Violence* and *Prosecution*, it will tend, should administration venture to bring them to an impartial Trial, to promote effectually the misuse in which this Society has embarked, and clear it from ill-founded and undeserved imputations!

10thly. That, therefore, so far from shrinking from observation, or courting obscurity, the Members of this Society pledge themselves to maintain the same uniform conduct which has ever distinguished them, and are ready to answer singly, at the *Bar of Justice*, to any charge legally brought against them, whenever it shall please their country to call upon them for their vindication; at the same time solemnly declaring, that they will sooner yield their LIVES than desert their PRINCIPLES!

FINIS.

N.B.[80] *As these Resolutions are distributed Gratis, those who wish to promote the welfare of the Community will, perhaps, after perusing them, take a pleasure in lending and recommending them to the attention of others.*

207. Report from spy Groves: LCS Division 2, 9 June 1794

Source: TS 11/954/3498

Report of Meeting of Division No. 2 Compton Street Monday 9th. June 1794

Citizen Brooks called to the Chair Le Maitre stated the Number of Members made the last Week to have been 9 –

That the Committee of Delegates had rejected the Recommendation of Four Divisions for calling a General Meeting, &

That they recommended a speedy Subscription for Citizen Gerald, who was daily

80 This postscript occurs only on a copy in TS 11/956/3501.

expected to be sent off for Botany Bay

That a Subscription be opened for the Wives and Families of those Citizens who were in Custody and stood in need of it

Jones (Tottenham Cot Road) rose and stated what had passed in the Commee of Delegates relative to the Resolutions he had drawn up & submitted to them – that the Commee had approved of them & that he had got them printed in the Morning Post only, not having Money enough to pay for Advertisements in the Post & Chronicle – as the Post charged 15s. & the Chronicle wanted a Guinea

He then read the Resolutions to the Division, which were recd. with Applause Having stated the necessity of publishing them in a more extensive manner he moved that they be printed on slips of paper and distributed

This, (after a confused conversation, respecting this mode of publishing & advertizing them frequently) was agreed to, & the Number to be 10,000 –

A Citizen moved that the Resolutions be printed in all the papers –

Another opposed it, because all the papers would not insert them –

Another moved that they be inserted in Three Morning Papers only – the Post, Chronicle & Courier – This Motion was seconded –

It was opposed on the Ground of want of Cash –

Jones put an Amendment to the Motion, by adding, that they be inserted in the Morning Chronicle only

A Squabbling Conversation for an Hour & an half ensued respecting the Order of putting the Motions, vizt. Whether the Motion for printing the Resolutions in all the papers, Whether the Motion for Printing them in three papers, or the last Motion for printing them in One only should have precedence –

It was insisted that the Motions should take place in order as moved –

Jones stated the regular mode to be to put the Amended Motion first & the Original Motion afterwards, and quoted the practice of the House of Commons –

A Citizen (who was a Visitor) was very warm – he said that the Movers did not understand their own Motions, and that they were all Stupid

He was called loudly to order, & the Good Sense of the Division No. 2 was defended by Citizen Groves – He said it was highly indecent for any Citizen who had neither a right to Vote or even to make a Motion, to charge a Division with stupidity, especially when that Division was known to have been looked up to as the Organizing power of the whole L. C.

Society – that in point of Numbers it was far more respectable than any three Divisions and as for Abilities, it was well known the Citizens of that Division, fell short of none, & he charged the Author of the Calumnies on that Division with coming there for the express purpose of creating a Confusion

Le Maitre insisted that he ought to be voted out, and said it would be a glorious triumph for Pitt and Dundas if they should learn of such a clamour and quarrelling amongst the Members –

Several personalities passed which occasioned great heat – Jones was up several times to calm & conciliate – but he could not be heard – Some Citizens went away

The Chairman loudly called to Order Groves said that he would never sit still & hear the Members of his Division so rudely attacked without properly animadverting on the Author and that the Charges of a Want of Understanding and of Stupidity attached only to those who could not understand the proceedings of that Division; that if they did [not] understand the proceedings it proved them to possess a narrower Understanding & a Stupidity in the highest degree, if they could imagine the Division was to [be] confused by so shallow an Artifice – He called for an Apology –

The Chairman said it ought to be made & it was made accordingly

All parties shook hands

The Motion for the Morning Chronicle only put & carried

Jones then lamented the fate of his Motion respecting a General Meeting, in the General Committee – He made a long Speech respecting its immediate necessity – and said he should persevere till he had obtained it –

His only words worth remarking were That he had been early taught the necessity of a Meeting or a Convention for a Parliamentary Reform, by one William Pitt whom he then adored, but who had since turned out to be an *Apostate Hypocrite*

He called Mr Dundas an *Impudent Wretch*

He was not, he said, prepared to go the length of saying that he not only wished the Citizens to meet for that purpose, but also to meet *armed*; tho' he had no doubt but that a body of Men met together peaceably & Constitutionally Might, if they were attacked, repel force by force, which was the great Bulwark of Liberty – but this he would say that he was ready at all times to lose his life in so glorious a Cause – He then made a Motion for a General Meeting – it was carried Unanimously

Eleven Members present

The Inclosed Song Sold by Le Maitre at 4 for a penny –

Adjourned –

208. Report from spy Metcalfe: LCS Division 6, 11 June 1794[81]

Source: TS 11/956/3501

Meeting 6th Division of London Corresponding Society at the Parrott on Wednesday Eveng. 11th. June 1794

only 7 Attended

And the only business referred to the Divisions from the Committee of Delegates, being to consider of the propriety of calling a General Meeting, of which this Division had deled their opinion./ no business was this night done./.

209. Report from spy Metcalfe: LCS General Committee, 12 June 1794[82]

Source: TS 11/956/3501

Meeting of the General Committee at Citn. Dowlings in New St. Covent Garden on Thursday Eveng. 12th. June 1794

Citizen Le Maitre in the Chair

25 Members present among them *Citn. Baxter* Not more than 3 Divisions having returned any opinion upon the subject of calling a General Meeting the consideration thereof was postponed until the next General Committee &c

The return of New Members were only 3. The thanks of the Committee were voted to Citizen Barrow for having procured 2000 of the Resolutions of the last General Committee to be printed off at his own expence, to be distributed to the public

Citizen Worship produced a drawing of a design for the Societys New Tickets of admission, On One Side the figure of Justice on the other Britannia with the Cap of Liberty, at the top the hand in hand and at the bottom a Dove as the emblem of peace, with the Societys Motto. of Unite persevere and be

81 Government description: 'Meeting 6th Divn. of London Correspg Society on Wedy 11 June 1794'. This report is on the same sheet as the beginning of Metcalfe's report of the General Committee meeting on 12 June.
82 Government description: 'Meeting General Committee on Thursday 12th June 1794'.

free./. the same was approved off and Citizen Worship was desired to engrave a plate and print 1000 Tickets against the next Meeting of the Committee

Subscriptions recommended

The Money paid in by those Delegates who attended, as money subscribed for Citizen Gerald amounted to £1 18. 6.

Adjourned

A Conversation took place relative to the violence which had been exercised by the Mob, at the House of Lord Stanhope[83] and a proposal was made to go there but it was determined to seperate and not be seen in a body on any account, as the circumstance would be held out by the Aristocrats, as a proof of the Societys Wishes for Uproar and Confusion. &c.

210. Report from spy Groves: LCS General Committee[84]

Source: TS 11/965/3510A

London Corresponding Society

Report of the Meeting of the Committee of Delegates held at Dowlings New Street Covent Garden   Thursday June 12th. 1794

The time, till 10 oClock, was taken up in reading paragraphs from the Morning Post, the Morning Chronicle & Courier – On its being asked, if any fresh News had arrived to cause anor Illumination, Le Maitre said, Yes that Advices had been recd. that two French fleets, one from Toulon, the other from Port L'Orient, had sailed & formed a junction for the purpose of attacking Admiral Montague, & securing the safe Arrival of the expected fleet of Merchant Men from America –

A Delegate, whose name I know not, came in, & pulling from under his Coat a large Horse pistol, begged to be excused attending, as he

83 On 11 June, following the news that Lord Howe had (on 1 June) captured six ships and sunk two, windows throughout the metropolis were illuminated. Church and king thugs broke windows which were not illuminated and also illuminated windows of some reform-minded men, including Stanhope and Hardy. The next night they returned to attack the houses themselves (*MP* 13 June 1794, p. 3). Mrs Hardy, in an advanced state of pregnancy, had to climb through the back window to escape.

84 Government description: 'Groves Report of the / Meeting of the / Committee of Delegates / of the L. C. Society / 12 June 1794. / (one inclosure)'.

was going up to Citizen Hardy's to protect the House which had been threatened to be destroyed – he also said that there were a number of good Citizens there for that purpose

Le Maitre said that there was a party also of Citizens in Earl Stanhope's House for that purpose which also had been threatened to be pulled down

There being but Six Candles in the dining Room Windows a half penny a piece was collected to put up more lights –

A Delegate said that a Citizen who had, the preceding Evening, seen several footmen breaking Lord Stanhopes Windows had followed some of them home, & had given Information to his Lordship of it – That the same Citizen had also seen some Footmen, Yesterday, behind Carriages, had learned where they lived & that of both circumstances he had given his Lordship Information.

Le Maitre called to the Chair

Some of the principal leading Members of the L C. Society, who are Delegates, such as Hodson, Smith Jones & few others did not attend.

It was stated that they had absented in order to protect their Houses.

Citizen Cooper produced and distributed to each Delegate a Dozen of the inclosed printed Resolutions of the Society

[There follows a description of the proposed design of the new tickets.]

It was moved to print Three thousand of them – The Motion was amended & reduced to 2000   The Amendment was amended to 1000 – which last was agreed by shew of hands 10 pro: 10 Con – The Chairman gave the casting Vote –

These Cards will cost 20s. per 1000 & are to be distributed on the Expiration of the present quarter when all the Old Tickets are to be called in & the New ones delivered

The Reason stated for printing the New Tickets & calling in the Old Ones, is, that Mr Pitt, being in possession of the Old Tickets, might insert in the Blanks the Number of the Member & the Division, and by that Forgery introduce his Treasury Runners, which this plan it was said would effectually prevent.

The thanks of the Society were voted to the Citizen who had printed 1000 of their last Resolutions gratis.

A Motion was made in consequence of the Recommendation of One of the Divisions to the Committee that 10,000 of those Resolutions be printed at the Societys Expence

Another Motion that 5000 only be printed – A third Motion was made that 3000 only be printed – Agreed to

The several Delegates gave in the Collections of their Different Divisions   No. 2 was £1. 7s 0d   No. 11. was 14s. & of the Rest of the Divisions none exceeded 6s – the whole amounted to £4. 13s 0d

A Motion was made that for the future the Chairman of every Division wherein a New Citizen was made, should transmit to the Commee of Delegates the name Address & profession of the Citizen"

The reason assigned was to guard against imposition, as it had been, on enquiry discovered, that no such person resided where the Entry in the Societys Books had stated it to be –

Another reason was that the Delegates who lived in the Neighbourhood of the New Citizens might perhaps know them, or if not might easily be informed of their *Morals* & Civism –

The Arguments against the Motion were 1st. That a Citizen might not wish to give in his profession

2dly.   That every *New* Citizen was proposed by two Citizens before he could be admitted who were obliged to vouch for his Civism & *Morals*, – therefore the Motion was unnecessary

Motion withdrawn.

A Motion was made that there be no more *particular* Collections made among the Divisions, but that the Collections made should be for *General* purposes, & Subject to the Disposal of the Commee of Delegates

Agreed to

It was stated that several Divisions had not met at all – That in others only two   three or four had met, & that the Citizens seemed Panic-struck: it was necessary, therefore, to take the most effectual steps to rally them, and that it be recommended to the Tything Men of the Divisions to wait upon as many Citizens as they conveniently could, for that purpose

The business of a General Meeting was resumed –

It appeared that the Sense of Three or four Divisions were for it, & as early as possible – that in one Meeting where there were only four Members present 3 were for the Meeting and One against it

This was adopted as the Sense of that Division, although Seven Members, according to the Societys Laws, must be present before a Division could be formed –

The Argument for adoption was, The Emergency of the Case, & that that Law should, at, present be suspended – Agreed to

As it appeared that the sense of the Divisions had not been sufficiently ascertained a Motion was made That the Consideration of a General Meeting be postponed to the next Meeting, and, if possible, the Sense of the Majority of the Divisions in the mean time be obtained –   Agreed

Adjourned at 12 oClock

It was proposed to go *in a Body* to Lord Stanhopes and give him Three Cheers   It seemed, at first, the Sense of the Delegates – The proposition was altered that instead of going *in a Body*, the Delegates should go off in Couples, & give his Lordship three Cheers when they were met, as going in a Body might cause a Confusion and endanger the Delegates

The second proposition giving the Delegates time for reflection, & the Words Confusion and Danger being made use of, the design was abandoned.

I have, I believe, in several of my Reports, stated the general description of the people forming the London Corresponding Society, but I do not recollect that I have ever since I was chosen Delegate represented the general description of the Delegates now Meeting, of the London Correspondg Society

There are some of decent tradesmen-like appearance, who possess strong, but unimproved faculties, &, tho' bold, yet cautious – the Delegates of this description are but few

There are others of an apparent lower Order – no doubt Journeymen, who though they seem to possess no abilities & say nothing, yet they appear resolute and determined, & regularly vote for every Motion which carries with it a degree of boldness –

The last description among them, & which is the most numerous, consists of the very lowest order of Society – few are even decent in appearance, some of them filthy & ragged, and others such wretched looking blackguards that it requires some mastery over that innate pride, which every well-educated man must naturally possess, even to sit down in their Company./– And I have seen at one Oyer & Terminer at the Old Bailey much more decent figures discharged by proclamation at the End of the Session, for want of a prosecution. These appear very violent & seem ready to adopt every thing tending Confusion & Anarchy – Friday Morning

13th June

211. Report from spy Metcalfe: LCS Division 11, 13 June 1794[85]

Source: TS 11/956/3501

Meeting of the 11th. Division of London Corresponding Society at the Parrott, on Friday Evening 13th. June 1794./.

Citizen Higgins in the Chair

20 Members present but only 14 of this Division
One New Member made

The Delegate reported from the Committee of Delegates, that the expediency of calling a General Meeting had been referred back for the consideration of all the several Divisions and that the numbers for and against was to be taken down by the Delegate of each Division and reported to the next General Committee, that some judgement might be formed, as to the Numbers who would attend such General Meeting,

On the Question being put there appeared to be 13 for a General Meeting   1 against it.

On a Citizen Skinner informing the Division that he had been just told, the Lord Mayor and City Constables intended to pay a visit to them on this Evening, it was proposed to break up sooner than usual, and there being no other material business the Division adjourned

There was a Subscription made, to be sent to the Committee of Delegates, for their Disposal of to Citizen Geralds use, The amount about 10 or 12s.

Baxter did not attend this Evening as was expected

212. Report from spy Metcalfe: LCS General Committee, 19 June 1794[86]

Source: TS 11/956/3501

Meeting of the General Committee in New Street Covent Garden on Thursday Evening the 19th. June 1794.

Citizen Grove in the Chair

36 Members present
   Report from Delegates   7 New Members made

85 Government description: 'Meeting of 11th. Division of London Correspg Society 13th. June 1794'.
86 Government description: 'Meeting of General Committee of the London Corrg. Society 19th. June 1794'.

Subscriptions reced at the different Divisions £4 .. 6 .. 5
Citizen Hodson appointed receiver.

Ordered that 1000 of the last Resolutions of the General Committee be paid for, and that 2000 more be imediately struck off   A Motion was made that 1000 should be printed on a single sheet so as that they might be stuck up about the Town but this Motion was negatived for the present, upon Citizen Hodgsons intimation that it might militate against another paper which the Committee of Correspondence meant to bring before the public in a few days, and which paper was understood to be an application to the public on the behalf of the Wives and familys of their imprisoned Members.[87]

Citizen Lemaitre observed that Citizen Gerald had made complaints that the Society did not give him that regular and necessary relief that his Situation required, and that as it was uncertain how short his continuance here might be, he thought it incumbent upon the Society to prepare those necessarys which they had provided for Citizen Margarot, on his Voyage, he therefore moved that an account be made out of all the Subscriptions received on Account of Citizen Gerald including the money subscribed at Chalk Farm which he understood to be £18. 5s. and that the whole be imediately appropriated to the providing the necessarys for Citizen Geralds Voyage, and to support whilst he remained in Newgate

To this it was objected that the Society had

87 A handbill (16½ x 20½ cm) dated 19 June, headed 'A Subscription is Opened for the Relief of the Wives and Children of Sundry Persons detained in Prison by the late Suspension of the *Habeas Corpus Act*', lists the men authorized to receive subscriptions: John Smith, bookseller, Portsmouth St, Lincoln's-Inn-Fields; Richard Hodgson, hatter, 10 Broadway, Wstminster; John Williamson, shoemaker, Charles St, Westminster; Christopher Cooper, grocer, 67 New Compton St, Soho; Thomas Upton, watchmaker, 8 Bell-yard, Temple Bar; John Hill, turner, 10 Bartholomew Close; J. Hewitt, tinman, 72 Goswell St; William Worship, engraver, 3 Ball-alley, Lombard St; John Powell, baker, Goodge St, Tottenham Court Rd (Place Collection, vol. 36, fo. 127). In five months the subscription brought in £314 19s 3d. By 19 Nov., when the LCS issued an accounting, £284 7s 11½d had been expended (printed list of contributors in collection 'English Radical Societies' in Nuffield College Library; advertisement in *MC* 22 Nov. 1794, p. 1 lists subscription as £314 16s 9d). Place notes that 'the subscription was for the twofold purpose of supporting the families and providing legal assistance but as raising money for the latter purpose was illegal it was not mentioned' (Add MSS 36628, fo. 84v).

not been at all unmindful of Citizen Gerald, that to take an account of such subscriptions as had been paid solely for the use of Gerald would be impossible because Citizen Hardy was the person who alone could give any such Account and from him under the present circumstances no information could be procured, and it also was to be observed that previous to the Meeting at Chalk Farm Citizen Hardy was in advance to Citizen Gerald at least £25 and if what had been collected for Citizen Gerald was to be set against this claim of Citizen Hardy it was probable that there would not remain any thing in favor of Citn. Gerald, after much altercation Citizen Le Maitre's motion was negativ'd

Several Motions were then made for allowing a certain Sum Weekly to Citizen Gerald for his support, and the Question was put for 1 Guinea, 25s. and 30s., and it was ultimately resolved that Citizen Gerald should have a Weekly allowance of One Guinea during his continuance here and that on his receiving Notice of being sent away, all the Money in the Hands of the Treasurer should be imediately appropriated to his Use

The Committee next proceeded to take the Numbers of such as were for, and against, calling a General Meeting, from the Report of the several Delegates, but not more than 14 or 15 attended to make any Report on which Citizen Smith proposed to refer the Question but he was overruled and the Numbers of such as had been returned being cast up it appeared there was 142 against it 84 for it on which the Measure was rejected./.

Citizen's Burks and Higgins were desired to call upon Citizen Worship to expedite the compleating of the plate for the new Tickets

Motion to adjourn. Citizen Smith informed the Committee that persons had been observed lurking about the Door all the Evening as tho' they were looking after some one of them, and desired they would all go away in a body imedy. which they did, t'was said they should not meet there again./

213. Report from spy Groves: LCS General Committee, 19 June 1794[88]

Source: TS 11/965/3510A

Report &c

The proceedings of The Committee of Delegates of the London Corresponding

88 Government description: 'Mr Groves's Report / Recd. 24 June 1794'.

Society held on Thursday June 19th. 1794 at Dowlings in New Street Covt. Garden, divide themselves into three distinct considerations

1st. The Sense of the different Divisions respecting a General Meeting of the Society.

2dly. The Meetings of the Divisions, with regard to the Number of the Divisions which now meet, & the Number of Members meeting in those Divisions, And

3dly. The intentions of the Delegates in order to keep alive the Sentiments and Spirit which gave birth to the Society

With regard to the first Consideration, the result of an application from three or four Divisions made some time since recommending a General Meeting to the Sense of the Delegates turned out be a Majority of More than two to One *against* it – the Numbers, pro & con, of each Division were stated (i.e. of those Divisions which met at all) & also the Unanimous Sense of some Divisions, both for & agt. the Meeting.

The idea & Motion for a General Meeting originated with Jones immediately on the apprehension of Thelwall, and, in order to procure it he has left no Stone unturned, – All his Oratory and Activity having been employed, as well in the Committee of Delegates, as in the different divisions, to effect that purpose

Jones has abilities & is a Scholar – he has also a warmth about him that attaches the uninformed to his Sentiments; but the Citizens of a shrewder cast though they admire his flow of Words are too cool & too cautious to be drawn in by his impetuosity – Among this latter description I reckon Citizens, Hodson, Burks, Cooper, Smith, & Bone, who have taken as much pains to prevent a General Meeting, as Le Maitre McDonald, Seal, & another or two have to procure it

It is remarkable that Jones did not attend the determination of his favorite Motion

Respecting the second Consideration it appeared, on stating the Sense of the different Divisions for and against a Genl Meeting that Eighteen Divisions never met at all, so that the Opinion of half the number of Divisions was not taken at all

These Divisions were set down as *panic struck*. It likewise appeared that no more than 18 Citizens met in any one Division, and that the general numbers of the Divisions that met were on the average from 7 to 11.

From these circumstances. i.e the proposition for a General Meeting being rejected, and also the desertions of the whole body of 18 Divisions, and the thinness of the numbers of the Members attending those Divisions it is tolerably clear that either a timely prudence has withheld the majority of the Society from attending during the present posture of affairs; or, that Fear & a Sense of danger have sufficiently operated on them to make them totally withdraw themselves.

These deductions lead to the third Consideration, vizt, The intentions of the Delegates to rouse the lethargy of the Society & rekindle the former Spirit of the Citizens

For this purpose Hodson made a Motion seconded by Smith that a Deputation of Delegates be appointed to wait on the different Divisions in order to *rally* the Members of the Society – This was agreed to, & 18 Delegates voluntarily offered themselves

These were divided into four deputations but the Motion was prevented from being carried into effect by an Observation that the Residence of the Members could not be then made out, as the Books which contained them could not, at present, be found –

It was adjourned, therefore, till further information could be obtained on the Subject.

It seems clear, therefore, that it is determined that the Sentiments and Spirit which gave birth to the Society shall, if possible, be kept alive, and that every step will be taken to promote that design –

An Additional reason for this appears to be that at this Meeting of *Delegates* there were 24 present, notwithstanding the general defection of the divisions

The general business of the Committee for this Evening was, A Motion for a specific allowance to Gerald, which after some debate was settled at One Guinea per Week to be allowed him during his Stay in Newgate & to be paid him by the Commee of Correspondence

In this debate it was stated that he paid 7s. pr. Week for his Lodging –

It was also taken under consideration whether a certain Sum of Money should not be immediately laid out for his use in order to equip him with Stores for his Journey to Botany bay.

The reason of this was, Gerald had informed two or three Citizens that he expected daily to be sent off, & that he might perhaps be called on at Midnight; but as it was generally conceived that whenever he was taken from Newgate he would lay on Ship-board time enough for purchasing Stores, the Consideration of the Subject was adjourned

Six pounds One Shilling & 4d. were brought in as different Collections –

2000 more of the Resolutions formed by Jones were ordered to be printed, and 1000,

already delivered, to be paid for

These are given to None but Delegates who are to take care to disperse them

A Motion was made by Seal and seconded by McDonald to print 1000 of these Resolutions on a single Side & to be pasted up all over the Town

It was Opposed by Hodson & Smith, & Motion withdrawn –

N B. These two Delegates, Seal and McDonald are two of that description among the Delegates, which, in a former Report of mine I have stated as the lowest Order of Blackguards, & as always being for violent measures

Citizen Groves was chosen president for the Night and at ½ past 12 the Commee broke up.

McDonald sold the inclosed printed paper intituled A Blow at the Irons[89]

214. Report from spy Metcalfe: LCS Divisions 6 and 9, 23 June 1794[90]

Source: TS 11/956/3501

Meeting of 6th. Division of London Corresponding Society at the Parrot on Monday Eveng. 23rd. June 1794

Ten present, the Delegate Burks read his Report   no other business done./.

Went in Company with Burks and Davis to the Falcon in Gough Square, where Division 9 which had been nearly dispersed had been assembled, there was 30 present and it appeared to be an Evening of pleasure rather than business, many very Treasonable Songs were sung[91] and they did not break up until past 12 oClock.

Walkd part of the Way home with Citn. Hodson   Hatter   of the Broadway and learnt that the Committee of Correspondence were to meet at his House on Wednesday Eveng next

89 *A Blow at the Root* [not Irons], 1794, is a 12 pp. extract from Richard Price's *Civil Liberty*, with a preface stating the position of the 1794 parliamentary reformers had been advanced in 1776 by reputable men.

90 Government description: 'Meeting of 6th. & 9 Division on 23 June 1794 and some parlars concg *Ross & Kennedy* / Rx 24th / Mr Metcalfe's Report / (one inclosure)'.

91 Metcalfe enclosed one of them, 'Parody on the Song of Poor Jack'; after contemptuously dismissing Richmond and Burke, it concludes that the time is near when Britons 'shall assert their demands,' and that tyrants shall never rule this island.

Tuesday 24 June

Met *Ross* in the Strand who told me that two others were come from Scotland, one of them *Kennedy* for the apprehension of whom a Reward had been offerd, whom he said had been all about the Country, and wished to be introduced to the Society & told them a Division would meet this eveng at the Falcon in Gough Square where they promised to come about 9 o'Clock

215. Report from spy Groves: LCS Division 2, 23 June 1794[92]

Source: TS 11/965/3510A

Report &c

At the Division No. 2 Compton Street held on Monday June 23d. nothing was done but Electing a New Delegate and Subdelegate for the Ensuing Quarter when Citizens Le Maitre and Groves were re-elected the former Delegate, & the latter sub-delegate

There were 22 Members present & the Subscriptions amounted to 13s 9d.

Brooks in the Chair

216. Report from spy Metcalfe: LCS General Committee, 26 June 1794[93]

Source: TS 11/956/3501

Meeting of the General Committee of the London Corresponding Society at Thelwall's House on Thursday Eveng. 26th. June 1794

Citizen Higgins in the Chair

36 Members present

The Resolutions of several of the Divisions, recommending "That the Revised Report of the Committee of Constitution should be for the present adopted," was taken into consideration and after much Debate, was resolved in the Affirmative, and that 1000 Copies be imediately struck off for the use of the Society

A motion was then made "That 1000 of

92 Government description: 'Mr. Groves's Report / of the proceedings of division / No. 2. June 23. 1794 / Recd. 27th.'
93 Government description: 'General Committee at Thelwalls Thursday 26th. June 1794'.

the last Resolutions of the General Committee, be printed upon a single sheet in Order that they might be stuck up about the Town" this Occasion'd very long debate, but was at length carried in the Affirmative and Ordered accordingly

A Motion was made by Citizen Grove, that in future those Members who did not attend the General Committee by Eight oClock should be fined 1d. by 9 oClock 2d. and if they did not attend at all 6d., this was negativ'd, but it was recommended to the Members to be more early in their attendance./.

The report of New Members   6
The amount of Subscriptions   £2. 5. 7.

Citizen Smith observed that Citizen Gerald complained much that certain Sums which had been subscribed in some of the Divisions specially for his use, had not been paid to him. To which it was answer'd that if Citizen Gerald expected to receive all the money subscribed, from what fund was the Society to pay him the One Guinea p. Week they had resolved upon, Citizen Smith was desired to inform Citizen Gerald that any Sums subscribed in the Divisions could not be received as for him alone, because that would compleatly put an end to the Subscriptions to the Societys fund, but that he would be in the receipt of his Weekly allowance and be furnished on his being sent away with such stores and necessarys at the Society's expence, as had been furnished to Citizen Margarot.

Citizen Hodson in Newgate, complained of being treated by the Society with inattention and neglect. and threaten'd to complain to the people, Citizen Smith was desired to inform him that the Society were not to be bullied into any measures whatever, that his present Situation had been the consequence of his own folly and intemperate heat, that it was impossible for the Society to support every person who might get into Goal from a Conduct in which the Society was not at all interested or concerned, and that they did not think themselves bound to support him or give him any regular allowance,/.

Citizen Worship not having attended with New Tickets, Citizen Burks was desired to collect as many of the Old Ones as he could, and produce them on the next Committee Night.

Adjourned

The Committee of Correspondence meet, Tomorrow eveng the 27th. at Citizen Hodsons Hatter Broad Sanctuary

A Report of the finances to be made next Committee

217. Report from spy Groves: LCS General Committee, 26 June 1794[94]

Source: TS 11/965/3510A

Report of Committee of Delegates held at No. 2 Beaufort Buildings, Strand (Thelwalls) 26th. June 1794.

At 10 oClock in the Evening Nine Citizens being met the Commee proceeded to business –

Previous to going into business Citizen Hodgson, who had been waiting ever since half past 8, complained to Citizen Groves of the late hour at which the Delegates met, & of the lateness which, consequently, the Commee were obliged to be subject to, & requested Citizen Groves to bring forward some Motion on the Subject in order to remedy it in future –

The first business was electing a president. Higgins, Groves, & Metcalf were proposed. – it was carried in favour of Citizen Higgins

The Committee were then occupied in calling over the Numbers of the Divisions, & the New-elected Delegates answering to the Number of the Division for which they were elected & delivering in their respective Certificates, each Division having a Delegate & Sub-delegate

On calling over the Numbers it appeared that the greater part of the Divisions who had elected Delegates & Sub Delegates, had re-elected for the ensuing Quarter their former Deputies –

It appeared also that several Divisions had made no re-elections, from not having met at all, and that others had continued their old Delegates & Sub-Delegates from Necessity, owing to the thinness of the Meetings of the Divisions

The principal Members present were

Higgins	Le Maitre	Mc.Donald
Hodson	Groves	Seal
Burks	Metcalfe	Cooper
Bone	Smith	Oxlade (a Visitor not re-elected)

The Collections for the Relief of the distressed Wives and Children of the Prisoners under the Suspension of the Habeas Corpus Act were delivered in by the Different Delegates & amounted to 2£. 16s. 0d – (Vide inclosed Bill delivd. by Oxlade[)]

The Collections of 2d. each, were made, which, in the whole amounted to 5s. which goes to defray the Expence of the Room, Candles &c which Room was the Garret, & the Candles two of One penny each

The Report from the different Delegates shewed that Ten New Members had been made in the Course of the last Week

The first Motion made was from Divisions No. 9 & No. 14. which are incorporated

The Motion was "That the *Commee of Delegates adopt* the *Revised* Constitution & send it to the different Divisions as the Constitution of the Society"

There was added to the Motion a Liberty for the Divisions to propose such alterations and amendments from time to time as the practical necessity of it might require –

To understand this Motion clearly it should be stated that early in the Spring there was a Committee of Constitution appointed in order to draw up a form of Government for the Society which they did in Sixteen very close printed pages, in twelves, and which was submitted to the Consideration of the different Divisions

The Report of that Commee & the Form of Government recommended gave rise to great Jealousies & Animosities, as founded on principles incompatible with that Liberty which the Society was seeking for in the National System of Governmt. and as investing Powers & creating Offices & Officers among themselves which would infallibly render the Division a Cypher, and the whole management & Controul be placed in the hands of a few, & thereby their Government be Monarchical or something worse –

The Divisions having taken alarm at the whole of the new formed Constitution, in order totally to do it away, appointed a Committee of Revision, and ordered them to make a Report, to expunge the objectionable parts, & to introduce such others as might be thought proper in order to render the different Committees subject to the controul of the Society and destroy every attempt at an arbitrary usurpation of Power.

This Constitution so revised was brought in to the different Divisions, & had undergone much discussion, but before it could receive the final concurrence of the Divisions, the Society recd. a Shock from the interference of Government wch. put an end to all further consideration then, and effectually laid it to Sleep till the present Moment.

The increased operations of Government having excited a general panic, and the defection being so great as to threaten the Society with a total annihilation, and it having been

94 Government description: 'Mr. Groves's Report of the proceedings of the Committee of Delegates / 26 June 1794. / Rx 27. / (one inclosure)'. The enclosure was a copy of the appeal for funds, dated 19 June.

189

adjudged that bringing forward the Constitution again, in any form, rather than being without one at all, would serve to rally the Society, and restore it to its original vigour, the preceding expedient was hit on & the Motion accordingly submitted

All the Delegates agreed that some Constitution was necessary to their existence.
Hodson warmly favoured the Original Report of the Commee of Constitution

Smith argued against it & approved of the Revised Report.

Seal & Mc.Donald objected to the Wording of the Motion as arbitrary & unconstitutional as it invested the Commee of Delegates with a power of *cramming down the throats of the Citizens* any Constitution the Commee of Delegates pleased, & said that the Divisions ought to be left to themselves in the choice of their Constitution –

Bone was for the adoption of the Revised Constitution & desired that it might go as a *Recommendation* from the Commee of Delegates to adopt it or alter it as they liked

This idea met the general Concurrence of the Society, & the Question was put & carried on it.

Hodson moved that the Commee of Correspondence be empowered to make such enquiries as may be necessary amongst the Wives & Children of the imprisoned patriots & to afford such relief from time to time as the finances would allow. Agreed to

Mrs. Thelwall he said had declined for the present, accepting of any Relief, but Mrs. Hardy *he thought* stood in need of it – (She has made application)

A Conversation took place relative to sticking up the inclosed Resolutions, or distributing them – It was agreed to print 1000 & several Citizens agreed to stick them up – Throwing them down Areas, & leaving them in public Houses were approved of also.

Dr. Hodgson (in Newgate) who had made frequent applications for relief, again applied – It appeared that the Dr. had threatened to appeal to the people & to shew them what the London Corresponding Society were. The Commee took fire at this – Hodson called him a Madman – Groves said that such Men did the

Society a material injury & deserved no regular relief – This idea was concurred in, & a deputation was ordered to attend Dr. Hodgson & to inform him that the Commee had allowed his Wife 6s. pr Week, as long as their funds would allow it, and that when they could afford to send him relief he might not be forgot.

Seal made a Motion that the Commee of Correspondence be directed to write to the different Societies in the Country to open a Correspondence with them – to let them know the L C. Society was in existence, & to advise them to continue their Meetings & to send Answers how they went on –

Hodson said Norwich & Sheffield had been written to & as soon as they could find *proper ways & means for safe conveyance*, the others would be written to also – Motion withdrawn –

The Finances, it was agreed, should occupy the attention of the Commee the first Thing next Thursday Evg.

218. Report from spy Metcalfe: LCS Division 6, 30 June 1794[95]

Source: TS 11/956/3501

Meeting of the 6th Division of the London Corresponding Society at the Parrot on Monday Eveng. 30th. June 1794

Citizen Worship Chairman

10 others present
Citizen Burks reported the business of the last General Committee & Read a Letter from Sheffield, desiring the London Corresponding Society to attend to the wants of the three Citizens lately taken at Sheffield, as also an answer sent thereto

Citizen Burks Reelected Delegate
Citizen Hill Sub Delegate
Citizens Metcalfe
      Merryweather ⎫
          &   ⎬ Tything Men
      Davis   ⎭

95 Metcalfe's description: 'Meeting 6th. Division of London Correspg Society at parrot on Monday 30th June 1794'.

190

PART SIX

1794C
(July–December)

219. Report from spy Metcalfe: LCS General Committee, 3 July 1794[1]

Source: TS 11/956/3501

Meeting of the General Committee of the London Corresponding Society at Citn. Dowlings in New St. Covt. Garden on Thursday Evening 3rd. July 1794.

Citizen Metcalfe in the Chair

31 other Citizens present
Seven New Members made,

Citizen Hodgson reported the State of the Societys finances, since the time of Citizen Hardy's being taken into Custody. as follows

Cash reced from the several Divisions being Subscriptions for General Purposes. from the 29th. May to the 2nd. July inclusive	17	5	8½
Cash for Quarteridge's	4	3	
Cash being Subscriptions for the relief of the Wives & family's of imprison'd Citizens	6	1	
Cash paid to the Wives of Citizens Ashley, Hardy Francklow and Hilliard 1 Guinea each	4	4	
For printing bills	3	15	
For printg Narratives of Citn. Hardy's seizure, to Citizen Smith	4	4	
For the Use of Committee Room		10	
Cash supplyed to Citizen Gerald	6	10	9
To Citizen Bromehead from Sheffield	1	1	
To Citn. Scott late a printer at Edinburgh for printg		9	
To Citizen Cooper for 3000 resolutions printg ⟨&c.⟩	1	1	
For Candles for illuminations on Lord Howes Victory		3	9
There were some other small Sums reced &c. Making in the whole reced up to 2nd. July	29	2	2½
Paid	21		6[2]

Ballance £ 8 .. 1 .. 8½ in the Treasurers hands.

Citizen Gallant, reported that he had been informed by Citizen Davidson the printer, that the Society were indebted to him to the amount of £30 and that the Society not only neglected to pay him but had employed some other printer, this he complained was an ungrateful treatment of Citizen Davidson who was well known to be as good a Citizen as any belonging to the Society, part of the demand was of a Year's standing[3] and therefore he ought to be paid in preference to any other person, To which it was answerd by Citizen Hodgson that there was no doubt of Citizen Davidson being a very good and worthy Citizen, but that he well knew the Situation of the Society and that on account of the seizure of Citizen Hardy and his papers it had been impossible to make out the true Statement of the Societys finances previous to and up to that time, that however the Committee would endeavour to adjust Citizen Davidsons account and pay what was due as soon as they had the means of so doing.

Several Delegates reported from their Divisions, that the Resolution of the last General Committee to adopt "the revised Report of the Committee of Constitution" had given

1 Description: 'Meeting of Genl. Committee of the London Correspg. Society. in New St. Covt. Garden on Thursday 3rd. July 1794'.

2 The expenditures listed here total £21 18s 6d, not £21 0s 6d. Groves omits some of the expenditures on this list, increases the size of others, and has a correct total of £21 0s 6d. In other reports the two men sometimes have different figures.

3 In Oct. 1793 the Society's debt was £9 3s 6d, which grew to £29 16s 6d by March 1794. Davidson was paid £5 5s on 10 April. This protest to the general committee brought him £2 2s on 10 Sept. Davidson extended more credit to the LCS by printing 1000 copies of *Reformers No Rioters* on 22 Sept. for £2 19s (Davidson's account, TS 11/957/3502).

great dissatisfaction, it had been considered as an Act of great usurpation and Aristocracy and what was not authorized by the Constitution, it was in fact craming a Constitution down the throats of their Constituents without asking their Opinion and exactly like the conduct of the present Minister, &c. To which Citizen Hodgson replyed that he was aware the Committee had been guilty of some little usurpation in the adoption of the Revised Report, but that at the time of its being resolved every Citizen must well remember that it was particularly noticed to be a measure of necessity under all the circumstances of the Societys situation, rather than of choice, and that the words of the resolution plainly evinced that the Committee had no intention of craming that revised Report down the throats of their Constituents without their acquiesscence, and that it was a mere measure of expediency, the concluding Words of the Resolution being that the Revised Report should be adopted *subject to future consideration*, he however was no friend to the Revised Report he liked the Old Constitution much better, and as the Society at this Moment were acting under the regulations of the Old Constitution, and for the sake of doing away all animosity between the Divisions he would move that the Resolution of the last Committee to adopt the Revised Report, be rescinded, which being seconded was carried. in the Affirmative

There were several other Speakers upon this subject, among them Citizen Bone, who spoke in strong terms against the Usurpation of the Committee, and among other things observed that the French Convention had never dared to speak of a Constitution until it had been sanctioned by and had received the compleat approbation and concurrence of the people./

Resolved that 500 of the Old Address and Resolutions be imediately printed for the use of the several Divisions, and which it was considered would answer all the purposes under the present circumstances, of any Constitution which could be form'd

Great Complaints were made of the want of Tickets, and it was said the Society lost a great many Members, for want of them, members having refused to pay their Quarteridge, or to be admitted Members, on account of their being no Tickets to give them

Citizen Burks reported that he had seen Citizen Worship who had said the plate would not be ready in less than a fortnight but that he Burks, believ'd there was no dependance to be placed upon Citizen Worship, who seem'd

quite panic struck, and therefore he proposed that letter press Tickets should be imediately printed, for the Societys use, Citizen Williams, imediately proposed to make the Society a present of an Engraved plate if they would accept it and that he would present it to the next Committee, On the Motion being put to accept Citizen William's offer, it was carried in the Affirmative

Report of Money reced this Night
For General Purposes   4 . 15 . . 6
For Wives & Children &c.   1 . 19 . 6
31 Members present 2d. each   5 . 2

£7 2

Adjourned

220. Report from spy Groves: LCS General Committee, 3 July 1794[4]

Source: TS 11/965/3510A

Report of General Committee
Thursday July 3d. 1794
Citizen Metcalfe in the Chair

The Meeting of the Committee of Delegates which was on the preceding Thursday held at Thelwalls in Beaufort Building Strand was, this Evening held at Dowlings in New Street Covt Garden

The Reason assigned by Hodgson for quitting Thelwalls was, that Mrs. Thelwall was apprehensive of some danger arising to her husband, or her House, if she permitted the Committee to meet there; &, in consequence of those scruples, the Meeting was removed back again to Dowlings; which, from the smallness of the Room, the heat of the Weather, the Number of Delegates & Sub-Delegates, & from the Windows & Shutters being shut close, to prevent the Neighbours opposite from either hearing or seeing, was become dangerous to all who met there.

The first business taken under Consideration was, The State of the Finances of the Society.

Hodgson made his report, which was, that no Accounts whatever previous to the imprisonmt. of their Secretary, Citizen Hardy, could be laid before the General Commee, as the Books, proper ⟨to⟩[5] that purpose, were not, *at present*, to be found –

4 Groves's description: 'Report of General Commee of Delegates'. Government description: 'Groves's Report of General Commee July 3. 1794'.
5 Interpolated and conjectured words may have been in the original, for the ends of the lines of writing are sometimes worn away with the paper.

He further stated that the Situation of the Finances from the 29th. of May last to the 26th. of June last inclusive, both Debtor & Creditor could be ascertained, & therefore he moved that the Commee receive the Report of those dates.

This occasioned some inconsiderable debate, some were for postponing the whole till the whole report could be made – Others were for receiving it as made out –

The Reasons assigned for the first were, That if that Report was recd., nothing more would ever be heard of the Accounts previous to apprehending of Hardy, & the whole state of the Finances up to that date be totally smothered, which statement the Commee had a right to know, & there [were] strong reasons why they should know it

On the other hand – those who were for receiving the Report as made out, said, That the Receiving the Report from the 29th. of May to the 6th. of June did not preclude them from calling for any previous report, hereafter, & that [as] it was best to learn all they could on the Subject of Finance, that Report ought to be made –

Hodgson said that there was no intention of withholding any previous Report that could be got at, that there were great hopes of obtaining ⟨the⟩ account the Commee were so desirous of & that if they could be got at they would certainly be laid before the Commee; but that he thought it best for the Commee to know all they could upon the Subject

On this Assurance the Motion for Receiving the Report from the 29th. of May to the 26th. June inclusive was put & carried by a great Majority

It appeared by that Report that the Sum of 29£. 2s. 2½d had been collected in the Course of those Dates, in the follg. manner

	£.	S	d
For General purposes	17.	5	8½
For Wives & Children	6.	1.	
* For Renewed Quarterages	4	3	
paid in by a Delegate	1	12	6
	29	2	2½

* Adverting to the 4£. 3S. 0d, Renewed Quarterages, it is clear that only *Sixty Six* Citizens have renewed their Tickets since the last Midsummer Quarter out of the whole Body of the Citizens.

That there had been paid to Smith for printing (or getting printed) the Narrative of Hardys apprehension   4 . 4

To Smith for Money advanced to Gerald	2	17	3
To Printing Handbills for Subscriptions &c	7	19	
To Money paid Wives & Children	5	16	6
To Money paid for Illuminations at Citizen Dowlings on Accot. of Lord Howes Victory		3	9
	21	0	6

By which Statements it appeared that there was a Ballance of 8£. 1s. 8½d in favour of the Society, vizt.

Collectns.	29 – 2. 2½
Expendits.	21 0 6
Surplus	8. 1 8½

It appeared also that there was a Debt due from the Society to Citizen Davidson for printing done previous to the above date of

	£	S	d
	22.	0.	0
To another printer	12		
	34	0	0

So that deducting the Surplus of	8	1	8½
now in hand from the outstanding Debts there appears a Balle. *agt.* the Society of	25	18	3½
There was to be paid, in part of his demand, to Citizen Davidson	5	5	0
By which there remains only in hand	2.16	8½	

[Groves explains the discussion of a new plate for tickets.]

[b]ut the thanks of the Commee postponed till the Plate was produced

The adjourned Question of considering the *Revised* Report of the Constitution & sending it to the Division as the Constitution of the Society, pro tempore, then occupied the attention of the Commee.

[Groves's account of this discussion is similar to Metcalfe's. He adds one objection: 'That it was the Province of the Divisions to make their own Laws, & not to have Laws made for them, by their Servants the Delegates who had only a power to reject the Specific propositions of each Division, but not to institute a Government for them.' Groves identifies the old constitution to be reprinted as the 1792 version starting, 'Assured that Man'.]

After some trifling remarks 500 were agreed on to be printed

The only thing worth further remark on the proceedings of this Nights Meeting is
1   That there appears a very great Jealousy to ⟨subsist⟩ among the Citizens of their Delegates respecting Money Matters, & of their assuming an Authority over the Citizens &
2.   That there were only 7 New Members made in the Course of the preceding Week –

221. Report from spy Groves: LCS Division 2, 7 July 1794[6]

Source: TS 11/965/3510A

Report of Meeting of Division No. 2
Compton Street   7th. July 1794

Although it is a Standing Order that there must be Nine Citizens present before the Division can proceed to business, yet at 10 oClock there being only Nine and four of them Visitors from other Meetings Le Maitre moved that that Order be for that Night only dispensed with, which being done he made the Report to the Division of the proceedings in the General Committee

Having stated the Report of the Finances, the Resolution rescinding the sending the Revised Report to the divisions for their temporary Constitution & the Number of New Citizens (Seven) the Division adjourned

A Conversation took place respecting Guarding the Citizens against those who were always whispering about Spies & Informers, as being dangerous Citizens, who wished to ruin the Society by slanderous insinuations, in order to drive away active & virtuous Citizens –

It was agreed that this Conduct could proceed only from those employed by Government in order to disseminate distrust as one means of annihilating the Society

222. Report from spy Metcalf: LCS Division 6, 7 July 1794[7]

Source: TS 11/956/3501

Meeting of the 6th. Division of the London

Corresponding Society at the parrot on Monday Evening   7th. July 1794./.

Nine Members present

Burks the Delegate reported the proceedings of the last General Committee

Two or three paid their Quarteridge up to Michaelmas and renewed their Tickets

A Motion was then made, that this Division should meet with Division 11, the Delegate of each Division to preside alternately, which was carried unanimously and Citizen Burks deled the Names and places of abode of the Tythings to Citizens Metcalfe and Davis, that they might give Notice thereof to the several Members within their Respective Tythings &c. Merryweather the other Tything Man did not attend

Citn. Metcalfes Tything. are

Citns. Burks   No 3 Craven St.   Hoxton
    Worship   Ball Alley   Lombard St.
    Caney   No 82 Wood St.   Cheapside
    Savage   No 1 Maiden Lane   Wood St
    Eaton[8]   No. 94 Newgate Street
    Langthorne   No. 4 Poppins Court
        Fleet St.
    Child   No 15 New Street Hill   Shoe lane
    Brothers   No 6 St. Dunstan's Court
        Fleet St.
    Noon   No 3 St. Martins le Grand (now
        at Birmingham)

223. Report from spy Groves: LCS General Committee, 10 July 1794[9]

Source: TS 11/965/3510A

General Committee of Delegates
Thursday 10th. July 1794

Citizen Bone president

The last Weeks Subscription appeared to be

	£	S	d
For Wives & Children	6	11	6
Quarterage & Genl. purposes		1	16	10
The Collection in the Commee Room of the Delegates & Sub Delegs. &c at 2d		4	4
	8	12	8

It is seen by the last Article that the Numbers present were 26. But each Division having

---

6 Government description: 'Groves's Report of Division No. 2 / July 7th: 1794'.
7 Metcalfe's description: 'Meeting of 6th Division of London Corresponding Society on Monday 7th July 1794./'
8 Eaton, Langthorne, Child and Brothers were not on Metcalfe's tything list of 22 May.
9 Government Description: 'Proceedings of the Genl. Committee of Delegates of the London Corresponding Society. 10th. July 1794. / Rx 12th July 1794 / accompanied by a copy of Verses'.

Delegate & Sub Delegate, & there being now reckoned but 31 Divisions, had there been a full attendance there must have been 62 Delegates & Sub Delegs. present.

As each Division elects Tithing Men in proportion to their Numbers, i. e, One Tithing Man for every Ten Members, and which Tithing Men are admitted into the General Commee; and as there are at least, upon the Average, Six Tithing Men to every Division, were the Whole Number of Divisions to meet, the Tithing Men, with the Delegates & Sub De. would make a Body of 248 Members in the General Commee

But, as upon a close observation I find that half the Number of Divisions now only meet the other half being totally dispersed, and as the Divisions that do meet are but thinly attended the Number of Tithing Men are reduced considerably below One half of the Original Number, which, reckoning Six to each Division in full Meeting would be 186 – Taking the half of that Number 93, and deducting for the present defections from 93, 43 there ought to be in the General Committee 50 Tithing Men

Instead of which reckoning Delegates & Tithing Men there were only 26 in the General Commee, & Division No. 29 with Delegate, Sub- & Tithing Men made 6 of that Meeting

It is clear therefore that neither Delegate Sub Delegate or Tithingmen attend the Genl. Commee in any proportion to their estimated Numbers and that the Defection is about Seven Eighths

I do not know that I have any where stated the use of the Tithing Men – it is of a threefold nature, First to give all the Divisions an Equal Representation in the General Commee & 2dly. To look after those Members who have deserted or are, to use their own words *panic struck* & endeavour to rally them, & 3dly. In Case of an Emergency to call the Citizens together in a General Meeting, as the Genl. Commee might not have time to do it

It appears also that of the Existing Divisions now Meeting several of them are so few as to be incorporated into others, as for instance, Divisions 5 & 30 are incorporated, from 5 to 10 Members only Meeting.

These observations arose on the Presidents calling over the Number of Divisions in order to collect from the Delegates their Subscriptions, & Motions sent from the Divisions to the Genl. Commee

Citizen Smith in order to instil a Spirit of industry among the Delegates & Members of the Divisions with a view to rally the whole body of the London Corresg Society moved

"That it be recommended to the Divisions to instruct their Tithing-men to call on the different Members whose residences could be made out, & that they should inform them of the existence of the Genl Commee & Meetings of Divisions – to let them know what was going on & to do every thing in their power to bring them back to their different Divisions" which was after a few words unanimously agreed to

A Motion for raising the Price of Entrance One Shilling was also agreed to be recommended to the Divisions

An Anonymous Letter sent to the Commee was also read recommending moderate & prudent measures to the Commee, and cautioning them against violent Motions which could only tend to injure those in Custody already, & which were only made either by weak, or designing Members, to give Government an opportunity of taking further advantages of the Society, & the letter also complained that something already printed by the Commee had injured those in Custody –

This Letter was brought to the President by the Woman of the House, & read by Citizen Groves, the president not being able to make it out, it being a cramped & disguised hand but evidently written by a professional Man –

Citizen Smith & Hodgson pointed out what the Author of the Letter alluded to by what had been already printed – It was a passage in the Narrative of Citizen Hardys Seizure page 5 line 33 – & was thus

"The sole intent of[10] was to devise means of attaining a complete representative body on the principles of universal suffrage, equal personal representation, and annual election, and whenever, *OR HOWEVER* such a body can be attained it will not be in the power of all the placemen and pensioners in St Stephens Chapel to dispute its legislative authority"

Smith & Hodgson agreed that the Words *or however* were the Cheak-pears[11] to Governmt.

The principles of the Letter was highly approved & the Delegates directed to recommend them to the Different Divisions

Citizen Williams produced his promised voluntary Engraving for the New Tickets, and was honoured with a Vote of thanks for the patriotic Gift – It is in the follg. form

[See top of next page]

The Device – The Old Man and his three Sons with a Bundle of Sticks laying down at their

10 'of' was not in the *Narrative*.
11 Choke-pear: something difficult to swallow.

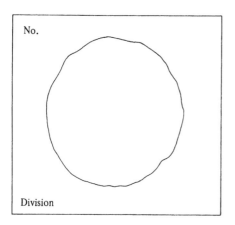

```
No.



Division
```

feet & the Old Man instructing them how to break the Bundle, by pulling one at a time & thus destroying that Body which could not be broke when tied together

The Allegory is The acquisition of Strength by Unanimity – Hodgson sold the enclosed for 2⟨d⟩ each – written by Eaton

Only One New Member had been made during last Week – The Commee met at Barne'ss in Compton Street – Adjourned

224. Report from spy Metcalfe: LCS Divisions 6 and 11, 15 July 1794[12]

Source: TS 11/956/3501

Meeting of the 6th. and 11th. Divisions of the London Correspondg. Society at the parrott on Tuesday Evening 15th. July 1794.

Citizen Cleets in the Chair

32 present.

Citizen Burks reported the proceedings of the last General Committee, at which Citizen Williams had presented the plate for the Society's admission Tickets which was much approved and for which the thanks of the Society had been voted to Citizen Williams./

Tickets from the New Plate were this Evening delivered to such Members as chose to renew them for the next Quarter

Two New Members were reported to have been admitted in the last Week

It was also reported that the General Committee had resolved on every General Committee night, to have the Names of all the Delegates Sub Delegates and Tything Men who attended taken down in Order to ascertain what Officers were attentive to their Duty and that the Names and places of abode of all the Officers of the several Divisions be taken down and delivered to the Committee of Correspondence, in Order that in Cases of Emergency that Committee might know where to send for them for their advise and assistance

This Created a very violent and personal debate. It was said by Citizen Blackburn to be a Measure of the most dangerous tendency and promoted he had no doubt by some one of Mr Pitts Spyes and Informers several of whom he had as little doubt procured themselves to be admitted into the Society and into Offices for the very purpose of marking out all those who approve themselves Good and active Citizens, as fit objects of the Ministers Vengeance and that it would be impossible to find persons to fill those Offices, if there Names and places of abode were to be known publickly in the Society, by which means they might be subject at all times to be seized upon and torn from their Wives and Familys to their utter Ruin, he therefore moved that it is the opinion of those Divisions that it is a Measure which ought not to be adopted and which after much altercation was at length carried in the Affirmative./

A Motion made in the General Committee and referred to the several Divisions, That in future there should be paid by every New Member on his admission the Sum of One Shilling in addition to the usual Quarteridge of Thirteen pence, this also met with violent opposition and was Resolved by these Divisions to be a Measure which ought not to be adopted

It having been represented to these Divisions that Citizen Burks had been on account of his attachment to the Society, turn'd out of his employ,[13] and that he was in great need of relief, A Motion was made that it be recommended to the General Committee to give Citizen Burks some small Relief Weekly from the Money subscribed for General Purposes, until such time as he could get into employ, on the Question being put, it was carried in the Affirmative *Unanimously*

Printed papers intituled "Revolution without Bloodshed"[14] was sold at penny's

13 At the East India House.
14 *Revolutions without Bloodshed; or Reformation Preferable to Revolt*, written by James Parkinson and published by Eaton and Smith, lists twenty-four changes which might result from a reform in parliamentary representation. They include changes in taxation, military recruitment, religious

12 Metcalfe's description: 'Meeting of the 6th. & 11th. Divisions of the London Corresponding Society at the parrot on Tuesday 15 July 1794'. Government endorsement: 'Rx July 16th'.

apiece, for the Relief of the Wives and family's of the imprisoned Citizens.

The Addresses and Resolutions signed by Margarot and Hardy were delivered this Evening to the several Citizens who were present.

Adjourned

225. Report from spy Metcalfe: LCS General Committee, 17 July 1794[15]

Source: TS 11/956/3501

Meeting of the General Committee of the London Corresponding Society on Thursday Evening 17th. July 1794 in New Compton Street

Citizen Smith in the Chair

26 other Members present

Report of New Members made last week — 4

[The divisions rejected, 133 to 5, the proposal to charge each new member 1s in addition to quarterage.]

Citizen Hodgson reported that the Committee of Correspondence had paid Nine Guineas from the Subscription for Wives & Children &c as follows. To Mrs. Thelwall 1 Guinea Mrs. Lovet 1 Guinea Mrs. Spence 2 Guineas Mrs. Hillier 1 Guinea, Mrs. Franklow 1 Guinea Mrs. Ashley 1 Guinea Mrs. Hardy 1 Guinea and Mrs. Baxter 1 Guinea,

He also reported that they had paid from the fund for General purposes £5 .. 18 .. – as follows To Citizen Gerald 1 Guinea To the Sheffield Men 2 Guineas for printing Admission Tickets 15s and for 1000 of the Addresses &c £2./.

He also produced a large parcel of the printed verses annexed which he said had been written by a Good Citizen for the relief of the Wives & Children of the imprisoned Citizens, and they were deled out 25 to each Delegate to be sold at ½ apiece, for that purpose.

Citizen Hodgson then read a Letter which the Committee of Correspondence had received from the Constitutional Society at Sheffield in which among other things it was stated that a Report had prevailed at Sheffield which had done considerable mischief for that it had created distrust among the Society and therefore requesting of the Committee of Correspondence to make enquiry's into the truth of such report, which was, That the three Citizens from Sheffield had been induced from threats or promises to desert the Cause and to give Evidence against that upright and Good Citizen *York*, whom *they* looked upon as having acted as the Organ of at least 40000 Staunch Citizens in and about Sheffield, &c. Citizen Hodgson reported that he had seen and conversed with those Men and that from his observation and belief there was no ground whatever for the Report and that he had reliev'd them with Two Guineas, and that the Committee of Correspondence were about to return an Answer to the Constitutional Society at Sheffield

Citizen Smith reported that the Sale of the papers intitled "Revolutions without Bloodshed"[16] had produced £3 .. 16 .., and that the expences of printing &c. being 2 Guineas, there remained a ballance to be carried to the use of the Wives & Children &c. of £1 .. 14 ..

He also reported that 400 of the New Tickets had been delivered,

Ordered that another 1000 of the Address &c. be printed A Motion was then made that none of the Addresses, or Tickets should be delivered but to Delegates at the General Committee which after some debate was carried in the Affirmative

Report of Money paid in this Evening by the several Delegates.

For the relief of the Wives &c.		£6 .. 1 ..
For General Purposes		3 .. 12 .. 7

Adjourned

I was this Evening applied to by Citizen Burks, who was deputed by the Committee of Correspondence for that purpose, to beg my advise and assistance in that Committee,

toleration and education of poor children. After describing the corruptness of Parliament, it ends (in large type) 'Traitors!! Traitors! Traitors!' – an allusion to the heading of pro-government handbills describing the 'treason' of the LCS. Parkinson, a physician and palaeontologist, wrote books on chemistry and medicine; he also identified Parkinson's disease.

15 Government description: 'Meeting of General Committee of the London Corresponding Society on 17th. July 1794 in New Compton Street / Mr. Metcalfe's Report / Rx 18. July 1794'.

16 'This paper I understand was written by Citizen Parkinson a Surgeon at Hoxton' (Metcalfe's note).

226. Report from spy Groves: LCS General Committee, 17 July 1794[17]

Source: TS 11/965/3510A

Meeting of Delegates

No. 3 Compton Street   17th. July 1794.

Citn. Smith in The Chair

The first matter that occupied the attention of the Committee was taking the Sense of the different Divisions on the follg. preceding Recommendation of the Committee, vizt.

"That an additional Shilling be paid by every *New* Member on his Admission"

[The tally of Divisions 2, 4, 5, 6 & 11, 7, 8, 12, 13, 18, 22, 27 and 29 showed that 142 opposed and 5 approved. Division 7 cast 5 votes; Division 13 cast 26 votes; the other divisions cast between 9 and 13 votes.]

Except No. 6 & No. 11 all the other Divisions were *unanimously* against the Motion

Two observations may be made on the preceding Statement

First, The Number of Divisions now Meeting

2dly., The Number of Members that now meet

This statement of the Numbers arises from Citizen Groves, who in the Commee moved that the Delegates in their report take down the Numbers on each side the Question, that the Delegates might not be left to report in the gross as they had been often found either partial or inaccurate –

There are now but thirty Divisions in existence, and therefore it is clear that out of that thirty, fourteen only can muster a sufficient Number of Citizens to make a Division, which is Nine. – It is evident that above one half are dispersed & that those that do meet are very few in Numbers

The argument against the Motion was principally That instead of increasing the Societys Finances it would tend to lessen them.

That the Society consisted chiefly of the poorer order of Men to whom 2s/1d wod. be a very material object (The admission being now 1s/1d) and that instead of raising the Admission, if a Motion was to be brought forward to reduce the entrance to 7d. it wod. meet the general sense of the Divisions as most likely to increase their Numbers & Finances –

The Collections & Subscriptions for the last Week were next Stated, which for Wives & Children of those in Custody, & for General purposes made near 14£.

The payments to Wives & Children for that Week were as under

[Seven guineas paid, one each to the wives of Thelwall, Lovett, Hardy, Ashley, Spence, Baxter and Hodgson.[18]]

Citizen Hodgson read a Letter addressed to the Commee of Correspondence from the Commee of Correspondence in Sheffield –

[Groves gives same account of the letter as Metcalfe, but names one of the Sheffield men as, 'Brummage' and adds that Sheffield will 'chearfully reimburse' the LCS for money given to their imprisoned members.]

It follows from this that Hodgson is *One* of the *Commee of Correspondence* whose names are kept very secret.

A Letter was read from Dr. Hodgson in Newgate severely complaining of the neglect of the Committee – stating his Attachment to the Society, & his sufferings for his principles – but it stated also that he had been *the Dupe* of the Commee – It concluded with wishing *HEALTH & FRATERNITY* & was dated from his *Bastille*, 1st. *Messidor* –

Citizen Metcalfe arose & moved that it be returned without any Answer which was agreed to

A Motion was made for re-considering the Motion for adopting the Revised Report

A Motion for Adjourning the Reconsideration to Thursday next was moved by Citizen Groves & carried Unanimously –

Adjourned

227. Report from spy Metcalfe: LCS Committee of Correspondence, 18 July 1794[19]

Source: TS 11/956/3501

Meeting of the Committee of Correspondence

18 Should be Hillier. Metcalfe's list adds Mrs Franklow and gives 2 guineas to Mrs Spence.
19 Government description: 'Minutes of the Committee of Corresponde / of the London Correspg. Society 18th July 1794 / Mr. Metcalfe / Rx. July 19th. 1794'.

17 Government description: 'Groves's Report of Meeting of Delegates / Compton Street / 17 July 1794. / ⟨Rx⟩ 21st'.

of the London Corresponding Society at Citn
Thelwall's house on 18th. July 1794

Present Citizen Hodgson
              Smith
              Burks
              Beck
              Higgins
              Bone
              Metcalfe

Citizen Hodgson who was to have drawn an Answer to be sent to the Constitutional Society at Sheffield, to a Letter received from them relative to Moody Gammage & Bromeheads having been prevaild upon to give Evidence agt. Citn. York, reported that he had visited those Men and had left with them a Copy of the Letter from Sheffield, and that not having had an opportunity of procuring their observations thereon, he therefore had not been able to draw an Answer, but said he would procure the necessary information from the Sheffield Men, and produce a Draft of a Letter next Wednesday Evening.

The Committee then proceeded to draw up an Address to the Public, to be incerted in the New Evening Paper, on behalf of the Wives and Family's of those persons who were confined in Goal in consequence of the suspension of the Habeas Corpus Act, and One having been compleated to the satisfaction of a Majority of the Citizens present, it was delivered to Citizen Smith who undertook to procure it's incertion in the Paper

Citizen Burks had then part of a Letter delivered to him by Citizen Hodgson, which he was desired to compleat by Wednesday next; and which was intended to be sent to Nottingham, to renew the Correspondence with the people there./.

The Original Letters received from Sheffield &c. are in the possession of Citizen Burks./.

228. Report from spy Groves: LCS Division 2, 21 July 1794

Source: TS 11/965/3510A

London Corresponding Society   July 21. 94

Meeting of Division No. 2   Compton Street –

The Report from the Committee of Delegates was made by Le Maitre to the Division

When that was done an Attack was commenced by Citizen Hunter, (Grocer, Compton Street opposite Barnes's) & two or. Members against Citizen Jones, of Tottenham Court Road, Surgeon & Man-Midwife, who is just returned from Margate – He has been absent about a Month & in that absence his name has been made very free with as a Spy –

He was denounced, last night, as above, on the ground of several violent Motions which had been made by him for the purpose of *entrapping* the Society – His Motion for calling a General Meeting – his Sentiments on the Subject of going armed, & his general inflammatory Speeches –

That such Motions & such Conduct proceeded only from those who wished Ruin to the Society & their Cause, & was the wish of Administration –

They attributed to his Eloquence the momentary Success which it generally met with, and to their deliberation their constant disapprobation afterwards –

Jones warmly defended himself, insisting on the purity of his intentions – if he erred, it was the error of the head not of the heart – the Cause of the Society was his Cause & he had none other

He took a temporary advantage of the absence of Citizen Hunter who, as soon as he had brought the charge, *slunk* away as Jones termed it –

The Citizens condemned Hunters Conduct, & his departure was reprobated –

Jones courted a Specific Charge, but as none was made the Matter dropped

This irregular clamour lasted an hour –

Citizen Groves rose & said that by the advice of several Citizens he had a Motion framed & which he wod. make –

He prefaced it by observing how irksome it was become to Citizens to know how to conduct themselves owing to the breath of Slander or the misconception of Citizens

If a Citizen made a Motion which seemed anyways spirited he was set down as a Spy sent among them by Governmt.

If a Citizen sat in a Corner & said Nothing he was watching their proceedings that he might the better report it, as alledged against Taylor – so that Citizens hardly knew how to act

He had, however, a Motion to make which was moderate, prudent, & he hoped, properly timed – it went to betray no persons name – nor was there any place or even Committee mentioned in it –

The Motion was read from the Chair

London Corresponding Society   July 21. 1794

The Members of the above Society are earnestly requested to meet at their respective Divisions during the ensuing Week

This he said could not subject any individual or the body collectively, to danger It might have the effect of rallying the Members & of increasing their Cash – He concluded that he hoped the Motion would be unanimously approved, – that he meant well – if it was taken ill he should be sorry for it, but as he was prompted to it from his regard to the Society he should make it, let it be taken as it might

The Motion being again read. He moved that it be submitted to the Sense of the General Committee, & if approved there, that it be recommended to be printed in such of the papers as were thought proper –

Several Citizens spoke for it Vizt. Brooks, Le Maitre, Hastie, Main &c – None against it – On putting the Question by shew of hands there appeared for it *20* – Against it – None –

Adjourned

229. Report from spy Metcalf: LCS Committee of Correspondence, 23 July 1794[20]

Source: TS 11/956/3501

Meeting of the Committee of Correspondence of the London Corresponding Society at Citizen Thelwall's on Wednesday Eveng. 23rd. July 1794

Present Citizens Hodgson
     Smith
     Beck
     Harris
     Higgins
     Metcalfe
     Burks (Secretary)

Citizen Hodgson produced a Letter in answer to one received from the Constitutional Society at Sheffield, relative to Camage Moody and Bromehead's having made some discoveries by which Citizen York would be materially affected &c. This Letter being approved was delivered to the Secretary to make a fair Copy of and to make up into a parcel with 50 of the papers intitled Revolutions without Bloodshed and to send by one of the Coaches directed to Allcock ink pot maker at Sheffield.

Citizen Smith produced a Letter he had received from Nottingham, without any signature, but which Citizen Smith said he knew came from a Good Democrat, this Letter was expressive of Good wishes for the Cause in which the Society are engaged and among other things desiring to open a Correspondence with them and requesting to be made acquainted with the Situation of the Society and of their opinion upon public Affairs &c. this Letter was refered to the General Committee./.

Citizen Burks the Secretary produced a Letter, intended to be sent to the people of Nottingham, full of very strong expressions against the Ministers and the Measures of Government, congratulating them on the successes of the French, and execrating the conduct of the Duke of Portland &c. for having deserted the people in his late Coalition with the Apostate Pitt and his infamous party

This Letter was the most violent and Treasonable I ever heard in the Society and I made some observations upon the danger of sending such a Letter, but Citizen Smith having assured the Committee that it would be conveyed in such a manner as to avoid any fear of it's being intercepted, the Secretary was desired to make a fair Copy to be transmitted to the People at Nottingham &c.

Citizen Smith produced the address which had been drawn up on the last Committee Night for incertion in the paper, which he said he had taken to the New Evening paper for incertion but was too late on which having advised with Citizens Burks and Higgins they had determined to endeavour to procure its incertion in the Courier, that he had been with the Editor of that paper who had said he had no objection to incert it but thought there was in one part of it some expressions which might be construed libellous, and recommended a revisal of it by the Committee, upon which he had brought the Copy back to the Committee, it was then read and after some debate upon the Motion of Citizen Hodgson was referred to Citizen Metcalfe for him to correct or to prepare another for incertion, by the next Committee Night.

Citizen Smith produced a few of the printed papers annexed which he said had been printed by a friend to the Cause at his own expence, he said there was 1000 printed, and proposed that the Society should whilst the press was set have another 1000 printed for their use which would only cost 7s., but on its being read It was determined that it was not such a paper as should go into the World as the production of or as issuing imediately from the London Corresponding Society.[21]

20 Government description: 'Meeting of the Committee of Correspondence of the London Corresponding Society on Wednesday 23rd. July 1794 / Rx July 24th'.

21 The sheet of c. 400 words is headed, 'What are all Mankind, but one Family widely scattered, and

Citizen Smith also produced some Songs, which he said had been written by Citizen Upton, and sold several at ½ each [22]

Citizen Burks applyed for a Letter book which Citn. Metcalfe offered to supply &c. Adjourned.

230. Report from spy Metcalfe: LCS General Committee, 24 July 1794 [23]

Source: TS 11/956/3501

Meeting of the General Committee of the London Corresponding Society on Thursday 24th. July 1794 in New Compton Street Soho./.

Citizen Robinson in the Chair
23 other Members present

Report of New Members in the last Week 7

The Delegate from Division 13 brought a Motion for a General Meeting. which was negatived

The Delegate from Division 22 brought a Motion, for a New Committee to be chosen, to examine the two Reports of Constitution, to select from them the most essential parts in Order to form a Constitution for the government and direction of the Society easy of Comprehension, subject however to future amendment &c. this Motion was referred to future consideration.

Citizen Grove from Division 2 brought a Motion, that there should be an Advertizement incerted in the Public Papers requesting the Citizens to attend their respective Divisions in the next Week, this after much debate was at length carried in the Affirmative [24]

Citizen Smith moved that such advertize-ment should be annexed to an Advertizement

GOD the Father of us all! ! !' It urges Britons to 'be no longer the dupes of K---s, Popes, and corrupt Pensioners', who send 'us to be slaughtered by thousands in order to restore Tyranny, Popery, Racks and Bastiles' on the French. It ends, 'GOD Save the PEOPLE'.

22 One of these songs, 'The Free Cockade', tells of a cowardly bishop who will boast of his conquests over the French. The song is signed 'T. J. U.'

23 Metcalfe's description: 'Meeting of General Committee of the London Corresponding Society 24 July 1794'. Government endorsement: 'Rx 25 July'.

24 Dated 24 July, it reads, 'The Engraved Tickets of this Society being now ready for distribution, the Members are requested to attend their several Divisions in the ensuing week' (*MC* 29 July 1794, p. 3).

which would appear in the papers in a Day or two on behalf of the Wives and Children of the Confined Citizens, but this was negatived, and it was ordered to be incerted in the Morning Chronicle, the Publicans Advertizer and the Courier as a distinct advertizement

Referred to the Committee of Correspondence to draw up the advertizement and procure it's incertion &c.

Cash received this Evening

For Genl. purposes £3 .. 1 ..   For Wives and Children £1 .. 16 .. and from the Members present at 2d each 4s.

adjourned

231. Report from spy Metcalfe: LCS Committee of Correspondence, 25 July 1794 [25]

Source: TS 11/956/3501

Meeting of the Committee of Correspondence of the London Corresponding Society on Friday 25th. July 1794 at Citizen Thelwalls

present Citizens Hodgson
Smith
Burks
Metcalfe
Bone
Parkinson
Higgins

Citizen Metcalfe produced the Draft of an Advertizement to be incerted in the public papers on behalf of the Wives and Families of the imprisoned Citizens, which after some small alterations was approved and Delivered to Citizen Smith to be incerted in the Courier the Morning Post and the Publicans Advertizer, It was also resolved on the Motion of Citizen Smith that three thousand copies of the Advertizement should be struck off to be distributed to the public./. [26]

25 Metcalfe's description: 'Meeting of the Committee of Correspondence of the London Corresponding Society 25th July 1794'. Government endorsement: 'Rx 25. July'. At the end of this report Metcalfe copied the advertisement of the subscription for the wives and families of the imprisoned men.

26 Dated 25 July, Metcalfe's appeal for donations stresses the needs of the 'Innocent sufferers, who have hitherto enjoyed the comforts of life through the Industry of their Husbands and Fathers'. Donations will be received by Smith, Hodgson, Cooper, Upton, Powell (all on the previous advertisement for funds) and D. I. Eaton, bookseller, 74 Newgate St (*MC* 4 Aug. 1794, p. 1; handbill in Place Collection, vol. 36, fo. 139).

An Advertizement was drawn up, requesting the attendance of the Citizens at their Respective Divisions in the next Week and Delivered to Citizen Smith for incertion in the papers pursuant to the Resolution of the last General Committee

Citizen Burks delivered a fair Copy of a Letter to be sent by Citizen Smith to the people of Nottingham as mentioned in the Report of the Minutes of the last Committee of Correspondence./.

Citizen Bone mentioned that he thought, if the Society turn'd their Minds to a Weekly Publication in the Nature of Paine's *Crisis* much good would result from it and each Member was requested to consider the subject by the next Wednesday Evening

Citizen Hodgson reported that he hoped shortly to be enabled to inform the Committee, that a Medium of Correspondence was setled with the Citizens at Bristol Leeds Manchester and several other places of equal import

He also reported he had that Day been refused admittance to the Sheffielders

adjourned

232. Report from spy Metcalfe: LCS Divisions 6 and 11, 29 July 1794[27]

Source: TS 11/956/3501

Meeting of the 6th. and 11th. Divisions of the London Corresponding Society at the Parrott on 29th. July 1794.

Citizen Heywood in the Chair

18 others present
The Delegates reported the proceedings of the last General Committee./

One New Member made.

The rest of the Evening occupied, by Citizen Burk's reading different parts of York's, Thoughts on Civil Government,[28]

The Speech of M. Moreau de St. Merry spoken in the Assembly of the Electors of

Paris July 29. 1789.[29] and other political papers, particularly one signed God save the people (one of which is annexed to a former Report)[30]

Citizen Burks reported the Tryal of Citizen Eaton for a Libel and that he had been found Guilty,[31] he said that the Jury were inclined to have given an imediate Verdict of Guilty but that Citizen Caney was upon the Jury and objecting, occasion'd their retiring near an hour before they return'd a verdict

adjourned

233. Report from spy Metcalfe: LCS Committee of Correspondence, 30 July 1794[32]

Source: TS 11/956/3501

Meeting of the Committee of Correspondence of the London Corresponding Society at Citizen Thelwall's on Wednesday 30th. July 1794./.

present Citizens Hodgson
Smith
Harris
Higgins
Bone
Metcalfe
Parkinson
Beck
Burks

Resolved that it would be very much for the interest of the Society, to publish a Weekly pamphlet in the Name of the Society upon political subjects at the price of One Penny and to have a public receiving box for Letters &c.,

27 Government description: 'Minutes of Meeting of 6th & 11th Divisions of London Corresponding Society at the Parrot / 29th. July 1794. – / Rx July 30th'.

28 Henry Yorke, *Thoughts on Civil Government: Addressed to the Disenfranchised Citizens of Sheffield*, 1794. This 76 pp. work attacks priests, aristocrats and primogeniture; it recommends education, equal suffrage and brotherhood. The readers are addressed once as *comrades*, elsewhere as *citizens*.

29 1790. The 8 pp. pamphlet starts with a rapture over the accomplishments of the French Revolution. It continues with a reminder that kings have been elevated for the general advantage and that the people are not bound to obey the king any more than he deserves to be obeyed. It warns the French to take warning from the visible decay in the British constitution.

30 See p. 202 n. 21.

31 On 29 July Eaton was prosecuted for publishing a libel on Lady Elizabeth Luttrel and her family in *The Female Jockey Club, or a Sketch of the Manners of the Age*. Eaton was ignorant of the contents of the book, written by Charles Pigott. Before the jury was given the case, the judge, Lord Kenyon, announced that in his opinion the work was clearly a gross libel (*MC* [30 July 1794?], in Place Collection, vol. 36, fo. 141).

32 Government description: 'Meeting of Committee of Correspondence of London Corrg. Society 30th. July 1794 / Rx July 31th'.

Resolved that such Measure be proposed in the General Committee, for their Sanction and to authorize this Committee to use the Society's *Name* to such Publication

Ordered that 5000 Copies of the Advertizement for the relief of the Wives and Children be printed in Order to distribute to the public and that two be inclosed in a Cover to each Democratic Member of the two Houses of Parliament

Citizen Hodgson reported that he had given to the Wife of Citizen Martin 2 *Guineas* she being in great Distress[33]

No Letter yet reced from Nottingham or Sheffield in answer to those sent by this Committee as mentioned in a former Report
adjourned

Hodgson informed the Committee that an Address would shortly appear to the Journeymen Hatters, who were a very large body of Men, from which he hoped great benefit would result to the Society, the contents he was not prepared to state.

234. Report from spy Groves: LCS General Committee, 31 July 1794[34]

Source: TS 11/965/3510A

London Corresponding Society
General Committee

Thursday July 31st. 1794
The principal business that occupied the attention of the Committee this Evening was "A Donation of Fifty Pounds given by a person unknown to the Uses of the Society and applied as follows

To Mrs. Hardy	10£.
To Mrs Thelwal	10£.
To Mrs Lovett	10£.

The remaining Sum of 20£. to be distributed amongst the Wives & Children of those Members of the L. C. Society who are in Custody exclusive of Mrs. Hardy, Mrs. Thelwal & Mrs. Lovett

33 Martin had been in King's Bench Prison since 11 Feb. because of inability to pay costs of an unsuccessful lawsuit on behalf of a man whose greedy brothers had locked him in a madhouse (*An Account of the Proceedings on a Charge of High Treason against John Martin*, 1795).
34 Groves's description: 'L. C. S. - proceedings of The Genl. Commee July 31st 1794'. Government description: 'Mr Groves's account of the Proceedings of the general Commee / July 31st 1794'.

The Account given by Hodgson of this circumstance was thus –
On the 29th. a Gentleman, accompanied by two Ladies called at his House, in the Broad Way Westminster, & gave to his Wife, he being from home, Twenty pounds for the above Purpose; saying, he had called on Mrs. Hardy & had given her 10£ That he had also called on Mrs. Thelwall & had given her the like Sum; but that not knowing Mrs. Lovetts Address he came there to enquire for it, adding, that he should also call on Mrs. Lovett & give her 10£. likewise

Mrs. Hodgson having given the Gentleman Mrs. Lovetts direction, he went away, saying, that perhaps he might call again another time on a similar errand –

Hodgson stated further that he had since called on Mrs. Hardy & found that the 10£. had been given her as stated by the Gentleman – that he had called on Mrs. Thelwall afterwards to make the same Enquiry but that Mrs Thelwall said she had not recd. any such Money or seen any such person – that he had made a like application to Mrs. Lovett, and recd. the like answer as Mrs. Thelwal had given him –

These two last circumstances, he said, had much surprized him; because, on the One hand he could not suspect the Gentleman of stating his Charity beyond the real extent of it, nor at the same time could he venture to suppose that Mrs. Lovett or Mrs. Thelwal had concealed the fact from him or told him a falshood – but, as it was a matter that required further enquiry he should postpone giving any opinion on it.

His evident meaning by this surmise was, that it was possible Mrs. Thelwall & Mrs. Lovett had recd. the donation but wished to conceal it from the Committee, by which means they might continue on the list of persons relieved; but that if they revealed it; the General Commee might withhold the present weekly allowances –

If Mrs. Thelwal & Mrs. Lovett should still deny the Receipt of the two ten pounds it is expected that on the next Commee night an Advertisement of Thanks to the Gentleman will be moved, for the specific Sums of 20£. to the General Body of Wives & Children & 10£. to Mrs. Hardy by which means it is probable that the facts may be discovered –

The Collections in the different Divisions during the Course of the Week amounted to Nine Pounds

The Number of Members who renewed their Tickets during that Week was 42 –

The Number of New Members made 7.

A new & particular question came before the Committee – It was stated that Citizen Burks who had held a Station in the India House, had been discharged from his Employment on account of his principles, & that he had been driven to this alternative, either to quit the L. C. S. or quit the East India House – that not choosing to renounce his principles, or of even seeming to do so, in order to retain his Situation, he had in a manly & patriotic manner boldly asserted his independence & chose rather to relinquish his situation than forsake the Society.

That this conduct had driven him into distress – that he had a Wife & Family & therefore, tho' he did not claim it himself yet his friend had proposed him a Relief in the Division to which he belonged, which Division had referred it to the discretion of the General Committee

This novel application opened a short debate – It was contended on one hand that Citizen Burks was a very worthy Citizen and deserving relief, and that his situation and conduct demanded it –

On the other hand it was argued, that tho' Citizen Burks really was a very good Citizen & had acted in a manner that strongly proved himself, yet if such Applications were encouraged, it would open doors to idleness fraud & imposition –

There was another ground started by way of Objection, vizt., Whether the Commee had such a power without its being the Sense of a Majority of the Divisions

In order, therefore, not to be guilty of indelicacy to Citizen Burks, the following question was referred to the Divisions

"Whether they would vest a power in the General Commee to relieve a Citizen, who may, on account of his principles, be in distress, but, at the same time, not in actual Custody on that account" – Adjourned

235. Report from spy Metcalfe: LCS Committee of Correspondence, 1 August 1794[35]

Source: TS 11/956/3501

Meeting of the Committee of Correspondence

of the London Corresponding Society on Friday 1st. August 1794 at Citizen Thelwalls.

Present

Citizens Metcalfe in the Chair
Hodgson
Bone
Higgins
Harris
Smith
Beck
Burks

Citizen Hodgson reported that a Gentleman & two Ladies had called at his House and had left £20 to relieve the wants &c of the Wives and Children of the Imprisoned Citizens, and had recommended Mrs. Baxter to be particularly noticed in the disposal of the Money, he also reported that the same party had paid to the Wifes of Citizens Thelwall, Hardy and Lovett. £10 each.

The rest of the Eveng, taken up, in paying Bills &c.

236. Report from spy Groves: LCS Division 2, 4 August 1794[36]

Source: TS 11/965/3510A

London Corresponding Society

Proceedings of Division No. 2

4th. August 1794 –   Compton Street

Le Maitre made the Report from the General Committee of the Sum given by a Gentleman unknown, of 20£. to the Wives & Children of those Members who are in Custody and also 10£. to Mrs. Hardy –

He mentioned the circumstance of the Gentleman having said he had given 10£. to Mrs Thelwall, & shod. give 10£. to Mrs Lovett, but that the two latter Sums had been said not to have been recd. which wod. be particularly enquired into.

He stated the Number of Members who had renewed their Tickets to have been during the last Week 42, & the New Made Members to have been 7.

He next mentioned the Referred question

35 Metcalfe's description: 'Meeting of the Committee of Correspondce. of the London Correspondg Society on 1st. Augt. 1794'. Government endorsement: 'Rx. Aug. 5th. 1794'.

36 Groves's description: 'proceedings of division No. 2. Augt. 1794'. Government description: 'Groves's Report of Proceedings of Division No. 2. 4. Aug: 1794'.

to the Division "Whether the Division would vest a power in the General Committee to relieve any Citizen who may, on account of his being a Member of that Society, be in distressed circumstances but not, at the same time, in Custody on account of his principles"

After some little debate between Le Maitre, Pearce, Groves, Main, & Brooks Pro & Con it was determined Unanimously, fourteen Members only belonging to that Division being present (the others being only Visitors & consequently having no Vote) That the General Comee should *Not* be Vested with any such Power

Citizen Pearce, who was lately discharged on Bail, made his first appearance there since that discharge

He stated that Taylor had perjured himself before the Select Commee, by having accused Pearce, on Oath, with making a Speech & Addressing the Meeting at Chalk farm –

He denounced a Citizen of the name of Webb, as being a Spy in the Pay of the Secretary of State, & added that Taylor recd. 1£. 11s 6d pr. Week

He also denounced another Citizen of the name of Gostling as a Spy in Pay, and Lastly

He denounced Citizen Metcalf who he said was a Delegate – That he well knew from his information that he was a Spy – that during his, Pearce's, Examination before the Secret Commee he had frequently seen Metcalf, about the Rooms there, & on the Stairs, who had, like a Jesuit, wished him success & to get well through it – He described Metcalf to be an Attorney, belonging to some Hall in the City – said he was a short Man, pale faced, light hair, & marked by the Small Pox, with an effeminate voice, and desired the Citizens to be on their guard against him – He also requested them to make enquiries after the Characters of Webb & Gostling, but Taylor in particular – adding that he lodged at or frequented a public House in Fleet Street called the Great Tom of Oxford

He concluded with stating that One of the Witnesses against Horne Tooke was a person who had frequently dined with Mr. Tooke[37] – that Horne Tooke knew who it was, & desired the Members to take care who they admitted to their Tables

Adjourned

237. Report from spy Metcalfe: LCS Committee of Correspondence, 6 August 1794[38]

Source: TS 11/956/3501

Meeting of the Committee of Correspondence of the London Corresponding Society on Wednesday 6th August 1794 at Citizen Thelwall's

Present Citizens Hodson
Beck
Burks
Higgins
Bone
Parkinson
Smith
Metcalfe

A Letter was read from *Camage* which had been forwarded to Citn Hodson through the hands of a Shopman at Mrs. Hardys where it had been left by a Messenger, stating that they were in great want of Cash and requesting relief, upon Motion this Letter was directed to be enclosed in One to the people of Sheffield and which Citizen Higgins undertook should be conveyed thither by a ffriend of his who was going to Sheffield on Monday next. The Committee very much suspected Camage's Letter to be a trap to ensnare Citizen Hodson, and the more partacly as it was deled by a Messenger. &c.

Citizen Burks reported his delivery of 4000 handbills on behalf of the Wives and Children of the imprisoned Citizens

Citizen Smith reported that a New Patriotic Newspaper would shortly be published twice a week, and requested the Committee to use their endeavours, to procure it an extensive patronage &c.

Citizen Smith reported that Citizen Peirce had attended the last meeting of the Second Division, where he had made a very long Speech, and had warned the Society to beware of Taylor whom he had seen attending the Privy Council and among others of Citn. Metcalfe whom he had heard was frequently at the Treasury but Metcalfe having anticipated any such observation by a long time since stating that he had a claim upon the Treasury which he could not procure a settlement of, this

---

37 Said to be John Wharton, M P, whose speech the LCS published in 1793.

38 Government description: 'Meeting of Committee of Correspondence / of London Corresponding Society 6th Augt 1794'.

report had no effect whatever upon the Committee, who replied that they had a perfect knowledge of the Circumstance, and that they knew very well Citzn Metcalfe, stood nearly in the same situation with regard to Government, that Citizen Frost had been under./.

adjourned

238. Report from spy Metcalfe: LCS General Committee, 7 August 1794[39]

Source: TS 11/956/3501

Meeting of the General Committee of the London Corresponding Society on Thursday 7th. August 1794 in New Compton Street

Citizen Upton in the Chair
29 other Citizens present

Six New Members made
A Letter was read addressed to the Chairman of the London Corresponding Society, signed Philanthropos, recommending unanimity and confidence in each other, that enemies to the Society endeavour'd to create distrust among the Members, and advising the Society to conduct themselves with caution and to keep themselves in their arguments within Constitutional bounds, &c.

A Letter of thanks from Mrs. Baxter was read, for the timely relief given to her by the Society.

A Letter from Nottingham was read, approving the conduct of the Society, and recommending a steady perseverance

The Committee proceeded to take into consideration the Referred Motion concerning the appointing of a Committee to revise the two Reports of Constitution and to select the material parts to be adopted by the Society for their future regulation, when after a long debate (of 2 hours) it was referred back to the Divisions for them to return their Affirmative or Negative, to this Question Viz.
Do they agree to authorize the General Committee to appoint from amongst themselves a Committee of Constitution for the purpose stated in the Motion &c.

Citizen Hodson reported the Opinion of the Committee of Correspondence that it would be for the interests of the Society to publish a periodical pamphlet at the price of One Penny, in the Name of the Society and at their risque, which was agreed to and the conduct of such intended publication referred to the Committee of Correspondence

Citizen Smith reported that a New Paper would shortly make its appearance to be published twice a Week, and which would be a compleat Democratic Paper, indeed the Society might call it their own Paper, and recommended it to the several Delegates to promote as much as in their power a General circulation of the Paper.

Citizen Higgins reported from his Division that it was their Wish, the Committee would take into their consideration the best means of defending the several imprisoned Citizens, whose Trials the *papers* said were to come on upon the 25th. of this Month, and Recommending the Committee to retain Council &c. Upon the Motion of Citn. Groves the consideration of this subject was adjourned to the next General Committee./.

A Motion was then made that an Account of the Monies Received for the relief of the Wives and Children of the imprisoned Citizens be forthwith published in some of the Daily papers, this was referred to the Committee of Correspondence

Upon the Question which had been sent to the Divisions for their Opinion "Whether the Committee should be authorized to relieve the necessities of distressed Members" the return was 4 for it   136 against any relief being given but to prosecuted Members and their Families./.

Citizen Hodson then reported that within the last Week Subscriptions had been received for the Wives and Children £17 . . – & for General purposes £3 . . 10 . . 7

Adjourned

239. Report from spy Metcalfe: LCS Committee of Correspondence, 8 August 1794[40]

Source: TS 11/956/3501

Meeting of the Committee of Correspondence of the London Corresponding Society on Friday 8th August 1794 at Citzn Thelwall's.

Present Citizens Hodson
Beck
Higgins
Harris
Bone

39 Government description: 'Meeting of the General Committee of the London Corresponding Society 7th. August 1794'.

40 Metcalfe's description: 'Meeting of the Committee of Correspondce. / of London Correspg Society 8th. Augt 1794'. Government endorsement: 'Rx 9th. Augt'.

Smith
Parkinson
Burks
Metcalfe

The whole of this Evening was taken up. in naming a very long list of Literary Men, to whom the Committee should apply for their Assistance, in furnishing matter for the intended Periodical Publication, and Citizen Parkinson was requested to write to Messrs. Gurney and Vaughan to furnish for the first Number An Essay upon the subject of The Privilege of Witnesses called to give Evidence upon Criminal prosecutions, and how far they [are] bound to answer Questions to criminate others, than the person under Trial, and how they should conduct themselves in resisting the impertinent questions of Council./. and also upon any other subject which may be useful in preparing and informing the people in general and particularly the Society many of whom it is probable will be subpoena'd to give Evidence on the several Trials, previous to their being called upon, that they may know how to conduct themselves upon that Occasion./.

A Letter was deled to Citizen Smith to be forwarded to the People of Sheffield inclosing the Letter from Camage mentd. in a former Report

Adjourned

240. Report from spy Metcalfe: LCS Divisions 6 and 11, 12 August 1794[41]

Source: TS 11/956/3501

Meeting of the 6th. & 11th. Divisions of the London Corresponding Society at the Parrott on Tuesday 12th. August 1794

Citizen Higley in the Chair
20 Citizens present

The Delegate made his Report from the General Committee
One New Member made
The Division proceeded to the consideration of the referred Motions (as mentioned in a former Report) concerning the appointment of a Committee to form a Constitution for the Society, when after considerable debate, those Divisions rejected the Motion and resolved that it be recommended to the General Committee to refer the revised Report imediately to the Divisions for discussion, that the Revised

Report had never yet been fairly considered and that it would be an insult to the Committee who drew up that Report as well as to the Society who appointed them, Not to enter into a fair and full discussion of that Report, before it was rejected, and that those Divisions are of opinion the revised Report is adequate for all the purposes of the Society/.

adjourned

241. Report from spy Groves: LCS General Committee, 14 August 1794[42]

Source: TS 11/965/3510A

London Corresponding Society

General Committee
Thursday Augt. 14th. 1794

Citizen Groves, President.

The attention of the Committee was first occupied by Information brought by Citizen Beck, the Receiver, that Citizen Hodgson of the Broad Way Westminster had experienced a very narrow escape from the Bow Street Runners, & Treasury Messengers, who having a Warrant against Hodgson for High Treason had, luckily for Citizen Hodgson, laid hold of a wrong person, which occasioned great mirth and gave great satisfaction in the Committee

Citizen Beck having also informed the Committee that he had seen Mrs. Hodgson & brought the necessary papers, the Commee proceeded to business.

On calling over the Numbers of the Divisions there appeared to have been made in the Course of the preceding Week 24 *new* Members, a number unusually large of late

The Treasurer's Accounts were next stated and preceding Subscriptions and accounts appeared as follows

	£.	s	d
Ballance in hand up to July 2d.	8	1.	8½
Subscriptions recd. for General purposes from July 3d. to Augt. 7th. incluse.	8	8	10½
By *Quarterages* during the sd. period	13	1.	11
The Sum total for Genl. purposes & Quarters.	29	12	6

41 Government description: 'Meeting of 6th. & 11th. Divisions of the London Corresponding Society / 12th. August 1794 / Rx Aug. 13th'.

42 Government description: 'Augt. 14. 1794. / Report of Genl. Commee / Mr. Grove's Report'.

By *Quarterages*, are to be understood the Renewal of the Quarterly Tickets at 1s. 1d. each Ticket

This account proves that from the 2d. of July last to Augt. 7th. inclusive, 241 Citizens had renewed their Tickets

$£$

The subscription during the above period for Wives and Children was	57. 2 3¼

Total of Subscriptions & Quarts. 86. 14. 9¼

Expended during that period for Tickets, Books, printing,	23. 2 9
Distributed to Suffering Patriots and their Wives and Children	30. 5 2

53 7 11

53. 7 11

Ballance in hand up to Augt. 8th. 33 6. 10¼

These three circumstances, vizt. The Number of New Members, The Subscriptions, the Quarterages and Expenditure, which prove the State of the Societys increase and the State of their Finances, are too striking too need any observation of mine – But a consideration arises out of the following part of their proceedings

A Motion of Citizen Grimshaws, which was made in the Commee of Delegates, "for a Select Committee to be appointed out of the General Committee in order to revise the Two forms of Constitution (already submitted to the Consideration of the Divisions) and prepare such an one out of both as may tend to unite and give stability to the Society", had been referred at the last Meeting of Delegates to the Divisions at large for their approbation –

The Answer returned by the Divisions to the referred Motion was, a Negative put on it by 113 Negatives to 22 Affirmatives, so that by this Answer it clearly appears that 135 Citizens met in the different Divisions in the course of the Week, vizt. Monday, Tuesday, & Wednesday last.

On calling over the different Divisions it appeared that the Number of those Divisions which had branched into 31 were reduced to 25, Six Divisions not meeting at all, or more properly speaking actually broke up, vizt. Divisions 1, 17, 19, 24, 30, & 31. That some Divisions, particularly Nos. 6, & 11 & 4 & 7 are united, the members in each being too small to even form a Division vizt. Nine Members. –

This annihilation is termed by the Citizens "Gone to Sleep".

These circumstances prove that the Society is most considerably diminished, especially when it also appeared that in 25 Divisions only 135 members met, which, upon an Average, proves also that little more than Five in each Division taking one with the other

The numbers that voted in the Different Divisions are as follow

No.		By this, the Number of
2 - - - - -	11	Divisions that may [be]
3 - - - - -	6	called Awake, prove to
4 & 7-16		be 14.
6, 11-24		
12 - - - - -	1	
13 - - - - -	13	The Remaining Divi-
18 - - - - -	16	Nos. 1 15 sions vizt.
22 - - - - -	10	5 16 are either
23 - - - - -	8	8 17 engrafted
27 - - - - -	10	9 19 into the
28 - - - - -	9	10 21 & other Divi-
29 - - - - -	11	14 24 sions or
		fallen fast
125 [43]		Asleep

The Reason why so large a Majority negatived Citizen Grimshaw's Motion was, a violent opposition to what the Divisions conceived to be an Aristocratic Measure in the Commee of Delegates, and an usurpation over the Democratic Body, vizt. the Elective Citizens.

A Letter was recd. from Citizen Hodgson addressed to the President of the General Committee of Delegates, & began thus "On the *Tramp*" Augt. 14. 1794

The Letter stated That the *Blood-hounds* had been after him, & that he narrowly escaped them – It strongly recommended the adopting a Constitution of some sort or other and with all possible speed – It gave advice how to proceed in it, assured the Committee of his Zeal in their Cause, and begged they would not impute his absence to fear, but to his desire of the safety of his person, on account of his Wife & Family, which he, notwithstanding could serve, in a measure, but not at all if in Custody, & concluded with wishing then Health & Fraternity –

A referred Motion, made by Citizen Smith of Portsmouth Street, for a New Weekly Publication at One Penny each, the expences to be paid by the Society, and the profits to be appropriated to use of the Society was resumed

It was agreed to, and referred to the Committee of Correspondence to Settle the Plan, to conduct & to revise it

43 Should be 135.

210

A Motion was brought forward from Division 2. as follows. – (Vide Inclosed papers)

August 13th. 94

That the General Committee appoint a Select Committee to examine and prepare[44] a Constitution and refer it to the Divisions for approbation

A: Main, Chairman

Affirmative   10
Negative   1

This Motion was considered as determined on already by the declared Sense of the Divisions

Ordered to be returned

A Resolution from No. 6 & 11 as follows
We do think that appointing any Committee to Revise the Constitution would be an offence to the feelings of the late Committee who were appointed to revise the first report, and an insult to the Society, without permitting the Society to discuss the Revised Report of that Committee, therefore we do propose that the Sense of the Society be taken on the Revised Report, as the discussing of it was desired to be suspended and never yet has been decidedly discussed

Referred Motion Negatived 14. for 10 agt.

W Higley Chairman

A Motion from Division 13.

That a Committee be appointed to take a Constitution into Consideration for this Society and each Division do send a Member to this Committee to bring forward that Constitution, and the respective Divisions do adopt it or reject it total

12 Augt. 94.   John Young President
Considered as disposed of already.

A Motion from Division 10

That the Society at Large enter into a public Subscription for the Benefit of Citizen Burks for One Evening only. That such Money collected may be remitted to the Committee & from thence to Citizen Burks for his Benefit

Stephen Cooper Chairman

Citizen Burks has been discharged from the East India House on Account of his being a Member of the London C. Society – He applied, before, to be relieved on that Account – The Committee were of Opinion they had no power to do it & referred to the Divisions "whether they should be invested with a power to relieve any Suffering Citizen, he not being in Custody" – This General reference was answered in the Negative by a large Majority of the Citizens, who were for *private* Sub-

scriptions for Citizen Burks as he was a Deserving Citizen – The Genl. Commee determined that the Answer to the present Motion had already been given by the Citizens & refused to refer the present application

Adjourned

242. Report from spy Metcalfe: LCS Committee of Correspondence[45]

Source: TS 11/956/3501

Meeting of the Committee of Correspondence of the London Corresponding Society at Citzn Metcalfe's on Wedy. 20th. Augt. 1794

Present Citzns. Metcalfe
                Hodgson
                Smith
                Burks
                Bone
                Harris
                Higgins
                Parkinson
                Beck

Citizen Burks reported he had just come from Shoe lane where he had heard the Riot Act read amidst the Groans and hisses of the Mob,[46] that he saw the Lord Mayor hustled and pelted, that a large party of Soldiers came, when the Mob ran down the Cross Streets, he saw several knock'd down by the Soldiers, he said he saw several Citizens among the Mob. whose Names he did not know. and Citizen Adams of division 6, he saw there Doctor Watson in company with one or two others and Young Eaton,

45 Government description: 'Committee of Correspondence of Lond. Corr. Society / 20th. Augt. 1794 / *some parlars of Riot*'.

46 The riots were in protest against the system of manning the army and navy by coercive recruitment. Victims were dragged or lured to houses of rendezvous or crimping houses and bullied or kept drunk until they could be formally enlisted. The riots started after a victim in a crimping house in Charing Cross committed suicide by jumping out the window. According to the Lord Mayor, Paul Le Mesurier, the intention of the rioters was 'to pull down every House which had been opened as a House of Rendezvous' (letter to John King, 21 Aug. 1794, HO 42/33). In a letter to the police magistrates Patrick Colquhoun accused the LCS of instigating the riots: 'I have strong grounds to believe that these riots are the result of a deliberate System originating with the Corresponding Societies for the purpose of introducing anarchy & Confusion into the Capital that they may with more ease carry into execution these designs which they are hatching for the purpose of overturning the Government' (22 Aug. 1794, HO 42/33).

44 Motion in HO 42/32 reads 'propose'.

that Eaton said he had put them up to it in Bride lane, Hodgson replied he was sorry Dr. Watson placed any confidence in such a babling prating Boy, he said also he had no doubt that the Exeter Street people were at the bottom of it, there appeared to be a System in the Mob's proceedings, he had no doubt some of the Exeter Street people were among the Mob. &c. it *was a fine opportunity if* it could have been properly managed and the people previously spoken to./.

The Committee proceeded to the business of the Society and Citizen Hodgson produced an Address he had prepared by way of prospectus to the intended periodical publication, on its being read much debate took place upon several passages, which seem'd to hold out the publication as a medium for discussing other questions than those which imediately related to a Reform in Parliament and universal Suffrage, and partarly to a part which courted a discussion upon the Merits and advantages of other Governments, at length the whole was referred to Citizen Parkinson for him to revise and modify against Friday Eveng next

Citizens Parkinson and Metcalfe were deputed to call upon Messrs. Gurney and Vaughan, to learn whether they would undertake the Defence of the several imprisoned Citizens and to have their Opinion, if it was lawful to advertize for Subscriptions to defray the expences of defending them, and by which the Committee would most probably procure some intimation with regard to their expectations of receiving regular ffees, or whether those Gentlemen would defend them without ffees. &c./.

Some conversation took place concerning the appointment of fit places to receive Communications for the intended publication but which was deferred determining upon &c.

Citizen Smith was requested to procure the Names and Initials of those who had subscribed towards the relief of the Wives and Children, to incert them in the public papers &c.

Citizen Jones was denounced as a person in the employ of Government, and who had given information at the Secretary of States Office, of all which had passed on the Monday Eveng. at Whitcomb Street &c.

A Report from Cin. Smith of the apprehension of Ross,[47] and that from the neglect of the Officer who took him in not searching him,

he had been able to secure all his private papers, which he had the next day, after his apprehensn. deled to Scott,[48] who went to see him in Tothill fields./.

243. Report from spy Metcalfe: LCS General Committee, 21 August 1794[49]

Source: TS 11/956/3501

Meeting of the General Committee of the London Corresponding Society in New Compton Street on Thursday 21st. Augt. 1794

Citizen Jones in the Chair
30 others present
Two New Members made

The return from the Divisions, upon the Question referred to them relative to the Constitution, was taken when it appeared that the Majority were for adopting the Motion, only three divisions being against it./.

A Motion from one of the Divisions "That all Letters containing Accusations against any of the Members of the Society should be signed with the Name place of abode of the person making the Accusation, and that Anonimous Letters should not be read or have any attention paid to them" was read, This created a very violent and long Debate, several Amendments were moved, and one by Citizen Smith "That anonimous Letters might be read in the Divisions to which they were sent, and then transmitted to the Committee of Correspondence" was carried, but it being suggested that the Committee could not controul the Divisions It was moved that the Motion and Amendment be referred to the Divisions, which was carried

A Letter was received and read, signed Peter Pindar Junius, stating the writer's inability to subscribe in Money towards the relief of

47 George Ross, formerly of the *Edinburgh Gazetteer*, had been assistant secretary of the British Convention in Edinburgh. After his arrest, he was sent back to Edinburgh and was in Tolbooth at the time of Hardy's trial (*ST* vol. 24, col. 1392).

48 Perhaps on the basis of this report, Scott was arrested. In return for release on recognizance and pocket money (3 gns) he turned government informer and was to report to the Lord Mayor on a new society, the members of which were to assemble at Eaton's house on 26 Aug. Since the list of members had been burnt, there was no meeting, but Scott provided information about who burnt the papers and who were said to be members (letters, Paul Le Mesurier to John King, 26, 27 Aug. 1794, HO 42/33).

49 Metcalfe's description: 'Meeting of General Committee of London Correspg Society 21st Augt. 1794'. Government endorsement: 'Rx Aug 22d'.

the Wives and Children &c. and inclosing an Acrostic of considerable length, which the Writer offer'd to the Committee hoping that the publication therof might produce something towards the fund for their Relief &c. upon the Motion of Citizen Groves that ["]the same together with the thanks of the Committee should be returned to the Writer for the entertainment his Verses had given" some debate took place, upon the indelicacy of returning the Verses, and likewise upon the impropriety of so doing, under the circumstances of the Society's being about to publish a periodical Work, to which the writer might hereafter contribute[50]

An Amendment to the Motion was then made and carried "That the thanks of the Society be returned to the Writer, and that the Verses &c. be referred to the Committee of Correspondence./

Citizen Burks then proposed that the Committee should issue some handbills, denying the Societys being at all concerned in the Riots now subsisting, declaring their detestation of such proceedings and advising the Members of the Society to be careful in demeaning themselves peacably and orderly and not on any account to join in the Mob's or from an idle curiosity be seen amongst them./" to which it was observed by Citizens Groves, Le Maitre & others that what the Members of the Society did individually was no concern of the Society, the Committee had no controul over the conduct of the Members as private Men and that to publish such a caution, would be to hold out to the World that the Committee were so conscious of the Riotous dispositions of their brother Citizens that it was absolutely necessary to publish a caution to restrain them from Acts of Violence,
            proposition rejected

One Citizen whose Name I could not learn, declared that he considered it would be honorable for the Society, if they were at the bottom of the existing Riots, or at all contributing to the demolition and extirpating of the infamous practise of Crimping and Kidnapping, and that he should feel no difficulty whatever in heading a Mob for such a purpose./

Reported from the Committee of Correspondence. That the intended publication was in great forwardness./.

Report of Cash paid to Wives of Imprisoned Citizens

50 He may have contributed later to the *Moral and Political Magazine* under the name of 'Tommy Pindar, Pet. Pind. Nepos'. The *Politician* did not last long enough to need his contributions.

7 Guineas
1 Guinea to Citn Gerald
Cash received since last Committee
                            £5 .. 17 .. 6.
            Adjourned

244. Report from spy Groves: LCS General Committee, 21 August 1794[51]

Source: TS 11/965/3510A

London Corresponding Society
        General Committee Augt. 21. 1794
            Citizen Jones President

The first thing that seems to lay claim to attention in the proceedings of the different Divisions during the Week is the very small number of New-made Members Vizt. Two only, and those were made in Divisions 18 and 22.

The Quarterages, or number of renewed Tickets were only four.

The Subscriptions throughout the whole Divisions for Wives and Children of the Citizens in imprisonment, for suffering patriots and for General purposes, amounted to only Eight pounds 7 Shillgs

From these three circumstances may be collected a material decline in the course of this Week as well in New made Members, as in renewed Tickets, as also in the state of the Societys funds, when compared with the several preceding Weekly Reports to the Genl. Committee.

If to these considerations be added the circumstance of the Weekly Expenditure by far exceeding the Weekly income, it may safely be said that the Society is in a very decreasing state

The Weekly expenditure amounted to Thirteen pounds nine Shillings so that the Weekly deficit is Five pounds 2s. a very considerable sum when speaking of the Finances of the London Correspondg Socy.

In the Word Expenditure is included the Monies paid to the Wives & Children, to Gerrald &c &c.

If to these Statements a reference is had to the Report of the proceedings given in by me last Week wherein may be seen that a large Number of the Divisions have been actually broken up, for want of a sufficient number of Members to constitute a Division, vizt. Nine,

51 Government description: 'Groves' Report of the General Commee / Aug: 21. 1794'.

213

the General Conclusion must be that the Society itself is very much on the decline, and that it will gradually drop off into a state of perfect annihilation.

The only idea that can operate against this conclusion is – Do the Members of the London Corresponding Society withdraw themselves only through fear and are they withdrawn in order to wait for times that may afford more favourable opportunities to carry their designs?

I am of Opinion that to the very great number that are panic struck, may be added a very considerable number indeed of those who are fully convinced that the principles of the Society are impossible to be carried into execution & have therefore totally withdrawn themselves – And also that the Society, at present, consists chiefly of the daring & the desperate

An Anonymous Letter was read subscribed Peter Pindar Junius to which the following Motto from Terence was prefixed

> Homines simus, et nihil humani a nobis alienum putemus

It was a poetical Rhapsody stuffed with Nonsense and, though long contained in an Acrostic, Six lines, the first two of which were

> George the third
> Upon my word

It was brought by Citizen Burks –

Citizen Groves moved that the Thanks of the Committee be returned to the Author with the productions, for the *Entertainment* it had afforded them –

Citizen Smith moved an Amendment by leaving out the latter part of the Motion – arguing that Authors ought not to be affronted, as the Society were about Establishing a new publication of their own.

The question that next took up some time in debate was

Whether Letters of Accusation against Members sent to the presidents of the Different Divisions should be read, and if Anonymous, no further notice taken of them

Citizen Metcalf compared such a conduct to the malice of an Assassin in the dark, and to an Adder lurking in the grass & darting his poison unseen.

Citizen Jones reprobated the reception of such Anonymous Slander

Citizen Groves urged that the Society by Admitting such Anonymous accusation to be read, was opening a door for Ministers to stir up a spirit of distrust among all the Members, & that thereby the most active & all those who had abilities would be sure to be the objects of Anonymous accusations which must be the ruin of the Society –

Several spoke for the reception & sending it to the Committee of Correspondence

It was at last agreed that Anonymous accusations should be recd. but that, after being read, no further Notice should be taken of them

Adjourned

245. Report from spy Metcalfe: LCS Committee of Correspondence, 22 August 1794[52]

Source: TS 11/956/3501

Meeting of the Committee of Correspondence of the London Corresponding Society on Friday 22nd. Augt. 1794./

Present Citizens Hodgson
      Smith
      Parkinson
      Higgins
      Bone
      Burks
      Beck
      Metcalfe

Upon Motion of Citn. Parkinson, it was resolved, to apply to some Literary Gentleman to write the prospectus for the intended periodical publication and Citn. Parkinson was desired to wait upon Mr. McIntosh,[53] to request him to do it and should he decline it, upon Dr. Towers,[54] Mr. Holcroft, and Mr Beaumont &c./.

Part of a Letter from Broomheads Wife, to her husband was read. requesting him to ask any assistance he might stand in need off. from any Sheffield people, and that if he would sign an Acknowledgement for such Sum as any ffriend might advance, she would take care it should be repaid, on which a Motion was made "That the Committee advance One Guinea to the Sheffield people and to take a Receipt for the whole which the Society had advanced, in Order to send such receipt to Sheffield to procure a remittance &c. and Citn Burks was desired to write a Letter requesting such remittance and to state the

---

52 Description: 'Meeting of the Committee of Correspondence of the L. Cor. Society 22nd. Augt. 1794 / Rx. 23d'.
53 Sir James Mackintosh replied to Burke's *Reflections* in his *Vindiciae Gallicae* (1791), but later became an admirer of Burke.
54 Dr Joseph Towers, a dissenting minister, was author of 3 vols. of political pamphlets.

inability of this Society to support their Members &c.

One Guinea Ordered to Citn. Gerald

Adjourned

246. Report from spy Metcalfe: LCS Committee of Correspondence, 27 August 1794[55]

Source: TS 11/956/3501

Meeting of the Committee of Correspondence of the London Corresponding Society on Wednesday 27th. August 1794./.

Present Citizens Higgins   in the Chair
                            Bone
                            Burks
                            Smith
                            Beck
                            Parkinson
                            Metcalfe

Resolved that Communications for the Society's intended periodical pamplet be received only at Citizen Smiths in Portsmouth Street Lincolns Inn ffields

Resolved that it be intitled 'The Politician'

Resolved that Citizen Smith procure a printer whose Name is not to be made public

Resolved that all Communications received, be regularly laid before this Committee for them to select such as may appear to them proper to be incerted in their Work

Resolved that *Citizen Smith*, procure an Editor for the Work to be paid by this Committee, and whose Name is not to be made public.

Citizen Parkinson reported that he had waited upon several Literary Men to procure them to write a Prospectus for the Work that Dr. Towers excused himself for the present on account of his particular situation, Mr. Holcroft had not time &c. he Parkinson had therefore delivered the one drawn by Citn. Hodson to Mr. Bayley, who had promised to revise and Correct it imedy. &c.

Citn. Parkinson reported that he had seen Counsellor Gurney upon the subject of its being lawful to advertize for Subscriptions to defend the imprisoned Citizens" and that he was of opinion any Subscriptions for that purpose must *be private ones*

Citizen Bone then produced a very long address to the public affecting to be a Denial only of a Charge that had appeared in the papers vizt. "that the Jacobin Societys were at the bottom of the late Riots" but which in truth is an address full of the most violent and seditious expressions & calculated to renew the tumults which so lately prevail'd   some of the expressions were too strong for the majority of the Citizens present, and the whole was referred to Citizens Parkinson and Burks to revise and modify, and to procure it forthwith to be printed, and published at the price of 1d.

Resolved that Citizen Smith be applied to, to get it in circulation by Saturday,[56] and that for the present. 1000 Copies be printed off.

Citizen Smith reported, that a Gentleman had (since the Committee met last,) left 10 Guineas for the Wives and Children of the imprisoned Citizens

adjourned until next Friday at Citn. Metcalfe's

247. Report from spy Metcalfe: LCS Committee of Correspondence, 29 August 1794[57]

Source: TS 11/956/3501

Meeting of the Committee of Correspondence of the London Corresponding Society on Friday 29th. August 1794.

Present Citizens Harris Chairman
                            Smith
                            Burks
                            Hodgson
                            Bone
                            Higgins
                            Parkinson
                            Metcalfe
                            Beck

Citizen Beck reported the denunciation of Citizen Groves in the General Committee, that he had been charged to have been the cause of Citizen Ross. being apprehended, that two Witnesses testifyed that he Groves had been seen in the Company of Williamson the Messenger from Scotland. on the Morning of his Arrival, that the Messenger lodged at his house, that he Groves was present at the Blackmoors head at the time of Ross's apprehension, some short time before which he left the room and returned, at which time it is charged he gave intimation to the Officers that Ross was there, that he followed the Officers aftwds to the Fountain, where he made enquirys concerning

56 30 Aug. *Reformers No Rioters* was not in circulation until 8 Sept.
57 Description: 'Committee of Correspondence of the London Corrg Society. 29 Augt 1794'.

55 Metcalfe's description: 'Committee of Correspondence of the London Corresponding Society on 27 August 1794'.

the business, as tho' he had been an utter Stranger to all that had passed, and lastly that he went off Arm in Arm with one of the Officers, all which (except that he was an Acquaintance of Williamson and had been so for 20 Years) he positively denied and parlarly that he had seen Williamson before the day on which Ross was apprehended, and he also denied that Williamson lodged at his house

The Committee were much exasperated much abusive language passed and he would have been excluded the Society at once, had not Citizen Bone proposed to defer the consideration of the business until the next Genl. Committee, at which time if they should be able to falsify any of the Assertions Citizen Groves had that night made there would then no doubt remain of his being the Rascal, that some of the Committee had long suspected him to be, and they would then treat him accordingly.

Citizens Parkinson & Burks produced, Citizens Bones Address to the people as revised and corrected by them, which was read And after considerable debate upon various parts of it, was at length approved and delivered to Citizen Burks to transcribe for the press imediately, under the title of *Reformers not Rioters* &c.

Citizen Parkinson reported that he had not been able to get back from Mr Bayley the prospectus for the intended periodical publication but that he would endeavour to do so before the next Committee, adjourned
Citizen Burks was desired to write Letters to the several Literary Men whose Names were delivered to him amounting to 48, requesting communications for their intended periodical Work, and that he be allowed 5s. for so doing &c.

A Recommendation from the General Committee, to write a Letter of condolance in the name of the Society, to Citizen Hardy upon the melancholy event of his Wife's Death[58] &c. was next considered and Citizen Bone was deputed to write such Letter.

Citizen Parkinson submitted to the Committee, Whether it would not have a very good effect for the Society to attend the funeral of Mrs. Hardy, I opposed the measure upon the Ground of its giving an opportunity to our Enemies to observe upon our calling together so great a Number of people as would attend that it indicated the Society's inclination upon every occasion that offer'd, to collect a Mob. and to renew the tumults and Riots which had

so lately prevaild &c. the Committee declined taking any measure to call the Society together upon the occasion but recommended to each Member who knew Citizens that meant to attend the funeral earnestly to recommend to them to behave peacably and becoming the solemnity of the occasion, and to disperse each to his own home imediately after the funeral is over./ Ordered that the expences of the funeral be defrayed by the Society, there was some other trifling business, concerning money matters, after which the Committee adjourned at 2 in the Morng

248. Report from spy Metcalfe: LCS General Committee, 4 September 1794[59]

Source: TS 11/956/3501

Meeting of the General Committee of the London Corresponding Society on Thursday 4th. September 1794./.

Citizen Williams in the Chair

29 others present

The Committee proceeded to investigate the charge against Citizen Grove, and no fresh Evidence appearing against him, he entered upon his defence, he denied any knowledge whatever of Ross. or of being at all privy to or assisting in his apprehension, and concluded by laying his hand to his heart and repeating in the most solemn tone of voice "by the God that made me I never saw Mr. Williamson until Sunday Morning after Ross had been apprehended"

He then produced a person of the Name of Dudley of the Bell & Horns at Brompton, a Mr Read[60] of No 34 Bridge's Street Covent Garden, Mr Banks Martlets Court Bow St. and Mr Edwead[61] who contradicted the Evidence which had been given against him, and closed his defence by producing two Affidavits appearing to have been sworn before Mr Justice Addington, by himself and Mr Williamson by which Affidts. they both positively swore they had not seen each other until Sunday Morning after Ross. was apprehended &c.

The Committee proceeded to take the opinion of the Committee seperately as to his Guilt, when there appeared to be 22 declaring him Not Guilty, 5 that he was Guilty, the

58 Mrs Hardy died on 27 Aug., a few hours after being delivered of a still-born baby.

59 Description: 'General Committee of the London Corresponding Society 4th. Septr. 1794'.
60 Reid, according to Groves.
61 Edwin, according to Groves.

other Citizens not having been present on the last Committee Night, declined giving any opinion./ he was then called in and acquainted with the decision in his favor. &c.

Report of New Members made in the last Week 5.

A Letter from Citizen Beck the Treasurer stating the Death of his Sister, and on that account his inability to attend the Committee was read. and desiring the Committee to appoint a Receiver for the Evening, on which the Committee appointed Citizen Burks Receiver for this Evening

A Long Letter was then read signed Pasquin, reflecting upon the Committee, which being known by the hand writing to have been written by Citizen Upton, he was called upon to say if he was the Writer which he acknowledged, on which a Motion was made to pass a Vote of censure upon Citizen Upton which was carried./[62]

Here a very violent dispute took place betwixt Citn. Upton and several of the Committee, much personal abuse passed and the Committee was wholly prevented from doing any further business.

A Motion from two Divisions to erect a Tombstone to the Memory of Mrs. Hardy with a suitable inscription, was referred to the consideration of the Committee of Correspondence./.

adjourned

249. Report from spy Groves: LCS General Committee, 4 September 1794

Source: TS 11/965/3510A

L.C. Society
General Comittee Septr. 4th. 1794

The hour appointed to hear further Evidence and the defence of Citizen Groves on the Charge preferred against him by Citizen Robinson (Foreman to Hardy) being Seven oClock Citizen Groves attended, with his Witnesses, to exculpate himself from that Charge –

The Committee waited an hour for the Accuser & his *further* Evidence when he not appearing Citizen Groves rose and requested the Delegates to proceed to business as every indulgence had been given the Accuser, & that one of Citizen Groves's Witnesses was much pressed for time, he being Steward of a Club that met that Evening at the Globe Tavern in the Strand

62 See account of the pop-gun plot, pp. 220-3.

The Delegates agreed that Citizen Groves was perfectly right and ought *now* to be heard –

Citizen Metcalf was nominated to the Chair & seconded –

Citizen Groves opposed Citizen Metcalf's taking the Chair, as he was not present when the Accusation was made and therefore could not be so competent a Judge as the Citizen who sat as president the preceding Commee Night – He did not object to Citizen Metcalf out of any disrespect, or dread of prejudice, but merely on accot. of his being a Stranger to the Testimony produced on the last Thursday Evg. & the consequent impropriety of presiding as president on a business, on which anor. Citizen had sat as president, and which business was only *Adjourned*   He therefore should move for Citizen Williams again taking the Chair as being the most fair and impartial mode of proceeding –

The Motion was seconded by Citizen Smith who declared the Motion did Citizen Groves much credit

Both Motions were put

For Citizen Metcalf's taking the Chair   1
For Citizen Williams   24

Citizen Groves then rose & desired to know if the Accuser & his further Evidence attended

The Accuser nor his Witnesses appearing Citizen Groves addressed the president.

He premised, that he stood in a situation more painful than any he had hithertoo experienced since he had known how to distinguish between a Sense of Honour and a Sense of Shame; but that he entertained not a Shadow of doubt but the result of this Evening and the decision of the Committee would obliterate every tincture of shame and greatly redound to his honour.

He observed that if Flight was a presumption of Guilt, a manly appearance to answer an Accusation was a strong presumptive proof of innocence, & he did not doubt but the liberality & good sense of the Committee would give that argument its due weight and force

He was not *bound*, he said, to attend that Commee, or enter into any Defence to the Charge; but from his feelings & his sense of honour, to establish which he came openly & boldly forward

How different was the conduct of his Accuser – He brought forward a Charge, which had been heard *in part*, & which was left for determination the present Evening. He had promised to bring forward his collateral Evidence! – had he done so? – No! – Did he appear himself? – No! What *had* he done? He had *skulked* from the investigation! He was convinced of the falshood of the charge and was ashamed to encounter the truly respectable Evidence that was to be produced in exculpation –

Taking then into consideration the conduct of the Accused and the Accuser, what was the natural inference – The accuser fled *from* the Charge, – the Accused *to* it – These Arguments he was sure would impress the Commee so forcibly in his favour that half the Accusation would be wiped away at least, if not the whole of it thereby.

He had experienced, he said, in the conduct of the present Chairman on the preceding Evening, a degree of liberality, candour, and impartiality, that gave him the most heart-felt satisfaction – He had experienced in the Commee the same degree of liberality candour and impartiality from a very large Majority indeed – to them he bowed with respect and thanks; but he was sorry to observe that in the minds of two or three there seemed a zeal that outstripped all candour, & a degree of inveteracy that sat impartiality at defiance –

Even these he trusted he should be able to convert in his favour & to expunge from their minds, in future, all low & illiberal prejudices –

To one Citizen, whether then in the Committee or not, he had a word to say in particular, because an expression had dropped from him the preceding Evening which called loudly for reprehension; and which expression could only be made by the mind capable of committing the Act.

"When, (said Citizen Groves) I produce my Witnesses I shall be able to exonerate myself fully & honourably" – The reply made was "It is easy to produce a false Witness for five Shillings"

I will leave it to the Committee, said Citizen Groves, to make *their* comments it is beneath me as a Man, a Gentleman, & a Citizen, to deign a further observation on the horrid imputation.

The Witnesses I have to produce to you this Evening, said Citizen Groves, are men of character & respect in life, & have always a Guinea in their pockets & *clean Shirts* on their backs

They will prove to you that I was out of Town when Williamson the Kings Messr. arrived in London to apprehend Mr Ross – They will prove I was never in the House I was charged. to have been in & consequently that I never could come out of it, as stated, at another door.

They will prove to you that there cannot exist a Man more zealous in the cause of the L. C. Society than the good & injured Citizen who stands accused – They will prove that I did not arrive in London till the Saturday

Evening about dusk at which time Ross was apprehended – they will prove to you that I never saw Mr. Williamson till the day after Ross was taken, & that it was on the Sunday Morning about 9 oClock, (the next day) that Williamson saw me.

They will prove to you that I am no Runner or Thieftaker at Bow Street, but a man respected in my Neighbourhood & of a far different profession to that of Thief-catching

The three points therefore of Accusation which were 1st. That I was a runner at Bow Street 2dly. That I pointed out Ross, and 3dly. That I went with the Thieftaker, into the House where Ross was taken & came out at anor. door will be perfectly done away – It is to your honour I commit my own, & I am sure I shall be happy in your decision

There is one thing, said Citn Groves which for form sake I must observe – It is That in no Court of Law whatever Evidence in Chief is allowed to be given after a prisoner has given in his Defense, & tho' I labour under no dread of such an attempt, I mean from the *absence* of my Accuser; yet I call on the Commee for the preservation of that eternal rule of Right & Justice which so universally & so honorably prevails in all Courts of Justice

The Commee signified their Assent

There was only one thing further, he said to Notice which was that he had applied to the Landlord of the House where Ross was taken to, to permit his Waiter to attend & prove beyond a possibility of doubt he never was in the House either that or at any time whatever – He was sorry to say the Landlord had refused & threatened to discharge his Waiter if he attended any such Society, and that all such Societies ought to be hanged – But as he had proof of the application to the Landlord & the refusal as stated he did not doubt & was sure that such proof would have all the force, if not more, than if the Waiter had attended personally –

Citizen Groves then called his Witnesses, whom he had introduced, by the Consent of the Committee *previous* to his Address and opening –

Mr Banks Master Taylor, of Market Cot. Covent Garden proved his calling up Citizen Groves on Friday the 15th. of August last, by desire, at 6 oClock in the Morning as Citizen Groves was going out of Town to Hemel Hempsted to see his Children, & that he saw Citizen Groves & his Wife get into a Chaise at ½ past 8. that Morng. & that he saw him return the next day about 7 in the Evening which was Saturday the 17th. –

That on Sunday Morning the 18th. he

brought Citizen Groves home two pair of Nankeen Breeches about ½ past 9 oClock when Citizen Groves was at Breakfast & a Mr Edwin, an Engraver & a Son of the late Mr Edwin Comedian, at Breakfast with him –

That at that time Mr Groves's Servant came into the parlour & said Sir, "Here is a Mr Williamson from Edinburgh at the door", that Mr G: jumped up in surprize met him & shook hands – expressed great satisfaction to see him, and asked him how long he had been in London – that Mr Williamson replied – he came on the Friday about 9 oClock in the Morning in a post Chaise & then lodged at the Black Bear in Piccadilly, of which lodging he much complained – that he was sure this was the first time Mr Groves had seen Mr. W since his arrival, and that Mr G. had recommended Mr W. to lodge with him wch. Mr W. did till he departed from London. and therefore that any suggestion that Mr Groves had been with Mr W. or seen him on the preceding Friday must be false. – Mr Banks concluded with observing that the Society cod. not have a warmer or a truer friend, that he had known Mr G: for 9 yrs. – that he never belonged to Bow Street & was too much of a Gentleman & too well respected to accept of such a disgraceful employment.

Mr Edwin confirmed Mr Banks in every particular

Mr Dudley of the Bell & Horns Brompton proved that on Saty. the 16th. & the day on which Mr Ross was taken he called at Mr Groves's where the Servant informed him Mr G: was out of Town –

That at 7 oClock in the Evening he called on Mr Reid Oilman in Bridges Street Covt Garden to order several things to be sent to his House – that he stood talking with him a considerable time – that all on a Sudden a Man was dragged across the Street in Exeter Street just opposite from the Blackmoors head to the Fountain – that he & Mr Reid directly ran over – that there was a great croud & that instant Mr Groves came up whom Mr Dudley asked what was the Matter – that Mr G: replied The Runners have got a thief, & that then Mr Dudley, Mr Reid, and Mr G: all went to the Blue Posts Tavern & Chop-house which is a House of Reputation, & there drank punch till 11 oClock when they parted – that Mr G: never went into the Fountain at all – that he was a warm friend to the Society & a good Citizen, a man always railing at corrupt placemen & Pensioners, & wishing for a reform in Parliament

Mr Reid confirmed this –

Citizen Jefferies, a Member of Division No.

2. proved Citizen Groves to be a Man always staunch to the cause of Freedom & Mr Fox and that he had known him 20 Years – that he was sure he never belonged to Bow Street, – that he was too much of a Gentn. to engage in such a profession & that he was a Lawyer

Citizen Upton who had called on Citizen Groves & met Mr Williamson there proved that Mr W. declared he never saw Citizen Groves till the Sunday after Ross was taken – that Mr W. said he knew Citizen Groves's Political Sentiments too well to intrust him with such a secret, & that that was the reason he wod. not call on Citizen Groves till his business was done

Citizen Upton declared that Citizen Groves was a worthy Member of the Society, & his Civism well known & approved of by all who knew him, – He attended he said to give that Evidence in favour of an injured Citizen –

The Evidence on the part of Citizen Groves being gone through, it was moved that the thanks of the Commee be given to the Gentn. for their attendance in behalf of Citizen Groves & for the fair, clear, & satisfactory Testimony they had given

It was agreed to & the thanks given

Citizen Groves then said he had two Affidavits to lay before the Committee & begged they might be read –

Agreed to –

The first was the Affidavit of Mr George Williamson & the substance was as follows

That he had known Mr Groves several years past – That on Friday the 15th. he came to London after George Ross & took him on the Saty. Evening – that Mr Groves neither directly nor indirectly in any manner of way or shape whatever was concerned therein or even knew of such a design till after it was effected – That Mr G. was a Man of such Political Principles he would not intrust him Therewith – that on his last arrival in Town he never saw Mr G: till the Sunday Morning after Ross was taken and that the accusation of Mr G: having pointed out Ross or being concerned therein or knowing any thing of it was false in every particular – And that he voluntarily made the Affidt. to do justice to the feelings, & the injured character, of Mr Groves

The Second Affidavit was of Citizen Groves himself who swore he never in his life belonged to any Public Office whatever in any Capacity – that he never knew or saw Ross in his life – that he neither was directly or indirectly concerned in taking him or pointing him out or knew therof – that he never was in the Fountain Tavern as accused of – that he never saw Mr Williamson till the Sunday Morning – that the Affidt. of Mr Williamson was perfectly true & just & the charge against him false & untrue[63]

The Defence being closed – Citizen Groves recapitulated the Evidence with pointed remarks on all its parts – the respect due to the Witnesses confirmed by the Vote of Thanks & commented on the Desertion of the Charge with much severity

Every Person then was desired to withdraw except the Delegates Sub-Delegates Tything Men, which they did –

It was moved that Citn. Groves shod. withdraw – He expressed his readiness & complied –

The Committee debated One hour & a half – Each gave his Opinion & his Verdict Guilty or Not Guilty – & his name was taken down –

When the whole had been taken Citizen Groves was desired to walk in – The President informed him That he had the Pleasure to acquaint Citizen Groves that the Committee had acquitted him of the Charge & deemed him perfectly innocent & that it was a great satisfaction to him to announce that Citizen Groves was considered as a good Citizen –

Citizen Groves returned his thanks to the President for the impartial manner in which he had conducted the business, & assured him that the communication was as pleasing to him as any thing that ever had been communicated to him, & that the manner of the communication enhanced the satisfaction it gave him, but he begged to know if the Sense of the Committee on the Matter was such as might be considered as flattering to him

The President replied "It was so in the highest degree"

There were .22 Voices for Citizn. Groves — 4 – against him

The president desired Citizen Groves not to entertain any resentment against the person who accused him, but to consider that it might arise from mis-information given & an over zeal for the Society –

Citizen Groves replied & said that he entertained no resentment against his Accuser, – that he was obliged to him for the Charge, & only wished the Accuser had been present to hear the Sense of the Commee on that Charge

250. The Pop-Gun Plot: 4 September 1794[64]

Source: See note 64

[A dispute in the general committee led to the revelation of the pop-gun plot, allegedly a scheme devised by some LCS members to assassinate the king by shooting a poisoned arrow through an air gun. For participating in this plot Paul Thomas Lemaitre, John Smith and George Higgins were arrested on 27 and 28 September 1794, kept in prison until May 1795, jailed again in January 1796, and finally acquitted in May 1796. Robert Thomas Crossfield, also an LCS member, was arrested when he re-entered the country in December 1795, was tried for treason in May 1796 and acquitted. All four acquittals were based on the report (denied by the defendants) that the chief witness against these men – still another LCS member – was dead.

The dispute which led to these arrests originated after the LCS, on 19 June, advertised for subscriptions for the families of the state prisoners. One of the nine men

---

63 Groves and his witnesses were lying, as his fellow spy Metcalfe indicated in a letter to Joseph White on 5 Nov. 1794: 'I submit to you whether any notice should be taken of my Reports of 29 Augt., 4th. & 5th. & 11th. September, from the circumstance of their noticing some very solemn Assertions of Groves relative to his not having seen Williamson the Messenger from Scotland previous to the apprehension of Ross, and upon which subject should I be examined, I should be obliged to contradict those assertions, which might injure Grove's credit with the Jury./.'

Metcalfe, Groves and Williamson must have been in collaboration in the arrest of Ross, for Richard Ford, writing about Ross and two other men, notes that Ross is now in Edinburgh and adds, 'whenever you think from Williamson, Groves & Metcalfe that the two last cannot be taken . . . give [Williamson] his Conge to depart' (letter, Ford to Wickham, 23 Aug. 1794, HO 42/33).

64 P. T. Lemaitre, *High Treason! Narrative of the Arrest, Examination, Imprisonment &c. of P. T. Lemaitre, Accused of Being a Party in the Pop-Gun Plot, or, a Pretended Plot to Kill the King!*, 1795; Lemaitre, 'Some remarks respecting the Supposed Origin of the Pop-Gun Plot', 1833, Add MSS 27808, fos. 121–31; Lemaitre, *Petition of Paul Thomas Lemaitre* to Parliament, 1846, Add MSS 27808, fos. 133–6v; John Smith, *Assassination of the King! The Conspirators Exposed, or, An Account of the Apprehension, Treatment in Prison, and the Repeated Examinations Before the Privy Council, of John Smith and George Higgins, on a Charge of High Treason*, 1795; trial of Robert Thomas Crossfield, *ST* vol. 26, cols. 1–224; examinations before the Privy Council of John Bone (PC 1/22/A37), George Higgins (PC 1/22/A36C), Lemaitre (PC 1/22/A36C), William Metcalfe (HO 42/33), Smith (PC 1/22/A37), Thomas Upton (PC 1/22/A36C and PC 1/22/A37); letter, J. Downes to Richard Ford, 28 Oct. 1794, HO 42/33.

appointed to receive subscriptions was Thomas Upton, a watchmaker. Shortly after publishing the advertisement, the committee of correspondence learned that Upton had been indicted for setting fire to his house in order to defraud the insurance office and had escaped prosecution only because of some defect in the law proceedings. The committee deputed Smith and Higgins[65] to investigate this charge. At the same time they sent Upton a note, written by Metcalfe, saying that they thought 'the interests of those families for whom the subscription is raised, require that his name should be omitted in the future bills; and as this will naturally excite some enquiries, by which Mr. Upton, however innocent, may be liable to receive injury; they think it will be prudent in him to withdraw his name from the society'.

Upton, in a great rage, went to Smith and demanded the names of the members of the committee of correspondence. Smith refused to give this information; he advised Upton to give a written reply to the reporter at the meeting of the general committee. Upton was introduced to the reporter, Anthony Beck; he abused the committee of correspondence to Beck and gave him, for the committee, a letter in which he explained that the grand jury had dismissed the indictment against him and that he had successfully prosecuted his accuser.

This explanation did not satisfy the committee of correspondence, and they sent Smith to make further enquiries.[66] Upton probably learned that the committee were still asking about the fire, because he attacked the committee in an anonymous letter to the general committee. This letter, signed Pasquin, was brought to a division meeting and then taken by the delegate, Lemaitre, to the general committee meeting on 4 September. The Pasquin letter, which dealt with the evils of bringing charges against members without adequate evidence, was read aloud. While the general committee puzzled over it, the committee of correspondence sat silent, suspecting that

Upton expected them to explain the meaning of the letter and thereby to reveal themselves and consequently be available for Upton's revenge. Finally, after a considerable pause, Bone rose and spoke. Lemaitre described the scene:]

"He should be sorry to see any of their time longer wasted, as he believed it in his power to explode the mystery, and relieve their anxiety;" he said "If he was not mistaken, the writer was then in the room, and as he doubted not but he could explain the reasons for so writing, there remained, likewise, but little doubt, but that he would have honor and integrity enough to acknowledge whether he had actually written it."

The cry of "name him" made him again rise; he said "The two o's conjoined constituted an 8, Yard or *Alley* was of small import, and as bell was often styled *tell-tale*, it required only the addition of Temple-Bar in lieu of Postern Gate, the signature was still easier explained;" he therefore believed, "Pasquin, No. oo, Tell-tale Alley, Postern Gate," was intended as "Upton, No. 8, Bell-Yard, Temple Bar." Upton was now asked whether he was the writer, and in a contemptuous manner replied in the affirmative. Higgins moved his censure, which I seconded and supported; declaring his behaviour could be compared to nothing better than a *vile assassin*, who not daring to meet his adversary openly, took this secret and base manner of stabbing him in the dark. This, with the following reflection, I call him "*that man*" for he does not deserve the name of "*Citizen*," put him in a violent rage, and rising he began to justify his conduct by reading a part of the afore-mentioned letter of dismissal from the Executive Committee; taking care to avoid mentioning that part relative to the report which had occasioned the same; and although the committee frequently called for the whole of the letter, he still obstinately refused to shew it. His answer to my comparison of his behaviour was by making use of the most injurious terms, "fellow, wretch," and "blackguard:" in fact, his countenance behaviour and language gave him more the appearance of a madman, than of one who but so lately had kept the most profound silence. His personal attacks on myself induced me to rise to reply. I assured the committee I believe the subject of his anger was the more painful to him, as it was a subject which his honor would not permit him to investigate. Were it *false*, as he affirmed, he certainly would not avoid even the most strict

65 This is the testimony of Parkinson. Bone and Higgins said that Smith alone was deputed; and Smith, who was probably lying, denied having any contact with Upton or his affairs, then or later.
66 He learned that the property was over-insured and that after the fire Upton absented himself until the insurance office advertised for him; whereupon Upton arranged for a friend to turn him in and they shared the £20 reward.

enquiries, when the censure must naturally fall upon the original aggressors. Were sufficient cause and foundation wanting, his insolence in attacking the other branches of the society, when he had complaints (as he styled them) only against one, and in such an unmanly manner, appeared to me fully sufficient to deserve *censure*. The outrageous defence he had made rather inclined me to support the question more eagerly. The whole committee appeared equally sensible of his insolent and unjust attacks; but the unruly conduct of Upton prevented many from delivering their sentiments which he justly suspected were not much to his credit. The committee being unanimous against him, to avoid the disgrace of hearing his own censure, he was drawing towards the door, when Higgins rose to inform the committee that if they were about to sensure Upton, they must be quick, as he appeared to be "hopping off." Chagrined at his designs being discovered, his mortification was considerably increased at Higgins's mode of expressing himself, "you wretch," said Upton, "that is a reflection upon my natural infirmities,[67] and you and more shall repent of it before many weeks are over." Higgins replied, "that if he was to retort upon him his own language, he would tell him *he lied*," but he would only say he did not speak with the intentions imputed to him. Higgins was called *to order* and asked pardon for having unwarily entered into what might be construed as personalities. The question for Upton's censure being now put, and carried nearly unanimously, Upton again arose, and reflecting upon the apology of Higgins, turned towards me and said "he never could or *would* rest satisfied until he had *revenged himself on Lemaitre*, and obtained satisfaction for the insult he had occasioned." Hearing which I gave him my address, told him I was ever ready to answer for my conduct to any man or set of men. That it was plain I was not as he was, *led away* by my *anger and passion*, and that although Higgins had apologised *I would not*; having acted in the same consistent manner I ever would on similar occasions; and should ever strive to prove the *dangerous tendency* of anonymous letters to society in general, by whom they were *as justly as generally reprobated*; and concluded by observing, if this would satisfy him, I never had any the most remote intentions to do as he had done to me, to give any personal insult, but my intentions were confined solely to reprobate his behaviour, which certainly deserved rebuke, if not execration. As Upton continued still unruly, a mem-

ber moved his expulsion from the society, which I likewise seconded, but it being represented that a little reflection might give him a proper sense of his conduct, this motion was withdrawn.

[Two days later Upton sent Lemaitre a letter challenging him to a duel in Lincoln's Inn Fields. (Lemaitre later thought the letter was sent only to secure a specimen of his handwriting on a reply.) Although he rejected Upton's challenge as childish, Lemaitre was visited about it by some alarmed LCS members he had never seen before. They said that if he did not become reconciled with Upton, the LCS might get the reputation of being a set of ruffians. To quiet their fears Lemaitre agreed to meet Upton that night to say he was sorry if he had insulted Upton personally and Upton to say he was sorry he had sent the letters in question. They met at Pearce's house, with Brooks present as a witness for Upton and Groves for Lemaitre. After they had apologized and shaken hands, Upton asked Lemaitre to introduce in the general committee a motion forbidding any member to accuse another unless he had direct proof. Lemaitre agreed and did introduce the motion, presumably on 11 September.

At the 11 September meeting of the general committee, there was a motion to censure Upton 'for seeking to destroy the confidence of the society in their Executive Committee'. Since Upton was not present that night, Lemaitre moved the adjournment of the motion and said he would oppose it as being included in the censure passed on 4 September. At the next meeting of the general committee (18 September), Lemaitre moved for the consideration of this adjourned motion. Upton, who was present this time, misunderstood Lemaitre's motives and began to make hostile comments about Lemaitre, who then called him to order and asked him to restrain his comments until he saw whether the motion would be supported. It was 'got rid of' without any debate.

At one of these two meetings of the general committee Parkinson recommended that the committee of correspondence reply to Upton's letter (presumably the letter about the indictment rather than the anonymous Pasquin letter). The general committee ordered this done and Parkinson was asked to write it. In his letter Parkinson repeated the suggestion that Upton with-

---

67 Upton had a club foot.

222

draw, but softened the request by saying that the committee had not charged Upton with any crime, but thought that his name on the list would lessen the number of subscriptions. Parkinson gave the letter to Beck, the recorder, who handed it to Upton at the meeting on 25 September.

During that meeting Lemaitre accused Metcalfe of being a spy and moved that a deputation of four be appointed to investigate his character and Groves's. According to Lemaitre, his accusation, his motion and the general proceedings of the meeting met with continued opposition from Upton, whose anger, which had been very visible before, was now at a high pitch.

Within the next two days Upton reported to government that Lemaitre, Smith, Higgins and Crossfield had ordered the construction of an air gun and had discussed shooting poisoned arrows to assassinate the king. He asserted that late in August Smith, Higgins, Crossfield and Peregrine Palmer (an attorney) decided to have an air gun made. Crossfield ordered a model from John Hill, a turner who was also an LCS member. On 4 September (according to Upton) Smith, Lemaitre and Higgins discussed using the gun to shoot poisoned arrows at 'Royal Game' and, as practice, at Pitt and Dundas in the theatre. About 11 September Smith called Upton out of the room where the general committee met (in Academy Court, Chancery Lane), pulled a two-foot long brass pipe from under his coat, told Upton that Lemaitre wanted an air gun made with it, and intimated that the committee of correspondence would pay for it. In the next two weeks Smith gave Upton two letters from Lemaitre about the gun.

When questioned by the Privy Council, Lemaitre said he knew nothing about an air gun. When shown the letters he supposedly sent, he admitted the handwriting was similar to his but denied writing them. (On one of them he saw the statement, 'Brass is not ready, nor poison prepared'.) Higgins testified that he hardly knew Upton or Lemaitre outside the committee room. Smith also denied all Upton's statements involving him in the plot. From other testimony, it appears that Smith and Higgins, far from conspiring with Lemaitre, distrusted him because he was friendly with Groves, who was widely denounced as a spy.

Upton and Crossfield did order a model air gun from Hill; Upton and another man (probably Crossfield) bought brass tubes.

Crossfield said that Upton wanted an air gun. And Upton, as recounted above, said it was Crossfield, Lemaitre, Smith and Higgins. Very likely, Upton was acting as an agent provocateur, encouraging Crossfield to treason.]

251. Report from spy Metcalfe: LCS Committee of Correspondence, 5 September 1794[68]

Source: TS 11/956/3501

Meeting of the Committee of Correspondence of the London Corresponding Society on Friday 5th. September 1794 at Citn. Metcalfe's

Present Citizens Metcalfe
                Hodgson
                Higgins
                Bone
                Smith
                Burks
                Parkinson

Citizen Hodgson reported that he had made some enquiry concerning a Monument proposed to be put up for Citn Hardy's Wife, but that he had not yet obtained full information, adjourned further enquiry to be made.

A proof was produced of an Address to the public upon the subject of the late Riots, intitled Reformers no Rioters,[69] Citizen Burks was appointed to correct the press. and to procure 500 to be delivered on Monday

A Letter of Condolence and Consolation from the Society to Citizen Hardy upon the Death of his Wife was produced by Citizen Bone, which being read was much approved, and Citizen Higgins was deputed to transcribe same and convey it forthwith to Citn. Hardy

Report from the General Committee of Money Reced. in the last Week
    For Wives and Children £4 . 4 . 6
    For Genl. Purposes   .. 9 ..
                             ―――――――
                          4 .. 13 .. 6

68 Description: 'Committee of Correspondence of the London Corresponding Society Friday 5th. Septr. 1794'.

69 *Reformers No Rioters.* This 8pp. pamphlet denies charges that the LCS instigated the riots of mid-August; it urges that blame for them be given to the men who connive at crimping and kidnapping; and it restates the LCS principles that 'the voice of the people ought to be heard in the councils of the nation' and that reason, firmness and unanimity were their only arms.

Ordered Two Guineas to be paid Davidson the Printer on Account

Report of Vote of Censure to Citizen Upton

Report of Acquittal of Citn. Groves Citizen Parkinson expressed his astonishment at Groves, acquittal, he said there could not be a doubt of his Guilt and that if this Committee did not pursue the matter to his exclusion from the Society he would attend at the next General Committee, and would tell him to his face he was a Villain, and that he never would quit him until he had procured his expulsion from the Society./ he also said that he would demand the two Affidts. produced on the last Genl. Committee to be deposited with the Committee in Order that they might undergo Minute examination and to ascertain whether they had ever been sworn as they appeared to have been before Mr. Justice Addington./

Adjourned

252. Report from spy Metcalfe: LCS General Committee, 11 September 1794[70]

Source: TS 11/956/3501

Meeting of the General Committee of the London Corresponding Society on Thursday 11th. September 1794 in New Compton Street

Citizen Ramsey in the Chair
29 other Citizens present

Report of New Members made since last Committee 8

After which a Motion from Division 27 was read, stating their opinion that the Evidence produced by Citizen Groves on the last General Committee night did by no means satisfy them of his innocence, and that he ought therefore to be excluded from any Office in the Society until he had proved by his Civism that he was a true friend to Freedom and humanity./.

Upon this Motion being seconded, a most violent debate took place, several speakers conceiving the Motion to be an insult upon the General Committee, charging them with not having done their duty &c. and Citizen Bone moved a Vote of Censure on that Division, &c. several Citizens spoke as warmly in favor of the Division, and particularly Citizen Parkinson who attributed the conduct of the Division to a laudable Zeal for the safety and Security of

70 Metcalfe's description: 'Genl Committee of the London Correspg. Society /11th. Septr. 1794./'

the Society, and which the late Verdicts in Scotland obtain'd by means of some of the Members of this Society[71] renderd it more than ever necessary, that they should be careful whom they admitted amongst them, the Debate had subsided nearly when Citizen Burks produced a Motion from Divisions 6 & 11 to nearly the same purport, this renewed the Debate with increased heat and much personal abuse passed, several Motions were made some for Censuring the Delegates of those Divisions some for censuring the Divisions, &c. Citizen Burks defended his conduct and said Divisions 6 & 11 had acted for themselves he was a Delegate and Obliged to bring their opinion to the General Committee, he said they were induced in a great measure to send the Motion he had brought on account of Citizen Groves not having deposited the Affidavits he and Williamson the Messenger had made.

71 On 3 Sept. Gosling and Taylor revealed themselves as spies by willingly testifying against the LCS at the trial in Edinburgh of Robert Watt for high treason. On 5 Sept. Taylor testified at the trial of David Downie. They testified only to Hardy's handwriting and the resolutions of the general meetings of 20 Jan and 14 April. There was no evidence that Hardy or any other LCS member had any acquaintance or correspondence with either of the accused men (*ST* vol. 23, cols. 1167–1404, and vol. 24, cols. 1–200).

Watt, who was executed on 15 Oct. (just two weeks before Hardy's trial opened), became a spy in 1791 and (so he confessed) a convert to reform in 1793. With the assistance of David Downie he planned a revolution by which Edinburgh, London and Dublin would be taken over in one night and Parliament replaced by a convention. In pursuit of this plan they ordered a quantity of pikes. Many LCS members and others believed that Watt invented this plan in order to collect a reward by betraying any other conspirators.

These trials are of special significance as revealing the argument government was to use at Hardy's trial two months later, that the LCS masterminded other reform activities. At the trials of both Watt and Downie the prosecution started with the letter of 17 May 1793 from Hardy ('who was secretary to a seditious society in London, of great magnitude') to Skirving asking what measures for reform the Scotch meant to pursue. The prosecution introduced other documents of the LCS and the minutes of the British Convention in Edinburgh in 1793. (Watt and Downie were accused of being members of a committee composed of men who had supported the British Convention.) Connecting the British Convention with Hardy's letter was a departure from the line of argument pursued in the earlier trials of men active in the British Convention (Skirving, Margarot, Gerrald). In those trials there had been no attempt to implicate the LCS in the deeds of the convention.

with the Committee that they might be strictly examined, if there was no loop hole no reservation in them and if they were regularly sworn &c. here Citizen Groves got up and laying his hand to his Heart exclaimed: *No By God there was no Mental reservation, he had sworn in positive Terms that he had not seen Williamson the Messenger or knew he was in Town until after Ross was apprehended*, Citizen Bone then made a Motion that Citizen Groves deposit the two Affidavits with the Society, which Citizen Groves acceeded to, after which upon the Motion of Citizen Le Maitre, the Motions of Divisions 27. 6 and 11 were delivered to the Delegates of those Divisions and they were desired to acquaint their Constituents with what had passed which it was hoped would satisfy them

Motions concerning a Monumental stone to Mrs. Hardys memory &c. adjourned

Report of Money received. £2. 4. 6

The Committee being in considerable confusion and much heat and altercation still passing. a Motion for adjournment was carried

> Not a Sylable passed concerning the late Verdicts in Scotland, but what was mentioned by Citn. Parkinson in the debate on *Groves* &c

253. Report from spy Metcalfe: LCS General Committee, 18 September 1794[72]

Source: TS 11/956/3501

Meeting of the General Committee of the London Corresponding Society on Thursday 18th. September 1794 in Academy Court Chancery Lane

> Citizen Metcalfe in the Chair
> 24 other Citizens present

Report of New Members since last Committee 7

Citizen Groves produced two Affidavits of himself and Williamson the Messenger from Edinburgh, concerning the Apprehension of Ross (as mentioned in a former Report) which were referr'd to the Committee of Correspondence./

Two Motions were received from Divisions 13 & 18 "that a Committee of 4 be appointed to draw up the proceedings of the General Committee that the Delegates by taking a Copy

might be enabled to make a just and full report to their several Divisions, the consideration hereof adjourned to next General Committee.

A Motion that "a Recommendatory Letter to the several Divisions for Subscriptions towards the relief &c. of the Imprisoned Citizens" was referred to the Committee of Correspondence

A Motion that all recommendations from Divisions upon the Subject of a Constitution for the Society be deposited with the Secretary until such time as all the Divisions had delivered their opinions thereon, was carried in the Affirmative

Motions from Divisions 13 & 27. That Citizen Groves be suspended from his Functions were upon the Motion of Citizen Le Maitre Ordered to be returned to the Delegates of those Divisions

Report from the Committee of Correspondence, that a Publication would make its appearance in a few Days concerning the Conduct of Taylor & Gosling upon the Tryals at Edinburgh &c.[73]

> Report of Money reced £1. 4. 6
> Adjourned

Citizen Bone applyed to me this Day, being directed by the Committee of Correspondence to request I would undertake the Defence of the several Imprisoned Citizens, in the Tower and Newgate./.[74]

72 Metcaife's description: 'Meeting of General Committee of the London Correspg Society on Thursday 18th September 1794'.

73 *A Vindication of the London Corresponding Society.* This 15 pp. pamphlet by Parkinson refutes attacks on the LCS in the newspapers, in handbills and at the trials of Watt and Downie. It also details the provocative activities of Gosling and Taylor in the Society. Denying that the LCS ever advocated force, it concludes, 'Reason is the only weapon which they have wielded, or proposed to wield.' At the end is a list of men receiving subscriptions for families of state prisoners: Eaton, Smith, Hodgson, Cooper, Hill, Powell and (new to the list) Burks, 52 Crispin St, Spitalfields.
Like Parkinson's other writings, this pamphlet is well reasoned and free from libertarian clichés. It was in print by 7 Oct. when Parkinson acknowledged his authorship to the Privy Council. While it was in press someone – perhaps Parkinson himself – thought it improper to publish the work before the impending trials. Accordingly, the press was stopped after only 250 of the projected 2000 copies (Parkinson's account of his examination before the Privy Council, in *Assassination of the King*, p. 59).

74 About this time Beck and Hodgson approached Thomas Erskine on behalf of Baxter and Lovett. Erskine agreed to represent them ('their inability to render me any professional compensation, does not remove them at a greater distance from me') and explained that they must apply to the

254. Report from spy Metcalfe: LCS Divisions 6 and 11, 23 and 30 September 1794

Source: TS 11/956/3501

Meeting of the 6th. & 11th. Divisions of the London Corresponding Society on Tuesday 23rd. September 1794[75]

15 Present

Report of Proceedings of last General Committee read
No Business done

Captain Morris Song, sold by *Burks*.

Meeting of the 6th. & 11th. Divisions of the London Corresponding Society on Tuesday 30th. September 1794 at the Parrott[76]

Present Citizens Burks
          Galloway
          Cuthbert
          Metcalfe
          Davies & 4 others

The business of renewing Tickets &c. was adjourned, the women of the House having been cautioned against receiving the Divisions any more at her house, and Citizens Burks undertook to provide a place for the Divisions to meet at on the next Week. On the breaking up of the Divisions I took Burks home to my house, where we enter'd into a long conversation upon the Subject of the apprehension of LeMaitre Higgins and Smith, Burks could not believe the Story of Upton to be true as there never appeared to be the least friendship between him and either of the prisoners, he believ'd it to be a Scheme of Upton's who was

court to assign him as their counsel (letter, Erskine to Hodgson, n.d., Add MSS 27813, fos. 3–3v). In the event, Erskine did not need to defend either man, but he did conduct the defence of Hardy and Tooke.
75 Description: 'Meeting of Divisions 6 & 11 of London / Correspondg Society 23 Septr. 1794'.
76 Description: 'Meeting of 6 & 11th Divisions of London Corresponding Society 30th. Septr. 1794'. This is the last report from Metcalfe, for he was revealed as a spy when government pressed him to help in the apprehension of the pop-gun plotters (letter, Metcalfe to Portland, 5 Jan. 1795, HO 42/34, fos. 11–12v). He may have been given one of the printed authorizations to collect subscriptions, dated 30 Sept. (Place Collection, vol. 36, fo. 168); for an LCS advertisement published 16 Oct. ends, 'Our friends are desired not to pay any money into the hands of W. Metcalfe, of Dowgate-Hill' (*MC* p. 1).

a needy Man, among other observations he let *drop that Citizen Hill had been with him since the*[77] *LeMaitre &c had been taken into Custody, very much alarmed and had told him that some short time since a Man whose person he was not acquainted with, had calld upon him and had given him directions to turn some thing like a Ruler, which the Man said was a Model for casting a brass tube*, and Hill was fearful it might be the instrument now said to be made for the purpose of Assassinating the King, and that he Hill would be Hanged and was out of the Way &c./

255. Report from spy Groves: LCS General Committee, 3 October 1794

Source: TS 11/965/3510A

Committee of Delegates
3d. O[ctober] 1794

Academy Court   Chancery Lane

Citizen Webb president

On calling over the Divisions in order to collect the Number of New Members, there appeared to have been only Two New Citizens made since the last Committee Night
    There were no Motions brought forward from any of the Divisions –
    The Order of the day was on a Referred Motion brought the preceding Committee Night by Citizen Callendar –
    Citizen Groves brought from No. 2 an Address produced in the Division by Citizen Corby (a Foreigner) with propositions, and a Resolution of the Division theron
    Vide the Address annexed[78] – It being read by the president, Citizen Bone moved – That the purport of it being correspondent with the Views of the Society, that it be referred to the Committee of Correspondence & the thanks of the Committee given to the Division theron –
          Resolved Unanimously
    The referred Motion was then read vizt.
    That it be referred to the Committee of Delegates to select four Delegates from the

77 This is the last word on the sheet; Metcalfe obviously intended a common noun to follow.
78 This address, dated 29 Sept., was obviously written in ignorance of the *Vindication* of the LCS, for it urges that the Society refute the calumnies spread about them and convince people of their good and just principles.

Committee in order to draw up the Report, to be made by each Delegate to his Division and that Copies of that Report so drawn up by the Committee of Four be sent to a certain place either on the Saturday Evg. or Monday Morning so that the Delegates might call for them and make *that* Report to the Divisions

The obvious meaning of the above Motion was, that from the inaccuracy of the Delegates in making the Reports, owing either to partiality or prejudice, when accusations were made made, each Delegate giving his own construction to the proceedings of the Committee; or, to a want of comprehension & inability to make the Report, whereby the Different Divisions could not understand the proceedings of the Commee, such a Committee of Four might arrange the Proceedings & thereby a true & fair statement be given, by which means the different Divsions and the Commee would be enabled to understand & act in unison with each other –

Citizen Groves rose & said, That most assuredly an arrangement of some kind was necessary; but that that arrangement ought to originate in the Divisions – for if the Divisions were to take the Report from such a select Committee, the Divisions would be directed by Four Delegates only, and that it was possible from a designed misrepresentation more injury might arise to the Society, than from any mistake that might be made by the free & unbiassed Opinion of each Delegate –

Besides – the Motion in itself seemed to convey a censure on the Delegates, & not only on them, but on the Divisions for choosing them, as it supposed a want of capacity in the Delegate & a sense of Discernment in the Division –

The next Objection was "Who would undertake the Task"? – The Committee sat always till Midnight – sometimes till near two oClock in the Morning – Each Delegate had his business to follow – perhaps obliged to be up at five oClock to work –

He confessed that in making a Report, especially when particular questions and specific determinations were combined, some discernment & abilities were necessary – but had not the Divisions Citizens of discernment & abilities among them? – If there was any fault the fault lay in the Divisions & with [them] the Correction ought to lay

Enter Mr Upton, followed by Mc.Manus, Jealous, Grant, Sleath, Kennedy &c &c &c

There was an immediate cry from two or three quarters "The Monster"!

Citizen Groves called To Order, & addressed himself to Mc.Manus asking If he wanted any

single individual or the whole Committee.

Mc.Manus replied, We want Mr Hodgson – Groves answered He is not here –

They all withdrew

A general confusion was ensuing When Groves called The Order of the Day & was Seconded by Calloway (Commee door kept open) Groves was proceeding when the officers re-entered with Upton who pointing to Burks said "That is the Secretary" – Burks was immediately secured

Mc.Manus & others began to seize the papers that lay on the Table Upton, pointing to Parkinson said "If there are any papers of consequence they are about that Man" – Parkinson was searched, as was also the President Webb –

The Officers withdrew with Burks & Calloway proposed an Adjournment, as the Runners might return & take somebody else – Seconded by Groves & Adjourned

Groves Calloway Ramsay & two or three others went to a public House in Butcher Row & there collected Six Shillings for Mrs. Burks

Calloway is to settle the place for the next Meeting of the Commee

[On 6 October a grand jury handed down indictments for treason against Thomas Hardy, John Horne Tooke, John Augustus Bonney, Stewart Kyd, Jeremiah Joyce, John Richter, John Thelwall, Thomas Wardle, John Baxter, Richard Hodgson, Thomas Holcroft and Matthew Moore.[79] They did not indict John Lovett, who had been arraigned with the others. The next day, the grand jury indicted John Martin, and two days later, John Hillier. When the jury reconvened on 16 October, they indicted

79 Hodgson and Moore were not imprisoned in 1794. Hodgson had been openly attending LCS meetings as late as Sept. He said that 'early in the business', presumably in Oct., he went to court to surrender, but the judges had gone to dinner. Intending to return after the judges had dined, Hodgson walked into the fields, where he met friends who persuaded him 'that to surrender would be foolhardiness'. Later, after the trials, he again went to the Old Bailey. This time he and a friend (Moore?) sat 'in a conspicuous place . . . though the judges saw us and knew us, there was no formal notice taken of us' ('Examination of R. Hodgson, before the Privy Council, 26th April 1798', *Proceedings of the General Committee of the London Corresponding Society on the 5th, 12th, and 19th of April, 1798, relative to the Resistance of a French Invasion . . . 1798*).

John Philip Franklow. On 21 October they indicted Thomas Spence, but not John Ashley, who had been in prison five months.

To prepare for the forthcoming trials, several LCS committees were appointed, probably by the committee of correspondence (Groves does not mention them in his reports of the general committee). On one of these committees was Francis Place, who had just joined the Society in June. Place's account of his committee work is, unfortunately, vague: 'I was very active and useful in directing others . . . those with whom I acted . . . were clever men in circumstances very superior to mine.'[80] John Pearce submitted the expenses of a 'committee of evidence' immediately after Hardy's trial. From the items on this bill and from the covering letter,[81] it appears that the committee of evidence served subpoenas for witnesses, arranged the expenses of bringing witnesses to London, searched for the will by which Gosling's stepson profited (the comparatively early disclosure that Taylor and Gosling were spies gave the LCS time to obtain evidence of Taylor's bigamy and Gosling's various shady activities). This 'committee of evidence' is probably the group designated by the spy James Powell as 'Hardy's committee', which met at No. 20 Old Bailey during the trials. The committee was composed of Burks, Bone, Dawes, Hobsworth (not mentioned until 1798 in LCS documents; he may be George Ebsworth, who was arrested in 1798), Moggeridge, Nash (not mentioned elsewhere), John Pearce the upholsterer, Seal, Webb, John Williams and Williams the engraver. According to Powell, the committee, but particularly Webb and Williams, examined potential witnesses and Pearce recorded their evidence in a book.[82] Finally, there is a 'committee for assisting in the Defence of the prisoners'. All that is known about them is that they deny writing an anonymous letter allegedly sent into court during the trials.[83] Possibly this is a general name for all the *ad hoc* committees helping the state prisoners.]

256. Report from spy Groves: LCS Division 2, 6 October 1794[84]

Source: TS 11/965/3510A

London Corresponding Society

Division No. 2

Monday Octr. 6. 1794

White Horse   Winslow Street   Oxford Street

Only fourteen Citizens met this Evening Seven of whom were Visitors from the other Divisions and the other Seven Members of the above Division –

It is manifest that from the general desertions of the Citizens at their respective places of Meeting, the proceedings of Government have struck a terror into some and a damp into others

Out of the thirty one late existing Divisions not more than fourteen now meet, & those in so few a number that the standing regulation of not proceeding to business till Nine Citizens have assembled is generally dispensed with

The very strong proof to support this is, the consideration that the Number of Citizens belonging to No. 2 amounted lately to very near 700 –

Division No. 2 was always considered as the leading Division, and which the other Divisions looked up to as the parent Division –

The number of Citizens who have renewed their Tickets in this Division for the ensuing Quarter, vizt., from Michs. to Christmas, amount to only Thirty – Of these Thirty Seven only met.

The Events, therefore, of the pending Trials, seem to me to be decisive of the Existence, or Non Existence, of the London Corresponding Society; at least so far as may tend either to continue a jealousy in the eye of Government, or to totally dispense with its fears and apprehensions on account of that Society –

Out of the Seven Citizens who met there were only four active ones, vizt Jones, Groves, Matthison & Candie – They made Necessity a Virtue & proceeded to business. Cn. Groves made his Report from the Committee of Delegates (to which he was Sub-Delegate) of the proceedings at Lunans in Academy Court, and the Apprehension of the Secretary (nominal) Citizen Burks.

The Division then proceeded to elect their Officers for the ensuing Quarter

80 *Autobiography*, p. 132.
81 Letter, Pearce to Burks, 7 Nov. 1794; 'An Acct. of Money expended in Subpoenaing Witnesses and Other incidental expences attending – The Trial of Thos. Hardy', Add MSS 27813, fos. 5–8.
82 'Minutes of James Powel's Informn.', TS 11/958/3503.
83 Draft letter, 'Sec' to P. Foulkes (i.e. Erskine's assistant), n.d., Add MSS 27816, fo. 579.

84 Government description: 'L. C. S. / Report of Division 2 / Octr. 6th. 1794'.

Citizen Groves was nominated & seconded, for Delegate.

Citizen Candie was put up in opposition – A Ballot took place & the Numbers were

> for Cn Groves   4
> for Cn. Candie   2

Groves was therefore elected Delegate

Citizen Candie & Cn. Jones were nominated as Sub-Delegates

On the Ballot there appeared equal numbers for both – the Chairman gave the Casting Vote for Cn. Candie

Jones was unanimously elected Tithing Man – He is already Secretary to the Division

There being no other business the Division Adjourned –

The Adjournment was moved for on the ground of an apprehension of a Similar Visit to the Division as was paid the Committee on the last Thursday Night.

257. Report from spy Groves: LCS General Committee, 9 October 1794[85]

Source: TS 11/965/3510A

London Corresponding Society
Committee of Delegates – 9th. Octr. 1794

On account of the events that took place at Lunan's in Academy Court Chancery Lane on the preceding Committee Night, when Upton and the Bow Street officers made their appearance, & also on account of a Note delivered to president Webb that Lunan was a Traitor, the Committee were under a difficulty of appointing a place for the next Night

Citizen Groves offered his House for the next Meeting – Cn. Candie offered his Apartments – Cn. Calloway was to let the Delegates know, in the mean time, where to meet –

As this information was not communicated till the Evening of the 9th. some of the Delegates went [to] Grove'ss & others to Candie's; but at last the whole (fourteen) met at the latters which is in Whych Street Drury Lane

The Conversation was chiefly upon the Subject of Upton (who is universally execrated) & Higgins & LeMaitre who are deemed innocent[86] –

Cn. Bone was called to the Chair   There were no New Members made nor any Motions brought forward.

The Collections for General purposes amounted 1£. 17s. 4d. for that Week

The Chairman moved that it be delivered to Mrs. Smith for the purpose of her conveying it to the Committee of Correspondence, & Citn. Ramsay was appointed for that purpose

Cn. Groves brought Twelve Shillings and Six Pence, being a Subscription of Five Gentlemen, for the Use of Mrs. Smith & her family, who has four small Children

He recd. the thanks of the Division for his exertions, & was desired to pay it himself to Mrs. Smith –

The Chairman in a short preface in which he adverted to the late Visit in Academy Court and also to the thinness of the number of Delegates present, & also to the expectations of another Visit of a similar kind, proposed an adjournment not only of the Commee of Delegates; but also of the Divisions, for a time – The Motion was seconded

It was opposed by all the rest on the grounds of its being

> 1st: A desertion, base & cowardly, of the Suffering patriots –

> 2dly. That it was now the identical time to shew their Zeal Courage & firmness, to support the principles of the London Corresponding Society, vizt. a Reform in Parliament –

> 3dly. That the Chief Justice had delivered his opinion that the Subject had a right to meet to consult upon such Reform, & legally & peacably discuss the form of Government – &

> 4thly. That if ever the Meetings of the Divisions were prorogued, or they should know that the Committee declined Meeting it would instil such a principle of fear, that they would never meet again, nor could all the efforts of the most zealous & active Citizens ever restore the Meetings, & the Society itself would be cut up, which it had pledged itself to the World, nothing should ever do, till their just & honest views were accomplished –

The Motion was withdrawn – The Chairman proposed an immediate Adjournment –

Adjourned accordy

85 Groves's description: 'London Correspg. Society / Report of Committee / of Delegates / 9th. Octr. 1794'.
86 An advertisement for subscriptions, published 16 Oct., implies that the LCS was contemplating a prosecution against Upton: The LCS 'have suspended their applications to a generous Public, while imputations of a horrid nature lay against some of the persons who were appointed to receive such contributions; and understanding that the prosucution of the persons accused is necessary in point of law to found a prosecution for the conspiracy which appears to have been formed against them, they patiently wait the issue' (*MC* p. 1).

258. Report from spy Groves: LCS Division 2, 13 October 1794 [87]

Source: TS 11/965/3510A

London Corresp Society — Division 2
Octr. 13th. 1794. -

Winslow Street   Oxford Street –

On this Evening there was a more numerous Meeting than had been for some time past – Twelve Members of the Division met, & an equal Number of other Members of the Society from other Divisions

The principals were Calloway, Ramsay Candie, Groves, Jones, Matthison, Cooper, Burks, Hastie, Thomas, Cordey (a Foreigner) & Seal –

Hastie was called to the Chair – Groves made the Report from the Committee of Delegates.

The concurrence (of all but Two) of the Committee of Delegates) to continue the Meetings of the Divisions & Comittee of Delegates met with unanimous approbation, & an Opinion given by the Reporter that the Committee, of Delegates being the Servants of the different Divisions had not a right to adjourn their Meetings without the consent of the Divisions, was much approved of

Matthison spoke to this effect, & said he should continue to meet altho' it cost him his Life

One New Member was made, which makes the Number of this Division exactly 31.

Fourteen Shillings for Renewed Tickets on the last and on this Division Night, were collected –

Citizens Matthison & Thomas were elected Tithingmen, so that there are now three Tithingmen to this Division, there being Thirty one Members

A desultory conversation on the Utility of Tithing-men took place, started by Cooper who argued against their Utility & stated them as inconveniences

He was answered by Cn. Calloway – Cn. Matthison said that as the Citizen who spoke last but one had decried the necessity of Tithing-men & stated that his Division (No. 5) had none, it was only a proof that No. 5 had neglected its duty, & that Division 2 was always looked up to as an example of order

and regularity, it was a proof also that Division 2 had done its duty –

Citizen Groves was called on, as Delegate, to explain the Meaning & Use of Tithing-Men

He said it was the Duty of Tithing-Men to rally the Members whenever occasioned called for a full Meeting, & to incite them, generally, to as due an attendance as business would permit the Citizens –

Another Reason for Tithing-Men he said was, to give each Division a proportionate share in the Representation in the Committee of Delegates, the Tithing-Men having voices there — For instance – if a Division consisted of 50, it had a right to send 5 Tithing-Men to the Committee, & so on if more or less – for as the institution of the Society was an adequate representation in the House of Commons, a similar principle held good in the Society itself –

He contrasted the Representation of Old Sarum with the Non-representation of Manchester & recommended consistency to the Divisions –

The Members of Division 2 took fire at the idea of any Member of another Division, presuming to interfere & direct in the choice of Officers, or to teach No. 2 its duty –

Citn. Cooper was called to Order

Cn. Jones, in a long speech – principally concerning himself & the hourly danger he stood in of being seized, & prosecuted as a marked victim of ministerial vengeance (by the bye, tho' a sensible Citizen, a scholar, & a very decent Speaker he is a compleat Egotist) said he had prepared a Hand-bill which he wished to be stuck up all over London – he said it was spirited & firm – In the course of his Speech he recommended attending the Trials in Numbers to shew respectability & perseverance, & respect to their imprisoned Bretheren.

Citizen Burks called to know if the Division could be indulged *then*, with the reading of it

Jones replied No, it was not yet compleat – He was requested by Callaway to compleat it by Thursday   Cn. Groves hoped that whenever it was produced it would be temperate & cool for every thing violent inflammatory & recriminating could never do the Society good, but might tend to injure those who were going to take their trials for their lives – that it ought to be laid first before the Commee, which wod. send it to the Divisions if it was approved. Jones appealed to his former productions as a precedent for his coolness & steadiness –

The proper Certificates for the Officers of the Division were made out to be delivered to the Commee of Delegates, & then the Division adjourned.

87 Groves's description: 'L. C. Society / Report of Division Two / 13th Octr. 1794'.

259. Report from spy Groves: LCS General Committee, 16 October 1794[88]

Source: TS 11/965/3510A

London Corresponding Society

General Committee –   October 13.[89] 1794

Held at Citizen Candie's

Citizen Seal in the Chair

On calling over the different Divisions for taking the Number of New-Made Members there appeared to have been Three made during the preceding Week

There were no new Motions brought from any of the Divisions

The Delegates & Sub Delegates appear to consist chiefly of those who have served the Officers the previous Quarter & who are re-elected –

Of Delegates Sub Delegates & Tithing-men there were 25 present.

An Adjourned Motion brought by Citizen Calloway to appoint a Deputation of Four in order to make out the Reports of the Proceedings of the Commee, in order to let the different Divisions have one & the same Report, & to prevent misrepresentation, was, on Motion, again Adjourned, – the Original Written Motion not having been brought by Citzen Burks the Secretary.

The Subscriptions & Collections for the Week amounted to 52 .. 6 . 8. exclusive of 1£. 0s 8d collected this Evening for General purposes – Secretary Burks informed the Commee that the Rt. Honble Chas. James Fox had sent a Donation to the Commee of Correspondence of 10£ – for which the Commee had voted him a Letter of Thanks & that it had been sent.

Citizen Groves enquired if Mr Fox had sent the 10£. as a present from himself, or from any one else, who had conveyed it to the Comee through the hands of Mr Fox

The Secretary replied, As a present from himself –

Cn. Groves thought that the present coming

from Mr Fox might have had another round 0 put to it which wod. have made it an 100£. –

Burks said perhaps it was sent at a time when Mr Fox was in a run of *ill luck* –

Groves answered that it would have been better for the Society if Mr Fox had postponed it to his *lucky* hour

Adjourned

Citizen Bone called upon Citizen Groves to state what had passed between him, Le Maitre, Upton, & Brooks, & Pearce, when the quarrel between Le Maitre & Upton was settled at Pearce's

The object Bone had in view was Whether the quarrel was terminated in a friendly amicable manner, & they appeared perfectly reconciled to each other, or, Whether it was made up between them on the principle that if the duel took place it would be a reflection on the Society & cause much mischief to it.

Cn. Groves explained

260. The trial of Hardy: 25 October – 5 November 1794[90]

Source: see n. 90

[On Friday, 25 October, Hardy and twelve of the other men indicted for treason were brought to the Session House of Old Bailey; the indictment against them was read; and all pleaded not guilty. The attorney general (Sir John Scott) announced that, since the prisoners intended to be tried separately, he would start with the trial of Thomas Hardy.[91]

Throughout the extremely long trial – eight days – Hardy was defended by Thomas Erskine and Vicary Gibbs.

The attorney general spent most of the first day of the trial (Tuesday, 28 October)

---

88 Groves's description: 'L C S. General Committee Oct. 13. 1794'. Government endorsement: 'Rx Octr. 18 1794. Mr. Groves'. This is the last report from Groves, for when the state prisoners received the list of government witnesses the LCS learned what some had long suspected, that Groves was a spy.

89 Thursday, the meeting day of the general committee, was the 16th, not the 13th.

90 'The Trial of Thomas Hardy for High Treason', *ST* vol. 24, cols. 199–1408. This version of the trial, taken in shorthand by Joseph Gurney, was originally published by Gurney (4 vols., 1795). There is another edition taken in shorthand by Ramsay and published by Ridgway (1794). Still another contemporary edition is that by Manoah Sibley (2 vols., 1795).

91 The decision to start with Hardy evidently reflects a change of plan. A long manuscript document entitled 'The King agt John Horne Tooke & others' refers throughout to 'Tooke and others'. In a different hand, Hardy's name has been inserted to go before Tooke's, and on the outside of the document is the note: 'Let Hardy be put first throughout' (TS 11/955/3499).

explaining the government's case against Hardy. The chief argument was similar to that used in the trials of Margarot and Gerrald (and repeated in Pitt's speech in Parliament when the *Report from the Committee of Secrecy* was presented): the real aim of the convention (in Hardy's case, the convention under discussion at the time of his arrest) was not to reform Parliament but to replace it.

Whereas in the trials in Scotland, the British Convention of 1793 was judged seditious on the ground that it was an attempt to overturn the constitution, at Hardy's trial the proposed convention of 1794 was presented as treasonable not by any difference in its aims but by a further interpretation of the notion of overturning the constitution: 'The life of the prince [is] so interwoven with the constitution of the state that an attempt to destroy the one is justly held to be a rebellious conspiracy against the other.' Scott pressed this point: 'This, I say, is a conspiracy to assume the sovereign power: it is a conspiracy therefore of necessity meant to depose the existing power, and of necessity to depose the king.' This conspiracy was alleged to have begun in 1791 or 1792 when 'someone' imported from France the plan to join together clubs and societies which were then to govern Britain upon the principles of French government. When the conspirators had diffused their ideas throughout the kingdom they planned to assemble a convention of delegates from the clubs and societies to assume the powers of government. 'You will find them inflaming the ignorant, under pretence of enlightening them.' In pursuance of this plan of diffusing revolutionary ideas, the leading members of the Society for Constitutional Information formed the London Corresponding Society. The London Corresponding Society aim of universal suffrage implies a government without a king. 'A representation of the people founded upon the principle of equal active citizenship of all men, must form a parliament into which no King, nor Lords could enter.'

This opening speech for the prosecution took Scott nine hours. That night when the Lord Chancellor learned that it had taken nine hours to outline the government case, he exclaimed, 'Then by God there is no treason.'[92]

After Scott's speech, the witnesses for the government began to testify.[93] Their testimony started on Tuesday, continued on Wednesday, Thursday, Friday and part of Saturday (29 October – 1 November). Many witnesses testified to seizing documents in the houses of reformers or to recognizing the handwriting of the documents or to hearing documents read at meetings. Large numbers of LCS publications were read, as were letters to and from the Society; also, minutes of meetings of the Society for Constitutional Information and letters to and from that society; and publications of the Sheffield Society for Constitutional Information. The spies Groves, Nodder, Sanderson, Gosling, Taylor and Lynam gave their accounts of meetings and of their conversations with LCS members. Metcalfe did not testify, though he was listed as a government witness.

Scott tried to connect Hardy with the arming societies in two ways. First, he had John Edwards and Samuel Williams testify to an indirect connection with weapons. For Edwards Hardy wrote on a slip of paper the address of a Sheffield pike-maker when Edwards was planning to start an exercise society. Williams asked Hardy if he knew anybody who wanted to buy a gun. Hardy did not, but he said that if he heard of anybody he would notify Williams. A couple of weeks later Hardy asked Williams for a gun, sold it, later sold two more for Williams. Hardy also gave Franklow's card to Williams, saying that Franklow was starting an arming society and needed someone to supply arms.

Franklow's arming society was the focus of Scott's second means of connecting Hardy with arming. Scott argued, despite objections from Hardy's counsel, that Hardy could be charged with the words and actions of any LCS member. Hence, Scott had witnesses testify about Franklow's exercise society. Government even carried the 'guilt by association' motif so far as to introduce evidence about the conspiracy of Watt (who had been executed in Edinburgh two weeks earlier). The argument was that since the LCS was associating with other reform societies to call a convention and since Watt (a member of one of these societies) was planning to arm people in Edinburgh just as Franklow was doing in London (and just as others were doing in Sheffield), there was obviously a conspiracy

92 *Memoir of Thomas Hardy*, p. 112.

93 Twelve days before the trial opened, Hardy had been given a list of the government witnesses, containing over 200 names.

to arm among the societies, including Watt's Friends of the People and Hardy's LCS. Watt had even said that he wished to write to Hardy.

The prosecution rested its case on Saturday afternoon. The weary jurors had been hearing testimony every night until after midnight, twice until after one in the morning. (At first, there had been a discussion of having the trial go on through the night.) On most of the nine days the trial resumed at eight or nine in the morning. There were two exceptions. On the third morning of testimony the court did not resume until eleven o'clock, perhaps out of pity for the jurors who had spent forty hours without taking off their clothes. On what little remained of the night between the first and second days of testimony (that is, between 12.15 a.m. and 8 a.m.) they had to rest on mattresses that the sheriffs had provided in the Session House. At the end of the next day's testimony, the jurors complained of this sleeping arrangement and the lack 'of the necessary refreshment of sleep'. They were then lodged at Hummums in Covent Garden and allowed extra time for rest the next morning. The extra time may also have been intended to give Hardy's counsel time to examine the papers presented by the prosecution. Two days later, at the request of Hardy's counsel, the court again opened later, this time at noon. Erskine said that he had been too ill to make use of the earlier period of extra time granted him. He pointed out that he reached home each night at two or three in the morning and had to be back in court a few hours later. He requested that court resume at noon the next day. Lord Chief Justice Eyre, the presiding judge, said that he could grant some time if Erskine would call no witnesses or would make no opening speech. Erskine rejected both alternatives. Alleging the fatigue of the jury, Eyre only reluctantly agreed to resume the trial the next day at eleven o'clock. Erskine again asked for the extra hour. Eyre replied, 'I feel so much for the situation of the jury, that on their account I cannot think of it.' A juror said, 'We are extremely willing to allow Mr Erskine another hour.'[94]

After the prosecution rested its case on Saturday, the defence of Hardy was opened by Erskine, who stressed that treason demanded that the accused intended to end the natural life of the king. (His cross-examinations of government witnesses in the LCS had shown that no one ever heard Hardy speak disrespectfully of the king, much less homicidally.) He also reminded the jury that the plan of reform laid down by the LCS was that advocated in the Duke of Richmond's letter to Colonel Sharman and accepted by Pitt in the 1780s. Erskine also reviewed the evidence brought against Hardy, ending with the attempt to lay Watt's crimes upon the shoulders of Hardy, 'though he never corresponded with him, nor saw him, nor heard of him, – to whose being he was an utter stranger'.[95]

Most of the witnesses for the defence testified (Saturday and Monday) to Hardy's good character: his former employer, his minister, tradesmen with whom he did business, a few present and former members of the LCS, men with the same interests in reform and men with no interest in it. Uniformly they described Hardy as quiet, reasonable, humble, peaceable. The Duke of Richmond produced his own copy of his famous letter. Sir Philip Francis, MP, and Daniel Stuart, of the Friends of the People, prominent men interested in reforming Parliament, testified that though they held slightly different views from Hardy, they did not regard the LCS as traitorous.

The closing speech for Hardy (Monday, 3 November) was made by Gibbs, who fainted after the first ten words of his speech. In a few minutes he recovered and continued. He reviewed the evidence, as did Sir John Mitford, in the closing speech for the prosecution (Tuesday). Mitford stressed similarities between the LCS and the French convention, LCS praises of the French, and LCS connections with the French. Lord Chief Justice Eyre then summed up the evidence (Tuesday and Wednesday, 5 November) and gave the case to the jury.

94 Years later Erskine said he had been told that Eyre was to be made a peer if he got a conviction in this trial (Lord Broughton, *Recollections of a Long Life*, 1865, vol. 2, p. 169).

95 Erskine's speech lasted seven hours. 'So prolonged and fatiguing were his exertions, that for some minutes before closing he was able to address the jury only in a whisper, and learning upon a table for support. . . . At the conclusion of his speech the audience broke into irrepressible acclamation, which was taken up and repeated by the gathered thousands without' ('Memoir', *Speeches of Lord Erskine*, ed. James L. High, 1876, vol. 1, p. 16). John Horne Tooke annotated his copy of Hardy's trial: 'This speech will live forever', quoted in *ST* vol. 24, col. 877).

They retired at 12.30 p.m. and returned at 3.35 p.m. with a verdict of not guilty.[96]

261. Narrative of LCS activities: October–December 1794

Sources: as notes

[News of Hardy's acquittal was cheered by the crowds that had gathered outside the Old Bailey each night of the trial. They huzzaed Hardy and his counsel, hissed and hooted the judges and magistrates. They also detached the horses from the carriages of Hardy, Erskine and Gibbs and drew these men to their homes (in Hardy's case, to his brother-in-law Walne's home). There were reports that the acquittal might be celebrated with illuminations, but the only one which the Lord Mayor saw was in Silver St in the window of a Mr Savage. The lights illuminated a transparency with the words 'The glorious Acquittal of Thomas Hardy'.[97]

But, as Pearce reminded Burks, 'the Business is not yet finished – further exertions must be made to restore the yet enslaved patriots to their Liberty'.[98] The only LCS exertions for which we have evidence is their paying the expenses of the witness in the trial of Taylor for bigamy[99] (he was convicted and fined one shilling). On the other side, government exertions in relation to the imprisoned men are clear: government was still trying to get a conviction for treason. John Horne Tooke was brought to trial on 16 November. Much of the evidence presented at Hardy's trial was repeated in the attempt to show that Tooke was the real leader of the SCI and that the SCI was responsible for what the LCS did. Tooke succeeded where Margarot had failed

and called as witness Pitt, who reluctantly admitted supporting reform meetings in the 1780s. Tooke was acquitted on 22 November.[100] Nine days later, starting on 1 December, Thelwall was tried on very much the same evidence as had been used in Hardy's trial. The weakness of the government case may be indicated by one new piece of evidence – a letter in which Thelwall asserted that he had 'been for 4 or 5 months past almost the sole labourer upon whom the fatigue, the danger and the exertions of the London Corresponding Society (the only avowed sans Culottes in the metropolis) have rested'.[101] It is hardly a letter with which to hang a man. On 5 December Thelwall too was acquitted.[102]

On 1 December, just before Thelwall's trial opened, Bonney, Joyce, Kyd and Holcroft (SCI members) were brought up for trial, no evidence against them was presented, and they were discharged. Baxter and Richter received the same treatment on 15 December. Also released on 15 December were John Edwards and Samuel Williams and the five Sheffield men who had been arrested in May (William Broomhead, Robert Moody, Henry Hill, George Widdeson and William Camage). Franklow, Hillier and Spence were released on 18 December. Hayward was bailed on 12 December.[103] These men had been in prison for seven months, knowing that their fate and that of men not yet arrested[104] depended on

100 Account of Tooke's trial in *ST* vol. 25.
101 To Allum, 13 Feb. 1794, TS 11/953/3497.
102 Account of Thelwall's trial in *State Trials for High Treason, Embellished with Portraits*, 1794.
103 The keeper of Newgate listed the lengths various LCS members had been in Newgate: Hardy, 13 days; Thelwall, 43; Richter, 53 (these three men were in the Tower before being moved to Newgate); Ashley, 155; Baxter, 161; Franklow, 200; Hayward, 202; Hillier, 208; Spence, 208; Smith, 212; and Roussel, 358 (PC 1/38/A117).
104 A few days after Hardy's arrest there was a rumour that 150 warrants for arrest had been 'backed by the Lord Mayor of London' (*Cambridge Intelligencer*, 17 May 1794, p. 2). Hardy had it on good authority that government had prepared 800 warrants of arrest, 300 of which were signed, some of them to be executed immediately if Hardy had been convicted (letter, Hardy to Place, 6 Dec. 1824, Add MSS 27817, fo. 128; this is repeated at the 1826 anniversary dinner celebrating Hardy's acquittal, fo. 138). Thelwall believed that government delayed sending Gerrald to New South Wales so that he could be indicted for treason if Hardy were convicted. Although Gerrald was convicted of sedition in March 1794, the order for his transpor-

96 The prosecutor, Sir John Scott (later Lord Eldon), never relinquished his belief in Hardy's guilt. Writing thirty years later, he explained that many thought the 'great Mass of Evidence' presented to the jury 'perplexed them so much that they were unable to draw the true Inferences from the Evidence'. (*Lord Eldon's Anecdote Book*, ed. Anthony L. J. Lincoln and Robert Lindley McEwen, 1960, p. 56.)
97 Letter, Paul Le Mesurier to the Duke of Portland, 6 Nov. 1794, HO 42/33. The Lord Mayor reprimanded Savage and, with considerable difficulty, put out the lights.
98 Letter, 7 Nov. 1794, Add MSS 27813, fo. 5.
99 Letter, Pearce to Burks, 7 Nov.

plot; Hardy, Thelwall, Richter, Baxter, Martin, Spence, Hillier and Franklow – indicted for high treason; Lovett, Ashley, Edwards and Williams – imprisoned for many weeks, but ultimately not indicted; Gerrald – convicted of sedition and awaiting transportation. In view of this large total of dependants and of the small number of active members, it is remarkable that the Society could still both survive and assume a role of leadership, as they did by renewing links with the Sheffield Constitutional Society (and perhaps also with other societies). A letter from Sheffield, dated 3 December, indicates that the LCS has approached them: 'The communication the Corresponding Society wished to open with us will be useful in promoting the cause of justice and truth.'[111]

The Society also tried to extend their influence by publishing the periodical, *The Politician*, which had been under discussion since July. The prospectus for the periodical was issued before 5 December, for an advertisement of this date states that the prospectus will be reprinted in the first issue.[112] The advertisement (probably written by Ashley, for a draft of it is in his handwriting[113]) states that the weekly

magazine 'is meant to disseminate Moral and Political Knowledge, to inculcate the Duties, as well as the Rights of Man'. At the end of the advertisement are two notes alluding to other matters. One is a further appeal for subscriptions for the wives and children of imprisoned members.[114] The other is a disclaimer of concern with any publications not directly in the name of the Society. In contrast to the Society's finances in June when they could not afford a single newspaper advertisement, they published this advertisement in nine papers at a cost of £4 6s 6d.[115]

The first number of *The Politician* was issued on 13 December. The eight page periodical ran for three more weeks until 3 January, when it was discontinued for financial reasons. The editors had assumed that if they avoided details and comments about contemporary events, they were liable to stamp duty of only two shillings per number, but the commission informed them otherwise. In the last issue the editor explained the reason for stopping publication and announced that when it was resumed *The Politician* would consist of a sheet and a half – that being the length not deemed libellous.]

111 William Chow to Hodgson, Add MSS 27813, fos. 11–12v.
112 *MC* 8 Dec. 1794, p. 1.
113 Place Collection, vol. 36, fo. 249.

114 Subscriptions will be received by Eaton, Smith, Burks, Richards, Hodgson, Powell, Cooper, Hill, Bone, Ashley and T. Emery, shoemaker, 41 Wardour St, Soho.
115 Place Collection, vol. 36, fo. 249.

PART SEVEN

1795A

(January–August)

Chronology

1795		Poor harvests and serious food shortages	Oct.	c. 15	Religious seceders form Friends of Religious and Civil Liberty
Jan.	3	The *Politician* folds			LCS adopts new constitution
Feb.	5	Habeas Corpus suspended to 1 July		26	LCS general meeting at Copenhagen House; Address to the Nation; Remonstrance to the King
March ?		LCS adopts new constitution			
March	6	Martin released from charge of treason			
	30	Division 12 secedes; forms London Reforming Society		29	Attack on king; opening of Parliament
April	5	Prussia makes peace with France		31	Proclamation offers reward for finding king's assailants
	6	Division 16 secedes; forms Friends of Liberty	Nov.	4	Proclamation against seditious activities
May		Lemaitre, Higgins and Smith bailed		5	Waltham Abbey outrage
	6	Martin released from prison		6	Grenville introduces Treasonable Practices Act
	15	Holland makes peace and allies with France	c. 9		*Reply of the LCS...*
June	23	Birmingham bread riot		10	Pitt introduces Seditious Meetings Act
	27	Parliament prorogued	Nov.–Dec.		Nationwide meetings and petitions against Pitt and Grenville Bills
	29	LCS general meeting at St George's Fields; Address to the Nation; Address to the King	Nov.	12	General meeting at Copenhagen House; petitions to King, Lords, Commons
July		Food rioting widespread in England		12	LCS correspondence published
	6–14	Crimping riots in London			
	15	Address to the King delivered to Portland	Dec.	7	General meeting at Marylebone Field; Address to the Nation; Petition to the King
	22	Spain and France make peace			
August	22	New French constitution; suffrage restricted		12	LCS adopts new regulations to circumvent 'Two Acts'
	31	Crossfield arrested for pop-gun plot			
Sept.	24	Division 27 secedes over religion		18	Pitt and Grenville Acts become law

262. The state of the Society: January–May 1795

Source: as notes

[Our knowledge of the activities of the LCS during the first half of 1795 is limited because there are no accounts of meetings before 2 July. Perhaps the Society preferred not to keep minutes, fearing that at some future time government might turn them against the Society. Government did try to replace the reports from the uncovered spies: Metcalfe made valiant efforts to recruit Burks as a spy. On 4 January, a Sunday, he went to Burks's home and told him 'that Government already had *one Spy* in the Committee of Correspondence, but they wished to have *another*, to report the proceedings, that they might be assured of his *fidelity* or *treachery*'.[1] Metcalfe returned on Tuesday and again on Wednesday; Burks was out both times. On Wednesday Metcalfe left word that Burks should come to his house. When Burks failed to do so, Metcalfe returned on Thursday and again pressed his proposals, offering to introduce Burks to Mr Ford at the Duke of Portland's office. Burks would receive an initial payment of 50 guineas and one guinea for each weekly report.

During the first six months of 1795 the membership, which had been declining since the arrests of 1794,[2] began to increase. The Society reported that there were seventeen active divisions at the beginning of March,[3] but the 'Treasurer's Acc't from April 9 to June 30' shows at most fourteen divisions sending dues during April.[4] In the first week of April eight divisions sent dues; by the last week, thirteen divisions. By the last meeting in June, sixteen divisions sent dues. There must have been divisions which were meeting but not submitting dues, for the minutes of 2 July show twenty-three divisions. 'The more thinking part of the common people', wrote Place, 'joined the reforming societies in great numbers.'[5]

While new members were joining the LCS, some old ones were dropping out, exhausted by their encounter with the full force of government. The most notable drop-out was Hardy, who never attended meetings after his acquittal.[6] He remained on good terms with the Society, on one occasion even suggesting a course of action for them, and Place, who probably did not meet Hardy until after his trial, became a close friend. After his release from prison, Hardy rented a shop at 36 Tavistock St and as early as 24 November 1794, was advertising as a boot and shoemaker.[7] Another who disappeared from the Society was John Lovett. After five months in prison, he found his hairdressing business had declined; and he emigrated to New York, where he operated a successful shop which combined a grocery shop, a tavern and a hairdressing establishment.[8]

Thelwall was a temporary drop-out from the Society but not from the reform movement. He explained that since he was tried for what Hardy said before he (Thelwall)

1 Letter, Burks to the editor of the *Telegraph*, 14 Jan. 1795, reprinted in Sampson Perry's *Oppression*. Metcalfe may have been eager to recruit a new spy in order to prove his continuing usefulness to government, which was planning to discontinue his annual allowance of £300 (Metcalfe's letter to Portland, 5 Jan. 1795). The spy on the committee was probably James Powell. It is astonishing that Metcalfe should reveal to the LCS the existence of a spy.

2 Place says that after the arrests of May 1794 the Society 'immediately increased in number' (Add MSS 27808, fo. 26). If so, it was a short-lived increase, as Metcalfe's report to government show.

3 'Prefatory Letter', *The Correspondence of the London Corresponding Society. . .* , 1795, p. 4.

4 Add MSS 27813, fos. 53, 63v–4v.

5 Add MSS 27808, fo. 28. Place estimated that by the end of May there were 2000 members regularly attending the weekly meetings (*Autobiography*, p. 140). This is too high a figure, but it does indicate a great increase over the number of members Place encountered at meetings the previous June when he joined the LCS.

6 Except to appear as a witness at a general committee meeting dealing with Martin's bill for representing Briellat in 1793.

7 *MC* p. 1. In 1797 Hardy moved to a shop at 161 Fleet St, where he remained until he retired in 1815. Place and Frend managed a fund to assist Hardy in his last years. He died in 1832.

8 *MP* 19 July 1797, p. 4; Add MSS 27814, fo. 74.

joined the LCS and Hardy was tried for what Thelwall said in his individual lectures, he decided he should quit either the lectures or the popular societies; otherwise one would be blamed for the other. Since he had a family to support, he chose to continue the lectures. Besides he believed he 'could do equal good with more security by standing independent'.[9] Therefore, he resumed lecturing at Beaufort Buildings on 4 February 1795.[10] He rejoined the LCS in November 1795, after the introduction of the Treason and Sedition Bills.

The activities of the Society before July are to be followed in the correspondence, published later in the year as *The Correspondence of the London Corresponding Society*. On 29 January, they wrote to Stanhope, thanking him for his protest against a motion of adjournment in the House of Lords on 6 January (this motion put an end to Stanhope's motion against interference in the internal affairs of France). This letter is signed by James Powell as president and J. Burks as secretary.[11] The Society's finances were strong enough to afford publication of this letter and Stanhope's polite reply in at least one newspaper.[12] On 15 February they wrote to the Duke of Portland, inviting him to send a representative (instead of spies) to meetings of the general committee.[13] On 9 May they wrote a circular letter 'to the Scotch Patriotic Societies', explaining that since the trials 'our sole attention has of necessity been turned towards the liquidation of our debts', and

'steady perseverance has now extricated us from every claim resting immediately on ourselves'.[14] The number of members, the letter continues, is rapidly increasing, and the Society intends to educate 'that part of our Countrymen who are ignorant of the true source of their sufferings' by means of cheap publications advocating universal suffrage and annual Parliaments; the LCS is discussing with some other reform societies the most effective mode of cooperating to obtain these reforms; when that is determined, other societies will be informed so that, if the plan meets their approval, they may agree to it. This letter is signed by John Ashley as secretary and Alexander Galloway as assistant secretary.[15]

This letter was inaccurate in stating that the sole business of the Society had been clearing its debts. In the time between the letters of 15 February and 9 May, the Society was in a state of upheaval over the constitution and, even more fundamentally, over the need for regulations in Society. 'Our unanimity was disturbed, and our very existence endangered, by the unhappy dissentions of some of the most active members [e.g. Baxter, Bone, Burks]; the result of which was the contending parties seceding, and forming two Societies', the London Reforming Society and the Friends of Liberty.[16] There are accounts of this quarrel in letters from two of the three seceding divisions and from the general committee to all the divisions.]

---

9 *Tribune* no. 15, reprinted as *Citizen Thelwall*. 'Advertisement', in *The speech of John Thelwall . . . November 12, 1795*, 1795, p. [i].

10 Advertisement, *MP* 4 Feb. 1795, p. 1. 'His lecture room', wrote Place, 'was a very large room fitted up with benches, so placed as to contain a great number of persons, the lectures were delivered in courses twice a week, on the wednesday and friday evenings. The price of admission was sixpence. The room was constantly crowded to excess. The lectures contained much loose declamation; they also contained many curious facts and statements but nothing which could be called either seditious or libellous, Thelwall entertained all the vulgar prejudices of the day. . . . These lectures had their share in producing and keeping up a state of irritation against the government' (Add MSS 27808, fo. 36). Thelwall's 1795 lectures are published in *Tribune*, 3 vols, 1796.

11 pp. 14–15.

12 *MP* 24 Feb. 1795, p. 3.

13 pp. 16–17. Also signed by James Powell and J. Burks.

14 The 'Treasurer's Acc't' shows (besides routine expenditures for candles, coals, stationery, door-keeper, Gerrald, Smith) payments clearing Davidson's long-standing debt, also 'Hawes clear'd off', and 'M. C. Brown pd off'. At the end of June the treasurer recorded a balance of £42 1s 4d. The expenses of the trials were being met by a subscription started in March by friends of reform outside the LCS.

15 pp. 26–7. Unless otherwise noted, Ashley and Galloway signed all letters and advertisements from the LCS from 9 May until 13 Nov. 1795, when Ashley alone is listed as signer. On 23 Nov. Galloway's name reappears with Ashley's on an advertisement. They co-signed documents until Feb 1796 when Ashley again became the only signer. Ashley probably signed all the letters of 1796, although the drafts do not contain signatures, nor do the copies published in the *MPM*. Ashley resigned as secretary at the end of 1796.

16 'Prefatory Letter', *Correspondence*, p. 4.

263. Letter: LCS Division 12 to General Committee, 30 March 1795[17]

Source: The Correspondence of the London Corresponding Society..., 1795, p. 18

CITIZENS,

With painful regret it is, that we the Members of the Twelfth Division, behold the dissensions that have so long continued to distract those Patriots who are associated for the salutary purpose of a "Reform in Parliament." When a calamitous War is continued, when corruption stalks abroad, when the Habeas Corpus Act is suspended, it is not a time for those whose pursuit is the good of their country, to cavil about trifles, or waste their time in futile disputes: – as such this Division has refrained, as much as possible, from entering into those personal disputes which have too long agitated the "Corresponding Society;" but they now find that you (the Committee of Delegates) have assumed power which never belonged to you; that you have treated our Delegate with contempt and reproach; that you have despised and neglected our motions, consequently have broken the laws of the society; therefore we determined to be just, and resolved not to establish a precedent of such base submission, do declare the social compact between us and you dissolved; and as we shall most probably institute another society, we hope that no other strife may take place between us, than "Who shall serve their country best." — But this Division, considering the embarrassed state of this society, will and do hold themselves bound to contribute their quota towards the annihilation of its debts, provided their subscriptions be applied solely to that purpose.

GEORGE STEAD, Chairman.
March 30, 1795.

264. Letter: LCS Division 16 to Members of the LCS, 6 April 1795[18]

Source: printed copy in Nuffield College Library, Oxford

A LETTER, &c.
TO THE MEMBERS OF THE
London Corresponding Society

As we have no doubt the tongue of slander and malevolence will be very active in misrepresenting our motives and intentions, we think it a duty which we owe, not only to ourselves, but to you, to make a fair representation of the circumstances which have led us to our present determination.

It may be recollected that at the period, when our fellow citizens were apprehended by warrants from the secretary of state; the Society had under their consideration the revised report of the constitution (and it deserves to be remarked, that the first report was made an article of accusation by the attorney-general; whereas the revised report was never mentioned on the trials, though they were found on several of those who were appre-apprehended) on the motion of Groves the spy, the further consideration of it was suspended till the fate of our imprisoned brethren should be made known.

The trial of Hardy developed a baseness of character which was hardly thought to exist in human nature; and to keep out of the Society persons of so infamous a description as those who appeared against him, it was thought adviseable to add a few more temporary articles for the admission of members to the original address and regulations, several motions to that effect came in to the general committee, who referred them to the committee of correspondence they again referred to Hodgson and Burks. Hodgson drew up what he called, A political creed; and to which nobody would subscribe but himself. Burks drew up six or seven articles which were submitted to the committe of correspondence, but the trial of Thelwall intervening prevented their deciding upon them. In the general committee an enquiry was made after these articles,

17 Address: 'To the GENERAL COMMITTEE of the LONDON CORRESPONDING SOCIETY'. Printed heading: 'SECESSION OF DIVISION XII'. This division seceded chiefly because it believed that John Bone, its delegate, had been badly treated: one division suggested he was a spy and another urged his expulsion from the Society (see next document and 268). After the secession, Div. 12 renamed itself the London Reforming Society. About the same time Div. 16 seceded, and another society of secessionists was formed, called the Friends of Liberty. James Powell, the spy, wrote a pamphlet (which I have not seen), the title of which suggests the contents: *The Immoral Procedure and Mental Despotism of the Seceding Members of the London Corresponding Society and the Cause of their Enmity* (listed in Place's bibliography of 1795 reform publications, Place Collection, vol. 37, fo. 3).

18 This division, after seceding from the LCS, formed the society of Friends of Liberty.

and no answer being made, Bone passed a very severe censure on the committee of correspondence for their neglect and delay, though he was a member of that committee, and knew what they had done, that they had been too much occupied in the salvation of that innestimable man, John Thelwall, to give them the necessary perfection for the general committee. Hodgson however informed them, that a citizen present had some articles in his pocket for their consideration, when Burks (rising) apologized to the committee for the imperfect state in which they were, and read them; the following is a copy. –

"Query. If a fortnight's enquiry would not be more eligible than the proposed one of a week?

I. Each candidate for admission to be proposed a fortnight previous to his election.
II. The proposer and seconder to be thoroughly acquainted with the political sentiments and general moral character.
III. The candidate to be proposed by a member of such division in which he is desirous to be enrolled, and the seconder to be a member likewise.
IV. That if a particular case should occur of a candidate being unknown to any but the proposer, the tything-men, or others nominated by the division, be deputed to enquire and this enquiry, if proved to be satisfactory, one of them shall become a seconder. This being deemed better than the mere formal seconding at present, too prevalent in the Society.
V. That on the night of admission, the name or names of the candidates be read by the president to the division, with the names of the proposer and seconder: he shall then ask each of them after the result of their enquiries, and the same to the vote of the division.
VI. Then if the candidate be accepted, the president shall address the new made members – perhaps in the words of the revised report, or any other that may be thought proper."

Whoever peruses these articles will clearly see that the object of the motions were provided for – that they required, or would admit of no alteration or improvement, we do not presume to say; but being short and confined to one object, and *that* the one required they might have been altered with very little trouble. Citizen Bone continued to throw out his censures against the committee of correspondence for not having brought them forward in a more perfect state; and when he had worked up the general committee to a sufficient degree of dis-

satisfaction, he then offered his service to prepare something that should be worthy of their acceptance, by the next Thursday. – He brought them forward according to promise; some of the members of the general committee were astonished at the production of such a voluminous body of articles, forty-seven in all, going into all the minutiae of constitution, and requiring considerable time and attention to come to any decision upon it. A majority however determined to proceed to the discussion, and went through sixteen that evening, leaving the rest to the Thursday following; accordingly they were resumed at past 12 o'clock, when several of the delegates had withdrawn; and to prevent their going who remained, the door was locked; and by 2 o'clock they got through the other thirty-one articles; to which was subjoined a recommendation to the divisions, "to adopt or reject them immediately, and return their answer by next Thursday night but some of the divisions had not seen them; 10th. and 16th. objectect them entirely, others required more time to consider them when, after agitating the Society for two or three weeks, in the course of which a great deal of animosity had been generated it was determined to adjourn their consideration, *sine die*. Prudence would have directed that they should have had a quiet rest but not so! for late one Thursday evening when some members had left the committee, and eleven only remained, one imprudent man re-agitated the subject, by enquiring after the new regulations: Bone (who knew the tender part), was determined not to lose this opportunity to dividing the Society: he therefore rose, and said. "Ah! the regulations – they ought not to be forgot – it is time that we should determine – if we wait for the refractory divisions, and those who have not yet sent in their answer, we shall never be able to decide upon them." It was moved by somebody, "that they decide upon them that evening," and seconded by Bone. This was objected to, but in vain; and when the question was put, that they be adopted as the regulations of the Society, six voted for them, the delegate of the 16th division against them; the delegate of the 10th had been instructed by his constituents to vote against them, but being in the chair, did not vote at all; the other delegates remained *neuter* because their constituents had neither approved nor rejected them; consequently they were carried by a majority. It was therefore reported they were carried by a majority of the divisions, and those which had not decided upon them, agreed to submit; not because they approved of them, but to prevent a schism. The 10th and 16th divisions contended that an artificial majority obtained in such a surreptitious manner, in the general committee, could not bind the Society, and was no proof that they were approved by a majority of individual members; an appeal was in consequence made to the Society, when those delegates who had supported the regulations in the committee, made use of every artifice and misrepresentation in their power, by visiting in different divisions, by asserting that we had no regulations to go by – that the Society would fall to pieces without these were adopted – that they were only to be temporary – and the best way to put an end to the present confusion was, by their immediate adoption – and that there was only two refractory divisions, who were fond of anarchy, that objected to them: by language of this kind, *perhaps*, a real majority was obtained. The 10th and 16th divisions still continue to object to the regulations, on the following grounds: 1st. It was not true, "that we had no regulations to go by," for there were the original regulations, which had served the Society in its most prosperous state, and led it through several storms; and which required very little addition to make it competent to every purpose we could want: there was also the revised report, which might as soon have been gone through as Bone's, both of which had this advantage, *his* was untried, *they* had gone throuh the law ordeal, and the attorney general found their composition too legal to admit of any objection: either of these would have "kept the Society from falling to pieces," consequently it was not *true*, that it was necessary to adopt Bone's for that purpose. 2ndly, Though we were told "They were only to be temporary," we could plainly see the faction who introduced and supported them, had determined they should be *permanent*; and to prove this beyond dispute, citizen Bennett, of the 16th division, put the question, and received for answer, "Certainly if they are found to answer our purpose they will be made *permanent*;" here the disguise was at once thrown off. 3dly, It appeared to us a most ridiculous, as well as false, assertion, that, "the best way to put an end to the present confusion was by their immediate adoption;" whereas it was them which had occasioned "the *present confusion*." Neither is it more true that "there were only two refractory divisions, who were fond of anarchy, that objected to them; for divisions 6 and 29, and some others rejected them also – (so much for the majority and manner in which it was obtained). 4thly, Some divisions having desired the addition of a few temporary articles for the exclusion of improper characters, it was the duty of the general committee to stop there: instead of that, regardless of their instructions, we have seen them bring forward a long system going into all the minutiae of constitution, and containing many exceptionable and dangerous articles; but what is still worse (if possible), allowing each division only one night to decide upon them, after hearing them read from the manuscript copy. 5thly, This copy, which contained forty-seven articles, was finally adopted without any alteration; yet when printed, there were but 45, thereby rerifying the observation, that "they who have submitted to *usurpation* in one instance, ought to prepare for it in another." 6thly, That though some divisions sent motions requesting the words, "Executive Committee," might be changed for Committee of Correspondence;[19] and other motions came for other alterations, all was lost in an overbearing majority, and that chiefly at the instance of a few individuals. 7thly, On a referred motion relating to the regulations, division 16th sent the following answer, "That having rejected the regulations *in to-to*, they could not consistent with their former resolution, take the question into consideration." When citizen Bone, assuming to himself all the power and judgment of the whole committee, took up their answer and cast it from him, with this expression, "They ought to be treated with something worse than contempt;" and so they were, for this insolent proceeding passed off unnoticed. On a motion from division 10th, he was pleased to say, "Shall we be dictated to by a few insignificant individuals, who, now that danger is over, peep from their lurking holes only to harrass and disturb the Society." Upon citizen Bennett's calling him to order, he said, "They had never met during the late prosecution;" this was contradicted by proving where they met and naming the delegates who attended for them during that period. At another time he said of them, "They were men without *honour* or *honesty*;" these repeated injuries and insults were suffered to pass off without any notice from the committee. 8thly, As citizens Hodgson and Burks had been appointed to prepare some articles for the Society, it was the duty of citizen Bone to have left it with them till they declined it, or the committee had taken it out of their hands: when the officious intrusion of his service was mentioned, he denied having

19 The implications of this change of name are more important than appears here: Stephen Cooper left the LCS because he disapproved of having an executive committee; though frequently asked to return, he refused (examination, 13 Jan. 1800, PC 1/3473).

any knowledge that Burks had drawn up, or was appointed to draw them up, at that time; though this is flatly contradicted by evidence who know that he saw them both in the committee of correspondence and general committee, where he passed the censure already mentioned.

During this period of altercation it was asserted that citizen Bone had several times been at the privy council, and the delegate of the 10th division was instructed to put the question to him, whether he had ever been there more than once? he at first refused to answer, "to gratify the insolence of that division;" but upon being told, the question was before the committee, and that it was a duty he owed them to answer it; he did so, by denying, positively, ever having been there more than once. This answer did not satisfy those who had entertained a suspicion to his disadvantage; it was therefore determined to bring forward an accusation in form. At the time appointed the parties attended, (and to throw out of our view every thing that is not immediately relevant:) citizen Bacon, who is a member of the 12th division, a member of the same congregation, and lives within four doors of citizen Bone, stated, "that he saw Bone's name among the witnesses who were to appear against our friends, and that no good citizen could do that;" this certainly amounted to nothing, because he might be subpoenaed: – he further stated, "that on Bone's being absent from meeting, one morning of the first day of the week (to use his own phrase), Bone was asked what kept him away, he replied to Bacon and another person who was present, that he had received an order to attend the privy council." Bone denied that any such conversation had ever taken place, or that he had ever been at the privy council on a Sunday. Bacon was asked if he could recollect the date, he replied, that having never expected to be called upon in that manner, he could not. – He was asked why he did not bring the other person with him; he replied, that he had no notice of coming there that evening, till seven o'clock, himself. – He was then asked the name of this person, which he refused to give aloud, as it might be a disadvantage to him in his business, but he would give it to the chairman and any other person, or any other two persons in an adjoining room, this was declined by the committee. Hodgson called him, an old fool, he was treated with contemptuous manners and language by some others, which served to irratate him; and he appeared both shocked and vexed at Bone's denying what he had so positively asserted, not from any motives of

ill will, but from a regard to the *truth*, and the safety of individuals.

It was proposed to the committee, that as the evidence was not sufficiently satisfactory to determine upon the case that night, it would be adviseable to defer it for one week; that citizen Bone's character could not suffer much by such a delay, neither could the Society; and in the mean time appoint two persons in whom they could confide for their integrity and impartiality, to get all the information possible against the Thursday following, and state it in a more concise and regular manner; for the evidence which had been given (abstracted from the ignorance and intemperance of the man who gave it) was by much too important lightly to pass over; more especially as it stood uncontradicted by any evidence but the naked assertion of the party accused; neither was it strong enough to convict. The general committee however did not think proper to accept to this proposal, but voted the accusation groundless, in as much, as it was the assertion of one man against another, and that citizen Bone deserved as much credit as citizen Bacon: by this means they shut the door against further information.

The 10th division when they heard the report of the general committee, saw they were determined to support a man, who on various accounts was a very improper person to be a member of such committee, resolved no more to send a delegate; the committee, when they were acquainted with it, on the motion of citizen Candy, sent them a deputation; unfortunately what was said by one of them only served to irritate the division from his defending Bone, and saying that the dissensions in the Society arose from a difference between Bone and Burks: whereas, they declared it arose from Bone alone; however the conduct of the other two was more conciliatory (and commands their respect and esteem) it drew from them a resolution to the following effect: "That if citizen Bone and his regulations were withdrawn from the committee they would continue with the Society." When this was laid before the committee it was treated with contempt; some said, Let them go, they are a set of disorderly men, we shall be better without them. Citizen Candy, who was one of the deputation, denied that they were more disorderly than any other division of the Corresponding Society and recommended it to citizen Bone to withdraw, so did citizens Vials, Ashley, and several others; but he declared his determination to keep his seat till he was expelled by the committee, or superceded by his division; consequently that division was lost to the Society by his obstinacy, and a majority in the committee.

The 16th division still continued to be a part of the Society but not less dissatisfied with Bone and the majority of the committee than the 10th. Still attached to the *body* of the Society they were anxious to preserve its union, and therefore sent the following motion, as their *ultimatum*, to the general committee it was drawn up with considerable care and attention, to avoid giving offence, and to prevent its being thrown out.

"That the general committee be requested to recommend to the divisions to change their delegates the ensuing quarter, as it may "tend to a reconciliation in the Society." On this motion they [p]assed to the *order of the day*; though as it related to themselves it was highly incongruous for them to decide upon it without such an appeal. They were in hopes by this motion Bone would be removed, and those who supported him; that a *change* of *men* would produce a *change* of *measures*; but that arbitrary and oblivious decree blasted their hopes, and left them without an alternative, but that of dwindling away by individuals, or separating in a mass: in one case they would be almost *lost* to the cause for which they has associated; in the other they are not without hopes of prosecuting it with more effect.

But this resolution was confirmed by the proceedings of the committee; on the Thursday preceeding a motion had been sent from division 3rd, requesting Bone might be expelled the committee, and another from division 5th, requesting he might be expelled *the Society*, and that they would support their motion by evidence. Accordingly citizen Davidson attended, and stated, that when he was at the treasury, a person came in, to whom Mr. Ford, in a very familiar manner, said, "Ah! Mr. Bone, how do you do? I am very glad to see you; but I am very busy at present, I shall be very glad if you will come tomorrow-morning. Mr Bone promised he would; and when he was going out at the door, Mr. Ford again repeated his request, desiring him not to fail; to which he replied, positively, he would not. The person who had Davidson in custody, asked him if he knew Bone: No, says Davidson; the other then said to him, He is one of your people, and comes here to give information.

Citizen Bone stated in his defence, that he went there in conquence of a letter he had received from Mr. Ford, desiring him to attend and enter in recognizance for his appearing at the pending trials, to give evidence, that he had the letter in his hand, and was three quar-

ters of an hour in conversation with Mr. Ford about it. This, Davidson positively contradicted, asserting, that he had nothing but his hat in his hand, that no more passed between him and Mr. Ford than he had already stated, and that he staid but a short time in the room. Though the general committee admitted there was some weight in what Davidson had stated; yet they were of opinion citizen Bone had given a very satisfactory answer; though there appeared some difference in their account, it might arise from the inattention of Davidson, who could not recollect the date: and at any rate, it was but the testimony of one man against one man; consequently ought not to be admitted as sufficient evidence. They therefore passed to the *order of the day*.

How the committee could come to such a decision, is to us astonishing. What sort of evidence do they want? Do they expect Mr. Ford to come to them, and declare the intercourse between him and Bone was only for the purpose specified? Is not the evidence of Davidson a flat contradiction of Bone? What credit is due to a man, who has been guilty of so much prevarication and falsehood? When he was asked if he had not been at the privy council more than once, he said, No; it is a poor evasion, to say, that the other times he was at the treasury, he only spoke to Mr. Ford; for we all know that Messrs. Ford, Wickham, Nepean, &c. were the persons who received communication from spies.

It is ridiculous, in the extreme, for the committee to say, it is but the evidence of one man against another. Have they not said the same of Bacon? And will they not say the same, if any number of individuals were to give evidence against Bone, when he has the effrontery to contradict them? What is this but a manouevre to screen a *guilty man*?

We cannot help remarking, that, from the conversation between Burks and Metcalfe, in which M. detailed the places of meeting, and proceedings of the committee of correspondence as a proof that government had a spy[20] in that committee and though he refused to give up his name, no doubt can remain on the mind of any man, that will exercise his judgment who *that* is.

The 16th division saw with concern the separation of the 10th from the Society; but

20 'Although we are under no apprehension, from what spies and informers may say of us, while they adhere to truth; the late trials have convinced us, it is not what we may say or do, but what they shall please to assert we have said or done, that renders caution necessary' - note in text.

247

they could not help admiring it, as a noble stand against the *usurpation, insolence*, and *treachery* of an individual, and those who supported him. Finding every effort of theirs ineffectual, to preserve the sinking credit of the Society, and to restore harmony and confidence to the committee, they chose to follow the example set them by the 10th division.

We regret the circumstances which have rendered indispensible our separation from men, with whom we have so long laboured for the common good: but, fully satisfied in our mind, that the measure we have adopted *is right*; that every man who had a regard for his personal safety, the principles on which the L. C. S. was founded, or the object it had in view will think and act as we have; that it is neither men nor names but principles, to which we should be attached; and when the Society have lost sight of them, it is a duty which we owe to ourselves and our country to separate from it, and pursue under another name and system, which promises to have more efect in the dissemination of knowledge, and a reform in the commons house of parliament.

Citizens we remain,
Friends of Liberty,   With all civic affection,
April 6th, 1795.   Yours
            STEPHEN COOPER, Secretary

265. Motion from LCS Division 7: 14 April 1795

Source: Place Collection, vol. 37, fos. 22v-3

London Corresponding Society
Division 7. April 14th. 1795

This Division having taken the late Disturbed State of the Society into their Consideration & it appears to them that it proceeded more from misrepresentation than any thing else, as at present there is scarcely two Divisions that has the Proceedings of the General Committee related to them in the same Manner –

In order to avoid the like for the future this Division Submits the following Resolution to the General Committee for their Consideration

Resolved   That 8 Persons be appointed to attend the General Committee regular, to take down their Proceedings but shall not vote, speak in, or be Members of that Committee four to set on each side of the Chairman

They shall set down all Motions, Recommendations vouchers &c-, brought to the Committee, as soon as they are delivered to the Chairman, leaving a Space between every one in Case any Motion or Motions should be made by any Member present

While the Motions &c, are discussing they shall write as many Reports as there is existing Divisions, & when discussed they shall mark each Motion &c. in what Manner it is disposed of, or if adjourned to what Time it is adjourned.

They shall compare all the Reports together to see if they agree & when the Business of the Committee is over, the Chairman shall read the Report to the Committee, which if not correct, he shall correct by taking the Sense of the Committee & when Correct all the Reports shall be signed by the Said Chairman & the Secretary as true Reports, & the Chairman shall deliver one to each Delegate, or sub Delegate when the Delegate is not present, & in Case of both being absent it shall be the Duty of the Secretary to convey a Report to that Delegate or sub Delegate, in Order that the Division may not be deprived of the Proceedings of the Committee.

It is also the Opinion of this Division that this Regulation should be put in practice immediately & not to be put of[f] till after the reading [of] the Circular Letter.

For if it should be the Resolution of the Society to set about forming another Constitution it is impossible to Say, or even think when such Constitution will be brought into Practice.

Therefore it is the Opinion of this Division that some mode should be established immediately so that the Report of the Committee should be given alike to each Division, & not for the Question to be put of[f] by saying it is a Constitutional Point, as by putting it off, we may be brought into the like Confusion as we have been for some time past   So that if the present Motion is found not to answer the Purpose intended, we move that the Executive Committee be ordered to Draw up a Plan & report in a week
Carried Unanimous   Nelson Chairman
in the Division

NEGATIVED in the General Committee

266. Letter: LCS to London Reforming Society (formerly Division 12), 27 April 1795 [21]

Source: *Correspondence of the LCS*, pp. 18–19
                                                April 27, 1795.
CITIZENS,
We received, with much concern, your answer to our deputation, containing your

21 Address: '*To the* LONDON REFORMING

reasons for seceding from the London Corresponding Society. We cannot think, that in forming this Resolution, you sufficiently considered the situation in which, from various causes, we found ourselves placed; but it is no part of our present purpose to renew the agitation of business already determined. We chiefly wish to cultivate that friendship which you offer, and to which we are greatly encouraged by the equitable conduct to which you have pledged yourselves respecting the pecuniary affairs in which we are mutually concerned.

We presume you intend chiefly to pursue the same political course with ourselves, namely, the diffusion, by means of cheap publications, of such knowledge as may tend to awaken the public mind to the necessity of Universal Suffrage and Annual Parliaments; and we doubt not you are well aware of the oeconomical advantage which attends the extensive circulation of any particular work, when compared with the attempting too great a variety. And as we apprehend no material difference will ever arise between our sentiments, we anticipate frequent opportunities of co-operation in this particular.

Wishing you success in the great cause in which we are mutually engaged, we conclude in the name, and by order of the London Corresponding Society.

JOHN ASHLEY, Secretary.

267. Letter: LCS Executive Committee to all divisions, 28 April 1795[22]

Source: Correspondence of the LCS, pp. 19–22

Committee Room, April 28, 1795.

CITIZENS,

You will have been informed by your Delegate, that the Division sixteen, previous to their secession, sent to the General Committee a request to be informed, when and how the present temporary regulations were to cease,

SOCIETY'. Heading: 'ANSWER TO THE SAME' (i.e. answer to the letter of secession, which was printed before this reply). MS copy in Add MSS 27813, fos. 50–50v, which contains non-significant variants in punctuation and capitalization, is headed, 'Genl Comee 23d April, 1795'.

22 Heading: 'CIRCULAR LETTER TO THE DIVISIONS, BY THE EXECUTIVE COMMITTEE'. MS copy in Add MSS 27813, fos. 51–52v is headed, 'General Committee Room April 23rd. 1795'. It contains minor changes in wording.

and a permanent constitution be established.

You will likewise have heard, that the Division six has sent a Motion of a similar import. – Your Committee, fully sensible of the justice of these claims, and likewise aware of the difficulty of the business, are of opinion, they cannot better consult the welfare of the Society, than by offering to all the Divisions, a few remarks on the nature of constitutions, and the effects they are intended to produce. You must all be sensible, that great pains have been taken by the advocates of Tyranny, to represent this Society as being composed of men who are destitute of any principles: and, however inclined we might be to treat the assertions of such characters with silent contempt, we cannot think the same conduct would be proper towards those who are only culpable for their giving credit where it is not due. No doubt exists that many well-meaning persons have long laboured under deceptions as to the true character of this Society, and it highly behoves us to take every step likely to remove such deceptions.

This, Citizens, we apprehend, cannot be better done than by giving to the Public an explicit declaration of our political principles; and having done so, we think it scarce necessary to observe, that the regulations of our own Society ought to be consistent with those principles.

Investigating with anxious care the causes of that dissention which has unhappily prevailed among us, on this subject your Committees find it has been generally occasioned by the want of a medium of communication between those Divisions, in of[23] which different doctrines have been actively propagated; and as your Committees cannot supply this defect, without describing in some degree the difference of those doctrines, they trust their so doing will not subject them to any suspicion of being actuated by personal considerations.

IN SOME DIVISIONS IT HAS BEEN MAINTAINED,

First. "That the only means of securing social happiness is by the general diffusion of Knowledge, and this being effected, all regard to constitutional or legal rules would become unnecessary."

Second "That, as human affairs are liable to exigencies which no discernment can foresee, and which will require measures peculiar to themselves, all constitutional rules may prohibit or retard the adoption of such

23 Illogical 'of' is not in MS copy.

measures, and ought to be considered as fetters on Society."

Third. "That as it scarcely ever happens that any two cases, whether civil or criminal, are precisely alike, it follows that established Laws, however numerous, cannot in their operation be perfectly equitable; and hence it is inferred, that all Law ought to be made extempore, and adapted to the particular case to which it is to apply."

In opposition to the foregoing, it has been maintained in other Divisions,

First. "That imperfection is inherent in human nature; and that no system of education would ever totally eradicate the passions and prejudices to which all men are more or less subject: That constitutional and legal rules ought to be the illustration of prudential and moral principles; and that under this description, they would form a great part of that knowledge which their opponents profess, in general terms to recommend.

Second. "That moments of exigence, being naturally attended with some perturbation of the Public mind, are of all others the least proper for forming new Institutions: That the baneful effects of institutions so formed, have in general proved them to be the offspring of Passion, rather than of Reason: – That a wise Society ought to provide as much as possible against every imaginable exigence; and that constitutional regulations, judiciously formed, are to be considered as beacons rather than as fetters."

Third. "That although civil Cases may be too various to be wholly provided for by positive Laws; yet that criminal cases not only admit of less variety, but being more generally interesting, are more subject to the interference of Passion and Prejudice: That jurisprudence (or a discretionary power in the administrators of public justice) wherever allowed, has generally been prostituted to private and partial purposes: and that explicit laws formed on general principles, without regard to any particular case, will always be found most effectual, either to protect innocence or punish guilt."

Thus Citizens, we have contrasted to you the extremes of the doctrines which have been propagated among us: – You will readily perceive, that the decision of the question which is the most proper, rests on the possibility or impossibility of attaining to moral perfection. If you find reason to believe that you have attained to such a state, you may be possibly right in adopting the first mentioned doctrines; But if such attainment is only matter of expectation, we think it would be preposterous to suffer your present conduct to be regulated by it: Much less would the adoption of such ideas be proper, if you are of opinion that moral perfection is unattainable by human nature. Under such a belief, it will be most indubitably adviseable to endeavour by prudent regulations, and the propagation of laudable principles, to guard against those follies and vices which have so frequently disturbed the happiness of Society.

Citizens, your Committee are fully aware that, in offering these comments, they are subjecting themselves to the charge of taking a part in the disputes; but they cannot suffer this apprehension to deter them from doing what they conceive to be a part of their duty, particularly as they will at all times be happy to circulate any comments which may be made on this subject, whether tending to confirm or oppose the foregoing ideas.

It is necessary to mention, that your Committees have received from several Divisions, motions relative to particular points of Constitution, and they trust the Divisions who have sent such motions will see the propriety of deferring the consideration of them under the present circumstances. In the motion of Division six, already mentioned, there is a plan proposed for the forming of a new Constitution, other plans for effecting the same object have been also proposed to your Committees; but as some doubts are entertained, whether the Society at large is desirous of engaging any farther in that pursuit, your Committees have thought it adviseable, previous to referring such plans, to request your answer to the following questions:

First. Are you of opinion that this Society can be conducted without any Regulations?

Second. Are you of opinion that the present Regulations, with such amendments as may be made in the usual way of reference by the General Committee to the Divisons, will be sufficient to answer the purposes of the Society?

Third. Are you of opinion that the appointing of any Committee for the special purpose of amending the present Regulations, or forming a new Constitution, is necessary?

YOUR COMMITTEES are anxious to have the sense of the Society, separately, as fully as possible, on the foregoing questions, for which reason they do not mean to take the reports until the 21st of May; and it has been recommended, that every Delegate should provide himself with a complete list of the Divisions which he represents; and rule in the front of the names, six columns, namely, one for the affirmative, and one for the negative votes on each question; by which means he will have an opportunity of taking the votes of individuals on any of the intervening nights of meeting; it it being understood, that every member may alter any vote which he may have given pending the discussion of the question.

Earnestly recommending amity and concord.

We conclude in name,
and by Order of your Committees,

JOHN ASHLEY, Secretary.

ALEX. GALLOWAY, Assistant Sec.

268. Letter: London Reforming Society (formerly Division 12) to LCS, 9 May 1795[24]

Source: Correspondence of the LCS, pp. 23–6

CITIZENS,

The pleasure with which we receive yours, is more easily conceived than expressed, being convinced that a clear and explicit understanding between men and men is the best means of preventing those party factions and antipathies which too often produce the most direful consequences. Our secession being the result of mature deliberation (not the sudden gust of passion) we still think every impartial man must justify us. Remember the patience we exercised during the trial and calumniation of our Delegate: we never sought *pretence* for secession; we exerted every effort to heal the breach which had unfortunately been made. Remember, that after you had declared the charges brought against him frivolous and vexatious, after you had honourably acquitted him, a minority of the Society started up, and demanded he should be expelled, or they would withdraw. This was too palpable an absurdity for you to do, after having acquitted him; therefore you sent a deputation for us to do it. Being reduced to this situation, we had only this alternative, either "to remain just and secede," or sacrifice justice, by "ejecting the man who had done his duty." Determined to to abide by principle, we chose the former in preference to the latter, though it was with the greatest reluctance we separated from that Society in which we had seen such tried patriotism: – but we wish not to look backwards, unless it be to profit by past misfortunes; we

look forward with pleasure, to a cultivation of friendship and unanimity, being determined that no misrepresentation shall separate us from you.

[The middle of the letter advances plans to circulate useful books without advertising costs. The major plan involves the scheme employed by the LCS the next year in the publication of the *Moral and Political Magazine*, namely, giving every member a publication regularly in return for his dues (and also encouraging other reform societies to order copies for all their members). In place of advertising in periodicals, handbills could be delivered to debating rooms and public halls. Every member should be encouraged to lend his book to one uninformed man. Every member who can do so should expose political books for sale, and patriotic booksellers should lend books.

After the receipt of this letter, Moore, Hodgson and Moody met with Bone and other members of the London Reforming Society to discuss this plan, part of which the LCS accepted and implemented by publishing an abridgment of the *State of the Representation of England and Wales*. It sold for 3d and 'several thousand' copies were circulated. The note containing this information concludes that 'since this conference, the Executive Committee have been so busily employed as to prevent the further acceleration of this excellent plan'.[25]]

This is accompanied with what we have collected towards the payment of the debt; and wishing you success in the great and good work in which we are mutually engaged, we are with much respect, by order, and in the name of the London Reforming Society.

JOHN BONE Secretary

May 9, 1795.

[The next known business of the Society is the public outdoor meeting held on 29

24 Address: 'To the London Corresponding Society'. Heading: 'Copy of a Letter from the London Reforming Society'.

25 Of side interest in the plan is the estimated size of reform societies taking these cheap publications. The letter calculates costs for a society (obviously the LCS of 1000 members and then assumes that if all the reform societies took one copy for each member, the total would be 20,000. These theoretical estimates indicate the increasing size of the LCS.

June, the desirability of which was debated in the Society. Some members were convinced a general meeting 'would stimulate its friends to come forward in its support, and also shew the nation at large, the London Corresponding Society still remained firm in asserting their undoubted rights to *universal suffrage and annual parliaments*'. Other members opposed a meeting, arguing that it would provide government with a pretext for a further suspension of the Habeas Corpus Act and 'by this rashness of ours, meet the censure instead of meriting the approbation of our country'. When the question was put to the divisions, they voted in favour of a meeting.[26]

On 22 June advertisements for the meeting appeared in the newspapers, stating that the general meeting would be held on the Gun Tavern's bowling green, Lambeth Rd, St George's Fields at 2 o'clock to consider the means of obtaining universal suffrage and annual Parliaments. Tickets to be had from delegates, from the secretary, Ashley, 6 Fisher St, Red Lion Sq., and from others listed in the advertisement.[27] Evidently the magistrates threatened the publican of the Gun with loss of his licence if he let the Society meet on his premises, for three days later, on 25 June, the LCS placed advertisements announcing that the meeting would be held not on the bowling green, but in an enclosed field near it (and that tickets were on sale for 6d).[28]

26 'Prefatory Letter', *Correspondence*, p. 4.
27 *MC* 22 June 1795, p. 1; *Telegraph*, 22 June, p. 1; *MP* 23 June, p. 1. The ticket-sellers are Eaton, Smith, Spence, Burks, Hodgson, Bone and Cooper – all on previous lists of one sort or another – and J. Lee, bookseller, 47 Haymarket; R. Hodgson, grocer, opposite Gun Tavern, Lambeth Rd; G. Ballard, bookseller, Bedford Ct, Covent Garden; D. Ross, 22 St Mary Axe, Leadenhall St; and J. Lovett, hairdresser, 4 Shepherd's Market, Mayfair. According to the *Morning Post*, Lovett's name was put on this advertisement without his knowledge or consent. 'This circumstance should serve as a caution to those who have been attached to the Popular Societies, to be careful how they assemble with *suspected characters*' (27 June, 1795, p. 3).
28 *MC* 25 June 1795, p. 1; *Telegraph*, 26 June, p. 1. There are some changes in the names of ticket-sellers: Lovett is not on this list, nor is Hodgson the grocer. New to the list are G. Riebeau, bookseller, opposite Buckingham St, Strand; and J. Hartley, shoemaker, 8 Prospect Place, South-side St George's Fields.

269. Accounts of LCS General Meeting: 29 June 1795[29]

Sources: as note

[At] about three o'clock, P. M. Citizen Jones, being appointed Chairman, rose and addressed them [the members] in the following manner: –

CITIZENS!

It is with infinite satisfaction that I behold here assembled, on this day, so very numerous and so respectable a meeting: it presents indeed to my view a spectacle at once sublime and awful, since it seems as if the whole British Nation had convened itself upon this extraordinary occasion to witness the propriety of our conduct, and testify for the legality of our proceedings. They will not, I believe, be disappointed. We meet for no other than our original purpose, a Parliamentary Reform, and

29 *Account / of the / Proceedings / at / a General Meeting / of / The London Corresponding Society, / Convened by Public Advertisement, / and Held in / An Inclosed Field, Behind the Long Room, / Borough Road, St. George's Fields, / On Monday, the 29th of June, 1795. / Citizen John Gale Jones in the Chair. / Price Two Pence.* 16 pp. The second edn is entitled *Narrative of the Proceedings at a General Meeting of the London Corresponding Society. / Second Edition, Revised and Corrected. / Price One Penny.* It contains minor changes in wording.

The field where the meeting was held was 'a large piece of ground, walled in between the Obelisk and the King's Bench Prison' (*Telegraph*, 30 June, p. 3). Estimates of the total crowd ranged from 50,000 to over 100,000. According to the *Morning Chronicle*, there were 12,000 to 14,000 who had paid 6d each to enter the enclosure and another 20,000 to 60,000 of the 'surrounding multitude' (1 July 1795, p. 2).

During the meeting people unconnected with the reform societies passed out handbills; one explained the Imperial Loan; another gave the first lesson for the 4th Sunday after Trinity; and a third contained a poem, 'No French Principles'. The meeting proceeded peaceably, with no tendency to riot; after it, the people dispersed in orderly fashion (*Telegraph*, 2 July, p. 2; *MC* 30 June, p. 3).

Government viewed the approaching meeting with great alarm. The Duke of Portland and undersecretaries of state called for assistance from magistrates of police offices, the Lord Mayor, the commanders of the Horse Guard and the military forces stationed at the Savoy and the Tower. Horse and foot guard were sent to protect the nearby King's Bench Prison from attack. Portland even drafted an order to disperse the meeting by reading the Riot Act (copies of orders in HO 65/1).

disclaim all intention of tumult or violence. I hope, by our firm, yet moderate conduct, we shall gain the good will and concurrence of all who are here present, and convince them that we are, as we ever have been, the sincere advocates and steady promoters of universal peace and tranquillity. The immediate objects to which I would call your attention are, – an *Address to the Nation*, another *to the King*, and a few Resolutions expressive of the present situation of the country, and our determination to pursue, by every legal and constitutional method, the best means of obtaining our natural Rights, Universal Suffrage, and Annual Parliaments.

Address to the Nation.
Friends and Fellow-Citizens!

After the lapse of more than a twelvemonth, replete with fearful agitation and alarm, the London Corresponding Society, still firm in its principles, and faithful to its original purpose, again offers itself to your notice, and solicits your immediate attention.

[While the slow progress of human improvement has produced an insensible revolution in opinion, mankind, unaccustomed to great changes, has been inclined to regard them as impracticable and to reject them. Hence the perpetuation of abuses; hence the servile disposition which prefers a partial evil to an uncertain good and which dreads innovation.]

But, with nations as with individuals, it sometimes happens, that the Hour of Danger is the Hour of Inquiry; and what would have been withheld from the calm remonstrances of reason is often yielded to the strong impulse of necessity.

[At such a time, deliberation is suspended and the shock of adverse powers becomes the only effectual means of redress. Happy the nation which is not compelled to so desperate a remedy. Everyone who would enjoy the benefits of civil society must preserve its tranquillity by warning fellow citizens of impending dangers. It is not enough to propagate principles; one must associate with those who share one's principles and be ready to die in their defence.

Four years ago we united, proclaimed our grievances, warned of the state of the country. We believed a parliamentary reform the only way to preserve our country from destruction. Now that the country is in a worse condition, should we desist? Surely not. Now, Britons, you are beginning to think; soon you will not permit your fellow citizens to be forced to fight against the liberties of mankind nor your families to be robbed of bread in order to feed foreign mercenaries.]

Away with cold calculations of safety or prudence – with paltry expedients and illtimed fears! It is necessary for all honest men to speak out, *the Times and the Country demand it!* Are we Men, and shall we not speak? Are we BRITONS, and is not LIBERTY our BIRTH-RIGHT! There is no Power on Earth shall silence the Voice of an injured Nation, or prevent the Progress of Free Inquiry! – Bring forth your Whips and Racks, ye Ministers of Vengeance! – Produce your Scaffolds and your Executioners! – Erect Barracks in every Street, and Bastiles in every Corner! – Persecute and punish every innocent Individual! – but you will *not* succeed! The Voice of Reason, like the Roaring of the Nemean Lion, shall issue even from the Cavern's Mouth! – The holy Blood of Patriotism, streaming from the severing Axe, shall carry with it the Infant Seeds of Liberty, and Men may perish! – but Truth shall be eternal!

While, among other terrible effects of the present cruel and disastrous War, gaunt Famine stalks along your streets, and haggard Wretchedness assails you in every shape; mark, Citizens, the shameful negligence and unfeeling conduct of those who hold that power which ought to be intrusted to none but your *real* Representatives! When a proposition to inquire into the cause of the present scarcity is coldly and reluctantly brought forward, it is in a moment, silenced by the insidious whispers of a Secretary of State, *"that such a Discussion would do more Harm than Good:"* Thus are you left to experience not only the *Humanity* of the present Ministry, in exporting your food to foreign mercenaries, but are compelled also to endure all the severe extortions of *private Avarice and Monopoly!*

Let us entreat you not to fall into those fatal errors which have so frequently misled our ancestors, nor rest your expectation on that delusive phantom – a Change of Ministers! With *such* an House of Commons, no Ministry *can* perform its Duty to the People! – YOUR CHIEF PERHAPS YOUR ONLY HOPE, IS IN YOURSELVES!

[We call on you to unite your exertions with ours and to endeavour, by every legal and constitutional means, to procure the natural and undoubted rights of universal suffrage and annual Parliaments.]

This Address having been twice read to the Members within the Field, was carried to the wall opposite the President, which afforded the greatest opportunity of communicating the proceedings to the immense multitude which surrounded the meeting: after which the following ADDRESS TO THE KING was brought forward:

To The
King's Most Excellent Majesty

Sire,
    Impressed with a sense of the numerous calamities with which our Fellow-Citizens are every where oppressed and overwhelmed, and conscious of the rectitude of our intentions, we feel it our duty, at this critical juncture, thus publicly to address you, and claim your favourable attention.

[We do not intend rudeness or incivility – but we speak as freemen, not servile slaves. We have been misrepresented as inimical to your person; the late trials have shown our innocence. If anyone is inimical it is those who try to pervert your understanding.]

Your Ministers have grossly and shamefully deceived you; – they have used your name as a pretext to enslave and destroy the people; and have staked the safety of your Crown for their own Political salvation: – they have set up to sale the Virgin Honours of the State, and violated the fair Fame of the British Constitution!
    But it is necessary, Sire, that you should be undeceived; and, if you have not an honest Minister, that will dare to speak the Truth, THE PEOPLE SHOULD INSTRUCT THEIR SOVEREIGN, AND SAVE HIM FROM DESTRUCTION!

[We have sought to preserve the people's love for you.]

But your Ministers, dreading lest you should have a common interest with the People, have basely slandered us, and represented a considerable part of the British Nation as disaffected and disloyal! By their infamous manoeuvres

they have betrayed you, and endangered even your safety! – The Nation itself stands tottering upon the Brink of Ruin, and YOUR EXISTENCE IS COUPLED WITH THEIRS!
    We conjure you, Sire, in the name, and for the sake of that Glorious Revolution, which seated the House of Brunswick on the Throne, to yield a timely attention to the Cries of a suffering People, and to exert that power with which the Constitution has intrusted you; – to give them that free and equal Representation, which can alone enable the British Nation to prevent future and remove the present calamities; – to dismiss from your Councils those guilty Ministers, who have so long with impunity insulted us, and betrayed our dearest interests; – to put an immediate period to the ravages of a cruel and destructive War, and to restore to us that Peace and Tranquility, which are so essentially necessary for YOUR OWN PERSONAL SECURITY, AND FOR THE HAPPINESS OF THE PEOPLE!

The Address to the King was, in the manner already described, communicated, as far as possible, to the company without.
    The two Addresses were then put to the Vote – That to the Nation was unanimously approved; but the Address to the King caused a considerable degree of debate; and which, in all probability, would have been much more extensive, had not the attention of so many of the most active Members been engaged in communicating the proceedings to the remote parts of the Company.
    In opposition to the Address it was contended, – That the Society ought to confine its efforts to the dissemination of Political Knowledge among their Countrymen in general; and that every other mode of attempting to attain a redress of grievances would ultimately prove delusive – That while every means were used to awaken national prejudices against the principles of Liberty, the Society ought not in silence to suffer the introduction of the principles of modern Germany; those principles, by which Soldiers, who, on all other occasions, are expected to exceed the courage of Lions, are, with respect to their Officers, required to sink beneath the submissiveness of Spaniels – That the late execution of *Parish* and *Cook*, two privates of the Oxfordshire Militia,[30] and the pains which have since been taken to misrepresent their conduct, and injure their characters, furnished no reason to hope any

30 In a ghastly ceremony on 13 June Parish and Cook were shot for attempting to prevent grain and flour from being sent away (*New Annual Register*, 1795, pp. 36-7, 40-1).

thing from the humanity of the executive part of our Government: it was also contended, that the idea of addressing the King was nugatory, it being understood that some late regulations preclude all possibility of presenting any Address immediately to himself; and that, in passing through the Privy Council, there could be no security that it would not be mutilated or suppressed.[31]

In support of the Address it was urged, that individuals, while forming but a Minority of a Nation, were in duty bound, whatever might be their private opinions, to regulate their public conduct by those institutions which had been sanctioned by the approbation or even acquiescence of their Countrymen – That if the system of Government established in this country was really defective, nothing could tend more directly to expose its defects than the inefficacy of measures adopted in compliance with its doctrines – That the power of reforming the Representation stated in the Address to be possessed by the King, implied, like all other Magisterial authority, a duty to exercise it for the general good – That the exclamations, now so common, that the King would pay no attention to the sentiments of the People, were premature, and would continue to be so until the Nation in general were prevailed on to require of him to use this part of his authority in a just and equitable manner; and, lastly, that if no other mode of presentment, except through the Privy Council, could be found, still the publication of the Address[32] would counteract any wish of theirs to mutilate or suppress it.

On the Question being put, there appeared a large Majority in favour of the Address: – and a Motion being made and seconded, that Citizen Earl STANHOPE be requested to present the same, it was carried unanimously.

A number of Resolutions were then pro-posed, which, after some Amendments and Additions, were severally put and carried, as follow:

[Resolutions one and two point to the lack of free and equal representation as the cause of the nation's distresses. The third resolution attributes the high prices and scarcity to the unjust war and calls for peace. The fourth resolution asserts that the state trials have proven the innocence of the Society and the guilt of their persecutors. The fifth resolution praises the conduct of 'Citizens Earl Stanhope and R. B. Sheridan' in Parliament. Resolution six assures their countrymen that despite malicious insinuations of their enemies and idle threats of ministers, they will continue to pursue parliamentary reform. The seventh resolution thanks Erskine, Gibbs, Clarkson and Foulkes – barristers and attornies at the state trials. The eighth resolution thanks the surrounding multitude for their orderly behaviour.]

After a Motion of Adjournment had been put and carried, the last Resolution was communicated by Citizen JONES, in the following manner:

FRIENDS AND FELLOW-CITIZENS!

I hope the event of this truly great and glorious day will fully prove to the world that a very large body of the people can, even in the most critical and perilous times, assemble to deliberate upon public measures, without the smallest violation of order or the slightest breach of decorum.

[It has been said that we should be dispersed by the military; this was an idle and useless threat. Were we surrounded by soldiers they would soon see the truth and justice of our declarations and if required to act would fight for, not against, the people. But I hope that the nation will never be reduced to such an extremity, that reason and remonstrance alone will produce the desired effects.

On concluding, Jones quit the chair, and the meeting voted him thanks.[33]]

31 According to the *Register of the Times*, someone in the audience said that since Mrs Nicholson's affair, his Majesty would receive petitions only through the Secretary of State. Inasmuch as the ministers were 'adversarious' to their cause, the speaker continued, they should not commit the address to them but to the people alone. In reply, it was stated that this condition was not the fault of the LCS, and sending the address would show how peaceable they were. This response was greeted with great applause (vol. 5, p. 460).

32 When it was agreed to print and distribute the addresses, one of the delegates informed the audience that the funds of the LCS, depleted by contributions to imprisoned brethren, were insufficient for such a motion (*Register of the Times*, vol. 5, p. 460).

33 The 2nd edn then gives Jones's reply to the vote of thanks. Both edns end with a statement that at the general meeting many persons appeared anxious to become members and that by leaving their names with any of the under-mentioned

270. Report from spy Powell: LCS Executive Committee, 2 July 1795 [34]

Source: PC 1/23/A38

Ex Committe Thursday July 2. 1795
Maxwell in the chair

Present Hodgson, Young, Ross, Ashley Galloway & Powell. Jones could not attend being very ill.

persons, 'they will, IF APPROVED, be admitted'. The undermentioned persons are Ashley, Hodgson, Smith, Lee, Hartley, Cooper, Riebeau, Ballard and – new to the list – J. Powell, baker, Goodge St, Tottenham Ct Rd; and R. Oliphant, tailor, 3 Angel St, St Matins le Grand. The 2nd edn adds the names of J. Shaw, bookseller, 4 Cranburn Alley, Leicester Sq.; and E Davenport, printer, 6 George Ct, Red Lion St, Clerkenwell.

34 Government description: 'Report of the Executive Committee July 2. 1795'. This is a report from James Powell of No 3 Ossulston St, Somers Town and also of Winkworth Buildings, City Road, St Luke's Parish; he was the most diligent spy during the second half of the Society's existence. For twelve years he had been a clerk in the custom's office ('Minutes of James Powel's Informn.', TS 11/958/3503). By avocation he was a writer, at one point leaving off spying and clerking to go to Margate to press for the production of a play. His pamphlet, *The Immoral Procedure and Mental Despotism of the Seceding Members of the London Corresponding Society and the cause of their enmity*, was published in 1795; and his short story, 'Such Things Are', appeared in the last issue of the *Moral and Political Magazine* (vol. 2, pp. 210–17). The story, which deals with the evils of war and of pressing and the cruelty of magistrates, was to be continued.

Powell was never uncovered as a spy. He seems to have escaped detection by appearing foolish. Place called him 'an easy silly fellow' and added, 'There was no absurdity no sort of proceeding among them that Powell did not eagerly go into nothing which any villainous spy could suggest that he would not adopt. . . . Powell was honest, but silly.' According to Place, he was an only son, who had been spoiled by his parents; he had married a woman of the town, who left him; and he lived with a young woman near Battle Bridge (*Autobiography*, p. 179; Add MSS 27808, fo. 92). It is difficult to tell when he joined the LCS, since references to Powell or J. Powell may refer to John Powell, the Goodge St baker. By Oct. 1793 he was a member, for he was called as a witness in the later investigation of the hiring of Martin to defend Briellat. Prior to the state trials of 1794 he was sufficiently in the confidence of the 'committee of evidence' to give government details about their activities. His being listed in

Resolved that the Address to the Nation to the King & the resolutions being extreemly short. A Narative of the Proceedings of the Day with the Debates & some pointed remarks theron be printed with them so as to fill one sheet to be distributed gratis to the members of the Society & sold to strangers at two pence each or less if possible it being found that distributing large numbers of publications to the public gratis had always kept the Society in debt, and now there being so great a demand for the proceedings of monday that they might be sold at any price. Ashly said that he believed upwards of a thousand people (not members) had called upon him for them.
The Telegraph sold 3000 thousand papers on Tuesday & were oblidged to reprint these narative Yesterday.
NB   The Societys Account with Addresses is to be published by Thursday next
The Secretary could not make a return of the Money received on Monday   The Persons who had Tickets to dispose of not having as yet

Jan. 1795 as president also indicates that he had established himself in the Society. He may have been sponsored by Thelwall, whom he had known since 1792 ('Minutes'). Thelwall described him as an intimate friend who knew all the evidence and arguments Thelwall was planning to use at his trial and who, three days before the trial, 'either from flurry and agitation on his own account, or from unguarded simplicity, was so indiscreet as to inform the Pricy Councellors of all that he was acquainted with' (Mrs Thelwall, *Life of John Thelwall*, p. 248). Thelwall, like Place, seemed to attribute Powell's behaviour to weakness of character rather than villainy.

During the arrest of United Englishmen and an LCS division on 18 April 1798, Powell 'escaped' and went to Hamburg. He was back in England in Dec. 1801, when he wrote to Richard Ford asking to have his salary for spying paid to his mother, as he was leaving London. A government note on the outside of the letter says that to keep Powell alert they accused him of negligence. In the letter Powell earnestly defends himself, explaining that he has been holding back from republican activities until someone else initiates them and that when Evans, Eastburne and others came to him for leadership, he told them he was wholly occupied with his new business (25 Dec. 1801 [misdated 1800], PC 1/3535). So successful were his tactics that Galloway, writing to Hodgson at Paris, describes Powell as 'our old friend' and adds, 'you know you can trust any thing by him' (24 Dec. 1801, ibid.). Powell, who was to take the letter to Hodgson, immediately sent a copy to Ford. During the Westminster elections of 1806 and 1807 Powell acted as an assistant to an unsuccessful candidate, James Paull.

made their returns he was certain it was a large sum above £100 –

Adjourned

271. Report from spy Powell: LCS General Committee, 2 July 1795[35]

Source: PC 1/23/A38

General Committe   Thursday
Place in the Chair   July 2. 1795

Quarterage 6 . 5 . 7½ Received from a Patriotic Society at Tewkesbury by the hands of Hardy £2 . . 2 . . –.
102 New members made last week.
This being the 1st meeting after the Quarter above an hour & a half was spent in reading the Certificates of new Delegates
Div. 6 resolved that the Thanks of the Society be given to the Ex. Com. for there asidious & patriotic conduct on & before the General meeting.
Div 23. That the Thanks of the Society be given to John Gale Jones for his truly Patriotic Conduct at the General meeting   There were many motions to this effect
But the thanks of the Society having been given at the meeting. the Committee passed to the order of the day on them all.
Div 29. Resolved That in the absence of the Delegate & sub Delegate the Secretarys of the Divisions should have a vote in the Genl Com.
     This being a constitutional point was referred to the Divisions
     Hodgson & Ashley reported an account of their Deputation to Counseller Vaughan on Account of Martins Application to the Society for the payment of £23 . 10 . – for the defence & subsistence of Carter the Bill Sticker whilst in prison. Vaughan was the Author of the Bill & had said at the time Carter was taken up that he would bear all expences.
the application of Martin to the Society.
Hodgson & Ashley were deputed to Vaughan – who said that Martin was in debt to him £60 & that he was very ready to set his demand off from that Debt. After a very long debate The Committee resolved that they could not accept Vaughans offer, for notwithstanding he was the writer of the bill it was approved off by the Society & stuck up by their order it therefore became there act & they could not suffer any individual that was appointed to draw up any paper for them to pay for the prosecution it might bring on & that Martin being certainly

employ'd by their Com. at that time had a just Claim upon them.
Resolv'd after an investigation of his account Martin be paid by the Society
Ashley then said that he had call'd on Hardy about the business   Who told that at the time of the 1st prosecution against Paines Rights of Man Subscriptions had been enter'd into at several places to defend it against the Crown. But that they were not applied to that purpose. that Boyd the publican had collected from his own friends £10. – Which Hardy understood he had given to Martin on Carters account
The Genl Committe then resolved to appoint a Com. of the oldest members of the Society to enquire into that business & investigate Martins account   It consists of Hodgson, Ashly, Moody, Moor, Cooper & Candy. The Committee voted £3 . 3 . – to be paid to Martin immediately to leave his distress it is to [be] considered as a part of the debt
Moggeridge informd the Committee that a new division would branch from No 5. to meet on Monday next at the New Public House the Corner of Frances Street & Thornaugh Street. The Com appointed a deputation to open it & Numbered it 26.
NB.   Since I made you out the list of the places of meeting several new Divisions have branch'd off & old ones changed their place of meeting   A new list was hung up in the Committe Room last night which I will make you a Copy of on Thursday next. After the report was given from the Ex Com by Young the reporter it was suggested that the Address to the King should be presented before the Societys publication of it.
Resolv'd That the Ex Com. be instructed to make a fair copy immediately & to appoint a depution from amongst themselves to wait on Ld Stanhope on that business
The appointment of the New Ex Committe then took place   It consists of Jones, Hodgson, Young, Maxwell Barton & Powell Ross & Fleming were ballotted out. Ashly & Galloway were reelected Sec. & sub sec.

Adjourned at ½ past 12.

N.B.   A letter was read from the patriotic Society at Norwich by Ashly desiring the Society to be firm in their principles & agreeing to cooperate with them in all their measures.[36] It is to be printed immediately with all the Correspondence since Christmas according to one of the Articles in the Regulations.
N.B   On the Conclusion of the Debate on

35 Government description: 'Report of Genl Comittee / 2 July 1795'.

36 26 June 1795, *Correspondence*, pp. 27-8. The LCS replied on 17 July.

Martins business Hodgson said that when Martin got the money he intended to take some spirited measures to get out of the King's Bench.[37]

272. Minutes: LCS General Committee, 2 July 1795

Source: Add MSS 27813, fos. 65v-7[38]

Genl Comee July 2nd. 1795
Citn Place in the Chair

Divn	Dele	Sub Dele	New	Present[39]
1. ab	Read & Jarvis		0	9
2			5	25
3	no report			
5	Binns & Cooper		6	50
6	Edwards & Dimes		0	17
7	Beck & Nelson		1	8
8 absent				
9	Stephens & Bray		5	30
10			2	10
11	John Williams & Savage		6	20
12	Ramsay & Neale		8	24
13			8	53
14	Wintrige & Simmons		2	11
16	Banting & Dukes		2	12
18	Ward & Brasington		3	17
20	Place & Purcehouse		7	30
21			1	
22 ab	Danton & Iliff		6	40
23	Browne & Pickard		1	18
24			11	30
27	Moody &		10	40
28	Wilson & Fife		6	18
29	Turner for 1 Night		2	23
			92	485

refer on other Page[40]
Deputations

1   Ward, Brasington, Protheroe, Bullock, Fife, Pearce

8   Neale, Ross & Wilson

22 Ross, Binns, Taylor, Davenport

Divn

14   A Motion for a deputation to be sent to them next Wednesday Deputed to Go, Williams, Fife, Jas Powell, Hodgson & Canty,

Mov'd Beck & sec'd Moody that vouchers be read before deputations are appointed – Affir –

1.   Mov'd to Wool Pack Jewin Street Tuesday.

23.   Resolved that it is the Opinion of this Divn that the thanks of the Society should be given to Ex Comee for their Assiduity & patriotic Conduct on the Genl Meeting –
Order of Day carried Affir –

16.   Moved to Bowling pin Old Street Square Wednesday –

7.   Reported Danton, Binns & Webster for neglect of Duty on deputation – Order of Day passed –

1.   Are unanimous of Opinion that the Secretary should have a vote in the Genl Comee when the Delegate & Sub Delegate are absent. Therefore we most respectfully recommend it to the Genl Come for their Consideration – reffer'd to Divns. –

29.   Resolved that the thanks of this Divn be given to Citn Gale Jones for his patriotic behaviour at the Genl Meeting this day – considered as their thanks only –

Read a letter from Norwich – by Ashley –
Stating that they having the same objects in view, & are enemies to tyranny & anarchy wherever established & are friends to truth wherever cherished – & requesting a close connection & correspondence

Citn Moggeridge admitted to the honours of the sitting & informed the Comee that Divn 5 wished to branch off to establish a Divn at the Corner of Francis & Thornhaugh St. – wanted no deputation – Granted & take No 26. – Report of Ex Com –

37 Martin was transferred from the Tower to King's Bench Prison on 12 Jan.; and on 6 March was released from the charge of high treason. He remained in prison because he believed the demand for bail was illegal. He was eventually released on 6 May on a writ from the Privy Council. In July he must have been in prison for a libel in publishing an account of the court martial of Samuel George Grant, sentenced to 1000 lashes on his bare back with a cat-of-nine-tails (Martin, *An Account of the Proceedings on a Charge of High Treason . . .*).

38 Another copy, almost identical, in Add MSS 27813, fos. 54-6v. The version given here has fewer abbreviations. The minutes of meetings of the general committee between 2 July and 10 Sept. are on fos. 54-129.

39 'New': members made during the previous week; 'Present': members attending their division meeting during the previous week.

40 A reference to the motion that the deputations to unrepresented divisions be made after the newly elected or re-elected delegates have presented their vouchers.

The address's to the People & the king both being short – they will publish the whole wth the Proceedings & debates – which will [be] deliverd Gratis –

Moody moved & sec'd – that the Ex Com be instructed to draw up & Publish the proceedings of the Genl Meeting as soon as possible   Affir

Hodgson reported as part of a deputation appointed to wait on Citn Vaughan, on acc't of Citn Martins application for a debt of 26£ Vaughan informed them that he had not paid Martin, but that he would strike it of a debt that Martin owed him – which M– hearing of, sent Vaughan a letter in which

He states that the applied for it with a view of extricating himself from his present troubles, & now finds that neither Judges, or Council will give him any Assistance towards obtaining Justice & States that he did not know when V lent him £60 it was only paying a debt due to him & that he finds himself hurt at not knowing of it before he made the application

Ashley informed the Comee that he had seen Citn Hardy who informed him, that while Paine's trial was pendg a subscription was raised at Boyds & that Boyd raised £10 among his own friends & that he did not pay it towards Paines trial, but paid it to Martin on Cater's Acc't –

Mov'd Moody & sec'd Wilson that the Society do accept of Citn Vaughans offer –   Neg –

Mov'd Moody & sec'd Binns that the Comee refuse Citn Vaughans offer to discharge the debt of the prosecution & support of the Bill sticker & that they take upon themselves to pay it after proper investigation & that a Comee be appointed for that purpose.   Affir

Moody, Cooper, Ashley, Moore, Hodgson & Smith, [to] be that Comee with full power to call any other Citizens

Movd Turner & Secd Beck that Martin be allowed 5 Gs on Acc't An Amendment that 3 Gs only be given   Affir

Div 22.   Thanks of this Divn to Citizens, Bone, Patten Iliff & other Citns for their Conduct at the Genl Meeting –

Ashley chosen Secretary – Galloway Assistant

Election of Ex Com – The old Members, Jones, Maxwell, Ross, Hodgson Young & Fleming –

Proposed

Davenport 8 Williams 3 Barton 8. Jas Powell 4. Oxlaid 4 Moody 11. Jones 16. Maxwell 12 – Ross 7. Hodgson 16. Young 8. Fleming 0.

Barton & Davenport having an equality of votes where balloted for again   When Barton had 11. Davenport 7.

The new Comee as follows –

Young
Jones
Hodgson
Maxwell
Moody
Barton

Quarteridge	6 : 5 : 7½
From Tewkesbury by Hardy	2 : 2 : 0
	£8 : 7 : 7½

273. Report from spy Powell: LCS Executive Committee, 6–9 July 1795[41]

Source: PC 1/23/A38

Executive Committe
Sittings of the 6th July, 1795.
Moody in the Chair

Present Hodgson, Young, Moody, Powel, Barton, Ashly, Galloway & Maxwell.

Hodgson, Ashley, & Moody inform'd the Committe that they had called at Lord Stanhopes House respecting the presenting the Address to the King. had found that he was out of Town. Resolved the Jones be deputed to write to Ld Stanhope in the Country immediately & he not being present in the Committe that Maxwell do call on him the next morning to inform him.

Hodgson said he had prepared his part of the proceedings of the General Meeting & left Blanks which noboddy but Jones could well fill up. that he had sent it to Jones who had promised to finish his part & bring it to the Committee either on the 8th. or 9th. Resolved that the Committe do meet again tomorrow evening & that Maxwell do request Jones to attend.

Adjourned

41 Powell's description: 'Report of the / Executive / Committe / Sittings of the 6th, 7th. 8th / & 9th. July 1795'.

Sittings of the 7th. July, 1795.
Maxwell in the chair

Present Hodgson, Moody, Barton, Maxwell, Powell Ashly, & Galloway

Hodgson said he had seen Citizen Joyce who told him that Lord Stanhope was going to sea in the Experiment ship which he had been so long constructing. That therefore the Society must give up the presenting the Address to the King for the present. – Jones not attending no business respecting the proceedings of the General meeting could be done.

Maxwell said he had call'd several times on Jones but could not see him.

Resolved that this Committe do meet again tomorrow & that Maxwell & Moody be deputed to Jones to urge his attendance.

Adjourned

Sittings of the 8th July 1795
Powell in the Chair

Present Hodgson, Barton, Moody, Maxwell, Powell, Ashly, Galloway,

Maxwell & Moody said they had called on Jones sevral times in the course of the day, could not see him   they had left a note for him.

Jones not attending no business could be done

Resolved that Hodgson do write a letter to Jones immediately to tell him of the consequence & necessity of his attendance on the morrow evening & that Moody do deliver it early in the morning. Resolved that this Committe do meet again tomorrow

Adjourned.

Sittings of the 9th July, 1795.
Hodgson in the Chair

Present Hodgson, Powell, Moody, Maxwell, Barton, Ashley, & Galloway.

Moody said he had called on Jones early in the morning could make noboddy in the House hear had therefore put the letter under the door.

Resolved that Barton be deputed to answer the letter from the Patriotics Society of Norwich.[42]

Resolved that Moody be deputed to write the letters to the Counsel & Jury of D.I. Eaton to

42 Galloway deputed, according to report in meeting of general committee. This reply to Norwich letters of 19 June and 16 July was dated 17 July. It repeats much of the circular letter of 9 May to the Scotch Patriotic Societies. It adds that over 400 joined the LCS last month and that over 100,000 attended the general meeting (*Correspondence*, pp. 28–30).

be sent with the silver metals agreeable to the vote of the General Committee.[43]

A summons to call the members of the Ex. & Gen. Comtes. to be engraved on plate was drawn up. N.B. It is exactly the same as the summons of the members of the Divisions only instead of the words your division the word Committe is inserted.[44]

Resolved that Barton be reporter to this Committe vice Young resigned.

Jones not attending & the members of the Genl Com. comeing in Resolved that his Conduct be reported to the Genl Com. & that this Committee do meet again tomorrow & that Hodgson be deputed to fill up the blanks in the proceedings as well as he can for the publication of them cannot be delayed any longer & they must possitively come out by Monday or Tuesday at furthest

Adjourned

274. Minutes: LCS General Committee, 9 July 1795

Source: Add MSS 27813, fos. 57–64v; a version of the first part of the report, which is almost identical, is on fos. 67v–8v

Genl Comee July 9th. 1795
Citn Beck in the Chair

Divn	New	Present	
1.	2	11	Jarvis & Martin
2 ab	1	15	
3	3	21	
5	24	65	
6	7	40	
7	12	42	

43 The letter to the jury, dated 26 July, explains that the LCS only recently received from government the medals (seized at Hardy's house in May 1794) commemorating Eaton's acquittal on a charge of libelling the king by printing Thelwall's allegory of the gamecock. The letter to Felix Vaughan and John Gurney (Eaton's counsel), dated 17 July, repeats the explanation of the delay in presenting the medals. A note explains that a deputation consisting of Ashley, Maxwell and Young delivered the silver medals and the letter. Gurney sent a thank-you reply to Ashley on 8 Aug. (*Correspondence*, pp. 44–6).

44 'Citns
    'You are hereby requested to attend the Comee of the LCS on the day of at O"Clock precisely on special business
                                                'Secretary
'The Comee meets at' – draft in report of general committee.

8	2	10	Hough & Thomas
9 ab	1	19	deputation already
10	2	11	attends
11	2	30	
12	14	50	Ramsay
13	7	40	
14	7	36	
16	1	14	
18	4	21	
20 ab	11	50	
21	2	13	Cavington & Bayley
22	10	70	Ham for 1 Night
23	2	15	
24	12	40	
26	13	40	Moggeridge & Hole
27	6	35	Stuckey & Brewer
28	9	40	
29	2	31	Turner & Jefferson
	156	759	

Deputations
Divn
 2 – Ward & Wm Nelson
20   Canty & Williams

Citn Moody introduced a friend which was not admitted to honours of sitting as he was not a Member

Divn   Resolved that it is the Opinion of this
11.   Divn that, if neither of the Delegates attend in due time the Secretary shall be impowered to Act a[s] Delegate that Evening & the delegates shall be incapacited for acting the Evening –

Resolved that it is the Opinion of this Divn that the thanks of this Society is due to Citns Hodgson & Jones for their Assiduity & Patriotic Conduct on the glorious 29 of June.

 1.   That the Secretary of any Divn should have a vote in the Genl Comee whenever the delegate & subdelegate are both absent –[45]

 5.   This Divn recommends to the Genl Comee to enforce the 17 Article of the regulations.[46]

21.   Unanimously that it is the Opinion of this divn that a large quantity of regulations & Cards should be printed for the respective Divns – That it is the Opinion of this divn that Citn Higgins do write out the regular expenditure of the Society & that a copy be given to every Delegate for the satisfaction of the divns & that the whole Acct of the number of Tickets that were issued likewise

It appearing to the Genl Comee that some neglect or misrepresentation had taken place in that Divn & the Delegate informing the Comee that it was the first night of his being a delegate he therefore wished to have a deputation [sent] to explain – as the Receipt & Expinditure [was] always bro't froward every Month & therefore that it must the neglect of the last Delegate – he therefore moved that a deputation be Appointed – which was put & there appeared   11 Aff- 11 Neg- & then the Chairn gave his vote in the Affir- Bantang Edwards, Pitcard & Dimes appointed   And to answer the last part of that Motion, a Motion was made That the Secretary make a report next Thursday Evening to the Genl Comee on the State of the receipt & disbursements on Acc't of the last Genl Meeting unanimously in Affir

Divn   Means to branch off to form a new
29-   Divn to meet on Wednesday at the Peacock Inn Houghton Street Clare market & requesting the Comee to appoint a deputation – deputed
Binns Jas Powell Oliphant, Ashley & Turner[47] – & the Number to be 4.

28.   Resolved that the thanks of this Divn be given to Citns Jones & Hodgson for their manly conduct for & at the Genl Meeting & this divn is of opinion they deserve well of the London Corresponding Society

18.   Resolved that the thanks of this divn be given to the Ex Comee for their noble & Patriotic exertions on the late Glorious meeting which must convince the Public & the nation at large of the object they have in view & defeat the various calumnies with which they have been loaded by the advocates of Tyranny & Oppression & likewise for that happy order which with their Assistance of the late Genl Comee they have established in this Society with regard to Deputations which are a happy means of conciliating the whole body & make them One & Indivisible & the strict attendance of the Members of Genl Comee & their Conduct thro' the last quarter.

45 Powell attributed the motion to Div. 27 and added that Divs. 12, 17 and 24 sent similar motions. Div. 17 had not been heard from since Feb. 1794; Powell must have misheard.
46 Powell reported that Divs. 6 and 21 also sent motions to print the quarterly correspondence of the Society.
47 Powell listed Davenport, but not Oliphant and Turner.

Divn 6. Approves of the referr'd Question as with the following amendment that the Delegate & Sub delegate attendg after the commencement of the business the Secretary shall continue the business of the Night –

18. Desires that all letters received from the Patriotic Societies in the Country be printed for the benefit of the Members agreeable to the 17 Article of the regulations

23. Resolved that it is the Opinion of this Divn the Secretary being in the Genl Comee in due time & the Delegate & sub delegate not being present shall be the head officer that that Evening

Recommend to the Genl Comee to put in force the 17 Article of the regulations as soon as possible

Movd & Secd that the Motions from Divns 5, 16, 23 be now taken into consideration   Negatived

Divn 27. That the Assiduous & attentive Conduct of John Barton our representative for the two last Quarters & now one of the Ex Comee merits the thanks of this division.

And in order that other Citizens may be stimulated to attain such honourable distinction – This testimony of our approbation be sent to the Genl Comee.

18 Resolved that the Secretary shall have a vote in the Genl Comee & if he attend in due time & the Delegate & Sub delegate be absent he shall be considered as the head Officer for that Evening –

12. Resolved that is the Opinion of this Divn that the time & enquiry is the proper time for information they therefore think that if the Duke of Richmonds Letter [to] Colonel Sharman & the state of the representation by the Comee of the Friends of the People were given gratis with the regulations to every new member, it would tend very much to advance the interests of this Society – Ramsay – stated that if the Above Resolution was put in practice his Divn thought it would be of very great benefit, as by that Means it would serve to enlighten the whole Nation, As they always hoped that if a new New Member had it given him, (& it might not be in the Power of some to buy them) it would not be confined to himself for that they hoped that it would be lent from him to many & therefore shew the necessity of a reform, in the first Place the Report of the Friends of the People would show to the Public what the

Present House of Commons was & in what manner the Nation at large is represented. & the Duke of Richmonds Letter would show them that Universal Suffrage & Annual Parliaments was the only effectual Mode of Reform that would Save the Country from ruin – he therefore moved That the Motion be now taken into consideration –

On the other hand it was stated that the arguments used were likely to prove some benefit, but that the financies Would not allow the Society to do it.

It was therefore Negative that the Motion be taken into Consideration be now

Citn Rock from Sheffield admitted to the honours of the sitting

[The report of the executive committee is substantially the same as that given by Powell.]

Enquired of the Ex Comee who was to present the address to the king, as Citn Stanhope was at Sea

Hodgson – answered that one of the resolutions stated the Publication of it was a sufficient presentation.

a Citn informed the Comee that a private petion had been presented to the king lately & had received redress –

Movd & secd that the Ex Comee do consider of a mode of presenting their address to the King –

Received a letter from Citn Rousel directed to Citn Ashley –

I shall esteem it a particular favour if you will represent to the Comee of the LCS my situation. the Attorney who has advanced the Money for my removal from the Kings bench – has applied to me for the money he has advanced, it is impossible for me to repay him unless the Society will releive me – as you know my Circumstances well.

I leave earnestly to you to speak on the Subject –

J B Rousel

Freemans stile
21st. Messidor
3 Year of Liberty   Rousel was impri-
on July 9. 1795   soned by Gosling
Slaves stile   Plots

Movd & secd that Ashley be requested to enquire of Rousel what the demand of the Attorney is   carr'd Affir

Divn 8. Informed the Comee that they were

destitute of a place to meet. for that last week, when some part of them went to their usual place of meeting they we[re] informed by the Landlord that a Justice of the Peace had called on him & told him that he understood that he had a Divn of the LCS met in his house – & he came there to inform him, that if he let them meet there that Evening – that he should lose his licence the next day – the Landlord therefore informed them that he could not let them meet there that Evening – They therefore retired to some other house as a Private Company – & transacted their business & made one new member

The Delegate was informed by the Genl Comee that the Mortar in the London Road would take them in – as the Landlord inform Hodgson that he should like to have a divn there – & Hodgson knew of some persons who would join that Divn if one could be established there –

They were recommended to go there

Citn Rock from Sheffield informed the Comee that the Sheffield Society wished to have a close correspondence & are ready to co-operate with us towards obtaining a Parliamentary & redress of grievance & he could give them a direction were to send – so that the letters might not [be] intercepted –

Requested to attend the Ex Comee
Quarterage – 9:7:5½.

275. Report from spy Powell: LCS General Committee, 9 July 1795[48]

Source: PC 1/23/A38

July 9th, 1795.
Genl. Committe
Beck in the Chair

156 New members. £12. . 17. . – Quarterage & Genl purpose money.

Treasurers Account for last Quarter. Money received £106. . 9. . – Expended by order of the Genl & Executive Committes £64. . 3. . – Ballance in the hands of The Treasuer. £42. . 4. . –

[The motions on printing the correspondence and on letting division secretaries act as delegates are reported, as are the admission of Citizen Rock and the branching of Division 27.]

The Deligate of Division 6 inform'd the Committe they had changed their place of meeting to the Woolpack Jewin Street Aldersgate street.

Div 14 to the Boatswain & Call   Maze Pond Southwark.

Div 21. Resolved that An account of the Receipt & Expenditure of the Societys money for the last Quarter with the Tickets issued at the General meeting be immediately made out & that Citizen Higgins being employ'd by the Society in writing should make a Copy for every deligate.

Hodgson rose & requested that this motion carrying a reflection on the Secretaries & Executive Committe should be taken into consideration immediately   Which after some debate was agred to.

Hodgson said that the Accounts of last Quarter was now hung up in the Room & that the Deligate of 21 might take a copy. With respect to the Account of the General meeting it could not possibly be made out till a return was made by the Deligates of the Tickets they had received   Ashly confirm'd this & said that he had as yet received only £32 . . 17 . . –

Upon this after some debate it was resolvd that no blame could attach to the Secretary & that he should make out his account as far as he could by thursday next & report those Persons who had not made a return of their Tickets

Resolved that a deputation be sent to Div 21. to explain the business.

The deligate of No 5 then made motion that the Motions from Divs 5. 6. & 21 be taken into consideration directly respecting printing the Societys Correspondence.

The Committe being eager to hear the Report from the Executive Come. negatived it. The Report from the Ex Com was now begun but I being in possession of that Report & being extreemly ill was obliged to leave the Com. Room & go home.

276. Report from spy Powell: LCS Executive Committee, 16 July 1795[49]

Source: PC 1/23/A38

Executive Committe   July 16, 1795

Sittings of the 12 Inst Present Moody Barton Ashley Maxwell Young Powell & Galloway. Young in the Chair

A Considerable Part of the proceedings of the

48 Powell's description: 'Report of the Genl Comitte / 9th July 1795'.

49 Powell's description: 'Report of / Executive / 16 July 1795'.

General meeting was read, approved & ordered to the Press

The Committe was of opinion that Citn Joyces letter not being official & satisfactory.

Resolv'd: the Citn Earle Stanhope should be officially waited on & that the information by way of letter would retard the business considerably therefore deputed Hodgson & Ashley to go to his Lordships House at Chevenning in Kent.

Sittings of the 14th July

Present Hodgson Ashley Maxwell Jones Powell Barton Moody Galloway & Jones Brother.

Maxwell in the Chair

Hodgson & Ashley reported that they had been to Lord Stanhopes house in Kent had found that he was out on Naval Experiments & that it was uncertain when he would return. The Committee therefore came to the resolution of Presenting the Address to the King through the medium of the Secretary of State & appointed a deputation of Jones, Barton Galloway, Moody, Maxwell & Jones's Brother to carry the same, appointed Moody reporter of the said Deputation.

Sittings of the 16

Present Hodgson Jones Moody Barton Maxwell Powell Ashly & Galloway   Barton in the Chair

Moody reported the Deputation to the Secretary of State

Thy met at the Ship proceeded to the Secretary of States Office were told the Counsel was setting Jones gave the letter ordered to withdraw & return was ask'd were the lettere came, said it was a letter to the King the Clark of the Counsel took it in. There was a number of Questions ask'd the deputation was ordered to withdraw & return several times once had got partly down the Staircase ordered back. Waited a considerable time in the lobby Galloway ask'd if, they might not have Chairs to set down whilst they were placing the Clark of the Counsel came out told them there was no Answer they might go.

The Committee allow'd the Deputation 5s/ for Expences[50]

Finish'd the whole of the proceedings of the Genl Meeting

Ordered 3000 to be struck off directly & the Press to be kept Standing   Resolv'd that a Reference to places were persons might apply to be admitted Members be printed at the end of the Proceedings

50 'conceiving that it was no way proper for Deputations to pay their expences' – report of executive committee in minutes of general committee.

Received & read letters from Birmingham and Coventry requesting Correspondence.

Adjournd

277. Minutes: LCS General Committee, 16 July 1795

Source: Add MSS 27813, fos. 69v–76

General Committee   July 16th. 1795
Citn Beck in the Chair

[The report starts with a tally of the 25 divisions, listing a total of 174 'New' members and 970 members 'Present'. Another column tallies the votes on the 'Refer'd Question' (whether the secretary of a division should be allowed to vote in the general committee when the delegate and sub-delegate are absent): 445 'Aff' and 111 'Neg'. No figures are listed for Divs. 15, 17, 19, 25 and 30. For three divisions there is a notation of delegate and subdelegate: Div. 5, 'Powell & Campbell'; Div. 12, 'Wilson Sub in place of Neale'; Div. 22, 'Ham & Reed, till Danton & Iliff returns'.]

Deputations

Divn		
2	Ward , Powell	Mov'd that Divn 6
3	Banting, Edwards	Report be left out
28	Jarvis & Pickering	as well as others that sent irregular Reports – Affir

Divn Branches off to the Black horse corner of Fishmonger Alley High Street 12 – Borough, requests Deputation & No Deputed Yates, Ramsay, Price, & Dukes – to be No 15

Divn Branches of to White horse in White horse Yard Drury lane requests No & 27 Deputation

Deputed Hodgson, Ham Canty, Purcehouse – No to be 17.

Citn Binns said he feard that Citn Canty found himself hurt at a Deputation being appointed to his Divn by wishing to go as a part of Deputation to the New Divn he therefore moved that Citn Canty be withdrawn from that deputation

Citn Canty informed the Comee that his Divn had been in the habit of having continual Deputations through the negligence of their former delegates – he found himself hurt on that Account as he did not wish to be placed with such neglectful People, As they were not worthy of the Confidence of any Divn –

A Citn stated that he hoped Citn Canty would withdraw from the deputation – for if he did not attend his own Divn that they would likewise be unrepresented next Comee night –

Citn Canty therefore withdraw himself –

Citn Binns produced the following Paper from Sundry inhabitants[51] of Greenwich, stating that they which to Join the LCS – & to have a Divn established at the White Swan Greenwich Road –

We the undersigned Inhabitants of Greenwich & its Environs wish to unite ourselves with the London Corresponding Society for the purpose of obtaining Universal Suffrage & Annual Parliaments. –

We therefore wish the General Comee of the above Society to send a Deputation for the purpose of assisting in forming us into a Divn agreeable to their regulations.

George Inkpen	Stephen Keatts
Richard Tyler	John Mead
John Jones	John Rowley
William Wenbo[r]ne	George Westall
Abram Abrahams	John Cunningham
Richard Baker	William Houghton
William Burt	John Stoneham
John Quaite	John Yates
William Sparrow	J Cranch
Jas Dunn	Jas Hawes Cranch
Richard Ellot	

The Divn to be No 30. Deputed the followg Citns to attend at the White Swan Greenwich Road on Sunday next,

Place	Binns	Waites
Hodgson	Moody	Mead
Powell	Binns Junr	Ramsay
Wintrige	Williams	Banting
Cooper	Price	Moggeridge
Ham	Edwards	

Divn
16.   Are for the reffer'd Motion for the Secretary to have a vote in the Comee when the Delegate & Sub Delegate are absent   7 Affir   5 Neg –

24.   This Divn is unanimously of Opinion the the Secretary of each Divn should have a vote in the Genl Comee in the absence of Delegate & Sub Delegate –

28   Resolved unanimously that it is the Opinion of this Divn that the Secretary should have a vote in the Genl Comee in the absence of delegate & sub delegate –

Mov'd & Secd that the Motion from Divn 12[52] – be now taken into Consideration   Affir –

Amendment that the Motion from Divn 12 be adjournd one fortnight   6 Affir   12 Neg

Motion of 12 taken into Consideration

Citn Ramsay stated the same as he did last week, & added in addition that the principle argument that was stated against it last week that the financies would not allow us to do it. Now he himself as well as his Divn was of opinion that it would great increase the financies & Numbers of the Society – On the hand it was stated that the Society had but about 50£ on hand, & that the Proceedings of the Genl Meeting was to be distributed gratis to Members – & the regulations were likewise, & that they were of opinion that it would cut the financies of The Society so low that we should be running into debt again

Question put & Carried in the Affir –

Mov'd that 2000 of each be printed & referr'd to Ex Come } Affir –

18.   Resolved that the Duke of Richmonds letter to Col Sharman be published & bound up with the regulations –

23   Resolved that it is the Opinion of this Divn that the Duke of Richmonds letter to Col Sharman should be printed & delivered to the Society gratis

11.   Resolved that it is the Opinion of this Divn that the Duke of Richmond's letter to Col Sharman & the State of the Representation & the regulation should be given to every new member when admitted if the financies will allow –

5.   Resolved that it is the Opinion of this Divn that the Duke of Richmonds letter to Col Sharman with the report of the Friends of the People be printed wth the regulations & distributed to the Members of this Society Gratis if the Financies will allow –

51 Powell identified them as 'Inhabitants & Housekeepers'; in the deputation to them he included Ashley.

52 That every new member be given a copy of the Duke of Richmond's letter to Colonel Sharman and of the LCS abridgment of *The State of the Representation of England and Wales*, originally issued by the FoP.

Divn Resolved that an Account of the
20. Number of Tickets for the General Meeting delivered to Individuals & the Sums
of Money & Tickets returned by such
Individuals together with the Sums
A received at the Meeting be laid before
the Society[53] – adjourned
Divn Recommends to the Genl Comee to
22 have the report of the Ex Comee delivered immediately after the appointing
of deputations to the unrepresented
Divns as we apprehend that Comee might
be more usefully employed at this great
press of business then attending the Genl
Committee till finished – adjourned –
29. Resolved that it is the Opinion of this
Divn that no Secretary or any Person
whatever except the Delegate or Sub
Delegate be admitted to the Genl Comee
except they come on business relating to
the Society – adjourned
Citn Cooper reported from the Comee
appointed to enquire into the Claim of
Citn Martin
He stated that they had made great progress – but not sufficient to state the
Particulars of the debt yet –
Report of Ex Comee

[The report contains the same information,
often the same phrases, as Powell's account.]

Read Statement of Tickets delivered for the
Genl Meeting with an Account of those settled
for & returned –

[A table listing the number of tickets 'Delivered', 'To whom', 'Returned', 'allowed', and
'£ S. D' shows that forty-eight people took
multiple tickets and sold all or most of
them – Eaton and Smith (the bookseller):
300; Galloway: 269; Barton: 202; Burks:
150; Lee and Cooper: 120; Aspinall, Bone,
Hodgson, Place: 100; Salter: 74; Fleming:
72; Danton, Oliphant, Pierce (Division 21):
50. The remaining persons took between 6
and 39 tickets, or took but had not paid for
tickets.]

53 This motion and the motions of 23 July which
are designated C, B and A are considered on 26
July. See no. 282.

Account of Tickets

Delivered		3008
Returned	513	
Allowed	60	
Bone delivered to J Pickard	16	
Jones not returned	2	591
		2417
Due not paid for –		373
		2044

[There follows a list of persons who owe
for tickets and of the number of tickets
each owes for, totalling 373.]

Received

2044	50:15:6
Taken at Door of Genl Meeting allowg 5/6 Bad	5: 8:6
	56: 4:0

Received Account of Citn Roussel's Attorneys
Bill amounting to £8:17:4 adjourned to this
day week –
Read the following letter from Birmingham[54]

[The associated friends to a thorough and
radical reform in the national representation
are pleased to read in the *Courier* the
account of your meeting on the 29th –
Besides the invincible weapons of reason
and truth striking the hydra of despotism,
all that is needed is for every friend to step
forward and unite, etc. – accept our con-
gratulations on the triumph of innocence in
the persons of citizens Hardy, Tooke and
Thelwall.]

The following Letter was read from Coventry

[Please send copies of your Address to the
Nation to be distributed to the swine of
Coventry, who now are convinced of the
necessity of the reform which the LCS pro-
motes.]

54 At the end of Add MSS 27813 there is a reference to this letter and the next, from Coventry:
'The Letter of July 10th. 1795 from Birmingham, Signed by John Kilmister, Secretary, No
13 St Martins Street Islington near Birmingham –
The Letter of July 2. 1795 from Coventry signed
by Thomas Prosser direct to him at Messrs Christ
& John Davies Coventry –' (fo. 148v).

Both Letters reffer'd to Ex Comee to answer immediately[55]

Quarteridge £11: 1: 5½ –

In consequence of being So many adjourned Motions it was moved & secd that an extra meeting of Genl Comee be called to morrow evening July 17th.   Negatived

Mov'd & Sec'd that an extra Meeting be called on Sunday July 27. at 6 O Clock in the evening precisely   Affir

adjourned

278. Report from spy Powell: LCS General Committee, 16 July 1795[56]

Source: PC 1/23/A38

General Committe 16 July 1795.
Beck in the Chair

174 New Members   £9 . 19 . 6 Quarterage

[Powell then named the deputations to divisions whose delegates were absent, reported the request of the inhabitants of Greenwich to join, and gave the vote on the referred question. He also gave the substance of the motions reported in the minutes given above. On the motion to print the three documents, he added:]

After a long debate The Secretary was calld on for his account of all the Money in hand that received at the General meeting & all when it appeared after all debts were paid the Society would have a Ballance in hand of upwards of £60. The Committee then Resolv'd that the Motions from Divisions 12. 11. 5. 20 & 23 should be agreed to & the Executive ordered to put them in Force immediately & to print 2000 at first & keep the press standing N B. The Printing of Genl Meetg Procdgs The Quarterly Correspondence & the Duke of Rds Letter with State of the Representation will take the whole of the above Sum if not more

Div 20   Resolv'd that the Account of the Money received at the Genl meeting be laid

before the Committe immediately with the Number of Tickets issued. This Motion having come last weeke & the Committe having appointed a Deputation to explain the business to them. That Deputation was call'd on when it appeard they had not done their duty. . . .

[T]he Genl Committee adjourn'd at 12 OClock N B.   Div 27 The Deligate inform'd the Committee they should Branch off to the White Horse, White Horse Yd Drury Lane to meet on Monday. The Committe gave them No 17 & appointed Hodgson, Ham & Purshouse to open it

Div 12   To Branch off to the Blackhorse Fishmongers Alley Borough to meet on Monday. The Committe Numbered them 15. & appointed Ramsey, Yates & Price to open.

Div 4 appoint James Powell their Deligate & Hecter Campbell Sub Delegate

Div 12 Wilson Sub Deligate.

279. Report from spy Powell: LCS Executive Committee, 17 July 1795[57]

Source: PC 1/23/A38

London Corresponding Society
Executive Committe Sittings of the 17th. July
Barton in the Chair

Held a Conference with Citn. Rock of Sheffield in consequence thereof ordered a letter to be sent to the Constitutional Society of that town Hodgson to draw up the same.[58]

55 Only the reply to Birmingham exists (*Correspondence*, pp. 32–3). Dated 17 July, it speaks of the orderliness of the general meeting, of the LCS reaction to recent riots against crimping houses, of the increase in the size of the Society (300–400 in the previous three weeks).

56 Powell's description: 'Report of the/ General Committe/ 16 July 1795'.

57 Description: 'Report   Executive Com. / Sittings of the 17 July 1795'.

58 The Sheffield reformers were evidently having the sort of internal dissension which the LCS experienced in March and April. The letter to them, dated 22 July, states that since the LCS has overcome its difficulties and acquired some experience, they offer advice. Suspicion and resentment are the passions most injurious to society. Suspicious men, if ever they condemn rightly, think they have authority 'to corrode every bond of Society, by disseminating doubts of every active character'. If anyone finds his fidelity doubted, 'he ought to consider it his duty to remove those doubts by amicable explanation, rather than exhibit a specimen of aristocratic pride, captiousness and punctilio'. A postscript adds that there are 41 divisions and that nearly 800 have joined within the last month. In addition there are two similar societies, the London Reforming Society and the Friends of Liberty, 'chiefly composed of persons who were formerly members of our Society, but who left us because the could not agree with each other'. The LCS is on good terms with both (*Correspondence*, pp. 33–6).

The letter to Birmingham read & approved & ordered to be sent with some of the Proceedings of the Genl Meeting Regulations, & report of the friends of the people.

Galloway produced an answer to the letter from the Norwich Patriotic Society. Read & approved ordered to be sent with Genl Meeting proceedings &ca as above

Moody, Cooper, Justice Jones, Young, & Maxwell appointed as a deputation to wait on the Council & jury of D I Eaton with the medals. to be allow'd 10s/6 for expences

The letter of the Duke of Richmond to Colonel Sharman with the Report of the Friends of the People sent to the Press.

Received & Paid the Carpenters Bill for erections in the Field for Genl meeting amount £7 . 6 . 9.

Bricklayers for repairing the wall &ca £3 . 7 . 1.

Adjourned

Present Hodgson, Jones, Moody, Barton Maxwell Powell, Ashly & Galloway

280. Minutes: LCS General Committee, 23 July 1795

Source: Add MSS 27813, fos. 76v–82

Genl Comee   July 23rd. 1795
Citn Moggeridge in the Chair –

[The report starts with a tally of the 28 divisions, listing a total of 179 new members and 1071 present at division meetings during the previous week. No figures are listed for Divisions 19 and 25. For four divisions there are notations naming delegates: Div. 2, 'Lemaitre sub instead of White superceded for Neglect'; Div. 9, 'Davidson sub dele'; Div. 15, 'Neale & Casey'; Div. 30, 'Morris – Jones'.]

Absent –
23.   Deputed Ward, Hough Graham –

The following Divisions branches & requests Numbers & Deputations

Divn   Branches to Scotch Arms, little
5.   Britain – on Tuesday – to be No 19 – Deputed, Binns Purcehouse, Moggeridge, Ham & Read –
20.   Branches to Marquis of Granby, Bennets Court Drury lane – Monday – To be No 25. Deputed Ward, Powell, Beck –
22 –   Branches to 2 Canns & Bunch of Grapes Goswell Street Friday – To be

No 32. Deputed Banting, Mead, Hough & Edwards –
13.   Branches to George, West Harding Court Fetter Lane, Wednesday – To be No 33. – Deputed Ward, Canty, Rawson, Hastie, Oxlaid –
28.   Branches to Talbot Inn – Grays Inn Lane – Tuesday – To be No 34. Deputed Neale, Wilson, Casey, Mead, Salter –
16.   The followg – To the Genl Com – Citns The under mentioned names is desirous of forming a Divn of the London Corresponding Society at the 7 Stars in Fleet Street Bethnal Green it being near their habitations & hope for you Approbation – Those Names marked wth Stars are members of the 16th. Divn the others have give their Names as members when they shall receive from you a Deputation & Number – to meet on Tuesday –

Thos Grace*	Wm Mills
Jas Grange*	Thos Pound
Danl Phillips*	Wm Eaton
Thos Linillin*	Wm Humphries
Geo Evans	Matthew Miller
John Matton	

To be No 35. Deputed Banting, Pickard, Canty, Oxlaid Williams

Informed by Assist Secretary that Citn Moody had applied to the Ex Com to establish a Divn at the Blue Posts Brewer Street Golden Sqre the Ex Com had given him the No 31. & requested the Genl Comee to appoint a Deputation & they Deputed Binns Wilson, Salter Mirfin Lemaitre –

Binns reported the following Defaulters of the Deputation to Greenwich   Moggeridge, Ham, Wilson Powell & Mead –

The Maidenhead Windmill Street Finsbury Square wished to have a Divn as soon as possible

Divn   Resolved that the State of the Repre-
4   sentation by the Friends of the People wth the Duke of Richmonds Letter to Colonel Sharman be given to ea member of this Society Gratis without exception if the finances will admit –[59]
   Resolved that the Ex Comee do wait on the Secretary of State for an answer to the address – as early as possible
5   That it is the opinion of this Divn that the report of Delegate respecting

59 Powell attributes this motion to Div. 1 and adds that it was 'resold. in the affirmative'. He also attributes the next motion to Div. 1.

the deputation with the address to the king should be revised by the Ex Com

That it is the Opinion of this Divn that ea member of the Society be furnished wth 2 Copies of the late proceedings of the Genl Meeting

8. Are of Opinion if the Society was to
C print the Declaration of the Bill of rights (meant the Declaration of Rights) & sold to Members & strangers at prime Cost, As it would be the means of diffusing knowledge amongst our suffering Countrymen

5.[60] It is the unanimous opinion of this Divn that the Insinuation cast upon Citns Ashley & Galloway is without foundation & that the above Citns have deserved the approbation of this Society

28. Resolved that altho' this Divn opposed the Genl Meeting yet the Conduct then pursued & that of the deputation in their manly & good conduct in the presenting the address meets their approbation & warmest thanks –

8. Recommend to the Genl Com to
B print the Duke of Richmonds letter to Colonel Sharman together wth the report of the sub Comee of Westminster to be delivered to the Members with the regulations

23. Resolved that it is the Opinion of this Divn that any person who shall assert or insinuate that Citn Galloway is guilty of Official Misdemeanor & refuse to accuse him in the Comee of Delegates shall be exluded the Society

18. Ordered the Secretary of this Divn to
A attend at the Genl Comee Room & take a copy of the last monthly Account & of the Genl Meeting Account – And it is recommended that other divisions should give similar orders to their secretaries as the means of preventing evil minded persons from spreading doubts & dissatisfaction. It is likewise ordered that the Secretary of this Divn do bring a list of the Divns with their several Days & places of Meeting –

Read a letter from the London Reforming Society directed to Citn Ashley – as follows –

[They are sending printed copies of their report for each LCS division. Signed J. Bone, sec.]

60 Div. 6 in Powell's report. The motion was approved.

A report delivered to Each Delegate –

Movd by Mead Secd Binns – That honourable mention be made of the London Reforming Society in the Minutes of this Society – & that the Same be transmitted to the London Reforming Society – by the Secretary & that Some Copies of the Proceedings of the Genl Meeting be sent at the Same time – Affir

Citn Draycott admitted to honours of sitting – he presented the following Letter –

Mitcham July 20th. 1795.

[Jas Pope of Mitcham informed me that you are connected with the LCS. I apply to you for information about your society. We are not yet ready to] apply to London for Admission. . : I had the happiness of being at the Genl Meeting in Saint Georges fields. So far as I could relate of the Proceedings it has met with General applause far beyond what I could have conceived as I find almost every Day new converts –

President desired to inform Citn Draycot – as follows which he did

That it would be most proper for him to inform his friend when Citn Pope comes to Town on Wednesday Week that he should become a Member & might then be admitted to the Sitting

Report of Ex Com called for, but the reporter being absent it was deferred a little later –

Mov'd & sec'd that the 1st. Motion from Divn 5 be now taken into Consideration Affir

Citn Mead begged leave to ask Citn Galloway what passed at the Secretary of State's Office when the address was presented – Galloway answered – That when Jones delivered the address to the clerk in the Lobby – he Asked where it came from & Citn Moody answered that it was a letter to the king – they then went away & was called back again – the clerk took the Letter (into the Council (which was then sitting) & bro't out word that it required no answer & that he saw it put into the kings private bag –

Mead stated his reason for asking as follows – That when he gave his report to his Divn he was contradicted & said that he had mistated it & he informed them that it was copied verbatim from the Report of Ex Com –

Binns the delegate of Divn 5 stated that when he gave the report of deputation as went with the address it was contradicted by Citn Jones – who said that they were received with all civility that could be expected & that they only was ordered back once & he therefore made the Motion that every Divn might have a true report – Binns mov'd & secd Beck that the Motion of Divn 5 be referrd to Ex Comee to correct the Report

Baxter & Burks Deputed from the Friends of Liberty & bro't the followg letter   admitted to honours of sitting
Order of Day mov'd on Motn of Div 5 neg –
Motion put wether it should be refer'd to Ex Comee   Affir –

Burks presented some resolutions of the Friends of Liberty & would have sent more – but but could [not] get any more ready in time as passed at a Genl Meeting which they held at Shacklewell near Kingsland on 20th July –

Mov'd that Honourable metion by made of The Friends of Liberty in the minutes of this Society, & that the same be transmitted to them by the Secretary & that some Copies of the Proceedings be sent at the same time Affir –

Burks returned thanks for the honour they had done & begged that he & Baxter might withdraw as they was obliged to attend at their Comee this Evening –

Comee Room July 23rd. 1795
To the Comee of the London Corresponding Society
Citizens –

[The Friends of Liberty send you the resolutions passed at their general meeting on 20 July.]

Pursue the Glorious tenor of your way – Perservereing stretch forward to the Goal – The Shouts of Victory shall be your reward! And the Trophies wrested from the strong Arm of Aristocracy shall invest your Brows with civic wreathes – Citizens if ought can add to the felicity of having restored to your Country the exercise of their rights to *Universal Suffrage & Annual Parliaments.*

The Society of the Friends of Liberty would request the privelige of being allowed to conjoin their exertions with *The London Corresponding Society* to procure so salutary & indispensible an object

It is true we are engaged under different Leaders yet being engaged in the same sacred cause – The same Standard must infallibly unite us all

	We have Citizens
	The Honour to be
Signed in Name	Your Fellow Citizens
& by order of the	The Society of the
Society	Friends of Liberty

Josh Burks Secy. –

The 2nd Motion of Divn 5 taken into Consideration Citn Mead rose & opposed the Motion as he could not see any Good it would [do], & likewise could [not] see why it could [be] wished for – for if it was meant to give one to a Friend – he [the] Citn could let him [have] [h]is own or the Person that was not a Member could surely afford to buy as the sum of 2d was so trifling, or if he could not he might lend his own – : & the sum of 2d could not make so much difference to the Person whom wanted it, as it would to the Society being obliged to Give one extra to each of its Members – as the Number of Members is now so large & is increasing so very rapidly – he therefore Mov'd the Order of the day on it – carr'd Affir –

Report of Ex Comee July 17

[The report is similar to Powell's. It adds that Ashley is to write the letter to Eaton's counsel and that Moody, Cooper and Maxwell are to write to the jury. Moody produced (probably at the general committee rather than at the executive committee) copies of the letters to counsel and jury. One other item is not in Powell's report:]

The Comee came to the resolution to recommend to the General Comee to call in all the Subscription Letters – has they have heard that there is money to a great Amount on them – the suggested to call them in by the 2nd Thursday in August.

The Secretary produced 2 Bills of Bricklayer & Carpenter for repairs done to the Field –

The Carpenters – 7:6:9
Bricklayers – 3:7:1 – 10:13:10

And stated that he had paid about 7:17:6 – has he thought they was extravagant charges & therefore thought that he could not over pay them by that

The Bills were examined, & was generally supposed to be rather extravagant – but that the wood was off the Ground, & the Bill so complexed that it would be a hard matter to tax it – he was therefore order'd to pay – & the Persons to do no more work for the Society

Citn Cooper Bill –

500 Tickets for Lectures	£	D
Printed by Seal		8:0
Cash in Pearce's hands	1	2:0

1:0:0 [1:10:0]

He stated the 500 Tickets was printed At the time of Delegates being sent to Edingburgh – & the Lectures was then given towards their support & that he paid Seale for them The Cash in Pearce's hand he stated thus That Pearce had received the Money for the Rent of Room in Compton St for Divn 2 – & that Cooper & Barnes having debts together he had paid the Room rent – & had asked Pearce for the Money whom told him, that the Society owed him a great Sum of Money, & that when that was paid he would pay him –

The Comee did not know of any debt due to him from them – & as there was always a Collection in Divn 2 for Rent – they could not see it just that Citn Pearce did not pay it to Cooper as he had paid Barnes – it was therefore to Ex Comee to examine the charge –

Quarteridge £11:3:11½

Citn Beck stated that he had heard several Members could not attend the Extra meeting on Sunday – he therefore moved that it be to morrow Evening – On the other hand it was stated that there were 2 Divns to meet on that Evening – & it would occasion 6 or 7 Members of the Comees being absent – that it would most proper on Sunday –

It was therefore Resolved to meet on Sunday Evening next at 6 O'Clock precisely –

281. Report from spy Powell: LCS General Committee, 23 July 1795[61]

Source: PC 1/23/A38

London Corresponding Society
General Committe 23d July 1795.
Moggeridge in the Chair

181. New Members, Quarterage £11. 5. 11½

Div 15. John Neale to be Delegate, Peter Casy Sub Del.
–   17. Thos Rawson Del. Martin Cockswain Sub Del.
–   30   Thos Morris Del, John Jones Sub Del.

[The rest of Powell's report is substantially the same as the minutes. He adds Galloway to the deputation to Division 23 and Powell to Division 34. After giving the motion that the general committee revise the report of the deputation trying to present the address to the king, he explains:]

61 Powell's description: 'Report Genl Committee / 23 July 1795'.

The reason of this motion was that from the Report of the Ex Com. it appeared that the deputation was treated with rudeness at the Secty of States Office   Jones who was present in the Div denied it & said they were on the Contrary treated with great politeness & civility & caused this Motion to be sent to the Genl Com.

[On the motion rejecting insinuations against Ashley and Galloway, he explains:] The insinuation alluded to is that he & Ashly had pocketed some of the mony receved at the Genl Meeting which is without foundation. . . .

[T]he Committe adjoun'd at one oClock –

282. Minutes: LCS General Committee, 26 July 1795

Source: Add MSS 27813, fos 82v–93v

Genl Comee July 26th. 1795
Beck in the Chair

[The report starts with a list of 35 divisions with 'ab' marked after numbers 9, 13, 20, 21, 27, 29 and 30. Some other division numbers are marked 'ab came in'. Notation after number 31: 'Jas McGuire   Jas. Fletcher, Thos Wilkins Secy'. Notation after number 32: 'Hewitt – Green – Huttley Secy to Meet on Monday instead of Friday'.]

Mov'd & sec'd that it be recommended to the General Comee on Thursday next to appoint Deputations to the absent Divns this Evening – Affir –

Divn 18. May 5. This Divn recommends to the Genl Comee in Case the Second referr'd Question should be affirmed to direct the Secretary to provide a Book for the Special Purpose of recording the Decisions of the Society on such Questions as may be referr'd relative to constitutional Points, in order in order that they may be inserted duly in the printed Copies – Affir –

It was stated the reason for this Motion being sent was – that they might be many questions at different times relative to constitution sent to the Genl Comee & referr'd to the Divn & affirmed – And it would be impossible to have the regulations alter'd every time – & therefore the Secretary should have a Book to keep them in – & then whenever there were more regulations wanting printing that they might then be duly inserted –

& if it were left to chance that they might be lost or forgotten –

The Motion put & Carr'd affir –

Divn 5   May 11th. That this Divn thinks it would be much the best for every Divn to depute one of its Members to draw up the address or any other Business for the Genl Meeting, as it would ease the Comee & bring forward the other members of the Society – answer by the Genl Meeting being over –

20.   May 13th. Resolved that the Genl Meeting [i.e. Genl Commee] do order the Ex Com to prepare & print the proceedings of the Society since the 5th. Nov 1794 for the use of the Members agreeable to the 17 Article of Regulations – Negative

It appeared to the Comee that the Divn had misunderstood the 17 Article – And it would be a very great expence & appeared to the Comee to be no utility – but they perfectly agreed with putting the 17 Article in execution – but was obliged to Negative the present Question –

5th.   July 6. This Divn recommends to the Genl Comee to enforce the 17 article of the Regulations – Affir –

16.   That it is the Desire of this Divn that the correspondence with all the Patriotic Societies in the Country be printed for the benefit of the members aggreeable to the 17 Article – Affir

23   Recommend to the Genl Com to put in force the 17 Articles as soon as possible – Affir –

Mov'd & sec'd that the Ex Comee do prepare & publish the same as soon as possible – Affir –

Divn 18.   June 2nd. It is the wish of this Divn that a list be printed of all the Members of The London Corresponding Society. that have been imprisoned bro't to trial & liberated with the Length of their imprisonment & charges bro't against them on their Trial or on examination wth a few remarks on the Constitutional & legal proceedings of the Society & the Illegality of their prosecutions believing it would form such a contrast as would be satisfactory to the Public & Society at Large –

It appeared to the Comee that the intention of this Motion – was no more than to shew Contrast of Our Proceedings & the Proceedings of the Ministry – & was of opinion that the acquittal on the late Trials was proofs enough of the legality of our Proceedings – & their

illegall proceedings – & was of opinion that if they would not convince the People at large that nothing would –

Order of Day was mov'd on it, but it was thought that was slighting the Motion therefore it was withdrawn

The Motion being put   8 Affir   12 Neg –

12   June 9. That a Subscription be raised for Citn Martin & that the Comee of Delegates give Direction to Ex Comee to send letters to the different Divns for that laudable purpose

The Delegate of that Divn address'd the Comee has follows –

That when this Motion came from his Divn Citn Martin was known to be in great Distress & had not made any claim on the Society of Cater's Acc't

It appeared to the Comee that Citn Martin had been releived with 5 Gs immediately after that Motion was made – & has since made a Claim on the Society for 20£ odd – & they admitted that he had a claim on the Society & had appointed a Comee to investigate the said claim – & thought that they ought to be just before they are generous – & if hereafter Citn Martin was in distress they should do whatever lay in the Power for him –

The Motion being Put – was negatived unanimous Mov'd & Sec'd that the Report of the Comee appoint to investigate Citn Martin's Claim be now Rec'd –

When the following was rec'd for Citn Martin –

Kings Bench Prison July 8th. 1795

Aggreeably to request send you the Expences of Cater's Acc't –

	£.	S.	D.
Law expences paid out of Pocket –	21:	0:	0
Cash give Caters in Bridewell 5s/0 & 3/0	0:	8:	0
When Bail	0:	5:	0
When convicted, Prison Fees & to get a lodging	1:	1:	0
To the Turnkey for civility Money –	0:	2:	6
Half Year allowance in Bridewell at 19 pr Week	27:	6:	0
Gave his wife when laid in	1:	1:	0
Do when christening	1:	1:	0
Expences of discharge & sureties for good behaviour	1:	13:	6
	53:	18:	0

Citn Martin send his Cr Acc't as
follows –

Subscription by Boyd	10:10: 0
Do for Some Divns	3: 3: 0
Rec'd from this Comee	3: 3: 0
Rec'd from Do	2: 2: 0
	18:18: 0

From the enquiry the Comee had
made, it appeared to them that Citn
Martin had rec'd £ 12: 1: 6. collected in
the Genl Comee at the time the prosecution was pending – which was clearly
related by Citn Field who related the
Persons who composed the Comee at the
Time & who subscribed – & what they
subscribed – & Citn Hardy related much
the same – Citn Martin was therefore
waited on & informed the deputation
that the Society must excuse any little
mistake if there was any found – for
when he was taken into Custody all his
Papers &c were seized – He recollected
something of the Subscription & therefore admitted the 12: 1: 6 – as been
paid –

His own Cr Acc't –	18:18: 0
The Subscription in Genl Comee –	12: 1: 6
	30:19: 6
The whole Expences of the Prosecution } –	53:18: 0
Paid him –	30:19: 6
Due to him at this Time –	£ 22:18: 6

Mov'd & Sec'd that the Ex Comee be
ordered to pay Citn Martin as soon as
possible –

The Genl Comee asked the Comee of
Investigation wether they was fully satisfied of the Justness of the Claim –

Moody & Cooper both Present
answered in the Affir –

Motion Put for the Ex Comee paying
it – Carr'd Affir –

Divn
20 June 10. This Divn considering the
great Benefit likely to result from a Distribution of the Report of the Friends
of the People

Resolved that a transcript of the Title
Page of the said work be stuck up in a
large Bill with the Price affixed   The
Delegate of that Divn informed the
Comee that his Divn was of Opinion that
the Report of the Friends of the People
would open the Minds of the Public at
large – & shew them that there was no
actual Representation in this Country –
& shew them the Corruption there was
by above two thirds of what is called the
Commons House of Parliament – is
chosen by Peers or there dependants &
likewise the Small Number of People at
even were represented then:

On the other side it was stated that Posting Bills was of no kind of Use – As there
were such quantity Bills posted every
where – that the Public at large would
Not look at them

It was therefore movd & Sec'd that The
London Corresponding be affixed at Top
in Large Letters – as by that Means it
would catch the Public's eye.

Mov'd likewise that the reference which
is at the End of Narrative – for Admission of Strangers where to apply & leave
their address &c –

Mov'd likewise That the Narrative of
Genl Meeting & Duke of Richmonds letter be added likewise

The Motion therefore Run thus –
That large Posting Bills be stuck up
advertising the Sale of The Report of the
Friends of the People, The Duke of
Richmonds Letter, & Narrative of Genl
Meeting & reference for Strangers to
leave their address &c – for Admission –
wth the London Corresponding Society –
at Top in large letters –   Affir

Reffered to Ex Comee to Execute the
Same

Divn Motion as Marked A July 23rd taken into
18 Consideration Considered as a Recommendation to each Divn to put in practice if they think proper

20 Motion as Marked A July 16th. taken in
Consideration   The motion is answered
by the Secretary having made one Report
on the State of Tickets &c – & will make
the other it is expected on Thursday
next –

8. Motion as marked B. July 23rd. The
Duke of Richmond's letter already
ordered to be printed – & they considered that there is very little more information in the report of Sub Comee of
Westminster, but what is fully explained
in the Duke of Richmonds letter & that
the financies will not allow us to print so
much – as we already passed resolutions
for printing &c – to above the amount of
60£.

8 Motion as marked C July 23rd. The Delegate rose & informed the Comee that it
was the Opinion of his Divn that there
were some very Good & instructing Parts

in the declaration of Rights – such as showing The Right of the People Petioning the king &c –

It appeared to the Comee that it would be very useful – but it was ill timed & that the Society had already taken as much on itself as circumstances will admit of at present

The Motion was put & Negatived[62]

Divn Wishes to Branch to Red Lyon Silver St
5. Golden Square to meet on Wednesday & requests Number & deputation – To be No 36. Deputed Beck, Lindley, England, Lapworth – Jas Raverty 3 Tunns Cross Street Hatton Garden – wishes to have a Divn meet there –

Beck stated that Treasurers Acc't was not correct – That it was £2 short in the Cash received –

Mov'd & Secd that Ex Comee do examine the Same & Report on Thursday Next

283. Report from spy Powell: LCS Executive Committee, 24, 27 and 29 July 1795[63]

Source: PC 1/23/A38

Executive Committe

Sittings July 24 Present Ashly Hodgson, Moody, Galloway Barton & Young.[64]
Moody deputed to draw up answer to the Friends of Liberty[65]
Galloway to the London Reforming Society[66]
Young appointed to examine the Gazette to see if the Address to the King was acknowledged as received.
July 27. Present. Jones Ashly Hodgson, Moody Galloway Young & Powell.[67]
Answer to the Friends of Liberty, produced,

amended and ordered to be sent with 50[68] Copies of Genl Meeting Proceedings. Hodgson, Young, & Moody the deputation to go with it.
Answer to the London Reforming Society produced amended & ordered to be sent with 50 Proceedings deputation as above.
Ashly deputed to examine into Pieces [Pearce's] claim on the Society. Not yet able to report.
July 29. Maxwell, Jones, Ashly Galloway Hodgson Moody, Barton & Young.
Received a letter from Bradford in Yorkshire full of strong civic expressions requesting correspondence & to know the Price of L.C.S. publications Jones deputed to answer it.[69]
And ordered that 100 Regulations. 50 Proceeding G.M. 12 Duke of Richmonds Letters & 12 Reports of the Friends of the People be sent with it
Hodgson Produced an answer to the Sheffield Society approved & ordered to be sent with 100 Regulations. 50. Proceedings G.M. 12 Duke of Richmonds Letter & 12 Reports of the Friends of the People
The Deputation with the medals to the Councel & Jury of D I Eaton Reported that they had deliverd them agreable to the Motion of Division 1.
Moody Galloway & Barton deputed to wait on the Secretary of State for an answer to the address to the King.

284. Minutes: LCS General Committee, 30 July 1795

Source: Add MSS 27813, fos. 87v–93v

Genl Comee July 30. 1795
Citn Place in The Chair

[The report opens with a list of the 35 divisions, the number of new members and the

---

62 'Motion from No 2' – LCS note.
63 Powell's description: 'LCS Executive Committe / 24th 27th & 29th July, 1795'.
64 'Absent, Jones, Maxwell' – version in report of general committee.
65 Dated 30 July, it thanks the Friends of Liberty for their resolutions and their commendation of the LCS, but denies the statement in their letter that 'we are ranged under different leaders'. '[D]epending only *on the correlative exertions of each other*,' the LCS recognize no leaders (*Correspondence*, pp. 41–2).
66 Dated 27 July, the letter thanks the London Reforming Society for the copies of their progress report (*Correspondence*, pp. 39–40).
67 Powell is not on the list in the report of the general committee, but Maxwell is.

68 300 copies, according to report of general committee; 'same Number' to be sent to London Reforming Society.
69 Letter from Bradford, dated 23 July 1795, states that twenty to thirty men have met to form a society and they ask the LCS for hints on the management of it. The reply, dated 31 July, describes some obstacles reform societies will encounter (ignorance, prejudice, calumny, suspicion and ministerial influence) and lists some advantages of political associations: besides facilitating communication of events, they tend to inspire goodwill and affection, to cement bonds of fraternity and love, and to cause men to discard 'all selfish and ungenerous ideas'. The number of new LCS members has been almost 200 each week (*Correspondence*, pp. 36–9).

number of members present in each division, totalling 216 new and 1353 present. Notations after division numbers: 14, 'Robson instead of Wintrige for Neglect'; 19, 'B P Binns T Lucas Anderson'; 25, 'Lymans Brown Whitehead'; 27, 'informs G C. that Citn Stuckey being obliged to retire on acct of ill health – they have chosen Citn Dixey Delegate Brittain Subd in place of Iliff – on Acct of Illness – Evans Secy'; 33, 'not formed'; 34, 'White Roebotham Pursey'; 35, 'John Gibbons, John Dyall'; 36, Mellows, Russel, Page'.]

Citn Simmons admitted to honours of sitting The unrepresented Divn were – & Deputed as follows –

Divn
8   Ward – Simmons
13 – Place – B Binns
22 – John Binns – Ramsay
33 – The Deputation of last Week informed the Comee that very few of The Members that was branch attended – & they that were there informed the Deputation that they would get a full attendance next week – & beg they would attend on them then – Part of the old Deputation informed the Comee that they could not attend – And that the direction was giving wrong – as it was the George East Harding St Shoe Lane instead of West Harding St Fetter Lane – The followg Deputation appointed Rawson, Davenport, Gibbons

Citn Beck stated to the Comee that it was recommended for the General Comee on Sunday Evening to appoint Deputations to the unrepresented Divns of that Evening – It was stated that Several of the unrepresented Divns had received the reports thro' Delegates of other Divns & that they could [not] see any good in give any Report twice to any Divn –

On the other hand it was stated that if they had received Reports it was [not] in any official way – & that the Comee could not be certain of their having rec'd any Report – & it was there duty to provide for the unrepresented Divns And if they did not appoint Deputations to the unrepresented Divns it would be showing a bad precedent – & might occassion Some time Delegates &c – to stay from the Comee & borrow reports from other Delegates &c – & that the Divns might be neglected –

Citn Lemaitre could not see any good that could accrue for sending Deputations to Some which had received the Report tho not official – He therefore moved That no deputation be sent the Divns that had recd the Reports of the Meeting of the Genl Comee on Sunday last – Negatived

Divn The unrepresented Divns were
9   Place
13 Place
21 Hewit
27 Ramsay instead of going to 22 – affir –
29 Danton

Defaulters reported of last Week
Binns reported Mirfin for not attend 31 – he was not in Comee
Beck – reported Ward – for not attendg 25 – who informed the Comee he had mistaken the Place – & was going of to Bunhill Row – but Meet the Delegate of Divn 8 who informed him he was going wrong – & he not having his minutes about – it was to late then to Go –
Beck also reported Lindley for not attendg 36 – not in Comee
Rawson reported Ward for not attendg – 33. – he informed the Comee that his wife was taken in Labour that Evening – The following Divns requested to Branch of – & to have Numbers & Deputations appointed –

Divn to Williams Eating house No 2 Fitzroy
29   Market Tottenham court Road – to meet on Wednesday To be No 37 Moggeridge, White Powell
24 – to Bee hive Durweston Street York Place Portman Square to meet on Wednesday To be No 38. Salter, Wilson, Evans –
28 – To Grotto Paradice Row Paddington St to meet on Tuesday
    To be No 39 – Wilson Salter, Jarvis Wingate

Divn To the Maidenhead corner of Windmill &
22   Castle Streets – City Road – to meet on Monday To be No 40 – Carrington, Read, Pickard, Banting
18 – To The Robinhood Milbanke St Westminster – to meet on Tuesday – to be No 41 – Ward, Denton Powell
4 – Changes to the Queen of Bohemia Wytch Street to meet on a Friday –
1 – The Delegate informed the Comee when the Members of that Divn [went] to there old place of meeting they were informed by the Landlord that they could not meet any longer there As he was in danger of losing his licence – they

have therefore moved to the Marquis of Granby – Knightsbridge – Wednesday

15. Moved to Kings Arms, King Street in the Boro' – Citn Beck desired to know wether the Ex Comee had revised the Treasurers Report – & likewise put in force the 17 Article of regulations as desired by Genl Come – The Comee was informed that multiplicity of Business had prevented them – but that it was there next Business –

21 – Moves to Punch Bowl Broker Row Moorfields
Report of Ex Comee

[The report is substantially the same as the report made by Powell.]

The Comee appointed to present the address to the Secretary of State for the home Department were Citns Jones, Barton Galloway, Moody, Maxwell & Robt Lloyd Jones –

Citn Jones gave the address to the Council keeper, who asked what they wanted & where they came from after some interval of Silence Moody answered it was a letter for the Duke of Portland, keeper than asked for who, Barton answered it was a letter for the Secretary of State, the keeper than asked who from, Jones replied Sir it contains a letter for the king. he answered Oh very well! very well! it is a letter for the king, the council is now sitting you may go. The deputation apprehended that if the Privy Council should know from whom the address came that it would never be seen by the king, & after Sealing it up enclosed it in a Blank cover directed The Secretary of State for the home Department, supposing the Council would not open the address itself, they did not expect any answer they therefore readily obeyed the keeper when he informed them they might depart, but while they were on the Stairs they were called back with great earnestness by the keeper, when they returned he observed, you said this was an address to the king. I will carry it to the Council & you must wait & see wether it requires any answer, he accordingly went into the Council Chamber & coming out again said Gentlemen you must wait, after waiting some time Galloway asked wether there was any possibility of being accommodated with Seats but received no answer. Soon after a Gentleman open'd the Door of the Council Chamber & appeared to survey the deputation, immediately after his return, the keeper with another Gentleman came out, the Gentleman having in his hand the address to the king which appeared un-

opened, he put it into the dispatch Bag & the keeper addressed himself to the Deputation & said Gentlemen it requires no answer & they immediately departed –

Signed

Moody, Barton, Maxwell, Galloway –

Report of Deputation appointed to carry Medals of D I Eaton's acquittal. The absentees where Moody, Cooper & Justice Jones, in consequence of which – Ashley was added to the deputation

The Report that they delivered them to Jury & Council – moved that the Country Correspondence & Booksellers be all Served with the Publications at the Wholesale Price – Affir – Divn Resolved that this Divn do think it

2 beneath this Society to follow the very unmanly method recommended by its regulations to ballot for their Officers – They think that Reformers should never be supposed conniving at Such proceedings & hope the Genl Comee will refer the present Motion to the Society at large to elect them in future by a show of hands – It was the Opinion of the Comee that they could [not] Do any [thing] with the present Motion put [i.e. but] refer it to the Divns for their Consideration –
Mov'd & Secd that it be referr'd to the Divns – affir –

22. Resolved that a ¼ part of the Income of this Society be set apart for the special purpose of forming a fund for the relief of such Patriots (members of this Society[)] who are now or who may hereafter be imprisoned for what a packed Jury may term Sedition. – We do not by this mean to encourage any to speak imprudently or unconstitutionally such conduct would meet our marked disapprobation – but after so late an example of tyranny in the condemnation of our worthy fellow Citn Henry Yorke[70] we think such a measure would tend very much to the Support of Parliamentary Reform –
Citn Denton as Delegate of that Divn informed the Comee this Motion was made in a very full Meeting & met wth their general assent –
It was stated on the other hand that in the present Mode the Motion stood it

70 On 23 July Henry Redhead, alias Yorke, was convicted of having used seditious words at a reform meeting in Sheffield fifteen months earlier, on 7 April 1794. He was sentenced to two years' imprisonment.

was a very Dangerous one & they believe Citn York a very worthy good Patriot – but was a man of a very violent Temper – but though he deserved every thing that lay in our Power to do for – & thought it would much best to refer the Motion back again to the Divn from whence it came to amend it –

Mov'd that it be refer'd to the Divns

Amendt   Moved & Secd that it be refer'd back to the Divn from whence it came to amend, & to be more cautious in their Words – Affir

32.   That this Divn do recommend Citn Yates the Landlord to change his Newspaper for the Telegraph & if he requires it the Divn to make the extra expence good. That our Delegate be desired to recommend the same to the Delegates of ⒞ⓐ Divn as it will be Public to the Inspection of all People who frequent those houses & must be productive of great Good –

Consider as a Recommendation to ⒞ⓐ Divn –

6   It is the Opinion of this Divn that refer'd Motion should not be passed over more than one Month before they receive the decision of the Society.

It was Stated by the Delegate of that Divn that the reason of this Motion being made was, that when motions were adjourned so long (as on Sunday last Motion were taken into Consideration of May 7th.) the object for which they were first brought forward where forgot – & the Delegates might Not then be Delegates –

Citn Beck states that it appeared to him that the Divn that [i.e. had] mistaken refer'd for adjourned Motions – therefore moved that it be referr'd back to the Divn for amendment from which it came – Motion made & Sec'd that it be refer'd back – Affir –

26   Resolved that this Divn think the present mode of publishing the proceedings to expensive to be beneficial to this Society – 2nd. That knowledge would probably be diffused more by printing the proceedings at one penny ⒞ⓐ – 3rd. Resolved that the Proceedings be printed at one Penny each & to be circulated as much as possible

It was Stated that this Society did not meet for the Purpose of make a Profit of Publications, but for the purpose of diffusing knowledge amongst our Countrymen, therefore as the present regulations

is or can be printed at or near about three farthings each, & as there will then be a sufficientcy then to pay for Trouble &c –

Motion Put & carried in Affir –

Read a letter Signed Roe – in his old Stile of writing railing against the Pickeringites, Wilsonites, Salterites &c – & raisd your Correspondite's &c

Citn Pickard inform the Comee that Citn Oliphant gave him the letter which he informed him came (undercover to him – Directed to The London Corresponding Society which he was very much astonished at –

The Secretary[71] then informed the Comee That the Narrative of Genl Meeting cost about £3 . 4 . 0 per Thousand – it was then Stated that there could be 3000 printed for £9 – Citn Williams then stated that he could Get 3000 printed for £8 . 10 . 0   Mov'd by Moggeridge & Secd That the Delegate of each Divn enquire of the Printers in his respective Divn concerning the Price at which they could print any Publications of this Society & that their proposals be sealed up – Affir –

Citns Hodgson, Young Moody than arrived in the Comee a Deputation appointed to the Friends of Liberty Hodgson wished to Report the result of their Deputation

Citn Galloway stated that As the Ex Comee appointed them on that Deputation they ought to Report back to them

Young then delivered Resolutions of the Friends of Liberty – Mov'd Moggeridge & Secd – that the Ex Comee do call a meeting of the Printers in this Society & that they lay before them such Publications as are now ordered for printing that they may send in their tenders sealed.

It appeared to the Comee that this would be a very troublesome way of proceeding – for when ever there was any work wanting publishing there must be the Size shewn to All the Printers & must have a Genl Meeting of the Printers called

The Motion was then put – Negatived

Citn Ramsay, stated that he understood the Deputation which had been to the Friends of Liberty, & some Business of importance which they could state to the Comee & he thought it was most proper not to delayed it   He therefore mov'd that they now Report to the Genl Comee the result of their Deputation

On the other hand it was still persistd in that they had no right to Report to this Comee before had to the Ex Comee –

Motion – put & Negatived

71 'Citn Moggeridge' crossed out before 'The Secretary'.

Quarteridge £11 .. 5 .. 9½

Citn Binns stated that as the Committee Room was to small for the Comee to meet he should move that the Ex Comee be desired to enlarge the same & make it Convenient for the Meeting It was stated that it need not be made a Motion of – As it was their duty to do it – as pointed out in regulations –
Citn Binns – then stated that the Secretary had been desired to Get Citn Roussel's Attorney's Bill – which had been laid before the Comee Three Meetings ago – & he thought it was neglecting it – He therefore moved that it be taken into Consideration on Thursday next immediately after the report of the Ex Comee
Adjourned

285. Report from spy Powell: LCS General Committee, 30 July 1795[72]

Source: PC 1/23/A38

General Committe 30th. July 1795
Place in the chair

216 New members. Quarterage £12 .. 5 . 9½
Div 34   D White Delegate.   D W Roebotham Sub Del   Heny Pusy Secretary
Div 27 I Dixey Delegate.
Div 25. James Lymans Delegate. Thos Brown Sub Delegate. D Whitehead Secretary
Div 28. Britton Sub Delegate. Evans Secretary
–   35 I Gibbons Delegate Jn Dial Sub Del.
–   36 Mellows, Delegate Russel Page Secty.

[Information about Divisions 1, 15, 29, 24, 28, 22, 18 and 4 changing meeting place or branching is the same as in the previous account.]

Div 14   I Robson Delegate instead of I Winterge superceeded for neglect of Duty.
Div 19   B. P. Binns Delegate   T Lucus S. D. J Anderson Secy . . .
Motions

[There are brief statements of the motions to vote by show of hands, to start a fund for for persecuted patriots, to solicit tenders from LCS printers, to answer motions within a fortnight (as against a month in minutes), and to charge a penny for printed proceedings of the general meeting.]

Citn Wood from Sunbury with a letter from a Society that was forming there who wishd to correspond with the LCS. Admitted to the honors of the Sittings & the Executive Committe ordered to answer the letter & send some of our Genl meeting proceedings. Publications &ca . . .
Adjourned

286. Report from spy Powell: LCS Executive Committee, 31 July, 4 and 6 August 1795[73]

Source: PC 1/23/A38

Ex Com. sittings of the 31 July 1795
Present Ashly Maxwell, Moody, Galloway & Powell[74]
Jones sent the Answer to the Bradford Society which after being revised was ordered to be sent.
The Deputation to the London Reforming Society reported That they waited on that Society who voted Thanks to the LCS. for answering their letter & sending them the proceedings. Also reported that the Committe of The above Society wish'd to be informd when it will be convenient for their deputation to confer with our Ex Com respecting the plan submitted by them for the more extensive circulation of political phamplets
They next waited on the Friends of Liberty.[75] they reported that our letter was twice read with applause on the 3d time of reading. Burks their Secty proceeded to make some remarks on that passage in their letter "It is true we are ranged under different leaders". He stated "that the Comitte had appointed him to draw up the letter in a great hurry which was the cause that this litte inaccuracy had slipp'd in had he been allowd time to revise it he cer-

73 Description: 'LCS Report of Executive Com. Augt 6th 1795'.
74 Powell omitted in report to general committee.
75 'on their arrival found the Comee had adjourned the members being informed of their admission resumed their sitting & appointed a chairman & received the deputation in form' – report to general committee.

72 Powell's description: 'LCS Report of the / Genl Committee / 30th. July 1795'.

tainly would have withdrawn that passage &
thought the LCS had acted very proper in the
comment they had made on it. Baxter also
appoligised for this passage & said the construction the LCS had put on it was extreemly
fair as it insinuated that they were under certain leaders which no person of sense could
possibly believe   He assured the deputation
there was not an individual in the Soc of the
Friends of Liberty but despized the idea of
Leaders after much conversation they requested
the deputation to state to the Genl Com. the
impropriety of printing either of these letters.
after this they voted their thanks to the LCS.
& the deputation withdrew.
Aug 4. Present Maxwell Moody Barton. Young
Hodgson. Galloway & Ashly. Jones[76] &
Powell.
Burks attended this sittings & after a conference respecting their letter the Ex Com
came to the resolution that in preference to
any other mode of proceeding it be recommended to the Friends of Liberty to send an
explanatory reply to our answers which should
be printed with our correspondence[77]
                                    Burks withdrew
The Ex Com after some deliberation do recommend to the Genl Com to audit the Treasurers
accounts publickly as the think it will be more
satisfactory to the Society at large & more
consistant with the 15 Article of the Regulations.[78]
Augt 6. Present Galloway Moody. Maxwell
Barton
Moody not having been present when he was
appointed as one of the Deputation to wait on
the Secty of State for an answer to the address
declined going which he said "he certainly
should have done at the time being perticularly
situated as not to have it in his power to comply with the request. Jones was appointed in
his stead the deputation was ordered to report
as soon as possible as the Society were im-
patient.
The parcells to Sheffield & Bradford were
sent –
                     Adjournd

76 'Absent' crossed out before this name.
77 This was recommended because it was too late
   to suppress the correspondence. A literal copy
   of the letter from the Friends of Liberty had
   been read and discussed in all the divisions
   (*Correspondence*, p. 43). The recommendation
   to the FoL was signed by John Young, chairman.
78 Art. 15, which specifies all the duties of the
   reporter (the liaison between the executive
   committee and the general committee), includes a charge to 'apprize the chairman of the
   [general] committee when the time serves to
   . . . audit accounts. . .'

287. Minutes: LCS General Committee, 6 August 1795

Source: Add MSS 27813, fos. 94–101

Genl Comee Aug 6th. 1795
Citn Binns in the Chair

[The report starts with a list of the 41 divisions, the number of new members in each
division and the number of members present
in each division, totalling 193 new and 1648
present. Notations after division numbers:
8, 'Smith Sub'; 14, 'Shirley instead of Simmons resigned'; 15, 'Ashford Sub Cresswell
Secy in place of Casey & Barker gone in
Country'; 20, 'Faulkener in place of Purcehouse resigned'; 33, 'Palmer Byron Troughton'; 37, Eeles Watkins Bridges'; 38, 'Allen
West Thomas'; 40, 'Everit French'; 41,
'Peirce Chambers Bury'.]

Unrepresented Divns to which Deputation was
appointed
13 – Peirce Rogers
      The Secretary of this Divn entered the
      Comee before the sense of the Comee
      was taken on Peirce & Rogers going –
      The Secretary therefore stated that has
      he was then there he did not conceived
      necessary to appoint a Deputation. Citn
      Lemaitre then stated has the Comee had
      not given their Sense on it – he thought
      it adviseable to not to send the Deputa-
      tion. On the other hand it was stated
      that the Deputation had been nomi-
      nated tho' the sense of the Comee was
      [not] yet taken whether they should
      go – therefore the sense of the Comee
      should be taken when it was there
      appeared   18 Affir 15 Neg –
20 – Roebotham & Russel
30.   Place to write report to be sent to them
39 – Russell, Place
Defaulters of last Week reportes
41   Powell for non attendance – he informed
      the Comee that he was very ill – & was in
      bed most of the Afternoon
33 – Oxlaid – for non attendance – as Secy of
      the Divn from which this branched – he
      informed the Comee that he did not
      know it was customary for the Secy to
      attend at a branch –
13 – place for Do he said he was on some
      Business for tickets for a supper – &
      waited so long at the Printers that he
      was to late

279

9. place for Do he said it was entirely neglect – & that he should willingly submit
to any censure they chose to pass on
him as he really deserved it
22 – The Secretary for not attending at a Branch
A Deputation appointed to Divn 29. to
endeavour to get them to appoint a Secretary conformable to the regulations
Powell, Brewer, Rawson – Affir
The following Divns requested to
Branch – & Desired Numbers & Deputations
5. Branches to 1 Tun in the Strand near
Hungerford Wednesday To be No 42 –
J Binns, Hough, Canty
5 Branches to the Ship little Turnstile
Holboren – Tuesday To be No 43 – J
Binns, Banting, Powell, Oxlaid
13 Branches to French Horn Lambeth
Walk – Wednesday To be No 44 Neale,
Peirce, Williams
27 Branches to the Cock Blanford St Man-
chester Sqre Tuesday To be No 45 –
Dixey, Brewer, McGuire
27 – Branches – to the Angel Inn High St St
Giles's Wednesday To be No 46 – B
Binns, Roebotham, Rawson, Brewer
24 Branches to the White Bear corner of
Newport & Lisle Street Newport Market
Tuesday To be No 47 – Salter. Lemaitre,
Allen
22 – Branches to the Nags Head St John St
Tuesday To be No 48 – Denton, Read,
French
The following Houses wished to have Divns
opened at them Citn Martins   Ben Johnsons
Head Westmoreland Buildings Aldersgate St
The Coach & Horses   Belton Street Long Acre
The White Hart Gravel Lane Southwark Earls,
The Red Lion Brownlow Street Drury Lane
Several Members of the Ex Comee wished to
speak but could not according to Regulations –
Citn Powell moved, sec'd Peirce that it be
referd to the Divns that the Members of the
Ex Comee be allowed to speak in the Genl
Come subject to the discretion of that Comeee
Amendt mov'd & Secd that all the words after
Genl Comee be left out
Powell withdrew that part
Citn Powell stated his reasons for makg this
Motion was that he thought the Members of
the Ex Comee being in the Genl Comee might
often throw some very good information at
times
On the other hand – the sense of the Motion
was not objected to but they did not think
that the Comee had that Power to refer any
Motion to the Divns without its having come
from some Divn

On the other hand it was stated – that any
time if the Genl Comee saw any thing good
that might be done for the benefit of Society –
they could not refer'd to the consideration of
the Divns without it came from some Divn
Motion put on its being referr'd – 24 Affir   8
Neg –
Report of Ex Comee

[The report for 31 July is substantially the
same as that given by Powell, except that it
adds one point:]

Moody & Galloway appointed to enlarge &
make convenient the Genl Comee Room, &
went there to form a plan – when they found
the workmen at work – but will have it ready
next week

[The report for the 4 August meeting is
substantially the same as Powell's.]

Aug 5th. Present, Galloway, Young, Moody,
Maxwell Barton   Absent – Jones, Ashley,
Hodgson –
Deputation appointed to wait on the Secretary of State for an answer – Moody not
having present when he was appointed, declined
which he certainly would have done at the
time being so particularly circumstanced as not
to have it in his power to comply with their
request.
It not being practicable to procure another
Citizen in Moody's place in the Ex Comee they
came to the resolution of recommending the
Genl Comee to fill up the vacancy – Citn
Hodgson answer'd that the vacancy was now
filled up Jones Barton Galloway –
Mov'd in the Ex Comee that the report of
the Ex Comee be revised by its members &
signed before delivered by the reporter –
The Sheffield & Bradford Letters both sent –
A Copy of Bradford Letter read –
The Sub Delegate of Divn 31.[79] entered &
informed the Comee that on Sunday last as
usual several Citns went to their old place of
meeting, after being there sometime 6 Constables of the Blackheath hundredths came in –
& said So you have got a seditious meeting
held here – & took very great Notice of the
Citns present, supposing to pick some out to

79 Must be Div. 30, which met on lower Greenwich
Road. Div. 31, meeting in Golden Square, would
not have been harassed by the Blackheath hundredths.

send aboard a Ship – at last fixed on the Sub Delegate asked him his name, he asked him what it was to him for he should not tell him Says do you know who I am – No Says he nor do I care who you are – You do not know who am – one of the Constables says to the Sub Delegate you need not been ashamed of your Name for Your name is Jones – & this Gentleman his the High Constable of the Blackheath hundreth's – he answered I am not ashamed of my Name for my is – Jones – mentioning his Christian as well – for I am only doing that which is right & I do [not] care who knows it – Then 1 of the Citizens want to go out of the Room & One of them set his back against the Door & said nobody should go out – they then all rose up & said that they would not suffer any person to be detained there against their consent – & after expostulating with they let him go about his business – & they then went away – The Landlord got information that the whole of the Constables of the Blackheath hundreths which amount to 24 – were Summoned to attend at the house – on the Monday Evening armed &c –

The Divn then thinking it would be most proper to remove their place of Meeting As they were sure there would be some mischief done As they had got some high spirit Plan amongst & they were sure they could not suffer them to interrupt them – it was therefore thought most proper to remove to some place out of the County – therefore removed to a private House the next door to the chapple – New cross turnpike opposite to the Dover diligence were – if they do interrupt them, they are determined to defend themselves – & they placed a Citn at their old place of Meeting where the old posse of Constables came as was expected & to their great mortification found only one Single man there – & the Landlady desired they would go & Search the house all over – which they declined, saying they were perfectly satisfied – he informed the Comee if it had not been for this dissaster – they should have about 20 New members

The Order of the day which was Citn Roussel Case, was then taken into Consideration – It was stated as Citn Roussel was taken up intirely for his attachment to the Society[80] –

& Government having kept him as long as they chosed of Treason – & supposed afters to have set his Creditors on him[81] – to lodge detainers against him – which is the cause of his present confinement – & this debt was contracted to keep him in the Fleet – as he should then be in a more central situation – & might get some little to do in his old profession – & that the money was due an Attorney who is himself a prisoner in the Fleet – & the whole or most of the Debt was money laid out of his pocket, & it was the means of Roussel's paying of it – & no doubt but Roussel depended upon us for it –

It was therefore moved that it be referr'd to Ex Comee to settle if the financies will allow – On the other it was stated they could [not] see that Citn Roussel ought to have made any application to us for it, & that we ought [not] to pay it as it would be encouraging any person in confinement that might contract Debts – to Send to The London Corresponding Society & would expect to have them paid & that there were many good Citns in the Society who through the hardness of the times wanted even a Shilling – & there were several good Citns who likewise thro the hardness of times could not even afford to belong to the Society at all – & was therefore was of Opinion that we ought not to give our Constituents Money away in this manner – by £8 at the Time – & the Debt itself was not contracted on Account of any part of his confinement for Treason – It was likewise stated that the Debts for which he is now in confinement was about £30 odds – & was contracted before his confinement for Treason but it was intirely thro' his confinement that the debts were not paid – as he was then in a very good way of livelihood & was encreasing very fast, therefore the debts would Soon have been paid if he had not been confined –

It was then moved that it be paid – It was then stated if this debt was not paid they could not remove him from the Fleet – & that they had better allow him some Sum of Money at times for his Assistance & not pay this debt –

It was then stated that it must make Citn Roussel very uneasy in his mind if we did not

80 In May 1794 Jean Baptiste Roussel told the Privy Council that he belonged to no societies. He had been in England since 1775, first as a silk merchant, then as a teacher of French language. He lived in Bury St Edmunds from 1788 until March 1794, when he left intending to go to France. Since he was arrested on 18 May 1794, there was not much time for him to

demonstrate his attachment to the LCS (examination, TS 11/963/3509, fos. 128–9).

81 This is the explanation given by Roussel in a handbill and newspaper advertisement (dated 23 May 1795) appealing for subscriptions, which could be left with Eaton, Burks, Lee, Hodgson, Ashley, Bone or Caney (Place Collection, vol. 37, fo. 30). Presumably the appeal in May did not bring in much money.

pay the debt – as it was the only means he had at present of paying it – & has it was all or most of it money paid out of the mans own pocket – & it not to be paid – & as it was means of keeping him from starving – as he had got some promises of having some employment in his profession –

Moggeridge was then stated[82] that he could not See any right that this Comee had to vote away the money of their Constituents in this manner – if it was refer'd to the Divns & they gave the consent to pay it – it was very well, but he did not think this Comee competent to do it –

He therefore moved that it be reffer'd to the Divns

Motion of Ex Comee paying it put – Neg –
That it be refer'd to the Divns & report this day week –
20 A – 12 N

Citn Burks admitted to honours of sitting –
Citn Seal admitted to Do –
Burks delivered from Friends of Liberty a letter which was read – further explaining the passage in their first Letter – "It is we are engaged under different Leaders –[83] Mov'd & Secd that it be refer'd to the Ex Comee Affir

Divn Resolved that it is the wish of this Divn
5   that the Secretary of the Society be directed to write Citn Henry Yorke to condole with him on the unfortunate termination of his trial & to offer him in the Name of the London Corresponding Society a pecuniary aid of £1 .. 1 .. 0 per week during his confinement if the financies of the Society will allow
36.   Do recommend it to the Genl Comee to enquire into the pecuniary circumstances of Citn Henry Yorke wth. a view to releive him if necessary, & expedient & to report as soon as possible for the information of the Society
16.   Resolved that it is the Opinion of this Divn that the publishing of a small dialogue[84] which was published in the Nottingham Journal 1783 will be the means of diffusing Political knowledge
6   Are of Opinion that adjourned Motions should not be passed over more than One month before they received the decision of the decision of the Society[85]

32.[86]   Resolved that this Divn do recommend to the General Committee to set a part a ¼ part of the Income of this Society for the purpose of forming a fund for the releif of those Patriots (Members of the Society who are & who may be imprisoned or otherwise punished for asserting the Right of Britons.

This Divn ever ready acknowledge the faults which they may have unwittingly committed & to profit by any past mistake which either intemperate & overheatead Zeal or any cause may have occasioned them to fall into. Do take this means to signify their approbation of the Conduct of the General Comee in that Business –

16.   Resolved that it is the Opinion of this Divn that a ¼ part of the Revenue of this Society should be funded for the benefit of Persecuted Patriots –
23.   Resolved that it is the Opinion of this Divn that a ¼ part of the Revenue of this Society should be funded for the benefit of Persecuted Patriots –
8.   Resolved that it is the Opinion of this Divn for the better regulation of the Comee that every Delegate shall attend the Comee tho' not constrained to stay the whole proceedings for the express purpose of delivering his Accounts in Money with their Number of New Members made &c – but if he cannot attend the Sub Delegate or Secretary must attend in due time, This may be accomplished by the Delegate giving due notice to the Sub Delegate & should he not attend which we hope will seldom occur he may state his objections to the Society that he may have Notice & in default of the person who takes cognizance of his proceedings unless something very material happens, he shall be supeceeded if the Comee thinks proper – this we think will forward the business of the Comee & prevent the delays occasioned
Divn by seeking deputations
Motion that no Member receive any of the Publications unless such Member have paid his quateridge –
Ballot for Ex Comee –
The old Comee were –
Barton
Jones –   36
Maxwell –   36
Young –   31
Hodgson –   11
Moody –   35

82 Originally: 'It was then stated that', etc.
83 They meant that the elected committees of the two societies were different (6 Aug. 1795, Correspondence, pp. 43–4).
84 'Dialogue Between a Clergyman and a Cottager'.
85 'decision of the Committee' in Powell's report.
86 '22' in Powell's report.

Read a letter from Hodgson stating that he wished to resign & recommended to enlarge to Ex Comee –
Citn Barton also resigned
New Members proposed for Ex –

Place –	Declined not in his power to attend[87]
Beck –	Do
Sellers –	17
Davenport –	26
J. Binns –	34

The New Comee

Jones –	36
Maxwell –	36
Young –	31
Moody –	35
Davenport –	26
Binns –	34

Quarteridge – 10 . . 8 . . 1½ –
It being recommend by Ex Comee to Audit Treasurers Account publicly –
Beck moved that they be orderd of Day of Thursday next – Affir –
Posting Bills enquired about – next business of Ex Comee

288. Report from spy Powell: LCS General Committee, 6 August 1795[88]

Source: PC 1/23/A38

L C S Genl Com. 6th Augt. 1795
J Binns in the Chair

193. New Members. Quarterage £10 . 16 . 7.

Vouchers for Officers.

Div	20.	J Falconer Sub. Del. vice Purse-house resigned.
–	40	Thos Evans Del. Thos French Sub Del.
–	39[89]	Farmer Del. Byron Sub Del Troughton Secty.
–	14	Thos Shirly Sub Del vice Symonds resignd.
–	15	Ashford Sub Del. Cresswel Secty vice Cary.
	8.	Smith Sub Del.

–	38	Allen Del. West Sub Del. Thomas Secty
–	41.	Price Del. Chambers Sub Del. Berry Secty.
–	37.	James Hales Del. Rd Watkins Sub Del Thos Brydges Secty.

[Report of divisions branching is the same as in previous report.]

The order of the Day was Roselles case who applied to the Society to enable him to pay an attornys Bill of £8 . 17 . 4 contracted to keep him in the Fleet Prison & prevent him from going to the Kings Bench.
After a long debate it was refered to the divisions.

[Motions from Divisions 5, 36, 16, 6, 22 (or 32), 16 and 23 are substantially the same as in the previous report.]

Div 8 Do recommend it to the Committe to put in force the 19th Article of the Regulations.[90]
Burkes Brought a letter from the Friends of Liberty explanatory of ther first. (vide Report of Ex Com)
Refered to the Ex Com.
A letter was read from Hodgson requesting to resign for a few months his situation in the Ex Com.
A letter from the London Reforming society was read with thanks for the Proceedings & wishing to know the directions to the Sectys of Country Societys. Referd to Ex Com
The letter in answer to the Society at Bradford was read
The Election of two members to the Ex Com then took place.
Hodgson & Barton resignd. J. Binns & Davenport were elected in their place
Adjournd

289. Motion from LCS Division 7: 11 August 1795[91]

Source: Add MSS 27813, fo. 146v

Divn 7 – Aug 11th. 1795.

It appearing to this Divn that the financies of the Society cannot be paid that attention too

87 But Place was present at some meetings: 'I had attended the sittings of the Executive committee before I became a member of it as, the Secretary Ashley – The Treasurer Beck and others of the five members were always desirous of my advice and assistance' (Add MSS 27808, fo. 26).
88 Powell's description: 'LCS Report of the Genl. Com. / 6th Augt 1795'.
89 Should be 33. Powell wrote 39 over 35.
90 Members of the executive committee 'shall be entitled to a Seat in the General Committee, but shall neither speak, nor vote, except their Reporter misrepresent them'.
91 This motion and one of 18 Aug. are put at the

which they deserve – They therefore recommend the following

That a Treasurer be appointed distinct from the Secretary, to whom all Publications shall be delivered & who shall be accountable to the Genl Comee for every single Pamphlet – without the gives reasons satisfactory to that Comee & shall report a state of financies every month on pain of being superceeded – He shall be in office three months & be eligible as long as the Genl Comee chuses to elect him.

We do not make this Motion by any means as throwing any reflection on our present Secretary, but are of Opinion that it is not in the Power of any one Citizen to pay that Attention to Secretary & Treasurer which they ought to be –

And we are of Opinion that our present Secretary deserves the thanks of this Society for his patriotic & just conduct We therefore return him our thanks & make no doubt but the other Divns will view his conduct in the same light & return him they thanks likewise

Lascelles Chairn

290. Report from spy Powell: LCS Executive Committee, 7–13 August 1795[92]

Source: PC 1/23/A38

Augt 7. Moody Davenport Maxwell Young Binns Young Ashley.[93] Binns was chosen Reporter

Received & Read a letter from Leominster Herefordshire requesting to be informd how they are to proceed for the purpose of forming a Society there to correspond with the L C S. Jones directed to answer it[94] & resolvd that 12 Regulations 12 Genl Meetg Proceedings 6 Duke of Richmonds Letter & 6 Reports of the Friends of the People be sent with it.

Augt 10   Maxwell Davenport Ashly Young Moody & Binns

Moved that the Committe do adjourn on account of the Absence of Galloway who was in possession of all the papers Motions &c of the Society & without which the Committe could not Proceed.

end of the minute book with other miscellaneous documents of 1795.

92 Powell's description: 'L C S Executive / Com. 13th Augt / 1795'.

93 'Absent Jones, Galloway' – report to general committee.

94 Letter from Leominster to Ashley, dated 2 Aug. Reply, dated 11 Aug., announces that enclosed regulations of LCS will show how to run a society (*Correspondence*, pp. 48–9).

Augt 11th   Ashley Gall. Maxwell Moody Young Binns & Davenport.[95]

Moved that the motion from Div 20 respecting public posting Bills with prices of the publications of this Society be referred back to the Genl Committee to be by them reconsidered.[96]

This Committe recommend Hand Bills

Moody Binns Maxwell & Galloway were deputed to arange the Correspondence of the Society & publish the same according to the 17th Article of the Regulations which will be carried into effect by the beginning of next Qarter & will include all Correspondence up to that Period

Read a letter from the London Refg Society Resolved that this Com. do not think themselves impower'd to inform them of the addresses of the Sectys of Country Societys. Also Resolved that this Com. being occupied in the publications already determin'd on by the L C S. cannot for the present attend to the plan submitted by the London Reforming Society. Binns deputed to answer their letter.[97]

Augt 12.[98] Resolved that the Members names be omitted in future who are appointed to answer any communication that may be sent to this Society

The answer to the Letter to Leominster read, approved & ordered to be sent

Davenport ordered to print 2000 Regulations & 2000 Genl Meetg Proceedings his estimate being the lowest. Binns added to the Deputation to wait on the Secty of State for an answer to the Address. Jones was chosen Reporter to that deputation.

Jones Report

About half past 2 oClock this day Augt. 13th. they went to the Duke of Portlands office & deliver'd the following letter.

Committe Room Augt 12th 1795.

May it Please Your Grace

We the undersignd being deputed by the L C S. wait on your Grace with a request to know wether the late address to his Majesty has been presented & wether he has been Graciously pleased to communicate any answer

Signd J G Jones. J Binns
J Barton. A Galloway.

·95 'Absent - Jones' – report to general committee.

96 Report to general committee omits this sentence and substitutes: 'As 1000 posting Bills will costing 29s Posting without printing & paper'.

97 Letter from LRS dated 30 July. Reply dated 14 Aug. (*Correspondence*, pp. 47–8).

98 'Present Jones Moody Young Ashley, Galloway,

On delivery of the above the Clark demanded to know what it was. Jones said it was a letter to the Secty of State & that they waited for an answer. The Clark told them the Duke of Portland was at St James but that he would give it to his Private Secty. In about 20 Minutes the Clark return'd & said the Private Secty could give no answer but that the letter should be immediately sent to his Grace. Galloway observed it would be necessary to have an answer & askd when they should call again. The Clark said it was uncertain but if they came that way in [a] day or two they might call. Jones replied "I should suppose the Duke might leave as an answer[99] when we think proper to call again. After this they withdrew.

291. Minutes: LCS General Committee, 13 August 1795

Source: Add MSS 27813, fos. 101v–7v

Genl Comee Aug 13th. 1795
Citn Powell in the Chair

[The report opens with a list of the 48 divisions, the number of new members in each division and the number of members present in each division, totalling 167 new and 1751 present. Notations after division numbers: 2, 'Constable Dele'; 3, 'Bustle in place of Davenport Richardson sub'; 7, 'Widdows instead of Nelson superceeded for neglect'; 10, 'Rogers, Harris'; 22, 'Morgan sub – instead of Read transferd to 48'; 39, 'Pilton Stewart Wilson'; 42, 'Ingram Davidson Ballard'; 43, 'Towerby Hethergill'; 44, 'Haselden Harrison'; 47, 'Constable Hasel Horton'; 48, 'Read Dennison Batchelor'.]

Unrepresented Divn
7 – Salter, Allen
Reported Defaulters last week
29 – Powell   reporter Brewer – The Divn chose a Secretary –
43 – Binns – did not – for was on Ex Comee that Evening –
Citns Edwards, & Davies – admitted to honours of sitting
Dimes – to keep the Door –
Divn Branches to Dog & Duck Bond St –
28 – Wednesday – To be No 49 – French Gibbons, Read, Hewit

Binns   leave of absence granted to Maxwell & Davenport' – report to general committee.
99 'leave a answer against the Time' – report to general committee.

3 – Branches to Ben Johnsons head Wetmorland Buildgs – to be No 50
29 – Are compelled by their Landlord to change their night of Meeting from Monday to Tuesday & was obliged for that Evening to meet in an upper Bed Room to accomodate a Society of Loyal Britons or a club of Church & King men who have taken our late meeting Room. The Landlord therefore obliged us to evacuate the same, during the whole Evening Citizens our Senses were charmed with those melodious Notes of God Save the king, Rule Brittania Britons strike home &c &c &c – But those tunes not being quite in unison with the under mentioned Citizens they therefore determined to branch of to form a new Division to meet on a Monday at the Bricklayers Arms Kingsgate Bloomsbury & request the Comee to appoint a Number & Deputation to open the Same –
The Citns who are here present have set down their Names
Turner Stacey Skale Stone Wenham Hanbury Sherman Anderson Parkinson Flyill
To be No 51 – Banting Powell, Place – Monday
Citn Moggeridge stated that the Justices had terrified the Landlord were Divn 26 meet that he would not let them meet there any longer – they had therefore moved to the Angel High St St Giles –
Coachmakers Arms Long Acre will receive Divn
Report of Ex Comee

[The report of the meetings of 7, 10, 11 and 12 August is substantially the same as Powell's. Both reports end with Jones's description of the deputation leaving a letter at the Duke of Portland's office.]

He then informed the Comee that he sent an exact copy of the Letter &c – to the Offices of the different papers – which would be inserted to morrow[100] – & hoped the Comee would approve of it – he then stated he could wish to speak on the propriety of sending another Deputation – but which to know the Sense of the Comee first wether he should speak   Citn Place then objected to his speaking as it was contrary to the Regulations – Dixey – stated

100 Printed as part of a news story in *Morning Chronicle* (14 August, p. 2). See cutting in Place Collection, vol. 37, fo. 57.

that he ought not to be allowed to speak, as it was contrary regulations for as we had got Regulations we ought to abide them till the sense of the Society altered them –
On the other it was stated as Citn Jones was apart of the deputation for that business he ought to speak As he must know more about it then the Comee as he had been –
Movd & Sec'd that he be allowed to speak on this Subject – Affir –
He then stated he thought & he made no doubt but it was the Opinion of the Comee that another deputation should go – but as to the propriety of allowing about week before they went or to go in a Day or two – for his part he should recommend a week – for these reasons first that it would not be hurrying of them – & Second it might be that the king did not think of sending an answer, as he might think the address would only be left there & thought no more on, but now seeing that a second Deputation had been – & the Letter going to The Duke of Portland – it might be the Means of the Duke of Portland stating to his Majesty that we had sent for an answer – & his Majesty seeing we expected to have an answer he might send one – Though it might not be to our Satisfaction – & if we did not receive any answer it would then be for our consideration to see in what plan the Society must pursue – but this he said he should not now trouble the Comee with as it was going from the Present question   Citn Oxlaid stated that he could not tell wether there lay any fault in the Ex Comee or not, but the Public was beginning to be very desirous to know the result of the Address – & it was delayed very much before the delivery – he therefore thought it would be most proper for the deputation to go in a Day or two –
a Motion made & Secd that the Same Deputation do wait on Secretary of State for an answer to the address – in the course of a week, & report to this Comee this day week – Affir

Recd the following Letter
                                        Aug 6th. 1795
To the Genl Comee

[We wish to form a division on 16 July at 2.00 p.m. at the Fox and Hounds, Sydenham, Kent. Signed 'Thos Holmes of Divn 27 Wm Bishop   John Sattam   Wm Saunders.']

To be the No 52 – Deputed Hodgson   Haselden

Place   Higgins   B.Binns   Saml Smith   Morris & Dyer[101]
Read the following Letter from Waltham Abbey sent to Citn Edwards of Aldersgate Street –
Citizen –

[I have no hope of forming a division here because the well wishers fear the magistrates. But we are holding a meeting on Saturday evening next; and if two or three more LCS members will come, we can use our utmost endeavours.]

It was stated this Letter was quite of a private Nature & that we could not anything with it –
Citn Edwards then stated the Citn who sent the letter to him became a member of the London Corresponding Society on Purpose (& was admitted to the honours of sitting in the General Committee) to establish a Divn there & he thought it the duty of the General Committee to Assist that Citizen all they could therefore they ought to send a Deputation –
Movd & sec'd that a Deputation of Citns Edwards, Dimes & Dowling – on Saturday next – & to carry some regulations some of Duke of Richmonds letter & State of Representation with them –[102]
Citizen Ward informed the Comee that he was informed there were a great many good Patriots about Derby & there was a Citn Venables in his Divn which could give a good of information about it – he therefore moved that he be requested to attend Ex Comee   Affir
The Divn 30 has moved to Citn Westfalls Tobacconist – in Greenwich – & requests a few of the Narratives of the General Meeting – Duke of Richmonds letter & state of Richmonds letter –
Movd & Secd that we do now adjourn till Morrow Evening 8 O'Clock –
         Amendt till Sunday 2 O'Clock – Neg
                              till to Morrow Evening – Neg

                              Carried forward

[There follow two tallies of the 48 divisions: 'The Decission on Refer'd Question to choose officers by Shew of hand'. 371 'Affir' and 608 'Neg'. 'Majority for ballot – 237'. 'Roussel Case', 391 'Affir' and 353 'Neg'.]

101 Pierce included in Powell's report.
102 To be Div. 53, according to Powell's report.

The following Answer relative to Roussels Case –

Divn 2. This Divn considering the refer'd question for the Payment of a debt incurred by Citn Roussel is of opinion that when such reference was made the whole state of the Case should likewise be pointed out otherwise they think it equally improper as impracticable to disscuss the propriety – & beg the same may be refer'd to the Divns before their return of the refer'd Motion –

9. It is the Opinion of this Divn that the debt of Citn Roussel be raised by subscription & not to be paid out of the funds – unanimous 22.

11. Resolved that is the Opinion of this Divn that Citn Roussells request ought to be paid by a voluntary subscription to be raised by the several Divns & recommend the General Comee to take it into immediate consideration

19. Resolved unanimously understanding for a Citn Visitor that Citn Roussel is a member of the Constitutional Society & that he has not applied to that Society for that assistance which he requests from us – In consequence of which it is the Opinion of this Divn that it is imprudent to advance him any Money until he has applied to that Society & has been refused

25. Do recommend to the Divns of this Society to make a general Subscription for Citn Roussel instead of taking it out of the Stock of the Society – 20 Affir – Neg 0 –

34. This Divn is of Opinion that the best Method to afford releif to Citn Roussell will be for the Genl Comee to recommend to the Society at large to enter into a Subscription for that Purpose – It is the Opinion of this Divn that the paying of the bill of Citn Roussel out of the fund would be establishing a bad precedent – but recommend that a subscription be raised in the Divns for assisting him to pay it – provided it is a proper & legal charge which we wish to be properly informed of –

No Number of Divn to this –

It appearing to the Comee that the Sense of Society had not been regularly taken on Citizen Roussel's Case – it was therefore moved that it be again refer'd to the Divns & for them to send in their Decision in writing signed by their Secretary & Chairman   Affir –

Treasurer's Acct adjourned

Quarteridge 10 . . 1 . . 9 –

Secretary informed Comee that Divn 8 had not paid any Money for 4 Nights – & had made new Members every Night

Divn 18 – had made new members but had paid no Money this Week –

292. Report from spy Powell: LCS General Committee, 13 August 1795 [103]

Source: PC 1/23/A38

Genl Comitte L C S. 13th. Augt. 1795
Powell in the Chair

New Members 173. Quarterage £10. 1. 9.

Div 28 Branch to the Dog & Duck New Bond Street   meet on Wednesday to be No 49. Willson, Constable   Pelton & Mc. Guire to open it.

Div 3 Branch to the Ben Johnsons Head   Westmoreland Buildings Aldersgate Street meet on Wednesday to be No 50. French, Gibbons, Read, & Hewit to open it

[The report of Division 29 branching and of requests from Sydenham and Waltham Abbey is substantially the same as the previous report.]

Numbers on the referrd Question to the Divisions. on the Question for chuseing officers by ballot on show of hands 472 for show of hands 794 for ballots

Roselles Case   It appeard that several Divisions did not understand this Question & the Deligates of several others not having taken an accurate account of the numbers. this Question after a very long debate was referr'd back again to the divisions to be reported on next Committe night.

The Debate on Roselles Case & the Report of the Ex Com. having taken up so much time no Motions were either read or debated.

Adjournd at 2 oClock

293. Motion from LCS Division 7: 18 August 1795

Source: Add MSS 27813, fos. 146v-7

Divn 7 – Aug 18. 1795.

It appears to this Divn that the members of this Society has & is encreasing so rapidly, that

103 Powell's description: 'L C S Genl Com. / 13th Augt 1795'.

it makes the Number of Members belonging to the Genl Comee so many & of course the Number of Divns is also so numerous that it is impossible to go thro' the Motions of the Week in one Night, & that Comee is so large that it is impossible to keep that decorum which ought to be kept in it –

We therefore Moved that the Number of Members requisite to make a full Divn shall be fifty & that they shall not branch till they consist of Eighty

It also appears to this Divn that it is impossible for the Chairman of the Genl Comee to take a correct report for his Divn & likewise that his Divn is unrepresented, as he cannot (or ought not) to take any part in the discussion, as a chairman ought to be impartial & he likewise cannot give any vote without there happens to be an equality of votes.

We therefore moved that a Chairman be chosen by the Genl Comee out of the body of the Society to continue in office three months – & be re eligible as long the Genl Comee shall think proper to elect him – he may be chosen from the Genl Comee but must vacate his Seat –

We move that the above Motions be refer'd to the Divisions

John Griffiths Chairn

294. Minutes: LCS General Committee, 20 August 1795

Source: Add MSS 27813, fos. 108–13

Genl Comee Aug 20th. 1795
Citn Beck in the Chair –

[The report starts with a list of the 53 divisions, the number of new members in each division and the number of members present in each division, with totals of 183 new and 1691 present. Notations next to division numbers: 4, 'no quateridge – Dele nor Sub not present by Secretary was & said the Dele had it'; 8, 'Hartley vice Iliff superceeded for neglect of duty –'; 11, 'Wallin sub vice Savage gone out of town'; 12, 'ab'; 16, 'Margetts vice Dukes who could not attend on acc't of distance'; 22, 'Wm Powell Secy in place of Goodwin resigned'; 26, 'Edey vice Hall resigned'; 27, 'no quarteridge – Delegate informed the Comee he did not come straight from home or should have pd it'; 30, 'Westfall Kates'; 36, 'Powell vice Mellows resigned –'; 39, 'ab'; 45, 'Price

Edwards Jennings'; 50, 'Hunter Evans Kennington'; 51, 'Travers Skimmell Haynes'; 53, 'Sheridan Nicolson Gregory – Waltham abbey'.]

Unrepresented Divns
12 – Deputed Neale – Ward
39 – Removed to Queens head High St
St Mary-le-bone deputed Salter Dixey

Citns		from Divn	
	Waite	from Divn	5
	Davies	from	20
	Milson	from	6
	Dreyson	from	42
	Trot	from	16
	Bowser	from	29
	Ham	from	22
	Hill	from	6
	Widdows	from	7

The above were admitted to the Honours of the Sitting

Divn Branches to the Queens head Charlotte
22: St Black Friars Road requests Number & Deputation – to meet on Monday To be No 54 – Deputed Ham, Danton Farmer Wm Powell

Report of Ex Comee

Aug[1]4.
Present Maxwell Moody, Davenport, Ashley, Galloway, Young,
Absent Jones & Binns –
Read a copy of a letter in answer to the London Reforming Society approved & order to be sent by post – Baxter Burks, & Bell from Sheffield waited on Comee as deputatn from the Friends of Liberty, were admitted to the honours of the sitting

Baxter, beg the Comee would dispatch them as soon as they conveniently could & as they were obliged to attend their Comee this Evening

Report of Ex Comee continued

Aug 18.
Present, Moody Maxwell, Young Ashley, Galloway Binns
Absent Jones & Davenport
Citn Venables attended agreeable to the request of the General Committee he informed your Committee that there were many friends to Reform in & about Derby, who wished to receive a few copies of the regulations of this Society & to correspond with The London Corresponding Society – a Member deputed to write to Derby & accompany the Letter with some regulations &c

A Member was also deputed to write to Sunbury Middx

Citn S Smith & Hodgson admitted to the honours of the Sitting

Deputation from the Friends of Liberty then heard Burks informed the Comee that he was directed attend The London Corresponding Society, by The Friends of Liberty, in consequence of having rec'd a Letter from Sheffield – stating that Citn Yorke was distressed for Money to print his Trial, which was of very great hurt to him (as he expected to have a very great sale for them at the ensuing York races) – As Ramsay who took it down in short hand refused to give the latter part of the Trial without he paid him £36. first – & the letter likewise stated the Birmingham Society had sent up £85 .. 10 .. 0 to the Comee conducting the State Trials which they intended solely for Citn Yorke – Burks then informed the Comee that he had waited on Mr Clarkson, who informed him that the Money from Birmingham sent to them was sent by Friends to impartial Justice but did not specify its being for Citn Yorke – he then asked Clarkson wether they could letter Citn Yorke having £36 as that was the Sum he wanted – he answer he could not, as there was [not] money enough subscribed to defray the expences – Ashley informed the Comee that a Person, supposed to be one of Mr Ramsays domestics had call'd at his house with a Letter from Mr Ramsay sent to him by Citn Yorke for £36 – & asked where Burks lived – which he was informed of –

Hodgson stated that there appeard something very mysterious in this affair – as this Society had Sent them a Letter & Parcel down Sometime before this Letter was Sent, & that they had not mentioned anything about receiving any Parcel for the London Corresponding Society, he said it appeared to him as if we had got a false direction, As the Ex Com were informed there were some differences existing amongst [members] of the Constitutional Society At Sheffield

It was then stated that has there appeared something very misterious in this business it would be the best way to request the Deputation to attend the Ex Comee & they might then make a full investigation

Citn Place stated he could [not] see anything the Ex Comee could have to do with it & likewise could not see anything we have to do with it as it was an application to The Friends of Liberty –

Baxter then stated he could not see any thing so very mysterious in this affair, for they had no occassion to say anything about having

rec'd a Parcel from The London Corresponding Society – as the Letter was sent to The Friends of Liberty – what differences there might exist at Sheffield he could not tell, but it was well known as might be seen in the Telegraph that the Constitutional Society at Sheffield had had a Public Meeting – when there was present about 10000 Persons & a Citn name Barrow, who was a Member of The Friends of Liberty who was going that way was President – And as the Sheffield [society] was so poor that they could [not] pay for a Room to meet in, but was obliged to meet in the open Air – they had applied to The Friends of Liberty for Assistance – & as the Friends of Libertys funds would not enable them to assist Citn Yorke which they should be very happ to have done if it had lain in their power they had therefore applied to The London Corresponding Society as being the most Numerous to see what they could do for him – Moggeridge then moved – & it was sec'd that the deputation be requested to attend Ex Comee

Moved & Sec'd that our Secretary Do write to Citn Yorke – & require an answer by return of Post –

Moggeridge's Motion put – 21 Aff   21 Neg – Chairn gave his vote in the Affir – of course the other motion fell

Divn   We have changed our night of Meeting
13.   from Monday night to Friday that being
       a night more convenient to the Land-
       lord & by which we shall be enabled to
       meet in away more agreeable to this
       Divn –
       Overtures have been made from Mitcham
       to cooperate wth the London Corres-
       ponding Society – Citn Simmons late
       Delegate of Divn 14 has engaged to go
       & form a Divn there & he requests –
       some Articles Proceedings &c
       Movd & Secd that Citn Simmons have
       some Articles &c given him – Affir –

Galloway was chosen Reporter to the deputatn that waited on Secretary of State –

Aug 19.
    Report of Deputation appointed to receive
    the Answer the address to the king con-
    formable to the order of the General Comee
        They appointed to meet on Wednesday
    the 19. Day.
    Present Binns, Barton Galloway,
    absent Jones on account of Illness – the
    Deputation came to the Resolution of
    drawing up a letter to introduce them – of
    which the following his a Copy – Comee
    Room Aug 19th. 1795

My Lord Duke –

We the undersigned being deputed from the London Corresponding Society wait on your Grace to receive any answer to their Letter delivered at this Office the 13th.

Signed

A Galloway, J Binns, J Barton

Galloway enquired of the Council keeper if the Duke of Portland was present & he returned for answer no, the keeper than asked what was there business – Galloway informed him – they had got a Letter for his Grace – the Council than requested the Deputation to leave it, on which Galloway desired him to take it to the private Secretary, on which the Council keeper readily obeyed the order & on his return informed the deputation that there was no answer, on which Galloway expressed he was very much surprised, as he conceived that an answer was there requested in possitive terms, & desired the Council keeper to enquire of the private Secretary wether the deputation was to consider the answer brought by the Council keeper to be his majesty's answer to our address or his answer to the present letter. – the keeper refused going with verbal messages from the deputation to the Private Secretary – on which Citn Binns asked the Council keeper if he was ordered not to carry verbal messages from the deputation – to which he replied I conceive Gentlemen you wish to sift me – Galloway than asked in what Manner the deputation might convey their sentiments to the private Secretary – he returned for answer Gentlemen you must write a Letter & presented the Deputation with paper &c for the purpose, on which they drew up a letter for the private Secretary of which the following is a Copy –

Sir

We wish to know if the answer brought by the keeper is to be considered as his majesty's answer to our address or your answer to the present letter – We take this way of communicating to you our request as the keeper informs the deputation that he cannot carry verbal Messages –

Signed A Galloway, J Binns, J Barton

Galloway then give this to the keeper & he returned for answer that the private Secretary was gone during the writing of the letter & requested it to be left for him till his return – the deputation refused leaving it. Galloway than asked when the Duke of Portland might be seen – he said it was uncertain & desired the deputation to wait on his Grace at Burlington House – The Deputation drew up a letter for that purpose & Citn Gale Jones was deputed carry the same – & he reported that his Grace was not at home therefore he did not leave the letter

Moved & Sec'd that the deputation do not go any more for an answer to our late address to the king –

Mov'd & Secd that it be referd to the Ex Comee to take it into their consideration

Movd & Secd that the deputation do go again

that the Deputation do not go again – Affir – The President informed the Comee that has there was now another Edition of Narrative of Genl Meeting, wether it would not be proper to print at the End – the reception which our address & deputation had met

It was mov'd & Secd – Carried Affir – The following houses wish to have divisions –

Angel Court Cecil Court St Martins Lane
Red Lyon Cross Lane Hatton Garden
Coach & horses Lisle Street
Golden horse Oxford Street
Tun Air Street Corner of Castle St Picadilly
Bull Christopher Street north end of Hatton Garden
Mitre Ely Court Hatton Garden
3 Tunns lower part of Cross St Hatton Garden
London Apprentice near Whitechapel Church
The King Harry's head Mile end Road

[Next follow two tallies of the 53 divisions' votes on referred questions. 'Refer'd Motion on Roussel Debt': 269 'Affir' and 412 'Neg'. 'majority agt 143'. 'Refer'd Motion of Ex speakg': 73 'Affir' and 496 'Neg'. 'Majority agt – 423'.]

Citn Place informed the Comee that a Motion had come from Divn 20 which was a constitutional Point, & As the Divns had not now got any thing before them – he mov'd that that Motion be now read & referr'd to the Divns for their Consideration Citn Beck – then informed the Comee that he stood in a very awkward situation as being Chairman & wishing to speak as to the propriety of referring two Motion which came from Divn 7 of this Evening – which are constitutional Point – to each Divn for their Consideration Salter Mov'd – Secd Allen – that they be referr'd to the Divns secd – Affir –

Divn | Resolved that this Divn do think it expe-
20. | dient that the Genl Comee should meet
on Thursday & Friday in each week &
that the 7 Article[104] should equally
apply to both meetings –
Divn | Mov'd that the number of Members
7 – | requisite to make a full Divn shall be 50
& that they shall not branch till they
consist of 80 –
Motion put for its being referd   Affir
Movd that a Chairman be chosen by the
Genl Comee from the body of the
Society to continue in Office three
Months & be re eligible as long as the
Genl Comee shall think proper to elect
him   he may be chosen from the Genl
Comee but must vacate his Seat –
Motion put of its being referr'd – Affir –
    Quarteridge – 10 . . 9 . . 5.
Movd & Secd that we do now adjourned
till Sunday morning –
8 O'Clock – Neg –
Movd & Secd – that we do adjourn till
Sunday evening
Six O Clock – Neg –
                Adjourned

295. Minutes: LCS General Committee, 27 August 1795

Source: Add MSS 27813, fos. 113v–21

Genl Comee Aug 27. 1795.
Citn Place in the Chair, Westfall vice President –

[The report starts with a list of the 54 divi-sions, the number of new members in each division and the number present in each division during the previous week, totalling 132 new and 1554 present. Notations fol-lowing division numbers: 3, 'no quarteridge Delegate said he did not come from home or should have brot it'; 10, 'no quarteridge – Secy attended & said the Delegate was ill, & he call[ed] at his house & his wife told him her husband had laid down & she could not disturb him'; 13, 'Evans delegate'; 14, 'Richardson sub delegate vice Shirley resigned'; 25, 'have changed their night from Monday to Wednesday'; 29, 'Palmer

104 Art. 7 specifies the duties of the chairman (and thereby the form of the meeting): collect-ing statistics on membership, taking motions presented in writing and reading them aloud twice, preventing interruption of speakers, making sure speakers do not wander from the subject and taking the sense of the assembly by show of hands.

Delegate vice Turner resigned'; 38, 'no quarteridge – Delegate informed the Comee that he lived at Chelsea & was in Town & thought it was too far to go back'; 53, 'did not meet this week, but would meet on Saturday next'; 54, 'Deputation of last week informed The Comee that only 4 Members of the Divn 22 were present, therefore did [not] open the Divn but promised they should have a Deputation next week'.]

The following Citizens admitted to the honours of the sitting

Mills from	35	Evans from	4
Waites	5	England	2
Sherriff	5	Iliff	22
Simpson	46		
Dreyton	5		
Incledon	40		

The following Divns being unrepresented – the following Deputations appointed
12 – Easter – Evans
15 – Haselden Robson
31 – Dixey Horton, Constable
34 – Bustle Canty
37 – Lemaitre Moggeridge
50 – French – Hewit
52 – Place to send a report – Sydenham
53 – Edwards to send – Do & he gave notice that they had removed to the Swan & Pike Enfield Lock – & that they did not meeting on Saturday last – as a justice had informed the Landlady that she had better not have any meeting at her house till after her licence was renewed which would be in a very short time – but they intended to meet on Saturday next –
54 – Ham, Palmer, Harris –
A Paper brot – as follows –
The following wish to establish a Divn at Fountain Virginia Row Shoreditch – Wednesday

Wm Weston	I Dykes
J Downing	I Keene
P Dykes	R J Lester
N Hammersley	N Clayton
J Drior	S Davies
Joseph Thompson	W Smith
Thos Carter	J Salter
D Barking	John Croft
J Young	C Hartley
J Jones	H Fox
John Kniblet	J Devonshire
C Bower	

A Citizen said that it would be best for those Citizens to enter into a Divn on the spot which there was one at Bethnal Green, & then they might branch to that house – And there was a Person name Dykes amongst them as he beleived was not a good Citizen as he belonged to the Loyal Britons[105]   On the other hand it was stated that we ought to appoint a deputation & let them establish a Divn for it we ought to give all encouragement possible to Citns wishing to become Members & that they had as good a right to open a Divn by themselves, as to run to some Place a distant from their habitations to join one

Citn Place said he had once being a Loyal Briton, but he did not think himself any the worse for it, & he said he knew that Dykes – & beleived him to be a very good Citizen –

Citn Wilson informed the Comee he had once belonged to the Loyal Britons – & he made no doubt but the Citn was fully convinced of his error

To be 55 Deputed B Binns Dyall, Cardinall Webb, Canty

Divn 26 – Branches to the 3 Brewers Lower Street Islington – Tuesday

To be No 56 – deputed Moggeridge, Banting Bowers Edey –

Divn 14. Branches to the Surry Arms   Surry Square Kent Road Near the Bricklayers Arms – Tuesday

To be No 57 – Haselden Hartley – Robson Citn Lemaitre informed the Comee that there were several Citns wished to formed a Divn – at the Red Lion Cross lane Long Acre – Tuesday Evening – there would 20 Citns from 1 Shop

Citn Cooper said the Divn 5 had intended to branch there this week but had deferr'd it till next week – which he supposed was the same

Citn Lemaitre said that this was quite distinct from any Divn which might be going to branch from 5 –

To be No 58. deputed Lemaitre Ingram, Rawson, Travers

The following Houses wished to receive Divns

The Nags head opposite the Castle & Falcon Aldersgate Street

Rose & 3 Tunns little Earl Street 7 Dials

The Old Black horse Borough

The Kings Arms Smarts Buildings[106]

The White Horse White horse Yard Drury Lane

The Fountain Red Cross Street – Room will hold 150

The Coach & horses Frith Street Soho

Johnsons – The Crown Hunt Street Mile end new Town

The Fleece little Windmill Street Golden Sqre

Maidenhead Ram alley Fleet Street

Report of Ex Comee
Aug 24.[107]

Present Moody, Young, Maxwell, Galloway Binns –

Absent – Jones – Davenport, Ashley –

Read a Copy of a Letter to Derby[108] amended & ordered to be sent

Burks & Baxter attended agreeable to the request of the General Comee, Burks read a letter from Citn Fell of Sheffield apologizing for not being able to attend the Ex Comee

Propositions submitted to the Ex Comee of the London Corresponding Society by Baxter & Burks in the name of the Friends of Liberty

1st. Respecting the precise purpose of the sum of £85 . . 10 collected at Birmingham

Answer the Ex Comee will immediately write to Birmingham for the special Purpose of enquiring into the same[109] & communicate information to the Secretary of the Friends of Liberty as soon as possible –

2nd To what Person the said sum of £85 . . 10 . . was paid in London

Answered by the Answer to the first –

3rd. What Sum we shall be enabled to afford Citn Yorke provided it shall be found he receives no releif from the £85 . . 10 collected at Birmingham in in his present necessity.

Answered – This Comee not being impowered to dispose of the financies of the London Correspondg Society

105 A pro-government society instituted on 10 Oct. 1793, their object was 'to assist the Executive Government upon every occasion . . . and prevent, to the utmost of our Power, the circulation of Inflammatory Pamphlets, Papers or Conversation; and . . . to hand down to the latest Posterity, our inestimable CONSTITUTION' (handbill in HO 42/26, fo. 701).

106 In Holborn.

107 Powell's report of this meeting is so close to the wording of this account that both must derive from a common source (PC 1/23/A38).

108 Robert Venables reported that some patriots of Melbourne (near Derby) wish to form a political society. 'As it is highly necessary all the Friends to Reform should act with unanimity', the LCS asks the 'precise views and sentiments' of these citizens and hopes the LCS's sentiments (which are stated in the letter) coincide (23 Aug. 1795, Correspondence, pp. 53–4).

109 J. Moody to —, 24 Aug. 1795, Correspondence, pp. 51–2. Moody, an early and assiduous member, has been identified as a spy: see Hone, For the Cause of Truth, pp. 63–4.

can give no precise answer to the 3rd
proposition
  Signed by order of the Ex Comee
    J Young Chairman –

Aug 25th.
 Present Young, Galloway Maxwell, Moody
 Ashley Binns
 Absent – Jones Davenport –
Read a copy of a letter to be sent to Birming-
ham approved & ordered to be sent –
Read a letter from Citn Callan, who attended
the Comee for arraigning the State Trials. The
Treasurer ordered to pay him 1 G – for his
attendance
Revised corrected & compressed the Report of
the deputation who waited on the Secretary of
State for an answer to the address which had
been presented his majesty
 True Report Signed
   Young, Galloway Maxwell Moody
    Ashley, Binns

Read a Letter from Birmingham in answer to
ours concerning the Request of the Friends of
Liberty – Wherein it stated that the Sum collected was by Messrs Clarkson's writing done
there[110] – was collected solely for the State
Trials & for no individual alone – likewise stating that they always thought Citn Yorke has a
Man of fortune – & stated that they could not
think who could circulate such a report as it
never was their intentions –
Motion made & Sec'd that the adjourned
Motions be taken into consideration first –
21 Affir 22 Neg –
Divn Resolved that an account of a deputation
19. appointed from this divn to wait on Citn
 Roussel to request a correct statement of
 his Case – They report they attended on
 him & received the purport of their mission
  Resolved that it is the Opinion of this
 Divn that it shall be read by the Chairman of the General Comee & that ea)
 delegate shall take a correct statement of
 the same for the information of his Divn
 Citn Cooper stated that has a subscription was set on foot – he thought the
 present statement unnecessary – he
 therefore movd the Order of the day on
 it –
 A Citn stated that has each Divn already
 had receive a fair statement of the Case

he conceive this to be intirely unnecessary –
Citn Dixey then stated that each Divn
had not received a fair statement of the
Case – & that there was scarcely two
Divns had received it alike – he therefore
thought the present Statement very
necessary –
 Order of the Day put – 23 Affir
14 Neg –
Divn That no Person be permited to speak to
8. one subject more than twice –
 The Delegate informed the Comee that
 it appeared to his Divn that the business
 would be much expedited by adopting
 the present Motion, as there were some
 Persons would speak three or four times
 to one question – when twice would
 answer the same purpose –
On the other hand it was stated that
many things might escape a person
while speaking & that it would very
unfair not to let them speak after –
 Order of Day moved & Secd – Carrd
Affir –
Divn Resolved that it is the Opinion of this
42. Divn that only one representative from
 each division be allowed to speak in the
 General Comee
 It appeared to this Divn that one representative from each Divn was quite sufficient to Do the business & that it was
 only prolonging the Business of the
 Comee
On the other hand it was stated that the
little Discussion that was taken up by
the sub Delegates & Secretaries was so
small that it did not retard the business
scarcely any –
 The Order of the Day was therefore
moved
 Movd & secd that they be referr'd to
the Divns
 The Chairman said he had [not] got
any motion to that effect –
Divn This is to certify that this Divn taking
27. into consideration the multiplicity of
 business of the General Comee & the
 great increase of Divns & consequently
 of Delegates do move that only one
 Officer from each Divn shall be permitted in the Genl Comee of Delegates to
 enter into any discussion upon any business whatsomever that is to say that
 neither sub Delegate or Secretary shall
 speak in the presence of the Delegate we
 think by this method a deal of confusion
 would be preventd & the business expedited –

110 The money was collected in Birmingham by
 Rev. David Jones and paid to Messrs Clarksons
 in London (John Kenrick to [Moody], 26
 Aug. 1795, *Correspondence*, pp. 52-3).

Order of Day move & Sec'd on each –
Citn Beck then stated that he conceived
that it was a very unfair way of dispos-
ing of Motions by the order of Day
being put on them – & it was showing to
the Divns that they were to lazy to discussion them – & therefore without looking into the merits & demerits of the
Case – to save themselves trouble pass
them over by the order of the day – he
stated he did see that the Comee had the
power of passing to the order of Day on
the present Motion As they were constitutional points & ought to be refer'd to
the Divns
Citn Cooper than stated the Divns could
not know the best way for the proceedings of the Comee & that the Comee
surely knew the best for their own
Order – & therefore ought to decide on
them first – for his own part he could
not see any great ill convenience for the
Sub dele & Secy speaking when present
which rarely happen he should therefore
give them his negative –

  Motions put – & Negatived

Divn This Divn is of Opinion that the Ex
2. Comee are highly censureable for allowing Citn Margarotts letters to be read in
the Westminster Forum & not allowed to
be read in the General Comee –
The Delegate of Divn 2 stated the letters
had been read by Citn Jones in the Westminster Forum & that they thought the
Ex Comee was highly censureable to let
them be read there & to be kept a Secret
from the Society at large
Citn Powell said has he conceived the
whole fault lay on Citn Jones – he moved
that a Vote of censure be passed on Citn
Jones – not secd –
The reporter of the Ex Comee stated that
every member of that Comee was allowed
to be in full possession of the letters as
he might not draw to haste a conclusion
wether they should be kept private or
not, he hoped the Comee would not go
to pass any censure on Citn Jones as he
no doubt did it in the debate when he
was very animated & unthinkingly did
to confute his adversaries – he therefore
hope the Comee would pass it over as
might lose a very active Member by it,
As he was a man which exerted himself
to the utmost towards gaining a Parliamentary Reform, for tho' he could not
attend the Ex Comee very constantly he
was still exerting himself at the Forum

he therefore hoped the Comee would
pass it over[111]
  The Order of Day moved & Secd –
  Affir –
Divn 23. Resolved that it is the Opinion of this
Divn that a Genl Meeting should be called as
soon as possible
Divn 48. Resolved that it is the Opinion of this
Divn that a Genl Meeting of the London Corresponding Society is absolutely necessary to
lay before the Society & the world at large the
Account of the proceedings of the business of
the address we agreed to at our last Genl Meeting –
Divn 9. Resolved that a Genl Meeting of the
whole body of the London Corresponding
Society be called as soon as possible in order
to point out some means for the address of
National Grievances & that a Genl Meeting of
all the popular Societies that we correspond
with be called on the Same day & notice to be
sent to the Societies in the Country to prepare
themselves for the said Meeting
Divn 3. This Divn recommends that a Genl
Meeting should be called as soon as possible
for the purpose of informing the Public of the
reception the London Corresponding Society's
address to his majesty has met with
Divn 16. Resolved that there be another Genl
Meeting as soon as possible
Divn 40 Are of Opinion that a General Meeting
should be called as soon as possible on account
of having no answer to our address to let the
Country at large know how we have [been]
treated
Divn 11. Resolved that it is the Opinion of this
Divn that a General Meeting ought to be convened as soon as possible for the purpose of
taking some immediate steps to forward the
Cause of Reform –
Divn 22. Resolved that it is the Opinion of this
Divn that in consequence of the contempt
shewn to the late address it would be very
beneficial to the London Corresponding
Society to call a General Meeting immediately
Divn 10. That a General Meeting be called of
this Society that we may have an opportunity
of expressing our Sentiments to the People on
our late address to the king –
Divn 33. It is the Opinion of this Divn that the
Public should be acquainted of the treatment
of the deputation respecting the address to the
king by a Genl Meeting –
Citn Cooper stated that he conceived it very

111 In Powell's report the motion was passed over
  because they were uncertain whether the
  letter was sent to the Society or to an individual.

wrong to call another General Meeting at present, as there would be nothing to lay before that meeting but the Result of our Address &c – & what would that be – nothing but a letter to the Duke of Portlands private Secretary & his answer – for we have no answer from the king neither have we had an answer from the Duke of Portland we therefore should move the Order of the Day on the Motions [112] – On the other hand it was stated by Citn Powell, that has the Motion had come from so many Divns he thought we should refer it to the whole for their consideration – he thought we ought to call a Meeting as the address did not go in the Name of the London Corresponding Society, only but in the Name of Sundry habitants of Westminster & its Environs beside – he therefore conceived it a duty we owed the Public to call another Meeting to inform them of the result of our late address – he therefore moved that they be refer'd to the Divns – It was then stated that the reception of the deputation who waited on the Duke of Portland for an answer to the address to the king was to be published in the next edition of the Proceedings of that meeting & that it was a

112 Place recalled that in the general committee the principal objections to the general meeting were 'that it would be used by ministers as an instrument to create a fresh alarm and . . . that the state of the societies funds . . . made the meeting inexpedient. These arguments had their weight in those divisions to which the delegates fairly represented them, but, as a great majority of the delegates were in favour of a General meeting it may be concluded that many of them did not fairly report the arguments used against the propriety of the meeting, and that some suppressed them altogether.' Place was one of those who spoke against the proposed meeting, which he later characterized as 'an injudicious proceeding'. His opposition was based on his beliefs 'that ministers would go on from bad to worse until they brought the Government to a standstill', that when this crisis occurred 'the people should be qualified to support those whom they might think most likely to establish a cheap and simple government', and that therefore 'the society should proceed as quietly and privately as possible'. Since very few members agreed with this analysis, the Society continued to act on the assumption that the House of Commons could be persuaded to reform the state of the representation (Add MSS 27808, fos. 37v-8). In this MS history of the LCS Place said that those who opposed the meeting refused to assist in plans for it; but in the *Autobriography* he recalled that he 'assisted to prepare the necessary arrangements, Resolutions, Petitions, Remonstrances and Addresses' (p. 144).

folly to have another meeting As that could be only business we have to lay before the Public –
The order of Day put & Negatived
For referring it to the Divns put & carried Affir
The Secretary then informed the Comee that Citn Thelwall would be in Town in a very few days – & he understood that the Lecture Room would be fitted up in a manner that it would be impossible to have the Comee there – but as Citn Thelwall was expected in Town on Friday – he should know therefore in case we should not be able to meet here   he thought it most proper for each Delegate to give in his name & place of abode – as he might then send each of them a notice where to meet – Each Delegate gave it –
Divn 32. Resolved unanimously that the Ex Comee do depute two of its Members to Weymouth to present the same address into the hands of the king with a preface informing his majesty the manner they was treated by the Secretary at the Secretary of States office & that they do report the preface verbatim to the General Committee for their approbation on the next Committee Night – It was stated that if we adopted this Motion we should [be] as far from having answer as at present As it was intirely at the pleasure of the king wether he would return any answer or not. –
the order of day was therefore moved on it – Affir
Div 26. Resolved that it is the Opinion of this Divn that the deputation appointed to attend for his majesty's answer to the petition of this Society ought not to cease their application untill they have obtained an answer thereto.
Divn 46. Moved that the Deputation do wait on the Secy of State untill they can obtain an answer to the address of the London Corresponding Society to the king –
Citn Moggeridge as Delegate of Divn 26. stated that it was the opinion of his Divn that we ought to apply again as by teasing them we might get any Answer –
On the other hand it was stated that if the king had meant to send an answer he would have done before now   they therefore moved the order of day –   Affir –
Divn 16. Resolved that the whole proceedings of the Deputation to the Duke of Portlands office be published in the newspapers & likewise by Posting Bills
Divn 23. Resolved that it is the Opinion of this Divn that the treatment the Society has rec'd relative to the address to the king from his majesty's ministers be printed in the Public Papers, posting & hand bills –

It was stated that it would be only throwing Money to adopted this Motion as it was already decreed to be printed at the End of the Narrative of Genl Meeting

The Order of the Day was moved on it –

It was then stated that as the address did not go in the Name of the London Corresponding Society we ought let the public at large know of the reception it had met with – It was therefore moved that these Motions be adjourned One Month –

Citn Beck then stated if anything was done the sooner the better, & has we should have the decision of the question on the Genl Meeting this day fortnight it would be decided then what step was to be taken he therefore moved an amendment that it be adjourned One fortnight

The Motion for adjourning it one Month was withdrawn –

Order of Day put & Negatived

Adjourn'd for 1 fortnight – Affir –

Divn 14. Resolved unanimously that it is the Opinion of this Divn that the report of the Ex Comee should be printed in Order to further the business of the Genl Comee

The Delegate of that Divn said they were of Opinion that it would save a vast time in the Genl Comee & would be of very little expence –

It was stated that it could not be done as frequently apart of the report was wrote in the Genl Comee & that the expence would be considerably greater than the trouble

Mov'd that it be referr'd to the Ex Comee & they report this day week – Affir –

Divn 39. Make this Motion That when any patriot stands in need of support of the London Corresponding Society – that 3 Delegates shall be appointed to wait on that Citn & enquire into the nature of his Case shall then communicate the same to the General Comee each Delegate shall take down his Case in writing & be signed by the Secretary & by that means it shall be communicated to each Divn by that Process each Divn will come to the truth of the statement.

It not being Signed could not be discussed –

Divn 48. This Divn is of Opinion that setting aside ¼ Part of the Income of the Society is a direct violation its Principle – as we ought to diffuse all the knowledge in our Power, & that we shall be ¼ Part as long again in Time before we gain our object –

Not signed –

Reporter of Ex Comee informed that we had not taken into Consideration the Motion of

Divn 20. that they refer'd back to us

Mov'd that it be order of the day on Thursday next – Affir –

Mov'd that it be refer'd back to Ex Comee to use their discretion –

Divn 18. Protesting against chosen officers by ballot –

Not signed –

Vote of censure moved on the Chairman of this Evening for delaying the business so long by reading the Motions not signed & Secd – Neg –

Rec'd 6 .. 5 .. 1½ Quarteridge
       2 .. 8 ..10 Roussel
       0 ..11 .. 0 2 letters
       1 .. 1 .. 0 by Citn Oliphant
                   by W & J – for
                   Publishg Pro-
                   ceedings of Genl
                   Meeting

296. Report from spy Powell: LCS General Committee, 27 August 1795[113]

Source: PC 1/23/A38

Genl Committe 27th Augt 1795

132 New Members. Quarterage £7 . 17 . 1½ Div 53 the Waltham Abby Div meet at the Swan & Pyke Enfield Lock on Wednesday. 23 Inhabitants near Shoreditch sent a letter requesting to form a Division at the Fountain Virginia Row meet on Wednesday To be No 55. Deputation B. Binns, Cardinal, Deal, Carrington, Webb Candy, & Waits.

[The information about the branching of Divisions 26 and 14 is substantially the same as that in the previous report. The list of houses wishing to receive divisions is also the same, except that Powell adds two not mentioned in the previous report:]

Golden Horse Oxford Road
London Apprentice White Chappell

[The motions from Divisions 8, 42, 27, 2, 23, 48, 19, 32, 26, 11 and 14 are briefly stated.]

113 Powell's description: 'Genl Com. L C S / 27. Augt 1795'.

PART EIGHT

1795B
(September–December)

297. Minutes: LCS General Committee, 3 September 1795

Source: Add MSS 27813, fos. 121v–5v

Genl Comee Sept 3rd. 1795.
Citn Place Chairman
Citn Moggeridge Vice do

[The report starts with a list of the 58 divisions, the number of new members in each division and the number present in each division, totalling 182 new and 1841 present. Notations next to division numbers: 1, 'Metcalfe Sub'; 5, 'Dreyton Secy vice Welsh resigned'; 10, 'did not come from home & had not so much about him'; 18, 'did not come from home'; 28, 'nor will not give any till they receive regulations &c'; 41, 'Chambers vice Peirce resigned Webb sub'; 54, 'Fowler, Ford, Ham'; 55, 'Hall, Evans, Webb';[1] 57, 'Thos Shirley, Joseph Goleston Philip Smith'; 58, 'Clarke Sheriff, Lemaitre'.]

The following Citizens admitted to the honours of the Sitting
Clayton
Cavry from Divn   15
Hodgson   18
Peter   2
King   47
Cole   5
Mckneel   17
Goleston   57
Dudley   17
Brest   7
Clinton   18
Unrepresented Divns
9   Hester Jas Powell, Ward
19   W Powell, Morgan Banting
34   Bustle, Dixey Canty, McGuire, Wm
      Brewer Jas Powell for 1 Month
52[2] Neild wl send a report to Waltham
      abbey –
55   Harris, Dennison Gibbons Dyall
51   Ward Harris
The Secretary informed the Comee that a Citizen Meeking of White's Row wished to become a Member of Divn – & requested the Delegate of that Divn to enquire into his character –
Smith from Divn 4 – admitted to the honours of the sitting
The following wished to establish a Divn at the Robinhood Windmill Street – Wednesday
Edward Laird   John Barlow, Charles Bowtell
John Wallis   John Wayland, John Naylor, Wm Phipps John Lawley Francis Langford Samuel Philpot Wm Irwine Wm Binns
These friends to Liberty wishes to engage the above house & hope it will meet with the approbation of the Comee

signed Joseph Clinton of Divn 18. –

To be the No 59. Deputed Ward, Horton
Constable Hodgson   Clinton Mckneell   Taylor –
Divn 28. Branches to the White Hart Market Street Oxford Market – Wednesday
To be No 60. Deputed Wilson   Rawson, Place, McGuire –
The Landlord of the Ship Charles St Westminster waited on & informed the Comee that the following Citizens wished to establish a Divn at his house, on a Wednesday
Mr Bewson, Rumens, Francis Dudley, Bailey, Wilmot, Robert St John, Jas Fisher, John Higgins
Hodgson requested to be taken from deputation to Windmill Street. –
Granted
To be No 62[3] – deputed Hodgson, Webb, Candy, Byron –
Divn 5. Branches to the Angel Cecil Court St Martins Lane –
Friday –
To be No 63.[4] deputed Dreyton, Dixey, Brewer, Bowers
Divn 23. Branches to the White horse Cloak Lane Queen St Cheapside Monday
To be No 63 – deputed Rogers Brown, Haselden, Banting
Citn Mason of Divn 4 – admitted to the honours of sitting

Report of Ex Comee

Aug 27th.   Present, Jones, Young, Maxwell, Ashley, Galloway, Davenport, Binns, Absent Moody

---

1 These three names should have been placed next to Div. 56, as Powell has them in his report of this meeting.
2 Error: Div. 53 was at Waltham Abbey.
3 Should be No 61. According to Powell, the deputation included Chambers, but not Webb.
4 Should be No 62.

The Comee took into their Consideration the necessity of providing a proper place of Meeting for the General Comee – Jones deputed to find a proper place of Meeting for the General Committee & report on Monday next –

Considered the Motion of Divn 14 on the propriety of printing the report of the Ex Comee – Neg –

Read a Letter from Davidson the printer on the subject of printing by estimate ordered to be read in the General Committee

Stating the unfairness of leting Davenport give in a second estimate in the Ex Comee after the others had been read, & if he had have printed them on coarse paper as they are he could have done them for less than Davenport, & his having printed for us in times of danger when nobody else would

Aug 31st. Present Jones Maxwell, Galloway, Young Moody Ashley Binns, absent Davenport –

This Comee recommends to the Genl Comee to rescind their resolution of printing by estimate the publications of this Society

Ashley added to Comee for accomodating the Genl Comee –

Sept 2. Present, Ashley Binns, Absent Jones, Galloway, Moody, Maxwell Davenport, Young –

Adjourned as not been sufficient to form a quorum

True Report, Ashley, Binns –

The reporter of the Ex Comee than informed the Genl Comee that it appeared to the Ex Comee that having the publications printed by estimate would be very troublesome – As we should not Get them fast enough to supply our wants, & further it was encouraging underselling –

It was moved that it be rescinded –

Citn Moggeridge stated that he could not see that it would by any means [be] troublesome – & has the Society was so large we ought to be very spareing – but he conceived the first Motion was not explanatory enough he therefore Mov'd –

1st. That the printers do send in their estimates to the Genl Comee –
2nd. That a Sample of the Paper be produced –
3rd. That they be delivered in 1 month after ordered –

The Motion put for its being rescinded 27 Affir. 17 Neg –

The Motion of Moggeridge's fell

Mov'd that adjourned Motion of Divn 20. be refer'd back to Ex Comee to do as they think proper – Affir –

Dawling mov'd that two Members be deputed to wait on Davenport & if Regulations &c are not ready – to supercede him Amendment to allow him 3 Days – Affir –

Chosen Ex Comee

The old

Jones	41
Young	30
Moody	30
Binns	42
Maxwell	40
Davenport	
Nominated	
Sellers	37
Rogers	17
Hiram Powell	16
Constable	29

Young & Moody 30 (ea) President gave for Moody

The New Comee as follows
Jones
Binns
Maxwell
Moody
Sellers
Constable

Hodgson informed Comee that Several Citizens wished to establish a Divn at the Coach & horses Turnham Green Sunday 2 O'Clock

To be No 64 – Hodgson, Ramsay, J. Powell, Limans, Seale Hester, Peters, Horton Kings –

Mov'd that adjourned Motions be taken into consideration first – Affir –

[There follow tallies of votes for three motions referred to the divisions: 'Motion of Divn 7 – for augmented No to make a full Divn'. 372 affirmative to 497 negative. 'Motion of Divn 20 for G C – to meet Thursday & Friday'. 168 affirmative to 641 negative. 'Motion of 7 for Chairn' of general committee to be elected for a quarter instead of a night. 577 affirmative to 326[5] negative.]

Read a Letter from Citn Vialls

Stating Some Persons wished to establish a

5 Negative should be 335.

300

Divn all housekeepers – to pay 2s. or half
Crown Pr Quarter –[6]
Order of day Movd
Movd that it be referd to Ex Comee Affir –
Motion from Divn 15 to be order of Day next
Thursday[7]
Place Chose Chairn[8]

Quarteridge   9. .2. .11
Roussel   1-4-5

298. Report from spy Powell: LCS General Committee, 3 September 1795[9]

Source: PC 1/23/A38

Genl Com. L C.S. 3d. Septr. 1795.

182 New Members   Quarterage £9. 2 11.
Div 57. T Shirly Del.   J. Gouldstone Sub
      Del   Smith Secty
    41   Chambers Del.   Pierce Resgd.
       Webb Secty.
    56   W Hall Del.   Evans Sub Del   Webb
       resgd.
     5.   J Drayton Secty.   Welch resgd.
    54   Fowler del   Ford Sub Del.   Ham
       Secty –

6   2 Sept. 1795, *Correspondence*, p. 55. John Vialls
    was secretary to Div. 27.
7   Another motion for managing the business of the
    general committee more efficiently. See 303.
8   Place recalled his election as chairman for three
    months: 'It was the post of honour and was
    eagerly desired by several others as well as by me.'
    He suggested reasons for his election: 'As it was
    found that I as Chairman [for the night] kept
    good order and dispatched the business in less time
    than most of the other member[s] who had pre-
    sided, I was frequently voted into the chair. The
    duty of chairman was arduous, frequently very
    difficult, it required, quickness to perceive and
    resolution to decide, combined with conduct
    which while it was preeemptory and inflexible was
    not calculated to give much offence. It may easily
    be supposed that among so many persons, of
    various dispositions no small portion of whom
    were eager to make speeches, and impatient of
    control that the office of Chairman was not an
    ordinary one, and that but few of the members
    were qualified to fill it. The forms of the House of
    Commons were as nearly as possible observed . . .
    I never permitted any deviation, from the course
    laid down. It was soon perceived that, this method
    accelerated the business and enabled the com-
    mittee generally almost always indeed to get
    through the whole of it at one sitting, which was
    sometimes not the case when another member was
    in the chair' (Add MSS 27808, fos. 28-9).
9   Powell's description: 'Report of the / Genl Com /
    L C S / 3 Septr 1795'.

58. A Clarke Del.   Sheriff Sub Del.   Le
     Maitre Secty

[Powell's account of the divisions branching and his report of the executive committee are substantially the same as the previous report.]

Genl Com. conclusion of the Report
A Motion was made to rescind the resolution
of printing by estimate. (*carried*)
A motion was made that the adjournd motions
be taken into consideration this evening (*car-
ried*) This motion was render'd nugatory as
the reelection of the Ex Com & the takin the
numbers on the 3 referrd motions took up
the time till 3 oClock in the morning.
Davenport & Young were ballotted out of the
Ex Com
Sellers & Constable ballotted in   the present
Com consist of Jones, Sellers, Binns, Moody,
Maxwell   Constable, Ashly & Galloway.

[The formation of Division 64 is next reported.]

The Numbers on the Referd Motions were
against the Genl Com meeting on Thursday &
Friday   a majority of 132. On the Divisions
being increased to 50 & not to branch to 80.
negatived by a majority of 400.
On the Chairman of Genl Com. being elected
for 3 Months carried by a Majority of 395.
Place was then elected Chaiman for the next
3 Months.
A letter was read from some members of Div
27 requesting they might form a a div of
Housekeepers only. to pay 2/6 or 3/ –
Quarterge –
    Referd to the Ex Com to write to them re-
fusing their request as it was directly contrary
the regulations but that they might form a
Society & correspond with us
                    adjournd –

299. Minutes: LCS General Committee, 10 September 1795[10]

Source: Add MSS 27813, fos. 126-9

Genl Comee Sept 10th. 1795

Marget to keep the Door

10   A copy of this report made by Hester and sent
     to Div. 52 in care of the publican of the Golden
     Lion at Sydenham, presumably where the divi-
     sion met, was intercepted and sent to government
     by the publican.

[The report opens with a list of the 64 divisions, the number of new members in each division and the number present at the division meetings, totalling 110 new and 1760 present. Notations next to division numbers: 2, 'England Sub'; 11, 'no Cash neither Dele nor Sub dele present'; 18, 'Hodgson sub Danby Secy'; 21, 'Geo Blyh[11] Sub H C Carrington Secy'; 23, 'Hogan Sub vice Pickard transfer'd'; 34, 'Wm Foster – Weston, Kniblet';[12] 58, ned'; 47, 'J Horton Dele, D King Secy'; 55, 'Wm Foster–Weston, Kniblet';[12] 58, 'Secy forgot Quarteridge'; 59, 'J Clinton J Barlow J Wallace'; 60, 'did not meet as the Landlord was afraid';[13] 61, 'Leonard Williams[14] George St John Francis Yates'; 62, 'Robert Malloy, Robt Stewart, John Scotney'; 63, 'John Pickard, Effey,[15] – & Solomon Chaffing'; 64, 'was not formed'; 65, 'John Rhynd Jas Hull & Aspinshaw'.]

Admitted to Sitting

Ellis from	24	Miller	16
Mitford	24	Ralph	13
Mckneell	17	Incledon	40
Pollard	17	Sutney	62
French	27	Cole	5
Patton	23		

Unrepresented Divns

27 – Deputed McGuire – Clinton
39 – returned to the Grotto – Wilson & Salter
52 – Sydenham Hester to write
53 – Waltham Dymes to write
56 – Thos Browne, Moggeridge –

31. The Delegate informed the Comee that that Landlord (where his Divn met) informed him they must get a fresh place to meet in, As he should [not] have his license renewed if he let them meet in his house – they therefore moved to the Fleece little Windmill St to meet to morrow & then change their night to Wednesday

Divn 21. Moved to the Paul Pindar corner of Half Moon Alley Bishopgate St[16]

11 Blyde in Div. 52 copy. In Powell's report Carrington is delegate and Blygh subdelegate.
12 Niblet in Div. 52 copy.
13 'not formed on account that the Publican could not take them in being [ap]prehensive of Loosing his Liscies' – Div. 52 copy.
14 Willmot in Div. 52 copy.
15 Eepey in Div. 52 copy. Heaphy, sccording to Powell.
16 'to Meet on Tuesdays' – Div. 52 copy.

51. have moved from Bricklayers Arms Kingsgate St to the Kings Arms Smarts Buildings[17] Monday
57. requested a deputation to go to Mitcham to morrow evening to meet at the Elliots head the other side of Newington at ¼ before 5 O'Clock To be No 60 deputed Haselden, Hiram Powell[18] B Binns
Morgan, Haselden resigned –
Movd & Sec'd that Citn Patton be heard – Neg –
Mov'd that 2 Members from Divn 24 do confer with the Ex Comee on establishg a correspondence in Cornwall – Affir
The following houses wished to have Divns
The Cart & horse little St Martins Lane
The Bricklayers Arms White cross St[19]
The 3 Tunns Horsleydon

a deputation from the Moral & Political Society, who bro't 70 Copies of their first production[20]
Movd & Secd that they be admitted to the Sitting – Affir
Siddon admitted to the Sitting

Report of Ex Comee

Sept 4th.
Present, Maxwell, Ashley, Galloway, Constable, Binns
Absent Jones
Binns reelected reporter
Read a Letter from Citn Sellers in which he declines the honour of being a Member of the Ex Comee
Citn Moody also resigned
Read a Copy of a Letter to be sent to Sunbury[21] amendd & ordered to be sent

17 'Holborn' added in Div. 52 copy.
18 J. Powell in Div. 52 copy.
19 'Cripplegate' added in Div. 52 copy.
20 'Messrs Hamilton Read [Reid] & Grimshaw' – Div. 52 copy. Predictably, the pamphlets they brought were 'to be dispersed amongst the society for the defution of Moral & Political Knowledge'. William Hamilton Reid left the LCS because he felt the Society was trying to force deism on the members. See 302.
21 From Citizen Wood the LCS heard of the patriotic society at Sunbury and was ready to cooperate to procure universal suffrage and annual Parliaments. 'All our present evils originate from the corrupt state of what is called Representation.' The most effectual mode of obtaining our goals is to diffuse knowledge by means of cheap publications tending to convince people of the necessity of forming societies. When the people are united they will find no difficulty in having their rights restored (10 Sept. 1795, *Correspondence*, pp. 65–7).

Read a Letter from Citn Vialls on the subject
of admitting housekeepers to form seperate
Divns & pay 2/6 quarteridge
a Member deputed to answer it – [22]
Citn Geo Ross requested to attend this Comee
next meeting night[23]

Sept 9.
Present Ashley, Galloway, Constable Max-
well, Binns
Absent Jones
Read a Letter from Citn Dowling wth a bill
for rent for the Divn 4 & 7 –   14 . . 3-6
                                                  3 - 10 –pd
                                                  ――――――
                                                  10 .13..6

Read a letter from Sheffield which was accom-
panied wth a Parcel[24] – a Member deputed
to answer it –
The Treasurer ordered to pay Citn Cooper – 8S
Read a Bill from Citn Davenport for printing
2000 copies of the Regulations – The Comee
came to the resolution of withholding the
Money till his bill has been adjusted[25]
A Member deputed to draw up a Letter to the
Friends of Liberty[26]
Gave the No 65 to a Divn to meet on a Wed-

nesday at the 3 Tunns Cross St[27] Hatton
Garden
Ashley informed the Comee that the deputation which had waited on Citn Davenport
agreeable to the orders of the Gen Comee –
with information that he had nearly concluded the Orders he had received for printing

2 Members of Ex Comee to be chosen
Nominated Hiram Powell   declined
                 Evans of Divn 4   38
                 Hester   25
                 Te S Price   36
Evans & Price elected
      Geo Ross sent a letter informed the Comee
      that he would print the proceedings of the
      British Convention if the Society would
      take 1000 – at 4½ ea) [28]
Movd & Sec'd that the Society do take
1000 copies at 4½d ea) to be sold to
Members at the same price Affir
Amendt that we take 2000 neg
Being some dispute about takg the Answer
to refer'd
Questions in writing only –
Movd that No returns but what are signed
by President & Secretary
                                                  28A. 22N

[There follows a tally headed 'Returned of
Refer'd Question for Genl Meeting'. The
totals are erroneously listed as 488 affirmative and 346 negative; they should be
498 and 365.]

Maxwell resigned his sitation in Ex Comee
Proposed Hester   42
        Jas Powell   12
              Hester elected
Several Motions being read relative to the
better arraingement of the Genl Comee
a Motion made & sec'd that they be referd to
a Comee of 5 & to report this day week
Amendt to report in a fortnight   Affir
Amendt that the Comee consist of 10   Aff
The Motion that they be referd to a Comee
of 10. & to report in a fortnight   Affir
Nominated
        Hodgson
        B Binns   declined
        Moggeridge
        Beck
        Maxwell declined
        Dowling

22 The offer of a division restricted to housekeepers
    'did not appear to meet with any degree of
    approbation' in the general committee. People
    making such offers imagine they will be more
    respectable. It is granted that men who do not
    have to labour for the necessities have greater
    opportunity of acquiring moral improvement
    and thereby becoming more respectable. But in
    every commercial country 'property is too
    much respected'. It may be evidence of industry
    and economy, but it is not a 'general test of
    moral rectitude'. No man appears truly respect-
    able who is not animated by sentiments of
    philanthropy which lead him to communicate to
    others the instruction or improvement he has
    acquired. 'This can never be effected while men
    of different descriptions are studious of keeping
    distinct companies' (17 Sept. 1795, *Correspon-
    dence*, pp. 55-6).
23 Ross had written 'that a friend of his had formd
    a society at Jedburgh that wishd to correspond
    with L C S. & who wanted to know how he
    might address a letter' – Powell's report.
24 'a Parcel of there proceedings at a Public Meeting
    held on Crookes Moor to be distributed to the
    Divs.' – Powell's report.
25 'Investigated' – Div. 52 copy.
26 The letter explained that the money collected in
    Birmingham was raised for the expenses of the
    treason trials, not for any individual, and that
    the LCS would assist Yorke by urging members
    to buy copies of his trial (17 Sept. 1795, *Corres-
    pondence*, p. 53).

27 'Kirby Street' in Div. 52 copy.
28 The work was to consist of four sheets (Div. 52
    copy).

Hiram Powell[29]
Cooper resigned
Banting
Morgan resigned
J Pickard
Wilson declined
Sherriff
Ramsay
W Brown
T Evans

Being 11 nominated that stood – moved that the Comee do consist of 11. – Affir – [30]
Mov'd that the Dialogue in the Nottingham Journal 1783 be now read – Neg –
Mov'd & Secd that the Treasurers Acct be printed Affir Amendt that they be audited first by a Comee – withdrawn
Movd that 250 Copies be printed – Affir
Citn Dowlings bill audited –

		Weeks		
1794	Divn 4 & 7 – from Feb 13. to June 30 –	21	at 7s ea̅	7. . 7. .0
	June 30. to Dec 9 –	24	at 3/6 ea̅	4. . 4. .0
1795	Dec 9 to March 25 –	15	at 3/6 ea̅	2. .12. .6

	14. . 3. .6
Recd	3. .10. .0
Due	£10. .13. .6

Movd that it be paid – Affir –
Beck movd that Motion of Divn 7 relative to Treasurer be referd to the Divns   Neg –
Beck movd that it be the order of Day on Thursday next –
Affir

Ashley gave Notice he must resigned to Michaelmas
Galloway – the Same –

Quarteridge	6. . 6. .6½
Roussel	1. .13. .1½

---

300. Copy of Minutes of LCS General Committee for Division 52, 10 September 1795 (extracts: items not in previous document)[31]

Source: PC 1/23/A38

Citizen Delegate
I am requested to desire you to return an answer of the progress you meet with and of the state of your Division in General
        Yours with Civic Affecition
                    Joh Hester

[from executive committee meeting of 9 September:]

Read a letter from Dundee in Scotland   A Member deputed to answer it.[32]

[from the committee of delegates:]

Read A letter from highwycomb in Buckinghamshire dated Sepr 2d 1795 wishing to unite with the London Corresponding society (it also stated that another division was forming

29 J. Powell in Div. 52 copy.
30 'To Meet at the hole in the wall fleet street on Fryday at 8 oclock Dowling reporter' – Div. 52 copy.
31 Address: 'To the Delegate / of Division 52 / Golden Lyon / Sydenham'. 'Delegate's Weekly Acct. / Divn. 52./ Golden Lion Sydenham'. Most of this report duplicates that in Add MSS 27813. It was sent by the publican (presumably of the Golden Lion) to the Greenwich Justices of the Peace, who forwarded it to the Duke of Portland. Government extrapolated some figures, noted on the blank parts of the sheets: '1639 – Old Members / 110 – New / [total] 1749', and 'voted – 921'.

32 The Dundee author, long imprisoned as secretary of the Dundee Friends of Liberty, and several friends wished to reorganize the society and asked how the LCS was conducted ([George Mealmaker] to [Citizen Gilchrist], 3 Sept. 1795, *Correspondence*, pp. 59–61; for identification of the author as George Mealmaker, see Michael Roe, 'Maurice Margarot: radical in two hemispheres', *Bulletin of the Institute of Historical Research*, vol. 31 (May 1958), p. 78n). The LCS reply acknowledged receipt of the letter by favour of Gilchrist, urged them to persevere in seeking reform and in encouraging a spirit of enquiry. 'It is through ignorance the world suffers, and in exact proportion to the want of knowledge despotism prevails.' Enclosed were copies of the LCS regulations and the account of the general meeting (23 Sept. 1795, *Correspondence*, pp. 61–2).

at Great Marlone)[33] was reffered to the Executive Committee

Read a letter from Truro in Cornwall stating that there was many friends to reform there, and wishing to receive instructions from the London Corresponding Society to know how they were to proceed as they was greatly Harrased by the Aristocrats there[34]

reffered to the Executive Committe

upon a Motion being made that no sopposed number should pass as real there Apeared

against	28
for it	22
	—
Lost by a Majority of Voices	6

301. Report from spy Powell: LCS General Committee, 10 September 1795[35]

Source: PC 1/23/A38

Genl Com L C S 10th. Septr 1795

110. New Members £6. .6. .6½ Quarterage

[Powell's information about Divisions 21, 31 and 51 changing meeting places and his list of public houses requesting divisions are substantially the same as in the two previous documents.]

57. Request a deputation to go to Mitcham in Surry on Friday evening to be No. 60. (This No given to a former division having no house to meet at the members transfd themselves to other divisions) Deputation Iram Powell, B Binns, Morgan, Ellford, & Milton – at the Bucks Head Micham

[The rest of Powell's report restates, in brief, most of the matter in the two previous documents. The majority in favour of a general meeting is given as 'near 200'.]

Adjournd ½ past 3 oClock

33 *Correspondence*, pp. 56–7.
34 To the president of the LCS, 8 Sept. 1795, *Correspondence*, pp. 63–4.
35 Powell's description: 'Genl Com L C S. / 10 Sept 1795'.

302. Report from spy Powell: LCS General Committee, 17 September 1795[36]

Source: PC 1/23/A38

Genl Com. L C S. 17th. Sept 1795.

109. New Members £6. .10. . – ½ Quarterage

A letter read from division 53 meeting at Waltham Abby informing the Com they had return'd back to the first place of meeting namely the Bullshead Waltham Abby on Tuesday – Also requesting the Committee would allow them to chuse a delegate residing in Town who might correspond with their Sub Del at Waltham Abby to whome he might send the Report & from whome he might receive motions to carry into the General Committe /

Moved & carried that a deputation of two persons do go down on Tuesday next to consult with them about it. James Powell & Travers to be the deputation, also moved that they be allowed 3s / each for expences/ carred/

Div 44 Change their place of meeting from the French Horn Lambeth walk to the Queens arms Kennington Lane meet on Wednesday

Div 10 from 14 Stairs Rosemary Lane to the Queens Arms Crutched Friars.

Div 42 from the 1 Ton Strand, to the Feathers Chas Court Strand

Div 21. Move to Citizens Sayers Mattrass Maker No 13 Willson Street Morefields

Div 10 return Harris their delegate, Thompson Sub. Del

Div 26 Branch to the Nags Head Kentish Town to be No 60/ that Number also not being form'd last week/ meet on Tuesday. Banten Eady & Brown deputation

Ex Com. Septr, 11

Evans Hester Price Galloway & Constable Citizens Milford & Ellis inform'd the Com that there were many frends of Reform at Truro in Cornwall who were anxious to correspond with the L C S. A member deputed to write to Truro.[37]

36 Description: 'Genl Com L C S 17 Septr 1795'.
37 The LCS rejoiced that Truro reformers wished to associate to obtain parliamentary reform. There will be a reform 'if the people with an united, solemn, and determined voice' demand it. To make this demand irresistible, 'it is necessary that the public sentiment should be explicitly and generally understood'. Therefore every good citizen must make his voice heard and his sentiments known. 'The man who does not join in

Sept 12.

Ashley, Galloway, Constable, Hester, & Price
The Com. resolved that on the next sittings
every member should bring with him in writing his opinion of the business to be brought
forward at the general meeting. A member
deputed to answer the letter received from
High Wickham.[38] The Committe investigated the tenders for printing in consequence of
which they requested Davenport to attend
their next sittings to explain his Bill.

Septr 16

Constable, Ashley, Galloway, Evans, Price &
Binns
Davenport attended, his bill examined &
ordered to be paid.
Read a letter from the Norwich Patriotic
Society. A member deputed to answer it (This
letter was also read in the Genl Com. it was
full of democratic expressions requested more
of the L C S publications for which they
would pay. it also informed the L C S. That
they (the Norwich Patriotic Society) increased
gloriously, they already amounted to 19 divisions & that they had enterred into a resolution to support no member of Paliament at
the next General Election but such as intirely
coincided with their Principles.)[39] Read a
letter from a female Citizen highly republican
& containd a Fable Personal on the King & by
inuendo advised the people to rise. (Read also
in the General Committee with applauses.) A
member produced a draught of a letter to the
Friends of Liberty, approved & ordered to be
sent by Evans & Price   A member produced
a draught of a letter in answer to the one from
Dundee / adjournd/.

Conclusion of the Report of General *Com.*

The Reporter of the Ex Com said he had left
all the adjournd motions at home. The *Com*

then went to the order of the day viz the
motion from Div 7. That a Treasurer be appointed distinct from Secretary to be chosen
out of the body of the Society or from the
General Com who shall be answerable to the
Ex Com. for all publications of the Society to
continue in office 3 months & to be reeligible
as long as the Genl Com. shall think proper.
Div 6   The like Motions./ *refered to the divi-
sions/*
Div 27   Resolved that there are in the Society
Atheists, Deists & other blasphemous Persons
who go about propagating the most horrible
Doctrines, contrary to every Principle of
Liberty, & which frighten all good Christians
from the Society. They likewise make use of
the most diabolical expressions such as calling
the Deity "Mr Humbug." "Damning the Bible"
Blasting all Christians & declaring the Society
will never do any good untill they are without
them. This division do recommend that the
President of the General [committee] do
severely repremand them for the 1st offence
& that they be expelld from the Society for
the second.[40]/ *passed to the order of the
day with contempt/*

40 This dispute between the religious and the non-
religious members must have been building up
since the publication of part 2 of Paine's *Age of
Reason* late in 1794. William Hamilton Reid,
who was active in the Society as early as June
1792, but who later denounced it in a work
tellingly entitled *The Rise and Dissolution of
the Infidel Societies* (1800), attributed the dissension to the attempt by the LCS leaders to
force Paine's deism upon the members. The
members, he argued, were prepared for Paine's
infidelity by the reading in the divisions of
Mirabaud's *System of Nature* and Volney's
Ruins of Empires. 'The adoption of Paine's Age
of Reason was not agreed, to in the London
Corresponding Society, without considerable
opposition, especially in the general committee;
but as zeal superseded judgment, in their discussions upon the subject, the epithets of d-m--d
fool, and d-m--d Christian ultimately prevailed.'
The attachment of the LCS to the *Age of Reason*
was so strong, according to Reid, that possession
of the book was regarded as proof of civism.
Bone and Lee, booksellers, 'were *proscribed* for
refusing to sell Volney's Ruins and Paine's Age
of Reason; and that refusal construed into a
censure upon the weakness of their intellects'.
A potential delegate would be recommended as
'a good Democrat and a Deist'; his recommender
might add as final praise 'that he is no Christian'. From the time when the LCS leaders
began to force their anti-religious opinions upon
the members, Reid asserted, the internal dissensions hastened the dissolution of the Society
more than any external obstacles (pp. 5–9).
Place confirmed these assertions that infi-

reformation, becomes an accomplice in the guilt
of his rulers' (26 Sept. 1795, *Correspondence*,
pp. 73–4).
38 The letter stated the need for good men to come
forward in the cause of reform, the belief that
the public was increasingly avid for political
knowledge and willing to associate (30 Sept.
1795, *Correspondence*, pp. 57–9).
39 The LCS reply applauded the plan to support
only MPs with the right principles, shared doubts
about the value of petitions, lamented that so ·
many people still regard 'artificial distinctions as
constituting the honor and glory of a nation',
announced an increase of 1500 members since
the general meeting, and regretfully refused to
send the names of the country correspondents
(23 Sept. 1795, *Correspondence*, pp. 64–5).

Div 4   That the question respecting calling a general meeting be again refered back for a fortnight discussion. /negatived/

Divisions 2. & 27.   Moved that those divisions who have not sent in a return on the question respecting a Genral Meeting be allowed to the 24th. Inst. /negatived/

Div. 14.   That the General meeting be held in 3 Parts of the town & at one time. Viz one for Westminster, one for Southwark, & one for Whitechapel & that the Ex Com do appoint presidents & speakers the same to be free. /negatived/

Div 45.   Recommend that the divisions Ticketts do admitt all citizens   Free at the next Genl meeting as the finances do not require it. / adjournd for 14 days./

Div 32.   Resolved that each division do appoint 4 of its most peaceable members to attend the General Meeting to patrole in every direction to keep the peace & assst the Civil Power if necessary – /negatived/

Div 22   That as many citizens as can shall attend the funeral of a deceased member /negatived/

Divs 63. 16. 29. 6. 65. & 23   Resolv'd that the General Secretary & assistant Secretary be allowed an annuel Salary. *Refer'd to the Divisions/*

Moved by Hodgson & carred that the following motion be refered to the divisions as an amendment on the former. Viz "That you will allow the General Committe the power of granting to every future Secretary, assistant Secrety & Treasurer such pecuniary reward as they shall think proper.

/adjournd 3 oClock in the Morning/

Genl Com L C S.
17 Septr 1795

303. Report from spy Powell: LCS General Committee, 24 September 1795[41]

Source: PC 1/23/A38

General Committe L C S
24th. Septr. 1795

85 New Members.   Quarterage   4£.6s.7½s
Div 34 meeting at Greenwich Branch to the Swan Charlton Kent to be No 67. Depution to go on Sunday 4th October of Hodgson LMaitre, Peckard J Powell, Place Hasledon & several others. A Society meeting at the Lukes Head St Martins Lane (to which a deputation was sent to hold a conference last week) sent a letter that they were willing to become a division of the London Corresponding Society. The Committe gave them the No 68 & appointed a deputation to open it.

Report of the Ex Committee. Sept 21.

A letter was sent the the Friends of Liberty which was civicly received. took into consideration the motion from Div 19 respecting the General meeting being held in the County of Middlesex resolved to carry the same into effect if possible.

Resolved that the General meeting be held on the 19th. of October next. Several members produced their opinions of the business to be brought forward at the said meeting   Read a letter from High Wickham requesting an answer to their former letter. Read a letter

41 Description: 'Report of Genl Com LCS. / Septr. 24. 1795'.

---

delism was common among the LCS leaders, but insisted that religious toleration was always practised: 'Nearly all the leading members were either Deists or Atheists – I was an Atheist . . . . This was also the opinion of many others – There were however a number of very religious persons in the society. If ever toleration in its best sense ever prevailed in any society it was in this. Religious topics never were discussed scarcely ever mentioned, It was a standing rule in all the divisions and in the committees also That no discussions or disputes on any subject connected with religion should be permitted and none were permitted. In private, religion was frequently the subject of conversation, and it was well known [that the] most conspicuous members were free thinkers but no exception was ever taken, to those opinions nor were they ever brought into discussion. Thomas Hardy was a religious man, John Bone was a saint, and a busy man at times in attempting privately to make converts among the irreligious' (Add MSS 27808, fos. 115-16).

Hardy, a dissenter, held an apocalyptic view of current history: he believed that Ezekiel 21 ('Her priests have violated my law . . . . Her princes are like wolves') was a reference to France (letter to Rev. David Bogue, 23 March 1793, Add MSS 27811, fos. 19-19v). The 'reign of the Beast of Civil and Ecclesiastical Power', he wrote, 'is almost at an end – Thanks to the Supreme Ruler of the Universe – for his great goodness hitherto – and the bright prospect before us' (letter to Henry Buckle, 12 March 1794, TS 11/953/3497).

The dispute over Paine's influence in the LCS continued: at a debate society on 12 Dec. John Gale Jones denied that the LCS forced the members to read Paine: 'the C. S did not officially circulate that pamplet [*Rights of Man*]; the C. S. always leaves it to the choice of it's Members to read what political pamphlets they think proper' (HO 42/37).

from Wychchurch Salop with an account of a Patriotic Society formed there which requested Correspondence with the L C S.[42] The Committee for arrainging the Correspondence of the Society Reported progress they were empowered to print 2000 thousand Copies & order the press to be left standing they were likewise empowered to draw up a preface to the same they will be ready next week. A member produced a letter in answer to that from Sunbury approved & ordered to be sent. The answer to the letter from Dundee approved & ordered to be sent. ordered 500 Copies of the Duke of Richmonds letter & the state of the Representation to be printed immediately. Adjourned.

General Committe.

The Deputation to Waltham Abby reported that the Division meeting there were very strong & were rapidly increasing They had appointed Citn Edwards to be their delegate residing in town who was to send the Report to the Sub delegate every week. They had also receved a request from sevral persons residing at Woodford to hold a conference & send them the publications of the Society. A like request from Cheshunt Herts. A letter was read from a numerous meeting of the Methodists belonging to the Society requesting the expulsion of Atheists & Deists from the Society & that they should not be reeligalbe 'till a twelvemonths probation. if this request was not complied with they said they would certainly secede from the Society. The Chairman said that this letter could not be taken into consideration not comeing from a division nor being a motion unless a delegate made it so. Dixey delegate of Div 27. immediately rose & moved that the request in the letter be complied with. A very long debate took place between the Methodists & their opponents. when the former finding they would lose their motion almost unanimously withdrew it & informed the Committe they would *immediately leave the Society.* (NB *I understand that by this defection the Society*

will lose six whole divisions besides several hundred members from others.)
Moved seconded & carried that a deputation be appointed to attend Div 27. (who had been the chief instigators in the business.) to endeavour to concilliate matters. (NB. *This deputation they refused to receive*)
The Committe of eleven appointed to form a plan for expediting the business of the Genl Com Reported that they had agreed to Nineteen Articles which would be laid before the Com. on the next meeting.

Adjournd

[There are no accounts of the next two meetings of the general committee (1 and 8 October). At these meetings were read a letter from and a reply to the Portsmouth Constitutional and Corresponding Society[43] and the 19 articles for the better management of the committee. One or more of these articles must have changed the method of producing reports to be read to the divisions, for there are no more full minutes in Add MSS 27813. The suggestions from the divisions indicate the problems that the committee of eleven tried to solve.]

304. Suggestions for Better Management of the LCS General Committee: 31 August–23 September 1795

Source: Add MSS 27813, fo. nos. as noted

London Corresponding Society
Division 15 – Augst. 31. 1795 – [44]

The very rapid increase of this Society,

42 'The late General Meeting of your Society has gladdened the hearts of all friends to the Liberties of Mankind.' Even in this aristocratic town men have listened to the voice of truth and wish to affiliate with your society, 'owning you our Political Fathers; as we never should have been converts to these principles [universal suffrage and annual Parliaments] but for your society'. We are forming a society 'founded on the principles of His Grace the Duke of Richmond, and your own!!!' (16 Sept. 1795, *Correspondence*, pp. 71–3)'

43 The letter from Portsmouth solicited advice from the LCS for their recently formed society. 'The London Corresponding Society; we behold with the filial respect of children to their parent accept us then as your offspring, give us your advice' (29 Sept. 1795, *Correspondence*, pp. 75–7). In reply the LCS sent copies of the State of the Representation and the Duke of Richmond's letter. 'They contain nearly all that is essential to a knowledge of the causes and means of correcting national grievances.' Among several admonitions was one to 'avoid the bane of religious controversy' (8 Oct. 1795, ibid., pp. 78–9).

44 LCS description: 'No 3 / Divn 15' (fos. 141–2v). 'No 3' presumably identifies this as the third proposal received for better management of the meetings of the general committee. The elaborate plan from Div. 50 (see below, pp. 310–11) is no. 10.

having so much increased the business of the General Committee as to render it impossible for them to go through their business in the usual time, unless some modes be adopted to facilitate their procedings; it is become indispensibly necessary that some arrangement should take place, which may answer this purpose –
The two Motions refer'd to us on this Subject, viz. One for enlarging the Number of persons necessary to form a Division – & the other for the Committee sitting two nights in the week; neither of them appear to this Division, calculated to answer the end proposed – This Division are of Opinion that a very large portion of time is consumed in matters of very little moment; whilst affairs of greater consequence viz. the Motions from Divisions &c. are adjourn'd for several Weeks together for want of sufficient time for the Committee to enter into the discussion of them – We therefore submit to the consideration of the General Committee the following

Plan for the better conducting the business of this Society in the General Committee. ——
Every Delegate shall, immediately on his entrance into the Committee Room deliver to the *Secretary*, an Account *in writing* of the Number of persons admitted into his Division the preceding week, together with the Money receiv'd & a receipt for the Secretary to sign – & in order that this part of the business may be done as soon as possible, the Secretary shall attend in the Committee room at ½ past Seven oClock
The President shall take the Chair precisely at 8 o'Clock & immediately proceed to business, by reading over the Motions, that every Delegate may take a Copy of them – whilst these are reading, the Secretary or his Assistant shall make out a List of those Divisions (if any) from which he has receiv'd no Report; which List he shall deliver to the Chairman, who shall call them over & if the Delegate, Sub Delegate or Secretary of such Divisions be not present, a Deputation shall then be appointed –
The Executive Committee's Report shall be printed to Wednesday in every week & a Copy deliver'd to every Delegate for the Divisions –
The next business shall be to take the Motions into consideration & the Chairman shall take the sense of the Committee on which Motion shall be first consider'd –
The Secretary or his Assistant shall cast up the total Number of Members made the preceding week, from the papers he receives from the Delegates – & shall report to the Com-

mittee the total Number of New Members together with the Quarterage –

Resolv'd Unanimously
That this Division do reccomend to the General Committee, that the foregoing Plan be immediately Refer'd to the Society
Litson Holliday Chairman
Robt Gospwill Secretary

Friday September 11th.: 1795

Division 4[45]

It is with regret this Division reviews the loss of time which the London Corresponding Society have sustained from the numerous motions which have been referred to the Divisions for altering its regulations; – a circumstance which, in the Opinion of this Division, tends much to increase the business of the General Committee as well as to defeat the object of the Society: inasmuch as the time of the Society is wasted in Cavils and disputes upon mere punctilios and questions of form when it might be employed to greater advantage in reading Political Books or discussing political questions; – To remedy this Evil in future –
It is moved that no motions that relate to the Constitution of this Society be discussed more than twice in every Six Months, and that the Executive Committee do appoint stated times for that purpose. –

ffor it	21	Hector Campbell Chairman
Agst it	4	T J Collett – Secretary

A plan under the second head of Regulation, Viz: to Divide the Committee[46]
The Secretary to attend at 8 O'clock, and proceed to Receive the Quarterage as usual, and take charge of the returns refer'd Motions & Certificates of Officers newly Elected, Motions only to be Submitted to the Chair
One Voice or Seat only to be alowed for a divn: which shall be numberd, and fill'd by either Del: S Del or Secy: The seats & the chair of the Committee to be taken by ½ past

45 fo. 136.
46 LCS description: 'Plan under Second head / by citn Evans' (fos. 134-5v). Above the description is a note, perhaps giving suggested headings of a form to be used at the general committee: 'Sertificates / Del Resignd S Del Resignd Sec Resignd'. Under these headings are words crossed out, perhaps imaginary names (one may be 'Hothead').

8 Oclock and the Committee declar'd to be Open'd for the Evening, the Secetary or Assistant shall emediately withdraw to an adjoining Room or such place as the Comte: shall apoint together with a certain Number of Officers (not Employ'd for the Night) where the Secy: or assist: shall call over the Returns of members Made and present (the same being Specified on the Receipts) and the Numbers for and against refer'd motions, and read the Certificates, the Officers to post the same in as many printed Numerical Tables as there are Divns. a plan of the Table to be seen anex't,[47] the Business of the Gen: Comte: to begin with the reading of the Report of the Ex: Com: and end with the apointment of Deputations –

Division 8[48]

This Division Recommends to the Society to appoint a Proppds Person as Secretary to attend the General Meeting to take the Report in a Concise manner & Imediately or As Soon as Can be Transmit a Coppy to Each Delegate & ⟨answer⟩ all Letters & do such other Business as is wanting in the Society for which he shall be allowed a Competent Sallary as shall be agreed on by the Society

19 Members for   W Thompson Chairman
  3 Against

                 A Graham Sect

14 Sepr 95

16 Septr 1795[49]

Division 36   Resolved, that for the greater Expedition of the Business of the General Committee that it is the Opinion of this Division that it would be very beneficial, That there should be four more Members added to the Executive Committee and That each

should Copy an equal Share of the report of the Ex- Com- for the Delegates which shall be delivered to them (ye sevl Delegs) respectively by the Secretary of the Genl Committee at the time they deliver in their Returns of New Made Members &c from their Divisions. card Unanimously

          G Welch President
          Thos. Sanders. Sub. Secty.

References, &c to Plan of Division 50
By the Secretary, a Compositor[50]

(A)[51] The whole of this Arrangement might be made while the Business of the Executive Committee was proceeding on, by the Reporter or an Amanuensis, which would save Delegate two or three hours of uninteresting Reporting. Delegate, Sub Delegate, a Secretary not attending to deliver their Returns in time to forfeit One Shilling each, to be expended on the Delegation. That this Business be last read (without copying) Deputations (if wanted) appointed) & a Copy delivered to the Printer

That a printed Form be furnished to Divisions, to be pasted or affixed in the Division Book, in this or a similar Manner – & for the Convenience of the Amanuensis, be written on a quarter Sheet of Fool's Cap Paper

47 The annexed table, headed 'Plan of the posted Table' and dated '12 Sep: 95', contains columns in which to record for each division numbers of new members, members present, votes for and against referred motions, and quarterage (dues), plus the subjects of the referred motions. Another table, headed 'Certificates of newly Elected Officers', contains columns for the names of delegates, subdelegates, secretaries and the men they replace in these offices. The imaginary names in the columns suggest there were some typical committee members in the LCS: 'Gabmuch, Shortwind, Sleepyhead, Knownothing, Forgetall'.

48 fo. 133.

49 LCS description: 'Divn 36 / 16 Septr. 1794 [1795] / RESOLUTION / yt 4 Members be added / to Ex: Com & yt ye Copy yt Report for / ye Delegates' (fos. 132–2v).

50 Titled (on a separate sheet in ornate lettering): 'Plan; &c for the Consideration of the Commission of Eleven'. Addressed: 'To Citizen Chairman of the Commission of Eleven'. LCS description: 'No 10 Kenningtons Plan' (fos. 130–41). The title, covering letter, samples of printed forms and contents are not in consecutive order. Between some of the items are pasted proposals from other divisions. The covering letter, headed 'Plan for printing Reports. From Division 50. By the Secretary, a Compositor' and signed 'John Franklin Kennington. Secretary to Division 50   No 2 Ben Johnsons Head   Westmorland Buildings   Aldersgate Street. Branched with & from No 3, Lord Cobham's Head, Clerkenwell', asks that the plan be introduced as that of Div. 50, not of Kennington, who last year had an information filed against him for publishing (under the name of Hunter) a weekly 2d pamphlet called the *Gleaner*. Since the sample form for the report of the executive committee gives the date of 4 Sept. and some minutes of that meeting, this plan must have been submitted after the general committee meeting of 10 Sept., at which the minutes of 4 Sept. were read.

51 'A' refers to a sample printed form headed 'Return of the Different Divisions' and containing columns for the numbers of new members, old members, total present, and for a list of the days and meeting places of the divisions.

London Corresponding Society . . . . . . Division

Monday &c.   Sep 17.

Division	Member made	Member present	Visitors	Total
51	5	39	16	50

Remarks – On ⟨Causes⟩ of more a less appearance –
On what may be⟩ Any Member persecuted, &c –
Other Business to follow

Secretary's Account
New Members – 5 - 0
Transfers . . .
Renewals . . .

————————

Quaterage

Tickets left ——
Articles Do ——
Proceedings ——
D of R Letter ——

State of Representation &c

President
Chairman
Secretary

(B)[52] The Society sent these books with an Intention of accompanying their plan of Admission, for the sake of gaining Subscribers; but not one Delegate in ten taking it down, we have only their Books, & they their Design frustrated   Some mode of having Abstracts, if not printing wholly, ought to be adopted, for every intelligent Delegate must lament his Attendance, when he cannot communicate such interesting Letters as read last Sitting to his Division – More essentially so of the Letters from Sheffield & High Wycombe – The volunteer Civism of the Mayor of Wycombe would have afforded a glorious Gratification to all Citizens if we could have presented it in its purity –
(C) The Whole of the Business of the Executive Committee might also be prepared by an Amanuensis a Reporter - And all the Blanks for Ballots Approbations, Elections &c. filled up as passed; & the Trouble, Formality & Expence of taking separate Reports done away by the Plan of printing

52 'B' and 'C' refer to a sample printed form for summarizing the business of the executive committee, including the letters received by the Society. The first sentence of 'B' is a comment on the following item on the sample form: 'Received a letter from the Moral and Political Society, accompanied with seventy books, for the use of the Society, entitled – Causes and Curses of War - 4 pages.' At the bottom of the form is handwritten, 'Specimen of Size, of Letter & Paper' and 'The following Blank is sufficient Space for original & all other Information of the Society.'

[There follow five points in the implementation of this plan for printing the weekly reports of the general committee: three copies would be printed for each division – one to be filed by the division and one each for the delegate and the temporary chairman. The printed reports would be delivered to the landlords of the divisions, the delegate paying a penny for delivery. Letters to be printed would be delivered beforehand to the printer; the reporter and an amanuensis would prepare all documents for the report, so that the delegates have only to discuss and vote. Extra copies of the weekly report would be supplied only on application to the executive committee.]

It is better that Citizens, & those who may become Members, come to the Divisions to hear & be enlightened by full Reports, than be allowed to have them printed; for a regular Supply might enable mercenary or proud people to form private Divisions - It might enable the housekeepers, referred to by Citizen Vials, to form Divisions themselves, while Reports are so interesting & authentic - At present, many are erroneous, ungrammatical, & in some instances, disgraceful

Lastly that it be recommended to the Commission to advise a trifling monthly Subscription, for defraying Citizens for filling the Offices of this Society . . . .

[Proposals from two other divisions present suggestions similar to those given above. Only part of the plan submitted by Sheriff of Division 9 remains. It, like the plan from Division 50, would have the delegates provided with printed copies of the proceedings of the general committee and the executive committee.[53]]

[The 'Plan proposed to expedite the business of the General Committee' recommends there be two secretaries with printed forms for statistics about the number of new and present members of each division and the votes on referred questions. These secretaries, appointed weekly, would arrive at 7:30 pm and receive from each delegate a paper containing this information. The delegate would give the secretary of the Society the money from his division and would then take his numbered seat. If the delegate were absent, the sub-delegate or secretary would take his place and retain it for the night; otherwise the sub-delegate and secretary would sit as spectators in another part of the room. The delegates would take minutes of the proceedings, but would be given printed copies of the report of the executive committee. At the end of the evening the appointed secretaries would give each delegate a list of the numbers of new and present members and the votes on referred questions.[54]]

305. Report from spy Powell: LCS General Committee, 15 October 1795

Source: PC1/23/A38

Genl Com. Octr 15. 1795.

115 new members. Quarterage £16. .–. 9½
A letter read from Chatham with information that 40 persons met at Rochester to form a Corresponding Society. to correspond with the L C S. it likewise said that in a few weeks they were certain of making some hundreds of members.
Refer'd to Ex Com.
Oliphant read a letter from his brother at Carlisle with a account of a Society form'd there
(Referd to Ex Com & moved & carried that Oliphant do cooperate with them

A letter read from 16 Persons meeting at the

Thatchd House Hammersmith. requesting to form a division of the L C S. (moved that a deputation do go on Tuesday next)

To be No 71. deputation Hodgson, Boay, Burt, Ellis Sael & Williamott.
A deputation brought a letter from the Religious Seceders saying they had form'd a Society. calld the Friends of Religious & Civil Liberty,[55] requesting to cooperate and correspond with the L C S.
A long debate took place Hodgson & many other members opposed corresponding with them on account of their conduct & the first article in their regulations. which said no members should be admitted but who pledged themselves to believe in the Scripturs.
   The discussion was adjournd for a week when the deputation were requested to attend again.
C Jeffrys attended & informd the Com. that a meeting of 7000 Persons had lately taken place on a Common in Glostershire   That another meeting would take place soon when he thought it would be proper to send a deputation down. He was ordered to attend the Ex Com & they were empowerd to give him 50 copies of Regulations   50 Copies of G M Narative & 50 Copies of 1st & 2d part of the Friend of the People to send down immediately

Vouchers for Officers

Div 12 Ramsey D. Bull S D. Cheswer Sy
70 Mellish. Redder. King.
14 Cicisen Jennings
20 Coates Sy
69 Moggeridge D. Roger S D. Hobson Sy
57.Allwinkle D.
63 Deal D. Lloyd S D. Chaffer Sy
11 Williams Do
35 Ingleton. D. Dormer. S Dial Sy.

Report of Ex Com.

The Reporter not attending Ashly gave it from his notes.
Octr 9. Present. Duhem.[56] Constable Evans & Gally.
Read a letter from the Com of arraingement requesting leave to be empowered to print 3000 copies of the Correspondence & the Press to be left standing. *Granted*
A letter from Do requesting that Lapwith of

55 They used their freedom to discuss religion: on 10 Jan. 1796, a spy reported that at one division of these 'citizens' the topic was the resurrection (PC 1/23/A38).
56 William Duane.

53 fos. 145-5v.   54 fos. 144-4v.

Div 31 might be added to that Com. *Granted* a member ordered to write to Martin informing him of the Resolution respecting his Bill for defending Briellitt.
Ordered 1000 Copies of Regulations 1000.
Copies of Duke of Rds letter to be printed.

Oct 12.

Ashly. Constable & Evans. leave of absence granted to Binns & Galloway. Read an answer to the Birmingham letter adjournd the discussion to the next sittings. Recd a letter from a Citizen stating his opinion on what he supposes ought to be the measures pursued at the Genl Meeting. The Com having adopted the outlines of their plan orderd the letter to be returnd.

Oct 14.

Ashly. Duhem, Constable   Evans. McGuire. Reconsidered the answer to the Birmingham letter amended & ordered to be sent.[57] A member orderd to draw up a letter to be sent to Wooburn in Bucks. The Ex Com do recommend to the Genl Com to request the Sectys of the Divisions to enter the names of all persons that have publications.

Genl Com.

Report on the 3 referrd Questions
That the Regulations drawn up by the Com of 11 be adopted in the Genl Com
Affirmative   661
Negative –   107
____
554 *Majority in the affirmative*
____

57 Perhaps amended again, because not sent until 23 Oct., the letter alluded to the dissension over religion, a topic not mentioned in the letter from Birmingham. This letter to the LCS announced the revival of the Birmingham society, and their admiration of the LCS. 'Britons might still have remained enveloped in the gloomy shades of ignorance and superstition, and have been ingulphed in the chaos of gothic barbarity; had not your Society cried aloud, "Let there be light!"', etc. (11 Sept. 1795, *Correspondence*, pp. 67–9). In their reply, the LCS 'earnestly recommend to all our associated friends to avoid themes of religious opinion . . . it would ill become us while complaining of political oppression ourselves; to lift the hand of intolerance against the conscience of any friend to Freedom . . . upon modes of faith it is not ours to discriminate' (23 Oct. 1795, ibid., pp. 69–71).

That Treasurer be only concernd with Cash
Af   779
N.   32
____
747. Majority in the affirmative

That the Secty be allowd £30 per annum
Affirmative   514
Negative   317
____
143 Majority in the affirmative.

That the Sub Sectry be allowd £30 per annum.
Affirmative   366
Negative   496
____
130 in the Negative.

Moved that he be allowed £25 per annum.
Referrd to the divisions

Moved & carried thet Ex Com. do concider of Martins Proposal for publishing a Constitutional History of England
Div 3. recommend that all the divisions do have a cheap civic dinner to commemorate the Acquital of Hardy on the 5 of Novr next
Div 63. That if the expence of the Genl Meeting be defrayd by subscription it will be very detrimental to the Society.
A long debate took place when it was pass'd to the order of the day & the following resolutions were moved by Hodgson & pass'd. .
1   That the Ex Com do take all the means possible to avoid an indiscriminate assemblage of People at the Genl Meeting.
2   Resolved that no subscription be taken on the Spot.
3   That the business to be brought forward at the Genl Meeting be previously discussed in the Genl Com & that the Reporter of the Ex Com do inform the Gl. Com by Thursday next when they shall convene them for that purpose   (adjournd at 3 oClock)

[On 21 October the LCS issued an advertisement for the 26 October general meeting, listing the business of the meeting – an address to the nation on the state of public affairs, a remonstrance to the king on the disregard shown toward the address of 29 June and sundry resolutions. Admission free. Members were urged 'to exert their usual efforts with strangers to preserve that order and decorum' which previously placed the LCS above slander and the intrigues of enemies.[58]

58 *MC* 22 Oct. 1795, p. 1. Government responded to news of the meeting with alarm but with less

The missing minutes for the general committee meeting of 22 October must have contained reference to two letters received by the Society. Robert Sands of Perth, who was arrested in May 1794 and imprisoned for a long time, explained that the reformers in his area did not contribute to the subscription for the expenses of the trials because they were supporting David Downie and Mrs Skirving. He added that they look up to the LCS: 'We know that the whole depends upon their exertions, and that without them nothing can be done.'[59] From Rochester G. Mascall and C. Yonans, secretary and chairman of a new reform society, reported their resolutions and motions, the first of which is to correspond with the LCS. They thanked the general and the executive committees for complying with their wishes; citizens Law (a delegate) and Horsey, for procuring them books. This letter from Rochester, headed 'London Corresponding Society', evidently needed more than a simple reply, for a copy is annotated, 'adjourned till Copy of former letter is got'.[60]]

306. PROCEEDINGS OF A GENERAL MEETING OF THE LONDON CORRESPONDING SOCIETY, Held on Monday October the 26th, 1795, in a field adjacent to COPENHAGEN-HOUSE, in the County of Middlesex[61]

Source: as n. 61

The Indifference with which the late Address from this Society to the King was treated;

the rapid approximation of National destruction, thro' the continuation of the present detestable War; – the horrors of an approaching Famine; – and, above all, the increased Corruption, and Inquisitorial measures pursued and pursuing, by those who hold the Country in bondage – obliged this Society to appeal once more to their fellow Countrymen . . . [Accordingly a meeting was advertised.]

Previous to the meeting, the *London Corresponding Society*, had taken into consideration numerous Communications from different parts of the Country, suggesting the utility that would result from the opening a more active and direct communication between the people in those several places, and this Society, by the appointment of Members on deputation to open and regulate Societies for Parliamentary Reform; which was likewise a measure submitted to the public Meeting.

About half an hour after twelve o'clock, the People assembled on the Ground, according to the concurring calculations of several persons, amounted to more than one hundred and fifty thousand persons,[62] at the same time that the Roads in all directions were still covered with people thronging to the Meeting.

[John Gale Jones opened the meeting by announcing that Citizen John Binns, 'a well known and long tried Patriot, and an Honest Man', had been nominated as chairman. After being unanimously approved, Binns took the chair and addressed the meeting, stating that he hoped the contempt shown to their last address would not provoke them]

but that you will now cooly and deliberately determine upon a further mode of proceeding, which shall enforce what has been done before, and convince those Ministers, that when the voice of a United People goes forth, it is their duty to attend to it; and if they do not

Citizens Binns, Thelwall, Jones, Hodgson, &c. / with the / Address to the Nation, / and the / Remonstrance to the King. / And the Resolutions passed by upwards of Two Hundred / Thousand Citizens, then and there assembled. / London. / Printed for Citizen Lee, at the Tree of Liberty, / No. 444, Strand, opposite Buckingham Street. This will be cited as Lee's *Account*.

alarm than in June: the Duke of Portland directed John King to issue orders to Lt. Col. Herries of the Westminster Light Horse Volunteers, to the Lord Mayor and to Col. Brownrigg to have their military forces in readiness; and to the police magistrates to retain extra constables and to send an observer to the meeting (23, 24, and 28 Oct. 1795, HO 65/1).
59 To Ashley, 19 Oct. 1795, Add MSS 27815, fos. 5–6v.
60 Rx 20 Oct. 1795, Add MSS 27815, fos. 7–8.
61 [No publisher or place of publication], 1795. This is the official LCS account of the meeting. Before it appeared, another account of the meeting was published: *(Price Two Pence.) / Account of the Proceedings / of a Meeting of the / London Corresponding Society, / Held in a Field near Copenhagen House, / Monday, Oct. 26, 1795; / Including the Substance of the Speeches of /
62 Between 40,000 and 100,000, according to other sources.

they will be guilty of HIGH-TREASON against the PEOPLE . . . .

[Three points will be brought forth for rejection, amendment or unanimous approbation: an address to the nation, a remonstrance to the king on the contempt shown to the LCS address presented to his ministers, and resolutions applicable to the present crisis.]

ADDRESS TO THE NATION.

Once more, dear friends and fellow citizens, in defiance of threats and insults – of base suggestions and unmanly fears – are we met in the open face of day, and call the heavens and earth to witness the purity of our proceedings. Amidst the dreadful storms and hurricanes which at present assail the political hemisphere of our country, with firm and unabated vigour we pursue our avowed and real purpose – the grand and glorious cause of PARLIAMENTARY REFORM!

[Every friend of liberty must boldly deliver his real sentiments. When citizens become indifferent to their rights or the choice of their representatives, the extinction of liberty and establishment of despotism are inevitable. The recent address to the king was either suppressed or passed over with contempt. If the former]

HIS MINISTERS have proved themselves GUILTY OF HIGH TREASON against the Lives and Liberties of the Nation! If the latter, *his Majesty should consider the sacred obligations he is bound to fulfil. . . .*

The history of the last few months presents indeed to our view, a rapid succession of ill-fated mismanagement, unexampled calamities, and unparallelled disgrace! . . . .

The comfortable and pleasing prospects resulting from an abundant harvest have turned out to be vain and fallacious. Monopoly, stimulated by insatiable avarice, and uncontrouled by those equitable laws which we might expect from EQUAL REPRESENTATION, frustrates the Beneficence of our Seasons, and forbids the industrious Poor, the immediate Necessaries of Life. . . .

What is this subtle and insinuating poison which thus vitiates our domestic comforts and destroys our public prosperity? – It is *Parliamentary Corruption*, which like a foaming whirlpool swallows the fruit of all our labours, and leaves us only the dregs of bitterness and sorrow.

Those whose duty it is to watch over the interests of the Nation, have either proved themselves indifferent to its welfare, or unable to remove the pressure of these intolerable grievances. Let them however be aware in time – Let *them* look to the fatal consequences – *We* are sincere friends of Peace – we want only *Reform*: Because we are firmly and fully convinced, that a thorough Reform would effectually remedy these formidable evils: but we cannot answer for the strong and all-powerful impulse of necessity, nor always restrain the aggravated feelings of insulted human nature! – IF EVER THE BRITISH NATION SHOULD LOUDLY DEMAND STRONG AND DECISIVE MEASURES, WE BOLDLY ANSWER – "WE HAVE LIVES!" AND ARE READY TO DEVOTE THEM, EITHER SEPARATELY OR COLLECTIVELY, FOR THE SALVATION OF OUR COUNTRY.[63]

We trust, however, that *Reason* and *Remonstrance* are alone sufficient to produce the desired effects. We have laboured long, and we hope not unsuccessfully. Our Numbers have increased beyond all human expectation: and many who once professed themselves our most inveterate Enemies are now converted into sincere and faithful Friends. A little more Patience, and a little Perseverance, Fellow Citizens, the Business will be accomplished, and our Triumph complete. The LONDON CORRESPONDING SOCIETY SHALL BE THE POWERFUL ORGAN TO USHER IN THE JOYFUL TIDINGS OF PEACE AND REFORM; AND UNIVERSAL SUFFRAGE AND ANNUAL PARLIAMENTS SHALL CROWN OUR SUCCESSFUL EXERTIONS!

JOHN BINNS, Chairman.
JOHN ASHLEY, Secretary.

The Reading of this Address was, from time to time, interrupted by such loud applauses as are but seldom heard, even in public places –and being ended amidst the warmest and most unanimous acclamations of approbation, the Chairman next proceeded to read,

63 Place, in retrospect, called this 'an absurd declaration'. The whole address he characterized as 'filled with common place topics'. The remonstrance to the king he thought 'better drawn'. As for the language of these documents, he felt the LCS 'did little more . . . than copy from their betters' in Parliament (Add MSS 27808, fo. 40).

315

THE REMONSTRANCE TO THE KING.

To the KING'S Most Excellent Majesty.

The humble and earnest Remonstrance of
Two Hundred Thousand, and upwards,
faithful, though greatly aggrieved, Subjects, associated and assembled with the
CORRESPONDING SOCIETY *of* London,
*in a constitutional manner, in behalf of
themselves and others.*

Sire!

When the treacherous duplicity, and intolerable tyranny of the House of STUART
had roused the long-enduring patience of the
British People, the expulsion of one restored
into their hands the primitive right of chusing
another, as their Chief of many Magistrates.

[At that period the privilege of remons-
trating with the Chief Magistrate was
established. When Queen Anne died without heirs, the public will called to kingly
office the head of the house from which
you are descended. The preservation of the
rights, reconfirmed at the Revolution, then
became part of the obligations of George I.
In spite of the smallness of the majority
which established the Hanoverian succession, the nation has supported the decision
of their representatives on that occasion.
The people of this country hoped that an
eternal gratitude would bind your house
(transplanted from poverty and obscurity
to dignity and opulence) to support the
freedom and happiness of this country.
Our present object is to renew a complaint delivered in an address to you, which
we put into the hands of the Duke of Portland on 15 July. In that address we expressed our belief that your ministers have
plunged the nation into its present calamities and should be dismissed; and that only
a reform in representation can restore this
country to vigour and happiness.
Our address was not attended to by
your majesty's servants as it should have
been. Are we to suffer and not complain?
What have we not to fear if there is an
impenetrable barrier between the oppressed and the magistrate? Alas, we hoped to
find the third sovereign of the Brunswick
line an example of royal virtue. We wished
you to consider whether your duty to your
royal progeny and to your people, whose
industry provides the funds for their
princely support, will be accomplished by
pursuing the measures of odious ministers
or by giving the people liberty, peace and
reform.]

*"Listen, then, Sire! to the voice of a wearied
and afflicted people, whose grievances are so
various that they distract, so enormous that
they terrify. Think of the abyss between sup-
plication and despair!* – The means of national
salvation are in your own hands – it is our
right to advise as well as supplicate: and we
declare it to be our opinion, that a Reform in
the Representation of the People, the removal
of your present Ministers, and a speedy
PEACE, are the only means by which this
country can be saved, or the attachment of
the People secured."

Signed by Order of the Meeting,
J. BINNS, Chairman.
J. ASHLEY, Secretary.

This being received with an equally unanimous approbation, the Chairman then read
the following RESOLUTIONS.

RESOLVED,

1st.   That the present awful and alarming
state of the British Empire, demands the
serious attention of our fellow countrymen.

2d.   That its unexampled distresses call
for immediate and effectual redress.

3d.   That we are fully persuaded the present exorbitant price of the necessaries of life,
(notwithstanding the late abundant harvest) is
occasioned partly by the present ruinous
war; but chiefly by that pernicious system of
monopoly, which derives protection from the
mutilated and corrupt state of the Parliamentary Representation.

4th   That the enormous load of taxes,
under which this *almost* ruined country
groans, together with its unparralleled National
Debt, (which has been and will be greatly
encreased by the present war) threatens the
British Nation with *total* ruin.

5th.   That the inflexible obstinacy of Ministers, in continuing the present cruel, unjust,
and disgraceful war – a war which has stained
the earth and seas with so much human blood
– calls aloud for the execration of every friend
of humanity.

6th.   That the present Government of
France, is as capable of maintaining the *accus-
tomed relations of peace and amity* with the
King of Great-Britain, as with the Elector of
Hanover.

7th.   That we remain fully convinced that
the permanent peace, welfare and happiness
of this Country, can be established only by
restoring to our fellow Countrymen their
natural and undoubted rights, UNIVERSAL

SUFFRAGE and ANNUAL PARLIAMENTS."

8th.   That we are determined, at the next General Elections, to support such Candidates only, as will pledge themselves to promote UNIVERSAL SUFFRAGE and ANNUAL PARLIAMENTS.

9th.   That the evasive conduct of his Majesty's ministers respecting our late Address, convinces us that our fellow Countrymen have little to hope from the Executive part of our Government.

10th.   That we believe the period is not far distant, when Britons must no longer depend upon any party of men for the recovery of their Liberties.

11th.   THAT THE ONLY HOPE OF THE PEOPLE IS IN THEMSELVES.

12th.   That the publicity of our conduct evinces the purity of our intentions, and is a testimony of our love of Peace, and of the sacrifices we would make to spare the blood of our fellow Countrymen.

13th.   That the events of every day are clearly proving we have gained the good opinion of our fellow countrymen, notwithstanding the opposition of our persecutors and calumniators.

14th.   That in order the more effectually to obtain the co-operation and assistance of the whole country, Deputies shall be sent from the Society to the principal towns in the kingdom, for the purpose of explaining to our fellow countrymen the necessity of associating, as the only means of procuring a Parliamentary Reform.

15th.   That strong in the purity of our intentions and the goodness of our cause – regardless of the calumny and threats of our enemies – we again solemnly pledge ourselves to the British nation never to desert the sacred cause in which we are engaged, until we have obtained the grand object of our pursuit.[64]

J. BINNS, Chairman.
J. ASHLEY, Secretary.

64 In anticipation of a large crowd, three rostra had been erected in the field. The Address, Remonstrance and Resolutions were read alternately from each rostrum and the vote of the surrounding crowd taken. They were then brought back to the chairman who put them to the vote once more (Lee's *Account*). Binns recollected the scene years later: '[W]hen, as Chairman of the meeting, I was about to take their opinions on the several questions ... [e]very face, every eye, was directed toward me; every voice cheeringly responded, and all who could make room raised their hands and clapped them heartily together' (*Recollections*, p. 54).

[Thelwall then spoke at considerable length[65] He explained his personal reasons for leaving the Society, but assured the meeting that his views had not changed. He warned the meeting against spies promoting tumult, insisting that zeal for liberty is consistent with humanity and benevolence. He urged them to avoid factions and animosities and to investigate facts and principles, by which alone they could know their rights and the means of obtaining redress. He then objected to the following passage in the Address: 'The comfortable prospect[s] of an abundant harvest have turned out to be vain and fallacious, *and were probably held out to lull the public mind into a delusive and fatal security.*' These (italicized) words, he thought, conveyed a censure on the pacific forbearance, on the tranquillity, of the people. Tranquillity was desirable, for it must secure the triumph of liberty and of annual Parliaments and universal suffrage. Thelwall then repeated the substance of his speech from the other side of the tribune.

After Thelwall sat down Hodgson addressed the meeting. As for the clause about the harvests, he argued that if it were true, as he had been told by eye witnesses, that the harvest was good, the LCS would appear to have been duped. He proposed replacing the objectionable (i.e. the italicized) words with the sentence, 'Monopoly ... Life' [cf. p. 315]. He suggested that the LCS, in refuting the charge of levelling, had stopped enquiring how much respect property has a right to claim. Even if possession of it might imply certain moral virtues, such as industry and economy, they are not the only virtues required in a representative. And there is no reason to require that a representative have landed property. This requirement produces legislators who make cobweb laws on imports and exports but do nothing to limit their unearned wealth by curbing monopoly.]

Several other Citizens addressed the Meeting from the other Tribunes; but from the length of their speeches, as well as the restricted limits of this narrative, a detail cannot here be given.

65 He had the shorthand writer, Ramsay, taking down his speech (c. 10,000 words), which he then published: *Peaceful Discussion, and not Tumultuary Violence the means of Redressing National Grievances,* ... 1795.

[The thanks of the meeting were voted to Binns as chairman and to Citizens Jones, Thelwall, Hodgson &c for their exertions this day.]

Both these Motions were unanimously past, amidst the greatest acclamations. A little after Five o'clock the Meeting broke up, when the immense Company that was present separated, and proceeded to their respective homes: the utmost harmony, regularity and good order prevailed during the whole time, each and every individual seeming to be impressed with the Idea, that it was a Day

SACRED TO LIBERTY.[66]

307. Report from spy Powell: LCS General Committee, 29 October 1795[67]

Source: PC 1/23/A38

Genl Comttee. L C S. 29th Octr. 1795

220 New Members   Quarterage £15.19.2.
McGuire, Binns & Constable gave in their resignation on the Ex Com.
B Evans. Skinner & Eady were elected in their room.
Div 40 Branch to the Bricklayers arms White Cross Street on Tuesday to be No 73   Incledon, French, Ralph & Colebrook deputation A letter was read from Toynton near Spelsbury Lincolnshire requesting the L C S to send them instructions for forming a Society there. Referd to Ex Com.

Sittings of Ex Com   Oct 27.

Present Ashly Dickens Constable & Evans. Proceeded to prepare & arrainge for the Press the Narative of the Genl Meeting

Octr 28

Ashly Binns, Galloway & Evans. Made progres in the Narative of the Genl Meeting for the press. Appointed a Deputation to present the Address to his Majesty[68]

A member deputed to answer the letter from the friends of Civil & Religious Liberty. Read a letter from Melburn near Derby.[69] A member deputed to answer the letter from Chichester. The Committe of Arraingement empowerd to advertise the Correspondence of the Society & announce its publication in a few days. A petition read from the Landlord of the French Horn Lambeth Walk who lost his Licence on account of a Division meeting there. A Deputation appointed to enquire the character of the House.
    Adjourned.

Genl Com

Moved & carried that the Ex Com do enquire into the practability of sueing the persons who apprehended the bill sticker on Saturday last & kept him illegally confin'd 'till Monday for posting the Societys Genl Meeting Bills[70] Matins claim respicting defending Briellit came on & after a long debate was adjourn'd till next week
This Committe do resolve to meet on Saturday week instead of Thursday on account of the Civic Oration on Hardys Acquital being given by Thelwall on that day
    Adjourn'd

308. *The Correspondence of the London Corresponding Society,* 12 November 1795

[Starting as early as 9 July, the divisions began pressing for the implementation of the 17th article of the constitution, which specified that all letters received by the executive committee and all sent by them be published quarterly, free to members. On 11 August the executive committee deputed Binns, Galloway, Maxwell and

better not come in the morning as I understand there's a jealousy against me by the new Delegates on account of my official situation' (PC 1/23/A38).
69 Thomas Skey, (formerly?) of Div. 22, Green Dragon, Fore St, answered the previous letter sent to Melbourne, but it miscarried. He now wrote to ask for copies of the LCS regulations, cheap political tracts and the 29 June address. Since the previous letter miscarried, this one was addressed to Citizen Venables to present to the LCS (*MPM*, vol. 1 (June 1796), pp. 34–5).
70 Jobson the bill-sticker was seized by Paul le Mesurier and detained in the Wood St compter until the moderate Lord Mayor, Skinner, was replaced in office by the harsh Alderman Curtis (*Tribune*, no. 47).

66 The *Proceedings* ends with a list of people to whom prospective members may apply: Ashley; Powell (the baker); Cooper; Smith; Oliphant; Davenport; Hawes; Hartley; Bone; Franklow, tailor, Pitt St, Blackfriars Rd.
67 Government endorsement: 'Rx. 29. Octr. 95'.
68 On 5 Nov. the deputation asked the Duke of Bedford to present the address to the king. Powell, who provided this information to government on 6 Nov., expected to give government the result the next day (Sat.). 'I think I had

Moody to arrange and publish the correspondence. This committee of arrangement reported progress on 21 September and were empowered to print 2000 copies and to draw up a preface. Two weeks later, on 9 October, they requested that James Lapworth of Division 31 be added to their committee and that 3000 copies be printed. Lapworth's name appeared with that of Moody and Maxwell at the end of the preface, dated 14 October. But there was confusion and dissension over his presence on the committee, for the last letter in the *Correspondence* was from the executive committee to Lapworth, explaining the situation.[71] From the letter (which is untypical of the *Correspondence* in dealing not with principles but with individual problems) it appears that Binns and Galloway were not doing their share of the work in arranging the correspondence for publication, and the executive committee voted to have them removed. (Probably Lapworth was added to compensate for their dereliction.) Before Binns and Galloway were notified that they had been withdrawn from the committee, Lapworth must have appeared at a meeting and been told that his election to the committee had been rescinded. Lapworth seems to have commenced a correspondence about his treatment and to have attended the committee of arrangement to complain. Since the letter reassuring him of his membership on the committee of arrangement was dated 30 October, this misunderstanding must have extended over three weeks.

The five page 'Prefatory Letter' is primarily a sketch of the Society in 1795 – the clearing of debts, the secession of members, the increase in size, the renewal of correspondence with other societies, the general meeting and the further increase in size. The letters included in the volume have all been cited except three letters from Margarot, two of them from Rio de Janeiro and one from Sydney. The four page 'Conclusory Address' stressed the 'rapid strides mankind are making in the attainment of useful information'. The 'Godlike task' of the LCS is to instruct their fellow men, since 'all the miseries that mankind suffer are in a great measure imputable to themselves, by their neglecting to obtain such information as might lead them in the road to their own happiness'.

At the end of the conclusory address is the wish, 'GOD SAVE THE KING', obviously added after the LCS was blamed for the 29 October attack on the king's carriage (for which see below).

According to a newspaper advertisement,[72] on 12 November was published *The Correspondence of the London Corresponding Society Revised and Corrected, With Explanatory Notes and a Prefatory Letter, by the Committee of Arrangement, deputed for that purpose: Published for the Use of Members, pursuant to the 17th article of the Society's Regulations.* 'London: Printed By Order of the London Corresponding Society, . . . Price One Shilling.']

309. The attack upon the king; the Pitt and Grenville bills; LCS reaction: 29 October–17 December 1795

Sources: as notes

[On 29 October as the king was riding to open Parliament, and later as he was returning, he was allegedly attacked. For these 'attacks' the LCS was widely blamed: they were accused of having stirred up disafection at their open air meeting three days earlier. The 'attacks' promply led to the introduction of legislation restricting the rights of assembly and free speech, legislation variously known as the Two Acts, the Pitt and Grenville Bills, the Treason and Sedition Acts, the Convention Bill. The passage of these bills hurt the LCS badly.

The 'outrage against his majesty' – as the 'attacks' were called – was an intensification of previous popular demonstrations against court proceedings. On earlier occasions spectators hissed and groaned as the king rode to Parliament. This year when there was a shortage of grain and an unpopular war, the people also called out, 'No Pitt, no War, Bread, Bread, Peace, Peace'. Then, as the state carriage drove through a narrow part of St Margaret's St, something was thrown against a window of the carriage and made a hole in the glass. This event was instantly translated into a plot to shoot the king. On his return from Parliament, the king changed from the

71 p. 80.

72 *MC*, 5 Nov. 1795, p. 1.

state carriage to a private one at St James's Palace and was proceeding to Buckingham Palace when someone allegedly tried to open the door of the carriage. This was interpreted as an attempt by the mob to drag the king out of his carriage.

Various witnesses were questioned and a reward of £1000 was offered, but no one was convicted of actual violence.[73]

According to Place, the door of the king's private carriage was touched (not opened) by an LCS delegate, John Ridley, a boot-maker. Ridley was returning home from Knightsbridge when he heard shouting and saw people running. Not knowing that the private carriage was the king's, Ridley stepped from the footpath into the road to get a better view. When he was close to the side of the carriage, his foot slipped; and to avoid falling under the wheel, he thrust his hand against the side of the carriage. Since his dress was accurately described in posting bills offering the reward, Ridley changed his coat and continued his boot-making.[74]

In opposition to this (allegedly) innocent involvement by an LCS member, is Binns's recollection that at a division meeting a member boasted of the attack, saying that he had seized the king by the collar and was dragging him out of the carriage when the troops galloped up.[75]

The proclamation offering the reward was issued two days after the supposed attacks; and on 4 November a second pro-clamation was issued, this one clearly allud-ing to the recent LCS meeting: 'Imme-diately before the opening of the present session of parliament, a great number of persons were collected in fields in the neighbourhood of the metropolis . . . and divers inflammatory discourses were deli-vered to the persons so collected . . . tend-ing to create groundless jealousy and dis-content.' Shortly after these proceedings came 'criminal outrages . . . to the imme-diate danger of our royal person'. There-fore, all magistrates, sheriffs, etc. are ordered 'to discourage, prevent and sup-press, all seditious and unlawful assemblies', to arrest 'persons delivering inflammatory discourses in such assemblies' and to bring

'to justice all persons distributing . . . sedi-tious and treasonable papers'.[76]

Two days later, on 6 November, Lord Grenville introduced in the House of Lords 'An Act for the Safety and Preservation of His Majesty's Person and Government against Treasonable and Seditious Prac-tices and Attempts'. This act extends the concepts of treason and sedition so that anyone speaking, writing or publishing words 'to incite or stir up the people to hatred or contempt of . . . his Majesty, his Heirs or Successors, of the Government and Constitution of this Realm' may, on second conviction, be punished by banish-ment, transportation or death.[77]

In the speech introducing the bill, Grenville referred to the LCS, saying that 'meetings were publicly held, at which dis-courses were delivered of a nature calcula-ted to inflame the passions of the multi-tude industriously collected to hear them. To that was to be ascribed the outrage that had lately taken place.' In his reply, Lauderdale made the identification with the LCS more obvious when he said that 'no connexion had been proved between the persons assembled in the fields near Islington, and those who had been guilty of the flagitious acts committed upon the person of their sovereign'. Repeating this assertion later in the same debate, Lauder-dale named the LCS, saying 'that he did not believe there was the smallest con-nexion between the London Correspond-

73 Five men were arrested for misdemeanours, in-cluding Kidd Wake, who made faces and shouted, 'No War'.

74 Add MSS 27808, fos. 47–9.

75 *Recollections*, pp. 55–6. Binns heard this at a meeting on 29 Oct. at the Green Dragon, Ches-wick St, Moorfields.

76 'State Papers', *Annual Register*, 1795. The *Morning Post* pointed out the connection bet-ween this proclamation and the LCS: 'The Pro-clamation . . . insinuates, that the Meetings at St. George's Fields, Copenhagen House, &c are illegal, without daring to make the unequivocal affirmative. It is only calculated to create alarm in the public mind, and can be issued for no other purpose, than to feel the pulse of the Nation, prepatory to some measure, which Government are at present fearful of putting in execution' (5 Nov. 1795, p. 2). The proclama-tion was timed to coincide with two anniver-saries associated with treason: the day in 1605 that the Houses of Parliament were to be blown up, and the acquittal of Hardy. To celebrate the acquittal a dinner (advertised as the celebration of the downfall of the system of terror) was held at the Crown and Anchor at 4.00 p.m. with nearly 300 (*Morning Post*) or possibly 800 (*Morning Chronicle*) present. Various reformist toasts were given, including one to 'The London Corresponding Society, the last hope of expiring liberty' (*MP* 6 Nov. 1795, p. 3).

77 *Parliamentary History*, vol. 32, cols. 243–4.

ing Society and the mob who committed the outrage in Westminster'.[78]

The LCS responded immediately to the assertions in Parliament and in the press that they had inflamed the populace to attack the king. The LCS response took the form of an address entitled, *The Reply of the London Corresponding Society to the Calumnies propagated by Persons in High Authority, for the purpose of furnishing Pretences for the pending Convention Bill.* This 1500 word address, signed by John Binns (as chairman of the meeting at Copenhagen House) and Ashley, condemned the calumnies against the LCS, stressed the lack of any evidence supporting the charges against the Society, and asserted the 'regularity and good order' of the LCS meetings. It stated that at the 'meeting so unjustly calumniated . . . strong arguments' were advanced 'to demonstrate that all tumult and violence were, in reality, favourable only to the views and objects of the Minister, whom we firmly believed (and it is now evident as the sun at noon, that our belief was well founded) only wanted the pretences, which such events might furnish, to make fresh invasions upon our Liberties, and establish Despotism on the Ruins of Popular Association'.[79]

On 10 November Pitt, in the House of Commons, introduced 'An Act to prevent Seditious Meetings and Assemblies'. This act specified that there may be no meeting (except that called by a civic official) of more than 50 people to consider addressing the king or either House about any change in established matters of church and state, unless previous notice be given and published in a newspaper and signed by seven householders. If, in a meeting held after such notice has been given, any matter should be deliberated purporting that anything by law established may be altered except by authority of king, Lords and Commons, a magistrate might order them to disperse; if twelve or more persons continued together an hour thereafter, they should suffer death. Anyone obstructing or resisting magistrates at such meetings should suffer death. Places for lectures or debates about supposed public grievances, where money was to be paid for admission, must be licensed; otherwise anyone using such a place might be fined £100. Justices might revoke licenses or grant them.[80]

Place recalled the temper of the times and the activity of the LCS: "No adequate idea can now [1824] be formed of the actual state of the country after the meeting of Parliament and while the bills were pending. The affair was made the most of both by ministers and the exclusively loyal all over the country The Newspapers howled treason . . . . Loyal addresses were got up in every possible way. Petitions in favour of the bills were handed about . . . . Threats, intimidation, persecution were all resorted to, all means were fair to persuade or to compel people to sign loyal addresses and petitions, while those who were known to be adverse to the conduct of ministers were calumniated in the grossest manner, and injured in every possible way.' About 30,000 signed petitions for the bills; 131,000 against. 'From the day on which the parliament assembled, the Executive committee of the London Corresponding Society met every evening, excepting the Thursday in each week on which night the General committee met. I was constant in my attendance, and was

78 *Parliamentary History*, vol. 32, cols. 244, 246, 250. The LCS was frequently named in the further debates over Grenville's and Pitt's bills, from 6 to 30 November and again on 3, 9, 10 and 14 December. On 13 Nov. Grenville reminded the Lords of the reports they had received about 'certain societies', i.e. the 1794 Reports of the Committees of Secrecy. 'Parties were afterwards prosecuted; and yet the proceedings of the London Corresponding Society were carried on with increased boldness . . . . These proceedings were inconsistent with the public tranquillity and ought to be suppressed' (col. 261). During these debates other speakers maintained that the principles of the LCS led to the attack on the king and that the LCS was affiliated with France.

79 Posting bill in Place Collection, vol. 37, fo. 103. Written by Thelwall ('Advertisement' to *The Speech of John Thelwall . . . November 12, 1795*, pp. ii–iii). It was widely believed that government had been waiting for such an incident to provide a justification for repressive legislation. In the LCS some believed that the attack on the king was planned and carried out by government. As they pointed out, Dundas acknowledged that government had been contemplating such legislation since the acquittal of Hardy and had been waiting for a favourable

opportunity; and in other countries such as Portugal fake attacks had been committed by persons hired by government (*New Annual Register*, 1796, 'History', p. 7; Add MSS 27808, fos. 41, 49).

80 *Annual Register*, 1796, Appendix to 'Chronicle'.

excused by my division from being present at its weekly meetings. A great quantity of business came before the committees   the correspondence was considerable, and every body who could assist was placed in requisition. Our sittings were now continued till midnight and frequently far beyond that time.'[81]

One of the activities of the executive committee was to write to Lord Stanhope, asking him to resume his seat in the House of Lords. Stanhope thanked the LCS for their good opinion, but declined, believing that the time had not come for him to appear on the public stage with utility.[82] The committee also sent a circular letter to the other reform societies announcing a general meeting to protest the Grenville bill and requesting the other reform societies to awaken their neighbours to 'a just sense of the dangers attending the present bill'. In London, the letter continued, the bill has brought about a union of the societies previously separated by 'distinctions which arose from differences of opinion as to the necessary degree of reform' and by 'personalities'. Whereas the constitution is 'a mixture of Saxon liberty and Norman slavery' with the people 'at one time freemen, at another slaves', the point now at issue is 'which of these principles shall be permanently established under the name of law'.[83]

The general meeting planned for 12 November was advertised on the 11th, after Pitt's bill had been introduced. Following the announcement of the time, place and purpose of this meeting of the 'Friends of Parliamentary Reform', is the admonition, 'Citizens! The Meeting is strictly legal, under the authority of the Bill of Rights; a Proclamation is not a law . . . attempts may be made to seize some of the persons assembled – do not resist. Ministry desire nothing more earnestly than tumult. For this purpose reports have been industriously circulated that some of the members of this Society mean to attend the meeting armed . . . . This is a snare . . . nothing can injure the cause of Civil Liberty so much as violence'.[84]]

310. Account of LCS General Meeting, 12 November 1795[85]

Source: as n. 85

[T]his day . . . upwards of three hundred thousand People,[86] most of them highly respectable . . . assembled . . . . The Meeting was appointed by the advertisement, to take place at eleven o'clock in the morning – but the immense crowds that appeared to be approaching from all quarters, loudly demanded, that, in justice to the importance and solemnity of the occasion, the opening of the proceedings should be for some time deferred. At half past twelve o'clock, Citizens Hodgson, Thelwall, and Ashley, from three of the rostra, erected at convenient distances, for the better accomodation of every one present, explained to the company the mode of proceeding which the Society had determined to adopt.

[The resolutions and petitions would be read from each rostra. Voting would be done as follows: when a white handkerchief was raised from the rostra, those voting affirmative should raise their hand. Then a hat would be raised and those voting negative should raise their hand. During the day not a single dissentient hand was held up.

At about one o'clock Citizen Ashley proposed Citizen Duane as chairman. After he was unanimously agreed to, Duane ad-

85 *Account of the Proceedings of a / Meeting / of the / People, / In a Field near Copenhagen-House, / Thursday, Nov. 12; / Including the Substance of the Speeches of / Citizens Duane, Thelwall, Jones, &c. / With the / Petitions / to the / King, Lords, and Commons, / Of Nearly Four Hundred Thousand Britons, / Inhabitants of London and its Environs; / Assembled together in the open Air, to express their Free Sentiments, / According to the Tenure of the Bill of Rights, / on the Subject of the / Threatened Invasion of their Rights / by a / Convention Bill*, 1795. This account, published by 'Citizen Lee', was not authorized by the LCS; however it is the only extensive narrative of the whole meeting. Thelwall's account of the meeting gives the prepared resolutions and petitions with his comments to the crowd before and after the reading of each: *The Speech of John Thelwall, at the Second Meeting of the London Corresponding Society, and other Friends of Reform . . . November 12, 1795*, 1795.
86 Newspaper estimates ranged from 10,000 to 100,000. According to Place, the crowd 'was probably the largest ever assembled' (Add MSS 27808, fo. 54).

81 Add MSS 27808, fos. 51–3.
82 Letter from LCS missing; Stanhope to members of LCS, 10 Nov. 1795, *MPM*, vol. 1 (June 1796), pp. 36–7.
83 *MPM*, vol. 1, pp. 35–6.
84 *Telegraph*, p. 1.

dressed the meeting. He reminded them that the Bill of Rights and the Magna Carta entitled them to petition and to resist encroachments on the liberties of the nation.]

He recommended measures of peace and firmness – but he said, that it would remain with the people of this country to determine, how long they would bear innovation on their liberties, an unnatural war, and the invasion of their domestic rights . . . by the detestable measures which were now attempted to be introduced. . . .

He then proceeded to open the matter before him, and read the Resolutions and Addresses which are annexed.

We offer the following as sketches (taken in short-hand) of the different Addresses; but will not vouch for their precise accuracy, though we can assert, that their spirit and substance is preserved.

TO THE KING's MOST EXCELLENT MAJESTY.[87]

It is with no small degree of diffidence and anxiety, that we approach you once more, to present to your Majestry the griefs and complaints of an over-burthened People, whom the misconduct and arbitrary counsels of your Majesty's Ministers, are rapidly driving to the verge of desperation.

[Twice before during the last five months we have tried to pour our grievances into your royal ear and tell you that the measures pursued by the administration are hostile to your real interests. We fear that our petitions have been prevented from reaching you. Instead of receiving redress, we are threatened with the extinction of our remaining liberties by these bills which make it felony and high treason to express our miseries. But before the enactment of these bills which threaten to overthrow the constitutional throne of Brunswick and restore the despotism of the exiled Stuarts, we assemble to express our fears of the consequences of these bills.

We conjure your majesty to distrust those who urge you to extend your authority beyond that prescribed at the Revolution; to recall the events which placed

your family on the throne; and to discriminate between your real and pretended friends. Those who are hostile to the rights of the people cannot be friends to the prerogatives of the Crown. The interests of the people and their Chief Magistrate ought to be inseparable; but how can this be when restrictions are put on the liberties of the subject during your majesty's natural life, especially restrictions founded on precedents from the despotic reigns of Tudors and Stuarts. Restrictions of the latter reign led to the Revolution. We hope the House of Brunswick will recall the principles to which it owes its elevation; we believe that Britons retain the love of liberty and the courage of their ancestors at that period. We conclude by petitioning your majesty to prevent the possibility of intestine commotion by directing your ministers to redress existing abuses instead of laying additional burdens and restrictions on the people. W. Duane, chairman, and J. Ashley, secretary.]

To the Lords Spiritual and Temporal in Parliament assembled.

MAY IT PLEASE YOUR LORDSHIPS,

The people having no immediate connection with that particular branch of the legsilature which is composed of your Lordships, further than as it forms a component part of the Constitution, it but rarely happens that you are addressed by *them*; or that they call for your assistance to vindicate their rights, or repel the threatened encroachments of Ministerial ambition.

[But in the present crisis, when most of what remains of the 1688 constitution is attacked by a bill introduced by a minister who is a member of your House and by another bill introduced by the Chancellor of the Exchequer in the House of Commons, we appeal to each of the branches of legislature. We express our concern for the threatened invasion of our liberties and remind our legislators of the reciprocal ties between government and the people, so that posterity will know we have fulfilled the duty of men who love peace and liberty.

We ask you to consider the alarming tendency and probable consequences of appealing (as the framers of these bills do) to the authority of the Tudors and Stuarts.

87 'These several papers', wrote Place of the petitions, 'were principally composed by Citizen John Thelwall and may even now [1824] be read with approbation' (Add MSS 27808, fo. 55).

If the conduct of the Stuarts deserves imitation, why was the succession of the House of Brunswick secured by driving the Stuarts to exile? How can you be attached to the House of Brunswick if you abjure the principles which put it on the throne? Is it not impolitic for you, at a time when you think there is prejudice against the House of Lords, to give such prejudice support by introducing a bill which repeals the provisions extorted from Edward III by the independent representatives of the people?

We entreat you to preserve the country from the dangers to which these bills may give birth. W. Duane, chairman, and J. Ashley, secretary.]

To the Honourable the Commons of Great Britain, in Parliament assembled.

MAY IT PLEASE YOUR HONOURABLE HOUSE,

Your Petitioners approach you, *once more*, to make their grievances and apprehensions known, in a legal and constitutional manner, to that branch of the legislature, which from its *legal style and firm* [form], was evidently intended to be the constitutional guardian of the people's liberties, and the champion of its rights and privileges!

[We approach you not to ask a remedy for existing abuses or to repeat arguments for parliamentary reform – had these claims been attended to, the cause of our present petition could not exist – but to conjure you not to drive the people to such despair as the bill before you will produce. Remember that the energies of the British constitution depend on freedom of speech and of the press, that the preservation of our liberties depends on observance of the provisions extorted from Edward III by the House of Commons. Invasions of these liberties have always had alarming consequences – they brought one Stuart to the scaffold and drove another from the throne. Recall the events that produced the Revolution of 1688 and the principles which established the House of Brunswick on the throne. Consider the compact between government and the people and the dreadful consequences of violating it. If these circumstances are considered, we are sure that you will reject the attempts by his majesty's ministers to stain the House of Brunswick by reviving the measures which

brought the House of Stuart into odium and produced the Glorious Revolution, upon the principles of which the House of Brunswick is entitled to the throne.

We ask you to dismiss with disapprobation the bill which would prevent popular assemblies for the purpose of political investigation, to guard trial by jury, to suffer no innovations on the existing laws of treason and sedition, and finally to believe that we reject tumult and violence because we know it is injurious to the cause of national and constitutional liberty. W. Duane, chairman, and J. Ashley, secretary.

Resolutions

The first two resolutions give thanks to Bedford, Lauderdale, Fox, Sheridan, Grey, Curwen and Sturt for their conduct in parliament; to the Whig Club for their recent resolutions against the proposed legislation; to all the persons who helped bring about 'the present happy unanimity among the Friends of Freedom'.[88] Further resolutions restate the LCS's abhorrence of tumult and violence, particularly the attack on the king, when misguided individuals directed their indignation against the king for the misconduct of his ministers. This delusion would not have occurred if the efforts of the popular societies to educate the people had not been counteracted by illegal persecution. Resolution five brands as gross calumny 'the assertions of certain persons in high station and authority' that the insult to the king originated in the LCS meeting at Copenhagen House. This calumny was invented to furnish]

a pretence for tyrannical usurpation, long before digested and determined upon.

Resolved, that we know how to cherish and to practice, in cases of the LAST EXTREMITY, the constitutional right of RESISTANCE TO OPPRESSION. We will exert our utmost endeavours on all occasions to repress all irregularity and excesses, and to bring the

88 After these resolutions of thanks, there was a cry of 'Erskine-Erskine'. Thelwall explained to his audience that Erskine was not thanked because he had not yet expressed in Parliament his opposition to the bills; he was waiting until he had read printed copies of them (Thelwall's *Speech*, pp. 14–15).

authors of such unjustifiable proceedings to the *just* responsibility of the law.

> Signed, W. DUANE, Chairman.
> J. ASHLEY, Secretary.

The several Resolutions and Petitions having been read, and unanimously agreed to,

Citizen Jones addressed the Meeting, in a most impressive manner. To attempt a detail of his admirable speech is more than the limits of our paper will allow, and we must, therefore, content ourselves with giving a mere sketch or outline of it.

[He reminded the assembly that the proposed act, if passed, would 'annihilate every grand and essential privilege' which Englishmen prided themselves on having. He noted the injustice of connecting the previous LCS meeting with the attack on the king: the LCS had always supported the people's rights in a peaceful and orderly manner; only by such methods could reformers hope to succeed. The administration's attacks on the constitution were reaching their acme; if they succeeded English liberty was doomed. The people must either submit 'to every degree of taxation and degradation' or resist these measures with determination. Just when the indescribable misery resulting from a ruinous war might be expected to lead the people to murmur and remonstrate, unheard of measures are proposed to stifle their groans, on pain of transportation. He was astonished that anyone would dare to infringe so far on the constitution, as settled at the Revolution of 1688, which gave the present royal family the throne. He hoped to see the day when the ministers who had advised such arbitrary measures against the rights of the people 'would answer for it with their heads.' He concluded by requesting that the people not rest until 'they had got rid of a monster' which aroused indignation and horror.]

Several other Citizens spoke, with considerable force and energy; and their addresses were received by the Meeting with the warmest and most unbounded applause. Citizen Thelwall was singularly happy in his allusions to and comments upon the *good times* from which the precedents were drawn on which the present Bills depending are founded, and shewed clearly that the reigns of the Tudors and the Stuarts are in perfect unison with the temper and disposition of the *immaculate heaven-born Minister* of the present day.

[Thelwall concluded a speech] which was received with abundant applause, by an earnest exhortation [to depart peaceably.] This advice was certainly very strictly adhered to.

[Immediately after the meeting, the Society set out to obtain signatures to the petitions. On the day after the meeting, 13 November, they issued an advertisement listing twenty-four places where people might sign the petitions and warning that 'delay or indifference may be fatal … a few days more, and it would be a crime at the discretion of Ministers'. The advertisement ended with a polite request for donations.[89] Shortly afterwards, but still within a week of the general meeting, the LCS issued a handbill explaining the dangers of the bills, listing the persons who will receive signatures, and footnoting their need for money. 'If the present Bills pass, Englishmen will be deprived of every Right that is valuable, and every Blessing that can be enjoyed. Every petty Justice will become an insolent Despot; and when they want the Honor of Knighthood, they will not fail to mark their Victims to the Laws of Sedition and Treason. … Theologists must no longer choose the Doctrines they may believe, nor the Founts in which they would worship: to differ from the Religion established by Law, will be called Rebellion against the State; and we may expect to see an Inquisition established, to persecute every Denomination of Dissenters. The Merchant, the Manufacturer, or the Cultivator must no longer meet to settle his

89 *History of Two Acts*, pp. 135–6. The advertisement probably appeared in the *Telegraph*, the office of which was one of the places where the petitions lay for signatures. The men receiving signatures (and money) were: Ashley, Ballard, Bone, Burks, Cooper, Eaton, Franklow, Hartley, Hodgson, Lee, Smith, Spence, Thelwall; and – new to the LCS lists – Cherton, 38 Bethnal Green Rd; Clayton, 66 Maiden Lane, Southwark; Lunan (or Lunam), 18 Whitcomb St, Charing Cross; J. Maxwell, cheesemonger, 39 Broad St, Bloomsbury; Meason (or Meeson), 8 New St, Walworth; Page, 14 Stangate St, Lambeth; B. Peacock, Globe Stairs, Rotherhithe; George Place, 6 William St, Walcot Place; Ridgway, York St, St James's Sq.; Rouse, staymaker, Colchester St, Whitechapel. The inclusion of Burks and Bone from the two secessionist societies is evidence of the union of reformers wrought by the pending bills.

commercial Concerns,' for he would run afoul of ministers if he needed to raise wages or the price of goods. 'And all Classes of Men will find, that they must suffer the Minister to tax them to the whole Amount of their Income, without complaining, or be punished for Sedition, or Treason.'[90] On 19 November, just one week after the general meeting, the Society issued an advertisement stating that since the committee had resolved to have the petition to the House of Commons presented on Monday the 23rd, the 'Citizens who have opened their houses to receive Signatures' should return the lists to the secretary and those wishing to sign should do so as soon as possible. A list of persons receiving signatures was given, followed by the polite request for donations.[91] Ashley alone signed these three documents.

As the requests for subscriptions indicated, the Society was in financial trouble. According to Place, they had never been out of debt: 'The Society had never recovered from the state into which the State Trials in 1794 had thrown it. It was in debt, but the debt had been reduced considerably before the meeting in October, which had again added thereto. Present circumstances demanded a continual expenditure . . . . There was however some increase of income, from the entrance money of members who joined the society and from the voluntary subscriptions of the members in their divisions.[92] Despite this increase, 'the income did not meet the expenditure and new debts were incurred'.[93]

While the LCS was collecting signatures, government was seeking whatever evidence it could find to damage the Society. The Duke of Portland sent for copies of all the publications sold or circulated at the 26 October general meeting together with

evidence, upon oath, of the sale or circulation.[94] It was probably from this group of documents that government found a pamphlet titled *A Summary of the Duties of Citizenship. Written Expressly for the Members of the London Corresponding Society*,[95] which was soon quoted in Parliament as evidence of the treasonable attitudes of the LCS.[96] On 18 November the LCS issued a denial of any connection with this work or with *The Duties of Kings*, both said to have been published for the Society by Citizen Lee. They declared that Citizen Lee had never been employed to print for the LCS and was not a member. They then listed the seven works printed for the Society from its beginning: 'The Duke of Richmond's Letter to Col. Sharman', 'The State of the National Representation', 'A Narrative of the Seizure of T. Hardy', 'A Vindication of the Society', 'The Quarterly Proceedings and Correspondence of the Society', 'The Regulations of the Society' and 'Five Numbers of a periodical Work, called "the Politician".'[97]

90 Place Collection, vol. 37, fo. 93, with signature of 'J. Richter' in upper corner. The list of houses for signatures omits three names from the previous list – Cooper, Page and Spence – and adds five – Frost, 16 Pepper St, Loman's Pond, Southwark; Morrice, 13 Pearl Row, nr the Magdalene; Robershaw, Orange Ct, Swallow St; Rouse, 3, nr Meeting House Walk, Snow Fields, Southwark; and Thomas, coal-dealer, Newington Causeway. A copy of the document in BL 806.k.i omits Maxwell.

91 *History of Two Acts*, pp. 331–2. The list contains the same names as the previous one.

92 Add MSS 27808, fos. 53–4.

93 *Autobiography*, p. 148.

94 John King to magistrates of police offices, 13 Nov. 1795, HO 65/1.

95 Written by a dissenter named Iliff, it had no connection with the LCS and did not name the Society (or any member) in the text. According to Hardy's annotation of his copy (now in the BL), Iliff had the names of the booksellers Smith and Lee put on the title page without their consent. On 30 November they were taken into custody. Lee escaped from a spunging house, while Smith was convicted. Iliff and Smith were LCS members.

96 Mornington had announced in Parliament that he bought from the 'avowed' printer and publisher for the LCS a book which recommended regicide, and that this proved a connection between the LCS and the attack on the king. In the debate on 23 Nov. Sturt announced that he had made enquiries about the printer Lee and had found that he was not then a member. He added that Lee had once been a member but had twice been turned out of the Society. Sturt went on to quote from Thelwall's exhortation at Copenhagen House to seek redress not by violence and tumult but by reason (*Parliamentary Register*, vol. 43, cols. 285–7). A note on the title page of *Rights of Princes* (BL copy) states that Lee was expelled 'for disagreeing with some of the members in religious sentiments. Lee is a Methodist.'

97 *History of Two Acts*, pp. 330–1. This list must have been compiled hastily, for its omits many LCS publications, including speeches by Stanhope and Wharton, the printing of which was authorized by the general commitee, as well as Hawles's *Englishman's Right*, to which the LCS added an appendix which was approved by the

The numerous attacks on the Society led them to issue, on 23 November, a handbill entitled *To the Parliament and People of Great Britain. An explicit Declaration of the Principles and Views of the London Corresponding Society*. In it they assert three principles:]

I. This Society is, and ever has been, most firmly attached to the principles of Equality .... Social equality ... appears to them to consist in the following things: 1. The acknowledgment of equal rights. 2. The existence of equal laws for the security of those rights. 3. Equal and actual representation, by which ... the invasion of those laws can be prevented .... In their ideas of equality, they have never included (nor, till the associations of alarmists broached the frantic notion, could they ever have conceived that so wild and detestable a sentiment could have entered the brain of man) as the equalization of property ....

II. With respect to particular forms and modifications of Government, this Society conceive ... that the disputes and contentions about these ... are marks only of weak and inconsiderate minds .... Their attention has been uniformly addressed to more essential objects – to the peace – the social order – and the happiness of mankind; and these ... might be sufficiently secured by the *genuine spirit* of the British Constitution. They have laboured therefore ... not to *overthrow*, but to *restore* and *realize* that Constitution .... Peaceful reform, and not tumultuary revolt, is their object ....

III. This Society have always cherished ... the most decided abhorrence of all tumult and violence .... at the same time, they do not wish to be understood as giving ... any sort of countenance to the *detestable and delusive doctrines of Passive Obedience and Non-resistance*. This is a system which none but *hypocrites* will *profess*, and none but *slaves* will *practice* .... To resist oppression (when no other means are left) even with the same arms with which it is enforced, is, they are

aware, not only a natural right, but a constitutional duty .... But resistance of oppression and promotion of tumult, are, in their minds, distinct propositions ... they trust that the Nation at large is equally sensible of the distinction; and that *if the dire necessity ever should arrive, when the liberties of Britain must be asserted not by the voice and the pen, but by the sword, Britons will rally round the standard of Liberty, not like a band of depredators and assassins, but like a Spartan Phalanx; prepared and resolved to a man rather to die at their posts, than to abandon their principles, and betray the Liberties of their country! ! !* J. Ashley, Secretary.[98]

[Such declarations of principle (as well as the popular petitions and parliamentary remonstrances) had no effect on the passage of the acts. On Friday, 18 December, the royal assent was given to the two bills, which were to be effective for three years from that day.]

311. Minutes: LCS General Committee, 24 November 1795[99]

Source: Add MSS 27815, fos. 19–19v

Genl. Comte. Room Novr. 24 – 1795
Thos Evans Delegate

Deputn. to Divn. 4 Limans 22 Williams
28 Russell & Bowtel
Divn. 29 Phellps 31 Russell 33 Evans
35 Dials 37 Welch 39 Phillips
40 May[100] 46 Windsor 47 Constable
50 Phelps & Chard & Edwards for a month
52 not formd 55 Dials & Harris 57 Haseldon
& Bo[rest of word torn off] & Jennings
61 Hodgson 62 May 73 not formd
74 Dials 40 Place

general committee. Hardy's list of tracts republished by the LCS also includes *Extract from the Appendix of ... Peace and Union*, by William Frend; an extract from Volney's *Ruins of Palmyra; An Explanation of the Word Equality*; Paine's *Letter to the People of France*; and Norman Macleod's *Letters to the People of North Britain* (Add MSS 27814, fos. 49–50, 54–5).

98 Place Collection, vol. 37, fo. 111. Place commented, 'This paper at the time it was written was thought a masterpiece. I have just read it (Oct. 1. 1824) and calling to mind the circumstances of the times, and recollecting who and what the persons, in whose hands the management of the affairs of the society was placed, am of opinion that the address is very creditable to them. That it was a manly spirited production remarkable well calculated for the time, and for the people to whom it was addressed' (Add MSS 27808, fo. 57v).
99 Most unusually, the general committee met twice this week: on Tues. the 24th and Thurs. the 26th.
100 Cancelled: '45 Millard'.

Moved in the Comte that no Del. shal have the priviledge of moving for the Honrs. of the sitting more than one person in a mo. Negative by the moving on amendment that no person sho[uld] be admitted to the sitting without they have business with the Comee. carried in the Affirmative

6. .7. .0½ Quarterage	6. .9. .8 ¾ Subscription
7. .7	10. .6
6. .14. 7½	7. .0. 2 ¾

Ex Comte. Sitting of Novr. 20. – 95 Present Bone Gall Ashley & Evans absent Oliphant Oxlade Duen & Newman –
a Deputation from the friends of Liberty submited to the Ex Comte. the following proposition in case the Conn Bill now pending in parliament should pass into a Law ought not the LCS and the Society of the friends of Liberty to devise some mode of opening a Conference, for the purpose of giving General assistance to the cause of Liberty Resolved that this Comte. is ready to open such a conference with the friends of Liberty
Drew up a refutation of the Calumnies of Mr. Pitt Ld. Mornington &c in the House of Commons which was inserted in the morning papers sitting Novr 23.
Present Bone Gall Ashley Olipant Evans absent Newman Oxlade & Duen Recd. a petition from Birmingham Signd by 3 thousand 4 Hunderd persons requesting this Society to obtain a member to present it Citn. Ashley deputed to wait on Citn. Sheridan who promised to do it[101] for them Recd a Letter from Sheffield inclosing the proceedings of their late G M. and requesting this Society to insert a copy thereof in the Corier[102] which was complied with draw up a Declareation of the principals of this Society order 5 thousand to be printed in the form of a posting Bill & one thousand Large Do the Comte. procured two Citns. to Delr. Copies of the Declaretion to each member of the House of Commons at their enterancie in to the house this day
Draw [up] a refutation of the Calumnies thrown out against this Society in a Large Bill posted up in different parts of the town against the insinuation that Thos Barrow a person Indighted for receiving stolen goods

101 Covering letter from Birmingham Society for Constitutional Information, 22 Nov. 1795, *MPM*, vol. 1 (July 1796), p. 88.
102 The general meeting of the Sheffield Society for Constitutional Information was held as a result of the exhortation in the LCS circular letter of 7 Nov. (20 Nov. 1795, *MPM*, vol. 1, p. 87).

was a Member & Del of this Society[103] 5 Hunderd orderd to be printed a Member produced a draft of an Ansr. to the portsmouth Letter[104] aproved and orderd to be sent with a parcel of the Decareations took into consideration the Busisnses of the next G M Members deputed to prepare the Business nesseresory to be brot forward at that M this Comte. has procured a place for the M more contingent to town than the last[105] but is not able at present to anounce the day the M will be held not being able to form an accurate opinion of the fate of the pending Bills but sufficient notice will be given as soon as the day is fixt upon this Comte. Received 5 Guineas from a friend to par Refm. by the hands

103 The refutation of the 'False, Scandalous, and Malicious Libel' also appeared in *MC* (24 Nov. 1795, p. 1) as a small advertisement, dated 23 Nov. In it the LCS solemnly declared that Barrow was not a delegate, had never been one, and was not a member. The report that he was a delegate emanated from the Lambeth St Public Office.
104 The Portsmouth Constitutional and Corresponding Society wrote on 10 Nov. asking the LCS opinion of the Grenville Bill (T. Jackson Board and Thos Dane to Ashley, Add MSS 27815, fo. 12). The LCS reply deplored the proclamation and the bills and added that 'our increase is considerably greater than at any period of our history' (Ashley to the Corresponding Society at Portsmouth, 20 Nov. 1795, *MPM*, vol. 1 (June 1796), pp. 37–8).
105 Place detailed the background of this change of meeting place: 'On the 2nd December the society gave notice of a meeting to be held near the Jews harp house in Mary-le-bone fields, now Regents Park. The reason for not holding the meeting where the two last were held was, that the money paid for the use of the field did not compensate the unavoidable damage done to it and the surrounding fields; by the immense number of persons who crossed them in all directions, making new paths, gaps in the hedges, and treading down banks. It was with the greatest difficulty any place could be procured and much time which could be exceedingly ill spared from our ordinary occupations was consumed in waiting on different persons, to obtain permission to occupy one of their fields. All the active men on the committees were industrious men, very few of them were masters and many of them had families wholly maintained by the work of their hands, to such persons loss of time was not only a great pecuniary evil but also in the discomfort neglect of business occasioned at home. These circumstances reduced the number of those on whom the burthen fell to a small number. It may be doubted by those who are friendly to the people that it was wise in any man to make such sacrifices as the condition in which the society was placed demanded' (Add MSS 27808, fos. 58–9).

of Citn. Hardy Citn Thelwall informd the Comte. that he had Recd. 14£ 1/6 by sub-scription at the doores for the use of the LCS the Comte. has been informed that 6£. . &c has been recd. this evening by Do. in addition – (finise), a letter was read from Chatham importing that Comistioner proby & others

Divn. 26	8	43	
69	34	33	Determinations of their
11	28	11	firm resolutions to stand
66	79	4	or fal with their Com-
10	20	22	mittees
32	17	13	
3	60	2	

312. Report from spy Powell: LCS General Committee, 26 November 1795[106]

Source: PC 1/23/A38

Genl Comtte 26. Novr. 1795.

New 176. since Tuesday   309 before   Members present in the Div 3576. Quarterage £6. .14. .7½
Subscription £7. .–.2 3/4
Div 66 Wish to know wether soldiers might be admitted in the divisions   They were told that they might.
Div. 10. Resolvd that all the divisions do meet one night in every week so that they may act in conjunction the Genl Com. to appoint the day

Referd

Div 19.
48
60
73
6
9
12
16
18
Resolved that the Committees do deserve the thanks of the Society for their truly patriotic Conduct & they are determined to stand by them whatever their determination may be, with their lives.

Ex Com Nov 24

Present Ashly Bone Newman Evans Oxlade Oliphant Galloway, Duen   Have provided a place for Genl Meetg
A member deputed to enquire when the peti-tions could be presented
The business to be brought forward at the G M. an address to the Nation   A petition to the King to dismiss his ministers. Resolution congenial to the Address.
A member deputed to draw up the form of an advertisement for the G M.

106 Description: 'Rept. 28 Nov'.

Two addresses are proposd in case the bills should or should not pass
Moved & carried that & 40,000 hand bills be printed to advertise the G M   1000 posting Bills & that men be employ'd to stand with poles in the Streets with posting Bills on them.

[On 2 December the Society issued an advertisement for the 7 December general meeting. After naming the date, place and purpose of the meeting, it addressed its audience, 'Englishmen! The moment is arrived when you must decide between a base dereliction, or a loud and full asser-tion of those rights obtained and handed down by your ancestors . . . . The Ministers . . . count on your servility . . . . Your character and your fate is at stake, and this one solitary opportunity is left to your hapless country, by exercising the humble privilege of petitioning.' Signed by Ashley and Galloway.[107]]

313. The LCS General Meeting: 7 December 1795[108]

Source: as n. 108

[The general meeting of 7 December was held in a field adjoining the Jew's Harp House near the top of Portland Road. Although it was organized by the LCS and advertised as their meeting, the chief speakers – Matthew Campbell Browne and William Frend – certainly were not leading members and probably were not members at all.[109] The meeting provided the op-portunity for prominent men to demons-trate publicly against the Two Acts (the crowd included many MPs, among them Fox). To accommodate the crowd two or

107 *MC* 3 Dec. 1795, p. 1; *MP* 3 Dec. 1795, p. 1.
108 There is no authorized narrative of this meeting. The chief source (from which I have drawn quo-tations) is the account in the *Telegraph* (8 Dec.), reprinted in *History of Two Acts*, pp. 643–54. Other newspaper accounts are in *MP* (8 Dec., p. 2), *MC* (9 Dec., p. 3), *Whitehall Evening Post* (6–8 Dec., p. 4). Place described the meeting in Add MSS 27808, fos. 59, 63–4. See also E. Phipps, *Memoirs of Robert Plumer Ward*, 1850, vol. 1, p. 31.
109 In naming the persons most active at the meet-ing, Place designated Frend and Browne as 'Mr', but Thelwall, Ashley, Binns, Hodgson and Richter were 'Citizens' (Add MSS 27808, fo. 63).

329

three rostra were erected at one o'clock; the speakers then announced that Browne had been nominated as chairman. The nomination was 'answered with loud and repeated plaudits'. Browne excoriated the proposed bills. From the rostra the 'Address to the People of Britian' was then read. It detailed the miseries of the nation, the cure of annual Parliaments and universal suffrage, the evils of the pending bills. Thelwall, 'who appeared emaciated, and labouring under severe indisposition', spoke several times. The petition to the king (signed by 15,000 people) was read. It asked him to refuse his assent to the two bills and to dismiss his present ministers. Next William Frend spoke against the bills and read and commented on three resolutions, which were moved and passed unanimously. Resolution one stated that the government of the country was based on the thirteen articles to which William and Mary agreed. Resolution two stated that the Pitt and Grenville bills violated the thirteen articles. Resolution three stated that anyone who, under pretence of legal authority, prevented a man from meeting or seized a man peaceably delivering his sentiments in conformity with the thirteen articles was a stirrer of sedition and a traitor to the king.

John Richter, 'in a very nervous and animated speech', introduced the resolutions of thanks, which were voted to members of both Houses who opposed the bills: Fox, Erskine, Bedford, Lauderdale, Sheridan, Whitbread and Mawbey.

The last resolution – that the LCS would never deviate from their original principles – occasioned some remarks from chairman Browne. He connected the LCS principles with those of Pitt and other reformers of the 1780s and discredited the 'good times' of the Stuarts, which were the precedents for the proposed bills. In conclusion, 'he had no doubt, that . . . their separation would be as peaceable and decorous as their meeting and continuance together had been'.]

314. Minutes: LCS General Committee, 10 December 1795

Source: Add MSS 27815, fos. 20-1

Genl. Comtee. Room Sitting of 10th. Decr. 95 Deptns. to Divn. 3 Kennedy 15 Boole at the Rising sun Rent Street 31 Rhind & Russell 34 Greenman St. Johns Lane St. Johns St. from the talbot Grays Inn lane Williams 43 Russel May & King 44 Nicholls 47 Constable 54 Evans 55 Dials & Junr Gibbins & Tompson 58 Mc.Norton Llody & Tooly 61 meets with 18, 62 May 64 Ballard 68 Dimes 74 Dials 76 broke up 77 Nicholls 78 Willson & Shirley 79 Boole & Shirley 80 Jay to write a report[110] Hodgson, Bone. Oxlade Williams Dials & Nicholls

Divn: 13 Protests against any Coalition of any political Society with the L C. S: unless they will associate for the purpose of universal Suffrag & Annual parliament[111] – renderd of no account as the whole was flatly contradicted – moved that an advertizement be printed to contradict the reports which was negatived

Members made	137 – 9	. . 1 . .5½	Quarterage
Do. Present	1669	1 . . 9 . .3½	Subscription
		. . 5 . .	Correspondence
		. . 1 . .6	British convention

10. .17. .3

Ex Comtee. Sitting of Decr. 8 – 95

Present Oxlade Oliphant Gall Bone & Ashley absent Duen Evans Newman Bone . . Reporter

110 Cancelled (presumably the delegates entered after this report had been written): '17 Llody 26 Mitchell . . . 37 Bowtel . . . 53 Dimes . . . 69 Mitchell 75 Nichols'.
111 A reference to the debate which took place at the Westminster Forum in Panton Street on 8 Dec. on the question, 'Are not the most probable Means left of saving the Country from the Despotism of the Minister – an immediate Junction of the Whig Interest and the Corresponding Society?' John Gale Jones, the chief speaker, defended such a 'junction' and said that 'a deputation from that respectable body [Whigs] lately waited upon me at my own house, desiring the assistance of the L.C.S and offering in return their Support to the C. S in opposing the Despotism of the present Ministers'. The debate was continued on 10 and 12 Dec. with at least two other LCS members recommending such a union. The vote was heavily in favour of the alliance. The *True Briton* repeatedly presented the union of the two societies as a reality: 'The recent Coalition of the dregs of the *Whig Club* with the *London Corresponding Society* . . . must be called to attention' (10 March 1796, p. 3; see also 25 March 1796, p. 3; 16 Jan. 1796, p. 3).

Resolved that two Hundd. & 50 Copies of the petetion to the King be printed to be left at the houses where the petition is to lay for signature orderd 250 large bills for the purpose of hanging at such houses ordered that a person be apointed to distribute the Sheets orderd that a narative of the G M of the 7th of Decr be printed but not that for the 12 of Novr. Recd. a letter of Resignation from Duen Recd. a Letter from Norwich thanking this Society for it's exertions proffesing their readiness to remonsterate against the Indecient hast the bills are hurried thro' the house wishing to know our intentions and promising to second our efforts Recd. a Letter from Watton Herts Requesting Citn. Hodgson to come down on Sunday ordered that a cirquilar be drawn up to send to cuntry corrispondence Decr. 9 Present Oxlade Oliphant Gall Ashley Evans Bone Absent Duen & Newman took into consideration a plan for the Organization of the Society –

[New organization of the Society]

[On Saturday, 12 December, the general committee agreed to seven regulations made necessary by the impending Treason and Sedition Bills.[112] Under this new organization the Society was divided into four districts, each to contain no more than forty-five divisions. Each division (of no more than forty-six members) was to send a delegate to a weekly district committee meeting. The district committee, in turn, sent deputies – one for every five divisions – to form a general committee. The Southern or Surrey District comprehended all places south of the Thames. They were to meet at Haseldon's in Walworth. The Eastern District included the area from Ludgate Hill to the east, and met in Brick Lane at a former Methodist meeting room. The Central District, also called Northern District, took in the area westward to Tottenham Court Road, and met at Thelwall's in Beaufort Buildings. The Western District, comprehending all places north of the Thames and west of Totten-

ham Court Road, met at the Royal Tent in Silver Street, Golden Square.

Place described the results of this change in the organization of the Society: 'The General Committee lost but little of its animation altho reduced to less than one half of its former number, it was occupied fully with the quantity of business which came before it. but the district committees soon became discontented and it was difficult to find members willing to be elected to them. As they had no legislative powers the persons who comprised these committees, had nothing to do but report to one another, this was unentertaining tiresome and monotonous. The consequence was that the district committees, were but badly attended and many divisions got reports from other delegates or remained in ignorance of what was going on, these things could not fail to produce dissertions and to drive away some of the best of the members.'[113]

315. Circular letter: Executive Committee to LCS members, 31 December 1795[114]

Source: handbill, Place Collection, vol. 37, fo. 159.

TO

THE MEMBERS OF THE
CORRESPONDING SOCIETY.

COMMITTEE ROOM,
DECEMBER 31, 1795.

CITIZENS,

After the Resolutions of various Divisions, after the Investigations of your Committees, and after the solemn Determination of your General Meeting of the 7th. inst. to persevere

112 Printed in Jan. with the heading, *Articles for Future Regulations for the London Corresponding Society, Recommended by the Executive Committee* (Place Collection, vol. 37, fo. 143). In Dec. Powell sent government an early version of the rules containing minor variations, such as the days each committee was to meet. Powell named the meeting places of each district committee (PC 1/23/A38).

113 Add MSS 27808, fo. 70.
114 Place recalled the circumstances which made this letter necessary: 'The terrible consequences which it had been predicted would follow the enactment of the new laws produced the result which ought to have been, but was not, forseen. No sooner had the bills recived the Royal assent than the reformers generally conceived it not only dangerous but also useless to continue to exert themselves any longer. The fears of some and the machinations of others reduced the number of members in every one of the Divisions, and caused several of them to abandon the society altogether. On the 31 of December the society published an address to the members calling upon them to keep the promises they had

in pursuing the Object of our Association, it appears to us inexplicable that a few Individuals should attempt to dissuade particular Divisions from Meeting.

We wish not to accuse these men of Arrogance, in attempting to prefer their private Opinions to the mature Deliberations of your Committees, nor of Timidity in falling short of the exertions of other Members, nor of treachery in wishing to promote the Views of the present tyrannous Administration: – On the Contrary, we hope every member of the Society will studiously avoid attributing to them any such motives: – We have thought it necessary to combat their Opinions, but we feel the most anxious desire to avoid every degree of personal enmity, trusting that farther reflection, and the example of other Members, may induce them to alter their Conduct.

To some, we are sensible the Bills lately passed appear much more formidable than any direct interpretation of them will warrant; that they are replete with ambiguities we readily admit, and we doubt not the ambiguities were meant to injure the Cause of Liberty in a greater degree than many of the Persons who have supported them ever intended. – but let us remember, that we are not *yet* deprived of Trial by Jury: – That English Juries have long been clebrated for their Opposition to cruel Laws, and that it is particularly unreasonable to fear they will give much support to the Edicts in question, because their existence is not only a contempt of the public Voice, but a violation of the fundamental Principles of the Constitution.

You are told that civil Liberty is annihilated, and that your only hope is in Arms. – We pretend not to say at what degree of depravity on the part of Government actual insurrection becomes the duty of the People.

We freely acknowledge our opinion, that in a Country which calls itself Free, it is the Right and Duty of every Individual to be constantly prepared to defend that Freedom: But though prudence may enjoin preparation, humanity requires that every civil means of obtaining redress should be tried, before recourse is had to Martial measures, – and we wish to ask how Men who are prompt to desert one line of Conduct, can possibly claim Confidence in another?

But it is said you dare not Speak, and therefore your Meeting must be in vain: We might possibly admit the inference if we thought the premises were justified by the Bills lately passed; – But Citizens ! let us request you to ask yourselves from what description of Men you hear this Opinion – Is it from any of those, who, by their steady perseverance in propagating by the calm language of Reason, those sound Political Principles which have contributed, notwithstanding all the efforts of Calumny, to raise the Society to its present degree of public estimations.? – Is it not rather from those whose habits of virulent personality have ever been a subject of Censure among ourselves? Think not Citizens, we mean to palliate the Restrictions now imposed on Conversation; – It is impossible for us to reflect on them but with abhorrence.

We wish only to remind you, that the chief purpose of our Association, was the diffusion of Political Knowledge, not only among ourselves, but among our Countrymen in general.

It would be a needless attempt to impress on your minds the powerful effect of your past exertions. In every part of the Nation, the Spirit of Liberty evinces itself with a vigour daily increasing, and the anxiety with which Ministry endeavour to effect your dissolution, is an indisputable evidence how sensible they are that popular Associations are incompatible with a System of Tyranny.

CITIZENS! Calumny has been repeatedly foiled; many of its supporters are branded with infamy and public Indignation; the approbation of your Conduct, and consequently the Spirit of Association is daily increasing, and ultimately cannot fail to bring into practice the just Principles of Universal Suffrage and Annual Parliaments.

Reviewing the persecutions which we have formerly suffered, and comparing them with the present, we cannot but conclude, that in a short time, the Members who have been prevailed on to neglect their Duty, will see the perseverance of the Society refuting the Opinions of rash and timid Men. It is, however, proper at the present juncture that every Member should not only be on his Guard against all Attempts to dissuade him from his own Duty, but that he should use every pos-

made, both publicly and privately to maintain and uphold the society. This address had some effect, it caused several divisions which had dispersed to rally, and reclaimed many who were falling off, but the society never again recovered either its number of divisions, or members. It never could raise money sufficient to discharge its current expenses to pay its debts. Its efforts were in more respects than one exceedingly injudicious and these embarrassed it still more and more, drove away its most judicious members and had nearly ruined it before it was finally suppressed by act of Parliament' (Add MSS 27808, fo. 67).

sible exertion to frustrate similar Attempts on the Minds of others.

Signed in Name and by Order of the
General and Executive Committees,

JOHN ASHLEY. Secretary
ALEX. GALLOWAY, Assistant Sec.

316. Additional correspondence: November and December 1795

[In addition to letters already noted, in November and December the LCS received letters from Dundee, Perth, High Wycombe, Norwich, Portsmouth and Worcester.[115]

The only extant reply is to a reformer at Worcester, who described a new society which wished to join with the LCS. The LCS expressed their pleasure at learning of this society based on the 'System of Association laid down & Recommended by the London Corresponding Society'; and they urged the new society to 'Persevere in that Line of Conduct which has Gained the London Corresponding Society that respect and Credit it has attained among the Friends of Freedom'.[116]]

115 Letters printed in *MPM*, vol. 1, pp. 87–90, 233-5.

116 Add MSS 27815, fos. 22-2v. Although the letter from Worcester was published in *MPM*, this reply was not. Perhaps the editor found it lacking in educational matter or abounding in vanity.

PART NINE

1796

Chronology

1796

Jan.	14	Crossfield, Lemaitre, Smith and Higgins indicted for pop-gun plot
	28–9	Stone tried and acquitted
Feb.	5–14/15	Binns's mission to Portsmouth
Feb.	?6–March 2	Jones's mission to Rochester, Gravesend and Maidstone
March	4	Binns and Jones deputed to Birmingham
	16	Binns and Jones arrested in Birmingham
	16	Death of Gerrald
	24	Binns bailed
	26	Jones bailed
May	11–12	Crossfield tried and acquitted
	19	Lemaitre, Higgins and Smith tried and acquitted
May	19	Parliament dismissed
June–July		General elections held; ministerial victory; Tooke defeated at Westminster; Tierney defeated in Southwark, challenges results
July	c. 1	First issue of *Moral and Political Magazine* of LCS
Aug.	19	Thelwall attacked at Yarmouth
Oct.	6	Parliament meets
Oct. 14–Dec. 18		Malmesbury's first peace mission
	18	Pitt proposes supplementary militia bill
Dec.	22	French invasion fleet at Bantry Bay

317. Report from spy Powell: LCS General Committee, 7 January 1796[1]

Source: PC 1/23/A38

7th Jany 1796

New members made in Western Section 15
                  Northern   2
But few divisions meeting Eastern   None
The Committe of the Surry Section Did not meet this week on account of some mistake in changing the night of meeting they also meet very thin
The whole of the business in the Section Committe the last meeting was choosing deputies to the Genl Committe
On account of the Society meeting so thin[2] (16 Divisions have not met since the passing of the bills)
The Genl Com came to the resolution of printing the enclosed circular letter one to be sent to each member.[3]
A General State of the Society has been made out from the Division Books it appears there are actually upwards of 10,000 names set down but this is a false account as vast numbers whose names appear have left the Society. There are also numbers who enter there names pay the /13d & never come to the Society again

The Account includes all the persons who were members during the State Trials & all who have enter'd their names since.[4]
There is still great talk of arms.
Hodgson is going to bring forward a plan to form the Society into a bank on the plan of Country Banks. he says he can get £5,000. – subscribed immediately.

NB I am sorry the inclosed circular letter is torn it was unfortunately done as I was folding it up to enclose it & I had not another

318. Report from unidentified spy: LCS General Committee, 15 January 1796[5]

Source: PC 1/23/A38

From a confidential person who has lately arrived from Birmingham it appears that the Societys in that Town are much decreasing and such Arrangements have been made as makes it almost certain that should any orders for Pikes or Arms be sent from London, intelligence will be sent to the Duke of Portland. –
Thelwall[6] proposes to recommence his lectures during Lent, which he says will be in strict conformity with the late Bills.

[After the arrest of Crossfield in December 1795, government prepared to try the alleged agents of the pop-gun plot. On 14

1 On 12 Jan. Powell sent this report with a covering letter addressed to Richard Ford, Secretary of State's Office, Whitehall. The information of the report, he explained, came from Evans, 'late Del of Div 13 but now one of the Deputies to the Genl Com.', who lodged with him. Powell had been too ill (violent cough) to go out and 'had noboddy I could trust to put it into the post on account of the Direction'.
2 Place described the Society's personal attempts to contain the scale of the defections: 'The business of the Society increased as the number of its members fell off. It was necessary in order to keep it from absolute ruin, to appoint deputations from the General Committee to the divisions whose delegates ceased to attend the District Committees as well as to those which were sluggish, or met in small numbers. This was an arduous undertaking I remember having to attend in this way as many as three divisions on one evening, having to harangue each of them on their neglect and to urge them to a state of greater activity' (Add MSS 27808, fo. 69).
3 The letter was antedated to 31 Dec. 1795.

4 According to another spy (see next report), the 'Account includes all who have ever belonged to the Society from It's Institution'.
5 Description: 'January 13th. 96 – London Correspondg. Socy. / one Inclosure'. The enclosure is the printed address to members, dated 31 Dec. 1795. This report from an unidentified spy repeats all the information from the 7 Jan. meeting of the general committee in the same order as in Powell's report. The extract given here follows the duplicated material.
    A spy reporting on a meeting of the Friends of Liberty on 15 Jan. included the following item: 'Resolvd. that a Subscription be Enter'd into to Support the prosecution against the Magistrate that Commtd Fletcher which the Corresponding Society. Intends to Support' (PC 1/23/A38). There is no record of the LCS supporting such a subscription, but in Feb. Fletcher left the Friends of Liberty and joined the LCS.
6 This paragraph is in another hand.

January 1796, a grand jury found a true bill for high treason against Crossfield, Higgins, Lemaitre and Smith. The latter three, who had been released in May 1795 after eight months' imprisonment, surrendered themselves and were imprisoned for another four months. Crossfield was tried on 11 May and acquitted the next day. A week later on 19 May, Higgins, Lemaitre and Smith were brought to trial. The prosecution introduced no witnesses, and the judge directed the jury to acquit the men.

On Monday, 18 January, the LCS (perhaps at a meeting of the executive committee) issued an advertisement expressing astonishment at the indictment and appealing for subscriptions for the families of Higgins and Smith (who had wives and children) and Lemaitre (whose 'relatives [were] equally subject to those distresses which these trying circumstances must produce'). The advertisement also noted that the LCS appealed to the 'generous Public' during the previous imprisonment of these men.[7]

Describing the labours of the general committee at this time, Place noted that 'the correspondence with the country was also very considerable, It was necessary to put the societies in the country in mind of the pledges they had given, steadily to continue their efforts.'[8] Such admonitions were necessary, for reform societies all over the country were declining. Probably the desire to invigorate the other societies impelled the LCS on 20 January to publish an 'Address to the People'. According to Place, it was 'sent to all the affiliated societies, in correspondence with the London Corresponding Society. It explained as the committee believed the causes of the proceedings of ministers, accused them of a wish to produce an insurrection, and failing that to find if they could an excuse for

attacking the people, in order to put them down by the sword, and thereby increase their own power.'[9]]

319. Report from spy Powell: LCS Northern District Committee, 29 January 1796[10]

Source: PC 1/23/A38

Northern district Com
29th. Jany. 1795 [1796].

16. New members. Quarterage £3. 6. –
Div 13 to Branch to the Falcon Fetter Lane to be No 90 Dep Evans. Rhynd MackNaughton to open it

Genl Com. 28th. Jany 1795 [1796]

44 New Members. Quarterage £13. 17. . –
Received a Letter from Friend of Cambridge proposing an advertisement respecting the Association with the Whig Club.
Pierce & Bullock of Div 49 inform'd the Com that a number of persons in the neighbourhood of High Wyckham. Marlow & Wooburn were in want of the publications of the Society. The Secty inform'd the Com they had been sent the day before   A letter from Rochester requesting a depution from the Society to go down there that they were willing to bear the Expence if it amounted to £4. 4. – per Week.[11]
A like Letter from Portsmouth with the same request.[12]
The Com. resolved on Thursday next to take into consideration the propriety of immediately putting in force the 14 Resolution enter'd into at Copenhagen house respecting sending deputies into the Country[13]

7 Newspaper cutting, dated 20 Jan., in Place Collection, vol. 37, fo. 176; probably from the *Telegraph*. Contributions were being received by John Ashley, shoemaker, 6 Fisher St, Red Lion Sq.; Thomas Hardy, shoemaker, Tavistock St, Covent Garden; F. Dowling, truss-maker, 24 New St, Covent Garden; John Thelwall, 2 Beaufort Buildings, Strand; Christopher Cooper, grocer, 67 New Compton St, Soho; J. Powell, baker, Goodge St, Tottenham Ct Rd; J. G. Ballard, bookseller, 4 May's Buildings, Covent Garden; D. I. Eaton, 74 Newgate St; Thomas Hartley, shoemaker, 4 Prospect Place, St George's Fields; J. P. Phelps, bookseller, Angel St, St Martin's le Grand; John Philip Franklow, tailor, 6 Pitt St, Blackfriars Rd; and the *Telegraph* office, 159 Fleet St.
8 Add MSS 27808, fo. 70.

9 fo. 71.
10 Description: 'N. D. Com. / 29th Jany 1796'. An almost identical spy report, also in PC 1/23/A38, carries the description: '29th. Jan. 96 / London Correspg. Society-'.
11 'N B. *Jones* will probably be deputed to go – addition in the other spy report.
12 'N B. *Bins* is fixed upon to go there' – addition in the other spy report.
13 The requests from Portsmouth and Rochester for deputations and the tentative assignment of Binns and Jones as deputies indicate that this resolution of the Oct. general meeting had been discussed in the Society before 28 Jan. According to Place, 'the question as to the propriety of sending deputies to the country had been referred to the divisions and had been carried in the affirmative for sending them, by an almost unanimous vote' (Add MSS 27808, fo. 73). This vote must have been taken earlier since Binns and

A letter from Waltham Abby complaining that the Committe had treated them ill in not assisting them to prosecute the persons who broke Gregory's (the Secty of that Div) Windows & the justice who had refused to take cognizance of it. The Secty was ordered by the Com. to answer it immediately & they appointed a deputation to go down on Sunday.[14]

Jones set off a week later, the day after the general committee officially decided to send them.

Retrospectively, Place was contemptuous of the decision to send deputies to the country: 'However, much this might have been approved when the society was increasing its numbers at a great rate and when nothing more seemed necessary to rouse the whole country and induce the people in every town to associate for reform of parliament, than such information as could be given to them in a very short space of time by deputies sent among them, the change which had taken place rendered the sending deputies not only unnecessary but actually absurd. It happened however that we cajoled ourselves, and each other with delusive expectation[s] which prove us to have been very silly people. It was expected that the eclat of the deputies would revive the spirit of the reformers in London, and send them back to their divisions. That the societies in the country would increase the number of their members, that new societies would be formed and that the country societies would willingly contribute enough to defray the expenses of the deputies. The members of the Committee were even persuaded [originally: 'We even persuaded ourselves'] that government would not molest the deputies. and on these absurd notions they [originally: 'we'] proceeeded' (fos. 71-2).

14 The deputation included Ashley, who took depositions at Waltham Abbey. In April the LCS explained to a correspondent the events at Waltham Abbey and the LCS's apportioning of blame: 'The Citizens of Waltham Abbey had in Consequence of their Principles rendered themselves obnoxious to the loyal Ragamuffins of the Town & early in November – Citizen Gregory, whom they consider'd as one of the most active among the Patriots, had 19 Panes of Glass broken by an unknown hand – on the 5th. of that Month they met to celebrate Hardy's Acquittal & another Citizen was grossly insulted & beaten by a Person whom they knew. – On the next Day the same Ruffian attack'd the same Citizen, & beat him – & Citizen Gregory had another Pane of Glass broken by a Person who was seen to break it – these Insults being accompanied by Threats that they should be repeated, Application was made to the Magistrates of the Town for Redress. & a Warrant was granted to bring the Offenders to an Account, but when the Magistrate understood that the injur'd Persons were Members of the Society – he tore the Warrant, & refus'd to give them a hearing. – Application was now made to our General Committee, who

The new organzation of the Society will be out in a Week.

320. Report from spy Powell: LCS Northern District Committee, 5 February 1796[15]

Source: PC 1/23/A38

Northern District Committe Feby 5. 1796

Report of Genl. Com. Feby 4th. 1796
26 New members   1094 present in the divisions. Quarterage 7£ . . 10s . . 10½d Subscriptions £4 . . 9 . . 6 Sale of Publications £1 . . 9 . 4.

consider'd this such a flagrant Instance of Injustice that they resolv'd if possible, to punish the Magistrate for neglect of Duty. – the Time when the Application was made, was however unfavourable to an immediate Process – it being just as the two Bills were introduc'd into Parliament. . . . two or three Months elaps'd. – We then consider'd what would be the most eligible Method of proceeding - our first Step was. to call upon the injur'd Citizens to state the whole of their Fate – which when they had done, it made a very different Impression from what it did at first. – We now found that though the Magistrates had refusd to punish the Agressors – there was reason to believe he had taken means to prevent any similar outrage – that tho' the Offenders had not been oblig'd to make legal restitution. – An Offer was made to one of the injur'd Persons to settle the Dispute amicably & that he had refus'd without knowing whether the Terms which were to be offer'd would have been adequate to the Purposes of Justice – or not. – they told us that when the Magistrate tore the Warrant, he desir'd Citizen Gregory to send the insulting Hero's Father to him. – this old Man was the Justice's Beadle – & very shortly after his Visit to the Justice – his Son call'd on the Citizen whom he had insulted, & ask'd him why they should continue at variance – & wish'd him to go over to the Public House & see if they could not settle it. – but the other would not consent. from this Statement, the Committee were led to doubt whether the Court in which this Cause would have been tried, would have approv'd – or censur'd the Conduct of the Magistrate. – whether it would not have attributed this Action to a litigious Desire of Revenge – & have found a Verdict for the Defendant. – When they consider'd the Consequences of the Society (while itself involv'd in Debt) risquing £100 in this Action – & compar'd it with all the Advantages which could be gain'd by obtaining a Verdict – they were decidedly of Opinion that it would be improper to commence the Action' (letter to Rochester, 29 April 1796, Add MSS 27815, fos. 51-1v).
15 Powell's description: 'Report of / Northern District / Committe / 5th Feby. 1796'. Government endorsement: 'Rx 7th'.

Balance in Treasurers hands at the end of last mont £43 . . 8 . . 9

Do on account of Smiths Higgins & Le Maitre's Subr £ . . 9 . . 7½ The Committee proceeded to elect the members for the Executive Com. The follg were reelected. Evans, Bone, Nichols & Finwick. Ross & Harold instead of Hodgson & Oxlade resgnd. Oxlade was elected Chairman of Genl Com for 3 Months. Citizen Hains refer'd to the Executive Com to receive publications to carry Nailsworth in Glostershire.

Report of Ex Com 26 Jany

Read a letter from the Rochester Society stating that their views & principles were exactly similar to those of the L.C.S. & that they had sworn upon the sacred alter of their hearts to support the L.C.S. even with their lives in asserting their rights to universal suffrage & annuel parliaments. Their Society was not form'd till the 28th October last when they increased but slowley but lately so rapidly as to make 6 Divisions, & that the people in General were friends to reform. Read an answer to the above letter informing them that we pursue the cause of Reform with as much zeal as ever are framing regulations agreeable to the letter of the late Acts.
That Deputies will be sent to the principle towns in the Country with as much expedition as possible & that one will be sent to Rochester in a few days.
A member deputed to write to portsmouth informing them a deputy will be sent there in a few days
The Committe resolved that the names of the Deputies & the time of their departure should be kept secret, as the contrary might give ministry an opportunity to frustrate the plan.
A member deputed to prepare a letter of instruction & another of introduction for the deputies to the Country Societey.
Read a letter from Birmingham requesting to know wether we met as usual & how we intended to proceed in future for that they would be govern'd by our conduct. A member deputed to answer it
Took into consideration *Friends letter respecting a junction with the whig club. After mature deliberation the Com determined that it is inconsistant with the views of the L.C.S. The advertisement recommended by Mr Freiend, as the whig club is too equivocal in its conduct to permit our assoceating with them in any manner as long as that ambiguity remains* A member deputed to write to Mr Friend to inform him of the same.
Read an answer to the Wocester letter Approv-

ing of its spirit & requesting the favor of a regular correspondance.
Received a bill from the proprietors of the Telegraph. A member deputed to wait on them respecting it.

Feby 3d.

Read the letter to Friend. Read an answer to the Birmingham letter informing them we continue to meet as usual; that the late Acts will rather be an advantage to us, as our divisions will become much more extensive & numerous. Read the letters of instruction & introduction to Country deputies refed the consideration to next sittings
Took into consideration a plan for the new orginization when the Com resolv'd 1st. that each District Come should give Numbers to new Divns. within their respective limits & that each district should begin with No 1. 2dly That no Div. should branch off till they had 60 names on their books. Adjournd a further consideration till next sittings

Genl Com.

Divns 69. 26. 5. 60 Recommed to the Com to cooperate with the whig club to procure a repeal of the Treason & Sedition Bills */Negatived/*
Div's 56. 36. 27. & 24 are of opinion that a discretionary power should be vested in the District Committes to negative all motions that they may think useless.
Div 78. Are of the contrary opinion.
Div 36 Recommends the District Committes shall be empowr'd to give Numbers to new Divs in their District & their Secty to be supplied with books for them   */Carried/*
Div 32. Resolved that it is the duty of the District Reporter to bring the Treasurers Monthly Account to his Com for the use of the Delegates
Div 7. Do   */Carried/*
Div. 24 Wishes the Quarterly correspondence to be published immediately.
Div 6 Are of opinion it would be better to report the letters monthly & not to put the Society to so heavy an expence
/Order'd the Correspondence of the last 3 months to be printd/
Western District Com. Recommend that the opinion of council should be taken respecting prosecuting the persons who committed the outrage at Waltham Abby.
/Negatived/
NB. *Binns went Portsmouth Friday evening Jones to Rochester Saturday morning*[16]

16 Jones published an account of this trip: *Sketch of a Political Tour through Rochester, Chatham,*

Maidstone, Gravesend, &c Including REFLEC-
TIONS on the Tempers and Dispositions of the
Inhabitants of those Places, and on the Progress
of the Societies Instituted for the Purpose of
Obtaining a Parliamentary Reform (1796). Jones
writes of the people he met in coaches and in
towns, with a stress on their attitudes toward
reform. The book has none of the harangue
which marks Jones's public speeches. Rather,
it sometimes reads like a sentimental tour: when
the town beadle starts beating a boy acting up in
church, Jones protests loudly, because he cannot
stand to see suffering. When he recounts the
death of Mrs Hardy, the landlady at the Falstaff
Tavern weeps aloud. After seeing a sailor without
an arm and discussing amputations performed at
sea, Jones exclaims over a world where men con-
sign each other to be mangled and destroyed. The
impetus to write this book may have been the
instruction that the deputies should keep journals
of their activities.

Fourteen instructions to the deputies and the
letter of introduction are printed in Jones's appendix (pp. 99–107). Instructions 1–4: Convince
the society you visit that our aim is reform of the
House of Commons and that meetings of 49 or
fewer are legal. 5, 6: Guard against those who
propose violent measures; convince the timid of
the legality of peaceable reform meetings. 7:
'Strain every power of your mind to awaken the
sleeping spirit of liberty; you are to call upon our
fellow citizens to be ready with us, to pursue our
common object, if it must be, to the scaffold, or
rather (if our enemies are desperate enough to
bar up every avenue to enquiry and discussion)
to the field, at the hazard of extermination. . . .
But to the end that we may succeed by the irresistible voice of the people, you are to excite
in every society the desire which animates our
bosoms, to embrace the nation as brethren.'
8: Caution the society not to divert their
thoughts from parliamentary reform to 'such
temporary and subordinate considerations' as
the Whig Club's call to the people to unite for
the repeal of the Treason and Sedition Bills.
9: If asked give, but do not impose, regulations
for governing a reform society. 10, 11: Invite
the society to send a monthly report, to adopt
the name of 'United Corresponding Society of
—' and to adopt the LCS regulations. 12: Invite
the society to contribute towards the expense of
the deputation. 13: Write immediately after the
first interview with a society and at least once a
week thereafter. 'In a word, you are always to
reflect that you are wrestling with the enemies of
the human race, not for yourself merely, for you
may not see the full day of liberty, but for the
child hanging on the breast; and that the question, whether the next generation shall be free or
not, may greatly depend on the wisdom and
integrity of your conduct in the generous mission which you and your fellow deputies now
take upon yourselves.' 14: Before leaving London get from the secretary the address to which
to send your reports.

In March when Binns and Jones went as

321. Report from spy Powell: LCS Northern District Committee, 12 February 1796[17]

Source: PC 1/23/A38

Northern District Com Feby 12. 1796

Genl Com.

20 New members   present 905. Quarterage
&ca 8 . 7 . 4½

Rep of Ex Com Feby 4.

The letters of introduction & instruction read
emended & deliver'd to the Country deputies.
Read a letter from Portsmouth expressing
their thanks & satisfaction for our intentention
of sending a deputation to them they had
already began a subscription for defraying his
Expences

Feby 9th

Received & read a letter from the Rochester
deputy saying that he was received with respect almost bordering on veneration   the
Society was in the most flourishing state   the
Town was full of good citizens they had a
patriotic mayor & magistrates.
Read a letter from the Portsmouth Deputy saying that he was received with respect when he
was introduced to the Society   there were a
number of strangers in the room   his letters of
instruction & introduction were no sooner
read than they immediately interrd into the
Society. They called themselves the Portsmouth united Corresponding Society

Genl Com. Feby 11th

Divs 84. 62. 42. 67. &. 51 Are of opinion that

deputies to Birmingham, their instructions included these fourteen points (with minor changes)
and two others: make sure you meet with no
more than 49 people in a group, and keep a journal of your proceedings (*Report of Committee
of Secrecy* . . . 1799, pp. 68–70).

The letter of introduction states that the
deputy will 'lay before you' his instructions,
and that 'nothing is wanting to obtain such a
Reform in Parliament as we demand, but a strict
union among those who are already convinced of
it's necessity . . . . In Britain, the first article of
the political creed is, that every individual who
is subject to government is represented, and has
a right to be represented, in the legislature. We
assert no more, than that the practice does not
at present correspond with the theory, and we
claim no more than the restitution of our rights.'
With minor changes, this letter was used in
March to introduce the same deputies to the
Birmingham reformers.

17 Powell's description: 'Report of the / N B Committe / Feby 12th. 1796'.

Councils advice should be taken respecting the outrage committed on the Citizens at Waltham Abby

> Carried & citizen Barr & a member of the Ex Com[18] ordered to draw up a case for Council

Div 9. 12. 13. Are of opinion that Genl meeting should be called soon to obtain a repeal of the Convention Bill
(referred the consideration to future sitting)
Div 29 Are of opinion that the taking of Quarterage should be abolished & that the Society should publish a monthly magazine to contain all the Correspondence & transactions of the Society with other patriotic matters & that Each member should pay 1s/6d per Quarter for which they would be entitled to three Magazines
> /referrd to a future sitting)

There were some other trifling motions which were negatived

NB   Ashly went to Portsmouth on Friday to inquire into the Report of Binns being prest[19] & to send him off to Chichester if the Report was not true as Binns was understood to be a marked man & his person well known at Portsmouth.[20]

322. Report from spy Powell: LCS Northern District Committee, 19 February 1796[21]

Source: PC 1/23/A38

North District Committe Feby 19th. 1796

18 D. Evans of 21 Old Boswell Court, Lincolns Inn Fields.
19 According to Binns, two members of the executive committee came to summon him back to London, as they had reliable information 'that orders had been given to have me impressed and sent on board one of the receiving-ships'. Binns fulfilled his speaking engagement that night (14 Feb. ?) and returned to London the next day (*Recollections*, p. 66).
20 Before his person became well-known his reputation had been spread about: When he sent to visit the prisoner of war camp at Porchester Castle, Binns and his companions were told that they could not be admitted without orders from the governor. Binns's companion remarked that this was a new regulation. ' "Yes", said the officer, "it is in consequence of some delegate from London, who has been sent to Portsmouth to set fire to the dock-yards and liberate the prisoners." ' On applying to the governor, Binns was admitted without difficulty (*Recollections*, pp. 64–5).
21 Powell's description: 'North District Com /

34 New Members   1120 Present Quarterage
£6. - 8½ Subn £2.3.3½ Publication £-.1.5

> Report of the Ex Com. Feby 12th.

Read a letter from Redbridge saying there were some citizens who wishd to form a Society there & requesting instructions how to proceed & wishing to receive some political phamplets. A member deputed to answer it.
Read a letter from Gravesend requesting the Society to send them a Number together with Tickets & publications as there were a great number of Friends to reform there who wished to form a division of the L C S. A member deputed to write to Gravesend to inform them that the Rochester Deputy would wait on them on his return from thence
The member deputed to draw up the new Constitution stated he had been unavoidably delay'd in the prosecution of the work but that it would be ready to lay before the Com on Wednesday next.
Read a letter from Binns the Portsmouth Deputy stating that the emissarys of Government were very active in obstructing the object of his deputation & from a paragraph that appear'd in the Portsmouth Gazette he had reason to apprehend some personal danger. The Committe resolved as their letters were liable to be intercepted a member should be sent to Portsmouth immediately to aid & assist the Deputy in his critical situation

> Extra sittings Monday 15. Feby

Agreable to the Determination of the Genl Com the Ex Com deputed one of their members to assist Citn Barr to take the opinion of Council on the Waltham Abby Outrage. Galloway inform'd the Com that he was with Jones at Rochester on Sunday last when he inform'd him that the Citizens of Rochester were active & bold in the propagation of the principles of Liberty among all descriptions of persons. That their divisions were both active and numerous & since his arrival two new ones had been form'd one in a small town of the name of Louton & the other in Rochester & that the inhabitants in General were flocking in a great number to join the Society. The Deputy transmitted a letter by Galloway in which he informs the Com that a person (whom he calls a Bobadile) had made frequent rude interrogations with much personal abuse either to extort information, or divert him from the object of his mission but that neither

Feby 19th 1796'. Government description: 'Report of London Correspondg. Society – / Rx. 20th'.

344

one or the other answer'd his purpose; He said Bobadil had made frequent applications to the Mayor to persuade him to disperse the Society for which he requested the aid of the Civil power to assist the Military. To which the Mayor replied that the Society conducted their meetings in a legal & peaceable manner & he could do nothing but give them his protection. Citn Jones requested more publications & a fresh supply of money with the use of two newspapers.[22] The Com granted him two guineas with the use of the Telegraph & True Briton & a sufficient quantity of publications and ordered him to return by Monday next.

Sitting Feby 17.

Resolv'd that no letter should be shown to any person whatever except the Ex Com when actually sitting. Binns appear'd before the Com & gave a report of his proceedings at Portsmouth when it was resolved he should attend the Genl Com & deliver the same. Resolv'd that the instructions of the Deputies be amended by inserting an article requesting each to keep a journal of his proceedings & deliver the same to the Com on his return. Resolv'd that it be recommended to the Genl Com to allow the Deputies two guineas per week as a recompense for their loss of time. Resolv'd that Binns have the thanks of the Com for his faithful discharge of his deputation at Portsmouth & his spirited behavior on that occasion Resolved that a letter of thanks be sent to Chas Brasset of Queen Street Portsea for his civic & generous entertainment of the Deputy. Resolv'd that the thanks of this Com be given to Ashly for his manly & spirited conduct in going to Portsmouth for the pur-

22 In a later letter Jones described another meeting in Rochester and one in Chatham. After he addressed the Rochester reformers for an hour and a half, they rose and 'professed their determination to live and die united with the London Corresponding Society'. After describing the meeting at Chatham, which was 'very numerously attended', Jones noted that 'the sending of a deputy from our Society has, if I am not mistaken awakened the whole county of Kent to a sense of its situation, and to a determination to assert its Rights' (extract of letter to Ashley, 16 Feb. 1796, in *Sketch of a Political Tour*, pp. 108–11). On 22 Feb. the United Corresponding Societies of Rochester, Chatham and Brompton met and passed resolutions, including one 'to act in concert with and pursuant to the principles of the London Corresponding Society' and another to persevere in 'the propagation of these principles [relating to reform of the House of Commons] even though it should be at the hazard of their lives' (pp. 111–12).

pose express'd in last sittings. Read a letter from Manchester stating that the Friends of Reform had resolv'd to form themselves into a Society there, it said that a Society of Gentlemen met in Manchester on the plan of the Whig club & that they reported the L.C.S. & the Whig club had united. They wish'd to know if the L.C.S had relinquish'd the cause of universal Suffrage & annuale Parliaments & that they should not join the Whig club of Manchester 'till they heard from the L C S The Com having reason to believe from the Manchester letter & others, that the Whig Club have circulated a report in different parts of the Country that they had united with the L. C. S. It was moved that a circular letter be sent to all the Country Societys to counteract such report. A member laid before the Committe the new Constitution for the future government of the Society Your Committee after a considerable discussion adjourn'd the deliberation to next sittings. Your Com will compleat it so as to lay it before the Genl Com next sittings.

Genl Com.

Motions from Div 6. 13. 32. Are of opinion that the Genl Com do immediately inquire into the conduct of the Ex Com for their deserting the Citns Smith, Higgins & LeMaitre. They having only received the most triffling sum out of the Subscription which is generally understood to have been collected for their use, and perticularly their having receivd the most unfriendly treatment in answer to repeated letters. (*Your Com after minute investigation resolved that they are perfectly satisfied with conduct of the Ex Com*)
Div 3. 34. 46. 48 That a magazine be substituted instead of Quarterage (*Refd to Ex Com.*)
Div 77. request the Quarterage to be done away & a voluntary subscription be substitutd. (*Refd to Ex Com*)
Div 21 Request Quarterage to be done away – & one penny collected weekly (*Refd to Ex Com*)
Div 56 Are of opinion that no member of the L C S the members of the Committes not excepted shall under any pretext whatever draw money out of the hands of the Treasurer or apply any money they may be entrusted with without leave of the Divisions
(*negatived*)
Div 32. Are of the opinion that the Secretary of each division shall inquire evry meeting night of ev'ry member wether he has chang'd the place of his residence that it may be inserted in the Division Books   (*carried*)
Moore & Parkinson elected to the Ex Com in

the room of Ross superseeded & D Evans resigned. Bone was elected assistant Secretary in the room of Galloway resign'd
McNaughton elected president in the Room of Oxlade resigned
Barr elected to the Ex Com in the Room of Bone.

323. Report from Magistrate W. Wright: Friends of Liberty meeting, 22 February 1796[23]

Source: PC 1/23/A38

Visited the 8 Sectn. [of the Friends of Liberty] a Deputation from the Corresponding Society, waited on them to know if they woud Join them[24] when fourteen of the Membrs. belonging to the Sectn. Joind & formd a New Division. No 74. Burks & Fletcher Chosen delagates and Bennett Secy. for that Divn the reason given for Leaving the Sectn. is the Corresponding Society haveing great Connections Can furnish them with arms on Emergency — Jones. & Binns are gone to Rochester to form Divisions in that Town –

Mondy feby 22d.

I am your
most Obt.
hble Servt.
W. Wright

23 Description: 'Friends of Liberty / Feb. 22d. 96'. The earlier part of this one page report briefly tells of Wright's visiting other societies and the general committee. At the meetings of the committee on 11, 17 and 18 Feb., six to eight delegates were present. At a meeting of section 8 on 10 Feb., thirty-eight members were present. The only reported activity of the society was a plan to give free lectures (the first to be on padlocks).
 This is the last mention of the Friends of Liberty, formed in April 1795 by the seceding Div. 16. According to one member, Stephen Cooper, the Friends of Liberty later joined the Sons of Liberty and took the name Sons and Friends of Liberty (examination, 13 Jan. 1800, PC 1/3473). LCS financial records list them as Friends and Sons of Liberty. Although Cooper said the combined society 'fell off', some of the FoL members named by him (Shepherd, Mills, Williamson) are mentioned in 1799 spy reports of Friends and Sons of Liberty, also called United Sons of Liberty or just Sons of Liberty (PC 1/44/A155).
24 Cooper was 'frequently solicited' to rejoin the LCS.

324. Report from spy Powell: LCS Northern District Committee, 4 March 1796[25]

Source: PC 1/23/A38

North District Com 4th March 1796
Genl Com. March 3d.

40 New members. 944. preasent in the divisions £2 . 11 . 4 Quarterage £ - 13 . . 3¼ Sub for Smith &Ca £ - 13 . . 4 for Downey £ - . . 2 . . 6 Publications.
Cherry & Williams elected to the Executive Com. in the room of Moore & Harold

Report of Ex Com Sittings Feby 26th.

Received & read a letter from Jones dated Maidstone Feby 24th[26] at which place he arrived the day before & lost no time in making his arrival known to the friends of Reform, he likewise informd the Com that prior to his leaving Rochester a general meeting of the members was call'd in consequence of a young man of the name of Newman a member of the Rochester Society who had absented himself in consequence of a warrent granted to apprehend him. The meeting enterr'd into some very spirited resolutions on the occasion expressive of their approbation of the conduct of Citizen Newman during the time he had been amongst them, of their determination to support & stand by him in his present critical situation & of the resolution of not abandonning the object of their association but with their lives, the above resolutions were orderr'd to be inserted in the Rochester journal. Read another letter from Jones dated Maidstone Feby 25 stating that he had met a very numerous & respectable assembly of the citizens of

25 Powell's description: 'Northern District Committe / March 4th. 1796'.
26 Two days earlier Jones wrote from Gravesend, which he reached on Saturday afternoon (20 Feb.). Despite the short notice fifty people were assembled before 8 o'clock. Jones spoke to them for an hour, after which sixteen new members were made. He was told that if his arrival were generally known, 'almost all Gravesend would assemble' (extract of letter to the executive committee, 22 Feb. 1796, in *Sketch of a Political Tour*, pp. 113–14). Three weeks after Jones's visit to Gravesend, the society there reported having twenty-one members who were determined, in defiance of the mayor and the incorporated body, to 'steadily adhere to the principals laid down by your executive Committee' (letter, R. Cooke to Alexander Galloway, 15 March 1796, Add MSS 27815, fos. 33–4v).

Maidstone at the Castle Inn, he addressed them for near two hours & was heard with great attention, they came to the resolution of forming themselves into a Society to obtain universal Suffrage and annual parliaments. Jones wish'd to be permitted to stop with them a day or two to assist them in orginizing themselves he says they have a great many friends in Maidstone among the rest Mr Taylor the member for the town who wish'd him success they were to have another meeting on Wednesday evening when he was to lay before them our regulations & they were to proceed to elect a committe of orginization. A Mr Smith the brother in law of Mr Taylor was in the chair the proceeding evening at whose house he was when he wrote this letter. Read a letter from the Wocester United Corresponding Society they acknowledg'd the receipt of our last & considered it as an act of the greatest friendship in the L C S to correspond with them they declard that the cause of Universal Suffrage & Annual Parliaments is the cause nearest their hearts & that they are determin'd to support it at the hazard of their lives. The committe appointed a member to prepare an answer.[27] An Answer to the letter from Manchester was produced & ordered to be sent.[28] Binns was order'd to write to Chas Brasset of Portsea to request him to use his

27 The brief answer thanked 'their Brother Citizens' for their letter of 18 Feb.; approved their reform sentiments and their 'intention to distribute such Publications as tend to enlighten mankind'; enclosed, as requested, twelve dozen copies of the *Torch* (an extract from Volney's *Ruins of Empires*); and recommended a weekly publication (by Bone), the *Politician* (letter approved by executive committee on 4 March, Add MSS 27815, fos. 24-5v).

28 Letter from Manchester and reply lost. On 3 March J. Shaw of Manchester wrote, asking about a letter the Manchester reformers had sent a month earlier in care of J. Barton of the Red Lion, Grosvenor Square. After identifying himself as the citizen who helped found a society at Bradford and Halifax, Shaw continued: 'Altho the Church and King Club or Rabbel are very Vilant and party runs very Igh yet with grate trouble whe have formed our selves and in three weeks are near four Hundred Strong but whe want Corespondance and with out that our Socity will fall to the Ground and the Letter I perswaded them to Send not being answered as put them out of Spirits thinking you are trimmed and have Droped the Caus so Glorsley began . . . if you will sind some littel a Count of the progres of your Socity it will Chear our Droping Spirits' (Add MSS 27815, fos. 27-8).

best endeavours with the Citizens of Chichester to continue their meetings & not suffer the Society to fall to the ground.[29] Binns was likewise requested to call upon Thelwall to know if he had compleated the address to the people of Scotland. The Com resum'd the discussion of the Constitution & at a late hour adjourn'd it to the next Sittings

Sittings March 2d

Jones arrived from his mission and communicated to the Com that he had attended a committe of about 6 persons at Citizen Smiths at Maidstone who after some discussion declared their determination to institute a Society for Reform to correspond with the L. C. S. At the meeting at the Castle Inn as before reported on Feby 24 a motion was made by Citizen Moore & seconded by Rt. Mason that a meeting be held on Monday the 29th at the above Inn to take into consideration certain propositions and enter into resolutions to obtain Universal Suffrage and Annual Parliaments   J Smith Chairman J Moore Depty Citizens Evans and Barr acquainted the Com. they were proceeding in the Waltham Abby business.[30] The Com. orderr'd the Treasurer to pay Binns for his time agreable to the order of the Genl Com. The Com proceeded as before to discuss the Constitution & resolv'd that an article be added to the instructions of the deputies going into the Country, that no more than 50 persons assemble at one meeting or place. Resolv'd unanimously that the thanks of this Com be given to J. G. Jones for his able spirited & judicious conduct during his mission

Genl Com.

Motions from Divisions 9 & 33. The former approved of the allowance to Country deputies, the latter objected to it
Div 11. Also disapproved of the Sum & wish'd

29 In a letter thanking the LCS for sending Binns as a deputy, the Portsmouth society later reported that the Chichester citizens could no longer meet (from J. Jackson, received 9 March, Add MSS 27815, fos. 29-30).

30 This is inconsistent with a letter written this day (2 March) by D. Evans, saying that he had not met Barr, that Edwards recently informed him the division at Waltham Abbey no longer met, and that consequently he thought the LCS need not take any action on this matter. Evans enclosed the depositions taken by Ashley (letter to executive committee, Add MSS 27815, fos. 26-6v).

it to be referrd to the divisions (*after considerable discussion negatived*)

In consequence of motions from several divisions recommending that assistance should be given to Downey at Edinburgh Castle[31] it was determin'd that £5 . . 5 . . - should be sent him. Citizen Cherry undertook to advance the money to be reimburs'd him by a subscription to be set on foot for that purpose.[32] West district Com recommend that Citizen Ward be allow'd £2 . 2 . - to procure a copy of his indictment for selling a publication entitled the Scarlet Devils.[33] (*order'd*)

South District Com recommend the Genl Com. to call on the citizen who was to answer the Edinburgh letter which they conceived was neglected having been received in December last & not yet answer'd

(*referr'd to the Ex Com*)

31 On 29 Feb. David Downie (convicted of treason in 1794 but reprieved from the death sentence) sent Hardy a copy of a handbill, dated 2 Jan. 1796, which reprints his letters to the king and the Duke of Portland. These letters explain that he has to leave the country immediately after his release from jail on 12 March but that he has no money to buy passage abroad for himself and his family. In a note to Hardy, written in the margin, Downie said that he could send more of these handbills if they would be useful (Place Collection, vol. 37, fos. 205–6).

32 At the beginning of July the Society still owed Cherry £1 3s. A subscription for Cherry during the month brought in only 10s 9½d (*Treasurer's Account for July, 1796*, Place Collection, vol. 37, fo. 309; financial statement for July–Dec. 1796. ibid., fos. 319–21).

33 Francis Ward ran afoul of the magistrates in Nov. 1795 when he was charged with having painted on two sides of his sign board, 'Citizen Ward, Shaver to the Swinish Multitude'. The magistrate told Ward to take the sign down; Ward refused. The magistrate next went to Ward's landlord, who said he had no right to take the board down or to direct what Ward could put on his sign. Ward was again brought before the magistrate; this time Ward said he had taken opinion of counsel. Pressed to tell what that opinion was, Ward replied that his solicitor said 'he was a blockhead for putting the board up, and the Magistrates of Queen-square were blockheads for interfering to pull it down'. When he still refused to take it down, Ward was then charged with circulating the *Scarlet Devils*. According to the magistrate, the seditious part of the pamphlet alluded to the king, charged him with being a miser and riding in a rubbish cart (*MC* 16 Nov. 1795, p. 3; see Place Collection, vol. 37, fo. 29, for an advertising card which reads 'Citizen Ward / No 7 Orchard Street / Shaver to the Swinish Multitude').

325. Report from spy Powell: LCS Northern District Committee, 11 March 1796[34]

Source: PC 1/23/A38

Northern District Com.
March 11th 1796

N D Com March 11th.
J Powell of Div 90 elected to the Genl Com. in the room of Fitzgibbon Div 58 superceded for neglect of duty

Treasurers Monthly report for Feby.

Balance in hand at the end of Jany last	£43 . . 19 . . 1½
Received in Feby. with £5 . . 19 . . 1½ Subn from Portsmouth	29 . . 10 . . 7½
	73 . . 9 . . 8½
Disbursed –	38 . . 12 . . 6
	34 . . 17 . . 2½
Received on Account of Smiths Higgin's & Subn	10 . . -- . . --
Balance in hand at the end of Feby	44 . . 17 . . 2½

Genl Com March 10th

35 New Members 700 Present in Divs   Quarterage £3 . . 4 . . 8½.
Smiths Subn £- . . 8 . . 3½
Downeys Subn. £- . . 17 . . 5½
43 Divisions unrepresented in the District Committes last week

Ex Committe March 4th.

Nicholls reelected reporter. A member produced an answer to the letters from Wocester, approved and ordered to be sent. The Com orderd the Treasurer to pay J G Jones for his loss of time on mission in the Country agreable to the order of the Genl Com. The Com came to the resolution of withdrawing the letter from Edinburgh from the citizen who was deputed to answer it he having fail'd so to do, A member desired to prepare an answer to the same immediately. £5 . . 5 . . ordered to be sent to Downy at Edinburgh agreable to the order of the Genl Com.[35] The Com pro-

34 Powell's description: 'Northern District com. / March 11th 1796'.
35 Downie replied, thanking them and telling them not to apologize for the smallness of the gift. He added that since he had been released at midday

ceeded in further discussing the Constitution
adjourn'd the same to the next sittings.

March 8

The Com ordered the two papers the Times &
Telegraph to be sent to Jones & Binns on mission into the Country agreable to their request
The Com came to the resolution that any
member not appearing in his place in the Ex
Com by ½ past Eight in the Evening to proceed to business, should be reported absent.
The Com having taken into consideration the
refer'd motions from several divisions respecting the publishing of a Magazine, Are of opinion
that such a work by the Society would be servi-
cible to the cause of reform, and that it would
be proper to institute it in the place of all publications except the Regulations of the Society,
each member paying /4½d per month for the
same. That it is proper notwithstanding on
account of the importance of the Question to
refer it to the Divisions for their decision. That
a member be deputed to draw up a plan of the
work to be laid before the Genl Com & the
Divisions

March 9th.

The Com took into consideration the plan of a
Magazine as produced by the member who
was deputed to prepare the same, adjourn'd
the further discussion on account of its importance to the next sittings. The Citizens who
were deputed to prepare the Waltham Abby
case produced the same. The Com ordered it
to be laid before council. The Committe proceeded in the further discussing the Constitution adjournd the same to the next sittings. A
member produced an answer to the letter
received from Truro in Cornwall approved &
ordered to be sent.

Genl Com March 10th.

Edwards elected a member of the Ex Com in
the room of Williams resign'd.
Div 5. 1. & 10 of the Eastern District & 15
Western. Are of opinion the Sum to be allowed
the deputies going into the Country should be
refer'd to the Divisions   (negatived)
Div 2. West D. a motion from for fixing the
sum allow'd the deputies including their expences   (negatived)
Div 7. Western & 8 Eastern Districts. Are of

opinion that such members of the Genl & Ex
Coms as neglect to attend their Coms for two
nights should be superceded   (recommended
                to the attention of the District Coms)
Div. 27. Western D. recommend to the Com to
use their interest for the repeal of the Treason
& Sedition Bills.   (negatived)
Div 11. Western D. Think that the Genl Com
ought to thank Citizen Binns for his conduct
during his mission   (negatived as a bad prece-
                                    dent)
Div 8. Eastern D. Are of opinion that the members of the Ex Com ought not to have the
right of giving their opinion in the Genl Com
unless call'd upon, their being an article in the
regulations which provides for this.   (orderd
                        to be put in Force)
Div. 7. Western D. Are of opinion that the
Genl Com have exceeded their powers in giving £2 .. 2 .. – to Citizen Ward, & they think
no money should be given in future for the
like purposes without the consent of the Divisions   (carried)
Div 64. Northern & 11 Western D. Are of
opinion that the Genl Com ought to consist of
one representative for evr'y 3 members of the
District Coms as they conceive the number of
members that now attend the Genl Com is
much too small considering how much the
Genl interests of the Society are in their hands
        (Refer'd to the Divisions)
Div 1. Western D. Wish the Quarterage to be
collected weekly.   (Refer'd to the Ex Com)

326. The arrest of Binns and Jones: 16 March 1796

Sources: as notes

[The deputation of Binns to Portsmouth
and Jones to Rochester, Chatham, Maidstone and Gravesend was so successful that
the Society decided to send them on a
deputation to Birmingham. On 16 March
they were both arrested and subsequently
charged with using seditious words. A year
later, on 9 April 1797, Jones was convicted
(but was never sentenced). Four months
later, on 30 March 1797, Jones was convicted
    The Birmingham deputation had its
origin on 24 January 1796, when the LCS
received a letter from the reform society at
Birmingham asking for advice. Presumably
the letter (now lost) contained an account
of the decline of reform ardour under the
threat of the Treason and Sedition Acts in

on Saturday, 13 March, and had to leave the
country within ten days, he was busy trying to
satisfy his creditors (to Ashley, 15 March 1796,
Add MSS 27815, fos. 31–2v). Downie reached
New York on 13 August (*New Annual Register*,
1796, 'Occurrences', p. 52).

349

a city where leaders of the 1790–1 'church and king' riots still swaggered in public houses.[36]

Soon after receiving this letter from Birmingham, the LCS sent its two deputies to Portsmouth and Rochester. The apparent success of these two trips must have determined the Society to respond to the Birmingham letter of January by sending both deputies to this important city. Just two days after Jones's return, he and Binns were deputed to go to Birmingham.

A few days before their arrival there was a reform meeting in Birmingham, about which the magistrates took depositions. These depositions convinced the Duke of Portland that seditious language had been used.[37] When the meeting with the London reformers was announced, the spies and the magistrates were in readiness.

This first public meeting of Binns and Jones with Birmingham reformers was on Friday, 11 March. News of their arrival brought out so many men that both Binns and Jones (they spoke at separate rooms) found it impossible to limit the number of auditors to forty-nine. Jones first read his audience a statement of the LCS's views and principles[38] and the instructions from the LCS to the deputies. He was then starting 'a statement of our situation' when a magistrate entered accompanied by two constables armed with pistols. When Jones explained that they were meeting to obtain a reform, the magistrate replied 'That Government were the best judges of the necessity of Reform'. One of the auditors of the lecture then took an oath that Jones had said, 'The people should choose their own Lawgivers' (later changed to 'Representatives'). Jones maintained that he had said, 'When laws are passed affecting life, liberty, or property, it is necessary they should be made by our own Representatives.' The magistrate read the proclamation, and Jones soon left the room.[39]

Meanwhile Binns addressed a meeting at the Swan public house in Swallow St. He

too read the declaration of the LCS's views and principles and the instructions to the deputies (as well as the form letter of introduction). Although a constable and a justice's clerk entered his meeting, it was not dispersed, and Binns spoke for a full hour.[40]

It was for statements made at this meeting that Binns was tried. His witnesses and government's witnesses agreed that Binns spoke of the importance of universal suffrage and annual Parliaments. According to two government witnesses, Binns said that the king and his ministers were convinced that universal suffrage and annual Parliaments were conducive to happiness, but they withheld them from the people. Binns was also alleged to have said that if the king and his ministers remained obstinate and if force should become necessary, he hoped that every citizen in the room would be willing to shed his blood; that if the soldiers were called out, they would refuse to fight against the preservers of their liberty. According to Binns's six witnesses, there was no comment about the king and his ministers witholding universal suffrage from his natural subjects. Binns stressed that annual Parliaments and universal suffrage were to be sought by peaceful means, by petitioning. After his remarks about this primary topic, Binns made a few comments about the Two Acts, pointing out that it was still legal to assemble, if the numbers were restricted to forty-nine. He then discussed the importance of trial by jury and the liberty of the press. In this connection, so testified his witnesses, Binns said that if these rights were taken away it would be proper for the citizens to use force and the soldiers, who had the interests of the country at heart, would not attack them.[41]

After receiving accounts of these first two meetings in Birmingham, the executive committee sent Binns and Jones a letter congratulating them on their courage and peaceable conduct and adding some regulations: have a shorthand writer or three or four intelligent men make a record of all that you say at meetings, make minutes immediately after a meeting, invite your auditors to respect the magistracy (Jones's audience wanted to hiss), do not prolong the meeting to a late hour, do not let more than forty-nine be present at a meeting.[42]

36 Binns, *Recollections*, pp. 68–71.
37 Letter, Duke of Portland to Birmingham magistrates W. Hicks, B. Spencer and W. Villers, 14 March 1796, HO 65/1, fos. 95–6.
38 This was the 23 Nov. 1795 document, *To the Parliament and People of Great Britain. An Explicit Declaration of the Principles and Views of the London Corresponding Society.*
39 Extract of letter, Jones to LCS, 14 March 1796, in LCS account of the deputation to Birmingham, newspaper cutting in TS 11/953/3497.
40 Extract of letter, Binns to LCS, 14 March 1796, in LCS account, cutting in TS 11/953/3497.
41 Trial of Binns, *ST* vol. 26, cols. 595–651.
42 15 March, in LCS account of the deputation.

Immediately after the meetings the Birmingham magistrates took depositions from men who had attended, and on the next day, 12 March, these depositions were sent to the Duke of Portland, who on 14 March directed the magistrates to arrest Binns, Jones and a Birmingham reformer named Francis Bathurst.[43] The magistrates acted promptly on these orders: on the 16th they arrested Binns while he was eating dinner with friends at the Hen and Chicken Tavern. They arrested Jones a little later that night.

On 18 March the executive committee received news of Binns's arrest, and on the 19th of Jones's. They immediately deputed Place to take twelve guineas to Binns and Jones and to arrange bail and legal assistance for them.[44] Place, who had never been thirty miles from London, much less to Birmingham, was directed to go first to John Kilmister for information and advice.[45] Government sent treasury solicitor Joseph White to the hearings; he and the LCS representative – this twenty-four year old journeyman tailor – found themselves in the same coach.[46]

White had been briefed by Portland, who was concerned that all legal formalities be carried out so that there would be no technical loophole at the ensuing trials of the men. The attorney general and solicitor general had advised Portland that Jones be discharged unless there was stronger evidence against him than that contained in the depositions.[47]

White and Place attended the hearing, probably on the 21st when Binns and Jones received copies of the warrants for their arrest, in which they were charged with attending illegal meetings and uttering seditious words (which were not specified).

Bail for Binns was given on 24 March; but that for Jones was rejected, and he was remanded until acceptable bail was found on the 26th.

The LCS, on 21 March inserted in the *Telegraph* a statement of their motives for sending the deputies to Birmingham. This statement includes the instructions to the deputies, the extracts from the letters of Binns and Jones, the reply from the executive committee and the letter of instruction to Place.[48] Three days later on 24 March, the Society issued an appeal for 'Patriotic Contributions towards the accomplishment of sending Deputies into the Country'. In this advertisement there is no mention of Binns, Jones, Birmingham, or the arrest.[49]]

327. Report from spy Powell: LCS General Committee, 24 March 1796[50]

Source: PC 1/23/A38

Genl Com L C S Sittings
Thursday March 24th. 1796

6 New members 826 present £1 . . 7 . . 6½ Quarterage 19s 6½d Downys Sub 3/4 Smiths ⟨&Ca⟩ Sub.

Ex Com Sittings March 18th.

Read a letter from a citizen at Birmingham giving an account of the arrest of Binns. Read

43 HO 65/1, fos. 95-6. Bathurst was indicted for allegedly addressing one of the meetings after either Binns or Jones had spoken: 'I very much approve what has been said; I wish you to acquaint the London Society that I believe I can answer for every person in this room, and for the major part of Birmingham being in favour of the London Corresponding Society. They [the people of Birmingham] can make arms, and will make arms, and will use them. I am prepared with a dagger' (*MC* 28 July 1796, p. 3; *True Briton*, 27 July 1796, p. 4; 28 July, p. 3).
44 Letter of instruction, Ashley to Place, 18 March 1796, in LCS account of deputation.
45 Draft letter, LCS to Kilmister, 18 March 1796, Add MSS 27815, fos. 35-6v.
46 Add MSS 27143, fo. 167.
47 Letter, Portland to Birmingham magistrates W. Hicks, B. Spencer and W. Villers, 18 March 1796, HO 65/1, fos. 96-7.
48 Cutting in TS 11/953/3496. The pro-government *True Briton* described this as 'a new Manifesto from the Corresponding Crew . . . containing an account of their proceedings for defeating the end of the two salutary Bills'. The instruction to encourage the affiliated societies to pursue their common object was described as 'this modest exhortation to open rebellion'. At the end of the article was a reminder (not the first) that one LCS member, Joseph Francis Bodkin, was executed for robbing his master (24 March 1796, p. 3).
49 *MC* 25 March 1796, p. 1. Subscriptions were received by Ashley, Cooper, Dowling, Eaton, Hardy, Hartley, Thelwall, the *Telegraph* office – all on the January list in the appeal for Higgins, Lemaitre and Smith; also by Hodgson, 10 Broadway, Westminster; Hughes, bookseller, Carthusian St, Charterhouse Sq.; Powell, baker, 8 Goodge St, Tottenham Ct Rd; Riebau, bookseller, opposite Buckingham St, Strand; the *Morning Post* office. The list excludes Ballard, Franklow and Phelps, who were on the January list.
50 Powell's description: 'Genl Com LCS / March 24'. Government description: 'Mar. 24. 1796'.

a letter from Portsmouth containing their thanks to the Society for deputing Binns to them it likewise expres that evr'y care had been taking respecting the Society at Chichester Ordered a general summons of the Com for monday next. Took in consideration the constitution, adjourn'd the same to monday

March 19.

Read a letter from a citizen of Birmingham giving an account of Jones being aprehended. The Com came to the resolution of deputing a citizen down to Birmingham immediately to give all the assistance in his power to Jones & Binns they likewise voted that he should take down with him 12 Guineas for their service.

March the 21st

Orderd agreable to the resolution of the General Com a general summons of all the members of the Society to attend their Divisions next week   a letter drawn up for that purpose ordered to be printed & distributed to the District Coms at their next sittings took into consideration the new constitution ordered six articles to be laid before the Genl Com & Divisions immediately. Orderared that the instructions given to Country deputies with an account of the arrest of Jones & Binns at Birmingham with the letters received from them at that place be published in the Telegraph immediately.

Sitting March 22d

Read a letter from Place the person deputed to Birmingham giving an account of his arrival & visit to Jones & Binns at the Birmingham Dungeon he stated that they could not tell for what they were arrested as they could not obtain a sight of their warrent 'tho' they had repeatedly demanded it   he had some difficulty in obtaining an interview with them & when he did two constables were always present. he stated they were visited by the most respectable citizens of Birmingham male as well as female who crowded to see them & their dungeon had absolutly become a political debating Room. A person said whilst he was with them "perhaps these citizens want mony." Two immediately went out & return'd in ten minutes with five guineas which was given to Jones. They told Place they would soon raise £50 – to pay the expences of Jones & Binns & also the expences of their prosecution.

Sittings March 23.

Read another letter from Place with an account of the examination of Jones & Binns before the justices when Mr White the Tresury Soliciter from London was present   The Chages against them were for seditious practices in delivering seditious harrangues to more than 50 persons   They were informd they might procure bail themselves in £500 & two other persons in £200 each   a number of names were given in when two were accepted for Binns & one for Jones   a number of other persons that evening offerd themselvs who would deposit the money if required. Orderd the letter to be read in the Genl Com.

Genl Com March 24

The last letter from Place at Birmingham read Div 8 Southern District. Are of opinion that the Society should be divided into tythings & the members should belong & attend the Divisions in the tythings nearest their Place of residence

(The Reporter of the Ex Com said that their was an article in the next constitution to that effect.)

Div 11. SD. are of opinion that the weekly allowance to the Country deputies should be refer'd to the Divisions   (*negatived*)

Div 54. N D are of opinion that portraits of distinguished patriots should be given in the Magazine   (*negatived*)

Ashly informd the Com That Place had arrived from Birmingham at 3 oClock this Day but having travell'd all night he did not think he would be able to attend the Com   he had brought two letters from Jones & Binns with copies of their warrent which he would read   The letters contain'd a wish that the Society would not drop the sending of Deputies to the Country on account of their arrest,[51] they wish'd after their enlagement which would certainly be on Thursday they might be

51 Although no further deputies were sent to the country, the Society did not immediately abandon the plan to send them. In a letter written in April, the LCS described the 'Business about which the Society is now employ'd'; first was 'organizing the Country by Means of sending Deputies', second was 'preparing a Magazine', and third was supplying the country with books cheaply (to United Corresponding Society of Rochester, written before 22 April, misdated 29 April 1796, Add MSS 27815, fos. 51–2v). Place, however, recalled that after the arrest and bailing of the Birmingham deputies, 'all were now convinced of the folly which had been committed [originally: 'the folly we had committed'], but the society were not at all dissatisfied . . . the members appeared to be satisfied because it was an act of their own', i.e. the divisions had voted almost unanimously to send deputies (Add MSS 27808, fo. 73).

permitted to stay a fortnight at Birmingham that the Society might be compleatly organized. Place here came into the Com. Room & read a long account of his transactions at Birmingham. The Ex Com who were in Room retired.
North District Com. Are of opinion that another week should be allow'd to obtain the returns on the referrd motion it being by no means compleat   (negatived)
On the returns of the Refer'd motion for electing one deputy to the Genl Com for evr'y 3 in the District – Coms then appear'd 369 in the affirmative 54 in the negative.
East District Com. Motion from. That in looking over the Treasurs account for the month of Decr last there appear'd £25 unaccounted for resolved the same be accounted for immediately
One of the Deputies of the above Com said that after the above motion was sent the had discoverd that elven Pounds of the above sum was accounted for & there only remain'd £14 collected at Thelwalls Door. Ashley said that Thelwall had expended the money & had not as yet sent in the account. /Orderd that Thelwall be waited on & requested to make out & send in his account as soon as possble
The Ex Com who had retired, now return'd & informd the Com they had had a sittings the substance of which their reporter would report.

Ex Com March 24.

Read two letters from Jones & Binns & Birmingham   ordered that 100 copies together with the warrents of their Commitment be printed immediately for the use of the Divisions & that they likewise be published in the Telegraph.

Genl Com.

Took into consideration the six articles of the new constitution laid before them by the Ex Com. After some dispute they were all agreed to. The first contention was about the name of the Society, when it was proposed that the words "Equal Representation", should be introduced before "Universal Suffrage". This being thought a question of importance The Ex Com were allow'd to speak. Fenwick contended "that Universal Suffrage contain'd Equal representation in the detail, That the Society could not conten'd openly for equal representation it being contrary to law & would be subverting the Constitution." Bone contended on the opposite side. "He said then the Duke of Richmonds letter went to subvert the Constitution," that the Society was associated certainly to subvert the Constitution or some of its parts. that it certainly was his inten-

tion. A protest was immediately drawn up against Bones words by Fenwick & sign'd by Fenwick, Nicholls, Parkinson, Powell & Place. Bone at the repeated request of the Com at last explaind that he meant if the Duke of Richmonds letter went to the overthrow of the Constitution he certainly went as far as that. This not being thought sufficient he at last finding that the Com thought he had utterd dangerous words he said he meant what the Crown Lawyers meant by the overthrow of the Constitution.   (The amendement was negatived)

There was some debate about dividing the town into tythings   (which at last was carred)

328. Report from spy Powell: LCS Division 90, 19 April 1796[52]

Source: PC 1/23/A38

Div 90 North district L C S. April 19th. 1796
Report Genl Com 14th. Apil
13 New members   822 present in the Divisions £5 . 9 . 6 Quarterge 5/7 Smiths &ca Sub 4s 11d Downey 2s 9d Birmingham Deputies
Received a letter from Sub Secretary Bone requesting the Societys assistance in the Circulation of a Weekly Publication call'd the Politician
(refd to the attention of the District Commites and Divisions)
Moved & carried that the mony collected for Smith, Higgins & Le Maitre be delivr'd weekly to their famillies.
Div 8. 84 & 86. Are of opinion the five half sheets should be given in the Magazine instead of six   (Negatived)
Div 12. 19. & 24 Are of opinion that the present disorganisd state of the Society proceeds from the unaccountable delay in the persons deputed to draw up the new Constitution.   (Refd to Ex Com)

Report of the Ex Com
Sittings Apil 11

The Comitte could not proceed to business on account of the absense of two of its members who were employd in preparing & regulating letters for the Magazine

Sittings April 13

J Binns elected reporter. *Read a letter from Truro in Cornwall giving an account of riots*

52 Description: 'Div 90 / LCS / 19 April 1796'.

by the Tinners at that place.[53] *A member deputed to answer it.*

The Committe came to the following resolutions respecting the Collecting Subscriptions to defray the expence of the prosecution of the Birmingham deputies
1st. That all persons willing to Collect Subscriptions should give in their place of abode to the Secretary
2dly That all such persons should have books given to them with the resolution of the Com authorizing them to receive Subscriptions printed on the first page
3dly That all monies collected should be deliverd to the Treasurer of the Society evry week
4th That no person collecting Subscription shall detain money in their hand more than one month on any account whatever
An Answer to the letter from Edinburgh read aproved & ordered to be sent[54]

53 This letter of 28 March and another of 6 April described the attack of 3000 desperate tinners upon Truro and the fear that they would return with 20,000 to 30,000 armed men. When some Truro reformers made friendly overtures, the tinners threatened to kill them (Add MSS 27815, fos. 39–42v).
54 Rightly labelled 'Letter of Apology to Edinborough', this was a reply to a letter (now lost) received in Dec. 1795. The LCS explained that 'the citizen who was deputed to answer the letter was prevented from executing the office by peculiar & temporary avocations; & the Ex. Com . . . . being acquainted with the fact deputed another Citizen for that duty'. A cancelled version of this explanation suggests some hostility in the executive committee: 'they [the executive committee] applied to him repeatedly for them and were constantly assured that they should be ready in a few days. Wearied by a repeated series of disappointments, they at length demanded your letter from him; he most faithfully promised to lay it before them at an early day which he named, but then like all his former promises he failed to perform. Resolved to be no longer trifled with, they immediately appointed another Citizn to prepare them.' (Since the second citizen was deputed on 4 March to prepare an answer 'immediately' but did not produce the answer until 13 April – almost six weeks later – the executive committee evidently had at least two sluggish members.) The body of the rest of the letter to Edinburgh contains lofty reform sentiments ('We can taste no pleasure, so exquisite as that of furthering the common cause in which we are embarked . . . . The all pervading sun of truth is dispelling mists of calumny & falsehood', etc.) and a description of the new organization of the LCS into divisions, district committees, general committee and executive committee. On another sheet, in another hand, is an interpolation reply-

A letter from Thelwall received & read with an account of monies collected by him for Smith &co & for printing the Decleration of the principles of the Society in which he brings the Socety in debt to him of upwards of £4 . . – . . –
(*refd to the Genl Com*)
There[55] is every reason to believe that the Society will advertise for a general public meeting of its members to be held in some open Spot near London about June next – they will advertise it, as for a petition for a peace, or will give notice to the Magistrates according to the provisions of the act, to which they say they mean to adhere

329. Report from spy Powell: LCS Division 15, 21 April 1796[56]

Source: PC 1/23/A38

Div 15 L C S
Genl Com 21. April 1796

18 New members. 732 present. 5.13. – Quarterage 10s 7d. Birmingham deputies Subscription. 5s 8d Smiths Do 1s 6d Downeys

Report of Ex Com Sittings April 15th

Read an Address to the people of Scotland[57]

ing to the assertion that the Edinburgh society 'dare not at present exist'. The recipient of the letter is urged to 'find a Companion to second your endeavours in bringing your Neighbours back to their Duty' (Add MSS 27815, fos. 134–6v; at the end of this letter is the note: 'Ashley to make a fair Copy').
55 This last sentence is on another folio of the paper and is in another hand.
56 Powell's description: 'Div 15 LCS / Sittings April 25th. 1796'. Government description: 'London Correspondg Society Rx 29th, April'.
57 This address was also motivated by the Edinburgh letter reporting the decline or disappearance of reform societies in Scotland. In the address the LCS 'call upon the Scotch Nation to rally round their Standard & assist them in the great work of restoring our Constitution to its original purity. So vast & arduous a task cannot be performed by any single Society . . . . Let not any Man say to himself, "Wherefore need I become a member of these political Societies? I can add but little to their strength." This is the most dangerous error, the most fatal delusion into which you can fall.' The LCS then remind the Scotch Nation of their 'illustrious Ancestors' and their 'tender Infants . . . demand[ing] their Birthrights'. The 'Scotch Nation' are then warned against two extremes: 1. those who argue that a change of ministers would be a sufficient remedy; 2. 'those who wod hurry you into intemperance & violence'. The address then describes the blessings resulting from a radical

aproved & ordered to be sent with the Edinburgh letter

Read an Address to the persons at Birmingham
who voluntaraly offerd themselves for bail for
the Birmingham deputies   approved and
ordered six copies to be made immediately &
sent with the publications of the Society to be
distributed at Birmingham

Read six more Articles of the new Constitution & ordered them to laid before the Genl
Com at their next sittings.

The person deputed to wait on Citizen Galloway to demand the papers of the Society
which he had in his hands informd the Com
that he had seen Galloway, & had appointed
a day when the papers were to be deliver'd up.

Sittings March 19th

Read an answer to the letter from Truro,
amended approved and ordered to be sent.

Read a letter from Helstone giving an account
of some persons there who wish'd to form a
Society there & requested instructions of the
L. C S how they were to proceed, they likewise wanted the regulations & publications of
the Society.

Read a letter from Gravesend giving an account
of some persons at that place who had been
very industrious in calumniating the London
Corresponding Society & its principle members. A member deputed to prepare an answer
immediately

Genl Com April 21st.

Took in consideration a motion that the Magazine should consist of five half sheets instead
of six.

                    Carried in favor of the latter

Took into consideration several Motions for
calling a General Meeting of the Society. The
Come. after the most mature deliberation are
of opinion That the *Society could not legally
call a meeting for any of the purposes set
forth in the motions & that such meeting
would be both imprudent & improper at the
present time*, but this committe when such
time should come that such meeting would be
proper & any purpose thought off for which
they could legally & constitutionally meet,

reform in the representation: the labourer in his
'humble thatch' eating 'good and wholesome
food; his children well cloathed, well fed, & well
instructed . . . the murdering sword of war'
sheathed. Finally, the Scotch Nation are reminded and exhorted: 'Your only hope is in yourselves . . . . Form yourselves therefore into
societies; let there not be a village without one'
(Add MSS 27815, fos. 43–4v).

will be happy to lend all their assistance to
bring about so desirable a measure

Six Articles of the new constitution laid before
this Com by the Ex Com, deferred the consideration them to the next sittings on Account
of the lateness of the hour.

The new numbering of the Divisions were
delivered to the Reporters of the District Coms
and ordered to be carried into effect immediately. Eeach district is to begin with No 1.

330. Report from spy Powell: LCS Division 15, Northern District, 2 May 1796[58]

Source: PC 1/23/A38

Div 15. N D May 2d. 1796

Report of Genl Com April 28th. 1796

6 New members 626 present £4 . – 6 Quarterage Smiths ⟨&c⟩ Sub 7s 6d. Birmingham deputies £1 . . 19 . . 6.

12 Articles of the new constitution were taken
into consideration approved off and ordered
to be laid before the divisions immediately
there Report to be made in a fortnight

Report of Ex Com 25 April 1796

There not sufficient members attending no
business was done

Sittings 27th April 1796

Read an answer to the letter from Gravesend
approvd and ordered to be sent.

Read a letter from Rochester respecting
money raised for Country deputies[59]   a
member ordered to prepare an answer immediately.

58 Powell's description: 'Div 15. N D. / May 2d.
  1796'.

59 In an earlier letter (now lost) the United Corresponding Society of Rochester must have asked
  about dissension within the LCS, especially over
  the treatment of the division at Waltham Abbey.
  In a long reply, the LCS explained (1) the events
  at Waltham Abbey and the reasons why the LCS
  decided not to act (see p. 341, n. 14), and (2) the
  current business of the society (see p. 351, n. 51).
  In a postscript they mentioned having had no
  report or subscription from Rochester, but having
  received a parcel containing copies of the *Politician*, which they conjectured came from
  Rochester (draft, misdated 29 April 1796, Add
  MSS 27815, fos. 51–2v). Rochester replied to the
  postscript and accused their secretary, Citizen
  Mascall, of duplicity in separating the money
  from the parcel (John Smallfield to [Ashley],
  letter addressed to Miss Willson, Mr Franzen,
  shoemaker, Holborn Hill, 22 April 1796, ibid.,
  fos. 45–6v).

Read a draught of a letter to the Country Societies requesting them to raise Subscriptions to pay the expences of the Trials of the Birmingham Deputies[60] approved and ordered one hundred copies to be printed and sent off to the Country Societies immediately Read a letter from the Society at Manchester. A member deputed to prepare an answer immediately[61]

60 After requesting money for the trials, expected to take place 'speedily', the letter explained the LCS motives for sending the deputies: believing that the only way to combat the 'enemies of the people' was enlightening the mass of the people, and expecting that some of the 'country brethren' would be deterred by fear or by misrepresentation of the situation, the LCS sent its deputies to Portsmouth and Rochester. The 'social state' of the country, the letter continued, was conducive to enslavement. All that remains 'to avert the force which would subjugate the few that are true to themselves and to human nature' is 'the unextinguished influence of laws conceived in better times'. Consequently, ministers are tempted 'to corrupt the laws in their source by legislation and in their current by a wicked administration of them. . . . And if they do make the attempt and succeed, . . . the nation will be placed in an alternative from which the bold may shrink, and in which the feeble will be utterly lost' (Ashley to 'the Societies in Great Britain in correspondence with the London Corresponding Society', May [date left blank], 1796, Place Collection, vol. 37, fos. 231-2; in the table of contents of this volume Place gives the date as 31 May, but copies were being sent much earlier in May).
61 The Manchester Society reported that they had printed their regulations, as the LCS had instructed them to do and that these regulations were almost identical with the LCS articles. To the LCS suggestion (made in a previous letter) of sending them a deputy, they replied by asking the LCS to wait until they wrote again when they were better known (Jonathan Ellison, secretary, to [Ashley], addressed to Mrs Mary Goodyear at Mr Jefferson Taylor's, Old North St, Red Lion Sq., received 26 April 1796, Add MSS 27815, fos. 49-50v). In reply the LCS thanked them for their regulations, expressed pleasure at hearing of the formation of a new society to diffuse political knowledge and urged them to be bold but temperate. In a large manufacturing town like Manchester, where artisans and mechanics cannot afford an education for their children, the ignorance of the masses 'lays them open to the insidious attempts of men who value not the happiness of the human race'. The Manchester reformers must enlighten the people by pointing out the 'lasting benefits' of a reformation of Parliament on the principle of universal suffrage and annual Parliaments (draft, Ashley to Manchester, 6 May 1796, ibid., fos. 57-7v).

Read an answer to the letter from Illstone approved and ordered to be sent.[62]

The 12 Articles of the new constitution were read in the division last evening by the Delegate there appeard very little variation from those the old Constitution except one article which was. That the divisions should meet at 8 oClock & as soon as the Chairman is elected he should appoint a door keeper whose business is to take care that not more than 49 persons are admitted into the room

331. Report from spy Powell: LCS Division 15, Northern District, 5 May 1796[63]

Source: PC 1/23/A38

Genl Com 5th May 1796

5 New members   669 present £2 . . 16 . . 9 Quarterage 7s 6d Smiths ⟨&c⟩ Sub 4/6 Downey 12s 4d Birmingham Deputies 8s 6d by Books for do

Report Ex Com May 2

Received a letter from Citizen Corne of Birmingham acknowledging the receipt of our letter of thanks for his becoming bail for Jones & Binns at Birmingham[64]
Received a letter from Dundee a member deputed to prepare an answer immediately
A member deputed to draw up a letter to enclose the circular one to the country Societies respecting Jones & Binns Subscription
A member deputed to draw up a letter to be sent to all the members of the House of Commons who were active in opposing the Treason & Sedition Bills.
Resolved that the Treasurer of the Society do attend the next Sittings of the Committe to lay before it a general state of the finances of the Society.

62 This answer is lost. It replied to a letter of 30 April asserting that it was impossible to start a reform society in a small town like Helston (in Cornwall) and suggesting that the LCS send a deputy to the miners of Cornwall (Add MSS 27815, fos. 53-4v).
63 Powell's description: 'Div 15. N D. L C S / Monday May 9. 1796'.
64 He added that the uprightness of Binn's and Jones's behaviour invited confidence in the LCS and in everyone associated with Binns and Jones (E. Corn to Ashley, 24 April 1796, Add MSS 27815, fos. 47-8).

Resolved that all members of the Society who have books for collecting subscriptions for the Birmingham Deputies do pay in the money they collect weekly. Members of the Eastern District to pay in to Citizen Morgan of Grubb Street. Southern to Bone of Weston Street Southwark. Northern to Ashly Holborn & Western to Powell of Goodge Street.

Sittings May 4th.

A member produced an answer to the letter from Dundee approved and ordered to be sent
Received and read a letter from Hereford with Three Guineas collected there by Subscription to be applied to the general purposes of the Society   a member deputed to prepare an answer immediately[65]
The Treasurer attended this sittings according to summons when on examination of his accounts there appear'd to be in his hands after all debts were paid £3 . . 17 . . 4.
A member deputed to wait on Citn Galloway the late Sub Secty to demand all the papers of the Society that were in his hands he having neglected to attend for that purpose on day that had been appointed
Took in consideration a plan for the more general distribution of Political Phampletts the heads of which are, That all the country Societies do raise a fund for that purpose; That they do immediately transmit to the Secretary of this Society. The easiest, cheapest, and safest mode of conveyance of parcels to their respective Secretarys or persons employd by them to receive said parcels
Deputed two members to wait on Citizen Rhynd to enquire into the reasons why he could not print the Magazine by the 1st of June & to take away the copy he had in his hands if they should think it expedient. Resolved that this Com do hold an extra sittings tomorrow Thursday morning to hear their report.

Extra Sittings Thursday Morn May 5.

The members deputed to wait on Rhynd reported that they had seen him, that he had been very dangerously ill & was but now recovering. That he stated as he wish'd to print the Magazine so as to do credit to the Society he would not trust the superintendance to any other person. That he had ordered a new type to be used only for the work but that the letter Founder had been unfortunately burnt out, that if the Society insisted on its being printed by the 1st of June he must give it up.
The Com came to the resolution (as there appered no neglect on the part of Rhynd & that the delay of a month would be sufficiently recompensed by a new type) that the Magazine be not published 'till the 1st of July next & that a letter be immediately drawn up to the divisions & the society at large stating the reasons of the delay.

Genl Com.

Thelwall, Ham & Ridley elected to the Ex Com in the Room of Bone & Parkinson resign'd & Moore superceeded
Moved & carred that all the papers in the hands of Rhynd the Printer be withdrawn from him & given to another printer. On the report of the Sittings of the Ex Com of this morning being read the above motion was suppressed.
Resolved that this Com do hold an Extra Sittings on Saturday next to take into consideration all the motions of this evening & all the refer'd ones of some time past.
Place elected Sub Secty[66] in the room of Bone resign'd.
NB The reason why Bone has resignd his situation as Suby Secy & in the Ex Com is on account of the Magazine he having violantly opposed it thinking it would injure a publication of his calld the Politician.

65 The letter from the Hereford Philanthropic Society included the names of the seventeen contributors and the sum each contributed; it also deplored the 'grumbling Egotists' who declaim against corruption but are backward in rewarding good principles (Charles Powis to Ashley, 2 May 1796, Add MSS 27815, fo. 55). In reply, the LCS thanked them for the 'Civic gift', enclosed copies of the printed letter requesting contributions, and announced (incorrectly) that Binns and Jones would be tried at the next Warwick assizes. 'If Ministers can obtain a Verdict in the present case, the most powerful & effectual means of rousing our brethren to vigilence in the cause of reform will be taken from us' (draft, n.d., ibid., fos. 56–6v).

66 Place's description of this election: 'The quantity of business in the London Corresponding Society had increased greatly and was fast getting into arrears, and this induced me after much solicitation to take the office of assistant secretary, for the quarter from Lady day to Midsummer day, and to take the quarters salary £3 2s 6d. This money I took with great reluctance, I had done business which if fairly remunerated would have not been overpaid even to a poor man like me with ten times the sum. Had I not been very poor I should have refused the money, as it was I often felt regret at having taken it' (*Autobiography*, pp. 150–1). The earlier draft of this passage adds that the secretary and assistant secretary were 'most badly paid' (Add MSS 27808, fo. 75).

332. Resolution: LCS Division 4, Western District, 23 May 1796[67]

Source: Add MSS 27815, fos. 59-9v

London Correspondind Society
Western District Division 4

May 23 1796

RESOLVED That this Division having duly considered the proposal of the General Committee respecting a GENERAL MEETING are of opininion that General Public Meetings such as we have formerly held would at this time be attended with such DANGER, EXPENCE and INCONVENIENCY as we doubt whether the probable benefit arising from such meeting could compensate

That was an *extraordinary meeting* to be called on each separate Division which every Citizen should be *generally* summoned to attend and where such resolutions addresses and declarations, as were prepared by the executive committee should be generally discussed and recieve the *general* sanction of this society; it would answer every purpose and be subject to none of the dangers attending a general public meeting

That the last general meetings did actually consist of 4 Divisions since all the proceedings were seperately discussed at each Tribune and we concieve that if we meet in 4 or 40 or a hundred Divisions the effect will be the same

That we have had public meeting sufficient to convince an impartial public of our numbers unanimity and love of Order which character we might lose by risking a general meeting in these critical times

That However the Prudence and good conduct of our members might be depended on, an illegal and hireling mob might mix in our assembly and commit riots and perhaps massacres in the name of the London Corresponding Society for which our best members might be persecuted and despotic laws might be made to destroy the little liberty Englishmen have left

That great part of a days attendance at a public meeting with the expence of refreshments a distance from home is a tax on the labours of poorer Citizens that we should not impose without evident necessity

for it   23   John Arnold President
against 0   Jas Hughes Secretary

67 Description: 'Motion for a General Meeting /
    Adjourned till after Jones & Binns are tried'.

333. Report from spy Powell: LCS Northern Division Committee, 24 June 1796[68]

Source: PC 1/23/A38

Northern District Comitte June 24th. 1796

Report of the Genl Com June 23

9 New members   459 present 15s/ Quarterage 9s/-d Country Deputies £2 .. 17 . 9 by Subscription Books

Lemaitre was requested to bring forward his charges together with his witnesses against the persons he wishes to be expell'd the Society on Thursday next.

Resolved that no members be entitled to the Magazine 'till they have paid up their arears of Quarterage

Moved that no member should have more than one Magazine at /4½d   (*negatived*)

Report of the Ex Com 20 June 1796[69]

Received a letter from Manchester a member deputed to prepare an answer immediately[70]
A member deputed to define, prepare, and

68 Powell's description: 'Northern District Com
    L C S / June 25. 1796'.
69 On the cover of the letter read at this meeting of
    the executive committee are three lines of notes,
    presumably minutes of the meeting: A[bsent].
    – Binns – Thlwll – Ridley/ Place to answer this
    letter / Fenwick shall Draw up the Pstng Bill'
    (Add MSS 27815, fo. 61).
70 From the LCS letter received on 17 May, the
    Manchester Corresponding Society concluded
    that an earlier letter to the LCS had not been
    received. They reported that their society was
    weak but increasing and that they would support
    the Birmingham deputies as soon as their circum-
    stances permitted (John Bradbury, secretary, to
    [Ashley], 11 June 1796, Add MSS 27815, fos.
    60-1). At the end of the letter is a draft of a
    reply in Place's hand. Place explained that the
    previous letter from Manchester had been re-
    ceived and answered, that a member had been
    deputed to send a copy of this letter but had
    been unable to find it, and that the LCS would
    like orders for their magazine, a prospectus of
    which he enclosed (fo. 60v). The mislaid letter
    was found and its contents incorporated (and
    polished) in the letter approved by the executive
    committee on 22 June. The only explanation
    the LCS could suggest for Manchester's not re-
    ceiving the letter of 6 May (here identified as
    that of 'the 10th Ult') was 'the neglect of the
    person who was charged with putting it into the
    post office'. The LCS also stated that they 'shall
    be happy to receve your remittance when con-
    venient' (June 1796, ibid., fos. 62-2v).

draw up the duties of the publisher of the Magazine.

June 22d.

Present Ashly, Place, & Binns. Receivd a letter from Rochester. a member deputed to prepare an an answer immediately.[71]
A member produced the answer to the letter from Manchester approved & ordered to be sent.
Resolved that all letters received by the Society be read in the Genl Com within one fortnight of the receipt of the same.

Adjourned

334. Report from spy Powell: LCS Northern District Committee, 31 June (sic) 1796[72]

Source: PC 1/23/A38

Northern District Com June 31. 1796
Genl Com June 30th

Moved that the Com do proceed to business at ½ past 8 and if any member comes in before

the deputations are appointed he shall [be] allow'd to take the report but not after
(carried)
Bussell[73] & Hodges elected to the Executive Com, Ashley & Place reelected Secty & Assistant Secty.
Div 22 S. D. Resolved that the thanks of this Society be given to J H Tooke & C J Fox for their conduct during the Poll
Div 36 Resolved that the Com ought not decide on Smiths Higgins & Le Maitre's case but that one member should be chosen from each division to try the same   (carried)
Moved that it be buried in oblivion
(negatived)
Moved that it be discust on Wednesday next
(carried)
Moved that the divisions who are concerned in the above case shall not sit in judgement but send a new delegate for that purpose.
(ordered)
Motion made that the Chairmen be chosen next Wednesday evening by ballot & that they proceed to business at ½ past 8 oClock
(carried)

Report of the Ex Com June 29th

Absent Place Rawlings Hasleden & Hardy.
Ordered 4 Advertisements for the Magazine one in the Times Morng Chronicle; Telegraph & Courier. deputed a member to draw up the same
Received a letter from Coventry,[74] deputed a member to answer it.
Received a letter from Melbourn Derby,[75] Deputed a member to answer it

71 The letter from Rochester announced the 'total annihilation' of the society, attributable to the disadvantages of the place, the preponderance of enemies to reform, the malicious report (about the LCS's treatment of the Waltham Abbey division), and the absconding of 'that Villain Jno. Mascall' with part of the society's books and all of its money, including money subscribed for Jones. The author, John Smallfield, promised to collect for the defence of Binns and Jones and to get subscribers for the magazine (to Ashley, 19 June 1796, Add MSS 27815, fos. 66–7). The LCS replied in a self-pitying tone: it was 'with more pain than surprise' that they read of the annihilation of the Rochester society. 'We were not surprized because we have lately witnessed so much of the weakness of Men who after promising to make rapid advances in the Cause have deserted on meeting the first difficulty that we now [rely] very little upon promises of Fidelity.' It is 'lammentable' that the cause 'should be obliged to rely upon such effeminate Beings'. The LCS sternly rejected Smallfield's explanations for the collapse of the Rochester society: the large number of the enemy should be an argument for redoubling vigour rather than repressing reform spirit; the 'malicious Report' (about Waltham Abbey) should not have influenced any member until he had refuted the LCS explanation; as for Mascall's villainy, 'it [is] a malancholy thing that one Traitor should be able to ruin a whole Society' (to Smallfield, n.d., ibid., fo. 58v).
72 Powell's description: 'Report / N D Com / June 31 (sic) 1796'; in another hand: 'Rx 5. July'.

73 Probably Russell.
74 The Coventry reformers received the prospectus for the magazine and the printed letter soliciting contributions for Binns and Jones. Since they had to subscribe for three men maliciously prosecuted by the mayor of Coventry they could not do much on behalf of Binns and Jones; but early next month they would send two guineas. They ordered forty copies of the magazine and six copies each of cheap editions of Paine's *Age of Reason* and *Decline and Fall of the English System of Finance* (Thomas Prosser to Ashley, 26 June 1796, Add MSS 27815, fos. 69–70v).
75 After receiving the LCS letter soliciting subscriptions, the 'Patriots of Melbourne' made a small collection. Since their letters to the LCS had been either stopped by the tools of ministers or ignored by the LCS, they were reluctant to send the money. They therefore requested to know whether their letters had been received and, if not, how they might send the money (James Mills to Ashley, 23 June 1796, Add MSS 27815, fos. 68–8v). The draft of the answer is lost, but the next letter from Melbourne acknowledged the LCS letter of the 27th).

Received a letter from Chevenning deputed a member to answer it.
The letter from Chevening complains they have no report.
That from Coventry concerns the Subscription.
That from Melbourn concerns the Magazine[76] & some letters that have miscarried. *adjournd*

Genl Com.

The return'd question on the Constitution was carried by a great Majority.
Moved & carried that only one Secty be obldged to attend the Ex Com at a time.
Moved & carried that all letters received from the country be sowed up in a book
Moved & carri'd that a short address be published at the head of the new regulations

Secty & Treasurers Report

9 New members 459. Present 403 paid for the Magazine.

Money received for the Mag. -	£10.. 9.. 8
Arears of Quarterage - - -	-.. 5.. -
For Deputies - - - - -	-.. 1.. 1
Subscription Books - - - -	2.. 8.. 11
Total of money received for -	18.. 11.. 8
Deputies	
	£21.. 1.. 5

Genl.[77]   North. Thelw.
  Westn. Rawl (Tent) Brewr St
    Long Acre
  Southern – Hasseldon paperstainer
    Walworth
  Eastern – an old Chapel – Brick
    Lane Spital Fields

335. Activities of the LCS from July to October 1796; support of Binns and Jones; publication of the *Moral and Political Magazine*

Sources: as text and notes

[Information about the LCS's activities during July, August, September and October 1796 – when Powell was not sending reports to government – is derived chiefly from the correspondence to and from the Society. For this four-month period there remain only two sets of minutes, one of them an investigation into events of 1793–4. The

events of the present which drew most heavily on the Society's energies were: (a) the forthcoming trials of Binns and Jones, which necessitated collecting money for their defence; and (b) the inauguration of an ambitious monthly periodical, *The Moral and Political Magazine of the London Corresponding Society*, the first number of which was issued early in July.

The support of Binns and Jones

A major activity of the LCS during this period was corresponding with societies which had contributed or which might contribute money for the defence of Binns and Jones at their trials. In response to a circular letter of 6 May (copies of which were sometimes sent by one country society to another) the LCS received one or more contributions from Exeter (£5 5s & £5 5s), Gosport (£4 11s 6d), Hereford ('a mite'), Manchester (£30), Melbourne (£4 4s), Norwich (£13), Perth and Portsmouth (£6).[78] The treasurer's reports for these months show contributions also from Coventry (£2 2s), Edinburgh (£7 19s), Gravesend (£3 3s), Helston (£3 9s).[79]
When the LCS heard of other towns or other societies supporting reform, they wrote them asking for money. When the Manchester contributors said that the reformers of Halifax were not contributing because they believed the Whigs would support Binns and Jones, the LCS immediately wrote to Halifax soliciting a contribution and stating that they had made no appeal to the Whig Club.[80] When the Society learned that Yarmouth citizens had befriended Thelwall (attacked at a lecture there), they wrote to Norwich and asked for the names of Yarmouth reformers who might contribute.[81] After they learned the existence of the Glasgow Reading Society, the LCS wrote to them for money.[82] When

76 There was no mention of the magazine in the letter. Powell has confused the two letters from Coventry and Melbourne.
77 These last four lines are in another hand.

78 Letters, all from Add MSS 27815, fos. 71–106v.
79 Place Collection, vol. 37, fos. 309, 312, 313, 315. Two later contributions complete the list of subscriptions from country correspondents: in Nov. £13 from Paisley, and in Dec. £3 3s from Stirling (ibid., fos. 316–17).
80 Letters, both in Add MSS 27815; John Bradbury to Ashley, 30 June 1796, fos. 73–3v; LCS to Halifax, 4 July 1796, fos. 78–81v.
81 Letters, both in Add MSS 27815; John [last name obliterated] to Ashley, 6 Sept. 1796, fos. 122–2v; LCS to Norwich, n.d., fos. 132–3.
82 LCS to 'Citizens of the Glasgow Reading Society', [12 Aug. 1796], Add MSS 27815, fos. 16–17v.

Wolverhampton 'patriots' wrote of possible assistance from citizens of Coseley and Sedgley, the Society immediately wrote to those towns.[83] There is no record that any of these groups responded.

At the end of June the total collected, according to the treasurer, was £18 11s 8d. But three days later the LCS announced that they had collected £60;[84] and on 16 July they reported a total of £90 collected.[85] The printed treasurer's reports for July to October record the following amounts collected each month:

	£	s	d
April	2	18	0
May	3	17	7¼
June	27	8	4
July	80	17	8
August	30	10	5
Sept.	6	6	0
Oct.	2	2	0

LCS total £154 0 2½ (should be 2¼)

Expecting that Binns and Jones would be tried at the Warwick assizes during the last week of July, the LCS set about retaining counsel and a solicitor for them. Erskine was approached, but he demanded a fee of 1200 guineas.[86] By 3 July they had retained counsel and by the 15th a solicitor.[87]

Binns and Jones left London for Birmingham on 9 July.[88] A few days later Binns, who handled the money for their expenses, wrote frantically to the executive committee: 'I have waited with anxiety to hear from you. I have not a Guinea to bring a Witness, to fee Counsel or give Mr Jones. You must feel my situation I leave Birmingham on Tuesday. I Entreat you will Remitt directly.'[89]

A certain hysteria might have been expected: Binns and Jones had not seen copies of their indictments, did not know

what seditious words they were alleged to have spoken, and did not know what witnesses would testify against them. Twelve hours before the case came up, they finally received this information (but not copies of the indictments). Accordingly, on 25 July, when they were brought to trial, they heard their indictments read, they pleaded not guilty, and their counsel traversed the indictment – i.e. postponed the trial. At that time the counsel for the crown by *certiori* moved the case into the court of the the King's Bench.[90] That manoeuvre enabled government to have the case tried by a special jury. Binns and Jones did not finally receive copies of their indictments until some time after 2 August. At the same assizes where the indictments were traversed, a grand jury refused to indict Binns and Jones for lecturing to a crowd of more than fifty.[91] The LCS told correspondents that the trial for seditious words would be heard in London, but a footnote to the August *MPM* (published early in September) stated that the trials would take place at the next Warwick sessions.[92]

The LCS ordered Binns and Jones to be back in London on 8 August to give an account of their expenses. On the 2nd, Jones wrote that Binns would give the account of their expenses, for he (Jones) planned to spend time with private friends and relations in Oxford.[93] Binns evidently did not appear before the executive committee with his account on 8 August, for the committee, on the 13th, ordered him to attend the next sitting. Although the LCS officially hoped for a 'happy outcome' of the trials, Binns knew he could not count on an acquittal (previous sedition trials generally resulted in convictions). Having decided to spend the interval before his trial in Ireland, he left England shortly after 17 August. On that date he wrote an open letter to the members of the LCS explaining his motives for joining the Society.[94]

83 Letters, in Add MSS 27815; John Bates Jr of Wolverhampton to 'Mr Johnson' of London, 31 July 1796, fos. 108–9; LCS to Wolverhampton, 6 Aug. 1796, fos. 114–4v; LCS to Coseley and Sedgley, n.d., fos. 110–10v.
84 Letter to Norwich, 3 July 1796.
85 Letter to Manchester, 16 July 1796.
86 ibid.
87 Letters, in Add MSS 27815; to Norwich, 3 July 1796; to Portsmouth, 15 July 1796. Samuel Romilly acted as counsel at Binns's trial.
88 *Telegraph*, 9 July 1796, p. 2.
89 n.d., Add MSS 27815, fos. 148–9v. The Tuesday mentioned was probably 19 July.

90 Letters, in Add MSS 27815; to Gosport, 31 July 1796; to Melbourne, 8 Aug. 1796, fos. 117–17v.
91 Letters; to Gosport, 31 July 1796; to Wolverhampton, 6 Aug. 1796.
92 p. 120. The trials were at Warwick, but not at the next quarter sessions. Jones was tried and convicted on 9 April 1797. Because there were not enough special jurors for another trial, Binns's case was postponed. On 15 Aug. 1797, he was tried and acquitted.
93 To Ashley, Add MSS 27815, fos. 111–12v.
94 *MPM*, vol. 1 (Aug. 1796), pp. 120–3.

The printed treasurer's reports show that after this period the Society continued to collect small sums for the deputies (between November and the end of March 1797 the total collected was £19 3s 1½d). Unfortunately these financial statements (which are not entirely reliable) do not give a clear picture of the expenditures for the deputies' defence. Most disbursements are listed as being to Binns or to Jones. Two small payments to John Martin (in December 1796 and January 1797) must be for 'stopping the Writs against the Bail' of Binns and Jones.[95] Since there are no records of paying Romilly or his two assistants (Reader and Fletcher) or the solicitor hired in July 1796, they must have been paid from some source not included in the LCS records, or counsel donated their services. The treasurer's reports do indicate what happened to large amounts of the money collected for the defence of the deputies: they were loaned to the Society for other purposes. Of £170 5s 2½d subscribed during 1796, the Society borrowed £92 3s 4½d[96]

The Moral and Political Magazine

The principal debtor to the deputies' fund was *The Moral and Political Magazine of the London Corresponding Society*, a 48 page periodical issued monthly from early July 1796 to June 1797. 'A better contrivance to prevent the society paying its debts could hardly have been devised,' reflected Place.[97] Ironically, the magazine was instituted to increase the Society's funds.[98]

This magazine was also intended to fulfil two interlocking aims of the Society: first, to publish the correspondence; and second, to provide other reformers and reform societies with inexpensive works of enlightenment.

There is no indication when the editor was chosen or who selected the title of the magazine. No editor is named in the magazine or in the minutes. The monthly treasurer's reports list payment only to 'The Editor'. Perhaps the Society preserved anonymity here to protect the editor from arrest if government prosecuted them for seditious words in spite of the Society's efforts to publish nothing actionable.[99] 'The Editor' seems to have been a literary committee responsible for the magazine and receiving payment for it. In December Fenwick offered to edit his part of the magazine gratis for two months. Presumably, then, the other subeditors (only William Williams, Hodgson and Crossfield have been named) were each responsible for one section of the magazine. In August there were five different payments to 'The Editor', two payments of three guineas, one of two guineas, and two of one guinea. This suggests a literary committee of five with varying degrees of responsibility.[100]

The title may have been selected at the last moment, for a June correspondent warned them that their title *The Monthly Magazine* was already being used by Dr Aikens's magazine.[101]

The animosities which developed over the magazine were hinted at even before the first issue was printed, for on 20 June the executive committee appointed a member to draw up the duties of the publisher. This clarification of the publisher's role must have been necessitated by complaints against Ashley who was the publisher as well as the secretary of the Society.

On 1 and 2 July the magazine was advertised in the newspapers. According to this notice, it would cost 6d and contain

A selection of Public Papers. A Review of Books on Morals and Politics. Original Essays on Morals and Politics. Memoirs

95 Treasurer's accounts show Martin received £1 8s 6d in Dec. and £3 5s 10d in Jan. (Place Collection, vol. 37, fo. 317; vol. 38, fo. 187). See executive committee reports for 23 and 30 Dec.

96 They borrowed £6 15s 7½d in May; £19 18s 1d in July; £29 12s 6d in Aug., for a total of £56 6s 2½d. The records do not itemize the loan of £35 17s 2½d during the last four months of 1796. In hopes of removing this deficit, the Society started a subscription for 'Liquidation of Debt', which first appeared on the Oct. treasurer's account. During the last three months of 1796, this fund acquired £22 1s 0½d. In Jan. 1797 a further £2 14s 8½d was collected. This fund was then discontinued or subsumed to another fund which first appeared on the Jan. account, a 'Subscription for Liquidating the Debt due to Deputies'. From the Dec. minutes it appears that not all the money from the first fund was being used to pay back the deputies' fund.

97 Add MSS 27808, fo. 75.

98 Letter to Gosport, 31 July 1796, Add MSS 27815, fos. 105–5v.

99 Letter to Gosport.

100 In November the fund to liquidate the Society's debt received a donation of £6 6s from 'The Editor'; very possibly two or more of the literary committee were returning their monthly salary.

101 Letter, Richard Dinmore and John Lightbody of Norwich to Ashley, 19 June 1796, Add MSS 27815, fos. 64–5.

of Eminent Persons. Strictures on Temporary Subjects, connected with Morals and Politics. Extracts from Foreign and English Publications. A concise account of Foreign and Domestic Transactions. Select Parts of the Correspondence of the Society. A History of the Society. Miscellaneous Subjects. And Poetry.[102]

This first issue consisted of short pieces, many pertinent to France or the Westminster election of June: a letter from G. Baboeuf to the Executive Directory of France (3½ pp.), a proclamation of Buonaparte (1 p.), memoirs of Buonaparte (2½ pp.), the history of affairs in France for the first half of 1796 (6½ pp.), the election advertisements of Tooke and Fox and a speech of Tooke to the electors of Westminster (6 pp.). There is also the first part of a summary–review of Inchbald's *Nature and Art* (7 pp.), selected LCS correspondence (5 pp.), a letter from Thelwall extolling heroic virtues and quoting Glover's *Leonidas* (2 pp.), a letter from Vice Cotis (not a member of the LCS) urging citizens to contribute to imprisoned patriots who have large fines to pay (2 pp.), a letter from William Williams refuting the charge that universal suffrage and annual Parliaments are illegal because not named in the 1688 Bill of Rights (2 pp.), a warning by Thomas Fry against certain tontines being advertised (1 p.), and two poems (1½ pp.). The remaining eleven issues of the magazine also consisted of short pieces – essays, letters, book reviews, political history and poetry.

The printing history shows the brief rise and the sharp decline of the magazine. Three thousand copies of the first issue (June) were printed, 3500 of the next two issues (July, August), 4000 of the fourth issue (September), 3000 of the fifth (October). There is no report of the number printed for the next issue (November). Of the seventh (December), 1000 copies were sold or sent to the country; it is not known how many more were printed. The last issue for which there are figures in the treasurer's report is no. 1 of volume 2 (January 1797), of which only 1750 copies were printed.

The price of the magazine was, as advertised, 6d to strangers, but was only 4½d to members of societies allied to the LCS. To make a profit from the magazine (or even to meet the expenses of it) the LCS would have to sell large numbers of copies to people outside the Society. In hopes of accomplishing this, they sent prospectuses to their correspondents in June, and in letters about the deputies they also solicited orders for the magazine. In July no money came from the country, probably because there had not been time for the country reformers to sell the copies and remit the money. But in August the money for the sale of the magazine in the country amounted to only £5 3s 4d. In September the total was 17s 1½d. In October there were no receipts from outside London.[103] Each month there was a greater disparity between the receipts for the magazine and its expenses. In July the Society took in £31 9s 3d for dues and magazines; the expenses of the magazine alone were at least £25 13s 6d. In August, the receipts for dues and magazines were £43 0s 11½d; expenses of the magazine, £48 6s ½d. In September, receipts, £27 3s 9½d; expenses of magazine, £39 18s 4½d. In October, receipts, £25 11s 6d; expenses of magazine, £39 18s 4½d.[104] Between July and December of 1796 the Society also contracted a debt of £63 13s to Elsee and Cotton, stationers; this must have been for paper for the magazine.[105]

103 Some of the money from other societies may have been lumped in with sales by the publisher. Since Ashley's receipts averaged less than 4½d a copy, he was not bringing the Society a profit from these outside sales.

104 The expenses: the editor received £10 10s each month except August when the payment was £9 9s. The printer was paid £14 9s in July, £13 6s in Aug., £13 14s 6d in Sept., and £3 3s in Oct. In Aug. and Oct. paper for the magazine cost £24 3s and £23 13s. The figures for the expenses of the magazine are derived from the printed monthly treasurer's accounts. These figures do not agree with a printed summary of the Society's debits and credits for July to Dec., issued in Feb. 1797 (printed copy of balance sheet in Place Collection, vol. 37, fos. 319–21, with MSS annotations; copy with explanation of finances in PC 1/41/A138). There the 'General expence of instituting the Magazine' is £10 13s 7d. The second edn of no. 1 cost £6 12s; no. 2 cost £2 18s 11¼d; no. 3, £9 6s 3d; no. 4 £20 4s 11d; no. 5, £14 0s 0½d (since no. 5 was issued early in Nov. some of its expenses may have been paid in Oct.). The total of the first five numbers, according to this summary, is £63 15s 8¾d. The total from the corresponding monthly statements is £142 12s 3½d.

105 Summary of the Society's debits and credits for July–Dec. 1796. During 1797 the LCS paid Elsee and Cotton a total of £77 2s, probably the original £63 13s plus interest. Elsee and Cotton had

102 *Telegraph*, 1 July 1796, p. 1; *MC* 2 July 1796, p. 1.

To retrench expenses, they changed printers, issued fewer copies and eliminated the editor's salary. In December they gave serious thought to discontinuing the magazine. When they finally agreed to end publication in June 1797 the decision must have been made after articles had been selected for the May issue, for it contains works to be continued, including the first part of a short story by the spy James Powell. This last issue contains no mention that this is the final publication.

Other activities of the LCS

Besides the affairs of the Birmingham deputies and the inauguration of the magazine, the correspondence during the summer and early autumn dealt with the activities of other reform groups, often the institution of reform societies allied with the LCS. James Digby reported that he and upwards of forty other men had just instituted the Leicester Corresponding Society, which would follow the rules of the LCS and correspond with them.[106] The LCS replied with copies of their rules and regulations, and with advice to beware of spies and informers, to recall that they associate for 'equal and general representation of the people', to respect the laws and the constitution and to avoid 'Republican conversations & ideas'.[107] Learning from the delegate of Division 33 that the 'friends to Liberty and Reform' at Ludlow wished to start a society on the plan of and in correspondence with the LCS, the Society sent them copies of the addresses and regulations.[108] When Charles Clay discovered that the works of Paine and the arbitrary measures of government had altered the aristocratic sentiments of people at Selby, he hoped to start a reform society there, and he wrote to the LCS asking for copies of their regulations.[109] The LCS replied, rejoicing in the change of sentiment in Selby and congratulating Clay on his patriotism.[110] On 29 August a reform society based on the principles of the LCS was started at Maidstone; a week later they wrote asking the LCS for copies of the regulations and other useful literature.[111]

While these societies were commencing, others were encountering opposition. A Portsmouth publican lost his licence for letting a division meet at his house; he wrote asking if anyone in the Society knew of a house in town to let.[112] From Morton upon Lugg John Mills wrote that 'the Hereford Philanthropic [Society] has long been dispersed'; that a few remained firm in the cause of liberty, and that they hoped to see Ashley in Hereford soon.[113]

to go to law to collect, for on 15 June the Society paid £14 14s for 'Law expences of Elsee and Cotton's account' (*Treasurer's Account for June 1797*, Place Collection, vol. 38, fo. 197). Ashley and Place apparently contracted for the paper for the magazine and were to pay for it with the proceeds of copies Ashley sold in his capacity as publisher of the magazine and secretary of the LCS. (Place recalled his connection with Elsee and Cotton: 'I was in good credit with a paper maker in Thames Street, in consequence of having had some transactions with him on account of the London Corresponding Society and having usually made payments to him for the Secretary': *Autobiography*, p. 159.) By the beginning of December the *MPM* was selling so poorly that Ashley and Place were not taking in enough money to pay for the paper. When they refused to provide more paper, the executive committee voted to indemnify them for the paper for the January issue. The money must not have been forthcoming, for at the end of December Ashley and Place refused to hand over any LCS publications until they were paid for debts contracted on behalf of the Society. Soon there were charges that Ashley was profiting from the *MPM*, and some delegates refused to take the magazine while Ashley was involved with it. The general committee decided to put the LCS publications in Bone's hands as soon as Ashley and Place were paid and had relinquished the publications. Early in 1797 Ashley was replaced by Bone as secretary and publisher. But Ashley did not give Elsee and Cotton the money due them, and they had him arrested. The £14 14s which the Society paid for law expenses in June was to extricate Ashley. The contention over the Elsee and Cotton account continued; in Sept. one division wanted Ashley to refund the £14 14s and another wanted to expel him (according to Place, Ashley was no longer a member and probably was in Paris). Money to clear the debt was given to Powell, who allegedly did not pay it to Elsee and Cotton. Their account was not settled until they received £36 10s on 18 Dec. – one year after the debt was contracted, and six months after the magazine ceased.

106 To Ashley, 30 July 1796, Add MSS 27815, fos. 107-7v.
107 6 Aug. 1796, Add MSS 27815, fos. 115-16v.
108 6 Aug. 1796, Add MSS 27815, fos. 113-13v.
109 To 'Citizen Edwards Junr.', 5 Sept. 1796, Add MSS 27815, fos. 120-1v.
110 20 Sept. 1796, Add MSS 27815, fos. 127-7v.
111 Owen Proben to Thomas Walter, 6 Sept 1796, Add MSS 27815, fos. 125-6v.
112 William Garnett to Ashley, 27 Sept. 1796, Add MSS 27815, fos. 128-9v.
113 To Ashley, 27 July 1796, Add MSS 27815, fos. 97-8v.

In a letter enclosing a contribution for the deputies, Perth reformers must have asked the LCS's attitude towards a petition and towards the Whig Club. In their reply (probably written late in August) the LCS said that, although it was degrading for a great nation to sue for its rights day after day, they had no objection to a petition when Parliament seemed willing to attend to it. The LCS also said that, contrary to rumour, they had not coalesced with the Whig Club. Although they were willing to join any group of men working for a radical reform, they would not sacrifice the principles of annual Parliaments and universal suffrage; the Whig Club would not declare their principles; until they did so, the LCS would not consider them allies.[114]

Finally, a letter from Norwich and the reply to it allude to the 19 August attack on Thelwall at Yarmouth, where he was giving a course of lectures on the laws and revolutions of Rome.[115] According to the letter from Norwich, twenty-two citizens from Yarmouth subscribed £50 each for the prosecution of the mayor and the ruffians who committed the outrage; Erskine was retained as counsel.[116] The LCS response, as noted above, was to wonder whether the liberal citizens of Yarmouth might subscribe to the fund for Binns and Jones. The Norwich reformers also reported that in a recent election for sheriff, the treasurer of their reform society had been narrowly defeated; that the court party, seeing that a 'patriot' would be elected, had supported a man friendly to their society. The LCS saw this as strong 'proof of the declining influence of Administration'.[117]]

336. Minutes: LCS General Committee, 18 August 1796

Source: Add MSS 27815, fos. 118–19

18 Aug. 96 G C Room Citn. Fenwick in the Chair

114 n.d., Add MSS 27815, fos. 130–1v.
115 A contingent of sailors broke into the lecture room, tried to drag Thelwall to the sea, plundered the hall and tore up his books, then decided to break into private houses. When asked for assistance in suppressing this riot, the mayor refused to leave the assembly and without his attendance the military could not act. Hence, his reluctant statement that Lord Spencer might send the soldiers if he pleased was useless (*MPM*, vol. 1 (Aug. 1796), pp. 130–3).
116 John [last name obliterated] to Ashley, 6 Sept. 1796.
117 n.d., Add MSS 27815, fos. 132–3.

Divns. Deputns. to absent Divisions –

3	Jacobs	from Scotland 8£
8	Mc.Norton	from Brrmhm. 13.5
16	Early	
25	"Royal Gorge Lower George St. Sloan Sr Chealsea Ward Dobson Leak & Williams	
26 –	Ward to wright a report	
29	Maxwell to write	
30 –	Mc.Norton to do	
32	Sanders	
34	Gallaway	
37	Oliphant	

Report of Ex C sitting 12 Aug 96 Absent Hodges fst. time Cn. B Binns attended the Comte. pursuent to order and Lay'd before them an account of the expences attending his Journey to Birmhm. orderd that he be alowed the 10£ for his expences resolved that the thanks of this Comte be given to B Bins for his patriotic Conduct during his mition read a Letter from perth Inclosing 8£ for the Depts. & requesting an address to the Inhabitants of that neighbourhood deputed a member to Ansr. it a member produced a draft of a Letter to the Glasgow reeading socy. amended and orderd to be sent a mem: produced a draught of a Letter to Birmhm. amended & orderd to be sent orderd the Carpenters bill to be paid 14£ Extra Sitg Monday Aug 13[118] Absent Jamsn. ft. time Hodges 3rd. time a mem: produced an ansr. to the perth Letter amended and orderd to be sent read a Letter from norwich dept. a member to draw up a Circular Letter to the Cuntry Socis. of the Case of Jons. & Binns Wednesday Aug 17 Absent Jamison 2nd. Time & Hodges 3rd. time a mem produced a draught of the Circular Letter to the Cuntry Soceys. amended and orderd to be sent orderd that the Secy. do purchase a book to keep a regular account of the Receipts and disburments of the Socy. to be Layd before this Comte. every sitting orderd that Citn Jno. Binns do attend this Comte. on next sitting

moved that the Editor & Sub D..be allowed to sit in the Comte of Visitors Carried –

G C moves that Secys. be allowed to sit as Representitavies in the Comte. in the absence of the Del & Sub Del Refd. to the Divns for their sanction to be returnd in a fortnight

moved that the Secys be alowed to sit for the night Carried unanimous

118 Wrong date: Monday was 15 Aug.

Citn. Hiram Powell Elected to the Ex C in the room of Ridley resign'd

Divn. 12 superseeded their Del for non attendance in the Comte. four Nights

an ajourn'd Motion was calld for respecting Citn Gerralds Child. information was giv'n by the Chairman that the Child was at boarding school Exeter

on the motion from the Divn. 9 was taken into consideration consisting of 4 Resolutions negatived that the money subscribed – be not applied to any other purpose Negative a motion from Divn. 17 the Del be supplied with a sufficient number

N. Mem	3 ..	
P.	449	
Q	1.. 1. .11 M	
Burks	11 . 2½	
Debts	6.. 7½	
Depts.	3.. 3	
Publ	1 9	
	1.. 4. 9[119]	

337. Minutes: LCS General Committee, 21 September 1796[120]

Source: Place Collection, vol. 37, fos. 225–67

Extra sitting of Wednesday Sept 21st – 1796 Convened to examine into the claim of Citn Martin on Brillats defence

Persons subpoened as Witnesses
Baxter

Wattson		Previous to every other
Cooper		business the Comte in
Hardy		consequence of so many
Moffat	Absent	absent divns came to the
More	Do	resolution of giving the
Field	Do	report to the G C the next
Hodgson		Evening after the rest of
Moody		its buss was over – – – –
Nichols		Martin was called on to
Black	Absent	state his reasons for this
Chaddick	Do	applycation. He began by
Jno Powell		stating that he had become
Jas Powell	Absent	a Membr of the Socy at a

119 Total should be £2 4s 9d.
120 Below the title of this document, Place noted: 'In the hand writing of Richard Hodgson'.

Oliphant	Do	very early Period. He was
Pickard		appointed Chairman of
Wenham	Absent	the G M at Lewis's Room
England	Do	at which place he first

new Brillat. The Socy through the interference of the Lord Mayor had been disappointed of Meeting at the Globe Tavern as was first intended. To prevent such inconvenience in future, Citn Brillat at that Meeting publicly declared that the Socy upon any other future occasion might meet upon his ground in the Hackney Road – A Genl Meetg was called some time afterwards for the purpose of appointing persons to represt the Socy in the British Convenn held in Edinboroug. The meeting in consequence of Brillats former invitation was held in his ground. When the regular business was over and the Meeting dissolv'd, Citn Brillat was taken up, Martin had previously proceeded toward Town, was overtaken by a deputation in West Smithfd & requested to come back, and render Brillat all the legal assistance in his power; which he immediately comply'd with. He then consider'd the socy as his employers. He says that B was prosecuted for words spoken 20 Months before, but believes that prosecution would not have taken place had B not suffer'd the Meeting on his premises. Having procur'd Bail Brillat secreted himself 3 Weeks at M Hous during which time M supplied him with every necessary relating to Board & lodging. Governt supposing Brillat had fled[121] from his bail, advertis'd a reward of 100£ for apprehending him. It was then agreed upon between B & M, That on the day of Tryal M was to deliver up Brilt. to John Wills the Wine Mercht who was a Membr of ye Socy & a Constable, by which means they were to get the 100£ which was to be consider'd to defray the expences of his Tryall, But which money M declares he never did recieve for upon applying to Mr White the Solicitor of the Treasury for payment, he told him That the Atty Genl was determind not to pay the Money – and should M think proper to bring his Action He would defend it. Martin intended to have brought his action and had nearly prepared his papers &c for that purpose when he was taken up and the business was of course droped. He farther says that he was called upon every Genl Comte Night to report on the Brillats business. That Brillat in all the conversations he Martin had with him never did give him the least reason to suppose that the Expences were to fall on himself but on the contrary that the Society were bound to defray it – in which opinion he Martin coin-

121 Or 'eloped'. One word is written over the other.

cided That Brillat had given Mrs Martin 5
Guineas as a compensation for 3 Weeks Board
& lodging, and 2 Guineas to employ a short
hand writer to take his Tryal down as he
intended to publish it – and that was all the
Money he recieved either directly or indirectly
from Brillat – That he knew nothing whatever
of Brillat – and went on with the prosecution
believing the Socy would see him paid – And
He believes it was likewise the opinion of the
Leading Membrs of the Socy at that time –
When Martin was first taken up on the charge
of High Treason he was prevented from seeing
into the business – but as soon as opportunity
would permit he sent John Pierce his Articled
Clerk to Brillat with the Bill. Brillat was so
much enraged, that beside using much indecent
& uncivil Language threatned to kick him out
of his room – When Cooper with Moody &
Field waited upon him as a Deputation from
the Comtee Martin declared his intention of
sending Brillats Bill with Carters But was
disuaded therefrom by Coopers advising him
to send only Carters first and the other at some
future period, as by sending so large a demand
togeth the Magnitude of the sum might astonish
and confound the Comtee and he might get
nothing – He declared that altho he had always
considerd the Socy. Dr to him in this affair –
yet nothing but his great distress could have
induced him to make the demand –

Baxter was called – He perfectly recollects
Brillats offering his ground to the Socy at the
Meeting in Oxfd Rd – When the Meeting for
sending Deputies to Edinbg was determin'd
upon, Citn Baxter was requested by the
Comtee being a neighbour of Brillats to apply
to him for the ground, which was granted –
After the business was over Brillat was taken
up He had retd, and knows of nothing which
took place on the spot but from hearsay – He
was in Court during the Tryal of Brillat, and
has every reason to believe that the words for
which he was prosed were not spoken by him,
and that he would not been prosecuted had he
not sufferd the Meeting to be held in his
ground – The Socy he believes never did pledge
them selves to pay it – twas a meer matter of
private conversation – Baxter & Brillat were
Membrs of the same division
Q – Did you believe at that time that the
Society were to pay the expences of the
Tryal? Ansr – I do not recollect – its certain there was no application made at
that time by Brillat or Martin for that
purpose – but it was expected Brillat would
apply, as he did not the matter drop. –
Q – It was a meer supposition that Brillat
was prosecuted for having the Genl Meet-

ing in his ground – Ansr   Twas not more
than conjecture
Q – Was you a Membr of Genl Comte at that
time – Ansr – Yes
Q – Do you recollect Martin being called
upon on the Comte Nights to report progress in the affair of Brillat   Ansr no –
Q – Was Martin called Back after Brillat was
taken up, by a Depetation   I refer you
to Citn Pickard for an Ansr

Watson called

He stated that he was a Constable, and in
habits of strict intimacy with Brillat at that
period, That he was called upon duty that day
and ordered to attend on Hackney Road –
That when Brillat was apprehendd Many of the
Citns ran upon the spur of the Moment for
Martin, to render him assistance   Saw Brillat
in Prison, in conversing upon the subject of his
apparent elopement and his subsequent resignation Brillt say'd what are you not up to
that? I resign'd myself up to Martin that he
might get the reward, to defray the expences
of Tryal – Brillat told Watson that Martin had
recd the 100£ and 10£ more – Constantly
attended B in prison who always told the same
story   He told Watsons apprentice the same in
the presence of Two other persons   Mrs
Brillat after Brillats departure told Watson
that Martin was doubly paid – having Recd –
100£ – 10£ – and had likewise sent in a Bill
which he intended to trouble him for
Q   You understood then that M Had recd the
100£ – Ansr Yes and 10£ as before stated –
Q – What Proff had you   Ansr   only B and his
Wifes own Words
Chrisr Cooper – Was at the Meeting in Hackney
road, knows nothing more than what they had
heard before from the preceeding Witnesses –
Cooper charg'd M with stating a falshood   He
declared that he did not advise Martins to bring
forward Bril Bill – but advisd him to wave it
altogether as he considered his claim was not
good and that if he persisted he probably wd
get nothing – – – – – – – –
Hardy – Said he could scarcely recollect any
particular circumstances – After the Meeting
he went with Brillat & 20 or 30 More to an
adjoining Public House to refresh themselves,
after which he went homeward with Martin
and others, – In Chiswell Street they were overtaken by some Membrs who informd them of
Brillats apprehension, M went back; saw
nothing more
Q   Do you recollect any order of the Comte
for M to defend Brillt
Ansr no order he was sure was given – or Motn
Made in the Comte for that purpose it was

367

private conversation – Q Was M order'd by the Socy to defd Carter Ansr think not – Q Was Martin orderd by the Comte to defd Margarot – Ansr I am not clear, but blieve Margt employ'd M himself – Questn by Martin – If 10 or 12 Members Was to ask me to defend any Person do you think I should have done it Ansr Yes you would I suppose – Q Do you think at that time I should have waited for a formal order Ansr No – Quesn to Martin – Did you suppose the Socy was bound to pay you Margarots expences, in consequence of his orders to you Ansr Yes Carter was prosecuted I was not ordered to defend him by the Society, yet the Socy Paid me – – – – – Baxter said that between (Jan 7 & May) he enquird of Brillat if M had recd the reward Brillat told him, no, He saw Brillat repeatedly after but never heard him mention Martins having reciev'd it – Quesn to M – Do you expect to recieve it Ansr No Did you ever forget the Society owed you the Bill, Ansr No that was impossible – – – – – –

R Hodgson

Was president at the G M in Hackney Rd heard of Brillt being taken – was then in company with 10 or 12 Persons Most of them Delegates who orderd Martin to be brought back – Always considered the Socy was to pay – corroborated and subscribed to what Baxter had given in Evidence – Believes no oficial report of was given by M to the Comte But was the topic of Genl conversation – Brillat did not apply to the Socy for payment & the socy being Poor did not offer – Hodgson being apprehensive Brillt might hurt his bail and bring disgrace on the Socy by secreting himself – Martin & Gray told him of the Maneuvre for obtaining the 100£ – Hodgson considered it as ridiculous – and Meeting with M some time afterward M told him there was no hopes of obtaining it – – – – Hodgson had now left the Genl Comte and knows nothing more than from hearsay – Q Did the persons who sent for M employ him for the Moment only or for the whole suit – Ansr They considered themselves as the G-C and employed M as their Solicitor – they considering the Society attacked – and after Martin came back Hodgson Margat and Hardy were very anxious Martin should undertake the defence and instructed him so to do – Q Did yo[u] consider the Society as being bound to pay the expenses – Ansr The Society as well as himself were of opin that Brillat was in circumstances, sufficiently prosperous to enable him to defray the Expence, but that in case of failure on his part, the Socy were Bound to pay it – Q. Do

you Recollect wether on the first G Comte night after, which was on the Friday following, whether the Comte Confirm'd the appointment of M for Defending Brillats – The Socy Consider'd M & B both in good Circumstances and that of course they could not suffer the expence to operate upon the Socy – besides it was hinted by M & B that, no charges would fall on them – – – – – – –

Moody called

He said he was a Membr of the Socy at the time but not present at the Genl Meeting – Was on a Deputation to Martin last Summer in company with Cooper & Field – Martin was then drawing up a Bill upon the Society containing 3 separte Accounts Viz Brillats – Carter & Margarots – Moody advised M to withdraw the Claim of Brillats – or he thought the whole would be rejected Could not charge his memory with particular conversation – But did not hear Cooper advise M to bring in his Bill at a future time – Martin had not the particulars of Brillats Acct but gave it in a lump at 30£ – Moody was intimate with Brillet, and have heard him say in conversation with him that the Society ought, not only to pay the expences of the Tryal, but, that they were Bound in Justice to pay his fine likewise

John Powell called

He said he was at the Oxfd St. Genl Meetg, Heard Brillat offer his ground to the Society. He was at the Meeting in Hackney Road. Heard that Brillat was taken; heard Margarot tell several persons to go after Martin and bring him back, He with Margarot & White was at the examination, at Mrs B's request He called upon Martn after Brillat was in prison, He thought it would be exceeding hard upon B to bear the expences himself Recd from Brillet Letter for Subscriptions which he took to several of the Divns He offerd to Subscribe 1 – 1 – 0 toward but did not think the Society was bound to pay it, Brillat told Powell, Martin had used him very ill, That he had paid him a great deal of Money, he hinted likewise M had recd the 100£ – – – – Q Did Brillat tell you that he had paid Martin for his defence,? Ansr he positivly did and showd me a List of payments he had made him to a very large amount nearly 100£

Pickard

Was a Membr of G Comte at the time, Margarot requested him to go after M, Pickard overtook him in Chiswell Street, Martin immediately went – – – declares upon his Honor that, M was never called on to report in the Commte. as stated by Martin ·

Q was any person with you when You over-took M – Ansr No

Q did you in going back meet any person in search of M   Ans No   Q You never heard of Martin being orderd to report   Ans   No such orders were given – – –

Hodgson Said he went next day to procure bail supposing the socy would approve of it – – –

Quesn to Hodgson Are you of opinion that if Brillat had forfieted His bail they consider'd themselves bound to Indemnify – Ansr   Yes

Nichols

Recapitulated the former proceedings of Genl Comte relative on Martins business, Went with Black on a deputation to Martin asked him why he did not send Bs bill in with Carters – He furthermore says that when Carters Bill was paid the Comte understood M had another Claim on the Socy – When Brillts Bill was sent it was rejected – but the Comte dismissd the Claim and voted him 5 Guineas to relieve his present distress

Finis
The Claim was negativd

338. Letter: spy Powell to government (excerpts), 28 October 1796[122]

Source: PC 1/23/A38

... From my first being employ'd by you Sir I am certain I have done evry thing in my power to fulfil the duties of that employment. During the whole of the last year the greatest part of which time I was in office in the Society I am sure Sir I was always regular in my reports to you & anxious to do evry thing in my power for the service of government ... At the time of the great generl meetings you always found me ready to do evry thing you wish'd & during the passing of the Treason & Sedition Bills when the Committes met three or four times in a week (& you yourself blieved Sir had I been discovered it would have been attended with much personal danger) & continued sit-ting 'till four & five oClock in the morning I never neglected 'tho my health suffer'd materi-ally & it brought on a violent cough & spitting of blood which oblidged me to resign my dele-gateship for a time, as soon as ever I was able to go out I attended my division was immedi-ately elected to the district Committe & shortly after to the Genl Com. when Sir you

122 The letter was probably sent to Richard Ford.

had my reports regular, it was during the time of Jones & Binns deputation into the Country. on my last attending that Com I was so bad with my cough that I was oblidged to leave room as I absolutely disturbed the business; The next evening I was not able to attend the district Com. The reelection of deputies to the Genl Com was not regularly to come on till the Wednesday following but the district Com not having much business to do it was moved & carried that they should be reelected on that evening accordingly I not being there was not included indeed allmost all the old deputies were in the same situation for not expecting the election to come on few of them attended. I could not force myself into office again the division had chose their quarterly officers in whome they had confidence it was not then as last year when the Society was at the height & new divisions branching evr'y week   I was no sqoner out of office in one Division when I had only to branch to a new one & I was sure to be elected it was not so this year instead of branching off two or three divisions were join-ing again into one   finding that I had not any liklyhood of getting into office till the next Quarter & thinking the Society in its then decayd state not so much an object to govern-ment. I applied to you for leave to go to Mar-gate supposing it materially to my Interest. how it has turnd out I hope you'll not think me impertinent in relating.

[Powell relates in detail his unsuccessful efforts to have his play licensed for pro-duction at Margate and the financial dif-ficulties which delayed his return to Lon-don.]

Had you but wrote me half a line Sir: that I was wanted in town I would have set off at any rate   I am sure Sir you always found me ready & eger to obey any command of yours. With respect to my losing my place I could not do otherwise   I was evry day told that I should be discharged on account of my belonging to the Society & had you interfered I know from the principles of some in those office it would have soon been divulged & I should not have been able to have done you any further service. In the Society it was a continuel subject of suspicion against me the old members said I could not be honest in keeping my place so long for it must be known that I belonged to the Society which would alone be sufficient inducement to discharge me as had been invari-ably the case: whilst the new members think-ing also I could not be honest to keep it as it was supposed I had some small private fortune of my own. I lost my election three times to the executive Committe 'tho each time by a very small majority on this very account I found it impossible to retain both my employments & thought it more to my interest to retain yours Sir. . . . All I wish Sir is that I may still be continued in my employment still have my £10 per month you will find Sir I shall be of greater service from my absence as it must do away evry lurking suspicion against me (& there were certainly some). . . . I am certain Sir you will find noboddy so ready or willing & from situation I may say abillities has it so much in his power to serve government as myself

October 28. 1796   I am Sir & ever shall be
No 3 Ossulston Street   with the greatest respect
Somers Town   Your Humble Servant
                        James Powell

P S May I beg the favor of line Sir as I shall not trouble you by calling on you 'till you send for me tho I shall send you all the information in my power

339. Report from spy Powell: LCS Division 9, 7 November 1796[123]

Source: PC 1/23/A38

Div 9. L.C.S. Novr 1796
Report of Ex Com Sittings Novr. 1

Mitchell Absent. 1st time
The Treasurer & Secretary informd the Com that the actual sale of the Magazine being now pretty well ascertaind that had fixed the Number to be printed at 3,000 & that 3,000 of No 3[124] had been printed accordingly.
                                        (*approved*)
Resolved that a circular letter should be drawn up & sent to evr'y member of the Society requesting them to pay sixpence instead of 4½ for the magazine to enable the society to pay its debts. Citizen Bone protested highly against this measure, which however after some contention was carried in the affirmative Recieved information from a member of a person who had received Subscriptions for the Society & not yet accounted for them.   (The member received the thanks of the Com).
An answer to a letter from Paisley read, approved & ordered to be sent.
Citizen Rhynd sent in another bill but it not

123 Powell's description: 'Div. 9 L. C. S. / Novr 7. 1796'.
124 Must be no. 6; no. 3, August, was printed two months earlier.

according with the request of the Com he was ordered to attend the next sittings.
No further information having been received respecting the future meeting place of the Genl Com the consideration was adjournd to a future sittings.

Sittings Novr 2d.

Rhynd attended to explain his bill when he said he could not follow the instructions of the Com, it being contrary to the rule of trade, whose secrets he was bound not to disclose
                        (*Bill ordered to be paid*)
Received & read a letter from Leicester a member deputed to answer it.
Received & read a letter from Portsmouth a member deputed to answer it.
An answer to a letter from Rochester read disapproved & ordered to be recommitted
An Answer to a letter from J. Binns at Dublin read approved & ordered to be sent.
Receivd & read a letter from Citizen Lesly at Edingburgh a member deputed to answer it, & the Committe came to the resolution that no more Magazines should be sent to him for the present. Lesly received 300 Magazines monthly but a dispute having arose about the mode of payment the Com. came to the above resolution.
A member of the Society being strongly suspected of immorel conduct, two members were deputed to enquire into the same.

Genl Com. Novr 3d.

Received & read a letter from Citizen Wm Williams stating that as the subject of Religion had been introduced into the Magazine contrary to the General order of the Society he begged leave to resign his office of sub editor.[125] The Com after a long debate which

125 The Oct. issue of the *MPM* (published early in Nov.) contained two anti-clerical articles to which Williams may have taken exception. 'On the Doctrine of Passive Obedience and Non-Resistance', by John Rhynd, the printer of the magazine and an active LCS member, attacked the Roman Catholic clergy, charging the priests of pre-revolutionary France with lasciviousness and the priests of James II's reign with hypocrisy. An anonymous article described the invention of automatons which could replace clergymen by reciting the words *death, judgment, eternity, damnation* and *hell* at set intervals in appropriate tones, ending with *amen* in a deep bass (vol. 1, pp. 209-10, 218-19). Although Williams was persuaded to continue as sub-editor, religion continued to creep into the magazine. In the Dec. issue George Dyer described his sect of semi-Quakers, who did not believe in titles (vol. 1, pp. 292-4); he continued the subject in the Jan. issue,

took up most of the evening, were of opinion that as it appeared to them Citizen Williams objections were without foundation another Sub Editor should not be appointed for the present: but that the Secretary should wait on Williams and request him to withdraw his resignation.

The following persons were returnd to serve in the Executive Com for the ensuing month. Hodgson, Bone, Fenwick, Mitchell, Powell, & Biggs.

Treasurers & Secretarys report 5 new members 320 present in the Divisions Magazines £3. .5. .6. Publications £. – .2.3. Subscriptions £1. .15. . – Total £5. .2. .9.

340. Report from spy Powell: LCS General Committee, 10 November 1796[126]

Source: PC 1/23/A38

Genl Com Novr 10. 1796

Deputations to absent Divisions 2. B Binns 7 Haydon 12 Nicholls 13 Early 14 Bagnell 16 Earley 25 Parsons 26 B Binns 30 McNaughton 32. Mayn 37 Eastbourn

Report Executive Com Sitting Novr 4th

Absent Green first time. Mitchell attended and admitted to the honor of the sittings not having been inform'd of his election till last night, & not at all of his being superseeded. Jobson's bill for Bill Sticking signd by all the members present. A letter from Citn Willson advising of 50 Copies of Tookes speeches at the late election as a present to the Society. Resolved that each delegate have one for the use of his division This letter also contain two copies of a prospectus of a work entitled Theories of

explaining that his aunt, who taught him from the bible, glossed a passage in Luke by telling him that in biblical days titles were unknown (vol. 2, pp. 7–10). Also in the Jan. issue W. D. (William Duane?) argued that Gibbon was incorrect in attributing the golden rule to Isocrates: Tobias expressed the same idea 150 years earlier; but no matter who stated the maxim first, it was best stated in the gospel (vol. 2, pp. 24–5). In the Feb. and May issues George Dyer again alluded to the absence of titles in the Bible (vol. 2, pp. 77, 207–10). Finally, in March there was a return to the anti-clerical article – Robert Watson reprobated the Catholic clergy on the continent for condemning to death anyone who did not agree with their beliefs (vol. 2, pp. 115–16).

126 Powell's description: 'Genl Com LCS / Novr 10th'.

Governments antient & modern by Chas Sinclair. Deputed a citizen to request a sufficient number of the prospectus to furnish each division with one & to return thanks for Tookes speeches.

On the division of a question relative to a question for altering the constitution the order of the day was moved seconded & negatived. Fenwick & Bone protested against the division. Resolved that it be recommended to the Genl Com to consider wether it will be expedient that persons elected into the Ex Com shall not enter on office till one week after election nor quit till one week after being superseeded in the ordinary course of election. A letter to Portsmouth read emended & ordered to be sent. Resolved that the Editor of the Magazine be recommended to insert this letter & as much as he may find convenient of the letter to which it is an answer in the next number of the Magazine.[127]

Sittings Novr 9.

Bone & W Powell absent first time. Citn Salter attendd the Com. & laid before them a letter which he had received from a citizen of Manchester the letter contain matter relative to this Society, a citizen deputed to wait on citizen Hardy relative to the contents of the letter above mentioned. Bone came at ½ past nine A letter from Stirling dated 6th Septr which has laid some time at Eatons read & a member deputed to answer it. (tis about the Magazine). A letter from Maidstone read a member deputed to answer it. A letter from Melbourne read, a member deputed to answer it. Bone reported progress in explainning to division 17. the Accounts of the Society Two Citizens reported progress in examining the report of cash in the hands of citizen Hall. Bone reported his having explaind to W Williams the Editors explainations of those parts of the magazine which he had objected to; that W Williams had in consequence withdrawn his objections. Resolved that this Com do hold an Extra sitting Tuesday

127 The Jan. issue (vol. 2, pp. 42–4) contained the LCS answer, dated 4 Nov. 1796. Evidently the Portsmouth letter reported that dockyard managers threatened to discharge anyone who belonged to a reform society. The reply regretted that the LCS had 'too many enemies and too many embarrassments to overcome among ourselves to relieve your pitable situation – farther than by our counsel – which is – PERSEVERE.' The LCS attributed this suppression of political discussion to the minister's fear of the public voice. They then warned their Portsmouth allies not to believe they must be subservient to the political beliefs of the person who employed them.

the 15 Inst to receive and audit the Accounts of the Society than to be posted into the ledger.

Genl Com

B Binns elected Chairman. Sellers & Crossfield nominated as Sub Editors of the Magazine   Crossfield returnd by a majority of two. The Reporter of the Extra com. reported they had no Candles to do business by.
Motion from Div 20 which stood for the order of the day. That it is the opinion of this div that a deputation be sent to Galloway to demand the papers of the Society in his hands in the state they are at present   (*Carried B Binns & Evans deputed*)
Div 15   Thinks it extravagant to have a door keeper.   (*negatived*)
Div 21. Resolvd that it is the opinion of this division that the delegates be allow'd some of the publications on hand & the divisions to be responsible.   (*Moved that this be referrd to the divisions negatived*) *This was considered to negative the original*)
Div 9. Resolved that no member of the Society shall be served with any magazine out of the Div under /6d. as much detriment has accrued to the Society by allowing members to be served at /4/- who consider themselved members of the Society tho they never attend their divisions   (*referd to divisions*)
3 New 305 present Mag – – 19s. 4½ Profits – 2s. 1½ Sub 3s/. Publications 4s/3d Total £1. .8. .8½

341. Report from spy Powell: LCS General Committee, 17 November 1796[128]

Source: PC 1/23/A38

Genl Com Novr 17. 1796

16 Divisions unrepresented in the Genl Com

Executive Com Novr 11th.

Not sufficient members attending to form a Committe no business was done

Extra sitting Novr. 15th

Hodgson & Ashley informd the Com that they had proceeded in posting the ledger but had not been able to compleat it. The Committee therefore adjourned.

128 Powell's description: 'Report of the Genl Com L. C. S. / Novr. 17th. 1796'.

Sitting Novr 16th.

Not sufficient members attending to form a committe no business was done.

Genl Com Novr 17.

Evans & B Binns the deputation to wait on Galloway informd the Com that they had got the journal & part of the papers from him. The papers consisted of vouchers & motions.
Moved, seconded & carried that the vouchers be immediately burnt & the motions deliverd to the Secty for the use of the Executive Committe.
Moved & carred that the deputation do continue in force 'till the whole of the papers are procured.
Div 9. Resolved that the money collected to liquidate the debt of the Society be applied solely to that purpose & no other giving a priority to the debt due to the deputies, & that the Secty or Treasurer do not apply or pay any of it except in the presence or by order of the Genl Com & that it also be requested of the delegates to perticularly specify the money they pay into the hands of the Treasurer for that purpose.   (*carried unanimously*)
Div 22. Resolved that it is the opinion of this Division that the 16th Article of the Regulations should be amended thus. "That all letters received & *approved* by the Executive Com shall be read in the Genl Com.["]
                    (*refer'd to the divisions*)
Div. 1 & 9. Resolv'd that officers elected to the Ex Com ought not take the seat till one week after election nor quit till one week after being being superseded & that the Ex Com did not act contrary to the rules of the society by recommending the above to the Genl Com & do request the Genl Com to rescind their motion on that head.   (*Moved & carried that the motion be rescinded*)
Resolved that it be referrd to the Divisions wether the Executive Com shall have the power of recommending to the Genl Com.

209. present 1 new member. Quarterage & Magazins 16s/- publications /10d. subscription for Deputies 2s/- Total 18s/ 10d.

342. Minutes: LCS General Committee, 17 November 1796

Source: Add MSS 27815, fos. 140–0v

Genl. Comte. Room Sitting of Novr. 17 . . 1796

Absent Divns.	On Deputation
2	Binns
3	Evans

Absent Divns.	On Deputation
5	is none
7	Evans
8	McNorton
12	Nicholls
14	Bagnell
16	Nicholls
17	Binns
18	Fenwick
21	Bailey
30	McNorton
32	Nelson
34	Vials
35	Pringle
36	broke up
37	Sterling

[The reports of the executive committee are the same as Powell's except that names of absentees are given – 11 November: Powell, Hodges, Hodgson, Green; 15 November: Powell, Biggs; 16 November: Powell Hodgson, Green, Bone. The rest of the minutes are also substantially the same as Powell's.]

1 New   209 Present Q M 16. .4½
                    Dep – 2
                    Pub – 10
Refd. Qn. 35 aff. . 53 Neg –

343. Report from spy Powell: LCS General Committee, 24 November 1796[129]

Source: PC 1/23/A38

Genl Com L.C.S 24 Novr. 1796.

Deputations to absent Div 3 J Powell   12 Nicholls   14 Bagnell   16 Earley   18 Fenwick 26 Nicholls   30 McNaughton   31 Pringle   32 Main   35 Pringle
Div 9 J Powell chose delegate   T Evans Secretary

Executive Com Friday Novr 18.

Absent Hodgson 2d time   Wm Powell 5th Hodges 2d. Read an answer to the letter from Melbourne Derbyshire amended approved & ordered to be sent   Read an answer to Leslys letter from Edinburgh approved & ordered to be sent   Read an answer to the letter from

129 Powell's description: 'Report of the Genl Com. / L C S. Sittings Thursday / Novr 24. 1796'. Government endorsement: 'Rx. 25. R. F.'

Sterling amended & ordered to be sent. Read an answer to the letter from Maidstone adjournd.
The Protest of Citn Green as a member of the Ex Com "I Protest against the vote of Citn Ashley being admitted in the Committe 1st. Because the Ex Com was not competent to grant that privilege to Ashley. 2d Because it is directly contrary to the 11th. Article of the Societys Regulations. which declares he shall attend in that Com. but not vote.["] Sigd H Green

Wednesday Novr 23d.

Absent W Powell 6th. time. Moved that the letter to Melbourne pass'd last sittings be reconsidered. (*negatived*) Hodgson protested against said letter "1st. Because it refuses to answer the Citizens of Melbourne two questions, one of which has been explicitly answer'd to another society. 2dly Because the mode of refusal appears to amount to an accusation of impertinence against the said Citizens 3dly. Because such refusal in any mode would be improper in as much as all National concerns either Civil or military are inseparably connected with the question of parliamentary reform. Acts of Parliament & the measures of Ministry sanctioned by Parliament characterize the existing system of oppression, they argue experimentally in favor of reform   4thly Because the said letter is nearly barren of all political sentiment, therefore unworthy of being sent in the name of this Society perticularly to a respectable body of citizens.["] Signd Rd Hodgson   Moved that the progress in arranging the accounts of the Society be reported   (*ordered*).
Hodgson reported that he had open'd the several accounts in the ledger that appeared to him necessary; that he had nearly arranged the several articles of income & expenditure for the month of July under their several Accounts, that the whole of the affairs of that month would have been arranged but that some parts require explanation; that after the attainment of such explanation & compleating the arrangement of that month. The Secty or any other member would be able to compleat the ledger next week if not delayd by want of explanation. Citn Biggs promised to assist & promised to meet at the Genl Com tomorrow night. The Genl Com may therefore expect to have the ledger compleated by next Thursday. Directed Ashley to write to the member who was deputed to enquire for a place of meeting for the Genl Com. Determin'd to accept the offer of Wm Bosville Esqr of attaching a song with the musick to the next Months Magazine free

of expence to the Society or diminution of printed copy; & to advertize the next months Magazine in four different papers.[130] Resolved that the thanks of this Society be given to Citn Bosville for said offer. Read & amended a letter to Maidstone & ordered it to be sent. Read a letter from Birmingham, two from Nottingham one from John Binns at Dublin & another from Leicester.[131] appointed four members severally to answer them. (Adjournd)

Genl Com.

Leslys letter read. It stated. "that in order to make a general circulation of the Magazine throughout Scotland that he was forced to send them to persons in the country on long credit that he was so good a friend to the cause that he wishd to get no profit on them; but that from expence of portage carriage &ca every Magne. cost him 7d. the other publications he could get much cheaper carriage paid. They must therefore contrive such a plan as to clear himself & give him time to collect the money from the persons in the Country or appoint some other person at Edinburgh to vend the Mag.["]
The answer stated "That the funds of the Society would not allow of long credit nor could they be sent on any other plan It therefore requested he would return the numbers unsold & remit the money in his possession. It stated some surprize that he had not mentioned £3. 3. – paid into his hands from the Stirling Society some time since for the use of the L.C.S 'tho they had received several letters from him since that period. supposed it must have slipt his memory.["] The letter from Stirling stated. "They had sent £3. 3. – to Cit Lesly for the use of the L.C.S. they would have sent more but they were few & poor it

stated they had none of No 2 of the Mag 'tho they had sent to Lesly for them.["]
The Answer stated they had received no account from Lesly of the £3. 3 "Urged them 'tho they were few & poor to stand firm like the unriven & knotted oak 'tho assailed by the turbulent storms of oppression. requested to know wether there were no persons in their part of the Country who would vend the "Magazines.["]
The letter from Melbourne stated "that they encreased 'tho but slow. a Dep. of 4 persons had waited on them from Castle Donnington saying that a number of Citns wishd to form a Society there & requested to know how to proceed. A Dep of 4 persons had waited on them from the Leicester Society one of whome was Citn Parry Bookseller there They requested to correspond with the Melbourne Soc, said they correspond with the L.C S. The Citns of Melbourne wishd to know that fact, as they would not begin a correspondence 'till that was assertaind. they also wishd some of the L.C.S. regulations as they would abide by them. They wishd to know the Societys opinion of Mr Pitts Militia Act[132] & how they should act on it. Likewise on Ld Malmsburys mission[133] & wether they did not think it only a deception.["] The answer stated. They were glad to hear they increased wishd "success to the Citns of Castle Donnington the L.C.S. were happy in the Correspondance of the Leicester Society. But begged to be excused from given any opininion on the Militia Act & Ld Malmsburys mission.["]
Citn Greens protest in the Ex Com taken into Consideration A warm debate ensued Green stygamatized the Ex Com as having acted in a dirty underhand manner said they were governd by Tyrents & dictators & that the Society ought no more to be governd by a Tyrant minister, than a Tyrant Citizen
Fenwick & Hodgson defended the Ex Com &

130 Songs were the only items named in the advertisement: Tooke's 'The Birthday of Liberty' in the Nov. issue (out 'tomorrow') and Bosville's 'O'er the Vine-covered hills' in the next number (MC 3 Dec. 1796, p. 2). Bosville's song, which was sung on 5 Nov. 1796, at the dinner celebrating Hardy's acquittal, extols the rise of 'the Day-Star of Liberty' in France.

131 The society at Leicester asked about a rumour (from Nottingham) that the LCS had 'deserted the *standard of* UNIVERSAL SUFFRAGE – for the *partial and unjust one of having the franchise extended to every* HOUSEDWELLER ONLY' (12 Nov. 1796, MPM, vol. 1 (Dec. 1796), pp. 320–1). In reply the LCS denied the rumour and described the Society of Taxed Housekeepers (formed in 1793) and conflicting LCS opinions about extending the franchise to taxed householders (n.d., ibid., pp. 321–5).

132 The Supplementary Militia Bill was designed to augment the militia forces in order to prevent or repel invasion. A pro-government newspaper report envisaged infiltration by the reform societies: 'We learn with real alarm, that the Members of the numerous *Corresponding Societies* throughout the kingdom have formed the resolution of putting themselves as much as possible in the way of being ballotted into the *Supplemental Militia*, of 60,000 men.' The reformist *Morning Chronicle*, which quoted this allegation, scoffed at it; but the LCS may have had it in mind when they refused to comment on the Militia Act (MC 25 Oct. 1796, p. 3; 3 Nov., p. 1; 10 Nov., p. 2).

133 In October Lord Malmesbury went to Paris as minister plenipotentiary to discuss terms of peace.

said Ashly was only suffer'd to vote on Literary subjects & letters which he signd & was accountable for the contents.

Ashly was very warm. & gave notice that he would positively resign his office of Secty on Thursday next & requested the Com to look for another.

The Com passed the following resolution. That it is the opinion of this Com. on considering the protest of Cit Green. that such protest is well founded: but at the same time think it would be well if the 11th Article were reconsidered & that it be referred to the Div wether the Secty be allowd to vote on Lity subjects only in the Ex Com. Fenwick resignd as a member of the Ex Com. The Protest of Powell as a member of the Genl Com. "I do protest against the Genl Com. for allowing members of the Ex Com to speak in the Genl Com diectly contrary to the 16th Article of the Regulations which possitively says they shall neither speak or vote unless their reporter misrepresent them.["]

Hodgsons Protest on the Melbourne letter taken into consideration Green who appeared to be the author of that letter was very warm calld Hodgson a Tyrant & Dictator. Hodgson was warm in reply. The following resolution was moved That the letter to Melbourne be sent. (Carried)

Hodgson & Biggs immediately resignd their situations on the Ex Com.

Moved That the letter be copied in the report & carred to the Divisions (Negatived).

Leake. Seal. Stucky. & Mitchell. elected to the Ex Com in the room of Hodgson, Fenwick, Biggs & W Powell, resignd

A Deputation of 3 members from the Extraordinary Com waited on the Genl Com to entreat the Deligates would urge their divisions to send members to that Com, as meeting so thin, they could not do any business.

Div 19. 17. 22. 6. 23. 33. Resolvd that it is the opinion that absent members on reenterring the Society should be admitted on paying for the Magazine only. (referred to the Div)

On the referred motion wether the Mag should be sold to members at 4½ only in the divisions there appeared in the affirmative 106 Negative 61. Majority in the affirmative 45

Treasurers & Secty Report

3 New members. 217. Present. Quarterage & Magazines 11s/ Sub. 1s/- Publications 1/3. Total 13s/3d

Executive Committee Men – 25. Novr 1796[134]

134 In another hand on verso of penultimate folio.

Bone
Green
Mitchell
Leak
Stucky
Seal
Hodges.

344. Report from spy Powell: LCS General Committee, 1 December 1796[135]

Source: PC 1/23/A38

Genl Committe LCS Decr 1st. 1796

Deputations Div 7 Powell 12 Nicholls 16 Nicholls 18 B Binns 24 B Binns 26 Nicholls 30 McNaughton 31 Pringle 34 Vialls 35 Hodgson 37 Walker.

Executive Friday Novr 25th

Absent Hodges, Bone, Stucky, Leake, Seal. Only two members attending there was no Committe

Wednesday Novr 30

Absent Hodges & Stucky 2d time. Bone was chosen reporter. Read an answer to the letters from Nottingham amended & ordered to be sent. Read an answer to the Birmingham letter amended & ordered to be sent. Read a letter from Norwich deputed a member to answer it. Read a letter from Citn Place Sub Secty informing the Com that he would no longer be answerable for the paper for the Magazines for the reasons before stated to the Committee (Adjournd)

Genl Com

The letter from Birmingham Read. It stated that a new Society was formd there unconnected with any other Society in that town the reasons were the great difference in religious opinion. Amongst the other Societies, the present were religious men they agreed with the principles of the London Corresg Socity & requested to be supplied with publications. They were willing to render pecuniary assistance to the L C S. for promoting the cause of Reform. They had taken the name of the Civil Society they already amounted to 65 members & were divided into four Branches

The Answer stated that no difference in religious opinion could make any alteration in the cause of universal suffrage & annual parliaments

135 Powell's description: 'Report of the Genl Com L. C. S. / Decr 1st. 1796'. Government endorsement: 'Rx. 2d. R. F.'

which was the inherent right of Britons, requested them to be steady & firm Thankd them for the offer of pecuniary assistance which was accepted & should be expended for the benefit of the cause & the happiness of millions, desired them to exert all their interest in promoting the Sale of the Societys Magazine First letter from Norwich read it was from an individual of the name of Black to an individual of this Society It containd an account of a new Society formd at Nottingham requested instructions how to proceed, the wishd to unite with other Sociesties, said the cause of reform proceeded rapidly there, "for hard usage from fools to slaves did much. The late election proved how much that city was against the present system of corruption.["] The second letter was from the Society itself it stated they wish'd to open a correspondence with the L.C.S. & their instruction in promoting a general diffusion of knowledge, requested our articles to go by, gave orders for the Magazine said they had call'd themselves the Bulls head Clubb for the improvement of knowledge. The answer stated the Society were happy in openning a correspondence with them, inclosed a copy of the articles wishd them success & requested them to promote the sale of the Magazines.

The Reporter stated he could not read the letter from Norwich it having been given to a member to answer There were two printed handbills inclosed in it some thousand of which had been distributed at Norwich which he would read. The first was said to be answer to the numerous handbills publish'd there by the vilest aristocracy that ever infested & distressed an unhappy country & the second was against the Militia Act & sign'd a Poor Englishman.

Moved & carred that the Ex Com do in their answer return thanks to the writers of the above Hand Bills

Div 3. Resolv'd that it is the opinion of this Div that the refusal of an answer to the citizens of Melbourne relative to the Militia Act & Ld Malmsbury mission was highly improper & they earnestly request the Genl Com to reconsider their resolution on that business

A long debate ensued during which it appeard that the letter had not as yet been sent Ashley having refused to sign it The following resolution was moved & carried. "That the letter be referr'd back to the Executive Com for reconsideration & that the whole Com be summoned for that purpose

Div 17 Resolvd that the Genl Com do instruct the Ex Com to draw up a circular letter for the purpose of stimulating the attendence of the absent members & that each Division be supplied with a sufficient quantity for the use of the same. Refd to Ex Com.

Moved & carried that the Accounts do stand for the order of the day next Thursday.

Moved & carred that Ashley be requested to continue his office of Secty 'till next Quarter day. (*Ashly consented.*)

Hodgson gave notice that he resignd the Sub Editorship of the Mag. *The Election was adjournd till next week*

4 new members 181 present Quarterage & Magazines 2£. 19s. 2d Profits 1/10. Publications 2s/ Sub 2s/. Total £.3. 3. 2[136]

On the Refd Question wether the Ex Com should have the powers of recommendation to the Genl Com There was 71 Affirmve 47 Negative Wether the word approved be inserted in the 16 regulation. 115 affirmative 15. Negative. (Div 3 have chosen Hodgson delegate.)

345. Report from spy Powell: LCS General Committee, 8 December 1796[137]

Source: PC 1/23/A38

Genl Com L C S Decr. 1796

Thelwall having been obliged suddenly to leave his house the Com adjournd to a public house opposite

Deputations to absent Divisions. 2 B Binns 12 Earley 13 Nicholls 14 Biggs 16 Earley 21 Powell 24 Arnold 26 Nicholls 30 Mallison 32 Mc.Naughton 35 Pringle 37 Hodgson

Report of the Executive Com Friday Decr 2d

Absent Stucky & Green 1st time Mitchell Hodges. not sufficient members attending to form a Com (*adjournd*)

Wednesday Decr 7. Absent Stucky, Mitchell & Hodges

Read two letters to Norwich ordered to be sent. Read a letter to J Binns ordered to be sent. Received a letter from Liverpoole in which were enclosed six copies of a Phamphlet on Government, requesting the Society to get the opininon of council on them & also to give their own opinion. The Ex Com were of opinion that it was inconsistant with the Societys present circumstances to employ council but resolv'd that each member of the Ex Com should take a copy to report his

136 Should be £3 5s.
137 Powell's description: 'Report of the Genl Com / L. C. S. Thursday Decr 8th / 1796'. Government endorsement: 'Rx 9th R. Ford'.

opinion on Friday. Ashley informd the Com that Cit W Williams had calld at his house & that he had given him a copy without consulting the Com & requested his opinion. The Com voted Ashly honorable indemnity for so doing. Leake resignd on the Ex Com. Resolv'd that the letter to Melbourne be sent without alterations.[138]

A letter from Norwich was read It was from an individual who stated 'tho he was firm in the cause he was obliged to be cautious as he was overseer to an aristocratic printing office it containd a number of democratic publications printed at Norwich & a copy of verses for the Magazine he stated notwithstanding his situation he was able to get publications printed for the Society at a triffling expence besides paper as no charge would be made for labor & that the Society might have no fear if they were what ministry call'd inflammatory as only one person (whom he could depend on) would be concernd beside himself.

The Answer thankd him for his offer which was refused as the sending publications to Norwich to get printed would be attended with considerable trouble. The verses were given to the Editor of the Magazine

A letter from J Binns at Dublin read It stated that he heard that his conduct had been extreemly calumniated & that he had given authority to Oxlade to enquire into the subscription for the Deputies which he denied he advised the Society to be unanimous, for by unanimity they could only succeed. It gave no account of the state of Politics in Ireland.

The Answer said they had heard no calumny against him & what he stated about Oxlade they believed to be false said the cause whent on well but not rapidly. The Society had had accounts of four new Societies having been formd within the last four weeks.

Ashley informd the Com that the 2d Letter to Norwich could not be read as the answer was in the hands of a member to make a fair copy

A Handbill sent from Norwich was read It was against the Militia Act & signd "One of the 80,000 incorruptable citizens".

Hodgson rose & said he was surprized to hear in the Report of the Ex Com that on the Wednesday they had not proceeded to business only 3 members attending not being sufficient to form a Committe, & that on Friday only the same number attending they did proceed to business & took into their reconsidderation the Melbourne letter when the whole Com were ordered to be summon'd there on

A long & very warm debate took place, Hodgson & Ashly contending that the Ex Com had acted very improperly & that the Questions in the Melbourne letter ought to have been answerd, Bone & Seal on the contrary.[139]

Hodgson Moved. That the letter to Melbourne be not sent on account of its refusing an answer to the questions on Ld Malmsburys mission & the Militia Act. (negatived)

Hodgson moved That it be immediately followed by another giving an answer to the two questions (The Com divided equally on this motion it was negatived by B Binns the Cairman casting vote.

Ashly informd the Com that they could no longer meet at Thelwalls, & that if all the property & papers belonging to the Society were not moved off the premises tomorrow morning they would be lost to the Society. The Com Resolved that B Binns be empowerd to employ the proper people to remove the same.

Took into consideration a future place of meeting for the Genl Com.

B Binns informd the Com that Citn Thos Evans No 14 Plow Court Fetter Lane had a room which the Com might have the use of. Resolved that the Com do meet there on Thursday next.

138 Leake's resignation seems to have been motivated by dissatisfaction with the executive committee's handling of this letter at a previous meeting, for he wrote them protesting 'their illiberality towards myself inasmuch as the only objection made to altering the Letter was the incapacity of the Comme to answer the questions [in the letter from Melbourne] – this I pledg'd myself to do if allowed 'till Friday Night – (and surely to plann to correct what 3 Weeks had been found too little to amend was no immodest request!).' Clearly, he was not given until Friday night; he left the meeting early. 'I explained in a most explicit & direct manner the necessity of my leaving the Comme. at the Hour I did & yet with shameless effrontry and false statement by the report of your last Sitting I find myself accused of abruptly leaving the Committee' (15 Dec. 1796, Add MSS 27815, fos. 144-4v).

139 Leake also reprobated the executive committee for meeting without a quorum, for voting to send the letter which did not answer the questions about the Militia Act and Malmesbury's mission, and for allowing the man who drafted the letter to vote on sending it (letter, 15 Dec.). On the same day that Leake sent his protest, Thelwall wrote to the Society suggesting that instead of wrangling they should spend their time 'in reading & political discussion'. To facilitate this he sent twelve copies of his latest work, The Rights of Nature (a retort to Burke's Thoughts on the Prospect of a Regicide Peace), and suggested that twelve men be appointed to read the book – 94 pp. – to the respective divisions (15 Dec. 1796, Add MSS 27815, fos. 142, 143v).

Reelection of the Ex Com. Leake, & Mitchell resignd. Biggs, J Powell & Oliphant were proposed. Biggs & J Powell were elected. The present Com consists of Seal Bone, Stucky. Green Hodges, J. Powell & Biggs
The Order of the day being the Accounts of the Society Hodgson & Biggs were call'd on. They stated they had not being able to proced any further for want of Accounts & vouchers for October & November. Ashly & Beck pledged themselves that the Com should have printed accounts for those months by Thursday next. Moved by Watling that Hodgson be incapacitated from holding any office in the Society except Diligate for one twelvemonth,
(negatived unanimously)
6 New members 188 present   Quarterage & Magazines £2. . – . .6½ General purposes £ – . .2s. 3d Profits £ – . .3s. .1½ Publications £ – . .1s. . – Total £2. .6. .11.
Herbert, Lloyd, Davies Esr of Cardigan in Wales and in the Commission of the Peace there, was admitted a member of the Society in Division 9 meeting at the Pitts Head Old Baily on Monday last.

346. Report from spy Powell: LCS Executive Committee, 9 December 1796[140]

Source: PC 1/23/A38

Executive Committe L.C S.
Sittings Friday Decr 9. 1796.

Absent Stucky & Hodges. Present Seal, Green, Biggs, Bone J Powell & Ashley. Seal in the Chair
Read a letter from Maidstone   J Powell appointed to answer it. J Powell elected reporter.
Resolved That the names of the members of this Com appointed to write or answer Letters or to do any other business for the Society be reported to the Genl Com.   (*carried.*)
The above motion was made by J Powell &

140 Powell's description: 'Report of the Executive Committee / L. C. S. Friday Decr 9th / 1796'. On 10 Dec. Powell sent this report to Richard Ford with a covering letter announcing his election as reporter of the executive committee – 'the principle officer in the Society, except the Secty, as all the correspondence & all the business of the Society must go through my hands'. He enclosed the letter from Maidstone (which Ford found unimportant) and the pamphlet on government from Liverpool, both of which he intended to reclaim by calling at Whitehall.

seconded by Green opposed by Bone his reasons were that in case of any prosecutions it would be a clue to the Attorney General to get evidence.
Resolv'd that the offer of Wm Bosville Esqr. be accepted of attaching that popular Song "Oe'r the vine cover'd hills." with the original musick, to the next months magazine free of any expence to the Society.
Resolv'd that the thanks of the Society be given to Wm Bosville for the above patriotic offer.
Ashly inform'd the Com that he had received £13. .0.0 from the Socety at Paisley by the hands of a citizen from that Place towards paying the expences of the Deputies.
Took into consideration the providing the paper for the next months Magazine. Ashley informd the Com he could not in justice to himself be bound for any more as only 1500 had sold of the last two numbers by which the Society sustain'd a considerable loss. Resolv'd that Citizen Beck the Treasurer be wrote to take upon himself that responsibillity This was afterwards negatived as the Com thought it unjust to request any individual to do that which might in the end be a considerable injury to himself. Resolvd that six members of the Ex Com do indemnify Ashly & Place for taking up £20 worth paper the quantity wanted for the next months Magazine And that when the Accounts were compleated it should be stated to the Genl Com wether it would be prudent to publish any other numbers. Resolved that the above be for the present kept secret lest the stationer should refuse to provide the paper.
Biggs appointed to write to Paisley acknowledging the Receipt of the £13. – . –
Adjournd.

347. Minutes: LCS General Committee, 29 December 1796

Source: Add MSS 27815, fo, 145

G C Sitting of Decr. 29. Citn Binns Chn.
1, Binns 2 Binns 3 Powell 4 Evans 7 Evans 12 Nicholls 14 Evans 16 Don't meet 19 Powell 20 Binns 21 Binns 24 Watkins 28 Watkins 32 Mc.Norton 33 Watkins 34 Vials 35 –

Report of Ex Comte Sitting of Decr. 23.96 Absent. Seal 1st Bigg 1st. Carr 1st. Letter from J. Binns Dublin read in Ansr. to the Last, an answr. to the Letter from bath read amended and orderd to be sent Cn. Green reported that if the Magn. was continued Cn. Fenwick would Edit his Part for two months gratis Namely Jany. & Feby. resolved that Cn. Place be impowerd to right to J G Jones demanding his attendance in this Comte. resolved that Cn. Ashley be Impowered to write to all the Persons of the bail of Jones & B to inform them of the proceedings in stoping the write of ⟨Cera Staccous⟩[141] and that he do preserve a copy for this Comte. on hearing a report that Cn. Green is forming another Socy. in oposition to the L C S and was very Industerious in his endeavours to gain over members to that Socy. from the L C S J Powell by athority of the Comte. put the following Questions to him Question the [First] "are You endeavouring to form such Socy. - ansr. various reasons have concurd in Inducing me to suppose that the Socy. was corrupt in its Conduct & that a man was bound to assert his freedom by withdrawing from tyrany if possible - I have often therefore ceriously thought of Quitting it and have concieved a plan of forming a new Socy. which may be more serviceable to the cause of reform Question 2nd. if so what are the principals of that Socy. - ansr. it apears to me highly improper to detail the principle of a Socy. which is not form'd if it is ever form'd and solicite the correspondence of the L C S they will then come properly forward Qn. 3rd. are You Indeavouring to seduce members from the L C S to form that Socy. Ansr. no - I challenge any man either in or out of the Socy. to prove the contrary in addition to the above Ansrs. I must also state that the Idea of establishing a Socy. in oposition to the L C S is in my idea mean & pitiful & I never did intend to Injure the L C S by any act or deed of mine

Read a letter from Maidstone expressing sur-

prise of not receiving the publications and an Ansr.

Referd to the Ex Comee. –

Read a Letter from Cn. Hardy wishing for publicks thanks to Geo. Tierny and the worthy Electors of the boro.[142]

that this Comee. Do Instruct the Ex C to take the subject of Cn. Hardys Let into their most serious Considrn. respecting their returning thanks to G. T & the Independent Electors of the boro. Considering this as a tryhumph for all the friends of Freedom and a beginning to the downfall to Slavery and Missrepresenta-tion Carried

140 Present 4½ magns.
2. 7 Deputies

Cn. Ashley & Place had resolved to retain the Magns. till the Socy. do indemnify them for the debts due
Resolved that Cns. Ashley & Place be alowed to retain the publications of the Socy.*
after the Balance is deducted that Cn. Ashley stands Indebted to the Socy.
* till the Paper bill is discharged & that this resolution be considerd to extend to the bill of Davidson Carried

resolved that the Members do pay an optional Weekly sum not less than one penny[143] and that this motion be referd to the Socy. for one week only –

LeCake Ward & Simpson Jnr.
Bone & Green & Carr

resolved that each divn. is requested to send in thier money subsd. with directions how it is to be aproperated to the Treasurer either for the Depts or towards the Liquidation of the Debt and that no resolution whatever shall order the money to be aplied to any other purpose

Carried –

141 There are no such words in eighteenth-century law dictionaries. The passage seems to mean that government tried to deny or cancel the bail of Binns and Jones and was prevented from so doing. At the meeting of the executive committee on 30 Dec. Martin was ordered to 'send in his bill of charges incurrd in stopping the Writs against the Bail'. It has been suggested that these words are meant to indicate *certiori*. When Binns and Jones were first brought to trial at the Warwick Assizes, in July, they traversed the indictment, i.e. postponed the trials, and the Crown was granted *certiori*, by which the trials were transferred from Warwick to London (Hardy writes that their trials will come on at Westminster next term). But when they were finally tried in 1797, the trials were held at Warwick. *Certiori* had been cancelled, or stopped.

142 Tierney, invited to stand for Parliament from Southwark, was defeated by George Woodford Thelluson. Tierney then charged that the election was illegal because Thelluson had spent money feasting the electors beforehand. Another election was held, and Thelluson again won. Tierney next charged that Thelluson was ineligible inasmuch as he had been guilty of an illegal act. Tierney then became the Member for Southwark.
143 Originally: 'resolved that the Members of the Socy. do pay a contribution weekly of any Sum optional'.

348. Report from spy Powell: LCS General Committee, 29 December 1796[144]

Source: PC 1/23/A38

Genl Com Decr 29

21 Divisions unrepresented in the Genl Com. Ballard brought a letter from Maidstone to the Genl Com sent to Hardys. likewise a letter to the Genl Com from Hardy. The letter from Maidstone was from a man of the name of Fellows a member of the L. C.S in London it stated that on going down to Maidstone he had visited the Society there & found them in great distress they told him they had written to the L. C. S several times & had received no answer had likewise sent orders for publications & Magazines which they had not received. They wish'd to know wether the Society was willing to send the publications regularly. Refer'd to the Ex Com to inquire into the above circumstances as a letter from Maidstone had been read last week in the Genl Com (acknowledging the receipt of parcels) with its answer.[145]

144 Powell's description: 'Report of Genl Com / L. C. S Wednesday / the 28. & Thursday 29 / Decr. & of the Executive / Com Tuesday 27th. & / Friday 30 Decr. / 1796'.

145 Henry Fellows (not previously mentioned in any LCS document) proselytized in Maidstone until he was arrested in May 1797. In March 1798 he was sentenced to two years' imprisonment for trying to stir up soldiers to be disloyal and to disobey orders. Government suggested that the LCS authorized Fellows's activities in Maidstone: among the letters from Fellows to Bone (seized in April 1798) was one ordering 100 more copies of the Ulster Address, which met 'the Approbation of the Citns here, particularly the Irish Soldiers'; 50 copies of Buonaparte's Address, of the Duke of Richmond's letter, and of Paine's *Agrarian Justice*; and some tickets. In this letter Fellows speaks of 'my last Week's Report' (in which he told Bone to charge the regulations, tickets and magazines to the Maidstone society) and of 'Beck's Letter' (presumably about the LCS magazine, which does 'not go of here, that is the Reason we send 7 Dozen back'). He ends with a 'Report of the Divisions: Divn 39: – 20 present: No new Members. Divn 39: – 20 sent: Do. [i.e. no new members]. The referd Motion in the Report, Negative . . . . With respect to other Divns, we have not been able to furnish them with Tiests, &c, but you shall here when we do.' Government identifies this as written shortly before Fellows's arrest (printed in Appendix 6 of the 1799 *Report of the Committee of Secrecy of the House of Commons*; other letters to Bone in PC 1/41/A138; see also *MP* 5 June 1797, p. 3;

Hardy's letter urg'd the Society to take some public notice of the Triumph of G Tierney in the Borough that the Constitutional Wiggs & other political Societies were about to do the same.
The Com came to the following resolution on it That this Com do instruct the Executive Com to take the subject of Hardys letter into their most serious consideration, respecting the returning thanks to G. Tierny & the independent electors of Southwark considering this as a triumph to all the friends of Freedom & a beginning to the downfall of corruption & misrepresentation.
Ashley & Place having refused to deliver up the stock of Magazine on hand, with the other publications of the Society. retaining them as a security for the debts for which they were bound.
After a long and violent debate (in which the conduct of Ashly was very much reprobated it appearing that whilst the Society was losing money by the Mag. he was making a considerable property of it. viz by advertisements on the Covers profits &a which he had retain'd for his own emolument & that he had likewise injured the Society by keeping back the accounts in which when brought forward the charges of management appeard extraordinary & extravagant.) the Com came to the following resolution.
   Resolvd that Ashley & Place be allow'd to retain the publications till the paper debt is discharged; after the Balance is deducted that Ashly stands indebted to the Society, & that this resolution be considered to extend to the bill of Davidson the printer.
On the last mentioned resolution being put only eight Delegates voted, viz four for, & four against it was carried in the affirmative by the Chairmans casting vote. several delegates immediately left the room declaring they would not attend the Com nor take a Magazine whilst they were in Ashleys hands.
Resolv'd that the members of the Society do pay a contribution weekly of not less than one penny at the option of the members.   (*Refd to the Div*)
Moved that a special Treasurer be appointed to receive the money raised to discharge the debt due to the deputies (*negatived*)
Resolvd that the delegates do pay into the hands of the Treasurer the money raisd to dis-

True Briton, 9 Feb. 1798, p. 4). Since Bone was a bookseller, the secretary of the LCS from Jan. to May 1797, and also a member of the United Englishmen (which administered a test oath to members), it is uncertain in which capacity or capacities Fellows was addressing him.

charge the debts of the society specifying what part is to be applied to the discharge of the debt due to the deputies & what to liquidate the other debts of the Society & that it be applied to no other purpose whatever, & that no other resolution of this Com shall be able to to alter that destination. *(Adjournd)* [146] At the Extra meeting of this Com Wednesday evening the only part of the Accounts considered were their state on the 7th July last when the ledger began. it appeared the Society were then £90. - in debt. the further consideration was adjournd to this evening (Thursday) but the business of Ashly & Place taking up so much time they were not brought forward   the Com sat till four oClock. Evans room in plow Court not being large enough the Com has taken a room at No 8 Wych Street Drury Lane   it is an old Building calld the Queen of Bohemias Palace. Le Coque. J Simpson & Ward were elected to the Ex Com in the room of Bone Elected Secty – Green & Carr. resgd.

124 present. 4½ Mag. 2s/7d to the deputies

Only two members attending the Executive Com on Tuesday evening no business was done.

Executive Com Friday Decr. 30.

Absent Seal 2d time   Simpson 1st. Hodges 1st. present – Biggs, Ward, Powell, Le Coque, Bone, Place. B Binns & Martin attend on business. The letter sent to the Bail of Jones & Binns read. The letter demanding the attendance of J. G. Jones in this Com read. (Jones did not attend) Receved a parcel & letter from Leslie

146 Place recalled that at the end of 1796 he, Ashley and other members of the general committee urged the Society to give up the magazine and concentrate on liquidating the debts. They offered to pay a shilling a week instead of 4½d a month and to go to each division persuading members to increase their contributions. Place and the others laid down two conditions, which were rejected: (1) that the Society use all money for the debts except that needed for current expenses and for necessary publications of no more than four octavo pages; (2) that the members be encouraged to increase their contributions and to collect money from others. Place and his allies believed that the Society's indebtedness was driving away members and preventing others from joining. If their advice were followed, the Society would receive money from members and non-members, would be able to pay all the debts 'speedily', and would 'flourish' (*Autobiography*, p. 153; Add MSS 27808, fo. 78).

the Bookseller at Edinburgh. The parcel contd 140 Mag returnd. 25 of each of the following publications viz "A pennyworth of Politics. Political Micellenies. – "Divine Origin of the British Constitution" "Sermon on Monarchy & £3. . – from the Society at Sterling for the deputies. Ashley had mislaid the letter therefore it could not be read. Martin stated that as the assizes began immediately after next Term it would be necessary to enter into the defence of Jones & Binns, it appeared that he (Martin) thought Toms the Solicitor was discharged on account of his neglect, & that he was employ'd in his stead. The Com told him they had no authority for so doing Toms being employd by J Binns. [147] Resolv'd that this business be deferrd 'till the Com hears from J Binns. Resolvd that Citn Martin do send in his bill of charges incurrd in stopping the Writs against the Bail immediately. [148] Took into consideration the letter sent to the Genl Com from Maidstone. It appearing that Ashly had been guilty of some neglect, Biggs was appointed to prepare an answer. Took into consideration Hardys Letter & the resolution of the Genl Com. thereon. Resolvd that they both be deliver'd to Hodgson for him to prepare a letter of Thanks to G Tierny & the independant electors of the Borough on their late triumph. Place was requested to wait on Thelwall to know wether he had finishd the circular letter to be sent to Absent members. Resolv'd that. Bone, Place & B Binns be empowerd to collect in the debts due to the Society, to be appled to the discharge of the paper bill so that the publications may be taken out of the hands of Ashley & Place & deliverd over to Bone   The Com took into consideration the present distracted state of the Society & came to the following resolutions moved by Bone, seconded by Biggs. 1st. That a special meeting of the Genl Com be call'd on Thursday next at 7 oClock to take into consideration the necessity of immediately calling a General Assembly of the Society to take into consideration the present state of the Society & the means of conducting it in future. 2d Resolvd that members be allow'd to introduce other friends of

147 But the LCS had to pay Toms £20 in 1797 (*Treasurer's Account for August, 1797*, Place Collection, vol. 38, fo. 203).
148 Martin's bill for £3 5s 10d was paid on 26 Jan. 1797 (*Treasurer's Account for January 1797*, Place Collection, vol. 38, fo. 187). During 1797 Martin defended another LCS member, Thomas Williams, until Williams refused to follow his advice to defy the judges (*MC* 6 Feb. 1798, p. 3). On 13 Jan. 1798 Martin died of apoplexy (*MP* 15 Jan. 1798, p. 2).

liberty who wish well to the Society & are interrested in its support 3d That a report of the present state of the Society be drawn up & printed to be laid before the said assembly.[149]

Resolv'd that Citizens Powell & Biggs do draw up the Report. The Com then drew up the following summons to be left at every division immediately.

Citizens

Your Executive Com feeling themselves call'd on to Act with energy in the preasant alarming state of the Society. have come to the following resolutions (*Then follow Resolutions 1. 2 & 3 as above*)

You are therefore earnestly requested to instruct your delegate to be punctual in his attendance at the Com Room No 8 Wych Street Drury Thursday next at 7 oClock in the Evening.

Signd by order of the Ex Com
J Bone Secty
F Place Asst Secty.

A deputation from the Extra Com attended to know wether the circular letter to absent members was ready they were requested to send a member to the Genl Com on Thursday next. Resolvd that the Extra meeting of this com call'd on Monday next do stand adjourned.

Adjournd

149 The report, which was not printed until Feb. 1797, shows that by the end of 1796 the LCS owed £242 1s 8¼d. The deputies' fund was the chief creditor (£93 17s 10¼d), followed by the paper manufacturers Elsee and Cotton (£63 13s). Other creditors included J. Rhynd (£29 4s), Davidson (£16 10s), Trow (£7 7s), Pace (£6 17s). Also, Thelwall (£9 16s 6d), and Beck (£2 8s 3d) (PC 1/41/A138).

PART TEN

1797

Chronology

1797

Feb.	22	French raid at Wales
	26	Order-in-Council suspends Bank of England cash payments
March	30	Jones tried and convicted of sedition; never sentenced
April–May		Meetings held nationwide to petition for dismissal of ministers
April	16–24	First Spithead Mutiny
May	7–14	Second Spithead Mutiny
May 12 – June 15		Nore Mutiny
May	26	Grey's reform proposal debated and rejected in Commons
June	?1	Last issue of *Moral and Political Magazine* of LCS
June	6	Bill to prevent subversion of armed forces passed
July	19	Bill forbidding secret oaths passed
	20	Parliament prorogued
	22–23	General meeting near St Pancras advertised
	29	Magistrates' advertisement states this meeting to be illegal and summons constables
July	31	General meeting dispersed; Ferguson, Stuckey, A. Galloway, Barrow, Hodgson, and B. Binns arrested and bailed; Address to the Nation; Petition and remonstrance to the king
July 6 – Sept. 15		Lord Malmesbury's second peace mission
Aug.	2	Members of Division 10 announce secession
	15	John Binns tried and acquitted of sedition
Oct.	11	Dutch fleet defeated at Camperdown
	13	Hardy's house attacked
	17	Treaty of Campo Formio; France and Austria make peace
Nov.	2	Parliament meets; boycotted by Fox and his followers

Activities of the LCS – January 1797

[Since Bone replaced Ashley as both secretary of the Society and publisher of their
magazine, Ashley had to settle his accounts
for the magazine. At least one of his debtors
was told to transmit the balance of his
account to Ashley by 10 January,[1] and
on 12 January a boy was paid 3d to fetch
the magazines from Ashley's house.[2]

John Bone, originally a muslin clearer,
had become a bookseller. During January
he moved from 8 Weston Street, Southwark, to a house at 120 Holborn Hill,
which was soon used for the meetings of the
the executive committee. On 26 January,
the Society paid him £6 2s 'for Fixtures',
presumably for fitting up his house as a
meeting place.

During this month one of the chief concerns of the Society was their debts. On 5
January the general committee unanimously voted to open a separate subscription for repaying the money borrowed
from the deputies' fund. This subscription
was remarkably successful, for at the end of
January it amounted to £16 7s 9d, including contributions from nine divisions and
Citizen Panther. The 'Liquidation of Debt'
fund, which had been started in October,
took in £2 14s 8½d, including 10s 6d from
'Citizen Powell'. In addition, 11s 0½d came
from contributions listed as 'Weekly Subscriptions', received on 12, 19 and 26
January, from Divisions 15, 4 and 9 each
time and from Divisions 13 and 20 once
each. These seem to be voluntary increases
in weekly payments, or a weekly passing of
the hat.

Dues, liquidation of debt fund, weekly
subscriptions – they were not enough to
meet the January outlay. The Society
had to borrow from individual members
towards the end of the month: on the 21st,
£10 10s from 'Citizen Welch' and £1 1s
from Watling; on the 26th £1 1s each from
Henry and Alexander Galloway; and 10s 6d
from Benjamin Binns, and 5s from Thomas

Evans. The crippling expenses of the month
were payments to Elsee and Cotton of £9
9s on the 12th and £21 on the 21st. In
addition Rhynd received £8 8s and Bone
(as noted above) £6 2s. The total expenditures for the month were £51 4s 7d.

Perhaps the shaky financial situation of
the Society caused the printer Rhynd and
the bookbinder Thomas Williams to abandon
some publication intended to enrich the
Society. On 20 January they wrote to Bone,
'We find it not convenient to proceed at
present with that Work which we had
formed some Design of going on with.'[3]]

349. Circular letter: LCS Executive Committee to defaulting members, 20 January 1797[4]

Source: printed copy, Add MSS 27815, fo. 154;
also Place Collection, vol. 38, fo. 6v

Fellow Citizen,

Your non-attendance at your Division
(together with other defaulters) has been of
such serious disadvantage to the Interests of
our Society, that we feel justified in reminding
you of the neglect – Presuming you were firmly

3 PC 1/41/A138. This letter may refer to the publication of the *Age of Reason*, for which Williams
was prosecuted. Place maintained that he and
Williams agreed to publish it jointly but that
Williams double-crossed him and published it on
his own (*Autobiography*, Appendix to ch. 10).
William Hamilton Reid believed that Williams was
'persuaded by the heads of the party, to undertake
a cheap edition' (p. 5). Perhaps Williams had
approached Bone about LCS sponsorship of the
edition and was now pulling away from them as
well as from Place.

4 This is the circular letter to absent members,
mentioned in minutes of executive committee on
30 Dec. 1796. If written by Thelwall, this is his
last activity in the LCS. Thelwall continued lecturing in other cities during 1797. After an unsuccessful attempt at farming, he returned to the
lecture tour in 1800. For several years he pros-
pered by teaching oratory and curing stammerers.
In 1826 his friends raised £1000 for a magazine
he wanted to start. In 1832 he complained to
Place that only thirty-four people contributed to
a fund to support him. He died in Feb. 1834 while
on a lecture tour at Bath (*Annual Biography and
Obituary*, vol. 19 (1835); entry in *DNB*; Add
MSS 36461, fo. 440; Add MSS 37950, fos. 131-2).

1 Undated letter, summarized as item 39 in government summary of documents seized in April 1978,
when the general committee of the LCS was arrested, PC 1/41/A138.
2 *Treasurer's Account for January 1797*, Place Collection, vol. 38, fo. 187. Other figures for expenditures are also from this account.

fixed in the principles of Liberty, and importance of Reform when you entered the Society; that it was *not* the silly effervessence of momentary zeal, but *sound conviction* which actuated your Conduct, we are staggered to guess at the cause of your lukewarmness – You profess to hope every thing from association *could it be but general.* Can it ever be accomplished if *associators themselves* grow *indifferent* – Are the principles of Freedom less beautiful, because you have oftener contemplated them? Impossible! to *reflect* on them *must* excite regard, and to anticipate their *enjoyment*-thrill every nerve and fire the manly soul – Is it then because your Calamities are less? – because Caprice no longer sacrifices your Fellow-Citizens at the shrine of bloated insolence! that Contractors, Placemen, and Pensioners no longer roll in the luxury of grinding taxes, squeezed from the toils of honest Artizans! that the pittance of the Labourer well provides him with Food, comfortable Clothes, and fills his little Cot with cir'cling Pleasure! – *No* cries of Want assail your Ears! *No* Misery wanders houseless and naked in your Streets! *No* Laws exist to bind the Sons of Liberty and bend you down to silent Slavery! *Ye dare not say there are not.*

Fly then to the standard ye have deserted, let not the Men who have braved the *Vengeance of Apostates* and all the *Rage* of associated Grandeur, be unworthy of their Trophies! Perseverance will give you every thing; and while every Village lifts its feeble Head and looks to be *foster'd* by *you* – deny it not – Rally in your Divisions – Instruct and be Instructed – Shine round your Country with refulgent light; be the admiration of the *living* Age and boast of *future* Patriots – then when they taste the sweets of Freedom unrestrained, their Hearts shall heave with grateful exultation and Joyful own – *they owe them all to* YOU.

Signed by Order of the Executive Committee,
John Bone, Secretary

Committee Room 20th, January 1797.

The Division No. meets at every Evening.

[Two documents from February give the names of the executive committee as B. Biggs, Thomas Harrison, W. H. Stather and T. Ward. The first of these documents is a letter of 6 February stating that Bone has replaced Ashley as secretary and publisher of the magazine and that orders should be

sent to Bone.[5] The second is an authorization from the executive committee to Beck to pay John Binns five guineas.[6]]

350. Explanation of indebtedness: LCS Executive Committee, 13 February 1797[7]

Source: printed copy, PC 1/41/A138

Executive Committee, February 13, 1797.

CITIZEN,

We lay before you an abstract of the pecuniary transactions of the London Corresponding Society, from the 7th of July to the 31st of December last, both inclusive. The Abstract consists of three seperate Statements; the first of which describes only the Debts and Credits of the Society on the 7th of July last; (there not having been any Accounts of Profit and Loss kept previous to that time) when the Balance against the society appears to have been 98l. 12s. 2d¼. from which deducting 12l. 15s. 10d. the value of Publications then on Hand, there remains 85l. 16s. 4¼d. actual Deficiency on the 7th of July, 1796.

The second is a statement of the Profits and Losses which have attended the several undertakings of the Society, between the 7th of July and 31st of December, beginning with the Balance of 98l. 12s. 2¼d. against the Society at the former Day, and leaving a Balance of 185l. 11s. 5¾d. against the Society at the latter, which agreeing with the Balance of Debts and Credits in the third Statement, they may both be considered as correct. The Publications on Hand are valued at 162l. 0s. 6d. which being deducted from the above mentioned Balance, leaves 23l. 10s. 11¾d. actual deficiency at the 31st of December, 1796.[8]

5 From executive committee, summarized as item 40 in government summary of documents seized in April 1798, PC 1/41/A138.
6 18 Feb. 1797, Add MSS 27817, fo. 45.
7 This explanation accompanies three pages of tables detailing the Society's finances from July to December 1796.
8 'It may be proper to remark, that the Magazines on Hand are valued at the wholesale Prices and the other Publications still lower. If by the civic exertions of our Members and Friends any considerable part of this Stock should be accounted for to the Society at retail Prices, this Deficiency will of course be lessened if not annihilated. The retail Prices are, Magazine Common 6d. Hot-pressed 8d. – Correspondence 1s. – British Con[v]ention 6d. – General Meeting at Copenhagen House 2d. – Indictments of Jones and Binns 1d' – LCS note.

388

Notwithstanding the decrease in the actual deficiency, our Friends, when they consider the prospect of our being very shortly called on to defend our Deputies, Jones and Binns, will readily conceive that our pecuniary embarrassments are at this time really greater than they were on the 7th of July last; and we cannot hope to see them make those exertions which are necessary to our relief, without obviating the Charge of misconduct in the contraction of our Debts.

To do this it is necessary to distinguish between those which were contracted previous to the 7th of July last, and the additions which have been made since.

While the Treason and Sedition Bills were in agitation, it is well known we were at a very great expence in holding General Meetings; for the purpose of exciting attention to their probable consequences, and stimulating our fellow Countrymen to those exertions which the privation of so large a portion of their natural and even constitutional Rights appeared to require.

In what degree our efforts contributed to produce that strong and almost general disapprobation which was evinced against those Bills, it is not our part to determine. But we hope that to every Friend of Liberty our intention in holding those Meetings will be sufficient to justify the Expence with which they were attended. It is of little moment to ascertain that Expence with precision, and at this distance of time it would be a matter of much difficulty; but we imagine that including the printed Accounts of the Proceedings which were sent into the Country, and otherwise given gratis, it would be found to amount to nearly as much as the whole of the Society's Debts at the 7th of July, 1796, and possibly exceed them.

Another cause of those Debts has been the sending Deputies into the Country: though this Measure was sanctioned in a General Meeting by Thousands and tens of Thousands, yet for some Months the Execution of it received no pecuniary support, except that of the attending Members of our own Society; and it is a painful, but necessary part of our Duty to state that their numbers were comparitively few, and rapidly decreasing.

We are aware that the Absentees endeavour to justify their Conduct by saying, the exertions of the nation at large respecting the Treason and Sedition Bills were so far inferior to what the Circumstances of the Times required, as to leave no hope but that the Cause of Liberty in Britain would continue to be retrograde.

If it were our business in this place to combat this despondency, we should need no other argument than the rapid increase of our Correspondence, and the continual formation of new Societies in the Country since that time; but supposing (not admitting) that the Absentees were right in their estimation of the national Character, we should not even then conceive their Conduct to have been proper in receding from a Measure, which they had sanctioned with such apparent cordiality. It appears to us, that if subsequent events had changed their Opinion, they ought openly to have advised their Fellow-Citizens to rescind their Resolution. As no such measure was ever proposed by any Division, nor to our knowledge, by any Individual, we cannot but think that a few Minutes reflection will convince the Absentees they are bound by every tie to renew or more properly to redouble their exertions at the present Juncture; – and with this Observation we leave this part of our Accounts.

Since the 7th of July last, the Society has depended solely on the Sale of the Magazine for a permanent Revenue; and the *hitherto* deficiency of that Sale has been the cause of the increase of our Debts.

The deficiency has, in a considerable degree, arisen from that despondency and consequent desertion which we have already noticed; and, if our observations on that Subject have any force, we may speedily hope to find our circumstances considerably improved.

We are aware that some of the earlier Numbers of the Magazine are objected to, as containing a considerable quantity of Matter not sufficiently novel. In opposition to this remark, it is but justice to the Editor and to the Work, to say that the parts objected to are allowed to be replete with Merit, and though currently known in the Metropolis some Months ago, were not in existence in a form easily preservable, or admitting extensive Circulation; under these circumstances it is obvious, that the force of this objection must daily decrease; – and we have received the most extensive Approbation of the later Numbers.

The Sale of the Magazine has also for the last three or four Months been much injured by a circumstance which ought, in our opinion, rather to have stimulated Citizens to promote its Circulation: what we allude to is its having proved, for the present, the means of undermining the Fund established for the defence of the Deputies. We are highly sensible this Circumstance is open to much misunderstanding on the part of our Friends, and much malevolent misrepresentation on the part of our

Enemies. In judging the moral propriety of any action, it is necessary to regard the intention, rather than the event. When the idea of instituting the Magazine was first suggested, the usual Quarterly income of the Society was rapidly decreasing, and the expectation of benefit from the Magazine, both as a source of Revenue to the Society, and vehicle of political information to the Country was so general. that we scarcely remember a referred Question on which the decision was so nearly unanimous. It was known that the small sum then in Hand toward the defence of the Deputies must be used to institute the Magazine, but the danger attending this measure was lost in the confidence of its being speedily reinstated; and we believe that if our Accounts had been then so arranged that we could readily have shewn the Profits on the first Edition of the first Number; the alarm respecting the Deputies would never have existed, and the sale of the Magazine in consequence, have been much increased. When it is considered that in the necessity of publishing a second Edition of the first Number, there was a considerable loss; (viz. the Expence of Resetting the Press) there can be no occasion for offering any apology for the conduct of our acting Members in printing a larger quantity of the Numbers immediately succeeding: They could not foreknow the decrease in the Sale.

Before we leave the subject of the Fund established for the Deputies, it may not be improper to remind our Members, particularly the Absentees, that when the proposal of instituting the Magazine was discussed, no Argument in its favour had greater weight than the probability of its proving the means of enabling us to use every pecuniary exertion in behalf of our Deputies, and an attentive perusal of the annexed Accounts must convince every Citizen, that if in place of puny Criticisms and groundless Alarm, the sale had been vigorously promoted, and kept up to that of the first Number, this effect would have been produced. It should also be remembered, that at that time there was not any extensive source of assistance toward the defence of the Deputies, on which we could rely. The Country had not then assumed that civic appearance which we have since seen with so much pleasure, and the solicitation of Subscriptions in Town was known by experience to have been productive of much injury; it would therefore be unjust in the extreme to blame our late Committees for entering into a measure; toward which they were so strongly urged both by the immediate necessities of the Society and the probability

of permanent Advantage. And tho the magazine has not yet fulfilled their expectations with respect to our finances yet we cannot admit it has been barren of favorable effect on the general Cause; since without vanity we may attribute to it some part of the present Appearance of the Country: But to obviate all objection to future exertions in behalf of the Deputies we have to state that by a Resolution of the General Committee on the 5th. of last month, all monies since received on Account of the Deputies, whether for the purpose of increasing the fund for their defence, or of paying the Debt due from the Society to that Fund, have been received by Citizen Beck, (Sadler, Oxford-Road,) as Treasurer for the Deputies, and not as Treasurer for the Society; and will hereafter be kept entirely distinct from the pecuniary Transactions of the Society and accordingly reported in the monthly Accounts for the Satisfaction of the Subscribers: In order to mark this distinction more strongly it was proposed that some other person should be appointed Treasurer for the Deputies, but those of the Members of the General Committee who had *avowed* the greatest Anxiety on Account of the Deputies, objected to the proposal, saying they knew no member more extensively known, or more unanimously considered as an Object of Confidence.

As the Editor's Salary has been the subject of much animadversion, we think it our duty to state, that for the last and present Month, it has been voluntarily relinquished. And however anxious the Society may be to give to Merit its due reward, yet as it will probably be necessary in the future conduct of the Magazine to use the most rigid economy, consistent with the obtainment of interesting Matter, we take this opportunity of earnestly soliciting the assistance of all our literary Friends.

The expence of Management having also been spoken of as being capable of retrenchment, we think it necessary to state that it has lately undergone a most rigid examination before the General Committee; when every article of Expenditure, which from the brevity necessary in printing the Monthly Accounts, had been deemed objectionable, was explained *even to unanimous satisfaction.* Respecting the permanent Expences which have been specially instituted by reference to the Divisions, we must remind those who object to them, that though the income of the Society has formerly been greater; its business was never so extensive and laborious as at the present Moment. Of the truth of this Remark and its application to the point in Question, those who have born the largest share in the labours of the Society (*themselves unpaid and wholly disinterested in the issue*) are the most capable of judging, and they judge accordingly: Of the present or any past Executive Committee, we know no Individual who does not agree but that the Salaries paid by the Society, ought in strict Justice to be rather increased than diminished, and very nearly the same unanimity prevails in the General Committee: This alone we believe will generally be deemed conclusive: but, waving personal confidence, let us ask, with how much difficulty do many Divisions find Delegates for the General Committee? and with how much greater difficulty do the General Committee find Members willing to undertake the greater labours of the Executive Committee? It must be remembered, that our Society does not contain many Men who can afford to give away any considerable portion of their Time. Of those who are most likely to afford it, many are deeply engaged in their private Concerns, and others have not a confidence of their possessing the necessary Talents. And were we otherwise circumstanced, it would bear a question whether a dereliction of our present mode would be consistent either with Justice or the true principles of Liberty. Since it is evident that our choice must necessarily be circumscribed to those Men in whom Talent and Confidence were combined with leisure.

To reward every Man according to his Works is the prevailing Sentiment with good Citizens, and we are sorry that even an Individual should shew any reluctance in applying this Maxium to the affairs of the Society; but we hope that farther reflection, or rather a closer intimacy with the Society's business will lead to a more equitable mode of reasoning.

We have stated that the increase of our Debt since July last, has arisen from the want of an adequate Sale for the number of Magazines which have been printed. We therefore request our Members and Friends to use their utmost Exertion toward circulating the Stock on Hand,[9] and we cannot think those Exer-

tions are likely to prove fruitless, since the enormous expence which would have been necessary to communicate general knowledge of the Magazine by means of Advertisements, has, in all probability prevented Thousands of good Citizens from knowing that we had engaged in such an undertaking.

It is almost unnecessary to point out the advantages which would result from placing the Society on a respectable footing at this Juncture. So general and rapid has the progress of popular Association lately been in the Country that our Society, like an aged Parent, broken by past toils, may be said to view its vigorous offspring with a mixture of rivalry and parental affection. But it may be doubted whether without a centre of Communication, these efforts will ever produce the effect of removing our present Oppressions from the mild and gentle operation of Reform, conducted on principles of universal beneficence, and the exclusion of partial advantages and factious enmity.

If it be true that the present Ministry have pursued a regular systematic Plan for enslaving the People: If it be true, that while taking more from the Liberties they have added more to the Burthens of the Country, than any preceding Administration, their enmity becomes the only necessary comment on our past exertions, It is not as they assert, occasioned by our being "the Great Revolutionary Engine;" but by our being the Constitutional Engine, likely to rouze our Fellow-Countrymen to seek their long lost Rights of Universal Suffrage and Annual Parliaments; by lawful and reasonable, but yet by firm and determinate means.

And shall this so laudable an attempt be suffered to fail for want of a little timely assistance. While it is on Record that our Association has braved the combined malice of Hords of public Plunderers; – shall it be said that it sunk into dissolution from the captiousness, the langour, or the selfishness of the Men who composed or professed to approve it. We hope otherwise: For should this be the event, it may be truly said, the Liberties of Britain were not undermined by the fraud of a Pitt or a Dundas; nor stormed by the sanguinary violence of a Burke or a Windham; but they went to ruin from the general depravity of the People themselves.

Signed by Order of the Committee,

JOHN BONE, Secretary.
J. POWELL, Assitant Secretary.

London

9 Perhaps it was in response to this appeal that fourteen members of Div. 31 signed a statement that they 'Acknoledge their responsiblitity to the L C S for as many Magazines as they shall take of the Socity not exceding fifty.' They authorized their delegate to bring three copies of the first six numbers, five of no. 7 and seven of no. 8. The signers include Anthony Beck (treasurer of the LCS) Robert Lascelles and Thomas Massie (undated, PC 1/41/A138).

351. Minutes: LCS General Committee, 9 March 1797

Source: Add MSS 27815, fos. 155-7

G. C Sitting of March 9 1797   Yong Chair

Depns		
3.	Steed[10]	10th Divn next door to the white port Newinton butts
13	Haseldon	————————————
21	Sheperd	Report of Ex Comte March
32.	Jameson	3 Present the Whole Comte.
	52 Greek St.	
38		read an abstract of a Lr.
39	Stather	from J. Binns requesting all
41		his Letters to the Socy
40	Evans	while on Depn. to ports-
		mouth and Birm. and the

Letters from the Birmingham Socy. of the 24 Jany. 96 and 50 Copies of Jones & Binns Indightments   Resolved that the Letters &c aluded to be sent the same Lr. Stated it to be necessary that 70 Guineas be ready before the commencement of the tryal 30 of which must be emediately paid[11]
resolved that Cns. Wadson & Bone do wait on Ashley for the amount of the Shares he prom-

10 Cancelled: '8 Drayton'.
11 Between 10 and 28 March 1797, the deputies received £46 13s; £31 19s 6d was given them before they left London for their trials, and £14 14s 6d was sent to them, presumably at Warwick. During March the fund to liquidate their debt received contributions of £38 1s 9d from the divisions, from individuals, from friends of members, from patrons of the Globe in Hatton Garden, from a supper at the Coach and Horses, and from Maidstone (*Treasurer's Account for March, 1797*, Place Collection, vol. 38, fo. 191). Place recalled that since John Binns was a friend to both him and Ashley, and Jones 'a very old acquaintance of Ashley's and rather an intimate acquaintance of mine and as we both of us had concurred in sending them to Birmingham, we thought ourselves bound to render them all the assistance in our power and we did so, as well in the society as in private' (Add MSS 27808, fo. 79). Neither Ashley's nor Place's name is listed as one who collected from friends. Probably they had subscription books, as had at least 111 people. Thomas Browning later wrote to Bone about his book: 'at the latter part of March or the beggining of april 1797 (to the best of my recoletion) there was an order from the Committee for mony to be raised for the Deputies in consequence of which order I brought all I had raised and should have brought it before had I not lost the subscription Book the sum was one shilling and seven pence and the person I paid it to took down my name and the number of the Book which was No. 82. and told me he would give the same to you as soon as you come in' (undated, PC 1/41/A138).

ised to collect on the Deputies account Resolved that Cn. Leak & B Binns do wait on Cn. Jones to consult on the appropriation of the 30 Guineas Examined the account of Cn. J Binns of the disposal of the money advanced him & the same proving to be expended for the Joint use of the Deputies this comte. is satisfied therewith   read a Lr. offering to convey a Lr. from the Socy. to Cn. Gerald[12]
a Lr. read to Nottingham
a Do. to Gerald
a Do. from Milburn

moved that the Latter part of the Melburn be taken down   Carried

[There follows 'the Latter part of the Melburn' letter of 15 June 1796, describing the resistance of the miners and of the author to the Militia Bill.]

Cn. Wadson to write one read a Lr. from norwich Bone to ansr.
read the ansr. to the norwich Lr. amended and orderd to be sent
resolved that a set of Magns. be sent with the Lr. to Cn. Gerald
recd. an account from Cn. Geo Williams of cash paid to the house keeper at Beauford Building 15 Weeks at 2/6 pr. week 1. 17. 6 order'd to be discharged in course 4 March Extve sitting absent Le-coak the 1st. time various Cns. of this Comte Deputed to wait on the Divns. not having yet contributed to the Liquidating the debt read a Lr. from melburn Cn. Williams to ansr. Crosfield apointed on the Literary comte.   Cns. Wadson & Bone reported that they had waited on Ashley according to Depn. he Informed them he had not collected any money for that purpose
8th. March absent Will 1st   Leak 1st   Lecoak 2nd.   Earley 1st.
recd. reportes from the Cns. who ware to wait on the Divns. on the Deputies account Divn. 6 2.2. – 8. – 10.6 – 19 2.4.6 – 20. – 2. – 32. – 12. – 40 – 1.9. – 27 – 9:1 [total:] 6.2.3   read a Lr. from Leiester ordering Magn   Wadson to ansr.   Bone orderd to send the Magn   read a Lr. to Cn. Gerald   aproved & orderd to be sent adjourned – true Report

Motions read from 14 Divn. 19 Do. 1 do 7 Do. 27 Do.

12 Although Gerrald died almost a year earlier, on 16 March 1796, the news of his death was not reported in England until 8 April 1797 (see cutting in Place Collection, vol. 38, fo. 40).

Depn. from the Sons of Liberty admited to
the Honour of the Sitting – Plade T. Wadson
G. Blyh B. Meath – united Sons of Liberty
Come. March 9th. We have apointed a Depn.
to the L C S by order of the Comte Williamson president the Depn are Instructed to enqr.
of the L C S if it is their Intention to hold a
G M 2nd to Enqr if the publick in genl are to
be Invited to the G M and if Societies are to
be admited to the M as Socys. or as Individuals 3rd. and perticulary to Enqr if the L C S
can consistant with their plan Inform this
Socy. of the Subjects that they propose to
submit to the public on that day 4th. to be
informd if any restrictions are Laid on Individuals or Socys. from Delivering theyr sentiments at the Meeting

Movd that the return on the Referd Questions
be taken   aff 213. 76 Neg   187 M
G. C Resolves that a Depn. Do wait on the
Sons of Liberty to give them every possible
Inform on the Subject of a G M carried
unanimous

Depn. Divn. 19. was herd on the subjec of the
Wig Intrest reterrnd satisfied —

---

it was next resolved that Cn Jones be herd

Resolved that Cn. J Jones & Bins have the
thank of the Socy. & that the Socy will do
every thing in their power for their support –
Carried –

---

6 Mar 358 Q M   £ 1.   2   8½
           P M   1. .16   –
           Dep -   15... 8.. 3
                     ————————
                     18. . 6 .11½

352. Minutes: LCS Executive
Committee, c. 23 March 1797[13]

Source: Add MSS 27815, fos. 151–1v

B. Binns Citn Benjn Binns has received from
different Subscription
   Books on Account of the Deputies as follows

13 Date conjectured from internal evidence.

B Binns

No	1	£0. 1. 0
	13	0. 4. 0
	12	0. 2. 6
	27	0. 1. 0
	85	0.11. –
	111	0.18. 3

Recd from
Citn. Barton   0. 3. 6
   &
from Citn
   Ballard   0. 2. 6
             ————
             2. 3. 9

Reced by Beck but not accountd for
in the Monthly Accounts
No 13 – £1. 1. –
   10   0. 9. 6
       ————
       1.10. 6

Reced by Wm Russell West-
ern District not accounted
for in Monthly Account

NB. in the No 28 ⎫ No 10   £0. 2. 4
there has been   ⎪   21   0. 6. 6
reced 19s/3 of   ⎪   23   0. 8. 3½
which there has ⎬   28   0. 5. 8
been paid to   ⎪   29   0. 1. 2
Treasure 13/7   ⎪   62
which is accoun- ⎪   Accounted for in
ted for   ⎭   monthly Accounts
                        3/3
                      ————
                      1. 3.11½

Reced by T Wallington not accounted
for in Monthly Accounts
No 27. £0.2.6
     ————
     0.2.6
Reced Nothing on
80. 81. 74. 68. 61. 72 70. 4

                      2. 3. 9
                      1.10. 6
                      1. 3.11½
                      2. 6
                      ————
                      5. 0. 8½

Citn. Mayne noticed to this Committee that rent for the room the Genl Committee meet in, being due next Saturday, viz 1 Quarter 1.19. 4½ –

Read the Letter to Norwich approved & ordered to be sent – (Powell)

Read the Letter to Loughbro', do do Watson
Read the Circulr letter (Watson) ordd to be taken into reconsideration next sitting

---

Resolved that this committee hold an extra sitting tomorrow evening at 7 Oclock

---

Deputed by Letter Cit Wilkinson who is now at Bath to receive of Cit Gould Books there whatever money he has recd on Acct of the Deps

---

Read a Let from Bath – (Watson) to be answd

[The trials of Jones and Binns]

[On 30 March John Gale Jones was tried at Warwick Assizes for his activities in Birmingham in March 1796, when he was a deputy from the LCS. His counsel included Samuel Romilly and Felix Vaughan. Jones was acquitted of four charges but convicted of using seditious words ('I want to know whether the people of Birmingham will submit to the treason and sedition laws'). No sentence was handed down, probably because the court was awaiting the outcome of John Binns's trial, scheduled for the next day.

Binns was prepared for his trial, but it was postponed to the next assizes because only ten jurors were accepted by both sides. The Crown rejected Binns's suggestion that two more jurors be selected at random from the group of thirty-two challenged jurors.

Binns was finally tried – and acquitted – on 15 August. Jones was never sentenced.[14]

14 On 6 May Romilly moved that judgment against Jones should be stopped. He argued that the words for which Jones was convicted showed curiosity rather than intent to stir up sedition. When the case came up at the beginning of July, the court postponed it until the next term. At that time (7 Nov.) Erskine produced an affidavit that Jones was too ill (haemorrhage) to be present. On 1 Feb. 1798, Erskine joined Romilly and Vaughan in again presenting arguments that no sentence should be passed on Jones. The court announced that they would give notice

The controversy with Sheffield over a general meeting

The decision to hold a general meeting in spite of the restrictions imposed by the Treason and Sedition Bills was taken in March (it may be the question on which the divisions voted during the first week of the month). But proposals for such a meeting had been made earlier, perhaps as early as December, when the Society discussed its debts and the continuance of the magazine. Place connected the discussion of the debts, the magazine and the general meeting: 'Many of the influential members were of opinion that if a public meeting was held, it would act as a stimulus, induce great numbers of persons to join the society, and others to assist it with money, and they had no doubt at all, that by this means the society would be soon in a flourishing condition. We on the contrary were as certain that a public meeting would ruin it. The matter was frequently discussed and it was at length resolved to continue the Magazine and to call a public meeting.'[15]

On 23 March the executive committee issued a printed folio letter to reformers, announcing the Society's resolve 'once more to call a public meeting of the friends of freedom, in the open air . . . to draw up a remonstrance to the king, in favour of peace; and request him to discharge his Ministers, they having lost the confidence of the nation'. As soon as the date of the meeting has been determined, the letter continued, notice would be given in the newspapers, and it was hoped that 'similar meetings will be held, in every town in Great Britain, on the same day'. The recipients of this letter were urged to discuss it with their fellow citizens and report their determination to the LCS. The letter, signed by William Williams, president, and John Bone, secretary, also detailed the misfortunes of the country in flamboyant rhetoric ('a despotic Administration, whose hands are dyed with the blood of innocence', 'mangled carcases scattered in every quarter of the globe', 'dying groans of your expiring Friends', 'your famished wives and weeping children') and urged the Society's fellow citizens to 'assume that undaunted courage, which characterized your fathers'. A post-

when they would deliver their opinion (*Cambridge Intelligencer*, 15 May 1797, p. 2; 17 Feb. 1798, p. 3; *MPM*, vol. 2, pp. 174–5; *MC* 8 May 1797, p. 3; 4 July 1797, p. 3; 8 Nov. 1797, p. 4).
15 *Autobiography*, pp. 153–4.

script reminded them that a meeting would be legal if seven housekeepers sign an advertisement in the newspaper of the town or county, specifying the purpose of the meeting.[16]

Less than two weeks later the 'Friends of Reform in Sheffield' communicated their determination, as requested. (Somewhat to the annoyance of the LCS this letter appeared in the newspaper three days before the LCS received printed copies of it.) The Sheffield reformers, in agreement with friends at Norwich, declared against an open air meeting to petition for peace and a change of ministers. They then detailed nine reasons for their opposition to such a petition: the lack of attention paid to previous petitions; the insufficiency of a temporary peace and a change of ministers; an unwillingness to have such a petition used by a political party which had not pledged itself to a change of measures; a conviction that the present administration had brought the country beyond 'palliative remedies', that 'an awful crisis' was near, and that those who had brought about the 'Mischief' should stay in place 'till the hour of retribution, that they may sustain the responsibility'.[17]

The LCS issued a printed reply three weeks later, on 24 April. In it they refuted the points made by the Sheffield reformers: they did not intend to have a petition, but a remonstrance, the basis of which would be the need for a radical reform, a fair and equal representation of the people; they have nothing to do with political parties and would not believe any pledges such parties did make; 'history and experience' do not show that bad rulers make way for the 'emancipation of the people'. 'We have nothing to do with futurity, the present is only within our grasp. . . . Will you wait till you are dragooned like Ireland – massacred like the Poles? . . . . The system of delay . . . is passive obedience in a modern dress. It may appear plausible to timid men; but it will never rescue our country from the gang of swindlers that prey upon its vitals.' Contrary to the Sheffield letter, Norwich has officially announced that it intends to cooperate with the LCS plan. One of the king's advisors has said that ' "some of the London Corresponding Society should be hanged and quartered, as examples to the rest" '. Why? For wishing peace and liberty? 'We solemnly declare, in the presence of Almighty God . . . that we have no views except the happiness of mankind, . . . and should the minister violate the constitution, and illegally attempt to deprive us of our lives and liberties, we swear . . . that, as we shall not be the first to take up arms, we shall be the last to lay them down – we shall either recover our natural rights, or lie buried under the smoking ruins of our country.'[18]

On 15 May Sheffield concluded this exchange with another printed letter, reasserting their conviction that meetings for the purposes of petition or remonstrance could have no tendency to establish the principles for which they associated. Such meetings only serve the purpose of political parties by pushing the INS out and the OUTS in. The reformers' abhorrence of the political corruption, their attachment to equality of rights – these sentiments have been sufficiently declared. Moreover, a remonstrance for peace and against ministers, even if heeded, would not eliminate 'the civil war of taxation' and 'Borough-mongering and Funding Systems'. The corruption must work its own cure, must go on until there were no longer means by which to patch up and piece together its detestable systems. Then ministers would be obliged to petition the people. Then the men who succeeded these ministers would find that the only way to go forward was with the people; 'in short they must feel that they are a part of the people, and nothing more'.[19]

16 Place Collection, vol. 38, fo. 33.
17 *Answer of the Friends of Reform in Sheffield, summoned to take into Consideration the Letter of the London Corresponding Society, on the subject of a Proposed Meeting, to petition the King to dismiss his Ministers, &c.*; signed T. Needham, chairman, and W. Camage, secretary; 4 April 1797; *MPM*, vol. 2 (April 1797), pp. 157–60. According to a spy sending government tidbits of old news in 1799, Thelwall wrote this *Answer* (PC 1/45/A164).
18 *Answer of the London Corresponding Society, Respecting a General Meeting to the Friends of Reform in Sheffield*, signed W. J. Early, president, and J. Bone, secretary; Place Collection, vol. 38, fo. 59; this copy belonged to John Richter.
19 *Reply of the Friends of Liberty in Sheffield, summoned to take into Consideration the Answer of the London Corresponding Society respecting a General Meeting*, signed William Dewsnap, president, and William Camage, secretary; *MPM*, vol. 2 (May 1797), pp. 228–32. Place shared the Sheffield view that government would collapse from its own corruption, as he indicated in his categories of LCS opinion on reform: some

The LCS intention to hold a public meeting was also announced in an address to Lord Oxford, dated 31 March, and published in the April *MPM*, which was issued at the beginning of May. (On 23 March Oxford moved that the Lords send the king an address urging peace; after this motion was rejected, Oxford filed a protest, giving his reasons for moving the address, including the need to remedy the abuses of 'the true spirit of the Constitution'.) The LCS address to Oxford speaks of their pleasure at reading his speech, of their indignation at his treatment by 'the King's Parliament', and of the admirable behaviour expected of 'the People's Parliament' if it existed.[20]]

353. Minutes: LCS General Committee, 19 April 1797

Source: PC 1/41/A138

G C Ap 19 1797 ⟨there⟩ was 7 Unrepresented Ds. which were regularly Supplied with Deputies the Deputation from Div 1 to Oppose the quetio[n] adjourned for 3 months: 10l ⟨57Pc⟩ quar 17. .11.

354. Minutes: LCS General Committee, 27 April 1797 (government summary)[21]

Source: PC 1/41/A138

Genl. Commee April 27. 1797 Motion from Rhynd requesting payment of his bill – refd.

members believed Parliament could be persuaded to reform itself; others believed that Parliament could even be persuaded to set aside the king and Lords; still others thought Parliament would never grant reform 'but that Government would be carried on, the abuses continually increasing . . . an explosion would be caused, and a representative government spring out of the Chaos, they who thought thus were strenuous in their exertions to have the people well instructed in the principles of Representative Government . . . . I and my most intimate friends, were of this opinion' (*Autobiography*, pp. 196–7). 'A very few were for using violence, for putting an end to the government by any means foreign or domestic' (Add MSS 27808, fo. 114).
20 Signed Robert Watson, president, and John Bone, secretary; vol. 2, pp. 155-6. Oxford's address and protest were published with the LCS address (pp. 152-5). On 13 April Watson, Williams, Leake and Powell presented the address to Oxford at his house in Portman Square and received his thanks.
21 This is item 52 in a government summary of

to Ex Commee[22] – from Citz Williams requesting assistance to procure copy of his indictment[23] – Citz. Beck promised to advance £5 for Citz Jones & to pay £3. 17. ordd. for Binns[24] – Bail for Citz Binns – Div. 14 for meeting on or before 19 May – 19 for – 40 – 8th. May – 21 – 15 May

355. Minutes: LCS General Committee, 25 May 1797

Source: PC 1/41/A138

Genl Comee. L. C. S. 25 May, 1797 –

Deputns. appd – Rept. Ex: Comee May 24th – Early in Chair; all prest. read Lr. to Norwich,
> apd. & ordd sent – recd Lr. from Manchester: – ordd. Ansr – recd Lr. from Shefd. with Cops. of their reply to our printed Lr. – Ordd. Lr. to be written to Sheffd. – Extra Sittg to be held tomw. Evg at 7 OClk

Do. to defer delivy of Oratn to Memy of Gerald till Conference held with Genl. Comee. – Adjd – 25th. – Lecoq in Chr. – absent Watson: – Took into Considn the Resolns. of 18th May & fully confirm'd the same: – But this Comee. havg no personal pique against Citn. Bone, the Secy & considg the Expce incurrd in the House in Holborn, recomd. in Case he shd. be no longer Secy that the Saly shd. be pd. him up to Michs. Next[25] & that the new Secy shll

documents seized in April 1798, when the general committee was arrested.
22 According to the treasurer's accounts, he was never paid.
23 For publishing the *Age of Reason*. If the assistance he sought was financial, there is no record that he received it.
24 The *Treasurer's Account for April 1797* lists undated payments from the deputies' fund: £3 to the deputies by Leake, £5 to Binns by Powell, and £2 2s to Jones by Herbert (a Coventry bookseller). These were probably sums sent to the deputies at Warwick. In addition Jones was given £5 on 7 April and Binns £5 16s 6d on 17 April. During April the fund to liquidate the deputies' debt took in £11 11s, including £5 from Thomas Brand, £1 1s from [William?] Williams, £3 from Leake, and £1 11s from Bath (Place Collection, vol. 38, fo. 193).
On 27 April Jones was paid £5 3s 7d and Binns £3 17s. At least for Jones, this cleared the Society's indebtedness for his expenses at Birmingham and Warwick, including coach hire ('Cit Jones's Acct', Add MSS 27815, fo. 124).
25 On 11 May Bone received a salary payment of £2 4s. This is the only entry of Bone's salary during the six months he was secretary. Discussion of paying him until midsummer was foolish.

do the business gratis. – Finis. –

Lr. to Norwich read. – Do. from Sheffd. with printed Lr.

The Ex Com: propd. to confer respectg Oratn (Gerald's.)

Divn. 6: – Object to confind mode of Dely & merceny appearance

    26: – Do —— Do —— Do

Wms. for Ex Com objd. to Sunday: – objd. to usg the money for other purposes while Socy in debt: – Sd. open Air could be apd. to if meetg too numerous but could not recede from open to Room. –

Ward & J. Binns objd. to Sentts. of Wms. & delay as prodve. of disappts.

Watson – Allusions to Thelwall & Binns: – Binns. – warmly Ansd. – Darke: confd. – do. Lemaitre do –

Lemaitre moved censure on Watson; Nichols seconded: – Watson in ansr. to them expld. that he had no allusion to Thelwall. – Binns & Lemaitre intimated to Watson to avail himself of interpretation of warmth of Debate: – Watson apologd. –

Motn. of Divn. 6: – Negatd. – Do. for open Air by Lemaitre: do. – Oratn to be Friday 1st[26] June as before resolved. – Tickets of Secy.

Darke enqd. about Genl. meeting. –

Letter from Maidstone: Fellowes in Maidstone Gaol: – No Warrant

    Threats against Divn. no avail but the contrary more numerous. –

Motn. by Binns denying sendg such parcel: – By Gl. Comee.: Ex Com: or Secy.

Motns. of Divn.

  20: Censg Ex: Comee. on 13 May usurpg

  23: Approvg – do. – do. – & thankg them

  40: Reprobatg Bone:

  22: Approvg Ex Com: up to 13 May inclusive

  26: Censg of Ex Comee. –

   3: Censg some members of the Ex: Com. –

   7: Reprobg both Genl. Comee. & Junto of Ex Com:

   6: Ex Com: forfeited Confidence particularly Watson. –

Much vague conversation. – Binns on Acct. of Health declin'd conductg ye business

Resolns. of Ex Com: of 18 May read: relative to supersedg Bone. – Williams in Explann. –

    Brasset consd. Bone official: –

Bone imprudent in bringg it forward: – Imperfect in copying Letters: Reserved to them & careless to others respectg private addresses. –

Bone in reply proved Watson & Kennedy depd to Portsmth; with Comn to form popular Socs.[27] – Expld. reserve & carelessness. – Trouble with Mag: & irregulr. meetgs of Ex: Com: – Accus'd Stather of divulgg the Business of Ex Com: prematurely. – The Ex Com: keep Accts? how. Watson kept parcel & misrepresented to Brasset.

Powell:, – sd. Bone had acted treacherously in professg to withdraw charges & yet in his defence had stated them. – Gave an instance of Bones want of literature & carelessness of Letters. –

Leake thought Watson going to Glasgow: – ? how was Portsmouth in the way to Glasgow:[28]

The Resignatns. of the Ex Comee accepted 8 to 3. –

Beck called for explanation of £5. . – . . –[29]

Leak sd pd. Sammell 2.10. –[30]

Powell interrupted him, sd: for Literary Committee

---

27 The animosity between Bone and Watson and two of the charges against Bone are indicated in a government summary of a letter from Bone to an unnamed person: 'A Letter signed John Bone complaining that Dr. Wats[on] with three other persons assuming the name of the Executive Committee had accused him of going to Portsmouth to commit Treason in the name of the Corresponding Society & that he had assumed the Character of Secretary to the L. C. S to procure entertainment at the House of the person addressed & desiring an answer to vindicate him from the latter part of the charge' (n.d., PC 1/41/A138).

28 At issue is the involvement of LCS members with the mutinies at Spithead in April and May. Apparently both Watson and Bone were at Portsmouth during the mutinies. Powell later testified that they were there together, but here Watson seems to have accused Bone of taking treasonable action in Portsmouth in the name of, but without the authority of, the LCS. Leake (probably a defender of Bone) questioned Watson's reasons for being in Portsmouth when he said he he was going to Glasgow. An associate of Watson believed that Watson was sent by the LCS to assist the mutiny, that Galloway was later sent to deny that Watson had authority from the LCS, and that, as a result, Watson quarrelled with the Society ('Extract from the further Examn. of Henry Hastings', PC 1/43/A152).

29 Probably the last item in the list of May disbursements: 'Balance due to Treasurer, including Ashley's Balance as per last. 5.0.5.' Ashley's balance in April was £3 5s 2d, presumably money he owed the Society for magazines he sold while publisher of the MPM.

30 Accounts for 1797 and Jan. 1978 show no repayment to Leake.

26 Must be wrong: 1 June 1797 was Thursday.

For Ex. Com.
   Ridley
   Thos. Jones
   Fenwick
   Lemaitre
   Galloway
   Jas. Powell
13 New Membrs. – 518 prest. –
   Mags   –.. 9.. – by Secy
   Qge   1.. 6.. 6
   Genl Purps   6

           1..16.. –

D. 3d. box T. M.
     J R

356. Letter: Powell to Bone, c. 15 June 1797[31]

Source: PC 1/41/A138

Citizen Bone

I am not able to attend the Comitte this eveng I have sent you the book by the 10th article in the constitution if not able to attend by giving you intimation you are to appoint a

---

31 Address: 'Joseph / Bowles / St. Margrets Parish'. Government description: 'Publi private / Letters'. Date conjectured: the punctiliousness of Powell's alluding to the precise article of the constitution which he is observing suggests he is writing at the time when Bone was being criticized for running the LCS affairs haphazardly. Note on verso in a third hand: 'his Distinterestedness ought to be pointed out'.

The absence of reports from Powell in 1797 and 1798 is puzzling inasmuch as he was both a delegate and a spy during this period. In an undated letter, probably written in June 1797, he assured Ford that he was not a double agent: 'I'm affraid sir that unfortunate suspicion, that I was sent to you by the other party still has influence against me, on my honor Sir there's not a person on earth not even my own family acquainted with my connection at your office besides myself.' In this long letter explaining his financial transactions with government (especially his need for £20 'immediately'), he described an activity involving LCS members: 'Just after his acquital, Thelwall established what was called a conversatione ev'ry monday evening at his house to which the principal men of the party were invited. I also for the purpose above mention'd [i.e. to 'ingratiate' himself with the LCS in order to provide information to Ford], knowing from the place I had then & your generosity I could afford it (indeed the expence was trifling bread & cheese & porter only being allowed.) mine was more numerously attended even than Thelwalls' (PC 1/23/A38).

---

person to take minutes of the Committes proceedings in my stead. Mather will do it.
             Health & Fraternity
Thursday Afternoon
                 J Powell
     —

N B If you have got a Geralds Trial to lend out send it.

[June–July activities]

[During June and July the country correspondence was kept up, letters from seven cities being paid for in June and from five cities in July.[32] These letters do not survive. A letter from Glasgow, intercepted by the Provost of Glasgow, suggests reasons why the unintercepted correspondence may have been intentionally destroyed: the writer described 'a Secret Union' of three thousand people in Glasgow who were in communication with 'nigh five hundred' other societies in Scotland and with 'our Bretheren in Ireland'. The Postscript admonished: It will be necessary that all Letters you receive from us be destroyed.'[33] This need for secrecy made another correspondent send his letter without a signature. He identified himself as a person who formerly corresponded with the Society. He now directed several small societies united as 'The Society of Universal Revolution'.[34]

About the first of June the last issue of the *Moral and Political Magazine of the London Corresponding Society* (for May) appeared, and three shillings was spent on an advertisement notifying the public of the 'dissolution of editorship'. The major expense of June was £14 14s listed as 'Law expences of Elsee and Cotton's account'. The total expenditures for the month were £17 10s 5d. Even with a donation of £5 5s from 'Citizen Everet', the Society did not take in enough money from dues, sale of magazines and from the fund for general purposes to cover these expenditures (£15 17s 3d).

---

32 *Treasurer's accounts for June and July*, Place Collection, vol. 38, fos. 197, 201.
33 Government copy of letter from Ralph Stevenson, president, and John Parcell to LCS, 14 June 1797, PC 1/40/A132.
34 Government summary of letter to Evans and Bone, n.d., PC 1/41/A138. Caution may not be the only reason that most of the correspondence has disappeared. Bone was probably less methodical about preserving it than was his predecessor, Ashley, assisted by the meticulous Place.

The subscription to repay the deputies' fund took in only 12s 9½d during June. Facing a bill from the solicitor Toms (paid in August), the Society made another appeal for money. This brought in £25 18s 9½d during July, of which all but £3 4s came from the divisions. On 17 July the Society issued another circular letter 'to the United Corresponding Societies of Great Britain' asking for money from societies which had not yet contributed.[35] They explained that the delay of Binns's trial caused 'a heavy train of law expences', that 'these trials have already involved this society in an expence of £400 from the delay above-mentioned', and that 'further expences . . . must necessarily be incurred'. An uncharacteristic appeal for contributions from the wealthy suggests how difficult it was becoming to get money from the members of reform societies: 'If there be any true patriots amongst the wealthy of your neighbourhood, a few such contributions as they might make would be far more desirable than drawing from a number of the poorer class, even the smallest portion of their too small pittance.' According to the postscript, remittances had to be made by 1 August (Binns's trial was scheduled for August). There is no evidence that any society responded to this appeal, unless it was the Friends and Sons of Liberty (1795 secessionists), who gave £2 2s.

With the *MPM* at an end, the Society returned to the short occasional publication. On 23 June they issued a three page pamphlet, *Thoughts on Mr. Grey's Plan of Reform; in a Circular Letter to the Popular Societies of Great Britain and Ireland.*[36] Grey's plan, which included some redistricting, proportional representation and a uniform poll day, was attacked for limiting the extension of the franchise to leaseholders and householders. The *Thoughts* denied the justice and the 'policy' of Grey's proposed franchise. The plan was unjust for it failed to give protection to the class of men who most needed it and gave protection to those least in need of it. Moreover, it was an insult to God to prefer 'an house or a field to his most perfect work'. The poor were in a state of slavery when they must obey laws in which they had no voice; but the poor were 'the most useful class of society, from their industry and labour come all the comforts, nay, necessaries of life; they fight all battles, they pay all taxes, in short they are the only men of consequence any country possesses'. As for policy, if 'we' deserted the poor, who are the most numerous class and whose energies were needed to effect a reform, we could not achieve even a partial reform.[37] Furthermore, could we believe Grey and his coadjutors are sincere? 'Oppositions have ever made a practice of avowing themselves friends to reform, while they continue in opposition. Mr. Pitt is a striking example. . . . [L]et us join in a phalanx, if possible, more impenetrable than hithertofore; then the Whig Club and all other bodies associated for partial reform, must of necessity be swallowed up in the tremendous but just vortex of public opinion. . . . The London Corresponding Society would not have troubled the country with this address, had it not been that every means have been tried to disunite the friends of universal suffrage, and entice them to join in support of Mr. Grey's plan, which we deem unjust and useless.']

357. Account of LCS General Meeting: 31 July 1797

Sources: as notes

The general meeting

[The major energy of the LCS during the summer was expended on the general meeting, finally held on 31 July. The date for the meeting seems to have been set only at the end of June. On 24 June a spy attending a meeting (probably of the United Englishmen) at Furnival's Inn Cellar[38]

35 PC 1/43/A152. The letter is signed by Alex. Galloway, president, and John Bone, secretary.
36 'Sold by Evans and Bone. . . . Price One Penny', Place Collection, vol. 38, fo. 108. This copy belonged to Richter. Grey's plan was debated and defeated in Parliament on 23 May (*Parl. Hist.*, vol. 33, pp. 644-735).
37 This is the first LCS publication in which the Society speak of the poor as a group different from themselves.
38 Furnival's Inn Cellar was a meeting place for reformers and radicals, and government kept a close eye on it. Coigly, of the United Irishmen, met people there when he was en route from Ireland to France (actually, en route from Ireland to the gallows at Maidstone jail). Thomas Evans told the Privy Council that 'Palmer, Crossfield, Hamilton, Powell, Despard, Binns, Hodgson seldom, Galloway seldom, Stuckey frequent the

reported that 'one Thomas Evans said it would not be long before there would be a Revolution, that all the Corresponding Societies would meet together within three Weeks. he believed in a Fortnight, that a Field was engaged already for the purpose & the precise time would be known about thursday next'.[39] On that Thursday, 29 June, the executive committee issued a printed circular letter announcing that the date of the meeting would be 31 July and that the objects of the meeting were an address to the nation, a remonstrance to the king on the impropriety of the war and on the right of the people to universal suffrage and equal representation (the exchange of letters with Sheffield obviously had an effect on this statement of purpose). The letter added that the LCS had little hope from any petition for the dismissal of ministers, since numerous other such petitions had already been presented. The recipients of the letter were urged to meet on the same day and to observe the legal procedures: seven housekeepers or two magistrates must sign a requisition specifying the 'immediate purport' of the meeting; the signed requisition must be advertised in one public paper at least five days before the meeting; and at the meeting 'no object must be introduced which has not been expressed in the advertisement'.[40]

On 14 July the Society issued posting bills listing the time, place and purposes of the meeting; stating the intent of the LCS to preserve peace and good order; and assuring the public that the meeting would be called under the provisions of the Treason and Sedition Acts.[41] In compliance with these provisions, the Society advertised the meeting in the *Courier* on 22 July and the *Sunday Review* on 23 July.[42]

Meanwhile, the decision to hold a public meeting was being opposed by both LCS members and by government. Place and Ashley resigned at the end of June because of 'the society being still determined on holding a public meeting'.[43] Even after the departure of these long-time members and after the advertisements for the meeting had been posted, there was still opposition in the general committee, for on 20 July – less than a fortnight before the meeting – Richard Barrow urged his fellow citizens not to revoke their decision to hold the meeting (see next document).]

Cellar' (examination, 14 March 1798, HO 42/42). The United Englishmen, more revolutionary than the LCS, were modelled on the United Irishmen. See E. P. Thompson, *The Making of the English Working Class*, 1968 edn, pp. 185-6.

39 Report of Thomas Milner to the Lord Mayor, PC 1/40/A132. A fortnight later, on 8 July, Milner reported from Furnival's Inn Cellar more talk connecting the general meeting and revolution: 'Ingleton & Ashley the Printer . . . were very Clamorous against Government said the Meeting would be on the 31st. of this Month & after that it would not be long before there would be a Revolt' (ibid.).

40 PC 1/40/A132. The letter was signed by Alex. Galloway, president, and Benjamin Binns, assistant secretary. The response of the country societies to this LCS proposal was minimal. The reformers of Wolverhampton planned to call a county meeting, but there is no evidence they did (government summary of letter, J. Bates to Bone, 18 June, 1797, PC 1/41/A138). On 10 July the Norwich Patriotic Society sent 'civic friendship' but no comment on a meeting, unless they alluded to a refusal to meet in the statement, 'Our conduct is not influenced by

sinister views but by public interest' (letter, Wm. Bossley, president, and Jas Darken, secretary, to Bone, Add MSS 27815, fos. 159-60v). In the end, the countrywide series of coordinated meetings amounted to only two – that of the LCS and that of the Nottingham Corresponding Society. See *Proceedings at a General Meeting of the Nottingham Corresponding Society, held in the Market Place, on the 31st of July 1797, in pursuance of a requisition from the London Corresponding Society . . . , 1797.*

41 Handbill in Add MSS 27817, fo. 50, signed by Galloway and Binns.

42 *A Narrative of the Proceedings at the General Meeting of the London Corresponding Society, Held On Monday, July 31, 1797, in a Field, Near the Veterinary College, St. Pancras, in the County of Middlesex, Citizen Thomas Stuckey, President*, 1797. Unfortunately, this official account is too long (31 pp.) to be included in this edition.

43 *Autobiography*, p. 154. Ashley soon emigrated to Paris, provided the French Directory with dubiously large statistics on the number of pro-French activists in London, and became a successful shoemaker. Government believed that he was a delegate from the LCS to the French government. Ashley died in 1829 (Goodwin, *The Friends of Liberty*, p. 437; Place, *Autobiography*, p. 156). Place managed the fund for the families of the men arrested in 1798 and 1799. In 1801 he opened a tailoring shop at 16 Charing Cross and was so successful that he retired in 1817. From 1807 to the end of his life in 1854 he was active in reform movements.

358. Letter: Richard Barrow to LCS General Committee, 20 July 1797[44]

Source: Add MSS 27815, fos. 161-2v

Bird Street West Square
July 20th 1797.

Fellow Citizens./

At a crisis so important as the present it appears to me the duty of every honest man & good Citizen to counteract, as far as possible, the efforts of Despotism; let them proceed from the prime Minister, the Opposition, or an overbearing minority of the London Corresponding Society. The agents of the two first oppose a General Meeting that they may ruin the Society, the last because their heads are too weake to see through the manouvres of corruption.

The question is not now shall we have a General Meeting? It is, shall we exist? a majority of the attending members of the Society have twice decreed there should be one. At the time it was debating in the divisions little or no opposition was made to it. for then the society could not have been ⟨hurt⟩ by the issue of the question. but no sooner are steps taken to carry the will of the Society into execution, the affiliated societies informed & preparing to meet, the day appointed & the time too late to revoke your former decrees, than it is thought fit to distract & harrass you, this is the time chosen to agitate the question, can such be the conduct of Patriots? can those love Liberty, who would wish its last & only hope the London Corresponding Society to appear childish, undetermined & contemptable in the eyes of the world? No they must hate Liberty, many, perhaps, hired to injure her sacred cause. There must be a time when discussion ought to end, can any time be more proper than the present concerning the General Meeting, when it can only do harm & no good. The majority has decreed a meeting should be called, the Country invited to co-operate with you, surely then every honest man will cease to oppose, & join the majority in carrying its will into effect.

Fellow Citizens, let me seriously invoke you to do your duties, & think of the fatal consequences which must attend on your not calling a meeting. You breake your plighted faith with the Country, & make yourselves the laughing stock of all your enimies   both Ins &

Outs, all reflective men will loose confidence in you, & thus Liberty will be cut of at the instant she is about to blossom by the cold & interested blasts of hireling Patriots.

Health & Fraternity.
Richd Barrow.

[Government had been preparing opposition to expected LCS meetings for several weeks before the actual meeting.[45] Then, when the date of the meeting had been advertised, the Duke of Portland responded to the LCS circular letter asking other reform societies to hold meetings on the same day: he ordered all police magistrates throughout the country to have military forces in readiness if reform meetings were to be held in their districts on the 31st. In London Portland ordered extra military forces to be in readiness.[46]

Two days before the meeting the Bow Street magistrates issued an advertisement stating that the proposed LCS meeting was illegal and ordering all constables to be in attendance. The executive committee met that day and deputed Samuel Webbe and one of the seven householders who had signed the LCS notice to take a letter to the magistrates. This letter, signed by Galloway, Barrow, Powell, Webbe and Evans, asked the magistrates to point out the illegality of the meeting. The deputation was received by Richard Ford 'with great civility', but he informed them that the magistrates 'did not feel themselves at all bound to explain particularly' why the LCS meeting would be illegal.[47] That same night the executive committee ordered advertisements to

44 Address: 'To the Chairman / of the General Committee'.

45 On 5 June the magistrates of eight police offices were alerted that 'separate Meetings of the London Corresponding Society are appointed for this day at Copenhagen House, Chalk Farm and in several parts of the Town'; the magistrates were ordered by the Duke of Portland to take precautions against any breach of the peace (HO 65/1). There is no evidence of any such meetings. On 16 June the police magistrates and the Light Horse Volunteers were ordered to be in readiness on 19 June when 'a numerous concourse of Persons chiefly belonging to the London Corresponding Society are expected to assemble at 5 O'Clock' (ibid.).

46 Orders, 21 and 28 July 1797, HO 65/1.

47 *Narrative*. The LCS letter with the substance of this reply is in PC 1/40/A132. Most of the details in this summary of the meeting are taken from the *Narrative*.

be posted all over town answering the magistrates. This posting bill, signed by Alexander Galloway, president, and Thomas Evans, secretary,[48] asserted that the meeting 'IS STRICTLY CONFORMABLE TO LAW, AND TO ALL THE PROVISIONS of the ACT 36 GEORGE III'.

On the morning of 31 July the executive committee met in a house in Somers Town to arrange the business of the meeting. At twenty minutes before two they were informed that magistrates and soldiers were in the field near the veterinary college at St Pancras. The assembled crowd consisting of a few thousand in the field and 'immense multitudes of spectators'[49] included, according to later LCS estimates, 2000 constables and 2000 soldiers with a further 6000 to 8000 soldiers nearby. On learning of the arrival of the soldiers, the committee hurried to the field, and the speakers ascended the three rostra, or tribunes. On the first were Galloway, Webbe, Stuckey and Robert Ferguson (who was not a member); Maxwell, Baxter, Barrow and Evans were on the second; and Hodgson, B. Binns and Rhynd on the third. With awesome irony, Powell was in charge of taking minutes of all that was said at the tribunes (he had six assistants).

At two o'clock, 'a white handkerchief being raised at the first tribune, which was immediately answered from the other two, the business commenced.' At each tribune a speaker explained the proceedings with the magistrates and read the advertisements from the magistrates and from the executive committee. As chairman the executive committee proposed Citizen Thomas Stuckey, a man of 'courage, firmness and impartiality'. He was unanimously elected. Stuckey then explained that the Address to the Nation 'being extremely long' would not be read but would be referred to the divisions and then printed. From the third tribune Hodgson also announced the omission of this address, but attempted to describe some of its contents. He said that much as he admired it he found it somewhat wanting in political morality and tolerance of those who differ as to the degree of reform. He hoped that the committee or the divisions might remedy this.

At the foot of each tribune was at least one magistrate. From his tribune Evans suggested that the auditors express their approbation by raising hands instead of clapping, so that the magistrates could hear everything. After enquiring if the proclamation had been read and learning that it had not, the speakers proceeded to read the Petition and Remonstrance to the king. At twenty minutes past two, the proclamation was read. When the men at each tribune learned this, they ceased the reading. The magistrates then arrested Ferguson, Stuckey, Galloway, Barrow, Hodgson and Binns. Hodgson told those surrounding him that the executive committee had anticipated this interruption and were prepared to have the legality of their actions determined by a jury. He reminded them that by law they had one hour to disperse.

After several hours of examination at Bow Street, the men were released on bail to appear at the quarter sessions.[50] Still on the same day, the Society issued as a handbill and as an advertisement a brief statement that 'it is our determination still to persevere in the same *peaceable* manner,

---

48 Posting bill in PC 1/40/A132. This is the first time Evans is listed as secretary. Bone must have vacated the office at the end of June, although he signed the 17 July appeal for subscriptions for the deputies. On 29 June, Benjamin Binns, as assistant secretary, co-signed a letter with Galloway. Presumably the office of secretary was then vacant. Place characterized Evans as 'a fanatic of a peculiar description, ignorant conceited and remarkably obstinate. Such a man could only have been secretary when the society had proceeded a long way in its decline and had greatly changed its character' (Add MSS 27808, fo. 105). When examined before the Privy Council in March 1798, Evans said 'that the reason why he became Secretary was that John Binns about the time he went to Birmingham owed [Evans] three Guineas and that he became Secretary in order that he might repay himself out of the money which was to pass thro' his hands to pay Binns two guineas a Week during his mission to Birmingham, and that he accordingly did repay himself' (HO 42/42). This explanation cannot be exactly true, for Ashley was secretary during the mission to Birmingham.

49 *MP* 1 Aug., p. 2.

50 Government immediately collected depositions as bases for a prosecution. After examining this evidence, the Attorney General (John Scott) and Solicitor General (John Mitford) on 17 Aug. submitted the opinion that a charge of using seditious words could not be proven. They recommended charging the men with a conspiracy to hold an illegal meeting for seditious purposes ('Case of the Persons apprehended at the Meeting on the 31st. July, with the Attorney and Solicitor General's opinion thereon', PC 1/40/A129). No such charge was ever filed.

while there remains any law to which we can look for protection'.[51]

The 'Petition and Remonstrance' to the king pointedly states that the LCS will not repeat their previous appeals to the king to dismiss his ministers since these appeals had no effect, despite the ministers' ruinous policies. Nor will the LCS dwell on the miseries engendered by the war (since they hope the peace negotiations will succeed). Instead they ask him to help restore the people's right to universal suffrage, annual Parliaments and equal representation. The origin of these rights in Alfred's time and their subsequent decline is summarized.

The 'Address to the Nation' has familiar themes: the cause of the nation's miseries is parliamentary corruption. The remedy is to unite for parliamentary reform. Only universal suffrage, equal representation and annual Parliaments can secure the people's rights. (A householders' franchise is rejected: the view that only those with property should share in government is sophistry; trade and labour, by furnishing subsistence, are property to those who follow them.) These three principles are found in the ancient constitution, and the decline of these rights since Saxon times is described. The reform efforts of the LCS and their persecution by ministers are reviewed.

The opponents of the general meeting must have sent an address announcing that if a public meeting were held they would secede from the LCS; for, two days after the general meeting they sent an official announcement of their separation. These men then formed the British Union Society.]

359. Announcement of secession from LCS: 2 August 1797

Source: Add MSS 27815, fos. 165–6

2d Augst 1797

We the subscribers hereunto in conformity to our last Address advising you of our determination to secede from the London Corresponding Society, should a General Meeting be held on the 31st. Ulto., now announce such our Secession, thro' your Office as the most public and universal medium of the Society. Secession has been held by us, a matter of the most serious consideration and only been

adopted as a measure absolutely necessary for the continuance of our support in the Cause of Reform –

We unanimously deplore the increase of factious spirit, the preference given to measures the most inconsiderate and violent, and the consequent hindrance to public Civism and State Reformation; We firmly believe those circumstances have much retarded the progress that might and ought to have been made in spreading political information; in drawing together in one strong and indissoluble Cement, those who are now anxious for Reform, and in encouraging and encreasing the present Country Associations: We do not mean by saying this to go into a detail'd examination of particular Measures which we have disapproved; We intend no hostile or angry opposition; We are ready to believe that generally your views were pure and well intentioned as our own; but as we find our difference in Opinion as to the Means by which we are to obtain the same End grows wider and more essential, instead of less'ning by Reflection, and harmonizing by explanation, We think it better to withdraw that Opposition which by promoting difference may increase Schism, be a constant source of uneasiness to ourselves, of malevolent joy to our Enemies, and clog the pursuit of Liberty –

Tho' we feel this our *Duty*, be assured we shall never forget or desert the *Principle* on which we first set out; *To obtain the complete emancipation of our Country*. For this purpose we have formed another Society on the same Basis with yours: Thus established we may receive those friends who differing with you on the Means, may yet approve ours, and that Secession which at first view seem'd an Evil may be very productive of Good –

Whenever the Measures of the London Corresponding Society meet our Opinion and Approval we shall be ready to give them any assistance in our power, and if our Success is proportioned to our Industry and present prospect, that Aid will not be immaterial –

Our Deputies shall never be neglected, We have voted for their Mission, We have approved their Conduct, and our hearts shall ever wish well, our hands shall ever be open to maintain and support their Defence

For the Society. To our Associates of that School where we first improved the virtue of Philanthropy, we shall ever avow and feel the most sympathetic Affection:

To that Altar where our first devoirs were paid to Liberty, our Hearts and Hands shall always bring their willing offering; jointly we'll sow the seed of Civic Truth, with anxious nurture cheer each drooping Bloom, and

51 Signed by Wm H. Stather, president, and Thomas Evans, secretary.

coupled reap in an united Joy, the common HARVEST of

OUR COUNTRY FREED,

John Nicholls Chairman
J. Leake
W Clark
David Conway Divn 10
Thos Cooke
Josh Deacon
John Butt
Davd Brent
Henry Galloway
John George
John Stroud
Richard Channer
Thos Wheelwright
James Thomas
John Merrell late of Division 7
Joseph Williamson   10
Thos Williamson   10
Wm. Williams   10
Robert Osborn   10
James Presland   10
John Parkinson

<u>21.</u>

Read 3d Augst – 97

R. H. [52]

360. Motions from LCS divisions: 1–21 August 1797

Source: all from PC 1/41/A138

Division 2 L. C. S. Augt. 7. 97

Resolvd that it is the Opinion of this Division that Citizens Ferguson – Maxwell – Burdett – Sturt – Stanhope – & Oxford – be admitted Honorary Members of this society they having shown the strongest attachment to the principles of Universal Suffrage & Annual parliments

                          H Newsham Secty
Carried Unanimous   R Spencer Prst
Adjd for 1 Mo   10th Aug

Divn 19 – Augt 8 – 1797

Is of oppinion that Each Divn of the L. C. S should appoint a Comtee from their own Body to inspect into each Monthly Account of the finances of this Society & Report to their Divn Monthly on the Same

                          Thos Oliphant Pr
                          Reid Secty

52 Richard Hodgson.

London Corresponding Society –

Resolved that Citizen McNaughton be appointed to attend the Executive Committee & take Copies of all Letters that in any manner concern the Society

Division No. 6 –   Jno. Mc.Naughton
July[53] 14th. 1797   Secrety
For the Motion 25   Wm St. Hone
Against it None   president

Read 17 Aug / 97 & moved but not considd[54]

London Corresponding Society   Division 26
                          August 15th – 1797

We are fully convincd of the benefits which have *resulted* and *are likely to result*, from our late General Meeting and in *consequence* of which we return the Executive and General Committees our hearty thanks for their *energetic, firm, and determined conduct* on that occasion. We further declare that we [at] all times will be for ward in combining our exertions with *such* Men who have set so *glorious and prasie worthy example* in the emancipation of our much injured and insulted Country –

                          John Pichot President
                          Chas Williams Secty

      Read 17 Aug 1797.

                          Augt. 15th. 1797
L C S Division 4

Resolved that this Division do recommend to the General Committe to put the recommendation from the Executive Committe concerning the Admission Tickets in force[55]

            For it   17 ⎫
            Against   0 ⎭
Read 17 Aug / 97 –   J Treherne Presedt
                          Jos Pape Secretary

Divn 19 . 97. Augt 15

Resolvd that we Recommend to the Genl Committe to Sanction the Publication of the address to the Nation Without Submiting it to the Consideration the Divisions, as we Con-

53 'July' must be wrong; there would not be a month between the origin of the motion in Div. 6 and its presentation in the general committee.
54 Originally: 'seconded'.
55 Probably the executive committee wanted to increase the Society's income by admitting to meetings only people with membership cards. On 3 Aug. the LCS paid 12s 6d. for '500 Admission Cards'.

404

cieve it would occasion Unnesseary Delay to the Prejudice of the Cause

Thos Oliphant Pr
E Edwards Secty

Present 17.

Read 17 Augst

L. C. S. Division No. 6

Resolved

That this Division is of opinion that all letters, which are in any manner interesting to this Society, be Copied & read in this Division and that we appoint a member to attend the Executive Committee to Copy them – or that the Executive Committe do appoint one of its own Body to attend this Division Regularly –

Augt 21st. 1797   Jno. Mc.Naughton Secrey.
For the Motion 27 Thos. Cole Chairman
against the motion none

Read 31 Augst 97 R H

[verso, also in hand of R H:]
'For Thursday 7 Septr'.

[August: other activities of the Society]

[A major concern of the Society in August was the trial of John Binns on the 15th, when he was acquitted of using seditious words. On the 10th the Society paid £20 to the agent of Mr Toms, Binns's Warwick solicitor. During August they also gave Binns directly £10 18s, and by Evans a further £4 5s 9d.[56] The Society met these debts by contributions from the divisions, by a donation of £5 from John King,[57] and by a loan of £2 2s from Galloway. The only contribution from another society was 10s from the Union Society (the men who had recently seceded from the LCS).[58] The circular letter of July still had brought no response.

Part of the money remitted to Binns may have been in response to his 19 August letter to the LCS from Birmingham: 'I trust you are aware that the money you sent me was very inadequate to the expences incurred. I am now bound in consequence of my inability to Discharge those debts which my situation made it necessary to contract. . . . Remit me some money to discharge those debts.' Binns added that 'Counr Vaughan . . . has remitted to Mr Jones the 20 Guineas which he recd as part of his fees; this sum has been put to the Credit side of your account.'[59] Binns's letter also indicated that the Society was continuing its attempts to keep the reform spirit alive in other parts of the country: 'You wished on my return from Birmingham that I should call at some places as well in the neighbourhood thereof as in Oxfordshire.'[60]

The other correspondence during the month included a letter to Binns's jurors, declaring the 'high esteem' of the LCS for them. 'If men like yourselves do not step forward, we are a lost People, victims devoted to be immolated at the Shrine of Ministerial rapacity, or as in Ireland hunted down by human Butchers, whose greatest recommendations are, the number of innocent men they have murdered.' This letter was signed by Thomas Goodwin, president, and Thomas Evans, secretary.[61]

An undated note to Bone directed him to deliver 'to our present Secy. all papers and documents relative to the society'. It was signed by Richard Barrow, president; Thomas Stuckey, Samuel Webbe, Alexander Galloway, and James Powell – presumably the members of the executive committee.[62] Of the eight letters to the LCS from other cities, payment for which was recorded, only that from the Melbourne Corresponding Society remains. They wished to know what steps the Society intended to take, so that they could act in concert with the LCS.[63]

During August the Society issued three printed documents. The first, dated 9 August, was a circular letter 'To the United Corresponding Societies of Britain' announcing that a narrative of the general meeting would be published in a few days, summarizing the government interference with the meeting, and praising the courage of the people at the

56 This may be the money that Evans siphoned off as repayment of Binns's debt to him.
57 King was a scoundrel ingratiating himself with the LCS for his own advantage, according to Place (*Autobiography*, pp. 236–9).
58 *Treasurer's Account for August 1797*, Place Collection, vol. 38, fo. 203.
59 The financial records to not show payment of any such sum to Vaughan or return of it to the deputies' fund. Here, as with the *MPM*, the accounts present a muddy picture of expenditures. It is not surprising that Evans was able to recoup his personal loan to Binns from the fund.
60 Add MSS 27815, fos. 170–1v.
61 31 Aug. 1797, Add MSS 27815, fos. 173–4v.
62 PC 1/41/A138.
63 Thomas Haimes to Bone, 18 Aug. 1797, Add MSS 27815, fos. 168–9.

meeting. 'Do not suppose, that because we were dispersed before we finished our Business, that we were defeated in our Object, – No; We have shewn the whole Country, that we *exist* and *act* as heretofore, and we think we shall also shew, that the Agents of a vicious Administration have committed a violation of their *own* Laws, by such an Outrage on their part. . . . We hope and trust that these Facts, in addition to the alarming and awful Nature of the present Crisis, will have the desired effect of inducing you to redouble your exertions in the promulgation of . . . Principles of Reform. There has been for some time past a relaxation in the exertions, as well as a despondency in the Minds of a considerable number of good intentioned Patriots.' This is signed by Richard Barrow, president, and Evans, secretary.[64]

On 19 August the Society issued a short 'Congratulatory Address' to the Nottingham Corresponding Society, which had met on 31 July, heard an address to the king, passed some resolutions and dispersed without interference from the magistrates. '[W]hile we applaud your exertions and felicitate you on your success, we cannot pass over in silence the singular instance of your good fortune in being situated among magistrates not anxious to exert *a vigor beyond the law.* . . . It is this combination of pleasing circumstances which has induced us to deviate from the usual mode of correspondence, and to send you this letter in the name of the General as well as the Executive Committee.' This address is signed by R. Hodgson, president of the general committee, and Evans, secretary.[65]

The final publication during August was a handbill issued by the executive committee at the 'Sitting of August 31, 1797', titled *The London Corresponding Society's Answer to a Member of Parliament's Letter.* The LCS assumed that the MP (whom they do not name) was sincere in 'professing to make Common Cause with the People' since he did so at a time when such professions were dangerous, as they were not when 'the smooth-tongued abandoned apostate [Pitt], under whose odious dominion . . . the country now groans, made his way by a similar conduct, to the seat of power'. The Society then argued against the MP's disapprobation of univer-

sal suffrage – "the only point on which we do not think alike". He opposed it as impracticable ' "in the present state of mankind. . . . history tells you so. . . . France has given it up." ' To this the LCS answered: 'If, when you say the *present* state of mankind, you have in view that spirit of inquiry which seems at this day to have spread itself far and wide, to have found its way into every mechanick's shop, and every peasant's hut, . . . as such inquiry must eventually shew them what are their own rights, and their reciprocal duties as Citizens, they will be far less likely in the *present*, than they were in a *former* state, to give up those rights themselves, or to forego the duty of claiming them for their Fellow Citizens. History . . . affords no fair example of Universal Suffrage. . . . As to the the abandonment of Universal Suffrage in the present Constitution of France as not being practicable . . . if they had no base intention, they were little read in human nature, to suppose it less practicable to secure the allegiance of the people to a government of which they were themselves, through the medium of their Representatives, the grand constituent part, than to one from which they were estranged, and in which they were contemptuously told (as in this country, by a sanctified monster, whom neither lawn sleeves, nor other ostentatious foppery, shall one day protect from the just vengeance which awaits him) they could have no other share, than to obey its ordinances, unless some lucky accident should enable them to *purchase* the *right.* . . . The dangerous experiment, therefore, for a government to try, is not the allowing to a people the exercise of their rights, but the withholding it from them.' If the vote were given only to those who pay towards the support of government, no one would be debarred since all pay indirect taxes on both necessities and commodities. This document is signed by Goodwin, president, and Evans, secretary.[66]]

361. Motions from LCS divisions: 11–26 September 1797

Source: all from PC 1/41/A138

September 11th. 1797

London Corresponding Society
Division 23. 1797

Resolved That the thanks of this Division be

64 Add MSS 27815, fo. 167; Place Collection, vol. 38, fo. 139.
65 *Proceedings at a General Meeting of the Nottingham Corresponding Society*, p. 5.
66 Place Collection, vol. 38, fo. 145 bis.

given to Citizen Moore and friends for their Patriact Conduct [in] acomodating this Division with the Spirited answer to the Member of Parlaments Letter

Thos Waller President
Citizen Farsent Secatary

Division 15 September 18 97

L C S
Resolved
    That it is the Opinon of this Division –
That Ashly has forfeited the title of Citizen, and such should be expelled this Society –

for it 12 agains it none   Frost Prisident
                                 Ford Secy

Read 21 Septr / 97

London Corresponding Society
Division 26   Sept. 19th. 1797

    From the Evidence collected by the Committee of Enquery, with respect to the sum of 14 Guineas encured by law exspence on a Claim between Elsee and Ashley; this Division is fully *convinced* from *such evidence*, that the *neglect originated* in *Ashley* and in consequence of which we are *decidely of opinion* that the Genl Committee *ought* to *resolve* that Ashley *refund* the sum of 14 Guineas being the sum expended[67]

Alexr. Galloway President
Chas. Williams Secretary

Read 21 Septr / 97

Division 20. Sep. 20th 1797

Resolved unanimously,

    That John Ashley having by his unjust and negligent behaviour in witholding the money due to Elsee & Cotton & not stating to the Executive Committee, their proceedings against him, relative to his arrest, but prevaricating & misleading them, by which means a great expence has fallen on those who so kindly undertook to be his bail, and ultimately on the Society's funds. – deserves for such conduct, the highest censure of this Society, and that it would derogate from the principles we profess to suffer such a Man any longer to continue as a Member of this Society,

Resolved unanimously also,
    That Citizen James Powell, by not paying the whole of the money he received for the purpose of defraying Elsee & Cotton's Bill – deserves the Censure of this Society – and this division recommends to the Committee to demand of Powell the balance he has not yet paid[68]

Cit ⟨Patten⟩ President
G Lamb Secty
Moon Delegate
Read 21 Septr 1797

Division 7 L C S   Septr 26 – 1797

It is the opinion of this Division that the Recent Conduct of the Bow Street Magistrates in not Prefering the Bills against the Citizens arrested at the last General Meeting must Clearly Prove to this Society and the Country at large the Illegality of their Proceedings wee therefore think another General Meeting should be Cauld as soon as Circumstances will Permit[69]
Past Unanimous 14 Present

H Dench, chairn
Thos ⟨D⟩yer Secretary

Read 28 Septr. / 97
Adjd 1 Week

362. Motion: 28 September 1797

Source: PC 1/41/A138

Resold – that it is the opinion of this Comee that all Monies reced for and on Accot of this

67 As noted before, in 1796 Ashley – as secretary of the LCS and publisher of the *MPM* – must have bought paper on credit from Elsee and Cotton (in Dec. the executive committee agreed to keep 'secret' the proposals to abandon the *MPM*, 'lest the stationer should refuse to provide the paper'). By the end of 1796, the LCS owed Elsee £63 13s.

68 On 18 Dec. the Society paid Elsee and Cotton £36 10s (*Treasurer's Account for December 1797*, Place Collection, vol. 38, fo. 217). Powell probably handled the funds during his short tenure as assistant secretary of the LCS. In March 1798 Evans explained to the Privy Council: 'James Powell was the Assistant Secretary he was superseded for not attending, & one Savage succeeded him' (examination of Thomas Evans, 14 March 1798, HO 42/42). Since the assistant secretary in mid-July 1797 was Benjamin Binns, Powell probably became assistant secretary at the end of July (when Evans became secretary) or later. The shortness of Powell's tenure in this office may be related to his handling of funds.

69 A similar motion from Div. 2 (with 13 present), dated 25 Sept., signed J. Sharpe, pres., and R. Spencer, sec.; another from Div. 22 (with 22 present), dated 25 Sept., signed Thomas ⟨Berren⟩, chairman, and T. Robertshaw, sec.; both in PC 1/41/A138. All three were read at the 28 Sept. meeting of the general committee and adjourned for one week.

Society should be paid into the hands of the Genl Treasure & that no special Treasurer be in future appointed. –

Passed 28 Septr /97.

[September: other activities]

[To meet the expenses of the 31 July general meeting, the LCS must have appealed to other societies, for early in September the United Sons and Friends of Liberty responded to a 'communication' with £1 1s and a letter: 'Citizens we have to lament that your request made to us in your last communication cannot be complied with to such an extent as your exertions deserve, or as we could wish.' They then explained that 'Democratical principles' have fallen to 'a low ebb', that members were slow to join and individuals backward in subscribing 'their mite to promote the general good'. The committee (which sent the letter) 'have had difficulty in forming their infant Society and . . . expence . . . in printing and distributing publications to them'. Besides, the committee intend to provide a small fund 'for the Relief of their future oppressed or imprisoned members – And should such an occasion happen, which may not be far distant – where then are this Committee to ask for subscription – Not from the Public because they are tired and unwilling to subscribe – Not to the Country Societies because they are called upon and do subscribe to the London Correspond Society – We cannot call upon the London Corresponding Society because they are soliciting the aid and assistance of others – We cannot call upon our own Society because the misfortunes of our Country have alas, almost at this moment rendered them to poor to purchase necessaries.'[70]

In reply the LCS executive committee, after polite acknowledgment, spoke of the calamities of the poor, 'which aristocracy . . . wish to increase, that they may allow no time to the Poor to think of their Condition, they [aristocracy] are aware that *Reflection* leads to *Action* . . . conscious of this, they resolve to allow them no respite from Drudgery'. The artisan and the peasant – 'their bodies rendered stiff by fatigue, their minds absorbed in the single Idea of procuring subsistence, & their feelings rendered callous by the objects of misery which surround them' – cannot perceive the 'real cause of their Affliction'. If the source of their 'scanty pittance' fails they must turn to charity or robbery, and their children are 'apprenticed to Vice & Infamy' in the parish workhouse. When they are grown, they must 'maintain themselves by fraud & violence or . . . the more vile profession of an inform[er]'. The LCS, according to this draft of their letter, agreed that 'association is the most likely Mode by which our object can be effected'; but a rejected version of this passage asked the Sons and Friends of Liberty to remember that partial association only pointed out to government the men to be sacrificed, whereas a general and united association shielded them from the arrows of persecution. The final passage, which was cancelled with a large X, urged them to 'Join then the Standard which the L C S has erected . . . it remains with you to determine how far – & whether the reincorporation of your Society with ours would not be the interest of both.' Signed J. Powell, president.[71]

At this time the Society may have been trying to invigorate the reformers in Kent. According to the Duke of Portland, 'the Inhabitants of Rochester . . . have had a second visit there from two Missionaries, of the names of Bone & Webbe, no business was done . . . great circumspection is necessary in the mode of their proceeding'. The name of Corresponding Society is so 'obnoxious' that they have assumed the title of Convivial Britons. '[N]o report has been made to the London Corresponding Society of the progress which had been made in the organization of a similar Society at *Maidstone*, since Bone (the missionary above mentioned) had been at Rochester.'[72] It is unclear how much the Society was active in Kent. The listing of Galloway's trip there as an expense of the general meeting is not explained. Henry Fellows, an LCS member who was detained in the Maidstone jail for passing out reform literature, may have been a 'missionary' from the Society or merely a radical loner.

On 30 September the executive committee issued a public statement about

70 Nathl Williamson, pres., and Thos. Cooper, sec., to the executive committee of the LCS, n.d., Add MSS 27815, fos. 146–7v. According to the *Treasurer's Account for October 1797* the money was received on 7 Sept. but the draft of the LCS reply is dated 6 Sept.

71 6 Sept., Add MSS 27815, fos. 177–8v. Powell must have been acting as president of the executive committee.

72 Letter, to Lord Romney (Lord Lieutenant of Kent), 30 Sept. 1797, HO 42/41.

government's failure to prosecute the men arrested on 31 July at the general meeting:]

THIS SOCIETY informs the COUNTRY, That no Bills being preferred by the Magistrates of Middlesex against the Citizens taken up at their last General Meeting, their RECOGNIZANCES were accordingly WITHDRAWN on Saturday, Sept. 23 – which clearly PROVES the LEGALITY of the said MEETING.

ROBERT DAWRE, President.
THOMAS EVANS, Secretary.[73]

[October: LCS activities]

[To stimulate declining enthusiasm among their allies, the executive committee, on 10 October, drafted a circular letter to the affiliated societies, expressing 'much surprise at not having heard from the Citns of —— for some considerable time' and reminding them of 'the necessity of drawing the bonds of fraternal affection as close as possible . . . by letter. . . . [W]e entreat an immediate answer, giving us an account of your numbers the state of the country & every circumstance appertaining to the great cause in which we are embarked. & this we expect to recive at least once a month. as much oftener as convenient. [I]n return the L.C.S. will write to you on every necessary occasion & every three months send you down the state of the Country at large, the progress of Liberty &c &c.'[74]

The decline of fervour in the affiliated societies paralleled that within the LCS itself. John Binns thought serving on the executive committee less needful than rousing the divisions. 'I learned with surprize . . . that the Genl Com. had done me the honor to appoint me a Member of the Executive Come I immediately acquainted the Secy that I could not serve. I was therefore astonished in last weeks report to find that I was regularly reported absent. . . . As I would wish the Society to know my reason for declining I now repeat it. That I had reason to hope my exertions in the Divisions would be of more service than my attendance in the Come I am inclined to believe that the line of conduct, which I have marked out will serve the Socy in a more effectually manner than any other I could adopt. I have promised to attend 3

Divisions in a week.'[75] In the same week the executive committee was threatened with the loss of another prominent member, Richard Barrow, who wrote, 'severe indisposition renders me unfit for filling the situation I at present am in . . . but if a member is not chosen in my place, no illness shall prevent my continuing until Thursday next'.[76] Since Barrow was still a member of the executive committee four months later, illness may not have been the only reason for this resignation. Two days after Barrow's note, John Baxter wrote that he would resign from the executive committee if it were not made functioning (see next document).]

363. Letter: Baxter to LCS General Committee, 19 October 1797[77]

Source: PC 1/41/A138

Citizens

Business of considerable importance lies before the Executive Committee, which has been adjourned from time to time, and is in no greater state of forwardness than when first proposed. In vain do two or three members meet – and the attendance of a competent number can only be enforced or secured by the authority of the General Committee. Permit me to suggest the only alternatives – these are, either to augment the E. C. to nine, three of whom to go out every quarter, and four to make a quorum; or the number to remain as it is, but to allow those who may be present, however few, to transact any business to which they may think themselves competent; and for the G. C. to censure, or remove any absentee, unless he shall previously address a line to the

75 Letter, to the chairman of the general committee, 12 Oct. 1797, PC 1/41/A138. Binns also called 'the attention of the Come to furnishing me with the means of paying the Debts which I were obliged to contract as their Deputy'.
   Binns's efforts in the divisions may have encouraged those with lax delegates to elect new ones: vouchers show that on 24 Oct. Div. 1 elected Adams as subdelegate, on 30 Oct. Div. 14 elected John Ayre and Wm Schofield as delegate and subdelegate, on 31 Oct. Div. 26 elected Wm Parker and Henry Frankling, on 13 Nov. Div. 2 elected Whitehead and Wm Reason (all in ibid.).
76 Letter, 17 Oct. 1797, PC 1/41/A138.
77 Address: 'To the / General Committee / of the / London Corresponding / Society'. LCS description: 'Letter from Citn. Baxter / 19th. Octr / 97 – Ansd'.

73 *Courier*, 3 Oct. 1797, p. 1.
74 Add MSS 27815, fos. 179-9v.

Secretary, signifying that he cannot attend that sittting, or assign satisfactory reasons for his absence to the E. C.

To augment this Committee, or permit two or three to transact business, are, both, disagreable expedients; but something must be done, or the concerns of the Society will be neglected. For my own part, I am desirous to employ every portion of my time to profit or improvement, I have none to waste in idle attendance upon men, who treat their colleagues with so much indifference. If my services are acceptable, I will continue in the situation to which you have appointed me, till the expiration of the quarter, provided some remedy is applied to the evil of which I complain - If not, I shall think it my duty, to resign, on thursday next, a situation in which, I can neither act with pleasure to myself nor profit to you.

Health and Fraternity
The General Committee   J Baxter
of the London Corresponding Society
October 19th. 1797

P. S. The Narrative is nearly out of print, and none have been sent to the Country except to Cradley. Two Guineas only have been paid to the printer towards the first Edition, and the second is stop'd for want of money.

364. Complaint from LCS Division 26: c. 14 October 1797[78]

Source: PC 1/41/A138

L C S Divn 26

This Division is some what surprised at the *neglect* of the Genl Committee in not communicating their proceedings to us for the last two nights as the cause of which neglect we hope they will explain to our Delegate

Wm. Parker President
J Wapshott Sec –

365. Motions from LCS divisions: October 1797

Source: all from PC 1/41/A138

London Corresponding Society
Octobr. 2ndth 1797

Division 17 / Resolved that it is the opinion of this Division, (as this Society was interrupted by the unjust interferance of the Magistrates –

78 Date conjectured.

of Bow-Street on the 31st of July) that it is a duty incumbent on the said Society, a gain to call a general meeting as speedy as Possible, In order to take into their Serious consideration, a Petition for Peace! a remonstrance to the King!! and an address to the world in the cause of Humanity!!!

Proposed by B. Coxon, Seconded by –
   P Edwards
      Signed   President – Jas Young Pres
      By   Secretary – Jno. Maxwell
                                    Secy.[79]

Present 16
Affirmative 6
Negative 3

L. C. S. Divn 10. Octr 3. 1797

Resolved it is the opinion of this Divn that it would be improper in the L. C. S. to call a General Meeting until after the Verdict of a Jury is obtained on the Conduct of the Magistrates[80]

Richd Barrow President
John Hodges Secry

For the Motion 9
Against   0
9. present

Divsn 19   Recommends to the Consideration of the General Committe wether Instead of A General Meeting which has Been Recommended by Difrent Divisions   A Civic Feast be Adopted as it would Answer Every purpose without being liable to its Ill conveniences, References for heach Person not to Exceed 1s. .6D

Citizn Edwards, Presnt
C. Jas Nash Secty

79 An undated motion from Div. 3 recommends that the general committee call a meeting, 'being of oppinion the Illegal means practiced in dissolving the last will not be again attempted. Cit. Aspinshaw, Chairman   J Bacon Secretary' (PC 1/41/A138).

80 Robert Ferguson attempted to obtain such a verdict against Sir William Addington, who arrested him at the general meeting. When the complaint came to trial on 19 Feb. 1798, the case was dismissed on a technicality, namely, that the notice of it did not contain the address of Ferguson's counsel. Government took the case seriously, for the Crown was represented by six legal counsellors. Since the time of limitations had run out, Ferguson could not bring the suit again (*MP* 20 Feb. 1798, p. 3, p. 4; *True Briton*, 20 Feb. 1798, p. 3).

Division No 17. L Corg Socy –

This Division are of opinion that if we wait for the end of a Prosecution agst the Magistrates, it will prevent a Genl Meetings for many Months if not for Years. They therefore wish that the question for calling a Genl Meeting be referred to the whole Socy for their opinion.

Affirmative   16   Soln Boreham Preset
Negative   0   Jno Maxwell Secy –

[verso] Referrd for one Month
             Negatived

Division 17 Octr 23 1797

Resolve'd
   That the Conduct of the General Committee, respecting a Motion from this Division for a General Meeting, to have been forwarded for the Sence of the all the Divisions, and on which they (the said Committee) have passed a Vote thereon. that it be considered that Day-Month, the Consideration of which does not belong to them but to the respective Divisions, it appears to us, that the said Committee have overstepped the Bounds affixed to their Duty

S Boreham President
Jno Maxwell Secy.

[verso]
A Deputation consisting of two Members viz. Cits. Whyth & Young is appointed to present this Motion to the Genl Comee

S Boreham President
Jno. Maxwell Secy

Negatived

366. Minute: LCS General Committee, 26 October 1797[81]

Source: PC 1/41/A138

Genl. Comee 26th Octr 1797

Resolved that a meeting be held in this Com-

81 This resolution was amended or replaced by a motion calling for each division to send an extra delegate to the 2 Nov. meeting of the general committee, at which time a declaration of loyalty was to be considered. Vouchers from several divisions list these extra representatives: Div. 1, Wm Seale; Div. 2, Wm Yeoman; Div. 7, Dobson; Div. 33, Potter. The enlargement of the general committee was repeated later in Nov., for vouchers show that on the 14th 'Divn. 1 appointed Biggs as its Member to the G. Committee on Thursday next' and on the 20th Div. 3 elected Rhynd 'Extry Representative for this Devision' (all in PC 1/41/A138).

mittee Room on Thursday the 8th of November, at which every member who shall have paid his Quarterage to Michaelmas last shall be admissible, for the purpose of considering the propriety of entering into a solemn engagement with each other not to relinquish the practice of popalar ascociation, under such description as may then be agreed on.

367. Minute: LCS General Committee, 2 November 1797

Source: PC 1/41/A138

L. C. S. Genl Comee 2d Novr 1797 –

Resolved that false or ill founded Reports have rendered it highly necessary that the Members of this Society should enter into and publish a Declaration of thier perseverance in the promotion of annual Parliaments & universal Suffrage by means of popular Asociation

368. Declaration of loyalty: LCS General Committee, 2 November 1797[82]

Source: Add MSS 27815, fo. 185

Copy of the Declaration Agreed to by the General Committee Novr. 2d. 97 wereas many weak minded persons have attempted to propagate an Opinion, that all Endeavours to promote the Cause of Liberty in Britain by means of popular Association must Necessarily prove fruitless, and have thereby prevaild on Some Members of this Society, who had not Rightely estimated the perseverance of their fellow Members, to Desert the Same or at least to become Remiss in the performance of their Duty, Now in Order to prevent the Spreading of Such Opinions, and to leave those who shall profess to act under them without Excuse, we Whose Names are hereunto subscribed do mutually engage ourselves to Each other for the full performance of the following Articles – first – that we will use all Legal and Constitutional Means to Obtain for the people of Britain Universal Suffrage and Annal parliaments. Article Second – that we will not Cease to be Members of the L. C. S. so long as the Measures thereof shall be Directed to the attainment of the rights above Mentioned

82 This must be a copy returned by one of the divisions with the signatures of the (pitifully few) subscribers. A draft of the declaration is in PC 1/41/A138.

Josh Whitehead No 8 Bishops Court Alesbury
Street
Wm Thearon – No 29 Castle Street Leicester
fields –
James Edwards No 7 Eyre Street Lether Leain
holbern
John Cave No 6 Newton St High Holborn
John Harrison – Ditto
Arch Loyon No 4 Berkeby St Clerkenwell
Robert Spencer No 9 William St Blk fryars
Road

369. Minutes: LCS General Committee, 9 November 1797[83]

Source: PC 1/41/A138

[The report starts with a column listing
twenty-three divisions, the number of members present at seventeen of the divisions (a
total of 168), and the number of new members (3). Next to two divisions which submitted no attendance figures are names,
probably of men deputed to visit these divisions: for Division 14, 'Kendall' and
'Edwards'; for Division 40, 'Moore'. Next
to Division 25 is the notation: 'Parker to
write'. Next to three divisions which did
submit attendance figures are names, either
of delegates or deputies appointed before
the delegates of these divisions arrived:
after Division 4 is the name 'Powell'; after
Division 22, 'Salter'; after Division 8,
'Hoope'. Above 'Hoope' is written 'Hereford'.
   On a separate sheet is the report of the
executive committee:]

Friday Novr. 3 Galloway ½ past nine Barrow
chair
Resolvd that this Committe do highly approve
of the resolutions of the General Committe of
last night and are determined to cooperate in
carrying them into effect
Barrow, Early, Dawe Mathews Baxter Galloway. Read a letter from Tunbridge appointed
Dawe to answer it   Red a letter Cradley
appointed Barrow to answer it   Resolvd that
a circuler to the Diners and Supper Hardy
Barrow

adjournd to Saturday 7 oClock

83 The minutes of the executive committee, more
coherent than the rest of the report – and on a
separate sheet – were probably copied rather than
recorded during the oral delivery of the minutes.

Saturday
Absent Mathews.[84] Early. & Baxter. Galloway Received the letter Hardy ordered 250
copies to be printed and distributed amongst
the Suppers and dinners[85]   Read a letter to
Cradley & orderd to be sent

Wednesday
Absent Early Dawe Chair   Read a letter to
Tunbridge approved and ordered to be sent.
Read amended and approved a letter to
Fox.[86] Barrow & Webbe to wait on him

84 John Matthews, of Div. 1, later resigned from the
executive committee, but did not date his resignation (PC 1/41/A138).
85 Probably a letter by Hardy, dated 30 Oct., correcting a letter in the *True Briton* from 'An Old
Inhabitant of Fleet Street', who described a riot
on 13 Oct. over illuminations in celebration of
Admiral Duncan's victory over the Dutch fleet.
According to 'Old Inhabitant' several leading
members of the LCS, who are named, were creating a riot in front of Hardy's house. The *True
Briton* refused to print Hardy's refutation. The
Morning Post published it on 2 Nov. (pp. 1 and 2)
and the *Courier* on 8 Nov. (p. 1). John Binns
placed members of the LCS, if not the leading
members, at the scene: when Hardy refused to
have any illuminations in his windows, the
royalists planned to sack his house. Word of this
plan having spread, 'about 100 men, chiefly
members of the society, many of them Irish,
armed with good shillelahs, took post early in the
evening in front of, and close to, the front of
Hardy's house'. An immense crowd gathered in
the street; there were violent attacks on the
house; and there were many wounds from fists
and sticks. The crowd did not disperse until
11.00 p.m., when a troop of horse arrived (*Recollections*, pp. 42–3).
86 On 10 Oct., at a large dinner celebrating the
anniversary of his election to Parliament, Fox
spoke at length of the attacks on liberty in
England and instanced the dissolution of the last
general meeting before the people had proceeded
to any business. Fox added that though he did
not favour universal suffrage he thought it ought
to be disccused (*MC* 11 Oct. 1797, pp. 2 and 3).
The letter from the executive committee to Fox
states that the LCS's detachment from party and
patron does not signify a disregard of 'superior
talents, for which, when joind with *integrity*,
they have the sincerest esteem'. The 'frankness
& candour' of Fox at the meeting of the Westminster electors 'leave us little room to doubt the
integrity of your heart. . . . You have again taken
occasion to express your disaprobation of universal suffrage . . . . its expediency . . . is certainly all
you contend for.' The LCS is persuaded that Fox
admits 'the original equal right of everyone to
Suffrage'. Signed Robt Dawre, pres. (10 Nov.
1797, Add MSS 27815, fos. 186–7).

with it Read a letter from Manchester appointed a Citizen to answer it. Read a letter from Ashton under line appointd Wednesday 15 Inst for the meeting to renmovate the Socity Read and approved a letter to Framlingham and ordered to be sent. Read and approved a letter to Leeds orderd to be sent.

Leeds.[87] Stead requestd [by the LCS] to promote a Socety [in Leeds. A society was] formed met twice admitted 100 members respectd [i.e. respectable, soon in numbers as the] Villages [are populous. The] Majority [of] Patriots [are] chiefly working mechanics astocratical [influence has] got trade undr their hands. oppress tradsmen publicly suppressed Society [which was formed here] 3 year since [The patriots are] coming to themselves [again. They] meet in private houses [They need] Tickets Regulations. 1000 Ticts 300 latter [i.e. Regulations. Also send] Political Songs and Tracts. Grays Plan of Reform Tickets like yours [or London &] Leeds united Request Correspondance often [Send parcel by the] Rockingham Coach

Cradley. Scots Plan Rich with with state of Representation[88] to be printd. Answer

Tunbridge wells A Society established E S A R request a letter the worst place for Democrats

Evans resgnd[89]

3 New[90] 161 Present 18/1 1s/6d Dep Extra Member

370. Minute: LCS General Committee, c. 9 November 1797[91]

Source: PC 1/41/A138

G C. Resolved that the Ex Comtee. be Instructed to draw up a string of propositions by which the Society shall address the Nation & petition

the King on the critical Situation of public affairs & call a special Sitting of the G C to consider of the Same

371. Letter: LCS Division 10 to Richard Barrow[92]

Source: PC 1/41/A138

Citizen you are requested to attend your Division this evening Nov. 13th. to answer to some charges from Citizen Macnaughton

By order of the Division

Thos. Barnes Delegate
Willm Slater Secretary

372. Motions: LCS Divisions 1 and 26, 14 November 1797

Source: all from PC 1/41/A138

Division 1 London Corresponding Society 14th Novr.

Is of opinion that an Advertisement should be inserted in the public prints – Stating that we are about to agree, addressing the Nation & petitioning the King on the state of the Country, and to request the members to attend their divisions, in order that we may be benefitted by their advice, on so *momentous* a Subject –

Carried Unanimous

Benjn. Binns Prest.
J-Ham – Secrey

Divn. 26   Novr 14th 1797

London Corresponding Society

This Divn consider that at this time it will be highly improper and unnecessary to *address* the Nation and much more to PETITION the King – We therefore hope the Genl Committee will fully weigh the nature of the case before

87 This paragraph is a summary of a letter from Benjamin Stead in Leeds, dated 16 Oct. 1797, but not received until 1 Nov. (Add MSS 27815, fos. 180–1v).
88 Cradley reformers must want copies of the minutes of the Edinburgh convention of 1793, *Thoughts on Mr. Grey's Plan of Reform*, the Duke of Richmond's famous letter to Col. Sharman and the LCS version of the *State of the Representation*.
89 But Evans was still secretary in 1798.
90 This and the following items are recorded on the verso of the minutes of the executive committee.
91 Date conjectured.

92 Address: 'Mr Barrow Surgeon Bird Street West square St Georges fields'. Barrow evidently had not responded to a milder summons the week before: 'Citizen You are requested to attend your division this evening Novr 6 at the Red Lion Brownlow Street Drury lane – By order of the Division.' These summonses to Barrow are items 21 and 24 in a government summary and copy of documents seized in Apr. 1798. Items 21 and 26 are headed, 'Barrows papers – taken 21 Apl. 98'.

they determine on the propriety of so important a measure

Alexr Galloway   Pret
John Wapshott   Sect

London Corresponding Society
Divn 26

Novr. 14th. 1797

Resolved, that this Divn *highly* approves of the declaration of the Genl Committee (of Novr 2d 1797) and we consider it *our* duty to give them *every* support in *our* power; and we are further convinced that the *steps* taken by the said Comtee. are *calculated to in a great degree renovate and give new live and vigour to the Society*

Alexr Galloway President
John Wapshott   Secty

November: other activities

[The *Treasurer's Account for November 1797,*[93] which shows receipts for dues of £4 8s 8d and disbursements of £1 4s 7½d, lists the Society as having in hand £26 8s 5½d, money probably being accumulated to pay (in December) the bill of Elsee and Cotton. There is no evidence that any of this money was used to repay Henry Galloway, despite his request: 'I send you this that you may inform the General Commitie that I hop they will be as ready and willing to pay me as I was to lend the Society the sum is one Guinea   you will wreit to me & let me know when I shall call for it as I am in need of it   I hop you will pay me within 8 or 10 Days.'[94]

The need for money to pay the bill for paper may have led Bone to press for payment of LCS publications sent on account. William Matthews of Nottingham wrote plaintively that after he was unable to col-

lect for pamphlets Bone wrote an abusive letter about him. Bone's letter led to charges that Matthews was pocketing the money, charges made by men who joined the Nottingham Corresponding Society just before the general meeting and who opposed it. Despite these charges, Matthews was unanimously reelected secretary of the society, which was being organized on the principles of the LCS regulations.[95]

December activities

During December the payment of £36 10s to Elsee and Cotton necessitated a special subscription to pay the quarterly rent of £1 19s 4½d for the room where the general committee met. The subscription on 7 December brought in only £1 15s 8d from ten divisions. As a result, the Society ended the month having disbursed £5 4s 6d more than they had in hand.[96] Their unsatisfactory records give no indication where the extra money came from (or what might still be owing to creditors).

Although the Society paid for letters from Leeds and Nottingham, the only letter of which a record remains is from Rochester, announcing the formation of a society called 'The Friends of Truth', which planned to correspond with the LCS.[97]]

93 Place Collection, vol. 38, fo. 215.
94 To Evans, 16 Nov. 1797, PC 1/41/A138. In Jan. 1797 Alexander and Henry Galloway each loaned the Society a guinea. In Oct. the Society repaid one guinea to Galloway, presumably to Alexander.
95 To Evans, 30 Nov. 1797, Add MSS 27815, fos. 188v–9v.
96 *Treasurer's Account for December 1797.*
97 Government summary of letter, John Smallfield to James Sykes, 3 Dec. 1797, PC 1/41/A138. Three frantic letters from Henry Fellows (arrested at Maidstone) to Bone and one to Martin make no reference to the LCS. They speak of 'money raised for the perpose of moveing' Fellows from Maidstone jail to Newgate and the assistance of Bone and 'the rest of my fellow Citizens', but these references are probably to exertions at Maidstone. Fellows's case had been put in the care of John Martin, who neglected to visit Fellows during the few days he was in Newgate. Fellows implored Bone to find him another attorney and described his unsuccessful attempts to be bailed. The letters seem intended for Bone himself rather than a committee (to Martin, 15 Dec. 1797; to Bone, 18 Dec., c. 25 Dec., 30 Dec. 1797; all in ibid).

PART ELEVEN

1798

Chronology

1798 — Massive recruitment of volunteers; preparations for French invasion

Jan. 30 — *Address . . . to the Irish Nation*

Feb. 28 — O'Connor, Allen, Leary, Coigly and John Binns arrested

April — Arrests of United Englishmen in Manchester

5–19 — General committee debates joining volunteers

18 — Thirteen United Englishmen and LCS members arrested in London; Evans and Roberts held to 1801 (others: Goodluck, Elson, Nagle, C. Williams, J. Galloway, Webb, Sacker, Clay, Edwards, Dight and Purnell)

19 — General committee arrested; Hodgson and Lemaitre held to 1801, Davidson to 1800 (others: Truchard, Crank, Cowell, Pendrill, Campbell, Rogers, Naylor, Probyn, Massey, Barnes, Heseltine and Phelps)

April 19–22 — Further arrests; B. Binns, Bone, Col. Despard, A. Galloway and J. Moore held to 1801, Spence bailed

20 — Royal message to Parliament denounces sedition

21 — Habeas Corpus suspended

May 11 — *Proceedings of the General Committee . . . Relative to a French Invasion*

21–22 — Maidstone treason trial: John Binns, O'Connor, Allen and Leary acquitted; Coigly convicted

23–26 — Outbreak of Irish rebellion

June 7 — Coigly hanged

14 — *Address . . . to the British Nation*

21 — Battle of Vinegar Hill; Irish rebellion broken

29 — Parliament prorogued

Aug. 1 — Battle of the Nile

22 — French invasion of Ireland

Sept. 8 — French surrender at Ballinamuck

Nov. 20 — Parliament meets

Dec. — Crossfield arrested; held to 1801

373. Motion: LCS Division 1, 30 January 1798

Source: PC 1/41/A138

| Divn 1 | Jany 30 – 1798 |

Resolv'd that it is the Opinion of this Divn that the Eight Pounds Subscrib'd for Citn Gerald should be given to his Daughter[1]
18 for none against

| Read 1st Feby / 98 | Harrison prest |
| & Adjd | J Purshouse Secty |

The Address to the Irish Nation

[On 30 January 1798, the LCS issued its last major document, the *Address of the London Corresponding Society to the Irish Nation*. Written by John Binns, who was a member of the United Irishmen, and signed by Robert Thomas Crossfield, another Irishman, and by Thomas Evans,[2] it expresses 'regret' for 'the enormous Cruelties which have with Impunity been practised in every Corner' of Ireland. After detailing the cruelties, the *Address* asks:] [W]hy has all

1 This subscription, not mentioned in earlier documents, is listed in the *Treasurer's Account for January 1798*. £10 18s had been collected, of which £2 17s 6d was 'in Ashley's hands' (Place Collection, vol. 38, fo. 241). This is the last printed financial statement of the LCS. Since Ashley emigrated to Paris in Sept. 1797, this subscription must have been started much earlier, probably in 1796 when Ashley was still secretary of the LCS. Concern for Gerrald's daughter was shown in minutes for 18 Aug. 1796.

2 Printed in *Report of Committee of Secrecy, 1799*. Although Binns wrote it (*Recollections*, p. 143), Place condemned it as the work of Crossfield and Evans: 'The address is quite characteristic of the men who signed it, but a disgrace to those who passed it, it is a rodomontade from the beginning to the end.' Evans, as noted above, Place described as an ignorant, conceited, obstinate fanatic. Crossfield he characterized as 'a man of learning and talents, both of which were most miserably misplaced . . . a drunken harum scarum fellow'. Place followed his comment on the address and its signers with an assessment of the LCS in 1798: 'What now remained of the Society was its refuse, with the exception of Galloway Hodgson, Lemaitre and a few other who from what they considered conscientious motives, still adhered to it' (Add MSS 27808, fos. 105-6).

this Inhumanity, this savage Barbarity been committed. 'Because', say your Governors, 'some Men formed Societies, calling themselves UNITED IRISHMEN, who swore in the most solem Manner *to persevere in endeavouring to form a Brotherhood of Affection among Irishmen of every religious Persuasion*, for the Purpose of effecting Reforms which we do not think expedient.' These are the Crimes of which you are accused, and to support these Accusations, Fire, Torture, and Death are to ravage the *once* peaceful Plains of Ireland. If to wish for that happy UNION of Mankind, when their *religious* Opinions shall be no Obstacle to the Performance of their *moral Duties*, be criminal, We also are guilty; and if to UNITE in the *Cause of Reform* upon the *broadest Basis* be *Treason*, WE with YOU are *Traitors*. . . .

Your Injuries have made a deep Impression upon our Minds, from a Consideration that as our Fellow Men in Ireland live under the same FORM of Government, and are in FACT governed by the *same* Men, we entertain the well-grounded Fear that what HAS been done in Ireland MAY be done in Britain. Penal Statutes have been multiplied against us as well as against you, and those Rights hitherto held most sacred have been attacked; yet have we not ceased from our Exertions; we *have* persevered and we *will* persevere, though Military Law be proclaimed and Trial by Jury suspended. . . .

[The armed Irishmen, addressed as 'soldiers', are urged not to engage in acts of cruelty and barbarity. British soldiers are urged to behave with 'manly firmness' rather than 'the Desperate Fury of Freebooters and Assassins', and Britons are reminded that] [i]f you massacre the Irish, will not the Irish in some Measure be justified in retaliating upon the British.

May Nations be instructed by your Example. . . . May your Governors be warned by historic Experience, and learn that Governments are made for the People, and not the People for Governments; that the Voice of God is always to be gathered from the congregated WILL of His rational Creatures; that the *just* Revenge of a People is ever *proportionated* to the Injuries which they have *received*; that the irritated Feelings of the injured cannot always be repressed;

that Forbearance beyond a certain Point becomes Cowardice; that a Courageous People may be driven to Despair; and finally that an UNANIMOUS, AN UNITED Nation never can rebel.

[May the] great Author of Nature . . . strengthen the feeble, invigorate the weak, encourage the timid, UNITE the DIS-UNITED, energise the virtuous, enervate the vicious, paralyse the Efforts of the wicked, and crown with Success the *Struggles* of the *brave* and *valiant*. . . .

374: Motions: LCS divisions, February 1798

Source: all from PC 1/41/A138

Divn. 17. Feby 5th – 98

We Request our Delegate may be supplied with 12 Admission Tickets & 12 Regulations
                    Jas Young Pres
        Recd. as mentioned
                    Jno. Maxwell Secy

L C S Divn 26   Feby. 6th 1798

This Division considers it their duty to give thier Thanks to Citn Beck (our late Treasurer)[3] for his steady and firm conduct in the execution of his office perticularly when this Society has been placed in situations of embarassment[4]
                              Alexr Galloway
    John Pichot Sect

Division 1   Feby 6th 1798

    Requests the attention of the Genl. Come to prevent the Exe. Come from ordering letters to be inserted in the Public Prints without the orders of the said Come agreeable to the Usage of the Society –
                    W. C. Cranke   President
                    J. Purshouse   Secty
Adjd till thursday Next[5]

3 When questioned by government, Beck said that he resigned as treasurer '[b]cause the S[ociety] was often borrowg. Money & I fear'd they might again – & I should not get Paid' ('Memorandum of Anthony Beck', Add MSS 27817, fo. 190).
4 Similar motions from Div. 1, W. Cranke, pres., and J. Purshouse, sec., 6 Feb.; and Div. 33, John Simpson, [pres.], and G. Welsh, sec., 8 Feb.
5 This disposition of the motion is written between the date and the motion itself. Between the first and second lines of the motion is written, in another hand, 'Early President'.

L C S – Division 39 Motion Febry 12th – 98

That this Division have full Proofs of[6] Mayho No 27 Wilsted Streett Somers Town Being In the Pay of Government and Employd As A Spie In this Society this Division his of Opnion that he Ought to be Exposed In and Expelld this Society[7]
                    Henry Whatcott President
15 Present   Jno Russell Sect for the Night

Divn 1 Feby 13 – 98

Resld that this Divn do returne there thanks to Citn Haselton for his Patriotic and Successfull endevours in promoting the Principles and Intrests of this Society
                    James Wilson Chairman
                    J Purshouse Secty

Feb 20th 98.

This Division No 34: hear Constantly from the reports the great number of Unrepresented Ds., which We Consider as a Disgraceful want of Zeal. in those Divisions Who for Months together have their Division Unrepresented they are very Sencible that the Conduct of Such Members of our Society do very much impede & hinder the Success of the Society and thwart their Vieus in Obtaining a parlamentary reform. they therefore recomend to the gen. Com. to Make a Standing Law in the Society. that every Division do elect their Delegates. one month at least before quarter Day.[8]
Nigtived
    on the 22d of Feby   Wilm Morgan Secy
Unanamous   Thoms Box chn
    21 prest

Divns. 3 & 7 Sitting of Feby 26 – 98

Resolved that we conceive a G. M. should be

6 Cancelled: 'Citizen'.
7 Div. 39 deputed Alcott and Hurst 'to Explain to The General Committee Concerning Mayho'. At the same meeting the division elected Alchorn delegate and Roberts subdelegate.
8 The difficulty in getting delegates to attend the general committee is also suggested by vouchers for mid-quarter changes of delegates: 'Citn Kenington not being able to attend the choice [of Div. 4] is fallen to Citn Thos Wetnall'. Signed by Jno Denison and Jos. Pape, sec. Div. 33 elected T. Dunn to replace Alchard, transferred to Div. 39. Signed by John Simpson and G. Welsh, sec. A voucher naming John Pichot as sec. of Div. 26 may have meant that he was also delegate. Signed by Alexr Galloway, pres., John Pichot, sec. (all dated 6 Feb. 1798).

called as soon as possible if the money can be raised out of the Society and that an advirtizement should be put in the papers calling upon the members to attend their Divns to consider the same -[9] in the affve. 10 – neg – 0

Dn 7 T. Evans President   Wm Webb Secretary
Adjd 1st March   W. Bacon Divn. 3
for one Week

L C S Division 15   Feby 26 – 1798
Resolvd

That it is the opinion of this Division that Mayo Shoemaker Lately discovered to be A Spy under the pay of the present Contemptable Administration & since expelld this Society. Should be more publickly Censured as Infamous, and Recorded in the Division book of each Secretary as A Traytor to his Country, together with A Discription of his Person and Wages

read 1st March / 98   John Flindale President
& special   H. J. Ford Secy
⟨adjournmts⟩ See
Minutes

375. The trial of John Binns for high treason, 28 February 1798

Sources: TS 11/953/3497; *ST* vol. 26, cols. 1191–1436; vol. 27, cols. 1–254; Richard Madden, *The United Irishmen* (1858), vol. 2, p. 308; *MP* 2 March 1798, p. 2; 26 May 1798, p. 2; W. E. H. Lecky, *A History of Ireland in the Eighteenth Century* (1892), vol. 4, p. 318; Binns, *Recollections*, pp. 78–139; Goodwin, *Friends of Liberty*, pp. 435ff.; E. Johnson's *British Gazette*, 21 April 1799, p. 4

[On 28 February 1798 John Binns was arrested at Margate together with four other Irishmen – Arthur O'Connor, James Coigly, John Allen and Jeremiah Leary. On 21 and 22 May they were tried for high treason. Coigly, a Roman Catholic priest, was convicted and executed; Binns and the other three men were acquitted.

The government, which had been following the movements of these men, charged that they had conspired to hire a boat to go to France so that they could help and encourage France to wage war against England; and that they had a concealed paper from the 'Secret Committee of England' to the Executive Directory of France, saying that 'myriads' of Englishmen would hail the arrival of the French and help them finish their campaign. O'Connor, Coigly, Allen and Leary were going to France with political intent, but at the trial they maintained they were merely individuals trying to flee the persecutions they had encountered in Ireland. Since it was illegal to go to France without a government licence, they had to arrange their transport surreptitiously. Binns, as a fellow Irishman but one with English connections, agreed to arrange the passage to France because he shared O'Connor's desire to 'emancipate Ireland from the thraldom and oppression of England'. With government agents close behind him, Binns went from London to Whitstable to Deal, where he finally arranged passage across the Channel for £60.

In his autobiography, Binns somewhat modified the account given at the trial: He did support the assertion that the accused were not confederates: he had never seen Allen until the day before they were arrested, and he had met O'Connor (at the home of Sir Francis Burdett) only a few weeks before the arrest. Allen was trying merely to escape persecution in Ireland. But Coigly was believed by his Irish political friends to have been on an important political mission to France. And O'Connor was en route to a meeting with Napoleon and General Hoche, who was expected to command the invasion of Ireland. O'Connor hoped to hasten and assist this invasion.

After the men had been arrested and brought from Margate to London and while they were awaiting questioning at the Bow Street police office, Coigly announced to the others that there was a treasonable address in the pocket of his greatcoat, which had been seized at Margate by the police officers. Binns's brother Benjamin later told him that Dr Robert Thomas Crossfield had written the address and given it to Coigly, with whom he was intimate, on the night before Coigly left London. This is more probable than another report, namely, that Crossfield planted the address on an unsuspecting Coigly.[10]

---

9 On 28 Feb. Div. 14 also resolved unanimously (23 present) 'that a general Mitting of the Society be called as soon as posable if the money can be provided for without the Society'. Signed by John Hal, pres., and Robt. Reid, sec.

10 The historian John Adolphus was 'reliably informed' that the letter was never intended to be delivered to France but that copies were to 'be scattered about, to frighten Pitt' (*The History of England from the Accession to the Decease of King George the Third*, 1840-5, vol. 7, p. 47).

Although Binns was acquitted, on the first ballot the jurors had voted 7 to 5 to convict him. The government had been hoping for this conviction, for they had offered Coigly his freedom if he would testify against O'Connor and Binns.

Binns was then free for ten months until 16 April 1799 when he was arrested and imprisoned without charge for two years. Shortly after his release in 1801 he emigrated to the United States.[11]

There is no evidence that Binns was acting on behalf of the LCS or that the Society was in any way connected with this unsuccessful attempt to cross the Channel. But it might be argued that leading members of the LCS were making and acting on decisions which were never communicated to the rest of the Society, including the general committee. If this happened, one must ask when a decision should be attributed to the LCS and when to individual men.[12]

The distinction between deeds of an individual acting alone, deeds decided upon by a few members of the LCS acting without authority from the Society, and deeds voted for by the general committee concerns not only Binns's involvement with Coigly but also Fellows's mission to Maidstone and Ashley's reform activities in Paris.

Fellows, awaiting trial and writing to Bone, seems to have no expectation of moral or financial support from men in London. When he asks Bone to consult an attorney on his behalf, he adds 'the Expence for such Addvice shall be Paid by my Brother. . . . I hope you will not Let me be Lost for want of [legal] Assistance.' He concludes with the request that Galloway 'and Some Other of my Friends' be notified of his transfer to London.[13] After his trial and conviction, he gives details of his sentence (two years in Maidstone Gaol and

two sureties of £250 each) as if Bone had no other way of knowing them. He ends with a personal appeal to Bone, 'I must Conclude with intreating you to Continue your friendship and Consult with Mr Gurney about Getting the Punishment mitigated.'[14] From the tone of his letters to Bone, Fellows appears to be relying on Bone as an individual rather than as a representative of a body of men. In contrast to Margarot in 1794 and Binns in 1796 and 1797, Fellows never writes as if any group has an obligation to assist him. He seems to be acting as a private individual.[15]

Ashley's situation is more ambiguous. According to Place, who lived in Ashley's house and was familiar with his movements, Ashley left the LCS at the end of June 1797 and departed from England for Paris in September 1797.[16] Married to an unattractive, shrewish woman, he became infatuated with a lodger in his house, 'a woman versed in intrigues. . . . Business was neglected and ruin seemed inevitable. Ashley ashamed of his folly and yet unable to extricate himself, resolved to go to France and seek his fortune there.' He urged Place to accompany him, for 'he had no doubt of obtaining assistance from persons whom he knew there'.[17] Place maintains that from the time of Ashley's departure until the arrest of the general committee in April of 1798 no one, not even his brother 'to whom he was very much attached', received a letter from him.[18] Place brands as 'base' the government allegation, in the *Report of the Committee of Secrecy, 1799*, that Ashley was the LCS agent at Paris.[19] Further, on the whole subject of secret machinations in the LCS, he asserts: 'I have

11 He first joined other emigrated reformers at Northumberland, Pennsylvania, the projected centre of a community of free spirits, which attracted Coleridge and Southey. Binns later became a newspaper publisher in Philadelphia.

12 Even if the financial records of the LCS are incomplete or inaccurate, they do show that by 1798 there was not enough money – the balance in hand at the end of January was 3s 1½d, and that only because they used money collected for Gerrald's family to make up the deficit from December – to tempt leading members to divert funds from the LCS to secret causes.

13 3 Feb. 1798, PC 1/41/A138.

14 16 March 1798, PC 1/41/A138.

15 That Fellows was not proselytizing for the LCS is suggested by his addressing (in Dec. 1796) a letter for the general committee to Hardy, who had not been active in the Society for over two years.

16 *Autobiography*, p. 173.

17 Add MSS 27808, fos. 83–5.

18 In April or May of 1798 Beck told government that he had not heard of Ashley's going to France. He would not be the first to learn of it, for he and Ashley differed 'in consequence of some part of his [Ashley's] conduct' and Beck had hardly spoken to Ashley 'for near a Twelve-month back' ('Memorandum of Anthony Beck', Add MSS 27817, fo. 190). Evidently Ashley's residence in France was not a topic in the general committee.

19 Add MSS 27808, fo. 109.

been most solemnly assured by several and by Hodgson and Galloway in particular, two men too honest to act in a secret society and too honourable to attempt to decieve any one, that the society, up to the day they were seized had no secrets whatever.'[20]

On the other hand, Place probably solicited these denials of secrecy in the 1820s, when survivors of the LCS wished to stress its respectability. Moreover, any conspiring LCS members would have known better than to tell their secrets to a man like Place, who informed treasury magistrate Richard Ford of a conspiracy involving his brother-in-law[21] and who proposed to expose the United Englishmen by threatening to tell Ford who and what they were and what they intended.[22]

Government had intercepted a letter from Ashley (unfortunately known to us only from a reference to it in a government memorandum of 1799).[23] And at the beginning of April 1798 Ashley was sending the French Foreign Minister information about the size of the crowds at the LCS public meetings and the probable number of men in London 'ready to co-operate against the Government when opportunity shall present itself'.[24] Finally, an undated list of LCS expenditures includes an entry of 16/9 for 'French Delagat'.[25]]

20 Add MSS 27808, fo. 108.
21 *Autobiography*, p. 134.
22 Add MSS 27808, fo. 92.
23 'Heads of Evidence to be produced in support of the Class No. 2', HO 42/45. This is a list of items of evidence connecting the LCS with the United Britons (United Englishmen), and the UB or UE with the United Irishmen, and all three of them with the French. Item 5 in this web is, '[t]he permanent residence of Ashley one of the leading members of the Corresponding Society at Paris as a delegate from hence'. Marginally is the note, 'The Duke of Portland is in possession of an intercepted Letter from Ashley at Paris.' Another marginal note states that '[t]he fact of his acting as a regular delegate can only be proved by Smiths testimony'. Smith, who figures throughout the evidence of this document, is probably the informer George Smith, who provided government with information about the United Irishmen (Hone, *For the Cause of Truth*, p. 90).

Since Ashley's intercepted letter may belong to late 1798 or early 1799, Place could be correct that no one in England received a letter from Ashley between Sept. 1797 and April 1798.
24 Quoted by Goodwin, *Friends of Liberty*, p. 437.
25 PC 1/41/A136. Other expenses are cash lent to

376. Note: Robert Dawre to President of LCS, 2 March 1798[26]

Source: PC 1/41/A138

Citn Prest
  I do hereby resign my situation in the Executive Comtee

Robt Dawre

Friday March 2nd. 98

377. Motion: LCS Division 19, 7 March 1798[27]

Source: PC 1/41/A138

Divn 19 (1798 March 7
Resolved
  That it is the Opinion of this Divn that a General Meeting be called as soon as possible as we conceive nothing tends more to forward the Cause of Liberty and that the above be refer'd to the Divns for their Opinion

J Nash Secty   Edwd Edwards
                                          Chair Man

[On 9 March the executive committee issued a letter or address to the 'patriots of Coventry', who had asked the LCS 'to arouse the energy of that city'. After deploring oppression and tyranny, the LCS exhort the patriots to form popular societies; as an aid the LCS send copies of their regulations, the Duke of Richmond's letter, the *Torch*, and the *Correspondence*. Signed in the name and by order of the LCS, Jasper Moore, president.[28]]

secretary and delegate of Div. 6, 12s; cash lent to Div. 31, 11s 6d; and books, 1s 3d. 'Cash in hand' was £6 10s 6d. It is possible that 'French Delagat' refers to a division delegate named French.
26 At the end of this month Dawre was returned to the executive committee (see 379).
27 This motion was made at the end of a day of tension for the LCS: 'Yesterday was pregnant with rumours of the seizure of persons on charges of Treason. Scarcely is there one conspicuous Member of the Corresponding Society, whom report had not made a prisoner.' There were believed to be warrants for eight individuals in London. These rumours were increased by the removal to the Tower of Binns, O'Connor, Coigly and Allen (*MP* 8 March, p. 2).
28 Government summary of documents seized in April 1798, PC 1/41/A138.

Three days later, on 12 March, the executive committee acted upon the motions recommending another general meeting. They issued an advertisement, published on 17 March,[29] publicly announcing the possibility of such a meeting:]

TO THE MEMBERS OF
THE LONDON CORRESPONDING SOCIETY.

CITIZENS,

You are hereby requested to attend your respective Divisions by MONDAY the 26th of this Month, when a question on the propriety of calling a General Meeting of the Friends of Parliamentary Reform in London (to finish the business of the late Meeting held at St. Pancras, or any other CONSTITUTIONAL subject that may be brought forward), will be submitted for the discussion of the whole Society.

Signed by order of the Executive Committee of the London Corresponding Society.

JASPER MOOR, President
JOHN MORGAN, Provisional Sec.

378. Query and Motion from LCS divisions: March 1798

Source: all from PC 1/41/A138

L. C. S. Division 6   March 19th. 1798

Resolvd that it is the Opinion of this Division that the Secretary of each Division should give their Tythingmen Lists of the Names of all the Members on their Division books, that they may summons them to attend to consider the propriety of calling a General Meeting of the Society

	T Barnes Secretary
passed nem Con[30]	J Atkinson Presedent
22 March/98.	

29 *MP* p. 1.
30 'News' of a public meeting reached the weekly *Cambridge Intelligencer* about the time the general committee was arrested: 'The London Corresponding Society have advertised a public meeting for next Monday' (24 Apr. 1798, p. 3).

Divison 1 –

Wishes to know what is the probable Means by which the Money to defray the expences of the General Meeting is intended to be Raised —
27th. March 1798

Andrsen Presd
Harrison Secy pro tempore
Read 29 Mar/98   R H C. G. C.[31]

Divn 19   March 27. 1798

this Divsn Recommends that the thanks of this Society be given to his Grace the Duke Of Bedford & the Other Patriots who Spoke so nobly in the House of Lords on the 22 Instant In Behalf of the People[32] & Likewise that it May be Published in the Newspaper

the Expences to be Defrayed by
Patriotic Subscription   C Clay President
Carried Unanimous   Jas Nash Secty
Read 29 March/98 – R H C. G. C.

379. Minutes: LCS General Committee, 29 March 1798[33]

Source: HO 42/42; similar version in PC 1/41/A138

G. C. Sitting of March 29th. 1798
Cn Hodgson in the Chair

[The report starts with a list of thirty-two divisions, eight of which are crossed out. For thirteen divisions there are numbers of new members and of members present,

31 Richard Hodgson, Chairman General Committee.
32 Bedford made a motion for an address to the king to change his ministers. The only other 'patriot' who spoke for the motion was the Marquis of Lansdowne. The motion was defeated by 88 to 11 (*Parliamentary History*, vol. 33, col. 1313).
33 In addition to the items in these reports, the general committee heard the motions of 27 Mar. from Divs. 1 and 19 and 'Cn. Vialls's Acct' (as a cancelled phrase in HO 42/42 labels it). Vialls's account, on a separate sheet in a different hand from either copy of the minutes, is headed,

'pamphlet[s] Delivered by order of the gen. Com. & signed also by the Chairman'. It shows that on 17 Jan. Hodges, delegate of Div. 28, received copies of 'Scotcth Convention' and 'Correspondence', for which he owed 3s 6d, of which 1s 10d was paid to Beck and by him to Hodgson; on 15 Feb. Parker, delegate of Div. 26, received copies of 'Scotcth Convn, Correspondence, rights of nature, impartial Addresses, Copenhagen', for which he owed 3s 6d; and on 20 Feb. Thomas Massey, delegate of Div. 31, received copies of all but 'rights of nature', for which he owed 3s. The account concludes: 'No moneys received by John Vialls on this account March 29th. 1798' and underneath, in another hand, 'read 29th March/ 98 R H C. G. C.' (PC 1/41/A138).

Verso of minutes in HO 42/42 contains matter about the United Englishmen, here called True Britons. Dated '1798. Mar 29', it gives the oath of the True Britons, thirteen names and addresses, a code and the description 'found in Evens Pocket'. This is the document in Evans's possession when he was arrested three weeks later, on 18 April. The oath: 'I —— do truely & Sinserely engage to defend my country should necessity require for which purpose am willing to Join the society of True Britons & to learn the use of arms – in order that equal rights & Laws should be established & Defended'. The names are 'Richd. Secker, Jerh. Vance, W Edwards, W Grimshaw, Tatlow Bespham, T Evans, (Fray.) Moore, Chas. Clay, Simon Walker, Reed, Chas Williams, Dennison, Jas Elsam, Cn Oliphant'. The code substitutes points and short lines for letters (a= ·|·, b = ·\·, c = ÷, d = ·/.).

Since these items have the same date as the meeting of the LCS general committee, possibly the True Britons met after the general committee adjourned. As the reference to arms in the oath indicates, the True Britons, or United Englishmen, made revolution part of their official programme. The shift of names from United Englishmen to True Britons to United Britons may relate to changing attitudes towards secret oaths, which were illegal. In Feb. or early March John Jones, who had attended three meetings of United Englishmen, was told by Evans that 'it was contrary to Law for any tests [secret oaths] to be given or united Englishmen formed . . . that all ideas of such a Society were given up' (examination of Jones, 8 March 1798, PC 1/41/A136). Evans may have mistrusted Jones. Or he may have found resistance to a society which sounded much like the radical United Irishmen (after which it was modelled). In changing the name to True Britons, Evans or his mentors showed an appreciation of irony: *True Briton* was the name of a pro-government newspaper with the motto, 'Nolumus Leges Angliae Mutari' – we do not wish the laws of England to be changed. True Britons seems to have been an interim name, soon followed by United Britons. But by the end of 1798 spy reports refer to the society again as United Englishmen.

totalling 2 and 230 (which should be 227). Next to the entries of six unrepresented divisions are names, probably of men deputed to visit the absentees: Butterfield, Hodges, Welch (twice) and Hodgson (twice). Next to the entries for Divisions 10 and 14 (for which there are statistics) are the names of Hodges and Dawre. Presumably the delegates of these two divisions arrived at the meeting after the deputies had been assigned.]

Ex C Sitting March 23rd. present Moore & Barrow[34] – there not being members sufficient to form a Comtee. adjourned the sitting to Wednesday
Sitting of Wednesday 28th. absent Hodges – Gally. prest. Cn. Moore repd that he had waited on Cn. Hardy – who paid him the sum of 3£. 17s. 0d being the amount of money collected at Exeter for Binns & Jones which sum he paid into the hands of the Treasure
This Comte. recommends to the several divns. the necessity of ordering the respective Tythingmen to call on all absentees to attend their divns. and collect the Quarterage   adjourned True report

---

Elected Citns. R Dawre & J Baxter members of the Ex Comte. in the room of Barnes & Crosfield[35]

Citn Oliphant re-elected Treasurer[36]

---

adjourned the Election of a Secy. to next week

Cn. Savage reelected assistant Secy.

Took into consideration a motion from Divn. 8 – requesting to be informed of the *Specific object* of a G[eneral] M[eeting] – Moved in Consequence that Divn. 8 be referd to the advertizement[37] – Carried

34 'Abs: Hodges & Galloway' – other version.
35 'Barnes resigned' and 'Crossfield non effve' – other copy. The executive committee consisted of Moore, Hodges, Galloway, Barrow, Baxter and Dawre.
36 'Chrmn Hodgson rechosen' – other version.
37 The speakers on this motion, according to the other version, were Hodges, Evans, Dawre, Davidson, Hodgson and Vials. Referral to the

moved for the Treasurers & Sectys. report.
    Quarge. 1. 14. 11½
    New 2 Present 2 [numerals inked out] [38]
    true report

380. Deposition from spy [Powell?]: c. 15 April 1798[39]

Source: HO 42/42

This Informant says that he has been for five years an active Member of the London Corresponding Society and has during that time been a Delegate from a Division, an assistant Secretary to the Society at large and one of the persons composing the executive Committee – he says at first by all but the leading Persons it was understood that the Society was formed for the purpose of bringg. about a Reform in parliament, by causing the members thereof to be chosen annually & by universal Suffrage, but that within these two years, that notion has never been mentiond. the Society having amongst themselves declared their Opinions in favor of a Republic and their hopes of being assisted by the French in such design – he says that they have at this time an Agent in Paris, John Astly [i.e. Ashley] who was for a long period their Secretary here, that he has written word to them thro' his Wife that they might expect assistance very soon from a french Army – Informant says that since the arrest of John Binns who was a very

principal & active Member, the imprisonment of many of the Society, they have not met so frequently, but that they do meet still, & that particularly on tuesday Night last the Executive Committee Met & debated as to the possibility of getting Arms to be in readiness to assist & cooperate with the French upon their intended Invasion of England. Informt. was not present, but has understood that such was the Subject of the Debate – [40] the Members of the Executive Committee are, A Galloway, Jasper Moore, Hodges, Baxter Barrow & Dawe –
    Informant further says that there now exists & has for these twelve Months existed a Society Calld. the United Englishmen, of which Society he is also a member, that the object of that Society is to form a republic thro' the Means of the French, he says that that Society has likewise received a very considerable Check by the late arrests, particularly as John Binns and OCoigly were leading Members of it, but that the Society is now again rallying, & that he was present at a Meeting at Evans's in Plough Court on Sunday Morning last, when Evans proposed to him one Walcot a Carpenter at Sommers Town a plan of organizing four Grand Districts of United Englishmen in London & Southwark, to be calld. the North East South & West Districts, & Evans assured them, that when they had so collected their Members they could form a Junction with the United Irishmen who are in London, & undertake together some great Design – Informant says he knows of Seven Sections of United Englishmen & that he is himself Captain of one of them, he says the Sections meet every week, that there are three near Pancras, they meet sometimes at one Bustle's a Hairdresser at Battle Bridge, at One Fletcher's a Scowerer No. 1. Pancras Place, & at one Rayner's a Hatter near Battle Bridge – he says there are two Sections that meet in Virginia Street Spital Fields, & two in Compton St. Clerkenwell[41] – in order to prevent detection the list

advertisement of 17 March did not satisfy Div. 17, which unanimously (13 present) resolved on 2 Apr. 'that this division do request the G C will state to the Society the principal object of the general meeting'. Signed Rob Cleets, chrmn, and Jno Maxwell, sec. The verso indicates that the general committee (presumably on 5 Apr.) voted 10 to 3 to refer this motion (PC 1/41/A138). Div. 17's motion may have been motivated in part by a report in the *True Briton* that day (2 Apr., p. 3) that the purpose was to urge the removal of government ministers.
38 '230' in other version.
39 Description: 'Secret Information from [beginning of a name thoroughly obliterated] taken by Mr. Ford'. Date conjectured: written before the arrests of 18 and 19 April and after Gray and Tankard were revealed as spies. Gray and Tankard gave information on 4 April in Manchester and verified it before the Duke of Portland on 15 April.
    Care has been taken to conceal the name of the informant. Usually the informant produced a deposition which started with his name and address and ended with his signature and was docketed with the informant's name. James Powell is the only man who fills the description given in the opening lines of the deposition.

40 The subject of arming had been debated earlier, for on 14 March Thomas Evans stated that he had seen a Mr Venner 'once on a meeting to propose a Corps of Patriots to defend the Country, it was about ten days before the King went to St Paul's' (examination of Thomas Evans, 14 March 1798, in HO 42/42. On 19 Dec. 1797 the king headed an extensive procession to St Paul's for ceremonies of thanksgiving for recent naval victories).
41 In Rotherhithe there was a section consisting, at least in part, of former LCS members: in Feb. John Scotson, a cotton weaver, accidentally met John Wheelwright, a seller of lemons and oranges, who had belonged to his district of the LCS.

of Members is kept by Initials only, & they
have signs by which they know each other, &
which are frequently changed – rubbing the
mouth with the left Hand is a sign at present &
the answer is closing the Hands & the fingers –
He says they have got Pike heads, & that they
are manufactured by Cook & Shirley who have
a forge at No. 20 Pancras Place – He says there
are many Societies of United Irishmen but as
they admit none but Irish to be members, he is
not in the Secret of that Body, he used to
hear a good deal of them from one Hamilton
who lately fled from England & is now said to
be in France in Company with Baily of Canter-
bury – that he believes they met at one Barton's
in Grosvenor Meuse, at the Black Horse in
Wild St. Lincoln's Inn, the John of Gaunt in
Duke St. Lincoln's Inn, the White Hart in
Grey's Inn Lane, two Houses in St. Giles's,
Whose signs he does not know, a House in
Wapping the Boatswain & Call in Little St.
Thomas's Head Southwark, that the two
Binns's are the principal Members of that
Society, as Evans & Galloway are of the United
English – he says both these Societies are
endeavouring to form similar Clubs under dif-
ferent Names in England, & that most of the
Societies yt used to correspond with the Lon-
don Correspong. Society, have adopted the
same plan – he says they communicate not so
much by Letters as by sending Agents backwards & forwards – He says that in many parts
of London there are Clubs calld. free & easy

clubs, open to all persons on payg. one penny,
that Songs are sung there & toasts given of a
very seditious Nature – these Clubs keep no
books, but out of them the Societies get many
Members – he says the Magistrates has stopt a
good many, but the Landlords find them bring
so much Custom, that they still keep them
secretly, under other Names – He says Evans &
Galloway have held many Conversations about
the Witnesses in the approaching Trials, & it
has been discussd. whether it would be proper
to assassinate them, but it has been determined
not to do so, as they do not apprehend any of
them have been *informers*, against whom they
denounce their utmost Vengeance, & whom
they distinguish from those persons who
merely act according to their Duty in their
several Situations – he says that they threaten
to destroy Gray & Tankard[42] & are making
Enquiries how they can know & get at them, &
that it has been said by Evans that Mrs.
Smith,[43] who they think gave the Account
to Government, might be seized & kept in a
cellar till the Trials were over – by an Informant they mean Members who give Information
against them – This Informant says that if it
were ever known that he had ever had the
smallest Communication upon this Subject
with any Magistrate or person in authority
that he is very confident his Life would be
shortly taken away – And this Informant further says that when the accounts of the Mutiny
on board the Fleet at Portsmouth came to London, the Society expressd. the greatest Satisfaction & actually sent delegates, namely Dr.
Watson & John Bone (the one being at that
time a Member of the Executive Committee of
the Corresponding Society & the other the
Secretary) down to Portsmouth to confer with
the leading Mutineers, and that when the
Mutiny also broke out at the Nore they endeavoured to communicate with sailors on board

Wheelwright said 'that he and others had formed
a new society and changed their Name, and that
they called themselves United Englishmen, and
asked [Scotson] to belong to it – [Scotson]
enquired if they had changed their principles, to
which Wheelwright answered, that they had not,
but that now they were determined upon the
point; that they met under the denomination of
a disputing Club at the Bull's head in Rotherhithe, near the Church'. When Scotson attended
on the next Tuesday he found thirteen men and
heard Wheelwright administer the oath to one
man. The oath, as Scotson understood it, was
'to keep secrecy, and to overthrow the present
Government, and to join the French as soon as
ever they made a landing in England'. Wheelwright then told the company that the king, the
Duke of Portland and Pitt should be murdered.
At subsequent meetings Scotson heard discussions of the punishment of tyrants and the benefits of a French invasion. Scotson added that
about the end of January 'he met one Bone who
was Secretary to the London Correspd. Society
who told [Scotson] that he was a United Englishmen, and had sworn, and that he hoped that
every man would soon be of the same way of
thinking' (deposition of John Scotson, 12 March
1798, HO 42/42).

42 Joseph Tankard and Robert Gray were spies and
agents provocateurs in Manchester. As a result of
the information given by these two men, Bow
Street officers went to Manchester and arrested
eight men on charges of high treason. They were
put into four carriages, in the custody of the Bow
Street officers and escorted towards London by
the Manchester and Salford Cavalry (*The Times*,
14 April, p. 3).
43 Mrs Smith and her husband, a printer, lived at
14 Plough Court, Fetter Lane, in the same building as Evans and Benjamin Binns. She had permission to take in a lodger or two, and had taken
in people recommended by Binns. Government
was interested in knowing whether she or Binns
had housed Coigly and other United Irishmen
(examination of Thomas Evans, 14 March 1798,
HO 42/42).

the Fleet there – and actually did so in one or two Instances.[44]

And this Informant further says that repeated attempts have been made to seduce the Soldiery from their Duty by dispersing seditious Hand-bills amonst them, in Hide Park & on the Parade & by encouraging the Members of the Society to enter into the Supplementary Militia, & the provisional Calvary –

Taken by me
Richard Ford

[Ever since the arrest of John Binns, Coigly and the others with them, there had been rumours that warrants were out for the arrest of numerous LCS members. These rumours became a reality during the last half of April, with extensive arrests through-out the country. Some of the men arrested were held for a few weeks; others, with the renewed suspension of the Habeas Corpus Act, were detained much longer, even until 1801.

In London the first mass arrest took place on 18 April when Thomas Evans was trying to organize a division of United Englishmen. Though Place is wrong in think-ing this the initial attempt to establish the United Englishmen, he is probably accurate in describing his contacts with the organizers of the 18 April meeting: Benjamin Binns, 'a man of much meaner understanding' than his brother, and Thomas Evans 'made an attempt to form societies of united English-men.... These two found some ten or twelve others to join them and having in consequence of their conversations with a man who was constantly about Quigley [Coigly] learned the details of the organiza-tion of the United Irishmen went immedi-ately to work, collecting people and prepar-ing papers. The object of this association was to promote a revolution, a more ridicu-lous project was never entered by the imagi-nations of men out of Bedlam. I attended two or three meetings when some half dozen others were present, and pointed out to them the extreme folly of their proceed-ings. They did not however desist, and I am fully persuaded that this was owing to

emissaries [i.e. government spies] who were sent among them. . . . An Attempt to estab-lish a society of United Englishmen was to be made on the 18 April, and many persons were invited to attend   I was invited, among others. With some of those invited I had a conversation when it was agreed among us that the project was equally absurd and mischivous, and that it ought to be put an end to. I was for doing this by sending for Evans, B Binns, and a foolish fellow their coadjutor named James Powell, and frankly telling them we would take means to stop their proceedings, by communicating to Mr Ford the Magistrate at the Treasury who and what they were and what they intended, so that unless they at once desisted, they should be prevented from involving others in mischief and disgrace and bringing punish-ment upon them. This was objected to, par-ticularly by Coln Despard as it would appear dishonourable, and it was proposed instead of sending for, Evans Binns and Powell, that we should go to the intended meeting and there shew its mischivous tendency."[45]

Place refused to attend.

Some of the men who did attend, includ-ing Joseph Nagle and William Webb, believed they were going to a division meeting of the LCS.[46] One such man gave government an account of his connection with the LCS and of the circumstances of his attending this meeting:]

381. Unsigned deposition: meeting of 18 April 1798[47]

Source: PC 1/43/A153

abrief acount from the first time ifell into political Company about the laterend of the year 95 iwent to the furnivals inn celer to get a pint of beer where iheard a gret deal of politi-cal discourse and a great many Songs it being on asaturdy night and iwas informd that alarg company asembled every saturday night which iatended for ashort time when ifellin company with two young men of my busness whom iknew which invited me to becom amember of their divison the house being very near my residence iacepted the invitation & became a

44 Government investigated and found no evidence that the LCS was implicated in the Nore Mutiny. Government were particularly interested in connecting Galloway and Beck with the muti-neers (letters, John King to A. Graham and D. Williams, 16 June 1797; Graham and Williams to King, 24 June 1797; both in HO 42/41).

45 Add MSS 27808, fos. 91-2.
46 Add MSS 27816, fos. 543, 548.
47 Description: '9 March 1799'. The author is neither Clay nor Nagle, specimens of whose hand-writing are in Add MSS 27816.

member after belonging to the divison about twelve months we were joined by a divison that evans belonged to that was secretary of the Society during the time ibelonged to the divison iserved the ofice of diligate twice but was never in the executive comitee or at a general meeting but being called upon ibeing a housekeepe[r] isigned the requisition for the general meeting according to law but did not atend about the later end of the year 97 the divison was movd to St Johns lane Green man were it continued till the later end of march 98 when it was moved to the Georg the corner of compton Street the wich hous iatended the divison two or three tims when evans called on me and told me there wold be ameeting on wendesday in the evening & desired iwould com and bring with me as many of my acquantance as icould iatended the meeting which ibelieve from the test found upon him he ment to to propose to be ameeting of true britains which test idid not take we being all takeing into custody five minutes after Evans came into the room.

[Considering that Place, Despard and others were invited, that the members of Evans's division (and perhaps of other divisions) were told to bring their acquaintances, it is significant that only fifteen men turned up, including Evans, the spy Powell, and (if Place is correct) men who came to oppose the United Englishmen.

The thirteen men arrested (two others escaped) included at least five LCS members: Charles Clay (LCS), John Dight, William Edwards, James Elson, Thomas Evans (LCS), John Galloway, Thomas Goodluck, Joseph Nagle (LCS), Charles Purnell, John Roberts, Robert Sacker, William Webb (LCS) and Charles Williams (LCS). In addition, the two men who escaped were LCS members: Powell and Aspinshaw.

Benjamin Binns was arrested the next morning, 19 April, at his lodgings in Plough Court. That evening the general committee of the LCS, as usual, held their weekly meeting in Wych Street; but before their business was concluded, Bow Street officers entered and arrested fifteen men: John Barnes, Duncan Campbell, George Cowle (or Cowell), Charles Crank, Alexander Davidson, John Heseltine, Richard Hodgson, Paul Thomas Lemaitre,[48] Thomas Massey, John Naylor, Charles Pendrill, Robert

Phelps, Thomas Probyn, Alexander Rogers, and Philip Truchard.[49] A sixteenth, John Vials, escaped.[50] Government believed that Jasper Moore (also arrested 19 April) had seen the warrants and had warned away members who would otherwise have attended that evening.[51] While the men arrested at the general committee meeting were being taken to the house of correction, John Bone was arrested at his house in Holborn. The next day, 20 April, Thomas Spence was arrested at his home in Oxford Street, and Alexander Galloway surrendered himself after learning that there was a warrant for his arrest. Col. Edward Despard was arrested on 22 April.[52]

Hodgson wrote a full account of the arrest of the general committee and of the two preceding meetings of the committee:]

382. *Proceedings of the General Committee of the London Corresponding Society, on the 5th, 12th, and 19th of April, 1798, relative to the Resistance of a French Invasion. Stated in a Letter to a Friend: intended to have been inserted in the Morning Chronicle (extract)[53]*

Source: printed copy in Nuffield College Library (n.p., n.d.)

PROCEEDINGS,

Newgate, State-side, April 30th, 1798.

On Monday the 2d instant, a motion was passed in the divisions of the London Corresponding Society, No. 3 and No. 7, recommending that the committees should advise

but hearing of the intention of the committee to discuss the propriety of offering themselves as a volunteer corps he went to his division and offered to go to the general committee as delegate to prevent the folly and mischief he apprehended' (Add MSS 27808, fo. 106).
49 PC 1/44/A158.
50 Add MSS 27816, fo. 578.
51 PC 1/41/A138.
52 Add MSS 27816, fos. 542-2v. Other arrests were made in London and the provinces. On 19 April everyone was arrested who went to Evans's house to enquire about him.
53 In an 'Introductory Letter to a Friend', dated 'Newgate, State-side, May 11th, 1798', Hodgson

48 According to Place, 'Lemaitre had ceased to attend the meetings of the Society for some time

states that he prepared this narrative with the assistance of some of his fellow prisoners, that they submitted it to the *Morning Chronicle*, which rejected it on three grounds: (1) it might be 'deemed an interference in a pending prosecution, and consequently subject the publisher to another prosecution'; (2) it might bring rigorous treatment on the men who signed it; (3) an address similar to that proposed in the general committee would soon be published. Hodgson's co-signer (not named) yielded to these objections and withdrew his name. Hodgson rejects the arguments against publication and knows of no intended address. He believes that publication of this narrative will counteract the effect of Dundas's suggestion in Parliament that the LCS sometimes assumed other names such as United Englishmen. (Dundas was quoted in *The Times* of 9 May (p. 2) as saying, 'Considerable societies and bodies of men, disaffected to the Constitution of the country, have formed themselves into assemblies, under the mask of Parliamentary Reform. They first apeared under the name of Corresponding Societies, but they have since assumed the appellation of United Englishmen, imitating the example held out to them by their colleagues in the work of anarchy and innovation in a sister country.') Hodgson denies the connection: 'Of the falsehood of this insinuation I am well convinced. Its absurdity must be evident from the constitution of the society. Every division has a weekly opportunity of sending to the General Committee new men, strangers to those with whom they are to deliberate. The General Committee, thus changeable in itself, has the same weekly power of sending new men to the Executive Committee. – Is a society so constituted capable of adopting a system of secrecy and duplicity? – Is it not rather manifest, that the publicity we have here ever avowed is interwoven in our very constitution? I never heard of the existence of a society of United Englishmen, till it was mentioned in the ministerial newspapers, a kind of evidence to which I am not apt to give much credit: but, if I am to believe them as to the existence of such an institution, it becomes a new question, whether they are to be believed as to its views and intentions. They say it is calculated to favour a French invasion, but, among the individuals who are represented as members of it, there are one or two with whom I was intimate, and they, I am certain, are decided enemies to any such event, and will be able to prove themselves such by the most satisfactory evidence.' A postscript suggests that the recipient of this document print a small number of narratives 'for distribution among those whose friendship, either from public or private considerations, may be depended on'. The friend to whom it was sent was probably Joseph Bacon, for the MS was among the papers seized at Bacon's house in 1801 (PC 1/3526).

The first two paragraphs of the *Proceedings* explain that the narrative is addressed to men of impartial judgment and give Hodgson's reasons for refusing to answer questions put by the Privy

the members what line of conduct to adopt, in relation to the bill, then pending, for the better resisting an invasion.[54] The motion came in course before the General Committee on the succeeding Thursday (5th inst.), and the president earnestly advised the committee to lose no time in taking it into consideration. His advice was adopted; and T. Evans, secretary of the society, having obtained permission to speak on the business, began by examining the internal condition of the French nation, which he stated to be widely remote from the enjoyment of liberty; in that the rights of the people to assemble and deliberate on public affairs, as also the liberty of the press, were completely annihilated; that the dignity and independence which ought to attach to the representative body, could not exist where the executive could seize and banish, without trial, every individual who might render himself obnoxious to their views: and having enlarged with much force of reasoning upon these topics, he next adverted to the conduct of the French Government, in relation to Holland, the state of Italy, and Switzerland, towards all of whom, he contended, they had acted with treachery and tyranny, and had shewn themselves more desirous of establishing an extensive military despotism, than of propagating republican principles. He therefore drew this general conclusion, that the committee ought to advise the members to resolve on acting strenuously in opposition to the French invasion. – Thus far he was heard with universal attention: but when he came to reason on the various modes in which the members might contribute to preserve the independence of their country, and mentioned, as the most signal way of avowing their sentiments, that they might collectively offer to form themselves into a military corps, disapprobation began to be manifested.

He was followed by Lemaitre, who avowed

Council. After the account of the meetings of the general committee, Hodgson concludes with a paragraph speculating that the real offence of the arrested men is teaching men 'that they are concerned in the laws of their country beyond mere obedience; that they have both rights and duties', etc. Following the narrative is Hodgson's account of his examination before the Privy Council on 26 April, when he refused to answer their questions because he was still under the 1794 indictment for treason.

54 On March 27 Dundas introduced in the House of Commons a bill dealing with measures to be taken in case of a French invasion. Its intent was to encourage the formation of armed volunteer corps and to assure compensation for those who might suffer by the attempts of the enemy (*Parliamentary History*, vol. 33, p. 1357).

himself taken by surprize, on a business which appeared intricate and important, and that he wished for time to consider of it. He agreed with Evans in reprobating the Government established in France, and its conduct toward the surrounding states; and generally ridiculed the idea of promoting liberty by foreign assistance, contending that it would only be established on the improvement of public opinion, and secured by public virtue, the basis of which he considered to be individual reform. He censured the idea of offering ourselves collectively; both because the offer was likely to be rejected, and because if accepted, it would put the members at the disposal of men in whose good will they had no reason to confide. He concluded with observing, the more he thought on the question, the more he was convinced it required further consideration. – Some other members spoke to the same purpose; but no plan was proposed, except that of a collective offer of military service, which was almost universally scouted: and some contended the question ought not to be discussed at all, since it could not be fully discussed with legal safety, and therefore moved "the order of the day" upon it. – Hasselden reprobated the idea of getting rid of such a motion by the order of the day, and supported the propriety of avowing our aversion to any foreign interference: that to stifle such a motion would be to use the divisions unfairly, as we ought rather to stimulate them to examine its merits. He acknowledged that it required consideration, and therefore proposed that it should be adjourned for one week, which was seconded by Lemaitre, and, being generally called for, the order of the day was withdrawn. – Lemaitre begged, before the question of adjournment was put, that he might be indulged in speaking again. He observed, that the warmth with which some members had brought forward their sentiments was highly improper; that if men could not habituate themselves to bear with patience diversity of opinions, even on the most interesting subjects, liberty was a vain pursuit. He presumed the adjournment would be carried, and hoped every member would exert himself in the ensuing week to acquire information and form opinions on the business; but cautioned them against that confidence in their separate judgements which would preclude a candid attention to the opinions of others, when in the committee, and thereby, in place of a calm and improving discussion, occasion mutual enmity and distrust.

The President, previous to putting the question of adjournment, observed, that he was as much a stranger to the motion as any member of the committee; for though it came in part from the division to which he belonged (No. 3), yet it had happened that on the preceding Monday, when it was proposed and unanimously approved, he had not attended the division; that this circumstance gave him great pleasure, because it left him more at liberty, in that place, to avow his high opinion of the merits of the motion, than if he had been originally concerned in forming it. He declared himself highly gratified by the just strictures which had been made on the French Government, which left him nothing to say on that subject; but regretted that the committee, instead of exerting their ingenuity to discover all the variety of advice which might be offered to the society, and selecting the best (which was the conduct really called for by the motion), had suffered their attention to be engrossed by one proposition, and that perhaps the worst that could have been imagined.

He said the latter part of Evans's observations had been misunderstood; or rather, that the strong antipathy which some members entertained against the advice which he chiefly recommended, buried all recollection of the circumstance that he did not mention it as the only practicable plan, but, on the contrary, had intimated that a variety of others might be suggested. He entreated the members to be very cautious how they made their reports to the divisions on this business; for if it should be represented to any part of them, that the motion from divisions 3 and 7 was for a collective arming, which they were almost sure to disapprove of, the society would be filled with dissention, or, what was equally bad, the business must be dropped, and their enemies would thereby have a plea for representing them as partizans of the French Government, which could not fail destroying their credit for ever. He acknowledged himself not prepared to offer any plan of advice; and that if he had a plan he should think it his duty to withhold it, both on account of the lateness of the hour, and the circumstance that so many members agreed in their general ideas of the business, and appeared inclined to avail themselves of an adjournment to mature their thoughts, which naturally led him to believe the business would be much better done on a future night. He concluded with earnestly recommending that not a syllable of Lemaitre's last observations should be suffered to fall to the ground. – The adjournment for one week was then carried almost unanimously.

It is in this place necessary to observe, that by the constitution of the society the transactions of the Executive Committee are weekly reported to the General Committee, and considered by it prior to any other business. And it happened on Thursday the 12th instant, the Executive Committee, among other business, produced to the General Committee an account book, in which the pecuniary transactions of the Society, for the three preceeding months, were stated upon a new plan. The explaining and examining this book occupied the attention of the Committee until something after ten o'clock, and by a regulation of the General Committee no member can be required to stay later than eleven. As soon, therefore, as the motion of 3 and 7, which stood for the order of the day in the General Committee, was brought forward, a farther adjournment of one week was immediately moved, and strongly opposed by Lemaitre, who argued that from the importance of the business, the general practice of the Committee ought to be waved. – G. Pickard said, he was as anxious as any man to shew his detestation of the French Government; but he would on no account consent to stay later than eleven, as late hours were not only injurious to him, but deterred many members from serving as delegates, which kept several divisions unrepresented, and occasioned their decay. – His observations were supported by Davidson and others; and it is obvious that every minute spent in considering the propriety of adjournment contributed to render it necessary. The business was therefore adjourned for another week.

Notwithstanding the caution given on Thursday the 5th, the motion from 3 and 7 happened to be misrepresented to the division No. 1, who conceiving it intended to form the Society into a military corps, and that the objections to that measure could not be fully stated with legal safety, resolved that the further discussion of it ought to be stopped; and (their delegate not being present) appointed a special deputation to support this resolution in the general committee.[55] The resolution, with the certificate of the deputation, were, as usual, given on Thursday the 19th instant, to the President of the General Committee, who took an early opportunity of declaring his great concern for the delays which had happened in the business recommended by the divisions 3 and 7; mentioning, at the same time, that he had that day seen in the Times a most infamous paragraph, the baneful effects of which would

have been completely prevented if the Committee had been more expeditious in declaring their attachment to the independence of this country, and their dislike to the present French Government.[56] He then said, that, notwithstanding the explanation which had taken place on the preceding evenings he was sorry to see, from a paper before him, the discussion was still likely to be intricate, and therefore advised the Committee to be as summary as possible on the business which must regularly precede it.[57]

The Reporter of the Executive Committee did not attend: we believe he was apprehended on his way to the General Committee. The adjourned business was therefore brought forward at an early hour; when the President, after reading the resolution and certificate of division 1, read also the motion of 3 and 7, and summarily recited the debates which had taken place on it, leaving it to the deputation from division 1 to determine how far the resolution of that division was in point. – Cranke, the only member of that deputation who attended, after some little enquiry and farther explanation, declared himself satisfied that the resolution of his division was founded on a

55 'We have appointed Citns Crank & Mathews to attend the Gen Comtee to oppose the discussion of a Question now before that Comtee on the propriety of Arming We considering such discussion as improper Harrison Pres J. Purshouse Secty' (17 April 1798, PC 1/41/A138).

56 *The Times* (p. 2) reports a rumour that the Duke of Bedford has invited some of his political friends to Woburn to discuss giving support to the government in the present crisis. It is about time, for 'a most foul, and we fear extended conspiracy, exists in the very heart of the country, to seduce the military from their allegiance; to assist the invasion of an enemy whose only object is plunder; and to set fire to the metropolis, as well as to other principal towns of Great Britain. . . . In the correspondence discovered at Manchester, it appears to have been part of the plan to set fire to London. In one of the letters found, certain persons, Members of the *Corresponding Societies*, complain *that they have no arms*, and that for want of them they cannot act with any considerable effect. In answer to this application, they are told by *their brethren* at Manchester, "The best arms you can employ, is fire." '.

57 One piece of business allegedly before the general committee that night was arranging to send arms to Bristol: William Bennett, who was arrested at Evans's house on the 19th, tried to obtain an interview with the Privy Council to reveal this information: 'Evan's wanted me to undertake a Mishan to Bristol – in order to Plant a Society there of United Britans I was to have been interduced that Evening I was taken into Custody to the General Committee of the London Correspondent Society in order to Carry a certain quaintity of Pikes to Bristol for that Purpose' (letter to William Wickham, Secretary of State's office, 30 April 1798, PC 1/42/A140).

mistake, and that he considered his commission at an end. – Phelps (delegate of division 1) dissented from the opinion of Cranke: he acknowledged he was not at the division when the resolution was passed; but as the motion from divisions 3 and 7 had produced no other plan of advice than that which was objected to by division 1, he thought Cranke in duty bound to oppose the discussion of it. He declared himself an enemy to a French invasion; and that if we were even to receive liberty from the French, it would be an eternal disgrace to us; that he had thought of entering into a volunteer corps, but was afraid to trust himself in a military capacity under the present ministers. He thought the Society collectively should have no concern with the business, lest it should appear like an approbation of the conduct of ministers, but leave every individual to judge for himself. – These opinions were opposed by Lemaitre and Hasselden, on the arguments of the first evening, and supported by Davidson and Massey. Other members also engaged on both sides of the question, whose names and several opinions we cannot accurately state, from the circumstance of their having been newly elected, and then but little known. – It was at length observed, that, previous to a decision whether or not the motion should be discussed, it was really under discussion; and Lemaitre having on this account suffered some interruption, the President observed, that to attempt a distinction between the discussion of the motion and the question whether or not it should be discussed, would only entangle the committee in frivolous questions of order, since the one must unavoidably involve the other, which he thought had been equally evinced on both sides in the course of the debate. He then noticed the argument of Phelps, that the motion of 3 and 7, after a fortnight's consideration, had produced no new plan of advice; and stated that it had been his intention to submit to the Committee a draught of an Address to the Nation on the present Situation of Affairs; but his private concerns not having allowed him leisure to commit his thoughts to writing, he would attempt to state the sentiments which he thought such an address ought to contain. And first, it appeared to him necessary the Society should in the most positive manner disavow any desire of a French invasion. It has been observed, that the influence of ministry was so great, and their agents so numerous, that whatever professions of this kind the Society might make, would only tend to bring on it a charge of insincerity; but he thought ministry would be barred from any chance of success in that way, if in addition to this avowal of our sentiments we were to state the reasons on which they were formed, and which, beside the general propriety of national independence, he said were contained in the strictures which in the course of the debate had been made on the French Government, and which he then recapitulated, with some additions.

[Hodgson's further objections to the French government are then detailed.]

After mentioning some other historical events, to the same purpose, he proceeded to avow his firm belief, that the sincerity of an address containing such remarks could not be questioned; and that it would have the effect of increasing the public confidence in the Society, and convincing the nation that they had suffered their most invaluable rights to be retrenched, and in some instances annihilated, on pretences totally false and slanderous. I believe (continued he) that hatred of the present ministers is almost universal. I believe that ministers are sensible of it; and as the only means of preventing the national voice from being collected against them, their hirelings are continually employed to raise alarming rumours either of foreign or domestic enemies. Let us do our duty: let it be our part to shew that these rumours, as far as they relate to us, are false: let us shew, that we are not to be deluded from the real principles of liberty by either personal or national attachments. While our country knows us only by ministerial descriptions, it will be out of our power to do any good, but, if we avow our real sentiments, I have no doubt the system of alarm, and with it the power of the present ministry must cease to exist: – they may be compelled to resign their authority into better hands: a state of popular union and energy may succeed the present jealousy, dissention, and sullen indifference; and this I believe would tend more to deter an invasion than any patch-work junction of incongruous parties. But if I could suppose the tide of prejudice against us at home too strong to be turned by such an address, I should still think it worth the publishing, for the benefit it may produce on the continent; it may rouse the states now in subjection to the French government to the pursuit of independence and real liberty; and shew the French nation the danger of suffering their neighbors to be enslaved, even by their own government. This opinion would look like vanity if it were addressed to a company of bigotted royalists, or even aristocrats; it may appear so to some of the new members of this committee; but its force will be felt by those who know that the publications of this society have made their way into the closest dungeons of Russia.[58]

But I know the basis on which I ground my opinions is not universally admitted. In private conversations I am frequently told that I form my opinions of affairs in France and the conduct of the French government from ministerial journals; without considering that however false their statements, no newspaper in Britain dares contradict them. —— I lament the restrictions of the press as much as any man I know; perhaps more; for I am certain they are productive of one ill effect, which I do not remember to have been noticed in anything I have either heard or read in favour of the freedom of opinion. In general they not only stop intentionally the progress of truth, but where they happen to be directed against error, they tend rather to confirm than to eradicate it. Men naturally presume there is something irresistable in the arguments which they are forbidden to publish, altho' perhaps, if published, nothing would be more easy than to refute them. —— An opinion is not necessarily good or wise, because it is an object of persecution to knaves or madmen. The contrary belief is an error against which I wish this committee to be particularly guarded. I do not form my opinion of French affairs from newspapers of any description, farther than they are corroborated by circumstances. I am persuaded that diversity of opinions is nearly as natural as diversity of countenances, and wherever in a numerous deliberative body no such diversity appears, I do not consider silence, except on self-evident propositions, as evincing uniformity of opinion, for that would be unnatural, but rather as a proof that their deliberative authority is merely nominal, and that they are in reality overawed by some superior power. When I look to France I see none of this natural diversity of opinion, either in those assemblies which ought to be deliberative, or in the sentiments avowed in their various newspapers; and though the vices of *their* government may be less likely to be permanent than those of *ours*; yet, considering only the present moment, I am perfectly satisfied liberty is at a lower ebb with them than with us. Nothing is more injurious to the cause of truth, or tends more to render political dis-

cussion useless, than the circumstance that when men are comparing two bad subjects, instead of examing them with strict impartiality, they insensibly become the defenders of that which they think least objectionable. I hope the committee will not suspect me of having fallen into this vulgar and hackneyed error. I am not the advocate of the present ministry: on the contrary, I think the address I am recommending should accompany the observations proposed on the French government, with similar strictures on the conduct of the British ministers: I say similar, because I believe them very near parallel. In several particulars of the means adopted for suppressing public opinion they are almost copies of each other: they appear to me exactly alike in the fabrication of plots, and in their endeavours to excite the minds of their respective nations, a rancorous spirit of enmity conducive to perpetual warfare, though nothing can be more obvious than that the real interest of both nations requires the cultivation of peace and amity. But though popular association is not shackled in this country so completely as in France, yet so many artifices are used to deter men from the practice of it, that I think the committee should avoid with the utmost caution every thing which is likely to excite dissention among the members which now attend. I am therefore of opinion the address proposed should not enjoin any particular line of conduct to the friends of liberty, relative to the French invasion, but, as has been already mentioned, leave individuals to judge for themselves; and after demonstrating the propriety of resistance, recommend that, however, in contributing to that resistance, their opinions may differ, as to the degree of confidence they may be inclined to place, either in the present or any future ministry of this country, they should anxiously cultivate their attachment to each other, which is essentially necessary to their co-operation in the pursuit of universal suffrage and annual parliaments; the sole object of this society.

But however much we may be convinced of the necessity of repelling a French invasion, one objection may be raised against our declaring that determination; and indeed I wonder much that it has not ever been hinted at in this committee. I think it my duty to notice it, because I apprehend it may be brought forward in some of the divisions, and possibly with considerable effect: I mean the chance that any such declaration might contribute to strengthen the savage system of coercion now pursuing in Ireland. This circumstance is worthy the most serious consideration, par-

58 'Of this fact several members of the society were assured in a conversation with the late celebrated Kosciusko' – Hodgson's note.

ticularly as it will require the utmost caution in stating our opinions. To judge rightly of it, I think we ought to enquire whether the political condition of Britain is at this time such as to give the people a full controul over their government. If it is not so; if the people are either excluded from that controul by defects in the system, or deterred from the exercise of it by false reports; it follows that the conduct of government cannot be fairly considered as characterizing the people. Indeed I am perfectly satisfied that deliberate cruelty forms little or no part in the character of the people of this country; and if, instead of suffering themselves to be disgraced and misrepresented by passive submission to the present ministry, they can be induced to avow their own sentiments, I have no doubt the effect will be beneficial to Ireland, and indeed to the whole world.

He concluded with repeating the arguments which had been used on the necessity of combating ministerial aspersions as the only means of promoting national union, and regretting the absence of T. Evans, who had supported the same opinion on the evening of the 5th.

Lemaitre, after expressing his concern that a draft of such an address had not been prepared, proposed that the motion from divisions 3 and 7 should be suffered to fall to the ground, pledging himself at the same time to assist in preparing some specific proposal on the business in the course of the ensuing week. – Cranke also stated that he would gladly contribute any assistance in his power. A desultory conversation for a few minutes ensued, and ended in a motion to adjourn the motion of divisions 3 and 7 for three months, which was carried with five dissenting voices. – Hasselden then observed, the committee did not seem sufficiently sensible of the value of dispatch in this business; that though they could not enter into it so fully as it was intended at their next meeting, they ought not to separate without agreeing to some general declaration, and giving the necessary directions for publishing it immediately. He was proceeding, when Davidson informed the Committee it was past 11, and he should depart. Two or three other members expressed their wishes to go, and it was moved that the Committee should adjourn; but the members shewing in general a desire that Hasselden should proceed, the motion of adjournment was withdrawn, and all but Davidson resumed their seats. – Hasselden had availed himself of this interruption to prepare a motion in writing, which he was about to submit to the committee, when Davidson returned, having been apprehended on the stairs by Townsend, one of the Bow-street run-

ners, who, on entering the committee-room, uttered a volley of horrid imprecations, and in an instant, without any provocation whatever, struck one of the delegates (Barnes) a violent blow on the head with a large stick; and, notwithstanding the expostulations of two of the king's messengers and three other runners who accompanied him (all of whom behaved with great civility), continued the same brutal behaviour, repeatedly declaring he cared for none of them, and would not be dictated to, till, much to the satisfaction of all the persons remaining, he was dispatched to Bow-street with part of the committee. All the books and papers in the committee-room were surrendered with the utmost readiness, and without the least attempt either of resistance or concealment. Among the printed works there were some of a small publication, which had been sent to the society in part of a debt. It is a very instructive extract from "De Volney's Ruins of Empires," *fantastically* named by the publisher "The Torch." This circumstance, we understand, has been made use of to countenance the report of an intention to set *London on fire*. But the principal part of the books were those printed by the Society, particularly the Duke of Richmond's letter to Col. Sharman in support of universal suffrage, and the Society's correspondence, among which will be found a letter to the Duke of Portland, disclaiming all desire of secrecy, and requesting the Duke to abandon the system of espionage, and openly appoint a person of good character to attend the Committee.

[The day after the arrest of the LCS general committee, the king sent a message to the House of Commons stating that preparations for an invasion 'are now carried on with considerable and increasing activity . . . and that in this design the enemy is encouraged by the communications and correspondence of traitorous and disaffected persons and societies in these kingdoms'. The king recommended the House of Commons to consider 'such farther measures as may enable his majesty to defeat the wicked machinations of disaffected persons within these realms, and to guard against the designs of the enemy, either abroad or at home'.[59]

The House responded the next day by suspending Habeas Corpus to 1 February 1799.

Shortly after these arrests in April, a subscription was opened for the families of the

59 *Annual Register*, 1798, 'State Papers', pp. 211-12.

prisoners. Place described his management of this fund: 'As soon as I could ascertain how the persons who had been seized were disposed of, I called a meeting of half a dozen men who had been or still were members of the London Correspdg Society and suggested to them the necessity and propriety of raising subscriptions for their families this was agreed to, but such was the terror, the seizure of so many persons had produced, and of the Habeas Corpus act having been again suspended that no one would either act as secretary, or allow his name to be taken down, I was therefore obliged to take the office of secretary. Memorandum Books were purchased which I signed authorizing the bearer to receive subscriptions The Books were numbered and registered, and a designation for each of the persons who took one was entered in the account I kept instead of a name. Thomas Hardy was appointed Treasurer.'[60]

At Place's suggestion, William Frend arranged a meeting with some of his friends, who agreed to collect money. Thus, there were two bodies of fund raisers with a common treasurer.

Place made a table of the persons in confinement, the size of their families, and their financial means. He then drew up a scale of allowance at the rate of 6s for each man, 4s for his wife and 2s for each child – less the family's other income. This scale was soon doubled and later increased again.[61]

On Fridays Place drew from Hardy the money for the weekly allowance, and on Saturday mornings the wives and daughters of the men in confinement came to him for their money. Towards the end of December 1798 the sum in the treasurer's hands was about £150, and the men in Newgate wanted it divided, but Place firmly refused. Despite complaints about his obstinacy Place continued to distribute the money until April 1799. Thomas Harrison then managed the money until the subscriptions ceased about the middle of 1800.

Most of the men arrested in April were released on bail at the end of the month or in August. But Benjamin Binns, Bone, Despard, Evans, Alexander Galloway, Hodgson, Lemaitre, Jasper Moore, Roberts and two men from Manchester were imprisoned until the expiration of the suspension of Habeas Corpus in March 1801. John

Binns, as noted before, was arrested again in March 1799 and held until 1801. Crossfield, arrested in December 1798, was also held to the end.[62]

The spy James Powell, who 'escaped' on 18 April while being taken to the house of correction, deceived both Francis Place and government. Two or three days after his 'escape' he came to Place, as Place recorded, 'almost in a state of despair', asserting that his house had been searched and that he was known to have been at the meeting. Place added, 'He was a very pitiful fellow. . . . Had this man been apprehended he would have said and done every thing government wished him to say or do.' Place concealed Powell at his home (four rooms where Place worked and lived with his pregnant wife and their two children), procured him passage to Hamburg, 'made him a suit of military cloaths, got him a cocked hat, & sent him to Harwich from which place he and the young woman who passed as his wife embarked and arrived safe'.[63] While Place was busy disguising Powell and procuring money for his trip, Powell must have been negotiating with government for the same trip to Hamburg. The letter which Powell wrote to William Wickham the morning he arrived at Yarmouth[64] indicates that government knew of his destinations to Yarmouth and then to Hamburg. This letter and one the next day list his expenses and urge speedy remittance. He suggests that £30 (to be sent to his mother) will be needed for a stay of two or three months. 'If I have not money to go about and spend with persons I meet at Hamberg I shall not

62 List of men arrested in London and Manchester, PC 1/44/A158 and PC 1/3536A. Men who were arrested in 1799 were also supported by the fund for prisoners' families. A chart of late 1799 or 1800 shows allowances made to Hodgson, Galloway, Lemaitre, Baxter, Eastbourne, J. Binns, Bone, Keir (arrested Apr. 19 at Evans's house), Davidson, Roberts, Moore, Heron and Crossfield (Add MSS 27817, fo. 200).
63 Add MSS 27808, fos. 93–4.
64 Place may have confused Harwich with Yarmouth, but more likely Powell played a double game and made Place think he was going to Harwich. Powell certainly seems to have let each side pay for his passage. Moreover, he probably padded the expense account he submitted to government. According to Place, Powell left London in the evening coach (*Autobiography*, p. 180). In submitting his expenses to government, Powell charges for the more expensive hire of chaises and explains that he was wrongly told there were no stage coaches to Yarmouth that day (letters to Wickham, 27, 28 April 1798, PC 1/41/A138).

60 Add MSS 27808, fos. 96–7. Place's entire narrative of this subscription is on fos. 96–104.
61 Add MSS 27816, fos. 564–8v.

be able to collect all the information I could wish You may depend on my useing evry endeavor & that I shall not mind running any risk or danger for the service of government.' Five days later Powell (still at Yarmouth) sent more hints for money, an apology for sending his mother to Wickham when she could not meet Mr Ford, and the news that a Leonard Bourdon is the agent at Hamburg for English and Irish refugees. 'I shall wait on him immediately on my arrival with a letter for Ashley & have not a doubt I shall soon be accridated in every way you could wish.'[65]]

383. Continuance of the LCS: May–June 1798

Sources: as notes

[At the end of March the Society had about fifteen active divisions with a weekly attendance of about 230 members. The discussions of arming in early April were more likely to have decreased than increased attendance, and the arrests of 18–22 April must have cut attendance even more severely than the arrests of May 1794 did. Nevertheless, some divisions continued to meet. Eleven members of a division met in Whitechapel on 5 May.[66] John Barnes's division met on Sunday, either 6 or 13 May, and collected 5s 6d for the subscription. Other divisions must have been active, for Barnes's friends report that '[w]e are Going to Opint Men to Go to Hall the Divisions in town Every Week' to collect for the subscription.[67] Hodgson and other prisoners wanted to demonstrate the continuance of the Society by publishing in the name of the London Corresponding Society an advertisement on behalf of the prisoners' wives. '[I]t's appearance under another form would imply a state of dissolution in the Society.' They were overruled about attributing the advertisement to the LCS but were told, '[W]e may convince the public that the society does & will continue

to exist by another advertisement immediately after the above.'[68]

On 14 June the last printed document of the LCS was issued, over the names of John Simpson, president, and George Picard, secretary. This *Address of the London Corresponding Society to the British Nation*[69] was delayed until after the trials at Maidstone, 'lest it might be said that we intended to prejudice the jury and pervert the course of Justice'. Now that the trials are over and Coigly has been convicted of having a treasonable paper purported to be an address from the secret committee of England, the LCS declare that Coigly was not a member and that they have no secret committee. Far from being secret, they invited the Duke of Portland, in 1795, to send a representative to the general committee, and they convened a public meeting in 1797 in accord with the new law (and were 'dispersed by an Armed Force, contrary to Law'). After such open and lawful conduct, they are surprised and concerned to hear Dundas describe them as disaffected, acting under the mask of parliamentary reform, assuming the appellation of United Englishmen. '[W]e declare that the principles we have ever maintained are the genuine principles of the British Constitution, and that we have not "assumed the appellation of United Englishmen." ... For the proof of our Declaration, we might refer to all our former Addresses, but on the present occasion, we think it necessary again to lay before the public, both our own principles and those of the British Constitution, that they may judge between us and our accusers.' The *Address* then restates the arguments about the role of the Commons, the inequality of the representation and the need for 'restoring the ancient Right of *Universal Suffrage and Annual Parliaments*', the advantages of a constitution restored to 'its original perfection'. The LCS are confident that when their committee members are tried, an English jury

65 Letter to Wickham, 4 May 1798, PC 1/42/A143. Wickham was Undersecretary of State for the Home Office and also private secretary to the Duke of Portland.
66 Letter, William Wickham to Richard Ford, 7 May 1798, PC 1/42/A143.
67 Letter, John and Sarah Figsby to Barnes, 14 May 1798, PC 1/42/A143.

68 Letters, Hodgson and eight others indicated by initials to 'Dear Frank', 14 May 1798; unsigned reply, undated; both in PC 1/3526. The earlier part of the letter from Hodgson *et al.* states the prisoners' approval of 'Frank's' arrangements for distributing the subscription money. A letter from Hodgson to 'Dear Frank' on 29 May (ibid.) also deals with the subscription money. Although the reply to Hodgson does not seem to be in Francis Place's handwriting, 'Frank' must be Place, who was distributing the subscription money to the wives.
69 n.p., copy in Nuffield College Library.

will find them not guilty. The LCS are determined to pursue by every peaceable and legal means a reform in the representation of the House of Commons.]

384. Report from spy William Gent: 31 August 1798[70]

Source: PC 1/42/A144

August 31st. 98

Sir,

In your absence I have been very diligent in my inquiries into affairs of the United Britons, and have been pretty successful, and those persons that I have thought has been the means of my not giving a right account I have had withdrawn from the Society, I last night being Delegate joined the Committee of the London Corresponding Society held at the Crooked Billet Shire Lane near Temple Bar, where Mr. Eastbourne was Chosen their President[71] and Mr Phillips their Secretary, but on their last Meeting night, there was some mistake concerning their future Meeting, some Persons came to the Crooked Billet on the night before, so there were only Ten that attended. All the Business that was done was the Regulating the Divisions and appointing the place of our next Meeting, which was agreed it should be at the same place on Thursday night next at 8 oClock. I have been much in Company with Eastbourne, Blythe, Vaughan and others and have heard something concerning Mr. Coigley; Eastbourne and others have been to see Crossfield. I asked how he was, they said he was well, and in good Spirits, but concerning the Letter that was found in his Pocket, I learnt sufficient to know who was the author of it, which I believe to be Crossfield himself as he said that there was no one that could come against him, that could testify the writing of it, since Coigley was

hanged and I rather think that Mr. Coigley was Ignorant of its being in his Pocket when he was taken.

I am yours &c.
Wm Gent

385. Report from spy Gent: 7 September 1798[72]

Source: PC 1/42/A144

Copy   Septr the 7th 98

Sir,

I met the Committee of the London Corresponding Society, held at the Crooked Billet Shire Lane   the Business was this, a Letter was read from the Friends of Liberty at Norwich, desiring to know why they had not heard from them so long, which was answered, and desired them to hold on with the utmost vigor, and not to be timid in the least, and to send them a few dozn. of the Addresses to the London Corresponding Society, with an Account of the seizure of the Committee in London – It was also agreed that Paines works be bought and distributed among the Friends of Liberty – Eastbourne also collected a few Names of Soldiers, who were in different Corps for the purpose of sending them such papers as may be for that purpose – It was also settled that we do meet early as possible on Sunday at the Crooked Billet Shire Lane and to have a Dinner dressed there so that we may spend the whole day in Exercise &c.[73] And then adjourned till that Night week 8 o'Clock.[74] Saw a quantity of powder at Eastbourne's, He was at Newgate all day yesterday.

W. G.

72 Description: 'Secret Inform – Un. Englishm. / 7, Septr., 1798'. After the salutation 'Sir' is faintly pencilled '(G. W'.
73 The Sunday meetings and the exercising with arms were activities of the United Englishmen. At a meeting of the 'Committee of Military' on 2 Sept., it was agreed to 'make no delay, but to overturn the present System by the force of Arms'. Three men were appointed 'to adopt a better Plan for learning the people Exercise', and the committee adjourned to the next Sunday. (letter from Gent, 3 Sept.). On that Sunday (9 Sept.) fifteen men, including Eastbourne and Simpson, spent the afternoon marching (letter, Gent to government, 10 Sept. 1798, PC 1/42/A144).
74 This sentence refers to the adjournment of the LCS.

70 Description: 'Information respecting the United Englishmen / Rx 4th Septr. 1798'. Gent, who attended meetings of both the LCS and the United Englishmen, often described meetings of both groups in a single report to government. Since some of the men he mentions belonged to both societies, the report may move without transition from a meeting of the UE to one of the LCS.
71 Eastbourne was also president of either a division of the United Englishmen or of the 'Committee of the Military', which was training people in the use of arms (letter, William Gent to government, 3 Sept. 1798, PC 1/42/A144).

386. Report from spy John Tunbridge: 8 October 1798

Source: PC 1/3119, fos. 49–50

8th. October 1798

On Saturday Evening last about 9 oClock J. T. went by Invitation of Dorman to the Unicorn in Shoreditch where he was informed there wou'd be some of the Corresponding Society. He found there a Mr. Child who seemed to be a leading Man and about six or seven more – Baxter came in at the time T. did. Dorman came afterwards and about 4 more whose Names – he does not know. They were in a back Room. The chief of them are those who used to meet at the Ben Johnson in Pelham Street. A general Conversation at first took place respecting Politics – Baxter afterwards proposed their going to Business. He was voted Chairman. Child took out of his Pocket a printed Paper and offered to have it read but Baxter objected to it and said it was not proper to be read that Night. Baxter took some writing paper and a Pen and Ink out of his Pocket & took down the Names of those present, he then said the Committee of Correspondents had received a Letter from Oxford from the Society there wishing to know if those in London were proceeding as usual as they wished to continue their Correspondence with them, & that the Committee had agreed to return them an answer. He mentioned that if those then met wished to hold themselves as a Society they must choose two Delegates. A Person (Stranger to T) observed that he had made up his Mind not to attend any Meeting at all but he thought it not right to drop it at this time as something must be done in a very little time. Baxter spoke upon this a long while respecting the state of the Public Mind for Six years past and said that if People's Minds were enlightened as much within the next 2 Years as they had in the last, they must expect to have Redress – That he had observed that Families of People who had not Bread to eat who wou'd applaud and say, God save the King, but that was to be imputed to Ignorance, their minds wou'd alter (when they were pinched a little more) in their Favor.

Proceeded to choose Delegates, Mr. Child was chosen for one, they did not fix upon any other. Child enquired of Baxter where he was to meet the Committee. Baxter said he must go to Little Shire Lane Temple Bar to the crooked Billet next Thursday Evening into the little back Room where Baxter woud meet him and introduce him up Stairs – After this

they choose 4 Officers as Servitors vizt. Dorman, Rogers, J. T. and the young Man who spoke before and said he had altered his Mind about meeting. It was agreed these 4 should take the Chairs in Rotation & they were to be assiduous in procuring Books and Pamphlets for the Members to read. Baxter said he wished the Members woud get Books of different Kings reigns James the Second &c that they might see how the people acted when they were oppressed, that it woud edify them and if they should be attacked in Conversation by any of the kings Party they wou'd be able to answer them in some of their ignorant Questions they put.

It was agreed they should meet at some House next Saturday. The 4 Servitors are to be there at 8 o'Clock to receive their Instructions from Mr. Baxter before the rest come. The Servitors are to look out for a Room at a private House it being thought best so, as they could not meet at Public Houses without bringing the Landlords into trouble.

J. T. thinks there has been no Meeting of the Corresponding Society or any committee except for the Relief of the Prisoners (since the Committee were seized several of whom are now in Newgate) until a Meeting held on Thursday last.

Dorman mentioned that the Men in Newgate had wrote a letter begging that a new Committee be chose and always to keep a Committee let government take them up as often as they chuse.

J T

387. Report from spy Tunbridge: 15 October 1798

Source: PC 1/3119, fo. 55

15th October 1798

On Saturday Night last J T. went to the Unicorn in Shoreditch to meet the Corresponding Society between 8 and 9 o'Clock. There came Mr. Rogers, Dorman, Vaughan, Wells, and 5 others whose Names are not known. Dorman was the Chairman. Baxter did not attend. As soon as Dorman took the Chair to proceed to business, Wells mentioned that he & Baxter had attended the Committee of Correspondents last Thursday Evening and produced a Paper which he read of the Number of Divisions that has met – No. 1, he said was Seven, No. 2 had ten Members   No. 3 had eleven (which was theirs at ye Unicorn) No. 4 had five – No. 5 had none – the other Numbers were

439

different, the highest had 15 Members – he stated as far as 10 Divisions. A young Man (a stranger) observed that he was happy to find the Divisions got forward – Vaughan said he was afraid before they could get their Ends it wou'd be a long while first. The other answered, he did not conceive it so for he had read a great deal and the Resources of the Country were very low indeed and particularly it is something in our favour as Mr Pitt was going to lay a Tax upon Gentlemens Property. Wells said that wou'd be a very good thing indeed for them. Dorman said it wou'd be a very proper thing to keep up a Connection if there were ever so far as they had plenty of Friends when once an Opportunity happened, – Their Friends were tired of meeting so long and nothing at all done, but he hoped every Member wou'd make the greatest Endeavours to keep up their Friends in Unity – That when the Opportunity happened it should not be lost a Minute for suppose the King was to die in a little time then the Soldiers Oath will be void & then will be our Opportunity to take care there should not be another King crowned and to down with a dozen or two of them who are our Enemies. Several spoke & said that Opportunity should not be missed by any Means for if they did it wou'd be all over with them.

After this Dorman produced a Book part of which he read to them. It treats of the government of their country sending to different Courts abroad at the beginning of the War to induce them to take up Arms against the French, and about the Duke of Brunswicks Proclamation and March to Paris. While reading Wells & the younger Man (the Stranger) made Observations upon particular Passages and pointed out the Villainy and Arbitrary Conduct of the Government in sending and forcing Men to fight to support their Tyranny.

When a great deal had been read the Book was put by till another Night – does not know the Title of it. Dorman then said they must choose a Chairman for the next Night & proposed J. T. which was put to the vote and carried. Dorman said it was J. T's business to look out for some thing to read to the Society next Saturday night & that if he was not provided Dorman wou'd furnish him.

Wells mentioned before this, in his Report, that the Committee had received a Letter from the Society at Norwich wishing to know whether the Societies were getting on again and that the Committee had written in Answer & that Baxter had got a Copy of the Answer. A great Conversation took Place upon a Proposition made that the Members should subscribe Money to buy Utensils to brew their own Beer and so avoid paying the Duty for what they drank – and also to purchase Meat Coals &c in the same way.

J. T.

388. Report from spy Tunbridge: 24 October 1798

Source: PC 1/3119, fo. 51

24th October 1798

J. T. on Saturday Evening last attended a Meeting of the Corresponding Society at ye Unicorn in Shoreditch where he was Chairman. The rest were Vaughan, Baxter, Wells, Dorman and about a Dozen more whose Names he is not acquainted with. Wells brought a Report from ye Correspondents Committee that there were 16 Divisions which now meet in London & that they were increasing, he said they mostly met in private Rooms but at the other End of the Town there was no Difficulty in getting a public House to meet at. Baxter proposed having Questions debated in the Society which upon Consideration they thought it not prudent at present as the Landlord wou'd learn for what Purpose they met. Rogers who was present Said they should look out for a private Room to meet in & then they could debate as they pleased only to be guarded in their Expressions they might understand one another without being too open. Nothing further of Business was done. They broke up about one o'Clock in the Morning.

[The concluding paragraph describes a meeting of the United Englishmen.]

J. T

389. Report from spy John Tunbridge: 2 November 1798[75]

Source: PC 1/43/A150

2d. November 1798.

On Saturday Evening last J: T: went to the Unicorn in Shoreditch and there met Rogers and Childs sitting in a back room they called T. back and said it was not agreeable to the

75 Description: '2d Novemr. 1798. / J. T – sent same day / Baxter'.

440

landlord for them to meet in the private Room as he had been informed they were a Club of Jacobins. In the Course of ten Minutes several more came and they agreed to go into the Room – They went in and it was proposed that the Servitors shod. meet on Wednesday night to provide a private Room some where else. After that they subscribed each 6 pence for a Prisoner one Blake who is going to be liberated from Newgate. A great deal of Conversation passed on political Subjects. It was agreed they shod. meet there one night more before they went to a private Room.

On Tuesday Evening met Blythe at the Punch Bowl Moorfields and Mr. Sayers, it being a wet Night none else attended – No Business was done. Blythe gave T. a Ticket for the Supper on the 5 Novemr. to commemorate Hardys acquittal at the Sign of the Saint Lukes Church ye. Corner of Wenlock Street St Lukes – he paid Blythe a shilling for it. Blythe told T. that the Societies of United Englishmen at the West End of the Town were getting on very much indeed – he said it was a nice Thing if they once could get Connections – the Committee had taken a nice Plan in order to form ye. Connections by circulating Letters different parts of the Country to those who laid dormant who were good Friends to the Cause.

On Wednesday Evening T. went as one of the Servitors of the Corresponding Society to Childs's House in a Court near George yard Shoreditch – Seven attended among whom were Rogers Childs and Dorman. Childs stated that there was a private Room which they could get in that Court which they agreed to take, and it was proposed they should get some Forms and a Table to furnish it – Rogers proposed T. to be a Delegate wth. Childs to the Corresponding Society and to attend Thursday Night at the Crooked Billet Little Shire. He was elected.

On Thursday Evening the 1st. Inst. J: T: went with Childs to the Crooked Billet – met about seven in all knew none but Baxter. A Chairman was chosen who asked if there was any Report. a young man the Secretary said no but they would proceed in collecting the Subscription Money. The Secretary then asked the Delegate of Divn. one, how many members met he reported 17 – the Subscription money 3s/2d – Division 2 reported nothing (that no members had met) Divn. 3 Twelve – the Subscription 4/8 – Divn. 4 Ten but no money – Divn. 5 no members but 1s/5d collected. Making in all 39 members and 9s and 3d. money subscribed. The Secretary reported that a Letter had been received from Nottingham directed to Newgate. That the Committee had written a Letter which the Secretary produced and which had been shewn to the prisoners in Newgate for their Approbation but they not approving it had written another for the approbation of the Committee. Both the Letters were read – Each of the Letters urged the Nottingham Society to persevere agt Government and mentioned about the Committee in London having been seized and imprisoned but they hoped soon to be at large and to be able to give them assistance and for them not to despair.

One of the Prisoners by a Letter wrote at the back of the other recommended the Committee to acknowledge the Nottingham Society as much as possible as they were the only Society in the Country that met at the same day the London did at Pancras. Baxter stated that he thought it necessary to mention the names of some Gentlemen who were in the habit of writing Questions for the Society to *debate on and enlighten their minds and named Mr. Ferguson Mr. Parkinson Mr. Wilkinson Mr. Cooper and two or three others* proposed that the Society should send them Letters soliciting their further Correspondence in returning Letters Questions and Pamphlets to amuse the Society and enlighten their Minds. A member (a Stranger) pulled out four Letters written to this Effect which were directed one to Mr. Parkinson, one to Ferguson, one to Wilkinson and to another Gentleman.

It was agreed that Baxter should write a Letter of Thanks to the Prisoners in Newgate for their Letter to Nottingham and to mention there wou'd be no objection to their writing any Letters in their own Names to any Friends in the Country, who were likely to be of Service to them. They broke up about 11 oClock – no Subscription was made – Each person paid for his Liquor – The delegates are to meet every Thursday night and they are to continue in Office about Three Months

J. T.

390. Report from spy Tunbridge: 9 November 1798[76]

Source: PC 1/43/A150

9th November 1798
J. T. on Saturday Night last met the Corresponding Society at the Unicorn in Shoreditch. Only Six attended viz. Dorman Childs Dodds,

76 Description: '9 Nov. 98. / J. T. Report'.

& two others with T. No Business was done further than agreeing to meet at Mr. Childs's House in a Court next the George in Shoreditch in future – each Member to pay one Penny per Week for the Committee of the Correspondents.

[Tunbridge then describes attending two suppers commemorating Hardy's acquittal. At one (at St Luke's Church) twenty-two were present, including Eastbourne, Baxter, Barrow, Evans, Williamson and Cooper Sr. At the other (at the Nag's Head in St John St) there were seventy LCS members. At the end of this report Tunbridge adds that sixty met at a commemorative dinner in Long Lane and one hundred and fifty at the Sugar Loaf in Queen St, Lincoln's Inn Fields.]

Last Night ye 8 Novr attended as a Delegate at the Crooked Billet in Shire Lane. Only 6 attended viz Baxter Childs, & 3 more. One a Stranger who seemed to be Secretary brought the Books Papers Pens &c – The first Business was the Report made by each Delegate – Divn. 1 had met 10 and brought 10 Pence Divn. 2 had met 3 & no money – Divn. 3 had met 8 – no money – Divn. 4 had met 6 no money – Divn 5 no Member or Money which were all. The Secretary produced the Letter proposed at the last Meeting to be sent to Nottingham from the Prisoners in Newgate – which was agreed shod. be written fair by the Secretary & sent in a parcel from one of the Prisoners next week – Baxter stated that he thought it not proper for the Prisoners to know about the Business of the Society – he mentioned that Hardy would take in all Letters for the Society. Nothing further particular passed. They seperated about 11 o'Clock.

J: T.

391. Report from spy Tunbridge: 1 December 1798[77]

Source: PC 1/43/A150

1st December 1798

J. T. went on Saturday night last to a Meeting of the correspondents Society at Child's House in a Court near George Yard Shoreditch. Only three besides Childs were there vizt. Dorman, Rogers, & T. No business was done they parted in about half an hour – agreed to meet this Night at Childs & to make a Proposal to meet in future at Public Houses as they found that the Members did not attend so readily at private Houses as in Public Houses. Saturday night week (the foggy Night only 3 met.) On Thursday in the last Week T. did not attend as a Delegate – He went last Thursday Evening in Company wth Childs to the Crooked Billet Shire Lane but no other Delegates attended. They staid till 10 o'Clock & then came away. Thinks the Reason no more attended was on Account of its being ye Thanksgiving day.[78]

   T. last Night called on Blythe at his House (by Blythes Desire) when Blythe informed T. that the United Englishmen were to meet at the Punch Bowl Moorfields on Monday evening, – hoped T. wou'd call on their Friends to get them to come as he wished the Division not to be dropt & that it was necessary they shod. keep up a Union. T. asked him how they went on at the west End of the Town Blythe said very well indeed & that if they persevered to fill his Division he could attend the Committee as a Delegate & bring them an Accot. of the Business that was done, for that without the Division being compleat he could not attend ye Committee.

J. T.

77 Description: 'Report from Corresponding Societies / 1. Decr. 1798. / J. T.'
78 Thanksgiving for the victory in the battle of the Nile four months earlier.

PART TWELVE

1799
(January–July)

Chronology

1799

Jan.   9   Habeas Corpus suspended to 21 May

        22 King's message proposes union with Ireland

March 10 Arrest of 19 United Irishmen at the Royal Oak

        15 Report of Committee of Secrecy

        16 J. Binns arrested; held to 1801

April 9 Arrest of 13 United Englishmen at Nag's Head; Baxter, W. Eastburne and G. Blythe held to 1801

May 20 Habeas Corpus suspended to March 1800

July 12 LCS, United Englishmen, United Britons, United Irishmen and United Scotsmen outlawed

392. Report from spy Tunbridge: 28 January 1799 (excerpts)[1]

Source: PC 1/43/A152

28th January 1799.

... Whelan ... Secretary for some time to the United Irishmen here ... told me that the United Irishmen here had such a regular Correspondence Kept up with those in Ireland as well as with the Corresponding Society by means of private Couriers that it was known here the very day that the insurrection was to take place in Ireland, and a similar one was to have taken place here at the same time in order to prevent Troops from leaving this Kingdom; and that they might distract the military force of Govt; but the failure of the insurrection here is attributed by the United Irishmen to the Cowardice of the Corresponding Society; who stated themselves to amount to 80,000 – but when brought to the point not one of them would turn out, tho' the Irish offered to convey to their assistance to London 40. or 50,000 men in various disguises, if the others would find them arms, and which they promised, but never performed. – I am rather disposed to think that the number above-mentioned is exaggerated; but I am convinced that it was the intention of the United Irishmen to send over a body of men to a very considerable amount – perhaps from Ten to Twenty Thousand Men. ...

I understand that Citizen Burks who has lately got out of Prison means shortly, in Contempt of Government to publish again openly another Pamphlet.[2]

393. Report from spy Turnbridge: 20 March 1799[3]

Source: PC 1/23/A38

J. T. reports that on Tuesday Evening he attended the Meeting of the Corresponding Society at the Nags Head in Saint John Street. Ten members met vizt. Baxter, Hill, Young, Barnard, Phillips, the other 4 were Strangers, by Name. The Chairman was one of the Strangers. Barnard stated that very little Business had been done at the General Committee as they met very thin, but there was Business before the   that   had not on that Account brought the state of their   that the Committee had answered a Letter   did not state the subject matter. One present   informed was a Hatter and lately discharged from (about 5 Months ago) produced a printed Publication or Book entitled Ar. O Connor's Letter to Lord Castlereagh[4] which was read by Baxter at the desire of the Society as far as 24 Pages. The rest was agreed to be read next Week. Baxter said it was a good Thing it was a pity it shou'd be lost. It seemed to give them great Satisfaction. No collection was made owing to Eastburn the Secretary not attending and the Members deputed to him not having been able to see him. The same 2 Members were desired to go after Eastburn again & to get him to come forward or to get the Books. The appointing Tithingmen was deferred till next Week. No other Business took place – about 500 more of Lord Stanhopes Address[5] were brought & distributed to them by Barnard.

The Person in the Chair mentioned to Young, that where he was Sunday Night he cou'd not get a Seat. T asked where it was. He said it was the Pitts Head the Corner of Old Street and they met there very strong in a Room up Stairs. He mentioned the Green Dragon ⟨Fore⟩ Street in the City where there was a strong Meeting ⟨Sunday night⟩ he sometimes went there. T. said he would   at the Pitts Head next Sunday

1 Description: 'Copy of a Letter from/ Mr. G. T. to Mr. Wickham/ January 28th. 1799./ (secret)'.
2 'This pamphlet apeared yesterday and is annexed to this paper.' – marginal note. Dated 24 Dec. 1798. Burks's four page pamphlet describes the bad treatment he received during his two-year imprisonment in Cold Bath Fields (for selling *The Duties of Citizenship*).
3 Description: '20 March. / Corresponding Society /
Report of "J T." as to / meeting at which / himself, Baxter, Hill, / Young, Barnard, / Phillips and 4 others / were present'. The missing words occur at places where the paper has rotted.
4 Dated 4 January 1799, this 50 pp. work consists half of O'Connor's account of his prison negotiations with government and half of his reflections on his conduct. O'Connor charged that Castlereagh broke an agreement made in July 1798, whereby government would allow O'Connor and other political prisoners to emigrate in return for their telling all they knew about the United Irishmen.
5 *An Address to the Nations of Great Britain and Ireland, on the Projected Union* (1799). Stanhope opposed the proposal to end the Parliament in Dublin and instead have a few Irish representatives in the Parliament in London.

Eveng. The other (said) T would find himself very comfortable for there were a great many Friends.

T. understands from Conversation with Young that some of the leading Men spend their Sundays with the State Prisoners in Newgate

J T.

394. Report from spy Tunbridge: 27 March 1799[6]

Source: PC 1/43/A153

27 March 1799.

J. T. reports that last Night he attended the Meeting of the corresponding Society No. 3 at the Nags Head in Saint John Street – There met the 14 members vizt. Eastburn, Currie who did belong to the guards a Shoemaker, Mr. Young, Mr. Phillips, whose Name T. mistook before and called Wilkinson and who attended the former Night with his Brother. The Names of the rest he is not acquainted with. *Barnard* who *belongs* to the private Committee and who was expected to make a Report did not attend. Phillips who also belongs to the private Committee mentioned that he had not attended them, being ill, but that he expected Barnard with the Report. Phillips pulled out of his Pocket some of Burks Affidavits respecting the Bastile as he termed it and sold some of them at a penny apiece. Phillips said that Burks had written this Week a Letter to Mr. Dundas demanding him to bring him to Trial that he might have an opportunity of proving what he had asserted. Phillips then pulled out of his Pocket one of the printed Reports of the Secret Committee of the House of Commons,[7] – asked the Members if they had seen it – said it contained a great many Falshoods – read several Passages – observed that

6 Description: '27 March 1799 / Report – J T / Copy / Maxwell / Eastburn'.
7 Ordered to be printed 15 March 1799. Though the LCS is attacked for its activites (from 1792 on), the main charge in this report is against the United Irishmen. The United Englishmen, or United Britons, are also described extensively and coupled with reform societies in Manchester, Glasgow and Hamburg as members of a large conspiracy to overturn government. The 1799 *Report* differs from the 1794 *Report of the Committee of Secrecy* in describing the words and actions of the LCS in highly charged language. The earlier report tended to let the documents speak for themselves. Perhaps the failure of juries to convict Hardy and Thelwall made government decide to direct the readers' reactions in this 1799 *Report*.

where mention was made in the Report that the apprehension of the Committee in Wych Street had tended to quite the Downfall of the London Corresponding Society – it was a damned Lie, for that he Phillips had always attended the Committees before and ever since, two or three present said they had attended Committees also.[8] Phillips said that tho' they did not meet so strong as formerly yet the Society was alive and their Friends had not forgot their Principles – he did not wish they shod. meet strong just at present only to keep up a Union amongst them – that Government had a strict watch over them – but the Times wou'd soon call them forward. Phillips is a very clever Man and devotes much of his time to the Society – Does not know where he lives.

Eastburn asked Phillips if he thought they were safe Meeting there so often – Phillips hesitating Eastburn added he thought they were not safe and, that he believed Government was looking out for them. Young replied to it that he thought it wou'd be best not to meet so often at one House. Eastburn asked if any one cou'd name another House. one of them mentioned the Pitts Head the Corner of Old Street. Eastburn said they might go there but the Landlord wou'd not allow them a private Room to themselves.

A member (whose Name T. recollects to be Maxfield a Shoemaker a Cutter out in Cornhill who attends regularly with his Brother) proposed their having a Hat Club or Clothes Club and then they might not find it necessary to move about – it wou'd deceive the Landlord & the Officers. This proposal was approved of by the Members present. It was agreed to be a Hat Club and to be for the Benefit of Hodson (now in Newgate) a Hatter. Maxfield said there were several Clubs held in that manner at different Houses by their Friends & that they held their Division Meetings under the Idea of Hat Clubs.

Eastburn was asked for his Books, he pulled one out of his pocket, a thickish Book in which the Names are entered, he put down the Names of some new Members, & then began collecting the Quarterage Money. As some had paid Barnard it was agreed not to collect any more then but Eastburn was desired to rule out the Book and enter the names a fresh against next Night, and then Barnard wou'd be there & the Money collected properly. Eastbourn was asked by Young to attend a little oftener than he had done. Eastbourn said he wou'd con-

8 Robert Oliphant also remained in the LCS until it was outlawed in July (examination, 2 June 1801, PC 1/3526).

448

tinue till the next Night but shod. then decline Secretary. The members pressed him to continue Secretary. He said he shod. decline for he thought they were in danger of being taken up.

Mention was made that the Officers had been sent into the Country to apprehend Persons supposed to be connected with those lately taken up. Currie said that the Affair of those apprehended near Red Lyon Square[9] was a very serious Business and that the Secretary wou'd be hanged as sure as he was born. T. asked if that was possible – Currie said that when the Secretary was seized his Box was secured and all the Writings. Nothing further particular passed.

J: T:

395. Report from spy Tunbridge: LCS General Committee, 5 April 1799[10]

Source: PC 1/44/A155

5th April 1799.

J. T. reports that being nominated a Delegate jointly with Blyth & John Carter at the last Meeting of the Corresponding Society at the Nags Head in Saint John Street, he attended the General Committee at the Crooked Billet Shire Lane. There met seven vizt. Blyth, Phillips, Mills, Williamson, a tall Man name unknown, and Barnard.

J. T. was appointed Chairman. The first Business was [the] State of the Funds of 2 Divisions No 1 and No. 2 Phillips who belongs to the private Committee, & is a Delegate from them produced a Book and read the account for those present to take the particulars & report to their several Divisions. In January last he stated there was in hand £2.8.1 and by different Accounts up to the 4th. April £3.11.5 – The Deductions were Postage of a Letter from Norwich 7 Pence, Paper for Baxter & Burks 5 Pence   Publications to Norwich 2s/5d including Booking at ye Inn

After this Statement J. T. reported that it was the wish of the Society he belonged to, that the private Committee shod. send one of the Reports of the Secret Committee of the

House of Commons to each Division and to be paid for out of the Funds. – Phillips opposed it, said it was proper there shod. be one in the Society but could not give his Consent to its being paid for out of the Fund, as the Fund was so low, but wished the Societys to subscribe for them, – that he would report it to the private Committee but he thought they would not approve of it as there were so many of their Friends in Confinement and if there was any Money to spare they ought to have it – he did not know how soon some of those present might be in the same predicament.[11]

Williamson and Mills did not attend as Delegates but as a Deputation from the Sons of Liberty. They were not introduced till the former Business was over. Blyth introduced them. Williamson delivered to T. a paper on coming into the Room written as follows

"April 3d. 1799

"Friends and Sons of Liberty
"Citzns. Williamson & Mills
"are deputed to wait on the
"Committee of the Londn Correpon
"Society
"Citzn. Richard Sheppard Presidt
David Rice Secrety.

He said their Deputation concerned Earl Stanhopes Address to the Nation. The Sons of Liberty did not know that the Correspondts. wou'd have wished to have any of them printed. The Sons of Liberty had had 1000 printed and after that they heard the Corresponding Society wished to have some they had desired the Printer not to break up the press, and that the Printer had agreed to print another thousand for 14s/. That Burks had agreed with them to pay them 1 Gūā for 1000 but he had not paid them. He said the Sons of Liberty wou'd not have been so particular about the Money as the Printer had agreed to give 6 Months Credit but since the Delivery, was very pressing for the Money – That he believed Cooper had now paid for them.

Phillips said in answer there must be a mistake for he understood from Burks that only

9 On 10 March, 19 members of the United Irishmen were arrested at a meeting at the Royal Oak public house in Red Lion Passage. Under the table was found a printed card celebrating the virtues of Coigly ('a willing victim at the shrine of selfish bigotry', etc.).

10 Description: '5th. April, 1799'.

11 Less than a week later, on 9 April, at a meeting of the United Englishmen at the Nag's Head in St John St the following men were arrested: John Baxter, Wallis Eastbourne, George Blythe, John Hill, John Maxwell, Stephen Cooper, Thos. Cooper, John Barnard, James Young, John Lewis, John Tunbridge, James Perkins, John Price. Baxter, Eastbourne and Blythe were imprisoned until the expiration of the suspension of the Habeas Corpus Act in 1801 (PC 1/44/A158).

500 had been ordered for the Corresponding Society and that he Phillips had fetched that Number and had paid 7s/0d for them. T. mentioned there was a mistake for the 1000 was to be only 14s/- and that Phillips had paid 7/- for 500 and that it was so mentioned by Barnard when proposed in the Society.

It was agreed for a Deputation of Barnard & Phillips with Burks to attend the Sons of Liberty Wednesday Evening at Williamson's House, to endeavour to settle the matter as to the price for the 1000 Addresses

The Reason of the Sons of Liberty requiring one Guinea for 1000 of the Addresses was that the first 1000 cost them printing £1.8.0

Williamson mentioned that Young Cooper had got the addresses printed

J. T.

396. Letter: Anonymous to Duke of Portland, 2 May 1799[12]

Source: PC 1/44/A158

London second may – 1799 –

My Lord

In giving your lordship the information I now do I wish to assure you it is fm. one actuated only by the future good will I intend towds the government of this country and that I do not do it fm. motives of rewd. nor enmity

to him I shall spake of. There now is – at the swan inn Lad Lane a young man of the name of OReyly Who is just returned (that is abt 3 Weeks ago fm france Where he has been on – buisness fm. the London Corresponding Society. and ⟨informs⟩ Us that – He has been there since march   he also told us he was going shortly – again and shewd us his credentialls as ambassadans – . . . he has been over for us twice before tho he is young the[y] send him because he passes unsuspected   he speaks french as well as english and is remarkably Clever   I think he could be brot to Make the most important discoveries – . . . I am myself a member of the society and shall continue in it – and will – if I find by yr conduct that the information I give your grace now is acceptable fm. time to time give you information of there proceedings – . . . they are now raising ⟨2⟩00 pounds to send him off – again – he stays in Lad Lane he says because he thinks the more publick he is the less suspicion . . . I shd think the best time – to get at his papers – would be early in the morning before he is up he generaly carries – a case of pistols abt him . . . he is acquint'd & Concerned with men of the 1st Property   his real Name is Michl Latting but has changed it while in town to – O Reyly . . .

I remain with the
highest – Respect – for my
king and – government

J. T[13] – a repentant Member of the L. C. S –

12 Address: 'To his/ Grace the Duke of Portland / at his office in London'. Description: 'information of importance/ 2d. May 1799/ Anonymous respecting Ryley'.

13 Probably Joseph Thomas, who reported to government in 1801 on the activities of the released state prisoners (PC 1/3526).

Postscript

[On 12 July 1799, the LCS was prohibited by name in 'An Act for the more effectual suppression of societies established for seditious and treasonable Purposes; and for better preventing treasonable and seditious practices'.[14] The punishment, if one were convicted by two justices of the peace, was either a fine of £20 or three months' imprisonment; if convicted upon an indictment, transportation for seven years. This act might not have deterred the men whom the spy Tunbridge met at LCS meetings, but most of them had been arrested in April. Probably some individual LCS members continued to meet informally as friends, as contributors to the subscription for the wives and children of the prisoners. There is evidence that in some formal way the LCS continued to exist, for as late as November 1800 there was an LCS meeting, on a Sunday morning, on Kennington Common.[15] Such a meeting presupposes a continuance of the Society, in some manner, after its banning.

To most members, the LCS soon became a part of their past rather than their present. Some of them emigrated to Paris (e.g. Ashley, Hodgson) or to America (J. Binns, Moore). Some of the extremists who were also members of the United Englishmen (Oliphant, Nicholls) pursued the revolutionary aims of the UE and in 1801–2 were involved in a conspiracy for which Despard was (probably wrongly) hanged in 1803.[16]

Still others became solid citizens working for change within the political system. It is this group that is best known, thanks to Francis Place's assiduity in retaining documents and recording political events. In the Westminster election of 1807 the committee which secured the election of Sir Francis Burdett included Place, Richter, Lemaitre and at least four other men who had been in the LCS, one of them the spy Powell. Alexander Galloway, presently the owner of a large engine factory, became a common councilman. Many of the former LCS members gathered each November to celebrate Hardy's 1794 acquittal (there were forty-eight such annual dinners from 1795 to 1842); when Place attended the dinner in 1822 he talked to twenty-four former delegates who were now 'all flourishing men', chiefly, Place said, as a result of their membership in the LCS. The most flourishing of the former delegates was certainly Place himself, who had become a prosperous master tailor, the friend of Jeremy Bentham, the advisor of reformers in Parliament. Place detailed the ways that he thought the LCS changed his life and the lives of other members: in the Society he met better-educated men such as Frend, Despard and Bosville, who visited him as he worked, talked to him, taught him. The membership in the LCS 'induced men to read books . . . to respect themselves, and to desire to educate their children. . . . The discussions in the divisions, in the sunday evenings readings, and in the small debating meetings, opened to them views which they had never before taken. They were compelled by these discussions to find reasons for their opinions, and to tolerate others. . . . It is more than probable that a circumstance like this never before occurred.'[17]]

14 39 Geo III, c. 79. The other societies named in the act are the United Englishmen, United Scotsmen, United Britons and United Irishmen.
15 Letter, Joseph Bacon to Hodgson, 12 Nov. 1800; 'Examination of Joseph Bacon Shoemaker, April 24, 1801'; both in PC 1/3526.
16 Marianne Eliot, 'The "Despard conspiracy" reconsidered', *Past and Present*, no. 75 (May 1977), pp. 46–61.

17 *Autobiography*, pp. 187–8, 198–9.

Index

453

464

Moore, Matthew* (*cont.*)
167; indicted for treason,
227; 251, 257, 259, 366
Moreau de St Merry, 204
Morgan, John*, calenderer, 285, 299,
302, 304-5, 357, 424
Morgan, William*, 420
Morning Chronicle, 71, 73, 91-2,
94n, 96, 104, 123, 126, 129,
178-9, 181-3, 203, 252n,
359, 430n
Morning Post, 59, 60n, 61, 63, 107,
120, 123, 130, 178-9, 181,
183, 252n, 351n
Mornington, Lord, 64n, 326n, 328
Morrice, 326n
Morris*, jackmaker, 90n, 142
Morris, Captain, his song, 226
Morris, Thomas*, 268, 271, 286
Morton, John, New Brentford, 86
Morton upon Lugg, 364
Muir, Thomas, Scottish reformer,
viii, 39, 82, 101, 108n, 110n,
111n, 113, 119n, 121, 124,
130, 134, 153
Munro, George*, spy, reports from,
27-8
Murray, Andrew*, 17, 19

Nagle, Joseph*, arrested 417, 429;
428
Nailsworth, Gloucestershire, 342
Nash, C. Jas*, 228, 410, 424
Naylor, John*, 299, arrested, 417,
429
Neale (Neild), John*, 258, 264,
268, 271, 280, 288, 299
Needham, T., Sheffield, 395n
Nelson*, William, 248, 258, 261,
285, 373
Nepean, Evan, under-secretary of
state, receives spy reports,
24n, 113n, 126n, 127n, 247
New London Coffee House, 112n
Newman*, 328-31
Newman, Rochester, 346
Newmills, Scotland, 119n
Newsham, H.*, 404
New South Wales, xvii, 101, 153;
see also Botany Bay
Nicholls, John*, master gardener,
330, 342, 348, 353, 366,
369, 371, 373, 375-6, 378,
397, 404, 451
Nicholson*, ? John, 288
Nicholson, Margaret, 255n
Nodder, Frederick Polydore*, spy,
botanic painter, 131, 137n,
144, 232; reports from,
131-2, 144-5, 148, 154,
158-9
Noon*, 169n, 196
Nore mutiny, 385, 397n, 427-8
Norfolk, Duke of, 54
Norman, John*, 117

Nottingham Journal, 282, 304
Norwich, 167, 258

O'Coigly, see Coigley
O'Connor, Arthur, 417, 421-2,
423n; *Letter to Lord
Castlereagh*, 447
Oliphant, Robert*, treasurer LCS
1798, tailor, 103, 256n, 261,
266, 296, 312, 318n, 328-31,
365-6, 378, 425; remains in
LCS to end, 448n; 451
Oliphant, Thomas*, UE, 404-5,
425n
O'Reyly (i.e. Michael Latting)*,
LCS courier to France, 450
Orr, George*, tailor, drills arming
society, 131; 144
Osborn, hotel keeper, 59
Osborn, Robert*, 404
Owen ?*, shoemaker, 59
Oxford, Lord, 396, 404
Oxlade (Oxlaid), John*, book-
binder, 189, 259, 268, 279-
80, 286, 328-31, 342, 346,
377
Oxley*, 132, 158

Pace, LCS creditor, 382n
Page, attorney, friend to the cause,
168
Page*, 275, 278, 325n, 326n
Paine, Thomas, xv, xvi, 14n, 15n,
23, 25, 27, 29, 31n, 47-8,
87n, 108n, 306n-7n, 438;
offers to write LCS address,
xv, 9; LCS starts defence fund
for, xv, 15-16, 257, 259; his
works disseminated in LCS,
xv; *Age of Reason*, ed.
planned by LCS, xx; 306n,
359n, 387n, 396n; *Agrarian
Justice*, 380n; *Crisis*, 204;
*Letter to the People of
France*, 327n, 364; *Rights of
Man*, xvi, xxv, 3, 14n, 58n,
82, 307n
Palmer, Peregrine*, attorney, 122,
163, 223, 279, 291, 399
Palmer, Thomas Fyshe, Scottish
reformer, viii, 39, 82, 101,
104, 108n, 110n, 111n, 113,
119n, 124, 130, 134, 153;
*A Narrative of the Suffering
of T. F. Palmer, and W.
Skirving . . . on Board the
Surprise Transport*, 153n
Panther, Jonathan ?*, coachmaker,
387
Pape, Joseph*, 404, 420n
Parcell, John, Glasgow, 398
Paris, 157
Parish, soldier, executed, 254
Parker, William*, 409n, 410, 412,
425n

Parkinson, James*, physician, *Revolution Without Bloodshed*,
viii, 198n, 199n; 80, 81n, 83,
203-4, 207, 209, 211-12,
214-16, 222-5; *A Vindication
of the London Corresponding
Society*, 225n; 227, 285, 345
353, 357, 441
Parkinson, John*, 404
Parliament, corrupt state of, 6,
10-11, 13; 165; petitions
for reform of, 39, 47, 48n,
49, 365, 395; to be reformed
from without, 166; private
committee to be killed, 167;
committee of secrecy, 167-8;
*Report from the Committee
of Secrecy* (1794), x, 138n,
168, 172n; 173, prorogued,
239; 253, 262, 273, 301n,
328; *Report from the Committee of Secrecy* (1799), x,
422, 448; *see* LCS aims,
petitions
Parr, Dr Samuel, xxii, 109n
Parry, Leicester, 374
Parsinnen, Terence, 'Association,
convention, and anti-
Parliament in British radical
politics, 1771-1848', 105n
Parsons*, Thomas, 371
Patriot, 15, 19, 25-6, 83
Patten, ? John*, 407
Patton*, 302
Paul, Charles, *William Godwin: His
Friends and Contemporaries*,
109n
Paull, James, parliamentary candidate, 256n
Peacock, Bartholomew*, stationer,
91n, 103, 105, 325n
Pearce, John*, upholsterer, 228
Pearce (Pearse, Pierce), John*, assist
ant secretary LCS 1794,
attorney, 83, 85n, 93, 103,
105, 114-16, 121, 122,
124-6, 129, 136n, 138, 139,
140n, 146, 147, 153, 155;
given journal night before
Hardy's arrest, 158; 159,
161, 163, 165-7, 169,
170, 172-5; arrested, 177;
207, 222, 228, 231, 234,
235, 258, 270, 271, 274,
367
Pearce (Pierce), John*, tallow chand
ler, 11n, 74; emigrates, 80
Pearson, John SCI, 133n
Pendrill, Charles*, bootmaker,
arrested, 417, 429
'A Pennyworth of Politics', 381
Perkins, James, UE, 449n
Perry, Sampson, *Oppression*, 241
Peter (Peters)*, 299-300
Peter, Pindar Junius, 212-14

467

Treherne, J.*, 404
Trenchard, John, 5
Tribune, 242n
Trot*, 288
Troughton*, 279, 283
Trow, ? printer, 382n
Truchard, Philip*, arrested, 417,
    429
True Briton, 330n, 345, 412n, 425n
Tubb, James*, weaver, 94
Tudor reign, 323, 325
Tunbridge, John*, spy, hairdresser,
    ix; reports from, 439–42,
    447–50
Turner*, 258–9, 261, 285, 291
Turner, Charles*, 47, 57n, 58, 64–5,
    74, 79
Turton, 72–3
Two Acts, *see* Treason and Sedition
    Bills
Tyler, Richard*, 265

Upton, Thomas*, informer, watch-
    maker, 140, 178n, 185n, 203,
    208, 217, 219; pop-gun plot,
    220–4, 226–7, 229, 231
Urquhart, William, Edinburgh, 67

Vance, Jeremiah, UE, 425n
Vassa, Gustavus (E. Equiano), xxii
Vaughan*, 438–40
Vaughan, Felix*, barrister, xxiii,
    11n, 23, 32, 35, 45–6, 83,
    89, 96, 103n, 117n, 123,
    161, 209, 212, 257, 259,
    260n, 394, 405
Venables, Robert*, haberdasher,
    58–9, 286, 288, 292n, 318n
Venner, 426n
Vial(l)s, John*, 246, 300, 301n,
    303, 311, 373, 375, 378,
    425n; escaped arrest, 429
Volney, Constantin Francois de,
    *The Ruins; or, A Survey of
    the Revolutions of Empires*,
    306n, 344; an extract: *Ruins
    of Palmyra*, 327n; another
    extract: *Torch*, 347n, 424,
    435

Wadson, T., SoL, 393
Waites, (Waite, Wait)*, 265, 288,
    291, 296
Walcot, UE, 426
Walker, ?Joseph*, 83n, 86, 375
Walker, Simon, UE, 425n
Walker, Thomas, Manchester, xxv,
    101, 129–30, 134
Waller, Thomas*, 407
Wallin*, 288
Wallington, T.?*, 393
Wallis (Wallace) John*, 299, 302
Walne, George*, tailor, 6n, 11n, 22,
    35n, 58, 62, 64n, 74–5, 78–9,
    83, 85n, 86, 92–3, 115, 117n,
    234

Walsh, James, Bow St officer, ⌐'6,
    137n, 138, 162
Walter, Thomas*, 364n
Waltham Abbey, 341–2, 344, 347,
    349, 355n, 359n
Wapshott, John*, 410, 414
war against France, 39, 64–67, 75–6,
    81, 84n, 106, 110, 123n,
    148, 153, 183, 239, 242–3,
    255, 314, 316, 323, 325,
    403, 417
'The War, or who pays the Reckon-
    ing?' 48n
Warbuton, John, Sheffield, 62
Ward, Francis*, hairdresser, 117,
    258, 261, 264, 268, 275,
    286, 288, 299; *Scarlet Devils*,
    348; 349, 365, 379, 381,
    388, 397
Wardle (Wassel) Thomas, SCI, 101,
    128, 144, 167, 227
Warren, barrister, 46
Warwick, 361
Watkins, John, and Frederick
    Shoberl, *A Biographical
    Dictionary of TheLiving
    Authors of Great Britain and
    Ireland*, xxi
Watkins, Richard*, 279, 283, 378
Watling*, 378, 387
Watson, ? John*, 366–7
Watson (Wadson), Robert*, physi-
    cian, 20, 22–3, 24n, 50, 73,
    211–12, convicted of posses-
    sing a seditious libel, 235;
    371n, 392, 394, 396–7, 427
Watt, Robert, Edinburgh, 101, 105,
    108n, 135n; tried, 224n,
    225n, 232–3
Watton, Herts., 331
Wayland, John*, 299
Webb, William*, 417, 421, 428;
    arrested, 429
Webbe, Samuel*, 108n, 116–17, 207,
    226–9, 292, 296, 299, 301,
    401–2, 405, 408, 412
Webster*, 258
Wells*, 439–40
Welsh (Welch), George*, shoemaker,
    299, 301, 310, 327, 387,
    420n, 425
Wenborne, William*, 256
Wenham*, 285, 366
West*, 279, 283
Westall (Westfall) George*, tobac-
    conist, 265, 286, 288, 291
Westminster Forum, 294, 330n
Westminster elections, 1796, 363;
    1806, 1807, 256n, 451
Weston, Williams*, 291, 302
Wetnall, Thomas*, 420n
Wharton, John, MP, viii, 71, 73,
    207, 326n; *Speech . . . on
    the Constitution*, 71, 74, 80
Whatcott, Henry*, 420

Wheelwright, Thomas*, seller of
    oranges and lemons, 404,
    426n–7n
Whelan, UI, 447
Whitbread, Samuel, MP, 123–4, 330
White*, 268
White, D*, 275, 278
White, Joseph, Treasury Solicitor,
    89, 351–2, 366
White, William*, 103n, 368
Whitehead, interpreter, 47, 57
Whitehead, D.*, 275, 278
Whitehead, Joseph*, 409n, 412
Whyth*, 411
Wickham, William, under-secretary
    of state, 135n, 140, 142n,
    149n, 154, 163n, 247, 436–7
Widdeson, George, Sheffield, 234
Widdows*, 285, 288
Wilkes, John, xxii, 165
Wilkinson*, 394, 441, 448
Wilkins, Thomas*, 271
Willby, Phillip*, 161n
William and Mary, 330
Williamott (?L. Williams)*, 312
Williams*, 163, 312, 327, 330, 346,
    349
Williams, Charles*, UE, 404, 407;
    arrested 417, 429; 425n
Williams, Captain Charles Turner*,
    142
Williams, George*, leather seller, 30,
    60–1, 103n, 113, 118, 119n,
    163n, 392
Williams, John*, wine merchant,
    103n, 105, 110, 112n, 118,
    194, 197–8, 216–17, 228,
    258–9, 261, 265, 268, 277,
    280, 366
Williams, Leonard*, 302
Williams, Samuel*, gun engraver,
    90n, 101–2, 131n; arrested,
    167; 228, 232; released, 234;
    236
Williams, Thomas*, bookbinder, 83,
    381n, 387, 396
Williams, William*, attorney, 55,
    362–3, 365, 370–1, 377, 392,
    394, 396n, 397; secedes, 404
Williamson, George, king's messenger,
    215–16, 218–20, 224–5
Williamson, John*, shoemaker, 131n;
    in arming society, 144; 185n;
    in Sons of Liberty, 393,
    449–50
Williamson, Joseph*, 404
Williamson, Thomas*, 404
Willingham, attorney, 174
Willson (Wilson)*, 258–9, 264,
    267–8, 275, 277, 285, 287,
    292, 299, 302, 304, 330, 371
Wilmot*, 299
Wilson, broker, 160n
Wilson, magistrate, 163
Wilson, Capt., arrest reported, 149n

Lightning Source UK Ltd.
Milton Keynes UK
UKHW030748080219
336879UK00006B/55/P

Also edited and introduced by Mary Thale
The Autobiography of Francis Place (1972)

Selections from the Papers of
the London Corresponding Society
1792–1799